SURVEYS OF INTERNATIONAL TRADE

SURVEYS OF INTERNATIONAL TRADE

Editors

Yin-Wong Cheung

Bharat R Hazari

City University of Hong Kong, Hong Kong

World Scientific

V JERSEY • LONDON • SINGAPORE • BEIJING • SHANGHAI • HONG KONG • TAIPEI • CHENNAI • TOKYO

Published by

World Scientific Publishing Co. Pte. Ltd.
5 Toh Tuck Link, Singapore 596224
USA office: 27 Warren Street, Suite 401-402, Hackensack, NJ 07601
UK office: 57 Shelton Street, Covent Garden, London WC2H 9HE

Library of Congress Cataloging-in-Publication Data
Names: Cheung, Yin-Wong, editor. | Hazari, Bharat R., editor.
Title: Surveys of international trade / edited By:
Yin-Wong Cheung (City University of Hong Kong, Hong Kong) and
Bharat R Hazari (City University of Hong Kong, Hong Kong).
Description: New Jersey : World Scientific, [2019]
Identifiers: LCCN 2018056453 | ISBN 9789813238596 (hbk : alk. paper)
Subjects: LCSH: International trade.
Classification: LCC HF1379 .S873 2019 | DDC 382--dc23
LC record available at https://lccn.loc.gov/2018056453

British Library Cataloguing-in-Publication Data
A catalogue record for this book is available from the British Library.

For any available supplementary material, please visit
https://www.worldscientific.com/worldscibooks/10.1142/10948#t=suppl

Desk Editors: Anthony Alexander/Lixi Dong

Typeset by Stallion Press
Email: enquiries@stallionpress.com

About the Editors

Yin-Wong Cheung is the Hung Hing Ying Chair Professor of International Economics at the City University of Hong Kong, and Professor Emeritus of the University of California, Santa Cruz. He obtained his Bachelor's, Master's, and PhD degrees, respectively, from the University of Hong Kong, the University of Essex, and the University of Pennsylvania. Cheung has published over 100 refereed articles in more than 40 academic journals, and co-authored and co-edited over 10 books. He is included in *The America's Registry of Outstanding Professionals,* the *Academic Keys Who's Who in Social Sciences Higher Education, Who's Who in Economics, Who's Who in America, and Who's Who in the World.*

Bharat Hazari is currently Adjunct Professor at the City University of Hong Kong. He obtained his PhD degree in Economics from Harvard University. He has taught at many universities, notably, University of British Columbia, University of Venice, Indian Statistical Institute and City University of Hong Kong. He has also delivered seminars at the University of Geneva, Sorbonne in Paris, University of Lille and Indian Statistical Institute. Bharat Hazari has published extensively in many areas of economics. He is the author of over ten books and more than hundred papers.

Contents

Introduction

Yin-Wong Cheung and Bharat Hazari*

International trade occupies a significant place in the corpus of Economics. It is taught in most universities, and the research in this area is prolific. Given its importance both in theory and applied economics, it has been surveyed by many prominent trade theorists. This collection brings together many surveys in one comprehensive volume. Not all surveys are included, for example, the important and pioneering survey by Richard Caves is not a part of this volume. The reason for this omission is that this survey is already available as a book and therefore cannot be part of this collection. The information in this book are from surveys which have been published in journals and not accessible in one place. Also included are some chapters that have been specifically written for this collection, to bring readers up to date on topics and to give the volume a better-rounded framework.

The first chapter in the volume is by the great Harvard trade theorist Gottfried Haberler. It was published in June 1950. It can best be described as a quasi-survey of trade theory highlighting significant problems in the pure theory of trade. The chapter presents

*We thank Vijay Mohan for extensive comments on this Introduction. Cheung gratefully thanks the Hung Hing Ying and Leung Hau Ling Charitable Foundation (孔慶熒及梁巧玲慈善基金) for their support through the Hung Hing Ying Chair Professorship of International Economics (孔慶熒講座教授(國際經濟).

a marvelous introduction to trade and distortion theory, which occupied an extremely important area of research for many years. The chapter is divided into five sections, each highlighting important problems. The emphasis is completely on the normative part of trade theory.

In Section 2, the two-country, two-commodity approach is used to geometrically show that in welfare terms free trade is better than no trade. This is a very old proposition in trade theory and dates back to the writing of David Ricardo. Haberler presents it in terms of the production possibility curve and the commodity price ratio. It eschews the use of social indifference curves as these were not discovered at the time this survey was written. It is important to note that this proposition has been proven with various techniques by many authors, for example, the use of geometry, or the use of the revealed preference approach and calculus. One can bring the most significant mathematical tools to address problems, but they do not change the nature of the basic insight that free trade in welfare terms dominates the no-trade position. More importantly, Haberler also addresses the issue of income distribution and free trade, highlighting that there are gainers and losers and that there is enough fat in the system to compensate the losers.

In Section 3 of the chapter, Haberler starts to move away from the ideal position to emphasize the significance of departures from the ideal conditions. The first problem that is addressed is that of factor immobility and factor price rigidity. It is shown that the free trade versus no-trade proposition is not affected by the presence of immobility. All that happens is that the production possibility frontier becomes a point giving rise to a kink but the proposition remains intact. The economy just loses the gains from trade from the production side but the consumption gains remain intact, giving rise to the gains from trade theorem.

However, factor price rigidity is a distortion and leads to a shrinkage of the production possibility curve and also to a possible non-tangency between the production possibility curve and the commodity price ratio. It shows how unemployment arises in real models (that is, models without any monetary phenomenon). Later, this kind of rigidity is fully analyzed and elaborated in various works on trade theory. More importantly, Haberler clearly points out that free trade cannot be ranked *vis-à-vis* no-trade. Trade theory has generally been built around inelastic supplies of the factors of production. However, Haberler clearly points out that it would be interesting to analyze the implications of work–leisure choice, which has also been attempted later in trade theory.

Finally, in Section 5, Haberler addresses the issue of non-tangency between the commodity price ratio and production possibility curve (without the shrinkage of the production possibility locus). Such a situation is associated with certain types of externalities. This has also been explored by many authors after the publication of this pioneering quasi-survey of trade theory.

The second survey in this volume is by Nobel laureate Robert Mundell. It is very interesting to note that in this survey no mention is made of the insightful and powerful quasi-survey of Haberler. The chapter by Haberler provided the foundations for many works later in trade theory. In spite of this, Mundell's survey is a class act and stands on its own merits. Its main emphasis is on providing a beautiful methodology to tackle the problems of unilateral transfers, productivity changes, export and import taxes, as well as production and consumption taxes in the context of the pure theory of international trade.

Section 1 begins with providing a very neat and elegant statement of the two-country, two-commodity model of international trade. Many trade theorists have used this as the foundation of their research. In later years, it became the standard practice in many models of trade to examine many propositions in trade theory. The use of P, the terms of trade, and its reciprocal in many functions is truly ingenious and shows how relative price ratios should be used in functions in a two-sector general equilibrium model. Mundell also points out other ways of stating the same model.

Section 2 of the survey details a procedure, that is, how to analyze the impact of parametric shifts on the movement of the endogenous variable in the system. This section should be useful for all backgrounds: undergraduate and graduate students, and trade theorists. In a way, it highlights how trade theory is an extended version of microeconomics, and how techniques from one area can be easily utilized in another area.

It is sometimes said that trade theory is poor man's general equilibrium as it extensively uses the tools of microeconomics. Section 2 is a perfect illustration of the latter point. The question that is being dealt with is how we go about analyzing a shift in a parameter (or policy change) from the point of view of comparative statics. The example used to illustrate the power of the technique is the impact of a parametric shift on terms of trade. The way this procedure works is as follows: let us first examine the impact of the parametric shift by computing the excess demand (at fixed terms of trade). This is followed by equating this excess demand to the excess supply. By equating these two the change in the terms of trade can be easily worked out. Of course, this procedure requires that the conditions of dynamic stability are met. Two examples of the use of this procedure are provided: (1) the Marshallian demand–supply system and (2) a simple Keynesian system.

The next section of this survey provides a very neat treatment of the Marshall–Lerner stability condition. It is a very clean derivation from the balance-of-payments condition. It is also shown that the stability condition can be expressed in terms of one good only. This is a consequence of the fact that the general equilibrium model used is a two-good model and only one market needs to clear for obtaining equilibrium. Therefore, stability in one market will ensure the stability in the other market. A diagrammatic illustration by the use of offer curves is also provided.

Having obtained the stability condition, the Mundell survey then addresses various other issues in trade theory. The first is the discussion of unilateral payments. The effect of these payments on terms of trade is determined by using the technique already outlined. The Leontief paradox, which established that the donor country could become worse off after making a donation, is analyzed, and it is established that this perverse outcome can only arise when the system fails to meet the stability condition. In later literature, it has been shown that the Leontief donor impoverishment result may occur in other types of models, for example, when there are three agents. In these models, the stability condition is satisfied.

Section 5 of the survey addresses the issue of productivity changes on terms of trade and welfare. The expressions are derived, and it is shown that the offer curve diagram may be used to separate income and substitution effects. This is nice for the reader as it shows how to apply microeconomic concepts in different frameworks, and how to use offer curve diagrams to separate such effects. It is an application of standard demand theory.

The survey then goes on to show how the change in productivity affects the terms of trade. The technique outlined earlier is used again to obtain an important expression. A great innovation here is to express the change in terms of trade as the annual rate of growth. This also extended to a two-country model where both countries are growing. The possibility of immiserizing growth is also discussed in this section. This arises from a trade-off between output growth, which is positive, and adverse terms of trade effect, which is negative. The balance between the two shows whether growth is positive or damnifying. Although it is shown that such an outcome may arise, it is not heavily emphasized as the conditions are regarded as quite strict. In later years, trade theory gets quite obsessed with the phenomenon of immiserizing growth. The survey then discusses the impact of taxes and subsidies on trade. Again, geometry and the excess demand technique are applied to derive all the results.

Section 7 deals with consumption and production taxes, as opposed to taxes on trade. This section is important in the development of trade theory, as a distinction is drawn between consumption and production effects of taxes. This is a distinction that was present in Haberler's survey in terms of his treatment of gains from trade. The distinction is now utilized in the context of these taxes.

Section 8 of the survey deals with other adjustment mechanisms, for example, fiscal policy and capital movements. So, it takes the system away from adjustments that occur via movements in terms of trade to adjustment mechanisms that are not dependent on price movements. A typical example of this would be the small-country assumption, which does not allow the terms of trade to adjust.

Finally, a generalized expression is produced that utilizes the balance of payments condition and that incorporates all the parametric shifts in one expression. This is a wonderful survey for teaching all trade theorists how to use a simple technique to obtain many important results.

The next survey in this edited volume is by the master of old trade theory Jagdish Bhagwati. This is indeed a famous survey and was described by Paul Samuelson as masterly. It is a comprehensive survey and stands in sharp contrast to the three-part survey by John Chipman. Both are comprehensive but with different emphasis. Both these surveys cover a large territory — one extremely intuitive and the other highlighting the mathematics of international trade.

The opening introduction of the Bhagwati survey is illuminating. First, it clearly states why we refer to this part of trade theory as "pure". Second, it highlights how one may view various propositions in trade theory: normative and/or positive, methodological equilibrium analysis, comparative static analysis, dynamic analysis and comparative dynamics. This is useful for all trade theorists as it shows how to examine and box various propositions in trade theory. The positive trade theory is divided into five sections, and normative theory into three sections.

The positive theory opens with the theorems on the pattern of trade. The Ricardian and Heckscher–Ohlin theorems of comparative advantage are discussed with great intuition and clarity. The discussion is mainly in the framework of two commodities and one factor in the Ricardian case, and of two commodities and two factors in the Heckscher–Ohlin case. In both cases, a second country is also in the picture. There is also a very fine discussion of the Linder theory of pattern of trade. The distinction between Ricardo, emphasizing differences in technology, and Heckscher–Ohlin, the role of endowments, is highlighted in an intuitive manner. In the Ricardian framework, the role of demand is also highlighted for determining the terms of trade. It is shown that the terms of trade are indeterminate without some sort of demand conditions and also the breakdown of the famous labor theory of value when the terms of trade do not coincide with the slope of the production possibility curve of the two countries involved in trade.

After the discussion of the pattern of trade, the survey moves on to discuss the factor price equalization theorem. This theorem had attracted a lot of attention from various trade theorists. Its importance arose from how trade in commodities with international factor immobility could lead to equalization of factor prices under some restrictive conditions. Attempts were also made to generalize the factor price equalization theorems to the case where the number of goods and factors is greater than two. The work of Samuelson, Kuhn and Mackenzie is surveyed in this context.

The survey then discusses trade theorems associated with comparative statics. Here an important distinction is drawn which is useful and independent of a time dimension, that is, it can always be asked in any trade model attempting comparative statics. The comparative statics may arise from two different sources: (1) from a change in policy, for example, imposing a tariff in either the small- or large-country case and (2) from changing one of the parameters of the model, for example, factor accumulation and its effect on endogenous variables. Under shifts in data, that is, a change in the parameters of the model (not policy changes), the main results considered are changes in international demand and the transfer problem. The effect of the transfer problem is extensively discussed. Note that this problem is discussed in the survey by Mundell, which also shows that the Leontief transfer paradox only arises in the presence of instability. The Bhagwati derivation of this result is slightly cleaner than that of Mundell.

From here, the survey moves on to changes in factor supply. The famous Rybczynski theorem is explained in this section although it is not linked to its dual, the Stolper–Samuelson theorem. The important papers by Johnson, Mundell and Ramaswami are all discussed in a succinct manner. The survey then moves on to discuss technological change, changes in non-trade policies and changes in international demand. As is the case with Bhagwati, major results in this area are lucidly summarized and important ones highlighted.

The survey then moves on to theorems in dynamics. This is a very short section as at the time of Bhagwati's survey not much had been done on dynamic propositions in trade theory. The next section of the survey is concerned with welfare propositions in trade theory. This section opens up with the theorem on gains from trade. A distinction is drawn between theorems that may be viewed from the point of view of national advantage and those that belong to the category of international advantage. The important result that free trade is better than no-trade is viewed as both a national and international advantage. On the other hand, an optimum tariff in the presence of monopoly power in trade is regarded as a result that belongs to national advantage. Mention is also made of the important work of Samuelson and Meade here, who provide alternative approaches to dealing with gains from trade.

The survey then goes on to discuss the problems associated with the presence of distortions, an area that is discussed in the short survey by Haberler (printed in this volume). The distortions may originate in the domestic economy and/or the foreign economy. The famous notation to discuss distortion in terms of the marginal rates of substitutions is introduced here. The first best is characterized as an equality between the Domestic Rate of Substitution, Domestic Rate of Transformation and Foreign Rate of Transformation (that is, DRS = DRT = FRT), and that the economy operates on the first best locus. Distortions, national and international, disrupt these equalities, and then appropriate policy measures are required to correct them. Some nice geometry is also provided to highlight the intuition. Increasing returns to scale are discussed, but not connected to intra-industry trade (this connection later becomes the new trade theory).The final section of the survey deals with the measurement of gains and losses associated with trade theory. This is a great survey that provides an overview of many problems in trade theory, as well as an enormous amount of intuition regarding trade propositions.

It is appropriate now to provide a brief summary of the monumental survey of trade theory by John Chipman. This is in three parts and was published in *Econometrica*. It covers the mathematical parts of trade theory and stands in sharp contrast to the survey by

Bhagwati. Enormous ground is covered in the three parts and the bibliography is just astounding. The classical part opens with a very interesting comment on Brouwer's fixed point theorem. Marshall's Pure Theory was written in 1897 and the existence of equilibrium there depended on this mathematical theorem. However, Brouwer's fixed point theorem was discovered after Marshall's important work. It is this kind of mathematical insight that is the hallmark of this survey.

The classical part of the survey devotes its attention to the Law of Comparative Advantage as propounded by Ricardo and Torrens. As mentioned in the Bhagwati survey, the Ricardian (Torrens) model relied on two countries with one factor, labor, in order to derive the Law of Comparative Advantage by introducing differences in technology. There is dispute as to who discovered the Law of Comparative Advantage first — Torrens or Ricardo. We are going to leave this issue aside and concentrate on the important mathematical part of the Law.

The major problem with the Ricardian theory of comparative advantage in the treatment by Torrens and Ricardo was that it explained the pattern of trade, but could not determine the terms of trade. Ricardo maintained that the terms of trade would settle halfway between the cost ratios of the two countries. There are two points to note here. First, no proof is provided about this assertion. Second, the existence of such terms of trade would contradict the labor theory of value. Later, John Stuart Mill tried to find an exact solution to this problem, and propounded the famous Mill's paradox. It is Chipman who provides a solution to the issue of terms of trade, as well as the conditions under which the terms of trade may settle at the midpoint.

Chipman poses the Ricardian model as maximizing a quasi-concave function subject to linear inequalities. To quote Chipman: "This is a problem in homogeneous programming (Eisenberg, 1961) and a special case of non-linear programming (Kuhn and Tucker, 1951)". By formulating it this way, all the Ricardian results can be derived. It just shows why mathematics in economics matters. The conditions of specialization, the determination of the terms of trade and the gains from trade can all be derived from the programming exercise. Chipman correctly remarks about Mill's Law of International Value: "In its astonishing simplicity it must stand as one of the great achievements of the human intellect". The theory is also presented geometrically. All this is followed by a treatment of later discussions of the Ricardian theorem by other trade theorists. There is also an elegant discussion of Graham and Haberler.

Then the survey moves on to discuss the works of Mckenzie, Whitin and others. McKenzie analyzed the Mill–Graham model in full generality, and showed how to solve trade models by quasi-programming techniques and removing all the indeterminacies in the simple Ricardian model. Mckenzie also considered the cases of multi-country and multi-goods in the Ricardian system. He showed a variety of solutions to the multi-good multi-country problems. There is ingenious use of programming and activity analysis techniques in this presentation.

An important contribution in this part of the survey is the treatment of Mangoldt (1863). The Chipman survey shows how to use the duality technique for solving the problems postulated by Mangoldt. So, implicit use of duality of linear programming is very old and implicit in the work of earlier writers. It is great that Chipman's survey brings all these ideas out and provides superb applications of programming techniques. The survey goes on to show how to treat intermediate goods in the programming framework and also discusses many results associated with intermediate goods in classical trade theory.

We will now proceed to discuss the second part of Chipman's survey, which deals with the neoclassical and modern parts of trade theory. This part starts with the introduction to two important and widely used concepts or geometrical devices in trade theory: (1) Marshall's concept of the offer curve and (2) Haberler's concept of the production possibility curve. These concepts were later developed by many authors: perfected by Meade and rigorously developed by Nikaido. After spending some time on these concepts, the Chipman survey then addresses the issue of the representative agent, a concept that is used not only in trade theory but also in many other areas of economics. This is great for readers, as they can understand the problems and solutions that are available when using the concepts of the representative agent and the community indifference curve in trade theory. The mathematical conditions relating to assumptions regarding homotheticity and distribution are elegantly discussed and the mathematics is presented in a beautiful manner. This section of the survey provides a treatment of the important papers by many famous economists like Leontief, Samuelson, Houthakker, Arrow and so on.

The next section of the survey deals with the production possibility curve (opportunity cost). The problem of obtaining a production possibility curve when there are variable factor supplies is also discussed. This goes back to work of Vanek. Caves and Kemp later addressed this problem and highlighted the problems associated with variable factor supplies, pointing out that one may obtain conflicting transformation curves and/or obtain linear surfaces. The most important point in this analysis is that these are not true production possibility curves.

In economics 101, we often teach students how to determine equilibrium in a market — showing that it is obtained at the point of intersection between well-behaved demand and supply curves. However, we rarely tell the students that we should be really talking about three problems: existence, uniqueness and stability of an equilibrium. This is even more important in trade theory, as the reciprocal demand curves on which equilibrium depend have income effects in them, and hence such effects can give rise to problems of existence as well as stability.

Chipman provides several examples of the non-existence of equilibrium in trade models. These examples are associated with Nikaido and Arrow. This section of the survey provides a clean treatment of what is required for the existence of an equilibrium. The existence requires applications of the Knaster–Kuratowski–Mazuukiewicz lemma and in some cases the use of Brouwer and Kakutani fixed point theorems. This section of the survey should be read by both trade and non-trade theorists as it clearly shows the mapping between these important mathematical theorems and international trade theory. These theorems are also used in other areas of economics. In this survey, the economics and mathematics are coupled with each other. Other important works of Bhagwati, Johnson, Arrow, Debreu and so on are also discussed in this part. All these works, showing conditions under which a trade equilibrium exists, are unique and stable.

The final section of the survey deals with external economies. This part does not contain much mathematics and the discussion shows the problems associated with such externalities in trade theory. The third part of Chipman's survey is titled Modern Theory. It should be noted that this is not a New Theory of Trade. It is very much in the tradition of old theory of trade. The focus in this part is rather interesting as it is devoted to the discussion of factor price equalization theorem, which was a very hot topic long time ago. Chipman, as usual, covers the mathematical aspect of this famous theorem in an admirable way. It is discussed with a historical perspective dating back to Wicksell (1919) and bringing it up to the work of Gale (1962). The fundamental questions here are the conditions under which the commodity price vector is uniquely related to the factor price vector, and whether the function $P = g(w)$ is globally invertible or not. There is an elaborate discussion of this requirement in this part of the survey. It covers issues like factor intensity reversal, the ACMS production functions, the role of number of commodities and factors, and the proximity of the endowments of the countries.

Then the survey goes on to deal with empirics of testing the Heckscher–Ohlin theorem. The Leontief paradox is expounded in this section and comments are made about the problems associated with testing the Heckscher–Ohlin theorem.

The rest of the collection is based on surveys that are not as sweeping as those by Mundell, Bhagwati and Chipman. So this introduction will provide a much briefer treatment of these surveys. There were two surveys on distortion and trade theory: one by Stephen Magee (reprinted in this volume) and the other by Bharat Hazari (1978). The latter is in a book form and like Maggee's survey contains many original results. Like Caves' survey, the Hazari work on distortions and trade theory is not printed in this volume as it is a book.

Magee's survey is mainly concerned with factor price differentials and their impact on trade theory. A factor price differential results in a non-tangency of the commodity price ratio and the production possibility surface, as well as shrinkage of the production possibility curve. Non-tangency leads to several important theorems in trade theory. First, all the gains from trade theorems collapse in this kind of framework. Second, growth is not necessarily welfare-increasing (immiserizing growth may occur in this type of a system). Third, the price output response may be perverse due to value intensity reversal. Fourth, from a policy point of view, a clear distinction can be established between the first-best and second-best policies. For example, a production tax cum subsidy policy is second best, a factor tax cum subsidy policy is first best. All these perverse phenomena are discussed in this survey by Magee.

The survey also discusses how distortions may arise either structurally or from the use of policy tools, for example, the imposition of a tariff in the small-country case. The distortions not tackled include Harris Todaro-type distortion, externalities, factor price rigidity (for example, minimum wage rates) and monopoly power in trade. There is a very extensive reference list at the end of the survey and also a complete and thorough discussion of various aspects of factor price differentials.

It is appropriate now to talk about the new trade theory. First, it is very important to draw a distinction between commodity trade and industry trade. Commodity trade occurs when we trade one commodity for another, for example, cloth and wine. Industry trade arises when we trade commodities that belong to the same industry, for example, a country may import and export cars. These cars are differentiated products and belong to the same industry. A large volume of trade consists of intra-industry trade. So trade theorists resorted to the idea of using increasing returns to scale as an explanation of intra-industry trade. This type of trade is not explained by the traditional models of Ricardo and Heckscher–Ohlin.

In this edited volume, we reprint the paper by Wilfred Ethier on returns to scale and the theory of trade. Ethier starts out by commenting that since World War II, trade has grown in the exchange of manufactured commodities between industrialized countries. The important work by Dixit and Stiglitz provided the foundations for incorporating increasing returns to scale and product differentiation into the theory of trade. Ethier's work sets out the production structure in Section 1. It concentrates on finished manufactures produced from intermediate manufactured components. The production relations are summarized in equations (2) and (2′). Equation (2′) is analogous to the utility functions used by Dixit–Stiglitz that is later adapted by Krugman and others. Having set up the production process, Ethier establishes the autarkic equilibrium and represents it using an innovative diagram. Ethier then moves on to establish the international equilibrium. Figure 2 in his work provides the geometric version of the equilibrium obtained in autarky and in the free trade situation. Ethier then discusses the validity of the standard theorems of trade in his modern version of trade theory. Factor Price Equalization, Rybczynski theorem, and its dual, the Stolper–Samuelson theorem, are all discussed in the context of the returns to scale model. The distinguishing features of these theorems in the context of modern theory are neatly analyzed and discussed.

The chapter also links the Heckscher–Ohlin theorem to the setting of returns to scale. Ethier draws two major conclusions in this survey article. To quote: "intra-industry trade in manufactures is complementary international factor movements" (p. 403). The second conclusion drawn is: "The present treatment gives national returns to scale a prominent place. The indeterminacy and multiple equilibria characteristics are still present" (*Ibid.*). More importantly, the parametric shifts result in "changes in the number of production units rather than in their size".

The next survey in this volume is by Elhanan Helpman on the structure of foreign trade. This survey starts with the well-known theory of comparative advantage by David Ricardo, and comments on the fact that it is difficult to build empirical studies for testing the Ricardian theorem. It then proceeds to analyze the Heckscher–Ohlin model. With Samuelson's exposition, this became the centerpiece of trade theory for many years.

The survey clearly draws the distinction between trade in goods and trade in factor content. Good and simple examples are provided for the meaning of factor content in trade. There is an elegant discussion of the Leontief paradox, which demonstrated that the Heckscher–Ohlin model was not empirically valid for US exports and imports. The attempts at generalizing the Heckscher–Ohlin model are discussed at length. These generalizations were empirically tested in the literature. However as pointed out by Helpman, they do not truly provide a test of the generalized Heckscher–Ohlin model. There is a wonderful discussion in the survey on all the testing methods of the Heckscher–Ohlin model.

After this, the survey discussion moves on to the treatment of the empirics of the new trade theory. The new trade theory is based on the concept of increasing returns to scale and product differentiation. The new trade theory is generally associated with Krugman. It is noted that the new and old trade theories are complementary to each other. The empirical techniques used for this complementarity are discussed at length.

The survey also discusses the issue of volume of trade associated with product differentiation. The concluding section of this survey is compulsory reading as it sheds light on the controversies in trade, between those who believe in the traditional approach and those who subscribe to the new trade theory to explain intra-industry trade.

It is now appropriate to discuss the chapter by Peter Neary with the exotic title "Of Hype and Hyperboles: Introducing the New Economic Geography". To quote from the chapter by Neary "on his website Krugman expresses the hope that economic geography will one day become as important a field as international trade. This sort of hype, even if tongue and cheek, is not to everyone's taste, especially when the results rely on special functional forms and all too often can only be derived by numerical methods". This is a very meaningful introduction to both new trade theory and economic geography as both are dependent on special functional forms.

In Section 2 of the chapter by Neary, the Dixit–Stiglitz model is presented in a very simple and elegant way. Figure 1 is very intuitive and of great help in understanding the Dixit–Stiglitz framework. In Section 2.2, Neary addresses the breakthrough of Krugman: extending the Dixit–Stiglitz framework to intra-industry trade. This is almost the beginning of new trade theory reliant on increasing returns to scale, love of variety and product differentiation as the source for gains from trade. The Krugman model is a modern glorified version of Ricardo, where there is just one factor of production with increasing returns to scale. Neary then goes on to discuss how this type of modeling is applied in economic geography. There is a discussion of economic geography and its associated problems in terms of core and periphery. Intermediate input and agglomeration are discussed in Section 2.4.

In Section 3, the extensions to the basic model of new economic geography are discussed, and several ideas for extensions and further explorations are provided. Section 4 discusses the limitations of the model, while Section 5 addresses the issues of old and new economic geography. There is a very nice thought expressed in the concluding section and we quote "focusing on a single cause of trade and location: technology in Ricardo, factor endowments in Huckster Ohlin, monopolistic competition in Krugman".

So far in this edited volume we have not included any chapter on the dynamic aspect of trade. The chapter by Jean-Pierre Laffargue fills this lacuna in the volume. It is a chapter on growth and trade with a Heckscher–Ohlin approach. Laffargue combines Ramsey's exogenous model of growth with Rebelo's model of endogenous growth. The chapter provides conditions for the convergence of factor prices, that is, factor price equalization theorem once again. However, Laffargue shows that the growth process does not necessarily lead to convergence of the outputs and per capita stock of capital across countries. A poor country may grow faster but remains poorer compared to advanced countries. Conditions for convergence are also discussed.

The penultimate chapter in this volume is on trade and economic growth in China by Tan Li and Larry Qiu. The implication of trade for economic growth has been discussed from both perspectives of trade theory and endogenous growth. Li and Qiu offer a succinct review on recent studies on links between the volume of trade or trade policy and economic growth. In addition, the authors use provincial data from China, an undisputed rising economic star in Asia and the world, to illustrate the contribution of trade growth to economic growth. It is also noted that the positive implication of trade for economic growth does not provide information on issues on, say, income inequality and welfare improvement.

The final chapter in this volume is by Vijay Mohan. Mohan looks at a subset of the strategic trade policy literature. James Brander had provided a very useful summary of strategic trade policy in 1995; however, since this is available as a book, we have not included it in this survey volume. Mohan's chapter revisits the relative merits of welfare-maximizing taxes versus revenue-maximizing taxes. Specifically, it outlines the role of delegation of strategic trade policy: welfare-maximizing governments can increase a nation's welfare by delegating to revenue-maximizing policymakers. Since this idea is closely linked to strategic managerial delegation within a firm, Mohan's chapter reviews that literature as well.

Last, but not the least, we would like to thank the contributing authors, as well as Anthony Alexander (production editor), DONG Lixi (in-house-editor), Alisha Nguyen and their colleagues from World Scientific Publishing Co. for their support in the publication of this collection.

Chapter 1

Some Problems in the Pure Theory of International Trade*

Gottfried Haberler

I

The present article discusses certain elaborations and applications of the now familiar and widely used presentation of the theory of comparative cost in terms of opportunity cost. It is largely an essay in welfare economics. I shall, however, not discuss the issue of real or labor cost *vs.* opportunity cost, because it would not serve any useful purpose. For, as Samuelson once said, "the doctrine of opportunity cost, properly stated, in no way contradicts the so-called pain cost theory of value. In fact, when stated with full qualifications, the doctrine of opportunity cost inevitably degenerates into the conditions of general equilibrium."[1] The issue seems to me no longer a live one, and its discussion can therefore be appropriately relegated to a footnote.[2]

*Originally published in *The Economic Journal*, 60(238), pp. 223–240.

[1] "Welfare Economics and International Trade," *American Economic Review*, Vol. 28, 1938, p. 263.

[2] Ten years later Samuelson seems to have forgotten what he had written in 1938. In June 1948 in the ECONOMIC JOURNAL he said: "Professor Viner has steadfastly maintained the more general equilibrium approach of Walras, Pareto and Marshall against his opponents Knight, Haberler and Robbins. And one by one they have

II

As is usual in such discussions, I shall use a two-country, two-commodity approach. One country may stand for the rest of the world, and the external terms of trade will be assumed to be given. This does not mean that what will be said applies only to a country of so negligible a size in the world economy that it literally cannot by its action influence its terms of trade. It only means that the country is supposed to act competitively and that the possibilities

---

either had to maintain an empirically gratuitous position (that all factors must be perfectly inelastic in total supply and indifferent between different uses) or else have had to reformulate the opportunity cost doctrine so that it becomes not only a rather awkward mumbo-jumbo but loses all novelty and distinctiveness as well" (p. 182).

It could be easily shown that Böhm-Bawerk himself had already in 1894 (see his article "Der letzte Massstab des Güterwertes"—1894, Reprinted in *Gesammette Schriften von Böhm-Bawerk,* ed. F. X. Weiss, Vienna, 1924, especially pp. 428 *et seq.*) extensively, though perhaps not quite satisfactorily in all details, discussed the simplifying assumptions stated in parenthesis above which Samuelson chooses to call a "gratuitous position." These assumptions can, therefore, hardly be characterised as subsequent concessions grudgingly made "one by one."

Viner himself admits that the opportunity-cost approach (in the narrow, unqualified sense) is superior to the real-cost approach "in the case of land use" where "real costs are absent or unimportant" *(Studies,* p. 520). He speaks of a "genuine contribution" of the opportunity-cost technique "to the treatment of land-use costs." Surely, what holds of land also holds of other factors to some extent even of labor (*ibid.,* p. 525). He insists that "the opportunity-cost form of the income approach has no obvious advantage as compared to an outright income approach" (*ibid.,* p. 520).

Now I never regarded the opportunity-cost theory as anything but an "outright" income approach, in fact nothing but a somewhat simplified general equilibrium approach; and it does not require excessive generosity and tortuous interpretations to see that this is also the attitude of the other (including the original) propounders of the theory. Everybody seems to be agreed, in principle, on which factors have to be taken into consideration as determinants of income or, better, of economic welfare. But not being sufficiently skilful mathematicians, most of us resort to simplifications and allow for factors from which we abstract in our simplified models by means of somewhat vague verbal qualifications. Without pursuing this matter farther, I would still say that the simplifications made in the (unqualified) opportunity-cost approach are empirically much less absurd than those resorted to by any real-cost or pain-cost doctrine; the opportunity-cost approach is more fertile, because it can be readily extended into a general

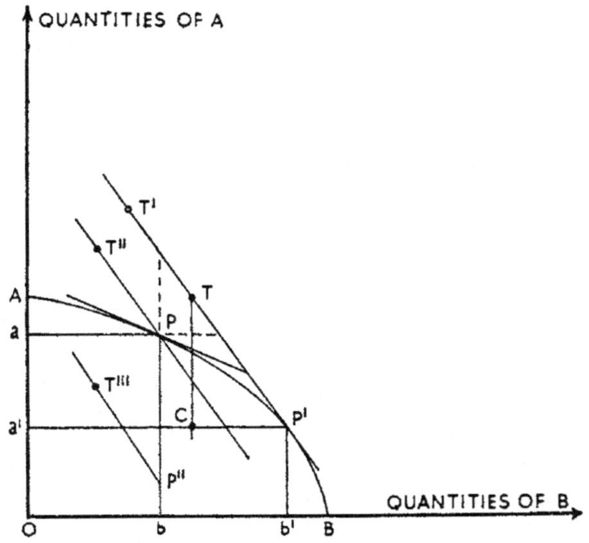

Figure 1.

of monopolistic doctoring of the terms of trade and oligopolistic or bilateralistic complications will not be discussed in the present paper. Dynamic aspects will also be ignored.

Let us now start with the familiar diagram (Fig. 1) showing a production opportunity curve *AB,* which represents the maximum combinations of *A* and *B* that can be produced. The curve is drawn under the assumption of constant (inelastic) supply of factors of production and of perfect competition in the factor and product markets.[3] The curve is drawn concave towards the origin signifying

---

equilibrium system. It is therefore not surprising that the opportunity- cost approach has gained more and more popularity, and that it is used even by those who, in principle, attack it. (See, *e.g.*, Samuelson in the very article from which the passage cited above is taken, and Stolper and Samuelson, "Protection and Beal Wages," *Review of Economic Statistics,* 1941.)

[3]The assumption of inelastic factor supply is made for convenience, but is strictly speaking not necessary. How the production-opportunity curve is to be derived from the production functions of the two commodities is shown in W. F. Stolper and P. A. Samuelson, "Protection and Beal Wages," *Review of Economic Statistics,* 1941, reprinted in *Readings in the Theory of International Trade,* Philadelphia, 1949. Stolper and Samuelson, too, assume inelastic factor supply. If

increasing opportunity cost of A in B and of B in A. Assume that in the absence of trade production takes place at point P, output (national income) being Oa of A and Ob of B. The tangent to the curve at P has then a double meaning: Its slope indicates (1) the exchange ratio between A and B, one unit of A being exchanged for two units of B (this is, of course, the reciprocal of the money price ratio and of the ratio of marginal money cost of A and B) and (2) the marginal transformation ratio : for one unit of A that is given up, two units of B can be produced.

It is very important to keep these two meanings apart, for only under special conditions will the two ratios be identical. These conditions are, roughly speaking, competition, indifference of factors with respect to the industry in which they are employed, and absence of external economies and diseconomies. If any one of these two conditions is not fulfilled, the exchange ratio (price ratio) and transformation ratio will diverge from one another and, as we shall see presently, very important welfare consequences flow from this divergence.

Assume now that trade is opened and the international-trade ratio is given by the slope of line $P'T$. That is to say, abroad one B buys about two As, while at home one B can be exchanged for only half an A. Our country will therefore specialise in B. Commodity A, which is cheap abroad, will be imported, while B, which is cheap at home, will be exported. The production point will travel from P to P', where the marginal transformation ratio is equal to the new exchange ratio, and by trade the country will then move to, say, T, exporting $P'C$ of B in exchange for CT of A.

How is the precise location of T on the line TP' determined? For our purposes it will be sufficient to answer: by demand conditions. Some writers prefer to say that the location of T is determined by the point of tangency of the trade line with an indifference curve. It must not be forgotten, however, that a shift in production will usually be accompanied by a redistribution of income. This precludes

---

they did not, they would need two additional dimensions, and their box diagrams would not work.

the uncritical application of community indifference curves, either as an explanatory device (we cannot say "the community" will choose the most preferred point on the trade line, because "the community" does not do any choosing except in a centrally planned economy) or as a criterion of welfare (we cannot simply say any point T on the trade line is "better" than P, on the ground that it obviously lies on a higher indifference curve). Things are not as simple as that. But we shall not pursue this matter any further, and the reader who wishes to think in terms of indifference curves may do so for the purposes of the present paper.[4]

But that point T is "superior," *i.e.*, represents larger "national income" or "economic welfare" than point P, can be established without making use of indifference curves. If T is above and to the right of P, a larger quantity of A and B is available after trade than before, and it is natural to call this a superior position. If T were, as it may well be, above P but to the left of it, say at T', there would be consumed after trade more of A but less of B. In what sense, then, can T' be said to be a "better" position than P? I reject the anthropomorphic argument to the effect that the society could have chosen T, which is superior to P, and since it actually chose T', this, *a fortiori,* must be better than P. This argument is unsatisfactory, at least for an individualistically organised economy. In such an economy what is to be regarded as a better position, a larger national income or superior welfare position must be defined in terms of individual incomes or welfare positions. Modern welfare economics has, however, shown that in the following sense the situation after trade can be said to be better than before: if income were appropriately redistributed, every individual could be

[4]T. de Scitovszky, in his article "A Reconsideration of the Theory of Tariffs" (*Review of Economic Studies,* 1942, reprinted in *Readings in the Theory of International Trade*) has made the only serious attempt, as far as I know, at constructing community indifference curves, taking into account changes in the income distribution. His solution of the problem is, however, not entirely satisfactory in my opinion.

made better off than before.[5] It is not necessary that income will actually be redistributed so that everybody will in fact be better off; there will practically always be some individuals who are worse off than before. But it is sufficient that everybody *could* be better off. That is the definition of what is meant by saying that one situation is better and constitutes a larger national income than another.[6]

III

What we have stated above is an ideal case which underlies much of the free-trade reasoning. Everybody knows, of course, that it is an idealised case which is never completely realised in actual practice. There are many types of frictions and deviations from the ideal conditions caused by monopolistic and oligopolistic imperfections of the market, external economies and diseconomies, price and wage rigidities, lack of information, irreversibilities of the various curves involved, etc. Each of these conditions *may* operate in such a way as to make certain deviations from the free-trade policy rational on purely economic grounds.[7] But these imperfections may just as well be such as to strengthen the economic case for free trade. A mere

[5]See especially Samuelson's formulation in "The Gains from International Trade" (*Canadian Journal of Economics and Political Science,* 1939, reprinted in *Readings in the Theory of International Trade*).

[6]It should be clearly realised that such a statement necessarily implies a value judgment on the part of the scientist, and in that sense is not entirely objective. But it seems to me that the formula in the text expresses clearly what we have in mind, when we say that trade (under certain assumptions) or something else, say technological advance (again under certain assumptions) increases national income and economic welfare. There are, of course, other alternative or supplementary valuations possible: for example, certain value postulates with respect to inequality of income distribution could be introduced. Moreover, it may be questioned whether a situation in which more goods are available for everybody is under all circumstances to be regarded as a better situation. But we need not go into these questions in the present paper.

[7]The above list is not meant to be a complete catalogue of cases in which a certain amount of control can be justified. For example, protection for the purpose of improving the terms or for changing the income distribution will not be discussed in the present paper.

enumeration of possible imperfections and deviations from the ideal case does not prove more than the possibility that certain controls might be beneficial (provided of course that they are efficiently administered—which amounts to assuming quite a lot). On this practically all economists agree. In order to prove that the restriction of international trade (rather than the opposite) is justified, it is necessary to show that these imperfections are persistent (in other words that there is not even a tendency for the ideal situation to work itself out) and that they persistently operate in such a direction as to weaken (rather than to strengthen) the case for free trade.[8]

I shall now illustrate this by discussing with the aid of our diagrammatic apparatus a few cases of real and imaginary deviations from the ideal type.

It is often said that perfect mobility of factors within each country is a necessary condition for the ideal classical model. The old classical assumption of international immobility *vs.* national mobility of labor[9] is undoubtedly responsible for this misconception.[10] It can be easily shown, however, that what really causes trouble and may make trade detrimental and justify protection is rigidity of factor prices, which may or may not be associated with immobility of factors.

If perfect mobility of factors between industries were required, the theory of comparative cost would indeed be useless. For it is obvious that land and other natural resources as well as manmade factors of production, such as fixed capital, are in fact immobile locally and occupationally. So is labor to a large degree, at least in the short run.

---

[8]Thomas Balogh does not betray any awareness of the complexity of these issues, and seems to believe that he has proved something by a loose and inexact enumeration of possible deviations from the competitive ideal. "The Concept of a Dollar Shortage," *The Manchester School,* May 1949, p. 188.

[9]Ohlin makes the same assumption as the early classical writers for his "region." His inter-regional trade is the same as classical international trade, for regions are characterised by internal-factor mobility. See his *Interregional and International Trade.*

[10]See, *e.g.*, Thomas Balogh, *op. cit.* This paper is a convenient and inexhaustible store of fallacies and misconceptions in this field. He says "there must be free internal mobility of factors" (p. 188).

In order to bring the basic principles out quite clearly, let us make the extreme assumption that there is no factor mobility whatsoever. (This assumption is, of course, even more unrealistic than the opposite extreme of perfect mobility. In any real economy there is a large amount of mobility, even if labor is occupationally almost entirely immobile, through the possibility of redirecting intermediate goods such as iron and steel and other materials and fuels, certain types of machinery, transportation services, etc., from one industry to the other.)

Under this highly unrealistic assumption the production opportunity or transformation curve shrinks to the broken line, aPb[11] (Fig. 1). If all factors are in inelastic supply (implying that their prices are perfectly flexible), production will take place at point P. Assume that before trade the exchange ratio between A and B is the same as before, *i.e.*, is given by the slope of the straight line drawn through P. (It is true we cannot now say that it is equal to the marginal rate of transformation, because there is none if there is a kink at P. But we need not discuss here how the exchange rate is determined. If we permit ourselves the use of community indifference curves, we would say that the slope of the indifference curve going through P determines the exchange ratio between A and B.)

Now assume foreign trade is opened at the rate shown by the trade line TP'. The production point will stay where it was, but the country will import a certain amount of A in exchange for B and move to, say, T''.

T'' is certainly inferior to T or T', and its superiority over P is not so obvious as that of T. Still it can be shown that with trade the country is better off than without in exactly the same sense as in the case of T': By redistributing income it would be possible to make everybody better off, although in fact the A-producers will be worse off and the B-producers better off than before.[12]

---

[11]It could be objected that in this case there is, by assumption, no transformation possible. This is quite true; still it is useful to regard the broken line, aPb, as a degenerate transformation curve.

[12]The redistribution of income will, naturally, be much more drastic than in the case of mobility of factors. In fact, it may socially be intolerable.

Now let us introduce in addition to immobility of the factors complete rigidity of factor prices, A-producers are, say, organised and their union does not permit any reduction of their members' real wage in the face of falling demand and a lower price of A. In that case, production of A will fall, and some (or all) A-producers will become unemployed. Production will fall to, say, P'', and the trading point may be T''', which is clearly inferior to P. Conversely, if by a tariff or some other protective device the *status quo ante* is restored, the result is a definite improvement. Protection thus may become highly beneficial.[13]

A number of questions remain to be answered. First, how is point P'' determined? Why is it not higher up or lower down? We may say that the extent to which production will fall depends on the shape of the marginal-cost curve. Production will fall to that point where marginal cost has fallen to the price level at which A is being imported. If the production function is homogeneous and all factor prices are rigid, constant costs will prevail and production of A will cease altogether. We need not, however, make such extreme assumptions. If the production function is not homogeneous or if some factor prices are not rigid (the price of land and of fixed capital equipment are likely to fall, in other words, these factors are likely to be in inelastic demand—barring dynamic complications, *e.g.*, expectations that the price change will not last) or if inefficient workers will be dismissed first or if efficiency all around goes up, as is likely to be the case when unemployment rises—in all these cases marginal cost will fall when output is reduced, and P'' will not move all the way down.

On the other hand, it is perhaps worth pointing out that the distributional aspect may be absent: Suppose A and B are in joint supply (although without any possibility of changing their proportion). Then it would be impossible to distinguish between A and B-producers.

In terms of indifference curves, it is clear that T'' is superior to P.

[13]If we make, however, the by no means unreasonable assumption that in the meantime wages of the B-producers have become rigid at the new real wage-level, a tariff will not carry us back from T''' to P. While production of A will expand, production of B will shrink, and we shall arrive at a point to the left and probably below P.

A second question is whether T''' is necessarily inferior to P. The answer is no, not necessarily, not even if production of A ceases altogether. Suppose that the international terms of trade are extremely favorable, that is to say, that the trade line is very steep, for example, bT'' (not drawn in the diagram). Then it would be possible to reach T'' or a still more favorable point beyond T'' on the line bT''. This is really obvious: If any commodity can be obtained from abroad almost without cost, it would be better to discontinue production altogether, even though it involves a lot of unemployment.[14]

What we have proved is the *possibility* of an unfavorable outcome, not its necessity. This possibility is, naturally, the greater the lower the production point (*i.e.*, the greater unemployment) and the less favorable (*i.e.*, the less steep) the trade line.

A third question concerns the implied change from the assumption of inelastic to that of perfectly elastic factor supply. For absolute rigidity of factor prices is equivalent to perfect elasticity of factor supply, while previously we assumed (for simplicity) inelastic factor supply.

Two kinds of supply curves of labor must be carefully distinguished: (*a*) The supply curve of the individual worker reflecting his subjective preferences for work (or income) as against leisure, and the market supply obtained by adding all individual supply curves; (*b*) the market supply curve as determined by union policy (or minimum-wage legislation or some other collective regulation). I suggest that failure to distinguish between these two meanings of labor supply has confused the discussion about voluntary *vs.* involuntary unemployment. What is really meant by involuntary unemployment is an excess of supply in sense (*a*) over actual demand,

[14]Of course, under the extreme assumption made with respect to complete factor immobility, it would be still better to let production of A continue *and* to import additional amounts. But that would require either flexibility of wagerates of A-workers or an arrangement by which some of the gains made by B-producers through cheap imports of A can be transferred to the A-producers so as to maintain their real wage.

more people wishing to work at the current wage than can be employed. This is quite compatible with supply in sense (*b*) being equal to demand.[15]

There would he complications from the point of view of the welfare interpretation, if contrary to our assumption the supply curve in the sense (a), *i.e.*, the subjective, individual supply curve of labor, were not inelastic. Although it is impossibly unrealistic, let us assume that labor supply in that sense is entirely elastic. (Assume, for example, that people have income from other sources and don't care for work below a certain wage-level.) In that case the resulting unemployment would have to be called voluntary. Point T''' need then not be called inferior to P. If namely, economic welfare is then defined not only in terms of products A and B, but also interpreted to make allowance for "irksomeness" of labor, the reduction in commodity supply implied by T''' as compared with P would be offset by more leisure.[16]

---

[15]We may put the distinction in the following way: from the point of view of the preference of the individual workers, that is to say, from the welfare standpoint, unemployment is involuntary; but from the point of view of the union it is voluntary, because the union voluntarily withholds labor supply at a lower wage. This does, however, not necessarily mean that the unions act against the wish of their members, not even of their unemployed members.

I think that our construction is in accord with, in fact gives life to, Prof. T. Haavelmo's forbiddingly abstract scheme: "The Notion of Involuntary Economic Decisions" (*Econometrica*, Vol. 18, No. 1, January 1950, pp. 1 *et seq.*). Haavelmo is troubled, as any theorist who values precision and clarity may well be, by the problem of how to interpret and to reconcile with accepted theoretical notions the concept of "involuntary" decisions and "involuntary" unemployment. He reaches the sensible conclusion that "the concept of involuntary decisions is related to the comparison of alternative economic systems, and not to the decisions within a given system" (*loc. cit.*, p. 2).

Applied to our case we would have to say, that in a system not characterised by wage rigidities employment would be larger, and the difference in the amount of unemployment between the two systems is "involuntary unemployment."

[16]It is a terminological question whether in this case we should distinguish between national income and economic welfare, the former being defined in terms of products only, while the latter makes also allowance for disutility of labor and similar factors. It may be also observed that the case takes on another complexion, if labor supply becomes very elastic (as is likely to be the case) at a very low

IV

We have proved for the extreme case of factor immobility and factor-price rigidity that trade may be very detrimental. It should be observed that no adverse multiplier effects depending upon a temporary excess of imports over exports are involved. The balance of payments is in equilibrium all the time. The detrimental effect of trade, the failure to reach an optimum, is entirely due to the fact that a static optimum condition is not fulfilled: the equality between the price ratio and the marginal substitution ratio is not preserved.[17] The exchange ratio (reciprocal of money-price ratio) is given by the slope of $P''T'''$, while the ratio of marginal transformation is given by the slope of Pb (as was explained above, aPb can be regarded as a degenerate transformation curve). Thus, because the price mechanism does not function properly, the price line cuts the transformation curve instead of being tangential to it.[18]

It will be instructive to apply now the argument to a less extreme case in which only some, not all, factors are immobile and only some factor prices are rigid.

In Fig. 2, we compare three cases, T, T' and T''. We have two transformation curves. The outer one APB is drawn under the assumption that most factors can be shifted and that the price system functions competitively. It thus portrays the "ideal" case. If P is the situation before trade, the country moves by production from P to p, and from there by trade to T.

Now let us start from the same initial position P, but assume that a number of factors are immobile. The reason for the immobility may be technological or unwillingness to move. Then we get a more

---

wage-level. It then would sound rather artificial, if not callous, to say that those workers who do not care for work at a very low wage "don't care" for work and "prefer leisure." But we cannot pursue this matter at this point.

[17]This is an optimum condition, because we assumed, for simplicity, the terms of trade as given. If that assumption were dropped we would have to substitute for the international price ratio what might be called the "marginal terms of trade."

[18]We may also say the ratio of private marginal cost, which determines, and is equal to, the price ratio (since the commodity markets are assumed to be competitive), does not reflect the social ratio of marginal substitution.

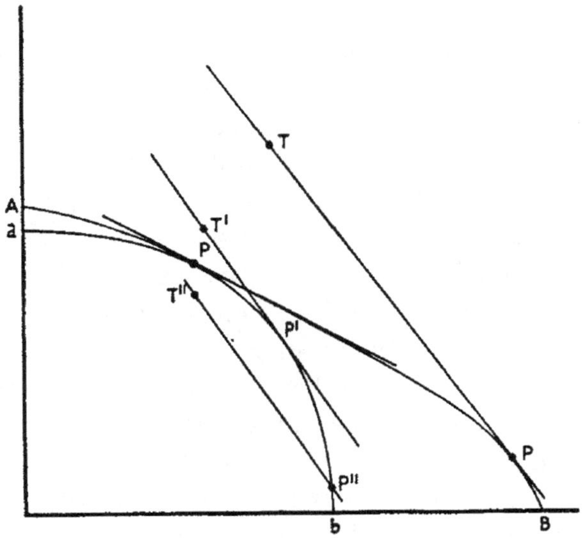

Figure 2.

sharply curved transformation line, *aPb,* inside *APB.* This curve might well be regarded as a short-run curve, inasmuch as in the short run factor mobility is in all probability much less than in the long run. We assume, however, that factor prices are still in inelastic supply, and that competition prevails, all prices including wages being perfectly flexible.

This case is then, in principle, no different from the preceding one. The country will move by production from P to p', and from there to T' by trade. T' is inferior to T, but superior to P. The inferiority of T' compared with T is due to the fact that owing to the reduced mobility of factors or, in other words, due to the lower adaptability of production, the output of B cannot be expanded so much as previously when the output of A is reduced. It should be also observed that when the production of A contracts, it is quite likely that certain factors of production will become idle; but only after their prices (imputed value) have fallen to zero. Suppose A is wheat growing, then marginal pieces of land will be abandoned. (On the other hand, in the B industry extra marginal factors may be drawn into employment.) The existence of unused free goods, extra marginal land, machinery, buildings, mineral deposits or even labor does, however, not constitute unemployment, although its emergence may constitute extreme hardship for the owners of the factors which have become worthless. The hardship is, of course, especially conspicuous in the case of labor, but is not necessarily confined to it. In the case of labor there is the further complication that its supply is surely not inelastic at low wages. Therefore labor will become unemployed long before its price has fallen to zero. But we come to this point presently.

The third case is distinguished from the second by the fact that in addition to immobility we assume price rigidity for some factors. We ought, then, to draw a third transformation curve more sharply curved than, and inside, the second one. But for simplicity I use the curve aPb again. It, thus, illustrates two alternative cases.

If the price mechanism does not work competitively, if certain factors used in the production of A cannot shift to industry B *and* refuse to accept a price cut, but choose to become unemployed, the price line will cease to be tangent to the transformation curve. The country will move by production from P to (say) p'', and by trade from p'' to, say, T''.

T'' is inferior to P, and trade is therefore detrimental. What was said in the preceding section concerning the precise location of p'' and the possibility of T'' being superior to P applies also to the present case.

Why the two cases (the case of mere immobility and the case of price rigidity) lead to different results can be explained as follows. In the "ideal" case we have the following equilibrium conditions: the money prices of A and of B are equal to their respective marginal cost. Each factor is remunerated according to its marginal productivity, and all factors that are willing and able to move receive the same remuneration in both industries.

Now suppose that output of A is reduced by one unit. A marginal cost's worth of factors is thereby set free. But these factors produce the same value in industry B. It follows that the price ratio is equal to the marginal rate of transformation.[19] No factor released

[19]This is, of course, true only if, as we assumed, the wage of those factors which can move is the same in both industries. Suppose factors can move freely, but that

from industry A becomes unemployed unless its price has fallen to zero, *i.e.*, unless its marginal productivity has vanished. Hence the existence or emergence of unutilised extramarginal factors does not affect the equality of the price and substitution ratio.

In the other case where some factor prices are rigid, factors become unemployed before their price has fallen to zero. Hence, when the production of A is curtailed by one unit, the production of B is expanded by less than the corresponding value because some of the factors go into unemployment rather than into employment in B. Therefore, the price ratio is not equal to the marginal rate of transformation. Expressed differently, the ratio of private marginal cost of A and B does not reflect the social ratio of marginal substitution, or, shorter, private and social cost deviate from one another.[20]

---

there exists a definite wage differential, wage-rates in one industry being, say, 20% higher than in the other; then the price ratio would not he equal to the marginal ratio of substitution. This is true whatever the cause for the existence of the wage differential. The welfare implications are, however, different according as to whether the wage differential is based: (*a*) on preferences of the workers (*e.g.*, the one type of work being more disagreeable than the other) or (*b*) on an arbitrary regulation. (See Viner's critique of Mihail Manoilesco's "The Theory of Protection and International Trade" in *Journal of Political Economy,* 1932, p. 121, and my *Theory of International Trade,* p. 197. This case could be analysed with the help of our diagrammatic apparatus. In fact Fig. 3 below could be used without any change to portray this case.

[20]In Pigou's terminology: Private and social marginal net product do not coincide.

The reader should remember that we have assumed inelastic supply of labor as far as the individual workers are concerned (as distinguished from the market supply as determined by collective action). This implies that our welfare scheme includes only alternative product cost and ignores other elements, *e.g.*, possible differences in the "irksomeness of labor" in the two lines of employment. In other words, economic welfare (national income) is defined in terms of products A and B only. We could, of course, introduce in addition to that disutility of labor. If the rigidity of factor prices, *i.e.*, elasticity of factor supply, were due to individual preference rather than to collective regulation, that is to say, if individuals preferred to go idle rather than to work below a certain wage, case 3 (T'') would not involve a welfare loss as compared with case 2 (T'), because the loss in terms of product would be voluntary: a certain amount of product would be voluntarily foregone in exchange either for more leisure or in order to avoid subjective or material cost of working.

We have established the possibility (though not necessity) of detrimental effects of trade in case of rigid prices and of beneficial effects of protection in the case of unemployment. It should be remembered that unfavorable multiplier reactions are excluded and changes on the income distribution ignored.

How important is the case here analysed? Is it a theoretical curiosum or a matter of practical importance?

It is dangerous to jump from such an abstract model to practical application, and there is room in an article not even for a sketch of how to fill the gap. Still I venture to say that, at least in the short run, it is a matter of serious practical concern. However, even in the short run certain qualifications would have to be made, protection would not be more than a *pis aller* and rational policy should not be concerned entirely with short-term considerations. But we cannot pursue these thoughts any farther at this point.

V

In this section two other cases will be briefly analysed which give rise to a deviation of price ratio from the marginal rate of transformation. Unemployment is not involved in either case.

The first case is the much-discussed case of external economies or diseconomies.[21] It is usually thought to be connected with the case of decreasing cost. Decreasing cost may be due to external economies.

To avoid misunderstanding, it should be emphasised that this construction does not neglect or minimise the hardship imposed on the owners of the factors whose income has fallen. These hardships may be severe, they may be socially intolerable. Compare what was said above concerning the neglect of income redistribution in the global welfare calculation. It is, of course, always possible to introduce additional value postulates concerning income distribution.

[21]The literature is fairly voluminous. See especially the famous controversy between F. P. Graham and F. H. Knight. Graham, "Some Aspects of Protection Further Considered" (*Quarterly Journal of Economics,* Vol. 37, 1923, p. 199 *et seq.*); Knight, "Some Fallacies in the Interpretation of Social Cost" (*ibid.,* Vol. 38, 1924, p. 582; Reply and Rejoinder, *ibid.,* Vol. 39). J. Viner has an illuminating review of the whole issue in his *Studies* (pp. 475–81). J. Tinbergen, *International Economic Co-operation* (Amsterdam–New York,

The assumption of external economies is, then, a way of making decreasing cost compatible with competition.

External economies (or diseconomies for that matter) need, however, not be associated with decreasing cost. Social as well as private costs may be increasing, and the underlying situation may therefore be quite stable and still there may be a deviation between social and private cost due to external economies or diseconomies, *i.e.*, due to certain cost-raising or cost-reducing factors which would come into play if one industry expanded and the other contracted—factors which for some reason or other are not, or not sufficiently, allowed for in private cost calculations.

This situation is depicted in Fig. 3. Production initially takes place at P. The true, social ratio of transformation is given by the slope of the transformation curve (line I). The international exchange ratio (again for simplicity assumed to be fixed) is given by the slope of line II. Commodity A being cheaper abroad ought to be imported in exchange for B. The country should move to p by production, and thence to (say) T by trade.

But now we assume that the ratio of private marginal cost of A and B and hence the domestic price ratio does not correspond to the true social-transformation ratio. Suppose it is given by the slope of line III. The exchange ratio overvalues B and undervalues A. This is due to external economies which could be realised and would lower the cost of production of B, if the B industry were expanded. These economies are, however, not recognised by B producers or for some other reasons fail to induce them to expand production.[22]

1945) devotes Appendix I, "Professor Graham's Case for Protection" (pp. 182–99) to a penetrating diagrammatic analysis of the subject.

On the broader issues about external and internal economies, private *vs.* social cost, the *locus classicus* is still Marshall's *Principles* and *Industry and Trade* and Pigou's *Economics of Welfare*.

[22]There is not enough space here for a thorough discussion of why this may be so. But let me say that it would be gratuitous simply to assume ignorance.

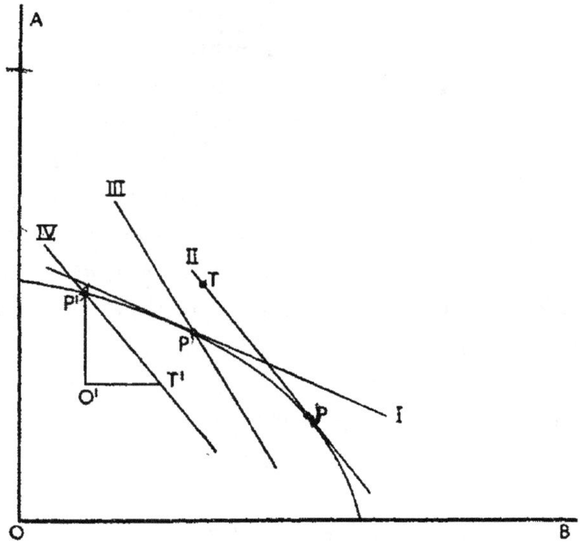

Figure 3.

If the discrepancy between private and social cost is as large as assumed in Fig. 3, the country will show a comparative price advantage in the "wrong" commodity. According to line III, B is cheaper abroad. Hence B will be imported and A exported. The production point will move to the left, to say p', where the ratio of private marginal cost (slope of line IV) becomes equal to the international price ratio (slope of line II). $p'o'$ of A is exported and

The reason may be that investments would have to be made the fruits of which cannot be appropriated by private individuals (*e.g.*, investment in the skill of the working population). On that point the literature mentioned above should be consulted.

It may be also noted, in parenthesis, that the existence of external economies involves a misallocation of resources in the absence of international trade. P would not be the optimum point. If I may be allowed to use briefly and inexactly community indifference curves, this could be demonstrated by pointing out that P is determined by the condition that an indifference line be tangent to line III, while the optimum point would be located at that point where an indifference curve is tangent to the transformation curve, that is somewhere to the right of P.

$o'T'$ imported. The new trading point, T', is inferior to P. This is, I believe, a correct representation of what Graham really meant.[23,24]

It is one thing, however, and an easy one at that, to point out the possible consequences of a divergence of private and social cost and to cite instances in which such a divergence is likely to arise. It is an entirely different and infinitely more difficult task first to demonstrate that such discrepancies do in fact occur frequently, persistently and on a large scale and to indicate concretely how these cases can be recognised and evaluated.

Most economists who have given serious thought to these problems have reached the conclusion that roughly, and as a rule, the ratios of private money costs do reflect the true social real cost ratios. Practically all economists recognise that there are exceptions to the rule, but they would insist that the burden of proof is on those who maintain that the exceptions are numerous, persistent, large, and, last but not least, practically recognisable and calculable.[25]

---

[23]If the discrepancy between the social and the private cost ratio is less extreme, *i.e.*, if line III is steeper than line I, but less steep than line II, the country would specialise in the "right" direction but not sufficiently. It would after trade be better off than before, but it would not reach the optimum point T. In that case an export or import subsidy (rather than a tariff) would be indicated.

[24]It is not, however, a literal rendering of what Graham said. Such a literal interpretation is not attempted. It presents considerable difficulties, because Graham was not too clear and seems to have changed his position in the course of the controversy. Cf. the literature quoted above, especially Viner and Tinbergen.

[25]We may again turn to Dr. Balogh's convenient store of all sorts of confusions to find an exception which proves the rule. He says: "It is wholly illicit to assume that *money prices* are proportionate to *long run social real costs.* We know that private money costs are not proportionate to social real costs, and neither are prices proportionate to private money costs" (*loc. cit.,* pp. 189 and 190. Italics in original). Dr. Balogh is, of course, unable to give any proof; he just asserts and states impressions. I would not blame him for that, because such a statement as his could, in the nature of the case, not be proved within the frame of a few articles. But he accuses me of "invoicing high authorities instead of proving" my contention that there is a rough correspondence between relative prices and real social cost. He seems to be not aware of the fact that the "high authorities," in fact practically all leading economists who have dealt with these matters, have, if not "proved" (such a theorem cannot be neatly proved like an arithmetical proposition), given plenty of reasons for accepting the contended proposition.

The theory of external economies is related to the reasoning underlying the infant-industry argument for protection, but the two are not identical.[26] The essence of the latter can, I think, be described with the help of our diagrammatic apparatus, as shown in Fig. 4. We start this time with a situation where trade takes place, the production point being P, the trading point T. Suppose now that by means of an import tariff on A, production is shifted from P to P' and the new trading point is at T'.[27] The new situation is inferior to T, which represents the fact that, with the assumptions made, protection is necessarily detrimental.[28]

They all treat deviations between private and social costs as exceptions to the rule of correspondence. This is, however, perfectly compatible with many shades of opinion about the relative importance or unimportance of these exceptions. Every leading economist who has dealt with these questions can be adduced (J. S. Mill, Marshall, Pigou, Taussig, Knight, Viner, etc.). Even Friedrich List could be read by Dr. Balogh with considerable profit. List was of the opinion that a manufacturing industry that cannot be kept alive on 20–30% tariff can be regarded as unsuited for the country concerned. (*Das Nationale System der Politischen Ökonomie,* Edition Berliner, 1930, p. 326.) Protection of 20–30% *ad valorem* has to be regarded as very moderate nowadays.

Dr. Balogh makes a lot of special risks attaching to foreign trade as an argument for protection and discrimination. It is true that the ultra-protectionist and chauvinistic economic policies advocated by Dr. Balogh which most countries have been now pursuing for many years (without waiting for Dr. Balogh's recommendations) have enormously increased the risk of investment abroad and at home for the purpose of building up export industries. But surely this fact cuts the other way than Dr. Balogh thinks. It increases the importance of expanding rather than of restricting international trade.

[26]On that I agree now with Viner (*Studies,* p. 482), while in my *Theory of International Trade* I held that Graham's case was but a variant of the infant-industry argument for protection. However, in view of the vagueness which attaches to much of the discussion and in view of the fact that different shades of each theory can be found, there would be not much point in a historical investigation about the closeness of their interrelation.

[27]The international terms are again assumed to be fixed. But that is not essential for the argument. The domestic terms of trade (internal price ratio including the tariff) is equal to the slope of the transformation curve at P', and the height of the tariff is given by the difference between the slope of the transformation curve and the slope of the trading line.

[28]If we drop the assumption that foreign demand is infinitely elastic and assume instead that the terms of trade for the protected country improve, protection may

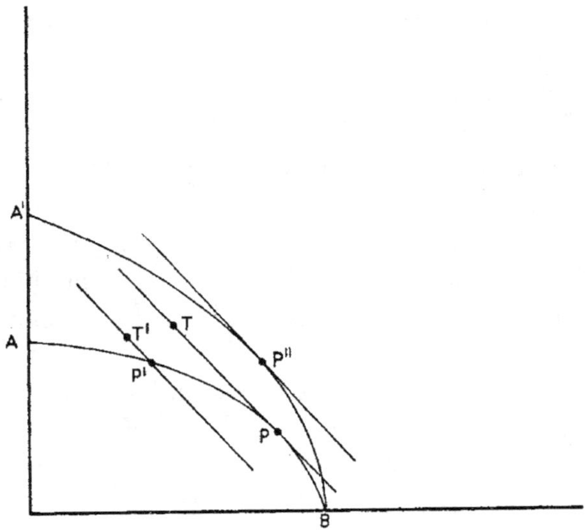

Figure 4.

The essence of the infant-industry argument is that a movement on the transformation curve will bring about an irreversible shift of the curve itself. Concretely, if the A-industry is protected and expands, methods of production will gradually be perfected, skills will be acquired, and so the short-run curve AB will assume the long-run shape $A'B$. The production point will shift to P''. In the new situation trade may or may not take place, and the country may export either A or B, *i.e.*, the trading point may be on either side of P'' depending upon "demand conditions."[29]

Again, it is an easy thing to state the assumptions, to derive the conclusions and to recognise that in principle the possibility must not be ignored that deliberate movements on the production-opportunity

be beneficial. This would be shown in our diagram by making the trading line steeper (not shown in the diagram). If it becomes sufficiently steep, T' may reach a position superior to T. In fact, as is well known, it can be shown that unless foreign demand is infinitely elastic there is always some tariff which makes T' superior to T.

[29]In terms of indifference curves: depending upon whether an indifference curve is tangent to the trading line at P'' or to the left or right of it.

curve may shift the curve itself. But it should also be remembered that, in principle, the shifts may be in either direction; there may be external diseconomies as well as economies, and the possibility of favorable shifts in production-opportunity curve is not confined to import commodities. Improvements may just as well be realisable in the export industries, in which case the opposite of a trade restriction would be indicated. In other words, the argument may cut either way, and it is a little suspicious that the argument is practically always used in one direction, that is to say for the justification of protection rather than of freer trade.

To go beyond the statement of possibilities, to generalise about the overall importance of the infant-industry effect, and to evaluate it in concrete cases is an extremely difficult task which requires not only theoretical acumen, but intimate empirical knowledge of industrial development and, above all, historical perspective. Most leading economists, beginning from J. S. Mill, Marshall, Taussig to Pigou and Viner, accept the principles. But those who made empirical studies, like Marshall and Taussig, became in the course of their studies somewhat sceptical with respect to the scope of the principle, and even more so concerning the chances of a rational application. It is to be hoped that the rapidly growing literature on the problem of developing underdeveloped countries will eventually add to our knowledge of these matters. But that is beyond the scope of the present paper.

Chapter 2

The Pure Theory of International Trade*

Robert Alexander Mundell†

The English classical model of foreign trade is the source of many propositions which form the body of international trade theory today. Despite attacks on other branches of classical theory it still survives as a basic tool of analysis. Its survival can be attributed to its applicability to leading policy issues in the country in which it originated, and to the power of its methodology: it was logically immune to the criticisms of general equilibrium and macroeconomic analysis.

The classical economists were content to establish the direction in which the terms of trade move as a result of such disturbances as dishoarding, tariff adjustments, devaluation, income transfers and productivity changes. Nowadays more refined methods make it possible to derive more implications from the model, implicit in their analysis, and to ascertain the quantitative extent of the change in the terms of trade. The purpose of this paper is to derive and summarize these results.

*Originally published in *The American Economic Review*, 50(1), pp. 67–110.

†The author is visiting professor of international economics at the Bologna Center, School of Advanced International Studies, The Johns Hopkins University.

Specifically, I shall construct an international trade model owing its origin to the classical school, and apply it to determine the exact effects on international equilibrium of unilateral transfers, productivity changes, export and import taxes, and production and consumption taxes. Many of the conclusions are already known, but it is believed that the methods employed will help to simplify the techniques used in this branch of international trade theory, and that the results established will provide a convenient survey of the subject. The first part of the analysis will be concerned with the implications of the two-country two-commodity model usually employed by the classical economists. In the final section an attempt is made to determine the validity of the results when there are many countries.

1. The Free Trade Model

Assume that there are two countries, A and B, in full employment, producing two commodities—X, which is exported by A, and Y, which is exported by B. Let capital letters denote production, small letters consumption, and subscripts, countries. Let T represent the capital exports (lending) of country A expressed in terms of X; let P denote the terms of trade, the price of Y in terms of X; and let D represent domestic expenditure.

The system can then be described by the following equations:

$$D_a \equiv x_a + Py_a = X_a + PY_a - T. \tag{1}$$

Domestic expenditure in A (in terms of X) equals national income minus net capital exports.

$$D_b \equiv x_b/P + y_b = X_b/P + Y_b + T/P. \tag{2}$$

Domestic expenditure in B (in terms of Y) equals national income plus net capital imports.

$$y_a = y_a(D_a, P). \tag{3}$$

The demand for Y in A depends on domestic expenditure and the terms of trade.

$$x_b = x_b(D_b, 1/P). \tag{4}$$

The demand for X in B depends on domestic expenditure and the terms of trade.

$$X_a = X_a(1/P); \tag{5}$$

$$Y_a = Y_a(P). \tag{6}$$

The production of X and Y in A depends on the terms of trade.

$$X_b = X_b(1/P); \tag{7}$$

$$Y_b = Y_b(P). \tag{8}$$

The production of X and Y in B depends on the terms of trade.

$$T = x_b - X_b - P(y_a - Y_a). \tag{9}$$

The net capital exports of country A equal the balance of trade of country A.

Variations in domestic expenditure in each country are assumed to depend on changes in policy. In the free-trade case the system is completed by the following equations:

$$D_a = D_a(T); \quad \text{and} \quad D_b = D_b(T/P).$$

We then have eleven independent equations in the twelve unknowns: $x_a, x_b, y_a, y_b, X_a, X_b, Y_a, Y_b, D_a, D_b, P$ and T, so there is one degree of freedom. Knowing the rate at which A is lending to B (i.e., T), we can solve for the equilibrium terms of trade (P); or, assuming that the terms of trade are fixed, we can find the rate of lending which will establish equilibrium.[1]

There are other, equivalent ways of expressing the same system. Equations (1) and (2) could be replaced by conditions stating that world production and world consumption of each good must be equal—these alternatives imply each other when combined with

---

[1]The system can be represented in one diagram by the Edgeworth-Bowley box diagram if production is fixed, and by the technique introduced by Meade [13] if production is variable.

The diagrams in the text provide an alternative proof of some of the propositions; but if the reader prefers to do so he can follow the argument without reference to the diagrams.

equation (9) expressing balance-of-payments equilibrium. Equations (3) and (4), the demand functions for the good which is imported in each country, could be replaced by the demand functions for the good which is exported since all income is spent—the part of domestic expenditure which is not spent on one good must be spent on the other good.

It will be convenient to define an import demand function for each country. The demand for imports is the difference between the quantities of the imported good demanded and supplied, i.e., $I_a = y_a - Y_a$, and $I_b = x_b - X_b$, where I_a and I_b are, respectively, the demands for imports in A and B. Then since the demand and supply functions depend only on domestic expenditure and the terms of trade, the import demand functions must also depend on these variables. Thus we have two more equations and two more unknowns:

$$I_a = I_a(D_a, P) \quad \text{and} \tag{10}$$

$$I_b = I_b(D_b, 1/P). \tag{11}$$

If we now substitute (10) and (11) in the balance-of-payments equation (9) we obtain

$$T = I_b(D_b, 1/P) - PI_a(D_a, P). \tag{12}$$

The task of the following analysis is to introduce into these equations various policy parameters, and to show how the equilibrium values of the variables are affected by changes in these policies. It is first convenient, however, to outline the procedure by which the effect of these changes may most simply be obtained.

2. Procedure

The purpose of comparative-statics analysis is to compare two positions of equilibrium distinguished from each other by a shift in some parameter. In this paper we call the parameter shift a "policy change." A policy change disturbs the initial equilibrium by causing an excess demand for one of the commodities which must be eliminated by an adjustment in some other variable at the new equilibrium. The adjusting or "equilibrating" variable may be another policy change, a reversal of the original policy change, or a process of adjustment which is sufficiently traditional—hence predictable—to be called "automatic."

In classical theory the adjustment mechanism was automatic. A policy change disturbed balance-of-payments equilibrium, induced a gold flow and, through changes in relative price levels, a change in the terms of trade. Today this mechanism is not so automatic, i.e., central bank and government reaction to disequilibrium in the balance of payments is less predictable. Besides the traditional inflation-deflation method of the gold standard a disequilibrium may be corrected by borrowing (in the short run), trade controls, tax changes, technological change (in the long run), or exchange rate adjustment. Most of these methods have been used by one country or another since the breakdown of the gold standard system to resolve balance-of-payments crises.

Because of this change in institutional response to disequilibrium any analysis of policy changes must be taxonomic. Questions like: "Do tariffs improve the balance of trade?" cannot be given an unequivocal reply—the answer depends on the other policies followed by the government. A tariff disturbs the initial equilibrium and therefore requires, for a new equilibrium to be reached, a change in some other policy; it may involve changes in any or all of the policies listed above.

But exploring all conceivable policy alternatives would be tedious and unrewarding; limits have to be imposed somewhere. For that reason I shall tentatively assume that the classical mechanism is operative, that the terms of trade "automatically" adjust to correct disequilibrium.[2] The first part of the comparative-statics analysis will therefore determine the effect of policy changes on the terms

[2]The terms of trade may be assumed to change by means of exchange rate or price level adjustments. If e is the price of a unit of B's currency in terms of A's currency, and P_a and P_b are the factor cost prices of exports in A and B, the terms of trade are $P = e.P_b/P_a$ in the free trade case. From a position of initial equilibrium an increase in e (devaluation by country A) would ultimately cause an offsetting change in P_b/P_a leaving the terms of trade and the balance of payments unaltered.

of trade. It will be shown later how the results can be manipulated to demonstrate the working of other mechanisms of adjustment.

The simplest way to derive the effect of a policy change on the terms of trade is to differentiate the balance-of-payments equation (12) with respect to the change in policy, and to substitute in the result the conditions necessary to satisfy the other conditions of equilibrium. A more intuitive way of getting the criterion, however, is to employ a device implicit in all comparative-statics analysis. This is to compute the excess demand caused by the policy change on the assumption that the adjusting variable (the terms of trade) is constant; and to equate this excess demand to the excess supply created by the actual change in the terms of trade. If, for example, we wish to find the criterion for the effects of a tax on the terms of trade, we first determine the excess demand caused by the tax at constant terms of trade and translate the coefficient of the tax change into the appropriate income or price elasticity; we then compute the excess supply of the same good created by a change in the terms of trade, translating its coefficient into the relevant elasticities. By equating the excess demand and the excess supply the criterion is established.[3]

One further point must be investigated. The adjustment mechanism implies a type of dynamic behavior and thus a condition

[3]This procedure, which may be called the "method of comparative statics," can be illustrated by two familiar examples drawn from economic theory. In the Marshallian demand-supply system, with mnemonic terminology, we have at equilibrium the condition that supply equals demand:

$$D(p;\alpha) = S(p) \tag{1}$$

where α is a parameter representing the position of the demand schedule. To determine the effect on price of a shift in the demand schedule first determine the excess demand caused by the shift at constant price; this equals

$$\frac{\partial D}{\partial \alpha}d\alpha. \tag{2}$$

The excess supply caused by an increase in price is equal to

$$\left(\frac{\partial S}{\partial p} - \frac{\partial D}{\partial p}\right) dp. \tag{3}$$

of dynamic stability. If the system is unstable it would not tend to approach the new equilibrium given by the comparative-statics analysis, and there would be little point in pursuing the comparative-statics analysis. On the other hand if the system is stable, a useful clue may be obtained from the stability conditions about the sign of the coefficient of the adjusting variable, the terms of trade.[4] The first step, then, is to examine the conditions of dynamic stability.

At the new equilibrium (2) and (3) must be equal so the criterion is

$$\frac{dp}{d\alpha} = \frac{\frac{\partial D}{\partial \alpha}}{\frac{\partial S}{\partial p} - \frac{\partial D}{\partial p}} \tag{4}$$

which is the criterion we set out to find.

In a simple Keynesian system we have, at equilibrium, equality of saving (S) and investment (I), i.e.,

$$I(\alpha) = S(y) \tag{5}$$

where y is income and α is a parameter representing autonomous investment. To find the effects of a shift in the investment schedule on income, first consider the excess demand for goods at constant income, i.e.,

$$\frac{\partial I}{\partial \alpha} d\alpha \tag{6}$$

and then the excess supply induced by a change in income, i.e.,

$$\frac{\partial S}{\partial y} dy = s' dy \tag{7}$$

where s' is the marginal propensity to save. At the new equilibrium the excess demand caused by the shift in investment and the excess supply created by the change in income must be equal. Equating (6) and (7) and rearranging terms we then get the familiar multiplier:

$$\frac{dy}{d\alpha} = \frac{\frac{\partial I}{\partial \alpha}}{s'}. \tag{8}$$

[4]By the correspondence principle [22, Ch. 9]. Thus in the first example cited in the preceding footnote, on the dynamic hypothesis that excess demand induces an increase in price, stability requires that:

$$\frac{\partial S}{\partial p} - \frac{\partial D}{\partial p} > 0.$$

Therefore the change in demand has the same sign as the resulting change in price.

3. Stability Conditions

An equilibrium is stable if a small displacement is followed by a return to equilibrium. I assume that the above system is stable if a displacement of the terms of trade from equilibrium sets in motion forces inducing a return to that equilibrium. Now a disequilibrium in the classical system induces a gold flow and a deterioration of the terms of trade of the deficit country: the system is therefore stable only if a fall in the terms of trade of the deficit country causes an improvement in its balance of payments. To find the stability conditions we need to compute the excess supply caused by a change in the terms of trade. This excess supply will simultaneously establish the coefficient of a change in the terms of trade for use in the comparative-statics analysis.

With no lending, and expenditure in each country constant, the balance of payments (B) of country A in terms of home goods can be written as follows:

$$B = I_b(1/P) - PI_a(P). \tag{13}$$

In equilibrium this must be zero. Now choose commodity units so that P is initially equal to unity; then at equilibrium the volume of B's imports equals the volume of A's imports so that we can write $I_b = I = I_a$ initially. Differentiating (13) we get

$$\frac{dB}{dP} = -\frac{PdI_b}{d(1/P)} - \frac{PdI_a}{d(1/P)} - I_a = I\left(-\frac{P}{I_b}\frac{dI_b}{d(1/P)} - \frac{P}{I_a}\frac{dI_a}{dP} - 1\right).$$

The first two terms in the bracket are, respectively, the elasticities of demand for imports in A and B; write these terms as η_a and η_b. For stability a fall in A's terms of trade must improve A's balance of payments so that the system is stable or unstable depending on

---

In the second example, on the dynamic hypothesis that income rises when there is excess demand for goods, stability requires that:

$$s' > 0$$

so an increase in investment induces an increase in income.

whether:

$$\frac{dB}{dP} = I(\eta_a + \eta_b - 1) \gtrless 0. \tag{14}$$

In words, the system is stable depending on whether the sum of the elasticities of demand for imports is greater or less than unity.[5] This is, of course, the familiar Marshallian condition.[6] (See Figure 1.)

The stability condition can be expressed in terms of one good only. To see this, recall equation (1) which expresses the equality of

---

[5]The dynamic behavior of the system may be approximated by the following differential equation:

$$\frac{dP}{dt} = k[PI_a(P) - I_b(1/P)] \tag{1}$$

which states that the speed of the change in the terms of trade is proportional to the discrepancy between foreign exchange payments and receipts. Expanding (1) in a Taylor series, omitting nonlinear terms, and choosing time units to make $k = 1$, we obtain

$$\frac{dP}{dt} = I(1 - \eta_a - \eta_b)(P - P^0) \tag{2}$$

where P^0, is the terms of trade at equilibrium. Equation (2) has a solution

$$P = P^0 + Ae^{-I(\eta_a+\eta_b-1)t}. \tag{3}$$

The equilibrium point is stable only if P eventually approaches P^0; this can only be the case if the other term in (3) disappears, i.e., if $\eta_a + \eta_b - 1 > 0$.

[6]Marshall's dynamic postulates differ from those described in the text and in the preceding footnote. The latter assumes that the budget equations in each country are instantaneously satisfied (each country is always at a point on its offer curve) but that markets are not necessarily cleared. Marshall's postulates are based on adjustments of offers toward the budget equations (offer curves) [11]. This difference corresponds roughly to the distinction made between instantaneous and lagged adjustments analyzed in Arrow and Hurwicz [1]. Marshall's adjustment process, which is rationalized by the varying profitability of export industries, admits the possibility of complex roots and therefore an oscillatory path to equilibrium. See Samuelson [22, pp. 266–68].

This discussion refers to the stability of an *equilibrium* rather than to the stability of a *system*. John Stuart Mill recognized the possibility of multiple equilibria without reference to stability (17, pp. 154–63], but his treatment was faulty. Marshall, in 1879, was aware [11, pp. 24–25] that a point of unstable equilibrium must be flanked by points of stable equilibria, that the number of equilibria must be odd, and that (therefore) if an equilibrium were unique it would be stable.

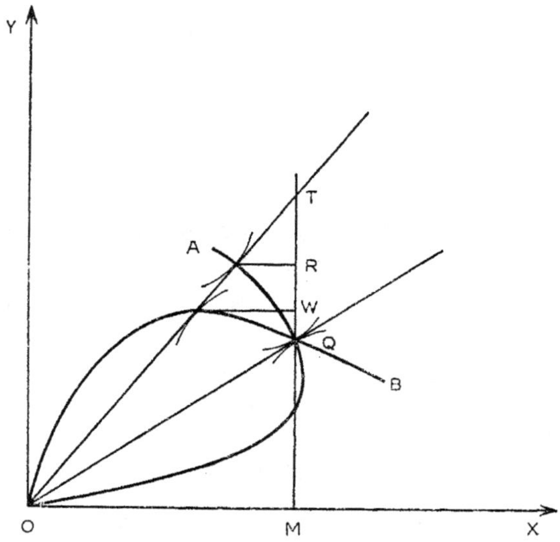

Figure 1. Stability Conditions.
The offer curves OA and OB intersect at initial equilibrium Q. A change in the terms of trade in the proportion TQ/QM in favor of A creates an excess demand for B's good and a deficit in A's balance of payments equal to RW (in terms of Y). The situation is therefore stable: Country A loses and country B gains gold, causing deflation in A and inflation in B until the gap RW is closed at the original equilibrium Q.

The stability conditions are derived as follows: Define the elasticities of demand for imports in each country,

$$\eta_a = \frac{RQ}{QM} \Big/ \frac{TQ}{QM} \quad \text{and} \quad \eta_b = \frac{TW}{QM} \Big/ \frac{TQ}{QM}$$

and the balance of payments deficit in A in terms of foreign goods,

$$\frac{dB}{p} = RW.$$

Then:

$$\begin{aligned} \frac{dB}{p} &= RW = QM \cdot \frac{TQ}{QM} \cdot \frac{RW}{TQ} = QM \cdot \frac{TQ}{QM} \cdot \frac{RQ + TW - TQ}{TQ} \\ &= QM \cdot \frac{TQ}{QM} \left[\frac{RQ}{QM} \cdot \frac{QM}{TQ} + \frac{TW}{QM} \cdot \frac{QM}{TQ} - 1 \right] \\ &= \text{(by definition) } I \frac{dP}{P} (\eta_a + \eta_b - 1). \end{aligned}$$

income (plus borrowing) and expenditure in country A. With lending zero this equation can be written:

$$X_a - x_a = P(y_a - Y_a) = PI_a.$$

i.e., offers of exports equal the value of imports demanded. Substituting in (13) and making a similar substitution for I_b, we can write the balance of payments (with no lending) as follows:

$$B = (x_b - X_b) - (X_a - x_a).$$

Differentiating and rearranging terms we get:

$$\frac{dB}{dP} = \left(\frac{d(x_a + x_b)}{dP}\frac{p}{(x_a + x_b)} - \frac{d(X_a + X_b)}{dP}\frac{P}{(X_a + X_b)}\right)\frac{X}{P}$$

where X is world production and consumption at equilibrium, and the arguments in the bracket are, respectively, the world elasticity of demand for X and the world elasticity of supply of X:

$$\left(\eta_x = -\frac{d(x_a + x_b)}{d(1/P)} \cdot \frac{(1/P)}{(x_a + x_b)}\right)$$
$$\left(\epsilon_x = -\frac{d(X_a + X_b)}{d(1/P)} \cdot \frac{(1/P)}{(X_a + X_b)}\right).$$

Hence:

$$\frac{dB}{dP} = X(\eta_x + \epsilon_x), \tag{15}$$

where units are chosen so that P is, at equilibrium, equal to unity. By similar reasoning

$$\left[\text{from the balance of payments equation, } \frac{B}{P} = (Y_b - y_b) - (y_a - Y_a)\right]$$

we find that:

$$\frac{dB}{dP} = Y(\eta_y + \epsilon_y), \tag{15'}$$

where η_y and ϵ_y are the elasticities of world demand for, and supply of, Y.[7]

The elasticities of demand for X and Y are defined to be positive provided that these goods are not Giffen goods; and the elasticities of supply of X and Y are defined to be positive provided that opportunity costs are not decreasing. It may then be seen that the system is necessarily stable if neither good is a Giffen good and opportunity costs are not decreasing. But even if the goods are Giffen goods, positive supply elasticities may yet make the system stable.

In the remainder of this paper I assume that the stability condition is satisfied, an assumption which, as the foregoing remarks suggest, does not appear very restrictive.[8]

4. Unilateral Payments

The first policy change we shall consider is a unilateral payment from one country to the other. This involves two parts: a *financial* transfer and a *real* transfer. The financial transfer refers to the accumulation and liquidation of debt on the part of individuals or governments in each country, while the real transfer refers to the induced movement of goods. Assume that A is the transferring country.

In the case of a private flow of capital (ignoring interest payments) lenders in A buy the debt of borrowers in B, the former financing the purchase out of an excess of saving over investment, the latter disposing of the proceeds by an excess of investment over saving. Because of the identity of income-less-lending and expenditure [equations (1) and (2)] the excess of investment over saving in B, and saving over investment in A, must each equal the transfer.

---

[7]Mosak derived stability conditions in terms of one good only [18, Ch. 4], See also Johnson [6, p. 98].

When trade is not initially in balance a slight adjustment is required in the stability condition. See Hirschman [5].

[8]Marshall's judgment is probably too strong: "...it is not inconceivable, but it is absolutely impossible" [12, p. 354].

In the case of intergovernmental transfers such as reparations payments or foreign aid, the government in A (the paying country) grants credits to B, the former financing the credits by means of, say, an income tax, the latter disposing of the proceeds by means of, say, an income subsidy. Again, because of the identity of income-less-lending and expenditure, the budget surplus in A and the budget deficit in B are each equal to the transfer.

Whatever the type of transfer and however it is financed and disposed of, domestic expenditure in A is reduced, and in B is increased, by the amount of the transfer. These changes in expenditure induce changes in demand which, at constant terms of trade, create disequilibrium in the balance of payments. The transfer problem may then be posed as the problem of determining the direction and extent of the change in the terms of trade required to eliminate the balance-of-payments disequilibrium.

The Terms of Trade. To find the effects of a transfer on the terms of trade we first determine the excess demand created by the expenditure changes at constant terms of trade. This can be done in terms of either good since an excess demand for one good implies an excess supply of the other good.

The reduction in domestic expenditure in A decreases the demand for Y in A at constant terms of trade by:

$$P\frac{\partial y_a}{\partial D_a}dD_a = m_a dD_a$$

here m_a is the marginal propensity to spend on imports in A. The increase in domestic expenditure in B increases the demand for Y in B by:

$$\frac{\partial y_b}{\partial D_b}dD_b = c_b dD_b$$

where c_b is the marginal propensity to spend on home goods in B. The excess demand at constant terms of trade is therefore the sum of these changes or:

$$m_a dD_a + c_b dD_b = (c_b - m_a)dT,$$

noting that the changes in expenditure in each country are equal to the change in lending, i.e., $-dD_a = dD_b = dT$. Now expenditure in each country is divided between home goods and imports so that the sum of the marginal propensities to spend on home goods and imports is unity; thus $c_b + m_b = 1 = c_a + m_a$.[9] We can now make use of this result to translate the above criterion into a number of equivalent forms. The most convenient for our purposes is the familiar one:

$$(1 - m_a - m_b)dT, \tag{16}$$

which states that transfer creates an excess demand for, or excess supply of, the good of the transferring country depending on whether the sum of the marginal propensities to spend on imports is greater or less than unity. Only in the special case where the receiving country increases its consumption of the two goods in the same proportion that the paying country does without them $(1 - m_a - m_b = 0)$ will no change in the terms of trade be required. If $m_a + m_b > 1$ the receiving country experiences a deficit; if $m_a + m_b < 1$, the paying country suffers a deficit. (See Figure 2.)

To correct the disequilibrium equal to $(1 - m_a - m_b)dT$ a change in the terms of trade is required. But we already know from the stability condition (14) that a change in the terms of trade causes an excess supply of B's good (or an excess demand for A's good, or improves A's balance, or worsens B's balance) by an amount equal to:

$$(\eta_a + \eta_b - 1)IdP. \tag{17}$$

The excess demand for B's good at constant terms of trade must, at the new equilibrium, be equal to the excess supply of B's good caused by the actual change in the terms of trade. Equating of (16)

[9]Differentiation of $D_a = x_a + Py_a$ and $D_b = x_b/P + y_b$ with respect to D_a and D_b yields:

$$1 = \frac{\partial x_a}{\partial D_a} + P\frac{\partial y_a}{\partial D_a} = c_a + m_a, \quad \text{and}$$
$$1 = \frac{1}{P}\frac{\partial x_b}{\partial D_b} + \frac{\partial x_b}{\partial D_b} = m_a + c_a.$$

and (17) therefore provides the general criterion for the change in the terms of trade:

$$\frac{dP}{dT} = \frac{1 - m_a - m_b}{I(\eta_a + \eta_b - 1)}. \tag{18}$$

It may be seen that the higher are the price elasticities of demand for imports the smaller will be the change in the terms of trade (a small change relieves a large excess demand). In the limiting case where one of the elasticities is infinite, no change in the terms of trade is required. Similarly, the closer to unity is the sum of the marginal propensities to import, the smaller is the excess demand to be eliminated by a change in the terms of trade, and so the smaller is the actual change in the terms of trade.[10]

Real Income. How is real income affected by a grant or gift from one country to the other? In the reparations discussions of the interwar period the view was widely held that the terms of trade of the paying country must fall, thus imposing an additional burden. The change in real income implicit within the change in the terms of trade was called the "transfer burden."

The change in real income due to transfer is composed of two effects—the direct effect of the change in expenditure, and the income effect implicit within the change in the terms of trade. Thus the real income of the receiving country improves by more or less than the transfer itself depending on whether the terms of trade improve or

[10]To obtain the criterion directly, differentiate the balance of payments equation:

$$T = I_b(D_b, 1/P) - PI_a(D_a, P)$$

with respect to T. This yields:

$$1 - m_b\frac{dD_b}{dT} + m_a\frac{dD_a}{dT} = \frac{\partial I_b}{\partial(1/P)}\frac{d(1/P)}{dT} - P\frac{\partial I_a}{\partial P}\frac{dP}{dT} - I_a\frac{dP}{dT}.$$

Expenditure changes are equal in absolute value to the transfer so

$$\frac{dD_b}{dT} = -\frac{dD_a}{dT} = 1.$$

Then by forming elasticities from the terms on the right, and taking P initially equal to unity, we get (18).

For a sample of recent literature on the transfer problem see [18, Ch. 4] [15] [7] [23]; and for a survey of earlier literature see Viner [24, pp. 290–3377].

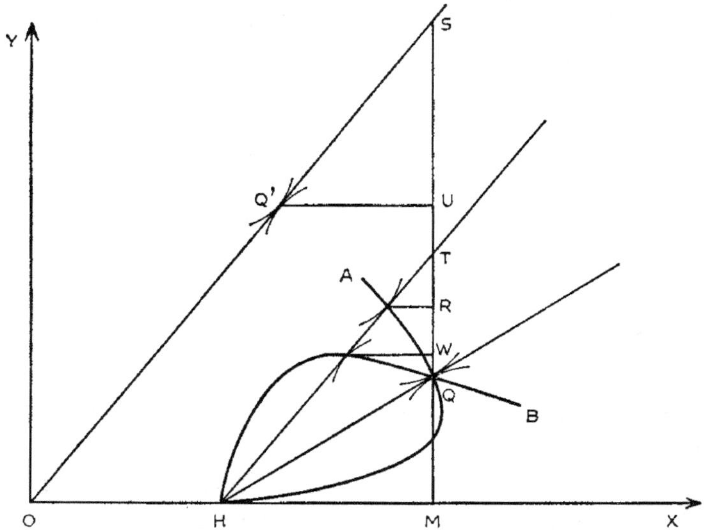

Figure 2. The Transfer Problem.

The pretransfer offer curves (not drawn) are assumed to intersect initially at Q'. Assume that country A makes a payment equal to OH of X to country B. Then at constant terms of trade expenditure in A is reduced and in B is increased by OH of X or ST of Y. These changes in expenditure induce A to buy UR less of Y and B to buy UW more of Y, creating an excess demand for Y and a deficit in A's balance of payments equal to RW. To eliminate this excess demand a deterioration in A's terms of trade is required until a new equilibrium such as Q is achieved. The new equilibrium Q is determined by the intersection of the new offer curves HA and HB which originate from the new endowment-position H.

The criterion for the change in the terms of trade following transfer may be derived as follows: Define the marginal propensities to import in each country,

$$m_a = \frac{UR}{ST} \quad \text{and} \quad m_b = 1 - c_b = 1 - \frac{UW}{ST} = \frac{SU - TW}{ST},$$

and the transfer

$$\frac{dT}{P} = \frac{OH}{OH/ST} = \text{ST in terms of } Y.$$

Then the deficit in the balance of payments of country A due to the transfer at constant prices (in terms of Y) is:

$$\frac{dB}{P} = RW = \left[\frac{UW}{ST} - \frac{UR}{ST}\right] ST = \left[1 - \frac{SU - TW}{ST} - \frac{UR}{ST}\right] \frac{ST}{OH} OH$$

$$= (\text{by definition})(1 - m_a - m_b)\frac{dT}{P}.$$

worsen. For small changes we can approximate the income effect of a change in the terms of trade by the change in cost of the initial volume of imports, i.e., by IdP. The change in real income as a result of transfer is therefore approximately:

$$\frac{dU_b}{dT} = -\frac{dU_a}{dT} = 1 + I\frac{dP}{dT} \tag{19}$$

where U_a and U_b are, respectively, the real incomes of A and B. Now substituting for dP/dT from (16) we obtain an approximate quantitative measure of the change in real income evaluated at pretransfer prices:

$$\frac{dU_b}{dT} = -\frac{dU_a}{dT} = 1 + \frac{1 - m_a - m_b}{(\eta_a + \eta_b - 1)}. \tag{20}$$

It will now be convenient to introduce a relationship between price elasticities and income propensities based on Slutsky's separation of price effects into income and substitution effects. A price elasticity of demand can always be written as the sum of a compensated (pure substitution) price elasticity and an income propensity. We can therefore write the price elasticity of demand for imports as the sum of the compensated elasticity of demand for imports and the marginal propensity to spend on imports. If the primes denote the compensated elasticities we have $\eta_a = \eta'_a + m_a$ and

---

Figure 2 (***Continued***).
On the other hand we also have, from Figure 1,

$$\begin{aligned}\frac{dB}{P} &= QM \cdot \frac{TQ}{QM}\left[\frac{RQ}{QM} \cdot \frac{QM}{TQ} - \frac{TW}{QM} \cdot \frac{QM}{TQ} - 1\right] \\ &= I\frac{dP}{P}(\eta_a + \eta_b - 1). \\ \therefore \frac{dP}{dT} &= \frac{1 - m_a - m_b}{I(\eta_a + \eta_b - 1)}.\end{aligned}$$

$\eta_b = \eta'_b + m_b$.[11] Since pure substitution effects are, in the two-good case, always positive the ordinary elasticity of demand for imports is always larger than the marginal propensity to import by an amount which depends on the size of substitution effects. (See Figure 3.)

Using this relationship we can manipulate (20) to get:

$$\frac{dU_b}{dT} = -\frac{dU_a}{dT} = \frac{\eta_a - m_a + \eta_b - m_b}{\eta_a + \eta_b - 1} = \frac{\eta'_a + \eta'_b}{\eta_a + \eta_b - 1}. \qquad (21)$$

From this criterion it can be seen that the real income of the receiving country can only decline, as a result of transfer, if the system is unstable.[12] Assuming stability, the higher are m_a and m_b (the

---

[11]Consider any demand function of the form $I = I(D, P)$ and differentiate with respect to P. This yields:

$$\frac{P}{I}\frac{dI}{dP} = P\frac{\partial I}{\partial D}\frac{dD}{IdP} + \frac{P}{I}\frac{\partial I}{\partial P}$$

after multiplying by P/I. Now $-P/I\partial I/\partial P$ is the (money-income constant) elasticity of demand, η, and $P\partial I/\partial D$ is the marginal propensity to spend, m. Thus:

$$\frac{P}{I}\frac{dI}{dP} = m\frac{dD}{IdP} - \eta.$$

A change in price can be associated with a change in real income approximately equal to the change in cost of the initial amount bought, *IdP*. If expenditure is adjusted to compensate for this change in real income, i.e., if $dD = IdP$, then $-P/IdI/dP$ becomes the compensated elasticity of demand, η', and we get

$$\eta = +\eta'.$$

If indifference curves are convex all substitution effects are positive, so $\eta' > 0$. From this it follows that the elasticity of demand for imports is always greater than the marginal propensity to import. A *fortiori* the sum of the elasticities of demand for imports is greater than the sum of the marginal propensities to import so that if $m_a + m_b$ is equal to, or exceeds, unity the exchange market is necessarily stable. Alternatively, an unstable exchange market implies that the sum of the marginal propensities to import is less than unity. J. E. Meade has made extensive use [14] of this relation; his stability condition is split into income and substitution effects and, in our notation, is $\eta'_a + \eta'_b + m_a + m_b - 1$.

[12]Leontief produced an example [9] consistent with convex indifference curves, where the change in the terms of trade in favor of the paying country is so great that the real income of the latter improves as a result of the transfer. Equation (21) proves that this cannot happen unless the system is unstable. The identification of this "Leontief Effect" with instability is due to Samuelson [22, p. 29].

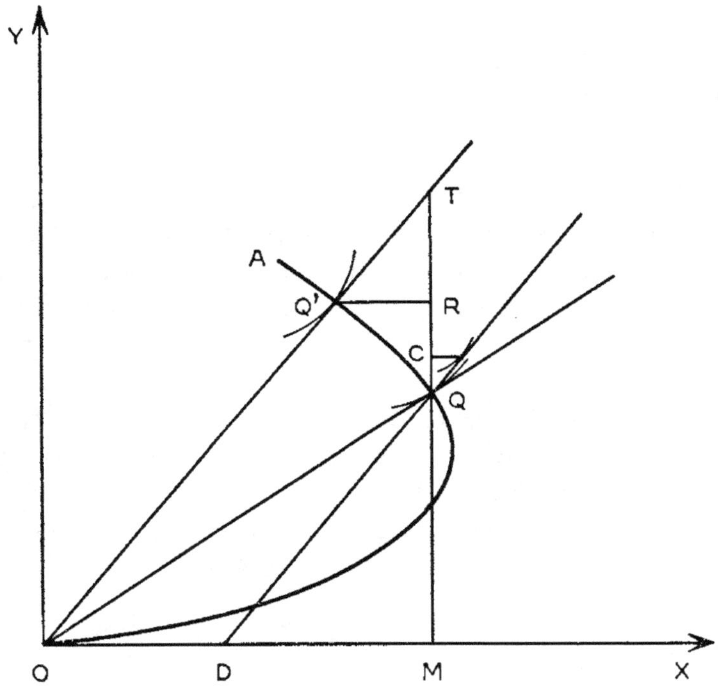

Figure 3. Income and Price Effects.
Initial equilibrium is at Q on A's offer curve OA. Suppose that the terms of trade change in the proportion TQ/QM, and that at the new terms of trade A trades at the point Q'. The income effect of this change in the terms of trade can be approximated by OD in terms of X or TQ in terms of Y, where DQ is drawn parallel to OT.

To prove the relation between compensated and ordinary elasticities: Define the elasticity of demand for imports in A,

$\eta_a = \frac{RQ}{QM} / \frac{TQ}{QM}$, and the marginal propensity to import in $A, m_a = \frac{RC}{TQ}$.

Then

$$\eta_a - m_a = \frac{RQ}{TQ} - \frac{RC}{TQ} = \frac{CQ}{TQ}.$$

But

$$\frac{CQ}{TQ} = \frac{CQ}{QM} \Big/ \frac{TQ}{QM},$$

which is the elasticity of demand for imports with the income effect removed, i.e., the compensated elasticity of demand for imports, η_a'.

marginal propensities to import) the smaller is the increase in real income of the receiving country, since income effects enter only in the denominator of (21).[13]

5. Productivity Changes

Assume that the country experiencing the productivity increase is completely specialized and that expenditure increases by the full amount of the increase in output. We shall first determine the effects of a change in productivity on the terms of trade, and then its influence on real income.

The Terms of Trade. To determine the effect of a change in productivity on the terms of trade we first determine the excess demand created for one of the goods on the assumption that the terms of trade are constant. If output in country A increases by dX^* then the change in demand for imports in A is

$$P\frac{\partial I_a}{dD_a}\frac{dD_a}{dX^*}dX^* = m_a dX^*$$

since expenditure (equals money income) increases by the full amount of the increase in output. Since at constant terms of trade no change occurs in country B, this is also equal to the *excess* demand for imports in A. This excess demand must be eliminated by a change in the terms of trade. The criterion is therefore:

$$\frac{dP}{dX^*} = \frac{m_a}{I(\eta_a + \eta_b - 1)}. \tag{22}$$

[13]Transfer analysis has many applications in economic theory. It applies to any redistribution of income between sectors, individuals or groups within a country. In the Keynesian problem of income redistribution a gift or tax-cum-subsidy from the rich to the poor increases or decreases effective demand depending on whether the marginal propensity to spend (MPS) of the rich is less or greater than that of the poor. In public finance theory an increase in government spending financed by new taxes stimulates effective demand if the MPS of the government is greater than that of the public. And in monetary theory a fall in the price level stimulates effective demand if the MPS of creditors is greater than that of debtors (including governments and central banks).

This result is obvious: an increase in the world output of X must lower the relative world price of X. The only exception (apart from constant costs and incomplete specialization, or perfect substitution in consumption) is the case where the country which has grown spends all of its increased income on its own good $(m_a = 1 - c_a = 0)$.[14]

Equation (22) can be translated into proportional changes by multiplying both sides by X (output) and dividing by P, with the following result:

$$\frac{dP/P}{dX^*/X} = \frac{m_a X/PI_a}{\eta_a + \eta_b - 1} = \frac{\sigma_a}{\eta_a + \eta_b - 1}, \tag{23}$$

where σ_a is the marginal propensity to spend on imports divided by the average propensity to spend on imports—i.e., the income elasticity of demand for imports. Alternatively we can express the criterion in terms of annual rates of change as follows:

$$\frac{P}{\dot{R}} = \frac{\sigma_a}{\eta_a + \eta_b - 1} \tag{24}$$

where $\dot{P}$ is the percentage deterioration of A's terms of trade per year and $\dot{R}$ is the annual rate of growth.

By following a similar procedure for country B we can find the annual percentage change in the terms of trade when both countries are growing:

$$P = \frac{\sigma_a R_a - \sigma_b R_b}{\eta_a + \eta_b - 1} \tag{25}$$

where σ_b and $\dot{R}_b$ are, respectively, the income elasticity of demand for imports in B and the annual rate of growth of B.

---

[14] To derive this criterion directly, differentiate $T = I_b(D_b, 1/P) - PI_a(D_a, P)$ with respect to X^* (output in A). With lending (T) constant and zero, this yields

$$\left(-\frac{\partial I_b}{\partial(1/P)} - \frac{\partial I_a}{\partial P} - 1\right)\frac{dP}{dX^*} = m_b\frac{dD_b}{dX_a^*} - m_a\frac{dD_a}{dX_a^*}.$$

Expenditure in B is constant (in terms of B's good) so $dD_b/dX_a^* = 0$; but expenditure in A increases *pari passu* with output, i.e., $dD_a/dX^* = 1$. Then, forming elasticities from the terms of the left, we get equation (22) above.

Real Income. A more interesting question is whether or not real income will increase or decrease as a result of a change in productivity. An increase in productivity affects real income in two ways which work in opposite directions. On the one hand real income increases by the full amount of the change in output at constant terms of trade; but, against this may be set the negative income effect of the actual deterioration in the terms of trade. We may very simply derive a measure of the change in real income by adding the effects of the change in real income at constant terms of trade, and the reduction in income due to the change in the terms of trade. The change in real income is $dU_a^* = dX_a - IdP$. Dividing by dX_a^* and applying equation (22) we obtain the following criterion:

$$\frac{dU_a}{dX_a^*} = 1 - I\frac{dP}{dX_a^*} = 1 - \frac{m_a}{\eta_a + \eta_b - 1}. \tag{26}$$

Real income will be increased by growth provided that $\eta_a + \eta_b > 1 + m_a$, i.e., if the sum of the elasticities of demand for imports is greater than unity plus the marginal propensity to import. Note that violation of this condition is consistent with stability. (See Figure 4.)

It will clarify the meaning of (26) if we make use of the relationship used in the previous section between "ordinary" and "compensated" elasticities of demand for imports—in particular, $\eta_a = \eta_a' + m_a$. Manipulating (26) we get

$$\frac{dU_a}{dX_a} = \frac{\eta_a - m_a + \eta_b - 1}{\eta_a + \eta_b - 1} = \frac{\eta_a' + \eta_b - 1}{\eta_a + \eta_b - 1}. \tag{27}$$

Thus real income will increase in the growing country if $\eta_a' > 1 - \eta_b$, i.e., if the compensated elasticity of demand for imports in the growing country is greater than unity minus the ordinary elasticity of demand for imports in the other country. This criterion may be simplified some-what by substituting in it the well-known relation between the elasticity of demand for imports and the elasticity of supply of exports (ϵ) : $\eta_b - 1 = \epsilon_b$ The criterion is therefore $\eta'_a + \epsilon_b \gtrless 0$.[15]

An alternative, direct method of getting this criterion is to apply the "method of comparative statics." To find whether real income in the growing country increases or decreases first determine the excess demand for imports on the tentative supposition that real income in A is constant. If real income is constant the terms of trade move against A so there is a pure substitution effect, $-\eta'_a IdP$, which measures the increase in demand for imports in A. On the other hand the increase in supply of imports forthcoming from B due to the change in the terms of trade is $\epsilon_b IdP$. The excess demand at constant real income is therefore $-(\eta'_a + \epsilon_b)IdP$. The deterioration in A's terms of trade which leaves A's real income unchanged is therefore too great or too little to relieve the excess demand due

---

[15]This relationship can be derived from the income = expenditure condition. From equation (2), with no lending, we have:

$$x_b/P + y_b = X_b/P + Y_b$$

$$\text{or} \quad Y_b - y_b = \frac{1}{P}(x_b - X_b)$$

$$\text{or} \quad E_b = \frac{1}{P} I_b$$

where E_b represents B's offers of exports. Differentiating, and taking P as initially unity, we have:

$$\frac{P}{E_b}\frac{dE_b}{dP} = \frac{P}{I_b}\frac{dI_b}{dP} - 1,$$

after dividing by $E_b = I_b/P$.

Thus $\epsilon_b = \eta_b - 1$, recalling that

$$\frac{P}{I_b}\frac{dI_b}{dP} = -\frac{1/P}{I_b}\frac{dI_b}{d(1/P)} = \eta_b.$$

Note that when the elasticity of demand is unity the elasticity of supply of exports is zero; this means that the same amount of exports is spent on imports regardless of the terms of trade.

A geometric proof of this relation can easily be got from Figure 3 or from Marshall's analysis [11, pp. 337–38].

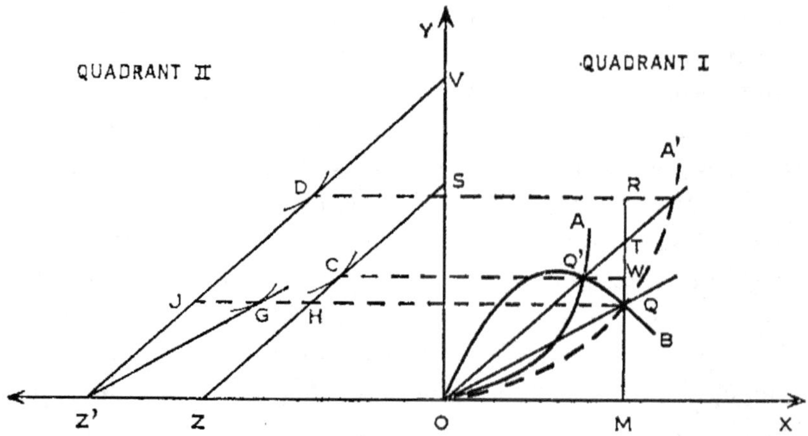

Figure 4. Productivity, the Terms of Trade and Real Income.

Quadrant I illustrates trade equilibrium with the initial offer curves, OA and OB, intersecting at Q'. Quadrant II illustrates production and consumption equilibrium in country A: Output in A is initially OZ of X; consumption equilibrium is at C (the length and slope of ZC is equal to the length and slope of OQ').

Suppose that output and expenditure in A increase to OZ' in terms of X. Then at constant terms of trade inhabitants of A demand more of both goods (in the absence of inferior goods), wishing to consume at a point like D. This means that, at any given terms of trade, A demands more imports than before the productivity change so that A's offer curve unambiguously shifts to the right (quadrant I). At the original terms of trade there is an excess demand for Y and a deficit in A's balance of payments equal to RW. The disequilibrium induces a flow of gold from A to B and a deterioration in A's terms of trade.

To connect the ratio of the change in the terms of trade TQ/QM to the increase in output ZZ', i.e., to derive a criterion for the change in the terms of trade, first define the marginal propensity to import in A. Since expenditure increases by VS at constant terms of trade and the demand for imports increases by the vertical distance between C and D, i.e., by RW, we have $m_a = RW/VS$. Now the deficit in A's balance of payments at constant terms of trade is:

$$\frac{dB}{P} = RW = \frac{RW}{VS} \cdot VS = \frac{RW}{VS} \cdot ZZ' \cdot \frac{VS}{ZZ'} = m_a dX^*/P,$$

where $dX^* = ZZ'$. On the other hand we know from the analysis of Figure 1 that:

$$\frac{dB}{P} = QM \cdot \frac{TQ}{QM}(\eta_a + \eta_b - 1).$$

It follows that:

$$\frac{dP}{dX^*} = \frac{m_a}{I(\eta_a + \eta_b - 1)}.$$

to the productivity change depending on whether $\eta'_a + \in_b \gtrless 0$. The criterion for the change in real income is thus established since, depending on whether the terms-of-trade change has been too great or too little, real income increases or decreases.

It appears then that a country may be worse off with, than without, the improvement in productivity. Growth may be "damnifying."[16] Too rapid growth of the export industries of one country, and the resultant attempt to push exports onto world markets, results in such a large decline in the terms of trade that the negative income effect of the change in relative prices is greater than the positive income effect of the increase in domestic output at constant prices. The case of the group of primary-producing countries readily presents itself. And, if the model were applied to different sectors within a single economy, it might be found that U.S. agriculture is another example.

Nevertheless, this possibility does not present a valid argument against growth. In the first place the conditions under which

---

Figure 4 (***Continued***).

It is easily seen that the shift in A's offer curve is greater the higher is the marginal propensity to import in A, and that if the latter is zero no shift occurs (all the extra expenditure in A is spent on home goods).

The change in real income in A, as a result of the productivity increase, is HG, measured at pretransfer prices. The criterion:

$$\frac{dU_a}{dX^*} = \frac{GH}{ZZ'} = 1 - \frac{JG}{ZZ'} = 1 - \frac{TQ}{VS} = 1 - I\frac{dP}{dX^*} = \frac{\eta'_a + \eta_b - 1}{\eta_a + \eta_b - 1}$$

is zero for small changes in output when Z'G-extended passes through C. The numerator of this criterion can be derived directly by examining the conditions under which a change in the terms of trade to $Z'C$ can be an equilibrium. Note that this result is not possible if OB is elastic.

---

[16]Mill was aware [17, pp. 150–53] that an increase in productivity would lower the commodity terms of trade and even the factoral terms of trade if foreign demand, in the latter case, were inelastic. Edgeworth interpreted [3, p. 10] Mill's passage as indicating that a country could be "damnified" by growth, supplying the necessary assumption to make Mill's analysis correct. The first derivations of criteria (23) and (26) are due to Meade [14, e.g., p. 153] and to Johnson [6] [8].

increasing productivity can affect real income perversely are quite strict: the foreign elasticity of demand must be less than unity and, perhaps, appreciably so if home substitution effects are high. Second (and more important), since world income as a whole increases, by compensation both countries (or sectors) could be made better off than before. Finally, the damnified country can always impose taxes on trade sufficient to reap at least some of the benefits of the productivity increase. Obviously the perverse effect is not possible if the growing country is following an optimum tariff policy since that implies an elasticity of demand in the foreign country greater than unity.

6. Taxes and Subsidies on Trade

A tax or subsidy on trade introduces a divergence between foreign and domestic price ratios. Equal taxes on exports or imports create the same divergence between foreign and domestic prices ratios (if trade is balanced) so that the *real* effects of import and export taxes are symmetrical. A tax on imports at constant terms of trade raises the relative price of imports in the taxing country and therefore *draws* resources away from export industries into import-competing industries. A tax on exports at constant terms of trade lowers the relative price of exports in the taxing country and thus *pushes* resources into import-competing industries. With balanced trade the revenues collected by the two taxes are the same. We may therefore speak of trade restriction or trade promotion without specifying whether the tax or subsidy is on exports or imports.[17]

[17]Marshall writes [12, pp. 180–81]: "... The considerations which can be urged for and against the levying of an import tax on a particular commodity differ widely from those appropriate to a particular export tax: and this is perhaps the origin of an opinion, which seems to pervade a good deal of economic discussion, that a general tax on all imports would have widely different effects from a general tax on all exports. In fact the two taxes would have the same effect: provided they were evenly distributed, equal in aggregate amount, and their proceeds were expended in the same way." He then shows how this can be proved. Bastable, Edgeworth and others were also aware of the symmetry. For a modern treatment see Lerner [10].

There are two analytic methods of disposing of the tariff proceeds. We may assume that the government spends the tariff proceeds on the two goods in a given proportion; or we may suppose that tax proceeds are redistributed as income subsidies to consumers. The latter method, which is used here, is simpler because it avoids the necessity of introducing a government demand equation, and does not give rise to asymmetries when dealing with trade subsidies. In the following analysis it should be remembered that we are in fact examining the effects of tariffs combined with this method of disposing of the proceeds.

The Terms of Trade. To determine the effect of a tariff on the terms of trade first compute the excess demand for imports at constant terms of trade. At constant terms of trade the relative price of imports in the tariff-imposing country (A) rises by the full amount of the tariff. Then, with t_a representing unity plus the ad valorem rate of tariff, the change in demand for imports before redistribution of the proceeds is:

$$\frac{\partial I_a}{(Pt_a)}\frac{d(Pt_a)}{dt_a}dt_a = \frac{\partial I_a}{\partial(Pt_a)}\frac{Pt_a}{I_a}I_a dt_a = -\eta_a I_a dt_a$$

assuming initial free trade ($t_a = 1$). To this change in demand must be added the increase in demand for imports occasioned by the redistribution of the tariff proceeds, i.e., $m_a I_a dt_a$. Adding the terms we get the excess demand for imports due to the tariff at constant terms of trade, i.e., $(-\eta_a + m_a)Idt_a = -\eta_a' Idta$. This excess demand must be eliminated, at the new equilibrium, by a change in the terms of trade. We then have the following criterion:

$$\frac{dP}{dt_a} = \frac{-\eta_a'}{\eta_a + \eta_b - 1}. \tag{28}$$

Tariffs normally improve the terms of trade.[18]

[18] To derive (28) directly differentiate:

$$T = 0 = I_b(D_b, 1/P) - PI_a(D_a, Pt_a)$$

The degree to which the terms of trade change following a tariff depends on the elasticities. The more elastic is the foreign offer curve the smaller will be the improvement in the terms of trade due to a tariff, and in the limiting case where the foreign offer curve is perfectly elastic, the terms of trade remain unchanged (the only exception). On the other hand if the foreign offer curve is elastic[19] the greater is the compensated elasticity of demand for imports at home the more effective will a given tariff be in improving the terms of trade; in the limiting case where η'_a is infinite the terms of trade will improve in the same proportion as the (ad valorem) tariff. Now both the above propositions are related to the classical notion about the division of the gains from trade between large and small countries. Because small countries tend to be more completely specialized than large countries, it was generally believed that the offer curve of a small country was less elastic than that of a large country. This means that the gain per unit of trade going to a small country was likely to be larger than that going to a large country. Then since the small country already reaped a large proportion of the gain from trade, opportunities for increasing that gain further through tariffs were small. On the other hand large countries, gaining little from trade, could exact a larger gain by imposing tariffs and forcing small countries to trade at a less favorable price ratio.

The Domestic Price Ratio. A common motive for trade restriction is the protection of import-competing industries. In order that

---

with respect to t_a. With D_b constant this yields:

$$
\begin{aligned}
(\eta_a + \eta_b - 1)I\frac{dP}{dt_a} &= P\frac{\partial I_a}{\partial D_a}\frac{dD_a}{dt_a} - \frac{\partial I_a}{\partial (Pt_a)}, \\
&= (m_a - \eta_a)I
\end{aligned}
$$

since $dD_a/dt_a = I$; i.e., expenditure in A rises by the value of the tariff proceeds.

The qualitative direction of change in the terms of trade was admitted by Ricardo and known to most of the later classical economists. The algebraic criterion can be got from Meade's analysis [14].

[19]Note that if the foreign offer curve is inelastic the terms of trade may improve by more than the tariff, provided that the home offer curve is not perfectly elastic; if the latter is perfectly elastic the maximum change in the terms of trade is equal to the rate of the tariff.

these industries be protected the domestic relative price of imports (inclusive of the tariff) must rise. We shall therefore develop a criterion for the change in the domestic price ratio following a tariff.

The domestic price ratio in country A is Pt_a (where t_a is unity plus the ad valorem rate of tariff). We are interested in how Pt_a will change as a result of an increase in t_a, i.e., in the sign of

$$\frac{d(Pt_a)}{dt_a} = P + t_a \frac{dP}{dt_a},$$

where P and t_a are initially equal to unity. Substituting for dP/dt_a, from equation (26) we obtain the following criterion:

$$\frac{d(Pt_a)}{dt_a} = 1 - \frac{\eta'_a}{\eta_a + \eta_b - 1} = \frac{\eta_b + m_a - 1}{\eta_a + \eta_b - 1}. \tag{29}$$

A tariff raises the domestic price of imports if the sum of the foreign elasticity of demand for imports and the domestic marginal propensity to import is greater than unity.[20] The only exception is the case previously mentioned where the home offer curve is infinitely elastic, in which case the domestic price ratio remains unchanged. (See Figure 5.)

The meaning of the criterion will be clarified if we consider the excess demand for imports on the assumption that the domestic price ratio remains unchanged. In that event the terms of trade improve by the full amount of the tariff, so that the change in supply of imports from B is $- \in_b Idt_a = (1 - \eta_b)Idt_a$. On the other hand the redistribution of the tariff proceeds and the resulting increase in domestic expenditure in A increases the demand for imports by $m_a Idt_a$. Subtracting the change in supply of imports from B from the increase in demand for imports in A we get the excess demand for imports at constant domestic prices, i.e., $(\eta_b + m_a - 1)Idt_a$. Now if the foreign demand is less than unit-elastic (foreign supply elasticity

[20]The classical economists, many of whom tried to determine whether a country gained more or less than the amount of the tax, generally employed the criterion $\eta_b \gtrless 1$, assuming, implicitly or explicitly, that the tax proceeds were spent on domestic goods, or that the tax was on the transit of goods that would be re-exported. For modern discussions see Lerner [10] and Metzler [16].

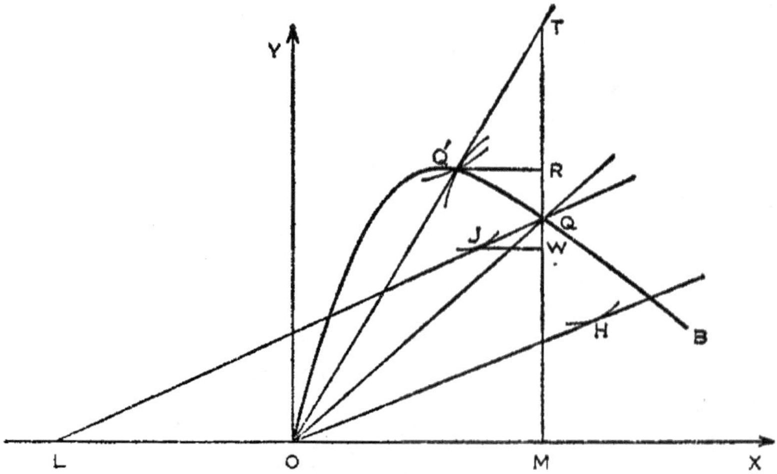

Figure 5. Tariffs, the Terms of Trade and the Domestic Price Ratio.
The offer curves of A (not drawn) and B (OB) intersect at the free-trade equilibrium Q Suppose that this equilibrium is disturbed by the imposition of a tariff by A's government. At constant terms of trade the price of Y in A rises by the full amount of the tariff LO/OM and trade equilibrium in A moves to a point on A's original offer curve, such as H. But when tariff revenues equal (approximately) to OL in terms of X are redistributed to consumers the demand for both goods increases. The equilibrium point for A at constant terms of trade therefore moves to a point on A's revenue-redistributed offer curve, such as J. At constant terms of trade the tariff-*cum*-income subsidy results in an excess supply of Y and a surplus in A's balance of payments equal to QW since the new equilibrium at J must be below Q if substitution effects are positive. Gold therefore flows into A from B and A's terms of trade improve until the excess supply WQ is relieved. Assume that the new equilibrium is at Q'.

The excess demand for imports in A at constant terms of trade is:

$$-\frac{dB}{P} = WQ = \frac{WQ}{QM} \cdot QM = \frac{WQ}{QM}\frac{OM}{OL} \cdot \frac{OL}{OM} \cdot QM = \eta_a' I dt_a.$$

On the other hand we have:

$$\frac{dB}{P} = WQ = WR - TR - TQ$$

$$= \left[\frac{WR}{QM}\frac{QM}{TQ} - \frac{TR}{QM}\frac{QM}{TQ} - 1\right] QM \frac{TQ}{QM}(\eta_a + \eta_b + 1) I \frac{dP}{P}.$$

It follows that:

$$\frac{dP}{dt_a} = \frac{-\eta_a'}{\eta_a + +_b - 1}.$$

is negative) an improvement in A's terms of trade results in an increase in supply of imports from B; but against this must be set the increased demand for imports in A resulting from the spending of the tariff proceeds. If the former effect is greater than the latter, the relative price of imports must fall. If, for example, the foreign elasticity of supply were $-.6$ (implying an elasticity of demand equal to .4) while the domestic marginal propensity to import were .5, the tariff would cause, at constant domestic prices, an excess supply of B's good equal to .1 Idt_a; to eliminate this excess supply of B's good, the relative (tariff-inclusive) price of imports must fall, and the terms of trade must improve by more than the tariff.

This possibility is consistent with stability. It means that a tariff may have an adverse protective effect. To protect the domestic industry imports must be subsidized instead of taxed! Under no circumstances, however, would a country ever find it beneficial in fact to subsidize imports to protect the domestic industry. For the adverse protective effect to occur the foreign demand must be inelastic, and in that case a tariff must always result in an improvement in national welfare (more imports are obtained for fewer exports). If an optimum tariff policy is being followed a further increase in the tariff always raises the relative price of imports in the tariff-imposing country and thus has a normal protective effect.

Tariff Changes in Both Countries. If both countries adjust their tariff rates the extent and direction of the disequilibrium depends

---

Figure 5 (*Continued*).
Note that η_α refers to the elasticity of the revenue-redistributed offer curve in A.

For the domestic price ratio in A to be unchanged at the new equilibrium, as a result of the tariff, the slope of the A-indifference curve at Q' must be the same as the slope of the indifference curves of A and B at Q. But in that case the marginal propensity to import in A is equal to RQ/TQ (for small tariffs); and since

$$\epsilon_b = \eta_b - 1 = -\frac{RQ}{QM}\frac{QM}{TQ} = \frac{RQ}{TQ},$$

it follows that $\eta_b = m_a - 1 = 0$. This is the borderline case. It is easily seen that the slope of A's indifference curve at Q' is flatter or steeper than that at Q as $m_a \gtrless \eta_b - 1$.

on the size of the tariff changes and the elasticities of demand. In bilateral tariff negotiations it may be useful to know what adjustment in the tariffs of both countries will leave the balance of payments unaltered. If, for practical reasons, changes in the terms of trade (through exchange rate or wage changes) must be ruled out, countries embarking on, say, a customs union experiment may need to know the rate at which each can reduce tariffs so as to leave the balance of payments unchanged. The answer to this question can readily be obtained from equation (28) making appropriate adjustments for country B. If we write P as the annual deterioration of country A's terms of trade, i_a as the annual change in A's tariff and i_b as the annual change in B's tariff we can obtain the following criterion:

$$P = \frac{\eta_b' t_b - \eta_a' t_a}{\eta_a + \eta_b - 1}. \tag{30}$$

In order to prevent any change in the terms of trade the numerator must be zero; tariffs must then be changed at a rate inversely proportional to the compensated elasticities of demand for imports. [Note that equation (28) applies with a changed sign to subsidies since subsidies are simply negative tariffs.]

Income Transfers and Trade Taxes. Suppose the authorities in one country wish to make a grant to another country but, for political or other reasons, are unable to make the gift official. Alternatively, suppose that one country wishes to exact a transfer of real income from another country without imposing a formal tribute. Can this be accomplished efficiently by changes in trade taxes? (See Figure 6.)

To show that it can consider first the relation between trade taxes and subsidies. Suppose that country A subsidizes exports (or imports) while country B taxes imports (or exports). In that case the same goods are being taxed, the only difference being that the customs duties are collected by officials of different nationality. Trade is subsidized in A and taxed in B. Now if the increase in trade subsidies in A is equal to the increase in trade taxes in B this combined policy is equal to a transfer of income from A to B equal to the value of the tax-subsidy payments. Since the tax in B cancels

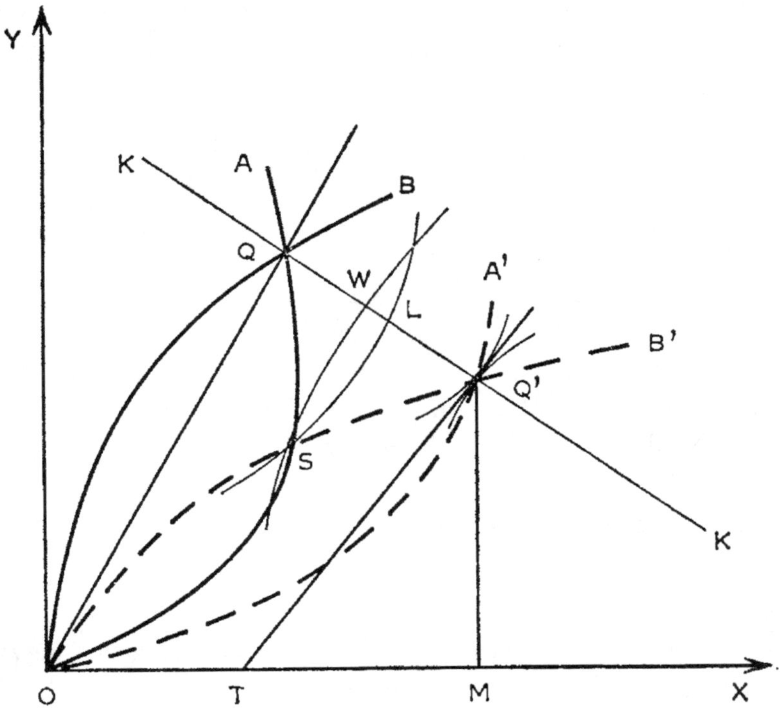

Figure 6. Income Transfers and Trade Taxes.

Initial equilibrium is at Q on the contract curve KK. Suppose that A subsidizes, and B taxes, trade at the same rate OT/TM. Then A's and B's offer curves bend down to OA' and OB', respectively, intersecting at Q' (they still originate from O). Since price ratios remain the same in both countries Q' must be on the contract curve. The slope of the indifference curves at Q' are, from the transfer analysis, greater or less than the slope at Q depending on whether the sum of the marginal propensities to import is greater or less than unity. The terms of trade are now OQ' necessarily worse for A if the system is stable. Real income in A falls to the same extent as if A had made a gift of OT of X to B.

Suppose now that only B has a tax (equal to OT/TM) so that trade equilibrium is at S. To restore efficiency (Pareto optimum), A can impose a subsidy equal to B's tariff, attaining the equilibrium (worse for A, better for B) Q'. A more interesting possibility is for A to bribe B to remove the tariff, the value of the bribe being the transfer necessary to effect an equilibrium between W and L (better for both than S). Or if A is already receiving gifts from B then tariff reduction in B and the elimination of gifts to A (i.e., "Trade, not Aid") can make both A and B better off.

the subsidy in A, price ratios in the two countries must be the same. The change in real income, evaluated at the original price ratio, in each country is given by:

$$-dU_a = dU_b = IdP = \frac{(-\eta_a' t_a + \eta_b' t_b)I}{\eta_a + \eta_b - 1}.$$

Now if $-dt_a = dt_b = dt$ we have:

$$\frac{-dU_a}{Idt} = \frac{-dU_b}{Idt} = \frac{\eta_a' + \eta_b'}{\eta_a + \eta_b - 1}. \tag{31}$$

But (31) is the same as the criterion for the change in real income after transfer [equation (19) above] if *Idt,* the value of the tax-subsidy receipts, is substituted for the transfer.

7. Consumption and Production Taxes

Taxes on commodities, as distinct from taxes on trade, make it necessary to distinguish between consumers' and producers' price ratios. A consumption tax or subsidy creates a divergence between the price ratio facing consumers in the taxing country and all other price ratios, while a production tax causes a discrepancy between the price ratio facing producers and all other price ratios.

There are eight taxes and subsidies in each country which are possible, but it will not be necessary to consider more than two. A subsidy is a negative tax so that we need only consider taxes. And a tax on one good is equivalent to a subsidy on the other good because of our assumptions about the disposal of tax proceeds and the financing of subsidy payments. Because of these assumptions an equal tax on the two goods has no effect on equilibrium; this follows because each tax is combined with an income subsidy, and an income subsidy has the same effect as an equal subsidy (or an equal reduction in taxes) on the two goods. But if an equal tax on the two goods does not affect equilibrium, then neither does a tax on one of the goods combined with the elimination of a subsidy of equal amount on the other good—hence it follows that a tax on one of the goods is equivalent to a subsidy on the other. Thus we need only consider one consumption tax and one production tax.

Consumption Taxes and the Terms of Trade. To find the effects of a consumption tax on the terms of trade first determine the excess demand caused by the tax at constant terms of trade. Let us suppose that a tax is imposed by country A on the imported good, Y. Then at constant terms of trade the price of Y to consumers in A rises by the amount of the tax. Before the redistribution of the tax proceeds the change in demand for y in A, at constant terms of trade, is

$$\frac{\partial y_a}{\partial(Pt_{cya})}\frac{Pt_{cya}}{y_a}y_a dt_{cya} = -\eta_{ya}y_a dt_{cya}$$

where t_{cya} is unity plus the rate at which commodity Y is taxed in A and η_{ya} is the elasticity of demand for y in A.[21] (P and t_{cya} are both *initially* taken to be unity.) Now the tax proceeds amount to $y_a dt_{cya}$ so that the increase in demand for y due to their disposition is $m_a y_a dt_{cya}$. Adding the two effects we get the excess demand at constant terms of trade,

$$(m_a - \eta_{ya})y_a dt_{cya} = -\eta'_{ya}y_a dt_{cya},$$

where η'_{ya} is the compensated elasticity of demand for y in A, i.e., the elasticity of demand for Y after consumers have been compensated for the change in real income implicit within the price change. We

[21]The elasticity of demand for the imported good is never larger than the elasticity of demand for imports. The exact relation can be derived from the definition of the demand for imports. From $I_a = y_a - Y_a$ we get, by differentiation,

$$\frac{\partial I_a}{\partial P} = \frac{\partial y_a}{\partial P} - \frac{\partial Y_a}{\partial P}$$

and

$$-\frac{P}{I_a}\frac{\partial I_a}{\partial P} = -\frac{\partial y_a}{\partial P}\frac{P}{y_a}\frac{y_a}{I_a} + \frac{\partial Y_a}{\partial P}\frac{P}{Y_a}\frac{Y_a}{I_a}$$

whence

$$\eta_a = \eta_{ya}\frac{y_a}{I} + \epsilon_{ya}\frac{Y_a}{I}$$

where ϵ_{ya} s the elasticity of supply of Y in A. (A similar result, holds for country B.) The elasticities η_{ya} and η_a coincide only when there is no home production of the imported good.

now have the following criterion:

$$\frac{dP}{dt_{cya}} = -\frac{y_a}{I}\frac{\eta'_{ya}}{\eta_a + \eta_b - 1}. \tag{32}$$

The compensated elasticity term is positive (it represents the elasticity of a consumption indifference curve) so that a consumption tax on the imported good generally improves the terms of trade of the taxing country. This conclusion is to be expected since a tax on the imported good diverts demand away from that good, thereby causing an excess world supply.

There are some special cases we may consider: (1) in the unusual case where η'_{ya} is zero—implying no substitution in consumption (a kinked consumption indifference curve at that point)—the terms of trade do not change; (2) if the foreign offer curve is perfectly elastic any excess demand can be eliminated by shifts in production or consumption at constant cost in the foreign country so there results no change in the terms of trade; (3) if the domestic offer curve is perfectly elastic (η_a is infinite) it is now necessary to know whether this is due to perfect substitution in production (incomplete specialization at constant cost) or perfect substitution in consumption; if the former is the case the denominator of (32) is infinite, so the terms of trade do not change; but if the goods are perfect substitutes in consumption both the denominator and the numerator are infinite so that the terms of trade change by the full amount of the tax; (4) if there is no domestic production of the imported good the tax has the same effect as a tariff (y_a = I and $\eta'_{ya} = \eta'_a$).

This analysis applies also to a subsidy on the consumption of the good which is exported and, with a change of sign, to a subsidy on the imported good or tax on the exported good.

Consumption Taxes and the Ratio of Market Prices. Does a consumption tax necessarily raise the market price of the taxed good relative to that of the untaxed good? By analogy to the effect of a tariff on the domestic price ratio we should not expect this to be so. The market (relative) price of importables is Pt_{cya}, which we assume to be initially unity. The change in this price ratio due to the tariff is:

$$\frac{d(Pt_{cya})}{dt_{cya}} = 1 - \frac{dP}{dt_{cya}} = 1 - \frac{y_a}{I}\frac{\eta'_{ya}}{\eta_a + \eta_b - 1} = \frac{\eta_b + m_a + \epsilon'_{ya}\frac{Y_a}{I} - 1}{\eta_a + \eta_b - 1} \tag{33}$$

where ϵ'_{ya} is the compensated elasticity of supply of Y in A, and represents the elasticity of the production transformation curves.[22]

[22]The compensated elasticity of supply requires some explanation. From the two relations:

$$\eta_a = \eta'_a + m_a, and\ \eta_a = \eta_{ya}\frac{y_a}{I} + \epsilon_{ya}\frac{Y_a}{I}$$

we can obtain:

$$\eta_a = \eta_a - m_a = (\eta_{ya} - m_a)\frac{y_a}{I} + (\epsilon_{ya} + m_a)\frac{Y_a}{I}.$$

It can now be shown that $\eta_{ya} - m_a = \eta'_{ya}$, the compensated elasticity of demand for Y in A; and that $\epsilon_{ya} + m_a = \epsilon'_{ya}$, the compensated elasticity of supply of Y in A. We have $dI_a = dy_a - dY_a$ from the definition of the demand for imports. Now dI_a contains an income effect equal to $-m_aI_adP$ where $-I_adP$ measures the change in real income of country A looked at as a whole. The term dy_a contains an income effect equal to $-m_ay_adP$, where $-y_adP$ measures the change in real income of people of country A looked at in their role as consumers alone. Finally the term dY_a contains an income effect equal to m_aY_adP where Y_adP measures the change in real income of producers of Y in country A. We now have the following relations:

$$dI_a = (dI_a)' - m_aI_adP; dy_a = (dy_a)' - m_ay_adP;\ and\ dY_a = (dY_a)' + m_aY_adP$$

where the primes denote pure substitution effects. Substituting in $dI_a = dy_a - dY_a$ we get

$$(dI_a)' - m_aI_adP = (dy_a)' - m_ay_adP - [(dY_a)' + m_aY_adP].$$

The income effects on the two sides cancel and the proof of the relation between compensated elasticities follows readily. Dividing by I_adP, multiplying by P, and changing signs we obtain

$$\eta'_a = \eta'_{ya}\frac{y_a}{I} + \epsilon'_{ya}\frac{Y_a}{I}$$

where the primes denote that the elasticities contain no income effects.

These elasticities have a simple interpretation: η'_{ya} is the elasticity of a trade-indifference curve; η'_{ya} is the elasticity of a consumption-indifference curve; and η'_{ya} is the elasticity of a production-indifference (production-possibility) curve. The identification is formally valid for small changes only.

Criterion (32) can be derived directly by differentiating:

Only by this term does the last criterion in (33) differ from the criterion for a change in the domestic price ratio after the imposition of a tariff [see equation (29)]. If a tariff will raise the domestic relative price of imports so will a consumption tax on the import good. The converse is not true. Even if the foreign offer curve is inelastic and the domestic marginal propensity to import is low, high substitution effects in production will be sufficient to ensure a rise in the tax-inclusive price of importables.

Production Taxes and the Terms of Trade. To find the effects of a production tax on the terms of trade first consider the excess demand caused by the production tax at constant terms of trade. If a tax on the production of the import good is imposed and the proceeds of the tax are redistributed to producers there remains only a pure substitution effect, a movement along the production-possibility curve. At constant terms of trade (which is also the price ratio facing domestic consumers) the excess demand for imports, after the redistribution of the proceeds, is equal to:

$$\epsilon'_{ya} Y_a dt_{pya}$$

where t_{pya} is equal to unity plus the tax, and ϵ'_{ya} is the elasticity of the transformation curve. This excess demand must be eliminated by a worsening of A's terms of trade. The criterion is therefore:

$$\frac{dP}{dt_{pya}} = \frac{Y_a}{I} \frac{\epsilon'_{ya}}{(\eta_a + \eta_b - 1)}. \tag{34}$$

Since with increasing opportunity costs ϵ'_{ya} is always positive the terms of trade of the taxing country fall. Again this applies to a production subsidy on the exported good and, with a change of sign, to a production subsidy on the imported good and a production tax on the exported good. This conforms to common sense. A tax on the production of any good decreases the production of that good

---

$T = 0 = I_b(D_b, 1/P) - P[y_a(D_a, Pt_{cya}) - Y_a(P)]$ noting that D_b is constant and that

$$\frac{dD_a}{dt_{cya}} = y_a.$$

and increases the production of the other good causing a rise in the relative world price of the taxed good.

Production Taxes and Relative Prices at Factor Cost. The price ratio facing producers is P/t_{pya}, which is initially taken to be unity. This will change as a result of a tax depending on the sign of:

$$\frac{d(P/t_{pya})}{dt_{pya}} = \frac{dP}{dt_{pya}} - 1 = \frac{Y_a}{I}\frac{\epsilon'_{ya}}{\eta_a + \eta_b - 1}$$

$$= -\frac{\eta_b + m_a + \eta'_{ya}\frac{Y_a}{I} - 1}{\eta_a + \eta_b - 1}. \quad (35)$$

The analogy to equations (29) and (33) above readily presents itself.[23]

Relation between Commodity Taxes and Trade Taxes. A tariff, at constant terms of trade, raises the price of imports to both consumers and producers in the taxing country by the full amount of the tariff. Any other system of taxes which does the same thing will have the same effect on the terms of trade as a tariff. Thus taxes on trade can be duplicated by taxes on commodities. We can establish these relations either by showing that the tax combination affects the price ratios facing consumers and producers in the same way as a trade tax, or by adding the effects of the criteria obtained above in each case. By either method it is readily shown that a tariff (on Y) or an export tax (on X) is equivalent in real terms to: (a) a consumption tax on Y plus a production subsidy on Y; (b) a consumption tax on Y plus a production tax on X; (c) a consumption subsidy on X plus

[23]Criterion (34) can be derived directly by differentiating:

$$T = 0 = I_b(D_b, 1/P) - P\left[y_a(D_a, P) - Y_a\left(\frac{P}{t_{pya}}\right)\right]$$

noting that

$$\frac{dD_a}{dt_{pya}} = Y_a.$$

To my knowledge the effects of consumption and production taxes on the terms of trade have not been formally treated in the literature before, although the general direction of their influence is indicated in many classical writings. See, for example, Viner [24, p. 363].

a production subsidy on Y; (d) a consumption subsidy on X plus a production tax on X. And because trade subsidies are negative trade taxes, an export subsidy (on X) or an import subsidy (on Y) can be duplicated by: (e) a consumption subsidy on Y plus a production tax on Y; (f) a consumption subsidy on Y plus a production subsidy on X; (g) a consumption tax on X plus a production tax on Y; (h) a consumption tax on X plus a production subsidy on X. From these relations it follows that: (1) the effects of devaluation can be duplicated or frustrated by changes in commodity taxes and subsidies (since devaluation is equivalent to an import tariff plus an export subsidy); (2) the optimum tariff can be duplicated by commodity taxes; and (3) income transfers can be duplicated by changes in commodity taxes in both countries. A further application is to customs unions; an agreement over tariff reduction has little force if it is not combined with agreement over the domestic tax structures.

Consideration of the commodity-tax structure is necessary before evaluating the desirability of tariff reductions. If there are commodity taxes and subsidies in each country none of the well-known welfare propositions of international trade theory holds. In particular from a "free-trade" (i.e., no *trade* taxes) position, it can be shown that, if there are commodity taxes and subsidies: (1) both countries simultaneously may be better off without, than with, trade; (2) a country may gain by a deterioration in its terms of trade even if the initiating cause occurs in the foreign country; (3) a small tariff may worsen the welfare of the tariff-imposing country even if the foreign offer curve is not infinitely elastic; and (4) the imposition of a tariff may simultaneously improve the welfare of both countries. These propositions follow because commodity taxes overextend or underextend trade.

8. Other Mechanisms of Adjustment

Thus far we have dealt with the effect of policy changes on the terms of trade, the latter adjusting through price-level or exchange-rate variations. It was argued earlier that authorities may adopt other policies which prevent, or render unnecessary, changes in the terms of trade. This would be the case if authorities pegged the exchange rate and stabilized domestic price levels, relying on, say, trade controls to correct disequilibria. The purpose of this section is to show how the results already obtained can be applied to other mechanisms of adjustment. The procedure to be followed is the same as before: First state the postulate on which dynamic behavior is based, deduce the condition of dynamic stability, and then examine the excess demands caused by the policy changes.

Fiscal Policy and Capital Movements. Suppose that authorities peg the exchange rate and stabilize the domestic price level in each country. The price level may be stabilized in a variety of ways but the simplest for our purpose is to suppose that authorities inflate domestic expenditure by means of a budget deficit when there is deflationary pressure (excess supply of its export good) and deflate domestic expenditure by means of a budget surplus when there is inflationary pressure (excess demand for its export good). We may assume that the deficits and surpluses are financed and disposed of by drawing on or accumulating credits with an international agency—say, the International Monetary Fund. Now since an excess supply of one country's good implies an excess demand for the other country's good it follows that one country will be borrowing at the time another country is lending; and because of the indentity of income (including loans) and expenditure, the rate of lending by one country is equal to the rate of borrowing in the other country, and both are equal (with appropriate signs) to the rate at which the budgets are out of balance.

Whether or not a system based on these rules is stable depends on the effectiveness of the deflation-inflation policy in relieving excess demand for the deflating country's good and excess supply of the inflating country's good. But it is easily seen that this is equivalent to whether a transfer from one country to another will cause an excess supply of the transferring country's good. The system is therefore stable or unstable depending on whether the sum of the marginal propensities to import is less than or greater than unity. The term $1 - m_a - m_b$ also gives the denominator of the criterion showing the direction and amount of lending required to eliminate a given excess demand. (See Figure 7.)

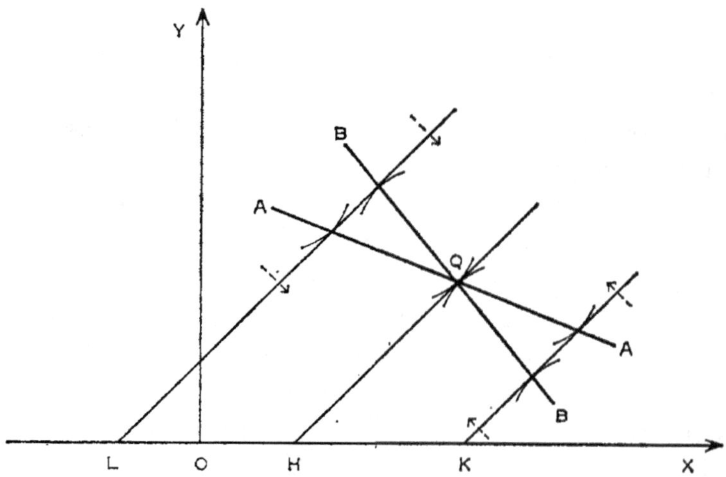

Figure 7. Stability of the "IMF System".

Let equilibrium be initially at Q with the government of A lending or giving to the government of B the annual payment OH. It is assumed that exchange rates are fixed and that each government, by means of fiscal policy, stabilizes export price levels.

Now suppose that the equilibrium is disturbed by, say, a private flow of capital of HL from B to A, and that this induces an excess of saving over investment in B, and an excess of investment over saving in A, equal to the transfer. Now if the sum of the marginal propensities to import is less than unity, as in the diagram, the Engel curve of A (AA) must be flatter than the Engel curve of B (BB); the capital flow therefore induces an excess demand for A's good and an excess supply of B's good, and a surplus in A's and a deficit in B's balance of payments.

To correct the disequilibrium, A's government deflates expenditure by means of a budget surplus and turns the proceeds over to the IMF; and B's government inflates expenditure by means of a budget deficit borrowing from the IMF. This process continues until the inflationary pressure in A and the deflationary pressure in B are eliminated, i.e., until the equilibrium Q and the net lending position OH are restored. By similar analysis it can be shown that a movement of capital from A to B in excess of OH (say to OK) will cause deflationary pressure in A and inflationary pressure in B, necessitating government action in each country to eliminate the disequilibrium. In either case the equilibrium Q is stable.

But if the sum of the marginal propensities to import exceeds unity the system is unstable. This may be seen by considering again a movement of capital from B to A of HL. This time the capital movement causes an excess supply of A's good and an excess demand for B's good. A's government therefore inflates expenditure and B's government deflates expenditure, moving the system ever further from equilibrium.

As a practical problem it would be necessary to distinguish between the Engel curves appropriate for different types of transfer.

To determine the effects of policy changes on lending in a system obeying the above rules we (as before) find the excess demand due to the policy change with no lending. For example, the excess demand for imports due to a tariff in country A is $-\eta'_a I dt_a$. The change in the trade balance and lending of country A is therefore:

$$\frac{dT}{dt_a} = \frac{\eta'_a I}{1 - m_a - m_b}; \tag{36}$$

if the system is stable the tariff improves the trade balance.[24] Or we may consider the change in lending and the trade balance due to an increase in productivity in, say, country B:

$$\frac{dT}{dY_b^*} = \frac{m_b}{1 - m_a - m_b}; \tag{37}$$

assuming stability, country A must lend to country B to maintain equilibrium in the balance of payments.

In a similar fashion we can find the effects on lending of all the policies discussed in previous sections. It may be helpful to consider two cases. Suppose that country A devalues its currency. Applying the same method we find that the criterion for the change in the balance of trade and lending is:

$$\frac{dT}{dP} = \frac{(\eta_a + \eta_b - 1)I}{1 - m_a - m_b}. \tag{38}$$

It should be noticed that (38) is the reciprocal of (18), the criterion for the change in the terms of trade after transfer. The interpretation is fundamentally different. In (18) the stability condition is that the sum of the elasticities is greater than unity, while in (38) the stability condition is that the sum of the marginal propensities to import is less than unity. In (18) lending induces—because of the "rules of the goldstandard- (or flexible-exchange-rate-) game"—a change in the terms of trade; in (38) devaluation induces—because of the "rules of the IMF game"—a change in the balance of trade and lending.

[24]This criterion has been used by Meade [14, p. 155] and derived geometrically by Ozga [21] although in neither case is a distinction made between stable and unstable situations. Ozga's analysis, which was presented to a seminar in London in 1956, greatly improved my own geometrical representations.

An interesting result is the following: If the IMF system is unstable the gold standard (or flexible exchange) system is stable; and if the gold standard (or flexible exchange) system is unstable the IMF system is stable. *Instability* of one system therefore implies *stability* of the other system, though not vice versa. This relation holds because the sum of the marginal propensities to import is less than the sum of the elasticities of demand for imports.

Finally, consider a trivial case. A change in capital exports has no ultimate effect on net lending! In the IMF system there is only one equilibrium rate of lending (in the absence of other trade policy changes), just as, in the classical system, there is only one equilibrium value of the terms of trade (assuming that the equilibrium is unique). This trivial case is cited for purposes of comparison with the classical contention that devaluation, from a position of equilibrium, does not change the terms of trade or the balance of trade: instead, it initiates price level changes which restore the equilibrium terms of trade. A displacement of the variable of adjustment from equilibrium initiates dynamic forces which induce a return to equilibrium.

Similar analysis can be applied to systems of adjustment based on tariff, tax or productivity changes.

9. Summary

The results of the preceding analysis may all be summarized by introducing all policy parameters into the balance of payments equation and differentiating. We obtain:

$$\begin{aligned}(1 - m_a - m_b)dT - I(\eta_a + \eta_b - 1)dP - I\eta_a' dt_a + I\eta_b' dt_b - y_a\eta_{ya}' dt_{ca}\\ + x_b\eta_{xb}' dt_{cb} + Y_a\epsilon_{ya}' dt_{pa} - X_b\epsilon_{xb}' dt_{pb} + m_a dX_a^* - m_b dX_b^* = 0\end{aligned} \tag{39}$$

where the same terminology is used as before except that *effective* tax rates are used. (Thus dt_a and dt_b refer to the effective rate at which trade taxes are changed in A and B; changes in trade subsidies are subtracted from changes in trade taxes. Similarly dt_{ca} and dt_{cb} represent the effective rate at which consumption taxes or subsidies are changed in A and B; a tax on the consumption of import goods combined with an equal tax on the consumption of home goods would leave the effective rate unchanged. Similarly for production taxes dt_{pa} and dt_{pb}.)

The policy equation (39) shows the relation between policy changes which are necessary to maintain equilibrium in the system; it can be used to show the policy changes which are necessary to offset the disequilibrium caused by other policies. Suppose, for example, country A wishes to know the rate at which it must tax import goods in order to relieve a disequilibrium caused by an increase in productivity in the foreign country. To find the answer set all policy changes except dt_{ca} and dX_b^* equal to zero. This leaves the equation

$$-y_a \eta'_{ya} dt_{ca} - m_b dX_b^* = 0$$

and the answer

$$\frac{dt_{ca}}{dX_b^*} = -\frac{m_b}{y_a \eta'_{ya}}.$$

The productivity change in B causes a surplus in A's balance which can be relieved by a reduction in the rate at which consumption of import goods (export goods) are taxed (subsidized) in A. Any other relation between two or more policy changes can in this way be determined.[25]

10. Extension of the Model: The Multiple Country Case

The propositions now established have been derived from a model consisting of only two goods and two countries. The traditional use of this model in international trade literature is based on a belief that it suggests "theorems which may be seen to admit of extension to more concrete cases" [3, p. 31]. In this final section general results are derived and it is shown that in at least one important case

[25] All of the criteria contained in equation (39) are capable of simple geometric proofs when the variables are taken two at a time.

The above analysis of policy changes has been expounded on the assumption that transport costs are absent; for a geometrical representation of transport costs employing Marshallian offer curves see Mundell [19].

the propositions previously established for two countries hold for an arbitrary number of countries.

Suppose that there are $n + 1$ countries, and let all prices and balances of payments be expressed in terms of the currency of country 0 (e.g., dollars). If prices (of export goods or currencies) are flexible then the balance of each country depends on all prices. The conditions of equilibrium can be written as follows:

$$B_1(P_1, \ldots, P_n; \alpha) = 0$$
$$\ldots\ldots\ldots\ldots\ldots$$
$$B_n(P_1, \ldots, P_n; \alpha) = 0 \qquad (40)$$

where a is a parameter representing a particular policy.[26] Note that only n equations are required since we are dealing with *normalized*

[26]Let x_{rs} and X_{rs} be, respectively, consumption and production of the rth good in the sth country, and let T_s be the capital exports of country s. Suppose that there are n countries and $m + 1$ goods. Then a general model can be expressed by the following equations:

$$Y_s - D_s \equiv \sum_{r=1}^{m} P_r(X_{rs} - x_{rs}) = T_s \qquad (s = 1, 2, \ldots, n) \qquad (1)$$

The national "budget" equations: Income—Spending=Lending, for each country. If these equations are satisfied each country is on its m-dimensional offer curve.

$$\sum_{s=1}^{n} (X_{rs} - x_{rs}) = 0 \qquad (r = 1, 2, \ldots, m) \qquad (2)$$

The market clearing equations: World Supply = World Demand, for every good. Notice that the excess supply function of the numeraire, commodity 0 (e.g., gold), is omitted; if equations (1) are satisfied, then the last equation in (2) can be deduced from the others (or vice versa).

$$x_{rs} = x_{rs}(D_s, P_1, \ldots P_m) \qquad \begin{matrix} (r = 1, \ldots, m) \\ (s = 1, \ldots, n) \end{matrix} \qquad (3)$$

Demand for the rth good in the sth country depends on the level of spending and the prices both expressed in terms of money, commodity 0.

$$X_{rs} = X_{rs}(P_1, \ldots, P_m) \qquad \begin{matrix} (r = 0, 1, \ldots, m) \\ (s = 1, \ldots, n) \end{matrix} \qquad (4)$$

Supply of the rth good in the sth country depends on the prices.

Domestic expenditure is assumed to be linked to lending and other policy variables. If we add to this system n equations of the form $D_s = D_s(T_s; \alpha)$,

prices; the balance of payments of country 0 follows from what may be called *Cournot's Law*.[27]

We wish to determine the effects of a shift in the policy α on the equilibrium set of prices so we differentiate equations (40) with respect to α. With appropriate choice of units of currencies or goods we get:

$$\begin{aligned} b_{11}\frac{dP_1}{d\alpha} + \ldots + b_{1n}\frac{dP_n}{d\alpha} &= -\frac{\partial B_1}{\partial\alpha} \\ \ldots\ldots\ldots\ldots\ldots\ldots\ldots\ldots & \\ b_{n1}\frac{dP_1}{d\alpha} + \ldots + b_{nn}\frac{dP_n}{d\alpha} &= -\frac{\partial B_n}{d\alpha} \end{aligned} \tag{41}$$

where $b_{ij} \equiv \partial B_i/\partial P_j$ is the change in the balance of the ith country due to a change in the price of the goods of the jth country. Solving for $dP_i/d\alpha$ we obtain,

$$\frac{dP_i}{d\alpha} = -\frac{\partial B_1}{\partial\alpha}\frac{\Delta_{1i}}{\Delta} + \ldots - \frac{\partial B_n}{\partial\alpha}\frac{\Delta_{ni}}{\Delta} = -\sum_{j=1}^{n}\frac{\partial B_j}{\partial\alpha}\frac{\Delta_{ji}}{\Delta} \quad (i = 1, \ldots, n) \tag{42}$$

---

where α is any policy, then we have a system of $2(mn + n) + m + n$ equations, and $2(mn+n)+m+2n$ unknowns. By specifying n parameters representing the capital exports of each country, the system becomes determined.

In the text the P's refer to the price level of each country's exports (exchange rates constant), or the price of each country's currency (price levels constant). If each country exports only one product, and the budget equations (1) are satisfied, then the partial derivatives $\partial B_i/\partial P_j \equiv b_{ij}$ [used in equation (42)] can be identified with the world elasticity of demand and supply of the exports of the ith country with respect to a change in the price of the exports of the jth country, making use of the following relations:

$$\begin{aligned} Bi &= \text{Value of Exports} - \text{Value of Imports} \\ &= (\text{Foreign Demand} - \text{Domestic Excess Supply})Pi \\ &= P_i(x_{i1} + \ldots + x_{in}) - P_iX_i, \end{aligned}$$

and differentiating with respect to P. Elasticities can then be formed by multiplying and dividing by X_i, leaving the typical term $\partial B_i/\partial P_j \equiv X_i(\eta_{ij} - \epsilon_{ij})$. (This assumes that units are chosen so that each P_j is initially unity.)

[27]Cournot made extensive use of the proposition that the sum of all balances is necessarily zero [2, Ch. 3].

where

$$\Delta \equiv \begin{vmatrix} b_{11} & \dots & b_{1n} \\ \dots & \dots & \dots \\ b_{n1} & \dots & b_{nn} \end{vmatrix}$$ and where Δ_{ji} is the cofactor of the jth row and the ith column of Δ.

Equations (42) provide a general framework into which specific policy changes can be introduced. But in order to evaluate any of the signs, $dP_i/d\alpha$, it is necessary to know the values, or at least the signs, of two kinds of terms: the coefficients $\partial B_j/\partial\alpha$ and the ratios Δ_{ij}/Δ. Now the coefficients $\partial B_j/\partial\alpha$ describe the change in the balances of payments arising from the policy change *at constant prices:* to evaluate these coefficients, then, we can apply the method of comparative statics. The ratios Δ_{ji}/Δ, on the other hand, indicate the interactions of price changes in multiple markets, and the effectiveness of price changes in relieving the initial disequilibrium. In the two-country case these signs were determined by the stability conditions; in the multiple-country case, however, it is easily shown that some of the ratios may be positive while others are negative without conflicting with the conditions of stability. It appears, then, that in evaluating equations (42) we will be left with some positive and some negative terms, and no general presumption about the sign of $dP_i/d\alpha$.

To make progress some restriction on the signs of the elements b_{ij} in the basic determinant Δ is required. The most interesting special case, for present purposes, is that where $b_{ij} > 0$ for $i \neq j$. This assumption means that an increase in the price of the exports of any country, other prices being held constant, improves the balance of payments of every other country; it also implies, by Cournot's Law, that a rise in the price level in one country worsens that country's balance of payments. From this assumption flow two important deductions: (1) the system is stable under the usual dynamic postulates[28] [1] [4]] [20]; and (2) every ratio Δ_{ij}/Δ is

[28]There are two approaches to the stability of international equilibrium. One approach is to treat the world economy like the domestic economy and postulate that the price of any good rises and falls in proportion to the excess demand and

negative [18, pp. 49–51], With this information we can evaluate the direction of change in the terms of trade resulting from many policy changes.

---

supply of that good. For example, the dynamic system may be written as follows:

$$\frac{dP_r}{dt} = k_r \sum_{s=1}^{n} (x_{rs} - X_{rs}) \tag{1}$$

where the summation is over countries. By linearizing (1) (retaining only linear terms of a Taylor series), and translating the resulting partial derivatives into demand and supply elasticities, we obtain:

$$\frac{dP_r}{dt} = k_r X_r \sum_{q=1}^{m} (\eta_{rq} - \epsilon_{rq})(P_q - P_q^0) \tag{2}$$

where the *own* elasticities of demand (η_{rr}) and supply (ϵ_{rr}) in the world as a whole are defined to be, normally, negative and positive respectively. The linear system can be stable only if the real parts of the roots of the following equation:

$$|k_r X_r(\eta_{rq} - \epsilon_{rq}) - \delta_{rq}\lambda| = 0 \tag{3}$$

are all negative (δ_{rq} is the Kronecker delta). The theorem on gross substitutes states that if all cross elasticities are positive (including the cross elasticities of demand for the numeraire good) the system is stable.

The above system focuses attention on world markets for particular commodities. Classical international trade theorists on the other hand (with the exception of F. D. Graham) emphasized the importance of disequilibrium in the balance of payments, gold flows and changes in the terms of trade. If we now let P_i denote the world price of the exports of country i we have the following system which is more compatible with the postulates of classical theory:

$$\frac{dP_i}{dt} = h_i B_i(P_1, \cdots, P_n \qquad (i = 1, \ldots, n) \tag{4}$$

assuming that there are now $n+1$ countries, and that prices are expressed in terms of the exports of country 0. Following the same procedure as above we find that stability requires that the real parts of the roots of the following equation:

$$|h_i b_{ij} - \delta_{ij}\lambda| = 0 \tag{5}$$

must all be negative. Again, stability is assured if all $b_{ij}>0$ for $i \neq j$. If prices were all constant and exchange rates were all flexible the system would be stable if all currencies were gross substitutes.

Generally the systems (1) and (4) are fundamentally different. Goods may all be gross substitutes while some currencies are gross complements, and vice versa. The gap between the two systems narrows, however, when only one country produces

Productivity Changes. Suppose that output and expenditure in country 0, the numeraire country, increase by dX_0^*. At constant prices, assuming no inferior goods, inhabitants of country 0 buy more of all goods, creating a deficit in their own balance and a surplus in the balance of every other country. The surplus in the balance of country i is $m_{i0}dX_0^*$ where m_{i0} is the marginal propensity to spend in country 0 on the goods of the ith country. The typical term in equation (42) is therefore

$$-\frac{\partial B_j}{\partial \alpha} = -m_{j0}.$$

By substitution, then, we get the criterion for the change in the terms of trade of the growing country

$$\frac{dP_i}{dX_0^*} = -\sum_{j=1}^{n} m_{j0}\frac{\Delta_{ji}}{\Delta}. \tag{43}$$

---

each good: In that case an excess world demand for a good implies an excess demand for the currency of the country producing that good.

I have said that the system (4) conforms more closely to the classical system than does system (1). This is not meant to imply that classical theorists would accept even as an approximation the rigid dynamic laws postulated. Consider, for example, the following passage from Marshall's privately circulated manuscript of 1879 [11, pp. 19, 25]:

> ...so that if we chose to assign to these horizontal and vertical forces any particular laws, we should obtain a differential equation for the motion of the exchange index.... Such calculations might afford considerable scope to the ingenuity of those who devise mathematical problems, but...they would afford no aid to the economist.
>
> For the mathematical functions introduced into the original differential equations could not, in the present condition of our knowledge, be chosen so as to represent even approximately the economic forces which actually operate in the world... Whereas the use of mathematical analysis has been found to tempt men to expend their energy on the elaboration of minute and complex hypotheses, which have indeed some distant analogy to economic conditions, but which cannot properly be said to represent in any way economic laws.

Every m_{j0} is positive in the absence of inferior goods, and every Δ_{ij}/Δ is negative if all exports are gross substitutes. Therefore *an improvement in productivity unambiguously worsens the commodity terms of trade of the growing country:* the prices of the exports of every other country rise relative to the price of the exports of the growing country.[29]

---

[29]Why has country 0, whose exports are numeraire, been chosen as the growing country? Suppose instead that country i grows by dX_i^*. Then substituting in equation (42) the terms

$$-\frac{\partial B_i}{\partial X_i^*} = m_i$$

(the aggregate marginal propensity to import in country i), and the terms

$$-\frac{\partial B_i}{\partial X_i} = -m_{ji},$$

when $i \neq j$, we obtain the criterion:

$$\frac{dP_i}{dX_i} = -m_{1i}\frac{\Delta_{1i}}{\Delta} - \cdots + m_i\frac{\Delta_{ii}}{\Delta} - \cdots - m_{ni}\frac{\Delta_{ni}}{\Delta}. \tag{1}$$

But $m_i\Delta_{ij}/\Delta$ is negative while all the other terms are positive. It would therefore appear that no unambiguous result is possible, and that the method of treating the change as occurring in the numeraire country is a special case.

Nevertheless the economist's intuition tells him that in static analysis the choice of numeraire cannot affect the ultimate change in *relative* prices; and that if the terms of trade of the numeraire country deteriorate when that country grows, the terms of trade of any other country must fall when it grows. He may therefore conclude that P_i must fall in equation (1), that the negative term dominates.

This is in fact correct. Making use of the definition of the aggregate marginal propensity to import, i.e., $m_i \equiv m_{0i} + m_{1i} + \cdots + m_{ni}$, we can rearrange (1) to get:

$$\frac{dP_i}{dX_i^*} = m_{0i}\frac{\Delta_{ii}}{\Delta} + m_{1i}\frac{\Delta_{ii} - \Delta_{1i}}{\Delta} + \cdots + m_{ni}\frac{\Delta_{ii} - \Delta_{ni}}{\Delta}. \tag{2}$$

Now the first term on the right of (2) is clearly negative. The other terms will be negative if the *principal* cofactor of Δ dominates each of the other cofactors, i.e., if $|\Delta_{ii}| > |\Delta_{ji}| (j \neq i)$. But by subtraction of the two cofactors it is easily shown that the resulting $(n-1)$th order determinant $\Delta_{ii} - \Delta_{ji}$ has all the characteristics of Δ (positive off-diagonal elements and dominant negative diagonal elements) except that its sign is opposite to the sign of Δ. (An analogous theorem has been proved by Metzler in analysis of the matrix multiplier.) All the terms on the right of (2) are therefore negative, so P_i must fall as a result of growth in country i.

To avoid these complications I have, in the text, supposed that the policy change occurs in the country whose exports are numeraire, though the result

Tariff Changes. Suppose that country 0 applies an undiscriminatory tariff equal to dt_0 on all imports. At constant foreign prices the tariff-inclusive price of all imports in country 0 rises by dt_0. On the assumption that the government spends the tariff proceeds on home goods, the excess demand for the goods of typical country j, at constant foreign prices, is $-\eta_{j0}I_{j0}dt_0$, where η_{j0} and I_{j0} are, respectively, the elasticity of demand for imports (with respect to own price) and the level of imports, from country j to country 0. The typical term from the general equation (42) becomes

$$\frac{-\partial B_i}{\partial t_0} = \eta_{j0}I_{j0}.$$

The criterion for the change in the terms of trade of country 0 is therefore:

$$\frac{dP_i}{dt_0} = \sum_{j=1}^{n} \eta_{j0}I_{j0}\frac{\Delta_{ji}}{\Delta}. \tag{44}$$

The elasticities are all defined to be positive (Giffen goods are ruled out by the assumption of gross substitution) so the conclusion is again unambiguous: *An increase in tariffs raises the price of the exports of the tariff-imposing country relative to the prices of the exports of all other countries,* on the assumption that tariff proceeds are spent on home goods.[30]

is perfectly general. The same applies to the analysis of tax and tariff changes analyzed below.

[30]If the tariff proceeds are redistributed to consumers an income effect must be added to each term in (44). The tariff proceeds are equal to I_0dt_0, where I_0 is the initial aggregate level of imports, so the typical income term is $-m_{j0}I_0$. The criterion then becomes:

$$\frac{dP_i}{dt_0} = \sum_{j=1}^{n} [\eta_{j0}I_{j0} - m_{j0}I_0]\frac{\Delta_{ji}}{\Delta} = \sum_{j=1}^{n} \left[\eta'_{j0}I_{j0} - m_{j0}\left(I_0 - I_{j0}\right)\right]\frac{\Delta_{ji}}{\Delta}$$

which makes use of the relation between net and gross elasticities, $\eta_{j0} = \eta'_{j0} + m_{j0}$. Notice that the sign of dP_i/dt_0 is not unambiguously determined; in both equations the coefficients of the cofactors are composed of one positive and one negative term, and we have no information about which term is dominant. It is

Consumption and Production Tax Changes. The effects of a consumption tax on import goods are equivalent to the effects of a tariff if there is no domestic production of these goods. If there is domestic production of import goods then the typical term, from the skeleton equation (42), is $\eta_{cj0}y_{j0}$, where η_{cjo} is the elasticity of consumer demand in 0 for the products exported by country j, and y_{j0} is the level of domestic consumption of these products. This assumes again that tax proceeds are spent on domestic goods. The criterion for the change in the relative price of the exports of the typical country i is therefore:

$$\frac{dP_i}{dt_{c0}} = \sum_{j=1}^{n} \eta_{cj0}y_{j0}\frac{\Delta_{ji}}{\Delta} \tag{45}$$

which is necessarily negative. Thus *the terms of trade improve with respect to all countries as a result of a tax on imported goods.* By similar analysis it can be shown that the terms of trade worsen as a result of an increased tax on the consumption of export goods. And by changing signs we get the criteria for the effects of subsidies on the consumption of import and export goods.

By similar analysis it can be shown that the typical coefficient of (42) resulting from a tax on the production of exportable goods is

therefore possible that some prices rise relative to the price of the exports of the tariff-imposing country.

This indefinite result differs from the two-country analysis where the net effect of the tariff is a pure substitution effect away from imports and to home goods. On the assumption that all exports are gross substitutes, and that no goods are inferior, all substitution effects are positive in the multiple-country analysis also; but it cannot, as far as I know, be proved that the net effect of the tariff is a shift of demand away from the imports of *every* country. A tariff applied to the exports of a particular country creates a deficit in that country's balance of payments equal to a pure substitution effect; but if, in addition, tariffs are applied to the exports of third countries, the income effect resulting from the distribution of the tariff proceeds of the third countries to some extent offsets or reverses the initial deficit in the first country's balance.

It should be possible to prove, however, that at least some foreign prices fall relative to the price of the exports of the tariff-imposing country, by making use of the proposition that net substitution must be away from imports and to home goods.

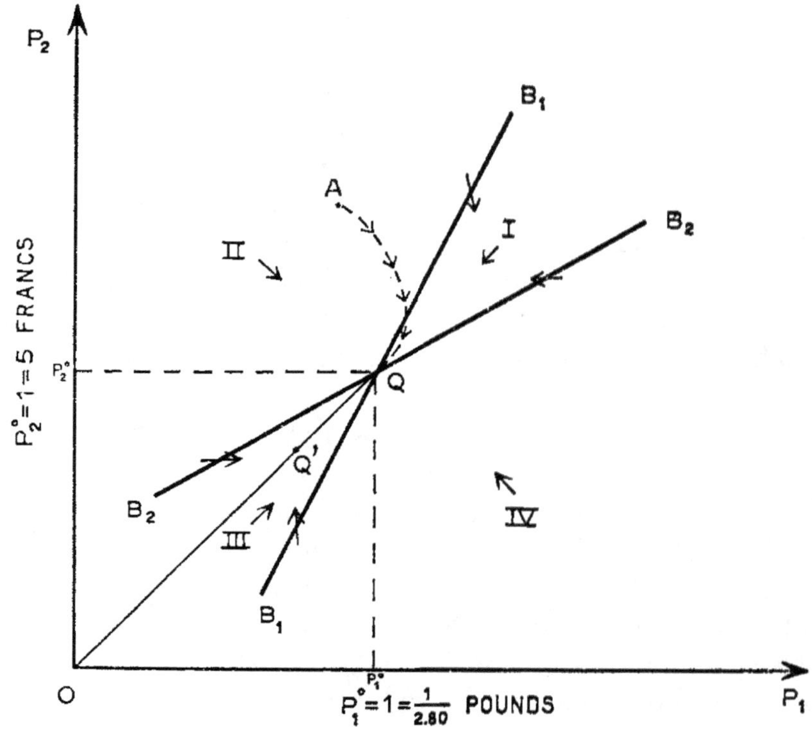

Figure 8. Multiple-Country Stability Conditions.

Assume three countries, the U.S. (0), the U.K. (1) and France (2) with the respective currency prices (expressed in dollars) 1, P_1 and P_2. Choose units of pounds and francs so that, at equilibrium, P_1 and P_1 are each unity. (If equilibrium ratios are $\$1 = 1/2.80$ pounds $= 5$ francs then $1/2.80$ pounds and 5 francs become the British and French currency units.) The two curves B_1B_1 and B_2B_2 trace the loci of pound-franc prices which allow equilibrium in the British and French balances. At Q both balances are in equilibrium implying, by Cournot's Law, equilibrium in the U.S. balance.

If all currencies are gross substitutes both curves have positive slopes: this follows because appreciation of the franc must be associated with appreciation of the pound to maintain equilibrium. Moreover, B_1B_1 has a slope greater than 45 degrees and B_2B_2 has a slope less than 45 degrees; this follows because of our choice of currency units and because appreciation of the dollar is equivalent to depreciation of the franc and pound in equal proportion; a movement along the line OQ from Q to Q' must improve the French and British balances and worsen the U.S. balance. Four quadrants can then be identified: east and west of B_1B_1 there are deficits and surpluses, respectively, in the British balance; and north and south of B_2B_2 there are deficits and surpluses in the French balance.

$\epsilon'_{pj0}Y_{j0}$, where ϵ'_{pj0} is the elasticity of supply in country 0 of the good exported by the jth country, and Y_{j0} is the domestic production (i.e., the production in 0) of the good exported by the jth country. The criterion is therefore:

$$\frac{dP_i}{dt_{p0}} = \sum_{j=1}^{n} \epsilon'_{pj0}Y_{j0}\frac{\Delta_{ji}}{\Delta}. \tag{46}$$

Thus if supply elasticities are all positive *a tax on the production of exportables improves the terms of trade of the taxing country with respect to all other countries.* [Note that each term in (46) is zero if country 0 is completely specialized.] The same criterion applies, *mutatis mutandis*, for production taxes on imported goods, or production subsidies. (See Figure 8.)

Unilateral Payments. Suppose that country 0 pays country S an annual tribute, or gift, or loan (ignoring interest payments). Then expenditure in 0 decreases and in S decreases by the amount of the payment. The demand for all goods in 0 decreases and in S increases if there are no inferior goods. At constant prices the deficit created by these expenditure changes in the balance of payments of the jth. country is $(m_{j0} - m_{js})dT_{s0}$, where dT_{s0} is the value of the transfer. The criterion for the change in the price of exports in the receiving

---

Figure 8 (*Continued*).

On the dynamic assumption that the dollar prices of pounds and francs rise and fall in proportion to the disequilibrium in the British and French balances, the arrows in each quadrant indicate the forces impelling a return to equilibrium. The reader may easily satisfy himself that the equilibrium position, once disturbed, will be restored. From the disequilibrium position A, for example, the path may follow the broken line AQ, becoming "trapped" in Quadrant I; or it may become trapped in Quadrant III and hence move to equilibrium.

To determine geometrically the movement of the prices as a result of policy changes it is necessary to indicate the direction in which the two curves shift. If U.S. output and expenditure increase, more British and French goods are demanded at constant prices improving both British and French balances; the two curves therefore shift away from the origin and the new equilibrium point moves to somewhere in Quadrant I. Similarly, for the tariff and tax changes analyzed in the text both curves shift toward the origin with an unambiguous improvement in the U.S. terms of trade.

country, relative to the price of the exports of the paying country, is therefore:

$$\frac{dP_s}{dT_{s0}} = \sum_{j=1}^{n} (m_{j0} - m_{js}) \frac{\Delta_{js}}{\Delta}. \tag{47}$$

[In the term $j = s$ the coefficient is $(m_{s0} - m_{ss}) = (m_{s0} - c_s) = (m_{s0} + m_s - 1)$ where c_s and m_s are, respectively, the marginal propensities to consume and import in country S.] The unilateral payment, through expenditure changes in the transferor and transferee, rearranges demand throughout the world in a way which does not permit any a priori generalization, a result which can be expected from the analysis of transfer between two countries.[31]

One special case, however, is of interest in view of recent discussions of foreign aid and "tied" exports. Suppose that country 0 makes a gift to a foreign country but requires that the gift be spent on its own exports. (It may be supposed that the gift is financed by taxation and that the financial transfer involves the grant of credits from an export-import bank.) In this case the price of the exports of the paying country rises relative to the price of the exports of the receiving country (all the terms m_{js} are zero). This does not imply, however, that the transfer "burden" is negative—that real income in the transferring country declines by less than the gift—since the prices of the exports of some of the third countries may rise. It further assumes that the receiving country does not re-export the tied exports to third countries.

Comparison of Two-Country and Multiple-Country Models. The foregoing account of policy changes in a system containing many national units naturally leads to more complicated conclusions than in the case of a system containing only two countries. Applying only the restrictions of stability, I have not been able to show that two-country and multiple-country systems lead to substantially the same conclusions. The difficulty lies in relations of gross complementarity

[31]The propositions in this section require modification if there are limiting cases such as infinite or zero elasticities, and zero or negative marginal propensities to spend.

among the exports of the various countries. Gross complementarity is consistent with stability in the multiple-country system but inconsistent with stability in the two-country system. The two-country model cannot therefore be expected to suggest "theorems which admit of extension to more concrete cases" when gross complementarity is involved.

However, when gross complementarity is absent—when all exports are gross substitutes—there is a remarkable similarity between the conclusions of the two models. Productivity, tariff and tax changes move the terms of trade in the same direction in the many-country system as in the simpler system. The explanation of this similarity lies in what may be called the Law of Composition of Countries. If all foreign exports are *perfect* substitutes for each other, the foreign countries can be aggregated into a composite country and called the "rest of the world"; in that case the conclusions of the two models will agree both qualitatively and quantitatively. But if foreign exports are only *imperfect* substitutes for each other exact results cannot be obtained by the use of a composite country. However, while the *quantitative* conclusions of the two models will in this case differ, the *qualitative* conclusions, with one qualification,[32] remain. There is a presumption, then, that the use of two-country models will not be subject to serious error provided that all exports are gross substitutes.

References

1. K. J. Arrow and L. Hurwicz, "On the Stability of the Competitive Equilibrium, I," *Econometrica,* Oct. 1958, *26,* 522–52.
2. A. Cournot, *Researches into the Mathematical Principles of the Theory of Wealth.* Transl. by T. Bacon. New York 1897.
3. F. Y. Edgeworth, *Papers Relating to Political Economy,* Vol. 2. London 1925.

[32]The qualification refers to the treatment of income effects examined in footnote 31.

The most important generalization of the classical system has been provided by Mosak [18].

4. F. HAHN, "Gross Substitutes and the Dynamic Stability of General Equilibrium," *Econometrica,* Jan. 1958, *26,* 169–70.
5. A. O. HIRSCHMAN, "Devaluation and the Trade Balance: A Note," *Rev. Econ. Stat.,* Feb. 1949, *31,* 50–53.
6. H. G. JOHNSON, "Economic Expansion and International Trade," *Man. School Econ. Soc. Stud.,* May 1955, *23,* 95–112.
7. ———, "The Transfer Problem and Exchange Stability," *Jour. Pol. Econ.,* June 1956, *64,* 212–25.
8. ———, "Increasing Productivity, Income-Price Trends and the Trade Balance," *Econ. Jour.,* Sept. 1954, *64,* 462–85.
9. W. LEONTIEF, "A Note on the Pure Theory of Transfer," *Explorations in Economics,* New York 1936, pp. 84–92.
10. A. P. LERNER, "The Symmetry between Import and Export Taxes," *Economica,* Aug. 1936, *3,* 308–13.
11. A. MARSHALL, *The Pure Theory of Foreign Trade.* London 1879; reprinted 1930.
12. ———, *Money Credit and Commerce.* London 1923.
13. J. E. MEADE, *A Geometry of International Trade.* London 1952.
14. ———, *The Balance of Payments Mathematical Supplement.* London 1951.
15. ———, "A Geometrical Representation of Balance-of-Payments Policy," *Economica,* Nov. 1949, *16,* 305–20.
16. L. A. METZLER, "Tariffs, the Terms of Trade, and the Distribution of National Income," *Jour. Pol. Econ.,* Feb. 1949, *57,* 1–29.
17. J. S. MILL, *Principles of Political Economy,* Vol. 2. New York 1896.
18. J. L. MOSAK, *General Equilibrium Theory in International Trade.* Indiana 1944.
19. R. A. MUNDELL, "Transport Costs in International Trade Theory," *Can. Jour. Econ.,* Aug. 1957, *23,* 331–48.
20. T. NEGISHI, "A Note on the Stability of an Economy where All Goods Are Gross Substitutes," *Econometrica,* July 1958, *26,* 445–47.
21. S. A. OZGA, "Tariffs and the Balance of Payments," *Quart. Jour. Econ.,* Nov. 1957, *71,* 630–8.
22. P. A. SAMUELSON, *Foundations of Economic Analysis.* Cambridge 1953.
23. ———, "The Transfer Problem and Transport Costs: The Terms of Trade When Impediments are Absent, I," *Econ. Jour.,* June 1952, *62,* 278–304.
24. J. VINER, *Studies in the Theory of International Trade.* New York 1937.

Chapter 3

The Pure Theory of International Trade: A Survey*

Jagdish Bhagwati

This paper[1] surveys that branch of international trade theory which, following Marshall, is generally described as "pure." This epithet separates it from "monetary" theory. It is *not* to be taken to imply exceptional esotericism and abstraction from the problems of the real world. Indeed, I propose, quite deliberately, to give prominence to that part of the growing, new literature in pure theory which attempts explicitly to bring the theory on to the ground—through empirical verification of testable propositions, through measurement of the gains and losses from changes in trade policy and through the formulation of analytical and operational models to assist the developmental planning that is rapidly becoming a key characteristic of the developing nations.

The pure theory of international trade represents essentially the application of the theories of value and welfare to questions of

*Originally published in *The Economic Journal*, 74(293), pp. 1–84. This is the fourth of the series of Surveys supported by the Rockefeller Foundation.

[1]This paper was virtually completed when I was with the Indian Statistical Institute. For correspondence and/or discussions, I am thankful to Professors H. G. Johnson, R. W. Jones, C. P. Kindleberger, B. S. Minhas, P. A. Samuelson and T. N. Srinivasan. V. Balasubramanian and R. Tagat have assisted with the computational work.

international economics.[2] Although the distinction between them has not always been clear in many writings, it is none the less true that two different species of problems have been the subject of analysis in pure theory. There are questions of "positive" or "objective" analysis: for instance, what determines the composition of trade; how will tariffs affect factor prices; what is the effect of trade on the terms of trade? On the other hand, there are questions in "welfare" or "normative" economics: among them, does free trade maximise world real income; are tariffs superior to free trade from the viewpoint of national advantage; how do tariffs compare with subsidies as forms of State intervention?[3]

The range of questions that have been asked is impressive. The recent literature which is addressed to them runs into several dozen books and over two hundred papers. This makes a brief survey exceptionally difficult, even if confined to the developments in the last two or three decades.[4] This difficulty is compounded by the fact that the subject has already been extensively, frequently and recently surveyed. We currently have a cogent and lucid survey in a brief monograph by Haberler [4], revised only in 1961; a nearly exhaustive,

[2]The pure theory of trade thus differs structurally from general theory in the kinds of questions asked, rather than in the kinds of assumptions made. This vexed question has been considered at length by Haberler [4, Chapter I].

[3]The distinction between "positive" and "welfare" questions is recent in trade theory and appears to have been stated explicitly and emphatically only as late as 1933 by Ohlin [34]. Ohlin, who distinguished between these two aspects, criticised the classical economists for muddling them. As Haberler [4, p. 3], however, has charmingly pointed out: "That his demand for not just a clear distinction between political evaluation and theoretical explanation, but for actual separation of these two areas by putting them into separate books or chapters, is easier postulated than accomplished is demonstrated by Ohlin himself. Thus, in an early passage of his celebrated treatise, in the midst of 'objective theory,' he proves in typical classical manner that interregional trade and division of labour results in an increased social product without making it clear that this statement implies a value judgment on his part and is not merely 'objective analysis."'

[4]Thus Lipsey's [7] concise and brilliant review of the theory of customs unions (part of the theory of discriminatory tariff changes) in this JOURNAL runs into several pages. And it deals with a comparatively recent field which forms only a small segment of the literature on pure theory.

full-length account in a 1960 volume by Caves [3]; an excellent, theoretical survey of some of the central analytical propositions of pure theory by Mundell [11] in 1960; and, most embarrassingly, a survey of some of the more impressive recent developments in pure theory by myself [1] as recently as 1961.[5]

To collapse the immense literature into a concise survey, to exercise the inevitable selectivity (with respect to both authors and problems of analysis) to maximum advantage, it is necessary to have a precise, logical frame. The structure of this paper is built squarely on the clear distinction between "positive" and "normative" pure theory.

Under positive theory, in turn, a distinction has been drawn between: (1) the propositions of "statics," which describe the properties of an equilibrium situation at *any given point* of time; (2) the propositions of "comparative statics," which concern the *differences* in the equilibrium values of variables between situations at *two different points of* (conceptual) time; and (3) the propositions of "dynamics," which involve time in an essential way.

The static propositions which have attracted the greatest analytical interest concern: (1) the pattern of trade: the determination of commodities as exports and imports; and (2) the configuration of factor prices. The analysis of the former question has further been enriched greatly by a recent, noticeable trend towards empirical verification. The propositions of comparative statics (which continue to be almost exclusively deductive) fall again into two classes: (1) those that concern the effect, on equilibrium prices and quantities, *under a pre-defined trade policy*, of an autonomous change in one of the following data: production functions, demand and factor supply; and (2) those that relate to the effect, on equilibrium prices and quantities, of a change in trade policy itself, while other data are constant.

[5]To these may be added Meade's celebrated works [8, 9, 10], which cover the entire field and the writings of Johnson [5, 6], which have done much to synthesis the literature on many aspects of trade theory. Mention may also be made of two papers: Lipsey's [7] 1960 survey of customs-union theory and the review in 1960 by myself and Johnson [2] of certain historical controversies in pure theory.

The development of pure theory has witnessed a synthesis and simplification of these propositions in comparative statics which eludes the few, though diverse, attempts at dynamic analysis. This synthesis has also been accomplished in terms of an analytical framework characterised by primary factors of production and integrated processes of production. This constitutes a central limitation of the theory in a theoretical world where this conceptualisation has been replaced generally by the more general approach of process analysis and in a real world where a large portion of the world trade consists of intermediates and capital goods and an increasing number of developing nations' imports are coming to consist almost exclusively of these commodities.

The parts of this paper dealing with positive theory have therefore been divided into the following five groups:

1. Section I: *Theorems in Statics: The Pattern of Trade.*
2. Section II: *Theorems in Statics: Factor Price-Equalisation.*
3. Section III: *Theorems in Comparative Statics.*
4. Section IV: *Theorems in Dynamics.*
5. Section V: *Central Limitations of Pure Theory: Intermediates and Capital Goods.*

In the theory of welfare and trade the classification has been easier. There is, on the one hand, the "traditional" theory which is addressed to *qualitative* propositions that rank different trade policies (*e.g.*, free trade is superior to no trade) and can be classified according to whether they satisfy Samuelson's superior-for-all-income-distributions criterion. On the other hand, there is a growing, important segment of the literature which aims at *quantitative* measures of costs and benefits — prompted by the objective of making economic analysis policy-oriented. At the same time the growth of centralised planning in many developing countries has raised the interesting questions of the *operational* use of trade theory's welfare insights and results as part of the complement of planning techniques; and some useful experience has been obtained.

The survey of welfare propositions in trade theory, therefore, has been divided into three major groups:

1. Section VI: *Welfare Propositions: Gains from Trade.*
2. Section VII: *Measurement of Welfare.*
3. Section VIII: *Trade Theory and Development Planning.*[6]

1. Theorems in Statics: The Pattern of Trade

The theory of comparative advantage (or cost), which concerns the determination of the pattern of trade, constitutes perhaps the oldest set of analytical propositions in pure theory. It belongs to the realm of "statics" because traditionally it has been formulated as a theorem concerning the determination of (traded) commodities into exports and imports in a static, analytical framework. This is certainly true of the two major theories, Ricardian and Heckscher–Ohlin [1], that have dominated this field.

There are, no doubt, different possible ways in which an "international economy" may be simulated by a theorist. Each such "model" could be used to deduce analytical propositions. Indeed, the literature on pure theory contains a large number of such idealisations, among the most celebrated being those of Yntema, Mosak and Graham [3].[7]

From the viewpoint of propositions concerning the pattern of trade, the two models of significance are those of Ricardo and Heckscher–Ohlin [19, 34]. Not merely have these models been used to derive "logically true" theorems concerning the trade pattern.[8] These theorems have also now been adapted to formulate testable hypotheses (based on factors stressed in the respective models). And these hypotheses have been subjected to empirical verification

[6]Although the paper falls neatly into these eight sections, there are inevitably some overlaps. None the less, I would maintain that the proposed classification is the most advantageous from the viewpoint of assessing the current state, limitations and trends of the pure theory of trade.

[7]For a summary statement of these and other models, Caves [3] is an excellent reference. A cataloging of such models however is of little interest as any number of models can be put down as one wishes. Only those models are of significance which have been used to yield theorems; and then it is only in considering those theorems that they merit discussion.

[8]The phrase "logically true" is used there in the strict mathematical sense: a statement that is true in every logically possible case is said to be *logically true.*

in a series of excellent papers. In consequence, new theories have now been devised, which provide *alternative* explanations of the pattern of trade. Prominent among these are the analyses of Kravis [22] and Linder [27]. These four theories concerning the pattern of international specialisation are discussed here, distinguishing clearly between the formulations as deductive, analytical propositions (which are logically true under a specified set of sufficient conditions) and formulations as testable hypotheses.

The Ricardian Theory

The Ricardian Theory can be construed in either of two ways: (1) as a highly simplified model which was intended to be, and served as, an eminently successful instrument for demonstrating the welfare proposition that trade is beneficial; or (2) as a serious attempt at isolating the crucial variables which can be used to "explain" the pattern of trade. There is little doubt that the former view is plausible. A careful study of the original texts yields supporting evidence; the most persuasive element is the fact that when both Ricardo and Mill discussed the "positive" (as opposed to "normative") proposition relating to the effects of cheap corn *imports* from the colonies on profits, wages and rents, and thence on the approach of the stationary state, they were using the full-fledged classical model characterised by three factors and diminishing returns [1]. And yet the impact of the Ricardian "constant cost" model in recent literature has been predominantly as an idealisation which affords a significant clue to the structure of foreign trade.[9]

[9]This has been the result of two factors: (i) traditionally the question whether the Ricardian theory should be construed as positive or normative has rarely been raised; it has always seemed "natural" to construe Ricardo as though he were genuinely attempting to explain the pattern of trade with his simple model; and (ii) the Ricardian "demonstration" of the benefits of trade, long since challenged as inadequate by Barrett Whale, has now been superseded by the elegant and more rigorous formulations of the new welfare economics and Samuelson's classic proof of 1939—so that it is no longer easy to see that the Ricardian preoccupation was predominantly with normative aspects.

On the latter interpretation the Ricardian theory can be deduced directly from the celebrated England–Portugal example in Ricardo's *Principles.* If it is assumed that there are two commodities, a single factor (labour) and constant returns to scale (in each activity),[10] the pre-trade commodity price ratio will be a function exclusively of the (scale-free) output-factor ratios contained in the production functions. The combination of a single factor with constant returns to scale ensures that neither demand nor the level of factor supply makes any difference to the equilibrium commodity price ratio in a closed economy.[11] Since Ricardo assumes a similar model for each country, it follows that the pre-trade commodity price ratio, and hence the composition of trade, is exclusively determined by international differences in relative output-factor ratios. If a_1 and a_2 are the output-factor ratios for country I and b_1 and b_2 for country II in activities 1 and 2 respectively, country I will export commodity 1 and import commodity 2 if $a_1/a_2 > b_1/b$, (as this will imply that commodity 1 will be cheaper, and commodity 2 dearer, in country I than in country II *prior to trade*). The algebraic condition is frequently written as $a_1/b_1 > a_2/b_2$, which states the condition in terms of "comparative factor productivities." If, however, the number of commodities is increased beyond two, while maintaining the two-country assumption, it is no longer possible to derive the "strong" Ricardian theorem that the trade pattern is determined exclusively by international differences in production functions (*i.e.*, by comparative factor productivities). The model now implies a weaker proposition: there will be a chain in which all commodities are ranked in terms of their comparative factor-productivity ratios such that *it will always be true that each of a country's exports will have a higher factor-productivity ratio than each of its imports.* The precise composition of exports and imports

[10]The last assumption listed here need not be implicit in the preceding one, since fixed factors like land may well be subsumed in the shape of the production function.

[11]The reason is that the resulting production possibility curve is non-strictly convex and characterised by a constant rate of transformation.

(*i.e.*, where the chain will be cut, dividing the exports and the imports) can be determined only by bringing demand into the model [20]. This proposition will continue to hold also in the more general framework of many countries and commodities, which represents a generalisation of Ricardo's two-country model by Graham. In an elegant generalisation of Ricardo's theory, drawing upon McKenzie's earlier work [78], Jones [69] has shown that, taking each pair of countries, only comparing the labour cost ratios of the commodities they are producing in specialisation, the Ricardian bilateral cost comparisons are necessarily satisfied. (These propositions relate, more generally, to the location of production in a free-trade world: their implications for the trade pattern are in conformity with the Ricardian theory.)

When international trade economists have attempted to formulate hypotheses, based on the Ricardian theory, and test whether observable trade conforms to the postulated pattern, the real difficulty has been that of trying to adapt the one-factor, Ricardian approach to the multi-factor real world. Two ways in which this adaptation may be made can be distinguished.

One way would be to focus on the fact that the Ricardian model emphasises the crucial role of comparative differences in *production functions* so that the testable proposition should be developed in these terms. For instance, if the technology in activity i could be characterised by $Q_i = \lambda_i^{\mathrm{I}} Q_i(K_i; L_i)$ for country I and by $Q_i = \lambda_i^{\mathrm{II}} Q_i\,(K_i; L_i)$ for country II so that the *only* difference between the two countries' production functions for an identical activity is a multiplicative scalar ($\lambda_i^{\mathrm{II}}/\lambda_i^{\mathrm{I}}$ in this case), then the Ricardian testable hypothesis could be construed to mean that

$$\frac{\lambda_i^{\mathrm{II}}}{\lambda_i^{\mathrm{I}}} > \frac{\lambda_i^{\mathrm{II}}}{\lambda_i^{\mathrm{I}}}$$

$$i = 1, 2, \ldots m \quad i = m + 1, \ldots n$$

where commodities $i = 1, 2, \ldots m$ are country II's exports and commodities $i = m + 1, \ldots n$ are its imports. This would be a

Ricardian hypothesis—as much as any other.[12] The possibility of testing such a hypothesis is not, by any means, remote. Minhas [33, p. 154] states, in a brilliant paper on the Heckscher–Ohlin theory, that "the isoquants in different countries, except for a pure scale change, look alike; and the marginal rates of substitution are unchanged at given capital: labour ratios" when homohypallagic production functions are fitted to the data for certain comparable industries in Japan and the United States. This empirical evidence seems to provide the means to test the kind of Ricardian hypothesis formulated here.[13]

The most frequent interpretation for the purpose of formulating a testable proposition, however, has been in terms of the factor productivities themselves. The comparative factor productivities, defined in terms of an arbitrarily chosen factor (almost always labour),[14] have been taken as providing the necessary clue to the trade pattern.

[12]The conditions under which this proposition is logically true could be established by an extension of the theoretical work on the Heckscher–Ohlin theory and on the effects of neutral technical progress [5, Chapter I and III]. For instance, if all the assumptions which are shown to be sufficient for the logical validity of the Heckscher–Ohlin theorem are made with the *only* difference that the production functions are not identical, but differ between countries in the manner postulated in the text, it follows that the (Ricardian-type) hypothesis in the text concerning the pattern of trade will be logically true.

[13]Minhas comes close to doing this, but does not see the problem in this way because he is focusing on the implications of such "neutral" differences in production functions for the Heckscher–Ohlin theorem. Credit must be given to him, however, for having seen the possibility of construing the Ricardian approach in the broader way (of differences in production functions) suggested here, as against the narrower approach of labour productivity ratios that is to be found in the literature.

[14]There is nothing in the basic *structure* of the Ricardian model which requires that this single factor be labour. It could be anything else. However, it has mostly been taken to be labour. The reasons for this exclusive preference may be that: (i) the historical context of the labour theory of value, in terms of which Ricardo's comparative cost doctrine has usually been understood, makes it inevitable that the formal identity between labour and any other factor, as noted here, should have been missed, and (ii) there has been, until recently, also a widespread tendency, in economic literature generally, to take labour productivity as the index of "productivity" rather than, say, capital productivity.

The intuitive and ultimate rationale behind this interpretation is easily stated (and, as will be evident later, has an important bearing on the procedure of testing). Since exports will take place only when domestic (pretrade) prices are lower than abroad, it follows that

$$\frac{\mathrm{P}_i^{\mathrm{I}}}{\mathrm{P}_i^{\mathrm{II}}} < 1$$

$$i = 1, 2, \ldots m$$

where $\frac{\mathrm{P}_i^{\mathrm{I}}}{\mathrm{P}_i^{\mathrm{II}}}$ refers to the price-ratio of commodity i, exported by country I, *prior to trade.*[15] Similarly,

$$\frac{P_i^{\mathrm{I}}}{P_i^{\mathrm{II}}} > 1$$

$$i = m + 1, \ldots n$$

where the commodity i is exported by country II. Hence

$$\frac{P_i^{\mathrm{I}}}{P_i^{\mathrm{II}}} < \frac{P_i^{\mathrm{I}}}{P_i^{\mathrm{II}}}$$

$$i = 1, \ldots m \quad i = m + 1, \ldots n$$

Now it is possible to write these prices (defined as equal to costs) in terms of three component factors:

$$P_i = a_i \cdot \frac{W_i}{L_i} \cdot \frac{TC_i}{W_i}$$

where a_i is the labour: output ratio, W_i is the wage bill (so that $\frac{W_i}{L_i} = w_i$ is the wage-rate) and TC_i the total cost (inclusive of profits, by definition) in activity i. If we now argue that it is, in practice, enough to focus attention on a_i and to ignore the other two factors (on the ground that either they are insignificant *or* they are identical between countries individually or as a product), then we could substitute

[15]Where transport costs are present, lower pre-trade prices are only a *necessary* condition for exports; where transport costs (and similar cost-raising factors) are ignored, lower pre-trade prices also become a *sufficient* condition.

a_i for p_i in the above price-comparison. This would give us the condition

$$\frac{a_i^{\text{I}}}{a_i^{\text{II}}} < \frac{a_i^{\text{I}}}{a_i^{\text{II}}} \tag{1}$$

$$i = 1, 2, \ldots m \quad i = m + 1, \ldots n$$

This is, in fact, the condition stated frequently as the Ricardian hypothesis.

This chain of reasoning also leads to a further formulation. It is possible to advance a variation of the hypothesis, which brings into the picture the structure of the wage-rates as well. This can be done by rewriting the previous hypothesis thus:

$$\frac{a_i^{\text{I}}}{a_i^{\text{II}}} \cdot \frac{w_i^{\text{I}}}{w_i^{\text{II}}} < \frac{a_i^{\text{I}}}{a_i^{\text{II}}} \cdot \frac{w_i^{\text{I}}}{w_i^{\text{II}}} \tag{2}$$

$$i = 1, 2, \ldots m \quad i = m + 1, \ldots n$$

This is, in fact, a statement of the Ricardian hypothesis which is in terms of comparative *unit labour costs* and not *labour productivity.* It is the hypothesis which is to be found in much of the empirical literature [1].

Although it appears relatively simple to go on from these formulations to their tests, there are some points of interest that need to be spelled out.

(1) To begin with, "indirect" tests of these hypotheses readily suggest themselves but can be treacherous. For instance, it has been customary to argue through an attempted demonstration of the international "similarity" of the inter-industrial wage-rate structure and the pattern of the total-cost/wages ratio. Caves [3, p. 272] has cited Kravis' [21, pp. 145–6] empirical results, which show that the ranking of industries by hourly earnings of workers is almost identical between Japan and the United States, to argue that these data lend force to the Ricardian hypothesis in terms of comparative labour productivity differences (as the determinants of relative price

differences).[16] However, such a deduction leaves out of reckoning the possibility that the structure of the costs–wages ratio may be largely dissimilar between trading countries and makes implicitly an unverified assumption of "similarity" of this structure. This procedure, in any case, is unsound, since, although each of the two structures (costs–wages and wage-rates) may be internationally "dissimilar," their product may be similar as a result of these dissimilarities being offsetting. A method which proceeds in terms of investigating the similarities of individual structures will leave out this possibility and thereby constitute an unduly restrictive and false test for the empirical verification of the Ricardian hypothesis in question.

(2) But then, if a direct test of the Ricardian hypotheses were adopted, examining whether the labour productivity or unit wage–cost ratios for the exports and imports for two countries (taken bilaterally) conform to the postulated relationships, would that be enough? I do not think so. Let me cast my argument in terms of hypothesis (1), which relates to labour productivity ratios—it is equally valid for hypothesis (2) relating to unit wage–cost ratios.

It will be recalled that hypothesis (1) is derived in two steps. (*a*) First, it is argued that the (pre-trade) prices are such that the relative price (defined as the domestic over the foreign price) of an exported good must be lower than the relative price of an imported good. This is a natural assumption to make; it merely reflects the assumption that the profit motive will direct the pattern of trade.[17] This, however, relates to the *pre-trade* prices. But the

---

[16]Similar data, showing similarity of industrial wage structures, have been produced for the United States, United Kingdom, Canada and (only a little less successfully) Sweden by Lebergott [23] None of this, however, adds up to anything impressive, since the coverage in terms of both activities and nations is severely limited.

[17]Theoretically, of course, one can think of cases where the pattern of trade does not conform to this rule. For instance, the contrary possibility can arise if there are domestic distortions (*i.e.*,divergence of the domestic rate of transformation in production from the commodity price-ratios) [112]. In anticipation, I may point out that this qualification does not apply to the *post-trade,* relative price comparison for exportables and importables, to which I proceed immediately in the text.

observed prices are inevitably *post-trade* prices. This should have posed an impossible difficulty in testing any proposition concerning the pattern of trade and prices. However, it is easy to get around the problem when one reckons with the fact of transport (and other) costs that lead to a difference in the post-trade f.o.b. and c.i.f. (landed) prices. This difference in f.o.b. and c.i.f. prices means that the price–trade proposition that the relative price of an exported good must be lower than that of an imported good will continue necessarily to hold (with the domestic price of a good defined f.o.b. and the foreign prices c.i.f for exported goods). The proposition is necessarily valid empirically in a world which is characterised by natural and artificial cost-raising factors. It therefore calls for no conscious attempt at verification. This is indeed a great gain. It is, however, an advantage not shared by the other postulate that must be made before the Ricardian hypothesis can be derived. (*b*) This other assumption consists in arguing that prices can be approximated by labour productivities. This proposition takes generally the strong form that the linear regression equation fitted to observed labour productivity ratios (for each activity in both countries) and corresponding price ratios would yield a 45 degree line from the origin.[18] This strong assumption, which is equivalent to arguing that the inter-industry structure of the total cost per unit labour is identical between the trading countries, is only a sufficient condition for yielding, along with the price–trade assumption, the required Ricardian hypothesis. It is also the condition that is most frequently found in the literature on Ricardian theories [3, Chapter X]. A weaker, but still sufficient, assumption would be to make labour productivity ratios a monotonically increasing function of price ratios. But the weaker this assumption gets, the more difficult it becomes to interpret it in meaningful, economic terms.[19]

[18]The labour productivity ratio here must be defined as the foreign labour productivity divided by the domestic; and the price ratio is defined as the domestic price divided by the foreign.

[19]In the tests of this assumption which I later attempt in this paper even the weaker hypothesis does not get through: the linear regressions yield very poor fits.

Since one does want to know why it is that the trade pattern is characterised, if at all, by the comparative labour productivity ranking postulated by Ricardian hypothesis (1), I would argue that it is also necessary to supplement such a direct verification by a further verification of whether labour productivity ratios exhibit the (underlying) hypothesised relationship with price ratios.[20] Unfortunately, neither the direct verification of the rankings of exports and imports (for a pair of trading countries) in terms of their comparative labour productivities or unit wage–cost ratios nor the necessary, supplementary test of the implied relationship between price ratios and labour productivity or unit wage–cost ratios has yet been attempted.

The empirical literature that exists, in some abundance, concerns itself with really different kinds of testable propositions concerning trade. These hypotheses do have some overlap with the Ricardian hypotheses (1) and (2), with the unfortunate consequence that the surprisingly good results that attempts at verifying them have turned up have been construed frequently as validating the Ricardian approach [3, Chapter X]. The pioneering study in this field is by MacDougall [28, 29], with follow-up by Balassa [13], Stern [40] and MacDougall [30] himself.

[20]Concerning the derivation of the Ricardian hypothesis (1) in this two-step fashion, however, there is just a little more that may be said. It may be contended that labour productivities approximate the *pre-trade* prices but that trade leads to boosted profits in the export industries with no imputation to wages and no impact on labour productivities. If so, one *could* find evidence for the trade pattern exhibiting the Ricardian ranking in terms of comparative labour productivities and/or unit wage–cost ratios, but *not* necessarily for the productivity or unit wage–cost ratios being related in any way to the price ratios. While, of course, this is theoretically possible (and such a theory would have its own further implications which should then be tested), I do not find it plausible. Why should labour productivity ratios, for instance, be a good approximation to relative prices before trade but cease to be so after trade? This asymmetry seems to have no rationale. In any case, the particular chain of reasoning used in the text, aside from being more plausible, is also the one generally subscribed to; and hence its implications have been fully spelled out.

Taking American and British exports of similar commodities to third markets, MacDougall [28, 29] has conducted analysis which is tantamount to investigating three hypotheses: $\frac{a_i^{\mathrm{II}}}{a_i^{\mathrm{I}}}$ is positively correlated with

$$\frac{E_i^{\mathrm{I}}}{E_i^{\mathrm{II}}}, \quad (i = 1, \ldots, k); \tag{3}$$

If

$$\frac{a_i^{\mathrm{II}}}{a_i^{\mathrm{I}}} \cdot \frac{w_i^{\mathrm{II}}}{w_i^{\mathrm{I}}} > 1,$$

then

$$\frac{E_i^{\mathrm{I}}}{E_i^{\mathrm{II}}} > 1, \ (i = 1, \ldots, k) : \tag{4}$$

and $\frac{a_i^{\mathrm{II}}}{a_i^{\mathrm{I}}} \cdot \frac{w_i^{\mathrm{II}}}{w_i^{\mathrm{I}}}$ is positively correlated with

$$\frac{E_i^{\mathrm{I}}}{E_i^{\mathrm{II}}}, \ (i = 1, \ldots, k) \tag{5}$$

where $\mathrm{E}_i^{\mathrm{I}}/\mathrm{E}_i^{\mathrm{II}}$ is the ratio of exports of commodity i by countries I and II respectively to third markets.[21] Stern has recently followed MacDougall's hypotheses and procedures closely, but introduced more recent data on productivity. MacDougall [30] has done the same. Balassa has tested hypothesis (3), using again the same new data on productivity, but does not consider hypothesis (4) and approaches hypothesis (5) differently, through multiple-correlation analysis.

Now, each of these three hypotheses has two main elements: (*a*) the adequacy of labour productivity (or unit labour-cost) ratios as an approximation to price ratios; and (*b*) the relation of price ratios

[21]Hypothesis (3) is clearly inspired by Ricardian hypothesis (I) and hypotheses (4) and (5) by Ricardian hypothesis (2). It should be made clear here that MacDougall's papers contain much *other* analysis of considerable interest and that the papers neither are confined to testing the hypotheses listed here nor approach those questions in the same formal manner as set out here.

(between prices of similar commodities exported to third markets by the United States and the United Kingdom) to quantity-ratios (of United States and United Kingdom exports of similar commodities).

It is easy to recognise the former as a proposition borrowed from the Ricardian analysis. The latter proposition, however, represents a departure from the Ricardian price–trade assumption. The assumption that the relative prices of exported goods will be lower than those of imported goods is now replaced by the postulation of some relationship between (United States–United Kingdom) price ratios of third-market exports and (United States–United Kingdom) shares in third markets. In hypotheses (3) and (5), for instance, the relationship takes the form of a negative correlation between the relative export prices; in hypothesis (4) the form is shifted: a country's exports are postulated to be greater when its price is relatively cheaper than its rival's, but nothing is stated about the effects of different degrees of relative price advantage on export shares.

Neither of the hypothesised price–trade relationships, however, seems to be plausible. It is difficult to see, for instance, the theoretical reason why the ratio of two rivals' third-market exports should, in a cross-section analysis, turn out to increase as the corresponding price ratio falls. The argument that relative prices of similar commodities and their relative sales can be correlated in *cross-section analysis* cannot be justified on the presumption that, for *any given industry*, a reduction in the relative price of a competitor will increase its relative sales. It is difficult to imagine that this presumption can be extended to cross-section data where different commodities will have varying "elasticities of substitution," depending on different degrees of product differentiation, quality differences, etc. as between different sources of origin (the United States and the United Kingdom in the present example).[22]

[22]This is perhaps what Caves [3, p. 269] also is hinting at in his critique of the MacDougall papers.

Despite these difficulties with the hypotheses (3), (4) and (5), the empirical verification is remarkably successful.[23] And yet, as already

[23]If one examines the evidence MacDougall [28, pp. 715–17] has produced one is astonished at the empirical support which is turned up for this hypothesis. For United States: United Kingdom export shares and price ratios, MacDougall produces supporting evidence, with twenty-three regressions and correlations, from 1913 to 1948; the lowest two correlation coefficients are −0.73. Fairly high correlation coefficients, with nicely negative regression slopes are turned up, moreover, for United States: United Kingdom, United States: Japan, United States: Germany, United States: France, United Kingdom: France, France: Japan, France: Germany, United Kingdom: Japan and United Kingdom: Germany. As for the evidence on hypotheses (3), (4) and (5) themselves, the results can be systematised as follows:

I. *Hypothesis* (*3*). The results of MacDougall, Stern and Balassa can be stated briefly:

Author		Sample	Year	Regression equation[a]	Correlation coefficient
MacDougall	(1)	25 industries	1937	Regression slope $= -4$	−0·70
	(2)	39 "	1950	$x = -2{\cdot}19 + 1{\cdot}89y$	0·61
Stern	(3)	24 (= MacDougall 1937 sample)	1950	$x = 0{\cdot}98 + 1{\cdot}65y(0{\cdot}57)$	0·52
	(4)	39 industries	1950	$x = -0{\cdot}68 + 1{\cdot}27y(0{\cdot}43)$	0·44
	(5)	25 "	1950	$x = 0{\cdot}91 + 1{\cdot}49y(0{\cdot}59)$	0·46
Balassa[b]	(6)	28 "	1950 and	$x = -1.761 + 1{\cdot}594y(0{\cdot}181)$	0·86
	(7)	28 "	1951	$x^* = -53{\cdot}32 +0{\cdot}721y^*(0{\cdot}103)$	0·80

[a]x and y refer to the logarithms of the United States: United Kingdom export ratio and United States: United Kingdom labour productivity ratio respectively. x^* and y^* in the last regression refer to the ratios themselves. MacDougall does not state his 1937 regression equation.
[b]The productivity data refer to 1950 and the source is the same as that used by MacDougall and Stern. However, the export data refer to values instead of quantities and are for 1951 instead of 1950. For the latter, the

argued, this has little to do with the empirical verification of the Ricardian hypotheses (1) and (2). While this is true, the authors

---

reason is that 1950 was an "abnormal" year. For the former, the reason is that it is very tricky to separate export prices and quantities. Balassa prefers to work with values and justifies this choice on the ground that, with the estimates of elasticity of substitution being high in general, a positive correlation between productivity and export quantities will exist, so that the tests proposed are not vitiated. This argument, however, rests on the estimates of high elasticities of substitution—which, in turn, are based upon the very same separation of prices and quantities which Balassa is shying away from.

The results, on the whole, seem clearly to support the stated hypothesis mildly.

II. *Hypothesis (4)*. Here only MacDougall and Stern have produced evidence. Two different approaches can be distinguished. (1) One is to examine the industries directly and see how many conform to the pattern laid down by the hypothesis. (*a*) Using only the *average* wage levels for the United States and the United Kingdom (instead of individual industry wages), MacDougall found for 1937 that "where American output for worker was more than twice the British, the United States had in general the bulk of the export market, while for products where it was less than twice as high the bulk of the market was held by Britain" [28, p. 698], while the average American wage was twice as high as the British wage. Thus, out of 25 industries investigated, 20 conformed and 2 more would have if the measure of productivity were suitably adjusted. (*b*) Stern, with the average American wage 3·4 times the British wage in 1950, found that from 24 industries (comparable to MacDougall's 25), 20 conformed to the expected pattern. (*c*) For the larger sample of 39 industries, the exceptions were only 5. These three, strikingly favourable results were obtained when the *average* American and British wages were taken. Both MacDougall and Stern, however, attempted to analyse the effect of taking individual wages for different products as well. (*d*) Owing to data limitations, MacDougall could attempt this only for 13 industries. His results showed a slight improvement: cigarettes became an exception, whereas pigiron, glass containers and hosiery held the line. (*c*) Stern, using the same sample, found a slight deterioration, although the expected pattern still continued.

(2) The other approach to examining hypothesis (4) is through statistical estimation procedures. Both MacDougall and Stern have estimated regression equations for logarithms of labour productivity ratios and export ratios, already listed earlier here. These are used to estimate the validity of hypothesis (4). (*a*) For instance, MacDougall found that his regression line, fitted to the 1937 data plotted on a double logarithmic scale, passed through the horizontal dividing line

of these empirical exercises have turned up a great deal of data on export prices and on labour productivities and unit wage-costs.

---

of 2 (*i.e.*, American output per worker twice the British) at a point considerably to the left of a vertical dividing line at unity, marking the point of equality in the two countries' exports. This implied that America tended to export only about *two-fifths* as much as Britain in 1937, when the American advantage in output per worker was exactly offset by the inferiority in advantage in average wage. (*b*) For the same sample of industries, Stern found in 1950 that America tended to export only about four-fifths as much as Britain when American output per worker and average wage-rates were 3·4 times higher. This clearly came closer to hypothesis (4). (*c*) For 39 industries, Stern's regression line passed almost exactly through the 3·4 point, appearing to verify hypothesis (4) totally. All these estimates are for data using *average* wage-rates. While this approach, on the whole and especially for 1950, appears to support hypothesis (4), it must be admitted that it represents an inadequate test from the viewpoint of hypothesis (4) itself: even though all observations conform to the postulated pattern, the estimated regression may register a deviation (from the point of intersection of the dividing lines); whereas the regression line may pass exactly through the point of intersection while the observed points deviate from the postulated pattern.

III. *Hypothesis* (*5*). This hypothesis, relating unit labour cost ratios and export shares, has been tested directly only by Stern and, with a different formulation, by Balassa. (*a*) For *average* wage data, of course, the regression and correlation coefficients for the estimated regression equations in the labour productivity hypothesis (3) should hold again, because all that happens is that the productivity ratios get each multiplied by a scalar (equal to the wage ratio). The results derived earlier, therefore, hold. (*b*) Stern, however, has produced the regression equation

$$X = 0{\cdot}01 - \underset{(0{\cdot}38)}{1{\cdot}40y}\,, \quad r = -0{\cdot}43$$

(where y is the logarithm of unit costs ratio), which lends some, though not very strong, support to the hypothesis being tested. (*c*) Balassa approaches the problem in terms of the question whether the introduction of the wage ratios as an *additional* explanatory variable (in a multiple correlation analysis) improves the explanation of export shares. Balassa's regression equation is

$$x^* = -181{\cdot}2 + \underset{(0{\cdot}167)}{0{\cdot}691^*} + \underset{(0{\cdot}102)}{0{\cdot}140\ z^*}$$

where x^* is the export ratio, y^* the productivity ratio and z^* the wage ratio. The multiple correlation coefficient is 0·81 (as against 0·80 in the simple correlation). The partial coefficients are 0·77 (for x^* and y^*) and 0·24 (for x^* and z^*); the

These data can be used to examine the proposition that relative prices can be approximated by comparative labour productivities and/or unit wage–cost ratios. This can only result in the verification (or refutation, as it turns out) of the prop on which the Ricardian hypotheses (1) and (2) are generally rested. A full-blooded test of these hypotheses, directly examining the ranking of (bilateral) exports and imports by comparative labour productivities and/or unit wage–cost ratios, is impossible to carry out with this information and must await further research.

For the limited test outlined here, I have used two sets of data. For the MacDougall sample of 25 industries (reduced to 24 in Stern's calculations for 1950), the necessary data are available for 22 industries for 1937 and for 16 of these for 1950 (Table I). There is a slightly larger and different sample of 25 industries, used by Stern for 1950 (Table II). There are certainly many limitations to these data. The most serious ones, from the viewpoint of the current analysis, are three: (i) the f.o.b. price reflects gross value, whereas the labour productivity refers to the final, value-adding industry; the results would surely be more in conformity with the spirit of the Ricardian approach if the *indirect* labour productivities were also computed; (ii) the f.o.b. prices also include transport and other costs which add to the ex-factory price, whereas the labour productivity figures are not adjusted for this when necessary; and (iii) in most

---

latter is not significant at the 5% level. For logarithms, Balassa's regression equation is:

$$x = -5{\cdot}164 + \underset{(0{\cdot}328)}{1{\cdot}457y} + \underset{(0{\cdot}566)}{1{\cdot}250z}$$

The multiple correlation coefficient is 0·88 (as against the simple coefficient of 0·86). The partials are 0·84 (x and y) and 0·11 (x and z); the latter is not significant at the 5% level. The explanation which comparative labour productivities provide is not improved by adding wage ratios as an additional explanatory variable. (It follows, therefore, that wage-structure differences between ratios do not have any systematic relationship with price differences.)

Table I. Labour Productivity Ratios and Export Price Ratios (United States/United Kingdom) for 1937 and 1950

	1937		1950	
Industry	Output per worker, U.S./U.K.	Price of exports, U.S./U.K.	Output per worker, U.S./U.K.	Price of exports, U.S./U.K.
1. Tin cans	5·25	0·68	—	—
2. Pig iron	3·60	0·84	4·10	1·33
3. Wireless sets	3·50	0·64	4·00	0·95
4. Motorcars	3·10	0·91	2·40	2·63
5. Glass containers	2·40	0·69	—	—
6. Paper	2·20	0·72	3·40	0·90
7. Beer	2·00	1·30	3·00	1·00
8. Linoleum and oil cloth	1·90	1·04	2·60	1·11
9. Coke	1·90	1·08	1·90	1·36
10. Hosiery	1·80	1·24	—	—
11. Cigarettes	1·70	1·08	2·50	1·08
12. Rayon weaving and making	1·50	1·19	—	—
13. Cotton spinning and weaving	1·50	1·03	—	—
14. Leather footwear	1·40	1·31	1·70	1·28
15. Woollen and worsted	1·35	1·42	1·80	1·44
16. Margarine	1·20	1·34	1·80	1·46
17. Cement	1·10	2·12	1·20	1·33
18. Electric lamps	5·40	0·51	3·60	0·92
19. Biscuits	3·10	1·01	2·40	1·24
20. Matches	3·10	0·86	—	—
21. Rubber tyres	2·70	1·12	2·40	1·42
22. Soap	2·70	1·24	2·50	1·10

Source: Stern [40, p. 278].

exporting industries a differential is observable between the average domestic price and the average foreign price [3, p. 281], so that the approximation of labour productivity ratios to relative (export) prices may have to be adjusted analytically for this phenomenon. Notwithstanding these limitations, however, I have carried out the analysis in consonance with the tradition of economists to catalogue the difficulties and thereafter to ignore them. The results, as already

Table II. Labour Productivity Ratios, Export Price Ratios, Unit Labour Cost Ratios and Wage Rates Ratios (United States/United Kingdom) for 1950

	Export prices, U.S./U.K.	Output per worker, U.S./U.K.	Unit labour costs, U.S./U.K.	Wage-rates, U.S./U.K.
1. Cement	1·33	1·16	2·33	2·70
2. Sugar factories and refineries	1·32	1·48	1·89	2·79
3. Tanneries	1·01	1·68	1·92	3·23
4. Footwear (except rubber)	1·28	1·71	1·68	2·88
5. Woollen and worsted	1·33	1·85	1·96	3·63
6. Metal-working machinery	2·64	2·21	1·79	3·96
7. Rayon, nylon and silk	1·15	2·26	1·51	3·42
8. Generators, motors and transformers	2·63	2·39	1·49	3·56
9. Tyres and tubes	1·23	2·41	1·50	3·62
10. Wirework	1·28	2·44	1·52	3·72
11. Soap, candles and glycerine	1·18	2·49	1·58	3·93
12. Rubber products (excluding tyres and footwear)	1·31	2·50	1·45	3·62
13. Tobacco manufactures	1·08	2·51	1·02	2·56
14. Linoleum and leather cloth	1·11	2·56	1·27	3·25
15. Bolts, nuts, rivets and screws	2·06	2·56	1·71	4·31
16. Breweries and manufacturing of malt	1·00	3·00	1·33	3·99
17. Pulp, paper and board	0·90	3·38	1·08	3·65
18. Electronic tubes	0·68	3·55	1·10	3·91
19. Electric-light bulbs	0·92	3·56	1·10	3·92
20. Paint and varnish	0·90	3·63	0·96	3·50
21. Basic industrial chemicals	0·95	3·72	0·91	3·38
22. Radio	0·95	4·00	0·85	3·39
23. Blast furnaces	1·33	4·08	0·72	2·96
24. Electrical household equipment	1·70	4·12	0·96	3·95
25. Containers, paper and card	1·12	4·28	0·96	4·09

Source: Stern [40, p. 288].

Table III. Relationship between Labour Productivity Ratios and Export Price Ratios

Data	Regression equation*			Coefficients
1937 (Table I)	$Y = 1{\cdot}72$	–	$0{\cdot}211X$	$r^2 = 0{\cdot}525$
	(0·2291)		(0·0450)	$r = -0{\cdot}724$
1937 (Table I)	$\log Y = 0{\cdot}252$	–	$0{\cdot}525 \log X$	$r^2 = 0{\cdot}0686$
	(0·1925)		(0·432)	$r = -0{\cdot}262$
1950 (Table I)	$Y = 1{\cdot}58$	–	$0{\cdot}169X$	$r^2 = 0{\cdot}129$
	(0·32605)		(0·1204)	$r = -0{\cdot}359$
1950 (Table I)	$\log Y = 0{\cdot}264$	–	$0{\cdot}611 \log X$	$r^2 = 0{\cdot}0912$
	(0·3769)		(0·5155)	$r = -0{\cdot}302$
1950 (Table II)	$Y = 1{\cdot}7044$	–	$0{\cdot}1470X$	$r^2 = 0{\cdot}0728$
	(0·3291)		(0·1095)	$r = -0{\cdot}2698$
1950 (Table II)	$\log Y = 0{\cdot}2056$	–	$0{\cdot}2773 \log X$	$r^2 = 0{\cdot}0906$
	(0·0816)		(0·1831)	$r = -0{\cdot}301$

*Y = Export price ratio, and X = Labour productivity ratio.

hinted at, are seriously prejudicial to the usefulness of the Ricardian approach: though, it should be emphasised, the verdict cannot be final in the absence of better and fuller tests.[24]

The linear regressions of export price ratios on labour productivity ratios are almost entirely hopeless, whether we take logarithms or not. The six regressions, listed in Table III, uniformly fail to be significant except for the unlogged, MacDougall sample for 1937. The failures clearly overwhelm the sucess in verification.

Testing the relationship between comparative unit labour-costs and export price ratios, we find the results to be equally disappointing. Table IV lists the two linear regression equations for the 1950 data (Table II). Both relationships are insignificant (though they register a negligible improvement over the regressions for export price-ratios and labour productivity ratios alone).

Handling the influence of relative inter-country wage-rates alternatively through the introduction of wage ratios as an additiona

---

[24]I am indebted to B. S. Minhas for assistance with the statistical analysis in this paper. The responsibility for any errors, however, is entirely mine.

Table IV. Relationship Between Unit Labour Cost Ratios and Export Price Ratios

Data	Regression equations*	Coefficients
1950 (Table II)	$Y = 0{\cdot}7227 \quad + 0{\cdot}4141X$	$r^2 = 0{\cdot}1233$
	$(0{\cdot}33194) \quad (0{\cdot}23021)$	$r = 0{\cdot}3512$
1950 (Table II)	$\log Y = 0{\cdot}03785 \quad + 0{\cdot}42113 \log X$	$r^2 = 0{\cdot}162$
	$(0{\cdot}0335) \quad (0{\cdot}1997)$	$r = 0{\cdot}40248$

*Y = export price ratio, and X = unit labour cost ratio.

explanatory variable in a multiple correlation analysis, further, we find that the results for the available data are again poor (Table V). The correlations continue to be insignificant (though they register a slight improvement over the simple correlation, for the same data, between export price ratios and labour productivity ratios alone).

These results, limited as they are, cast sufficient doubt on the usefulness of the Ricardian approach (as generally understood). Contrary, therefore, to the general impression (based on the MacDougall, Balassa and Stern results), there is as yet no evidence in favour of the Ricardian hypotheses. This is perhaps not as unfortunate as it seems. For ultimately the practical utility of the Ricardian hypotheses is somewhat limited. Labour productivity, after all, is not a datum in the sense that production functions are. The reliance of the prediction on labour productivity unaccompanied by any explanation of why the labour productivity is what it is, and how therefore it may be expected to change, restricts the utility of the prediction. Moreover, even if we could forecast changes in labour productivity, we could not tell exclusively therefrom that the pattern of imports and exports would change in a specified manner; all we could say is that, if the pattern of exports and imports changes in any way, the new pattern will also be characterised by the postulated Ricardian ranking in terms of comparative labour productivities and/or unit wage ratios.[25]

[25] I would not claim that *any* type of prediction concerning change in the pattern of trade is impossible. But even apparently simple predictions are not possible. For instance, if labour productivity increases in an export industry we *cannot*

Table V. Multiple Regressions between Export Price Ratios, Labour Productivity Ratios and Wage Ratios

Data	Multiple regression equation*			Coefficients
1950 (Table II)	$Y = 0{\cdot}5572$	$-\ 0{\cdot}2286X_1$	$+\ 0{\cdot}3905X_2$	$r^2 = 0{\cdot}191$
	(7·8)	(0·1140)	(0·2182)	$r = 0{\cdot}437$
				Partial: $X_1 = -0{\cdot}3931$
				$X_2 = 0{\cdot}3564$
1950 (Table II)	$\log Y = 0{\cdot}1646$	$-\ 0{\cdot}4304 \log X_1$	$+\ 0{\cdot}8011 \log X_2$	$r^2 = 0{\cdot}1850$
	(0·0599)	(0·2015)	(0·5018)	$r = 0{\cdot}4301$
				Partial: $X_1 = -0{\cdot}4143$
				$X_2 = 0{\cdot}3220$

*Y = export price ratio; X_1 = labour productivity ratio, and X_2 = wage-rate ratio.

The Heckscher–Ohlin Theory

An alternative approach to explaining the pattern of trade is attributed to the works of Heckscher [19] and Ohlin [34], but owes much to the work of Samuelson [38, 91]. Indeed, in its current form it has discarded so many of the variables which Ohlin explicitly listed as significant that it is almost certainly liable to be rejected by Ohlin as an adequate version of his original analysis!

This approach breaks away from the Ricardian model and works in terms of an analytical framework which is in striking contrast to its predecessor. As we saw, the Ricardian model assumes one factor, and therewith (through the supporting assumption of constant returns to scale) makes the factor supply irrelevant in determining the trade pattern;[26] on the other hand, as we shall soon see, the Heckscher–Ohlin model assumes two factors and makes international differences in factor endowments the crucial and sole

necessarily predict that the industry will continue to export its product (even if all oilier autonomous change in the trading countries is ruled out).

[26]This is, strictly speaking, not true in a model with more than two commodities. In this case demand must be brought in to "break the chain" of ranked commodities into exports and imports. But demand itself will be a function of the level of income, which will depend, among other things, on the factor supply.

factor determining comparative advantage.[27] Moreover, whereas the former attributes to international differences in production functions the explanation of comparative advantage, the latter explicitly postulates the international identity of production functions.[28] The Heckscher–Ohlin theory is also different from the Ricardian analysis in having been presented *explicitly* as a contribution to the "positive" theory, as an attempt at explaining the structure of foreign trade, rather than with a view to establishing the welfare propositions of trade theory.

The Heckscher–Ohlin theorem states that *a country's exports use intensively the country's abundant factor.* This is an eminently "plausible-looking" proposition. One would expect that a country should be able to produce more cheaply those goods that are intensive in the use of a factor when that factor of production is (physically) abundant in the country relative to its trading partner. Of course one can think of some exceptions immediately. For instance, it is clear that this presumption rests on the similarity of production conditions between trading countries. There could obviously be a contradiction of the Heckscher–Ohlin proposition if *production functions* for individual industries were different between countries. Alternatively, the country may quite well have an offsetting

---

[27]Viner [44] has attempted to demonstrate that the factor endowment approach is to be found in classical writings. But his contention is not persuasive, based as it is on fragmentary remarks which do not add up to systematic analysis.

[28]It should be emphasised that these contrasts, which are based partly on the distinction between production functions and factors of production, raise the well-known question as to the proper definitions of these two concepts. It is interesting, in this connection, to recall that Ohlin appears to have taken it as apparent that production functions would be the same everywhere, because the same causes everywhere (and at any time) produce the same effects. However, as Haberler [4, p. 19] has pointed out," if the concept of the production function is to be a useful tool of analysis, it cannot be identified with, or derived from, such unverifiable metaphysical propositions as 'the constancy of the laws of nature.' By hypothesising every conceivable circumstance which may affect output as a separate factor, the production function can, no doubt, be endowed with constancy, invariability, homogeneity, and what not, but at the price of emptying the theory of all empirical content and reducing it to a useless tautological system."

preference for the *consumption* of these commodities—so that the pre-trade (relative) prices of commodities may turn out to be higher (rather than lower) abroad—thus refuting the Heckscher–Ohlin proposition. Some qualifications are less intuitively seen. One of the theoretically interesting qualifications[29] follows from the fact that although, technologically, the production function for an activity may be identical between countries, the operative segments of it may be intensive in the use of a different factor in each country. Where such "reversals of factor-intensity" can occur the effect can be similar to that of differences in production functions and the Heckscher–Ohlin proposition need not hold.

Theorists have established a set of conditions which ensure the "logical truth" of the Heckscher–Ohlin theorem. These conditions differ, depending on the definition of "factor abundance." It is possible to choose between two definitions: the physical and the price definitions. Under the former, country I is abundant in factor x and country II in factor y when $(X/Y)^{\mathrm{I}} > (X/Y)^{\mathrm{II}}$, where X and Y refer to the quantities of factors x and y respectively and the superscripts to the countries.[30] Under the latter, the countries are similarly described when $(Rx/Ry)^{\mathrm{I}} < (Rx/Ry)^{\mathrm{II}}$ *prior to trade* where Rx and Ry refer to the rentals on factors x and y respectively.

When the physical definition is used the set of sufficient conditions for the logical truth of the Heckscher–Ohlin proposition is: (1) international identity of production functions; (2) non-reversibility of factor-intensities, such that a given commodity is factor x-intensive in relation to another at *all* relevant factor price-ratios; (3) constant returns to scale and diminishing returns (along isoquants) in each production function; and (4) identity of the consumption pattern

[29]It is also empirically possible, as Minhas' [33] study shows.

[30]The physical definition raises serious conceptual difficulties when applied to the factor "capital." As is obvious, it is impossible to collapse different varieties of capital equipment into a single index of "capital" in the same way as we reduce labour to man-hours. Of course, even with labour, the element of "human capital" raises equally knotty issues.

between countries at each relevant commodity price ratio.[31] Samuelson [38, 39] has established that, under perfect competition and profit maximisation in perfect markets, condition (3) will suffice to generate a strictly convex production possibility curve, characterised by a unique relationship between factor and commodity price ratios (except at positions of complete specialisation in production). Using these propositions, it is possible to demonstrate in a two-commodity system that where two countries, with identical production functions for each activity (condition 1) and non-reversible factor intensities (condition 2) have different capital: labour ratios in the aggregate, the capital-abundant country will have a higher ratio of capital-intensive: labour-intensive outputs at *each* commodity price ratio. When condition (4) is added to this result it follows that the pre-trade commodity price ratios will be such that the capital-intensive commodity will be cheaper in the capital-abundant country. Hence the Heckscher–Ohlin theorem will be logically true. This result is valid for a multi-commodity model as well:[32] as Jones [20] has demonstrated, commodities can still be ranked, from technological and factor-supply data, in terms of factor ratios, and are thereby uniquely ranked also in terms of comparative advantage, with demand being introduced (as in the Ricardian system) to "break the chain" into exports and imports.

---

[31]Identity of tastes, *i.e.*, the aggregate preference map, is not adequate, since two countries may be at different levels of income and hence at different positions on their preference maps. Unless, therefore, the maps have homothetic isoquants, the result can be different consumption patterns at identical price ratios. For a disaggregated economy, with many individuals, the conditions which give rise to such aggregate identity of tastes are quite restrictive [66, 67]. It is also necessary, of course, that transport costs for individual commodities are not such as would shatter this chain of comparative advantage when the c.i.f. prices are considered (as they have to be from the viewpoint of the determination of the trade pattern). The trade theorists generally disregard transport costs; the omission of "distance" as a factor in most trade models represents a serious deficiency which vitiates the utility of many conclusions.

[32]The definitions of "factor abundance" and "factor-intensity" in a multi-factor model, however, are not so intuitive; but one can always adopt a convention [35, 53]. The results, however, are both more restrictive and less intuitive.

When the price definition of factor abundance is chosen we can dispense with the condition of identity of consumption patterns. This is because, when the other assumptions are made, a country which is capital-abundant will, by virtue of the unique Samuelsonian relationship between commodity and factor price ratios, necessarily have cheaper capital-intensive output. The use of the price definition, while it has this advantage over the physical definition, correspondingly leaves less scope for "explanation."[33]

Where the theory is deficient is in its not having been extended to a multi-country, multi-commodity framework. The prediction holds when there are many commodities and two countries. However, when there are many countries and commodities it is not clear, in the absence of theoretical analysis, what conditions will suffice to make the Heckscher–Ohlin hypothesis true—in any of the several alternative versions that are possible in a multi-country framework: (1) the comparison of factor endowments may be between country I and the sum of *all* the other countries of the world; or (2) it may be between country I and the *sum* of *all* the countries directly in trade with it; or (3) between country I and the sum of *all* the countries directly or indirectly in trade with it; or (4) between country I and *each* of the countries in direct trade with it, so that the Heckscher–Ohlin hypotheses would hold for *each* pair of countries (*bilaterally*). There is little in the traditional analysis of the Heckscher–Ohlin hypotheses which affords a reliable clue to a meaningful choice among these different ways in which a Heckscher–Ohlin hypothesis can be interpreted in a multi-country framework. Nor need we expect the conditions under which each of these hypotheses will be logically true to be identical either with each other *or* with those that have been spelled out for the restrictive traditional frameworks.[34] This amounts

---

[33]Lancaster has proposed inadvertently a third definition which states that a country is abundant in that factor which is used intensively in the exportable industry [14]. From the viewpoint of the Heckscher–Ohlin theory, this is totally tautologous and leaves *no* scope for "explanation."

[34]For instance, it is clear that if country I is K-abundant in relation to country II and L-abundant in relation to country III, and the Heckscher–Ohlin hypothesis holds for each pair of countries (say, I and II, II and III), then it is *impossible*

to a deficiency in the literature (especially from the viewpoint of empirical testing, since the real world unfortunately constitutes a multi-country, multi-commodity international economy).

Empirical testing of the Heckscher–Ohlin hypotheses has indeed been attempted in the literature, starting with Leontief's pioneer attempt at ascertaining the factor-intensities of the average exports and competitive imports in the United States [25]. It is typical of his and other contributions that, while factor-intensities are carefully ascertained, the factorabundance of the country in question is usually left uninvestigated, except tangentially and vaguely. The result has been a failure to face up to the question raised by multi-country, multi-commodity analysis: how is factorabundance to be interpreted? By *implication,* Leontief [25, pp. 386, 399] seems to favour the *bilateral* interpretation: "A comprehensive, two-sided explanation of our economic relationships with the rest-of-the-world will not, of course, be possible before the internal economic structure of at least one of the most important of our trading partners has been studied as fully as that of our own." Recent studies by Bharadwaj [16] for India, Tatemoto and Ichimura [42] for Japan and Wahl [45] for Canada have also implicitly adopted the bilateral interpretation by considering, in addition to the factor intensities of the average *aggregate* exports and competitive imports (which necessitates viewing the country's

---

that the export and import commodities of country I can be ranked in terms of K: L ratios such that all exports are K-intensive in relation to all imports. The export and import commodities inevitably criss-cross, fouling up the strictly ordered chain on which the traditional Heckscher–Ohlin hypothesis and proof depend. However, if this chain cannot criss-cross under the usual assumptions, as Jones has demonstrated, we have a contradiction *in terms of the traditional model* and apparently the pattern of international specialisation in production and in trade will necessarily have to turn out such that the bilateral formulation of the Heckscher–Ohlin hypothesis holds in a multi-country world. Of course, what I have argued here is not intended to be a proof, in the strict sense, of an extension of the Heckscher–Ohlin hypothesis to the bilateral, multi-country formulation within the fold of traditional postulates concerning technology etc. The point I am making is really that the analysis of the Heckscher–Ohlin variety of hypotheses, in any or all of their possible versions in a multicountry framework, is not yet available and represents a serious lacuna in the literature.

factor-abundance in a non-bilateral way), the factor-intensities of the average exports to and competitive imports from *specific* trading countries or regions.[35]

While Leontief [25], and nearly all of his many followers, have left this crucial aspect unsatisfactory, Leontief's attempted test has been of significance—for the perverse reason that it turned up the startling result that the United States exports are labour-intensive and its competitive imports capital-intensive.[36] Since the United States may be conceded to be capital abundant by any definition, this result did seem to contradict the Heckscher–Ohlin hypothesis—provided the statistical information and procedure could be accepted. There *were* objections on statistical grounds. For instance, the agricultural capital–output ratio was considered unreliable [18], but recomputation under different assumptions did not reverse the findings. Balogh [12] voiced compelling doubts concerning the implications of aggregation in the input–output matrix (used to compute indirect capital–labour ratios). Thus, the labour-intensity of the American export industries might be spurious and attributable to the aggregation of capital-intensive exportable products with "similar," non-export, labour-intensive activities. No evidence was produced to support this objection [1]: yet, it leaves a degree of doubt.

While Leontief's exercise spurred the majority of the theorists on to a re-examination of the sufficient conditions for the Heckscher–Ohlin hypothesis [20, 36, 37], the plausibility of the Heckscher–Ohlin propositions is so powerful that some ingenuity was addressed to the task of rescuing it from the refutation that had emerged from Leontief's exercises (Leontief himself being one of this small group

[35]In each of these instances, however, there is no discussion either of the alternative ways in which the Heckscher–Ohlin hypothesis can be interpreted or of the theoretical implication of the specific (bilateral) form of the hypothesis that is chosen or suggested.

[36]The tests have uniformly used the two factors, capital and labour. This choice, as also the definition of capital, are necessarily arbitrary. This arbitrariness is inevitable, and its justification lies in the argument that the theory being tested represents an abstraction.

of analysts).[37] This task is not entirely hopeless, since, although Leontief's results may be accepted, it is possible for the economist, *not* to change the form of the hypothesis, but to retain this form while redefining the concepts used. This is a perfectly valid, scientific procedure: the hypothesis, with redefined concepts, can once again be subjected to empirical verification [1]. This is precisely what may be done with the Heckscher–Ohlin hypothesis, in the expectation that Leontief's United States results may be reversed.

There are many ways in which this can be done. For instance, one could argue that the factor-abundance comparison should refer to the quantities of factors employed in the traded-goods sector, since the original formulation of the Heckscher–Ohlin theorem is logically deduced in a framework assuming no non-traded goods [1]. Or it could be argued that, since the traded-goods sector in some countries represents merely a geographical extension of a country's activities,

[37]Leontief also produced subsequently another paper [26] which reworked the calculations in the light of criticisms addressed to his original work. For instance, instead of the inversion of only a 50-sector matrix earlier, he inverted a 192-sector matrix. Adjustments were carried out concerning agricultural data. None of this, however, reversed the findings concerning the refutation of the (unadjusted) Heckscher–Ohlin hypothesis. Leontief also went into some theoretical issues, such as the examination of a linear, input–output model for international trade. This has unfortunately been responsible for some confusion concerning the limitations of the empirical verification of the Heckscher–Ohlin hypothesis itself. For instance, Valavanis-Vail [3, p. 279] has objected to Leontief's exercise on the ground that "input–output models (except with rare luck) are logically incompatible with international trade." Whatever the analytical support for (any interpretation of) this statement, it is really irrelevant to the objective of Leontief's exercise and the methods used by him to achieve it. The input–output table is used by Leontief (along with the labour and capital coefficients matrices) merely to *compute* the indirect capital and labour requirements for unit exports and imports. The assumptions of input–output *analysis* are *not* necessary. Although Leontief loosely talks of "reducing" exports by a million dollars and seeing what capital and labour are "released" thereby, this is *not* what is actually required. All that is necessary, and this is really how Leontief's exercise should be construed, is to compute the total capital and labour requirements of the *current* (level and composition of) exports. And this can be done by a purely "notional reduction" of (a representative bundle of) exports and the corresponding, computed, notional "release" of capital and labour.

these sectors being really foreign enclaves based on foreign capital and dominated by foreign economic considerations, it is sensible in such cases to merge these enclaves with the foreign country in question for obtaining the data for the Heckscher–Ohlin test [18].[38] The most interesting attempts, however, have centred around the fact that labour embodies (human) capital, and its implications for both factor-abundance and factor-intensity.

The easiest way of handling this has been to argue that the human capital element should be allowed for in the factor-intensity comparisons. For the United States, this seems to provide an important escape from the refutation of the Heckscher–Ohlin hypothesis. As many of the commentators have noted: (i) American export industries employ relatively more non-agricultural labour,[39] and agricultural labour is likely to be less educated and trained than non-agricultural labour [18]; and (ii) American export industries pay an average wage in excess of the national wage (suggesting that they intensively use skilled labour)[40] [21]. Thus, this computation of human capital (from an analysis of the labour inputs in the exporting and import-competing industries) added to the capital employed in measuring factor-intensities may quite possibly reverse the factor-intensity findings for the United States. However, we should also have to adjust correspondingly the measurement of factor endowments,

[38] It is not necessarily correct to use such an adaptation of the Heckscher–Ohlin hypothesis. For the latter, what is relevant is the *availability* of factors of production *regardless of their ownership*. It is only in the extreme case where the investment is accompanied by full, complementary migration of other necessary factors to a piece of foreign territory (which itself does not serve as a factor of production) that it would be proper, from the Heckscher–Ohlin viewpoint, to adopt this approach. Not otherwise.

[39] The breakdown of labour (for a million dollars of exports and import replacements) between agricultural and non-agricultural labour was given by Leontief [25] as follows:

	Exports.	Import replacements.
Agricultural labour, man years	22·436	40·394
Non-agricultural labour, man years	159·872	127·069

[40] An alternative explanation, of course, is that they are the "dynamic," innovating industries, and hence pay higher wages.

adding the computed human capital to the measure of capital stock: a procedure which highlights the great conceptual difficulties that attend on both measuring capital meaningfully and comparing it between countries.

An alternative way in which the fact of labour efficiency differences between countries has been handled is by adjusting the labour supply itself by an efficiency factor.[41] Leontief [25, p. 26], in his original paper, argued that "labour" should be defined in "standard" units, after adjusting for varying degrees of efficiency. On this basis he asserted that the average American worker is three times as efficient as elsewhere and that "spread thrice as thinly as the unadjusted figures suggest the American capital supply per 'equivalent worker' turns out to be comparatively smaller, rather than larger, than that of many other countries."[42] Hence, the Heckscher–Ohlin theory could be rescued from an apparent refutation (on the implicit assumption that this efficiency factor concerning labour is not neutralised by a similar efficiency factor attributable to the other factor of production).

Leontief's procedure, however, is not valid, although his suggestion is valuable. He does not state how the efficiency factor of three was arrived at. Leontief's argument in support of the assumed efficiency factor of three is that if it were not so it would be impossible to "explain the comparative surplus of labour which our figures unmistakably reveal" [25, p. 28]. This argument is unpersuasive because (as I have already argued elsewhere [1]) "it already assumes that the Heckscher–Ohlin theorem provides a valid explanation of the American pattern of trade when, in fact, the question being asked is precisely whether it does"; and (2) "it also assumes that only the hypothesis about threefold efficiency of American labour

[41]This method adjusts the measurement of the labour input, whereas the earlier method alters the measurement of the capital stock.

[42]In the original paper [25] Leontief argued for this threefold efficiency, but did not make any differential adjustment for the efficiency factor in export- and import-competing industries. This implicit assumption of an identical efficiency factor for labour in both these sectors was removed by Leontief in his later exercise [26] by an explicit weighting of labour in each sector by its average wage.

can reconcile the results with the Heckscher–Ohlin type hypothesis when, in fact, there *are* other ways in which such reconciliation could be attempted." The most interesting analysis, which has a bearing on this issue, is by Minhas [33]. As noted earlier, Arrow, Chenery, Solow and he continuously found that for individual industries in different countries the only significant difference between the estimated homohypallagic (CES) production functions consisted of an overall efficiency term, which meant that whereas the isoquants continued to remain more or less the same, the scale factor changed. This means, as Minhas concluded [33, p. 159], that Leontief's requirement that the efficiency factor can be attributed to one factor *alone* is unsupported by his specific investigations.[43]

While these different ways in which the definitions of capital and labour have been adjusted, to explore the possibility of reconciling the United States pattern of trade with the Heckscher–Ohlin hypothesis, are of interest, perhaps the more significant innovations have emerged from the work of those who proceeded to apply Leontief's methods to the trade patterns of other countries. There have been four Leontief-type studies so far: Bharadwaj [15, 16] on India, Stolper and Roskamp [41] for East Germany, Tatemoto and Ichimura [42]

[43]Diab [18] also has attempted to test Leontief's conjecture, using Colin Clark's data. His results appear to sustain this conjecture. Diab's methods show that the United States has, in terms of "standard" labour, a lower capital: labour ratio than Canada, Great Britain, Netherlands, France and Norway. The procedure by which this conclusion is reached, however, is arbitrary. Diab assumes that: (1) labour is the factor which has to be reduced to "standard" units in each country; and (2) the Cobb–Douglas production function, identical for all countries studied, is known for national output, in terms of capital and "standard" labour. With this production function, national output and capital known, it is then easy to determine the single unknown, "standard" labour, with the one equation [1]. Diab postulates a hypothetical production function (with "standard" labour), uses observed values of output and capital to deduce his "standard" labour and then attributes the discrepancy between the quantities of "standard" and observed labour to an "efficiency" factor. This is surely an arbitrary procedure, which can yield no acceptable results. For instance, one could well use the procedure, assuming that capital, and not labour, is the factor which should be reduced to "standard" units. Out of curiosity, I did this: the United States turned out to be overwhelmingly "capital"-intensive [1]!

for Japan and Wahl [45] for Canada. These have now given us a larger range of evidence with which to attempt an assessment of the Heckscher–Ohlin hypothesis. For Japan, exports are capital-intensive and imports are labour-intensive—on the surface again, a black mark against the tested hypothesis. For East Germany exports are capital-intensive and imports are labour-intensive—the authors find this consistent with the stated hypothesis, since the East German trade is threequarters with the Communist block, where she is probably among the most industrialised of these nations. For Canada, exports are capital-intensive and imports are labour-intensive—presumably an unsuccessful verification, as Canadian trade is primarily United States-orientated.

Where many of these studies innovate is in departing from the Leontief method of taking the *aggregate* exports and competitive imports. They begin to explore the possibility of defining the Heckscher–Ohlin hypothesis in the *bilateral* form[44] (*i.e.*, for each pair of countries) rather than in terms of one country and (presumably) the rest of the world. Thus, Bharadwaj [16] goes on from the aggregative analysis to work out the factor-intensities of Indian trade with the United States, Wahl works with Canada–United States and Canada–United Kingdom trade, and the Tatemoto–Ichimura result is interpreted in terms of the geographic composition of Japanese trade. In the Indian case, when the Indo–United States trade is isolated for analysis, the factor-intensities are the *reverse* of those that obtain for total Indian trade. The Indian exports to the United States turn out to be capital-intensive and imports from the United States are labour-intensive, thus appearing to refute the Heckscher–Ohlin hypothesis. For Canada, the results again are identical with the aggregate results and refutation continues. For Japan, however, the result of disaggregation is beneficial. In the Japanese case the aggregative result is supposed to be attributable to the fact that 75% of Japanese exports go to the (presumably labour-abundant)

[44]This bilateral formulation, it may be recalled, is only one of several formulations of the Heckscher–Ohlin hypothesis that we can have in a multi-country world.

underdeveloped areas and only 25% to the (presumably capital-abundant) advanced countries. It is widely accepted in Japan that the Japanese economy is somewhere in the middle of the advanced and underdeveloped countries and the "disaggregated" explanation is only a logical consequence. Tatemoto and Ichimura have computed the capital–labour ratios of Japanese exports to the United States and imports from the United States and find the latter higher than the former. Unlike the Indian case, therefore, a disaggregated approach *supports* the Heckscher–Ohlin approach in the Japanese study. The Japanese result thus demonstrates the possibility of profitably adapting the Heckscher–Ohlin hypothesis so as to state it in terms of *each pair of trading countries* (instead of in aggregate terms).

When these diverse bits of evidence and arguments are added up there is little doubt that an attitude of agnosticism is certain to be left in the reader's mind concerning Leontief's original refutation of the Heckscher–Ohlin theorem.[45] Meanwhile, the empirical verification is

[45]It is of interest to note that the Ricardian hypothesis (in terms of comparative labour productivities) may be verified and yet the result may equally be in conformity with the Heckscher–Ohlin hypothesis. Thus, for instance, a capital-abundant country I may be exporting capital-intensive commodity x to country II in exchange for commodity y. Then, if transport costs are introduced and the necessary technological assumptions which underlie the Heckscher–Ohlin theorem are made, the capital–labour ratio in x will be higher in country I than in country II and therefore the output–labour ratio in x will also be higher in I than II. Similarly, the output–labour ratio in y will be lower in I than in II. Therefore, *both* the Ricardian and the Heckscher–Ohlin hypotheses will be valid in this case. A similar example can also be produced for the more sophisticated Ricardian hypothesis stated in the text (involving comparisons of production functions). For instance, assume that the production function is identical for commodity y in both countries and that country I has "neutral" advantage in producing commodity x such that the same capital and labour produce λ times more of x in I than in II. Assume x to be capital-intensive at all factor price ratios and I to be capital abundant. Then if the Heckscher–Ohlin thesis holds, so does the sophisticated Ricardian hypothesis automatically. Further, it follows that in free trade equilibrium (with zero transport costs), the capital–labour ratios in I will be lower in each activity than in II. Since constant returns to scale are being assumed, the labour productivity in both x and y would be lower in I than in II, except that the efficiency factor λ in the production of x in I would offset the

progressing apace and evidence is accumulating on either side. The most interesting recent result has been Minhas' [33] demonstration that, far from being a theoretical curiosum (as Samuelson [38, 39] believed it to be), the reversal of factor-intensity is an empirical possibility of some significance. Since his data relate to the United States and Japan, the results appear to furnish additional ammunition to those who are sceptical of the utility of the Heckscher–Ohlin approach.[46]

The Kravis Theory

While the Ricardian and the Heckscher–Ohlin approaches have dominated the thinking on comparative advantage for many decades, recently some original theories have appeared in the field. Kravis [22], for instance, in the early period of gloom after Leontief's paper [25], argued that the commodity composition of trade is determined primarily by "availability." Trade tends to be confined to goods which are "not available at home" [22, p. 143]. By this phrase, Kravis intended to describe goods which are "unavailable in the absolute sense (for example, diamonds)," and goods where "an increase in output can be achieved only at much higher cost (that is, the domestic supply is inelastic)." The reason for trade to be restricted to items characterised by such unavailability is that tariff policies, transport costs, cartelisation, etc., tend to eliminate from trade those commodities which are available through domestic production, although at "slightly" higher cost. The reasons cited for unavailability, as defined, are: lack of natural resources (relative to

fall in labour productivity due to lower capital–labour ratio. Assuming that this offset leaves the labour productivity in x greater in I than in II, the comparative labour productivity ratio in x will be greater for I than in y. Hence the Ricardian hypothesis will be sustained in its comparative labour productivity form as well.

[46] Minhas' demonstration of the possibility of factor-intensity reversals is quite serious, since it contradicts one of the premises on which the Heckscher–Ohlin hypothesis is traditionally based. In fact, the damage it does is fatal because, if factor-intensities *are* reversed between two trading countries, for exports and imports, it is logically *impossible* for *both* countries' trading patterns to pass the Heckscher–Ohlin test (though, of course, either can).

demand) or technical change and product differentiation which confer temporary monopoly of production on the innovating country (until the trading partners have learnt to imitate).

The theory appears attractive. However, it is noticeable that Kravis does not get down to stating precise, testable hypotheses. While he fails to do so, one can still derive several from his suggestive ideas. (1) For instance, one could seize on his idea of the "inelasticity" of domestic supply and state the refutable proposition that *a country's imports will be characterised by domestic inelasticity of supply.* (Such an hypothesis would, naturally have to be backed by an explicit definition of "inelasticity.") (2) Another hypothesis, based also on the concept of inelasticity, might be that *a country's imports will be characterised by the excess of foreign over domestic elasticity of supply.*[47] Both these hypotheses, and related formulations, however, neither get down below the surface *qua* explanations nor are capable of being tested without elaborate econometric estimates of supply elasticities. (3) A more interesting way of formulating Kravis-type hypotheses seems to be to go *directly* to the scarcities of natural resources and temporary scarcities through innovations. Kravis himself indicates that *a country's export-industries will show rates of technical progress higher than the national average.* (4) This could be turned into an alternative, plausible proposition, with traces of Ricardo [1]: *a country's export-industries will show higher rates of technical progress than the same industries in the trading partners.* (5) Perhaps the most promising approach would be to utilise Kravis' distinction between "unavailability" due to scarce natural resources and due to innovation. Thus, to the preceding two propositions, one could add a further clause: *or, will be intensive in the use, or consist, of raw materials which are relatively abundant in the country.*[48] Such Kravis-type hypotheses have, however, neither been

---

[47]Cf. Kravis' remark: "it is the elasticity of supply abroad and its inelasticity at home that gives rise to [the United States imports]." [22, p. 150].

[48]This, of course, begs the question of defining relative abundance. Some working definition would have to be devised. In practice, of course, it is relatively easy to identify the industries whose advantage consists in access to raw materials;

clearly formulated and analysed so far nor tested systematically with empirical evidence.

The Linder Theory

Another novel and ingenious approach is attributable to a recent Swedish author, Linder [27]. He begins by attempting to explain the pattern of trade, but ends up by doing something quite different— and it is precisely in this way that Linder makes a contribution of some significance.

Linder starts with the distinction between trade in primary products and in manufactures. The former is natural resource-intensive, and Linder accepts the thesis that such trade must be explained in terms of "relative natural-resources endowments" [27, p. 92].[49] Trade in manufactures, however, cannot be so explained. Linder explicitly rejects the analogy.

He despairs, however, of being able to predict the *precise* composition of trade in manufactures. This is a function of many factors: "technological superiority, managerial skills and economies of scale are perhaps the most important ..." [27, p. 103]. The results cannot be congealed into a precise, predictable pattern.[50] Economists, when confronted with questions that they could not answer, have usually changed the question. Linder likewise virtually gives up the traditional inquiry and argues that, while the precise

---

although, once again, the distinction between abundance in terms of price and physical units is relevant. For an interesting attempt at estimating the "resource-intensiveness" of activities entering trade in the United States see Vanek [43].

[49]Linder construes this as consistent with the Heckscher–Ohlin theory because he accepts the original Ohlin statement of his theory, which mentioned a whole host of factors of production, *inclusive* of natural resources. Of course, to the extent that other factors of production are also brought in, the theory both becomes less impressive as an abstraction and is less successfully tractable analytically because of the consequence, for the definitions of "factor-abundance" and "factor-intensity," of more than two factors of production.

[50]Linder, while he admits this, does not quite reconcile himself to the conclusion. He feels that *something* can still be said about the trade pattern. But his observations (*e.g.*,that Sweden will export paper because of forest resources or that Eskimos are unlikely to export refrigerators) do *not* constitute a theory.

composition of trade in manufactures cannot be forecast, what one *can* have instead is a theory concerning the *volume* of trade (as proportion of national income) between different pairs of trading nations.

Linder's central thesis is that the *volume of trade in manufactures of a country with each of her trading partners, when taken as a proportion of the corresponding national incomes of these countries, will be higher, the greater the similarity in the demand patterns of the pair of trading countries.* The "similarity of demand patterns" would be associated with the similarity of incomes *per capita*—although income distribution and similarity of taste patterns are additional variables. However, tastes are internationally not very dissimilar according to recent evidence [27, p. 95]. Hence, provided income distribution is ignored, the last clause in the thesis can be rewritten to state. "*the closer the pair of trading countries in their incomes* per capita."

Although Linder has not rigorously formulated his analytical framework, the chain of reasoning which leads to this hypothesis is available. (1) Firstly, the pre-condition for a non-primary commodity to emerge as an export is the presence of "home demand." This is attributed to several reasons: foreign trade is only an extension of domestic trade; innovation centres on existing industries and gives them export possibility; etc.[51] (2) Secondly, the existence of industry catering for internal demand implies that the internal demand pattern will determine the range of commodities that constitute potential exports. (Linder tries here to introduce the concept of "representative demand"—to narrow down the range of potential exports. The intention is to exclude those commodities for which the internal production is presumably not "large enough." But Linder really leaves this idea hanging in the air, without chiselling it down into clarity and precision.) (3) Thirdly, where the overlap in the

[51]One might add: the foreign market is risky (through Q.R.s and the possibility of entry which cannot be "controlled" with tariffs as in the domestic market) and the home market is not, so that producers generally do not wish to rely on the foreign market alone.

commodity-composition of the potential-export range of any pair of trading countries is *greater,* the possibility of a *larger* volume of trade will obtain. (4) Fourthly, the potential volume of trade will be larger, the larger the income-level of either trading country [27, p. 111]. (5) Fifthly, where the potential volume of trade is larger, the actual volume of trade will also be larger (though tariffs, transport costs, political connections which prompt discriminatory trade promotion, etc., may "distort" the relationship). (6) Sixthly, a similar set of arguments applies to imports. Linder qualifies only to the extent of stating that his "representative demand" concept is no longer necessary: this hardly matters, however, in view of its imprecision. (7) Hence the Linder thesis.

Many questions inevitably come to one's mind. Aside from, and related to, the looseness of concepts such as "representative demand," there is lack of precision concerning the concept of the potential-export range. Is it to be defined entirely in terms of the number of commodities with domestic production, or is one to assign weights to commodities in terms of their relative size in terms of some relevant index? What are the conditions under which the size of the trading countries can be expected to affect the volume of trade? And so on.[52] But, despite these limitations (which inevitably attend on pioneering analyses), Linder's work remains significant.

Our survey thus demonstrates that the theory of comparative advantage has been greatly advanced recently. New theories have emerged. And it has been the vehicle of the significant, recent trends towards empirical verification. This trend has synchronised with a more general investigation of the empirical validity of traditional theses about the structure of the international economy: among the

[52]Linder's brief attempt at empirical verification is also not fully satisfactory. The trade figures relate to aggregate imports, instead of imports of manufactured goods. The relationship investigated is with respect to *per capita* income, with no attempt at examining whether the explanation improves with additional variables like regional or fractile income inequality indices. The statistical analysis is halted short of the estimation of regression equations. Linder's hypothesis, while brilliantly suggestive, awaits both rigorous analytical formulation and empirical verification.

prominent contributions being Michaely's [31] study of concentration in world trade and Coppock's [17] analysis of the incidence of economic instability among the trading nations.

Meanwhile, analytical theory of the "traditionalist" persuasion, concerned with the statement of "logically true" theorems, has proliferated at a great pace. To this, we must now turn.

2. Theorems In Statics: Factor Price Equalisation[1]

The problem which has engaged the attention of many of the most distinguished trade theorists concerns the relationship between factor prices in different countries, under free trade in goods but factor immobility between countries.[53] The question dates back to the writings of Heckscher [19] and Ohlin [34]. They considered trade to be an equalising factor with respect to factor returns in trading countries, though they cited several reasons why *full* factor price equalisation would not occur in practice. In 1948 Samuelson [38] initiated the rigorous investigation of the conditions under which complete factor price equalisation would follow.

Samuelson [38, 39] stated everything that has ever been said subsequently as far as the restrictive case of two goods and two factors is concerned and, subject to certain sufficient assumptions to be noted shortly, managed to prove factor-price equalisation by

[1]I have had the invaluable opportunity of corresponding with Professor P. A. Samuelson in writing this Section. Although I have drawn freely on this correspondence, especially for the general case of many goods and many factors, the responsibility for any errors is entirely mine.

[53]I have referred only tangentially in Section I to one other problem, on which there is some, though scant, literature. This is the question of the pattern of international specialisation in *production* (as distinct from *trade*). The papers of McKenzie [78] and Jones [69] discuss this problem most elegantly in a Ricardo–Graham model with one primary factor of production and many countries. While I am on the subject of omissions, I should also note that I have not dealt at any length with the question of the stability of trade equilibrium, although I might have included it in Section IV. The interested reader will find useful and adequate discussion of the problem in the papers of Mundell [11] and myself and Johnson [2, Section IV] and in the volumes by Meade [9] and Vanek [93].

establishing a *unique* relationship between (relative) factor and commodity prices. In 1953 Samuelson [53], preceded by an investigation of Meade [50] into the two-factor, three-product case, offered the first serious analysis of the general case of many goods (n) and many factors (r), thereby extending the analysis to all the $n \geq 2 \leq r$ cases. In the process it turned out that the more general analysis was limited by the non-existence of the required mathematics, Samuelson having to content himself with the formulation of what were clearly overly-strong sufficiency conditions for uniqueness in the large (for $n = r > 2$). Subsequent to Samuelson's 1953 analysis, progress has been registered in this area in the following respects: (1) Kuhn [47] has added an alternative sufficiency condition for uniqueness when $n = r \geq 2$;[54] (2) McKenzie [49] has provided a basic theorem which seems to overlap with Samuelson's 1953 sufficiency theorem, without either implying or being implied by it; (3) Nikaido and Gale are reported to have discovered a basic flaw in Samuelson's mathematical proof of the sufficiency condition for the uniqueness of equilibrium in the large; and (4) Samuelson [54] has extended the analysis to an investigation of the conditions under which free trade would equalise not merely rentals but also interest rates between countries.

In contrast to the difficulties of the general case, the case where $n = r = 2$ is strikingly simple and, since Samuelson's pioneering analysis, has been extensively surveyed [[5] Chapter I; [3], Chapter III]. Samuelson used the following assumptions, which proved to be sufficient for the purpose: linear, homogeneous production functions in each good; (2) diminishing returns along isoquants for each good; (3) non-reversible and different factor-intensities of the two goods at all (relevant) factor prices; (4) identity of production

[54]Pearce [51], in an excellent paper which brings out the essence of the problem in an extremely simple fashion, has attempted to provide alternative sufficiency conditions. But apparently Professor McKenzie has produced an example which contradicts Pearce's conjecture and the mathematical results of Nikaido and Gale also have had a similar effect. Mention may also be made of Reiter's [52] contribution which demonstrates the intuitive, inverse theorem that identical production functions are implied by "universally observed factor price equalization."

functions for each good between countries; (5) perfect competition and valuation of factors according to marginal value productivity; (6) incomplete specialisation in production in each country; and (7) absence of transport costs. The last assumption ensures commodity price equalisation, under free trade, between countries. The first five assumptions ensure a unique relationship between commodity and factor prices, under incomplete specialisation in production, which obtains identically between countries. With assumption (6), ruling out complete specialisation, therefore, commodity price equalisation necessarily entails factor price equalisation.[55]

When the general case, $n \geq 2 \leq r$, is considered the analysis is the simplest for the case $n = r > 2$. The kernel of the argument can be summarised easily.[56] If x_{ij} is the quantity of the ith factor used in the production of the jth good, ϕ_j the output of the jth good and q_j its selling price, constant returns to scale ensure that

$$\sum_{i=1}^{n} p_i x_{ij} = q_j \phi_j \ (j = 1, 2, \ldots n)$$

The quantities x_{ij} of factors used are determined by factor prices p_i and commodity prices q_j so that the n equations can be thought of as equations in $2n$ variables, p_i and q_j. For uniqueness, therefore, it is necessary that there be only one set of p_i corresponding to each set of q_j, and vice versa. It can then be shown that uniqueness follows if $|x_{ij}| \neq 0$, which consistutes a sufficient condition for factor-price equalisation in the small. It should be noted that, in the $n = r = 2$ case, $|x_{ij}| \neq 0$ turns into the familiar factor-intensity-difference condition, and uniqueness can be established *both* in the small and in

[55]Of all these assumptions, the postulate concerning the non-reversal of factor-intensities has aroused the greatest analytical and econometric interest. The principal analyses in this direction were noted earlier, in Section I, when discussing the Heckscher–Ohlin theorem.

[56]Samuelson's [53] Appendix contains a lucid account of the argument concerning uniqueness. Pearce's [51] paper contains an easily comprehensible account, from which I have borrowed.

the large because every element of the determinant is essentially one-signed. For the $n = r > 2$ case, however, Samuelson [53] argued that the condition that $|x_{ij}| \neq 0$ was not sufficient and an *additional* sufficiency condition would be that there should be *some* numbering of factors such that the leading principal minors of $|x_{ij}|$ of *every* order should be non-zero. It is this "strong factor-intensity" condition which has recently been reportedly re-examined by Nikaido and Gale and found to be inadequate. However, a further strengthening of the factorintensity postulate, such that *every* principal minor is non-zero (for *all* naturally ordered sets, as distinct from only one, corresponding to *all* numberings of factors), appears to constitute a sufficient condition for uniqueness in the large (as per Samuelson's correspondence).

The cases where $n \neq r$ are more difficult and the results of the analysis more devastating to the prospects for factor price equalisation. Samuelson's results are most conveniently summarized as follows. Let the observed number of goods actually produced in both countries be $n^* < n$ and the factors actually used in production of these goods, and with positive prices, be r^*. Then, if $n^* \geq r^*$, and if for *some* subset of r^* goods of the n^* goods, the strong factor-intensity conditions of Samuelson-Nikaido-Gale (or alternatively Kuhn and McKenzie, not detailed here) are realised, then equalised goods prices imply equalised factor prices. If, however, $r^* > n^*$, factor price equalisation is generally not implied (though it may obtain under certain strong and bizarre assumptions).[57]

Although the bulk of the analysis has been centred on the question of the equalisation of the *rentals* earned by factors of production in a Walrasian general equilibrium system (with extension to intermediate products), the effect of free trade on *interest rate* equalisation has recently been subjected to analysis by Samuelson [54] in a hitherto unpublished paper. The analysis supports the

---

[57]Several illustrative examples could be produced. For instance, if $n = 1$ and $r = 2$, factor price equalisation will generally be forbidden.

inference that rental equalisation (except in certain limiting situations) will be accompanied by interest rate equalisation.[58] The possi bility of introducing intermediate products without invalidating the factor price equalisation theorem, while demonstrated by Samuelson generally in his 1953 analysis, has further been recently demonstrated by Vanek [55], whose $n = r = 2$ analysis dovetails neatly into Samuelson's more powerful work.[59] Laing [48] has, on the other hand, opened up the investigation of the effects of increasing returns to scale, though his results serve merely to support the implication of Samuelson's analysis that constant returns to scale cannot be given up without invalidating the logical truth of the factor price equalisation theorem. Although the subject is, therefore, both of historic interest and still continues to attract fresh minds, one cannot help feeling that perhaps too great a proportion of the intellectual energy of trade theorists has been directed towards a question of limited utility. Of greater importance are the propositions in comparative statics which we must now discuss.

3. Theorems in Comparative Statics

The bulk of the analytical literature in pure theory is concerned with the implications of *differences* between two general equilibrium situations–or putting it differently, with the effects of specific *changes* in a given general equilibrium situation.

---

[58]The inapplicability of the traditional models (used to examine factor prices equalisation) for the purpose of analysing the effect of trade on interest rates was suggested originally, by a reading of Harrod's [46] paper, to V. K. Ramaswami and myself at Oxford in 1958. We noticed Harrod's unwarranted transition from rental to interest-rate equalisation, while operating within the framework of Samuelson's 1948 and 1953 models. I wrote subsequently to Samuelson concerning this question, and he worked out the required analysis. Ramaswami also wrote independently a paper which is yet unpublished.

[59]Samuelson has drawn my attention to the fact that Vanek [55] has managed to prove the following intuitive theorem: that (where $n = r = 2$ and both goods also serve as intermediates) if the *direct* factor-intensities are in one direction, then the *total* factor-intensities (including indirect factor requirements as well) will always be in the same direction.

Two classes of questions can be distinguished. (1) On the one hand, the effects of a change in *trade policy* are considered while assuming as given, for the trading country, the general equilibrium "data" (*i.e.*, tastes, the distribution of ownership or resources and transfer claims, factor supplies, production functions and general economic policy plus a specific trade policy from the outside world such that the precise offers of trade at varying terms of trade which the country has open to it are known and given): for instance, the effect of a change in a country's tariff rate on its terms of trade may be analysed. (2) On the other hand, the effects of a change in these "data" may be considered, while assuming the trade policy as given: for instance, the effect of capital accumulation on the terms of trade may be investigated.

Naturally it is not true, *strictly speaking,* that trade theorists have always considered the given "data" (trade policy), in the context of which the stipulated change in trade policy (data) takes place, as independent of the change itself. Thus, for instance, Myint [83] has argued that a change in trade policy from no trade to some trade will change the country's taste pattern itself–though no formal analysis is founded on this observation. An interesting illustration of the change in trade policy when the "data" shift is furnished by Kindleberger's [73] brilliant study of the trade policy reaction of different European governments to the influx of cheap American corn in the 1870s. The only other, and the most formal, example of such interaction is provided by the analysis of tariff retaliation. A change in trade policy prompts retaliation which alters the trade possibilities open to the country. A full, sequential analysis is usually presented, with the response mechanisms of each country specified, which properly belongs to the next section on dynamic analysis [5, Chapter II]. Aside from these instances, the last of which belongs elsewhere, while the others are not formalised into theorems, it does continue to be true that the interactions between changes in trade policy and in "data" have not been the object of serious analysis in the comparative statics of pure theory.

The effects of the shifts in trade policy and in data have been studied generally with reference to certain variables which recur with varying frequency in the numerous analyses. The terms of trade, the internal commodity price-ratios, the factor price ratio, output levels, the composition of trade and the levels of individual exports and imports are among those that turn up almost regularly. Yet, even among them, frequently important extensions of theory have by-passed the analysis of the impact on some variables, leaving many gaps in the literature (which merely need patient and much tiresome work to be filled out).

The models in terms of which the effects of the stipulated changes on these variables are studied vary as well. And yet, it is true that, in the last three decades, an astonishing amount of synthesis has been effected and a large number of theorems worked out in terms of the model (already used in Section I) which, while inspired by the work of Ohlin and Heckscher, is very much the creation of Samuelson, springing directly out of his early work on the factor price equalisation theorem [38, 39] and, with Stolper, on the effect of protection on factor rewards [91].

This Heckscher–Ohlin-Samuelson (H.O.S.) model is characterised by two countries and (within each country) two commodities, two factors of production, production functions characterised in each activity by constant returns to scale and diminishing returns along isoquants, perfect competition and full employment of the given supply of the factors of production.[60] The supply of each commodity, in this system, is exclusively a function of the terms of trade between the two commodities. On the other hand, the demand for each commodity is taken to be determined by both the terms of trade and the level of domestic expenditure. A detailed specification of an H.O.S. type model for the international economy (but omitting the specifications concerning the number of factors) has been provided recently by Mundell [11], who has also furnished therewith an excellent summary of many of the principal results (excluding those that depend upon the H.O.S. specification concerning the number of

[60]For certain limited purposes, the assumption of international identity of production functions for each activity is sometimes made.

factors) in comparative statics of the pure theory of trade. Meade's [9] work on trade and welfare contains many formal statements and applications of the H.O.S. model.[61] Recently the H.O.S. model has been strikingly extended, with many of its "restrictive" characteristics removed. Among the more significant of these extensions are: (1) the investigation of the *multiple country* (and multiple-commodity) case by Mundell [11, pp. 101–9] drawing upon Mosak's earlier work; (2) the analysis of demand explicitly in terms of the pattern of income distribution associated with an equilibrium situation, in contrast to the standard H.O.S. practice of assigning to aggregate, community demand the same properties as to individual demand–an extension introduced independently by Meade [9] and Johnson [66, 67]; and (3) the relaxation of the assumption of fixed factor supply to include the classical case of factors *in elastic supply* with respect to their rentals by several writers: Walsh [95], Vanek [92], Kemp and Jones [72], and myself and Johnson [60].

The theorems derived with the H.O.S. model (and its recent extensions) and others, can be surveyed under the two main heads:[62] (A) *shifts in data (other than trade policy);* (B) *shifts in trade policy.* Under the former the analysis subdivides further into shifts in data internal and external to the trading country. Among the internal shifts are: (1) *changes in demand;* (2) *changes in factor supply;* (3) *technological change;* and (4) *changes in (nontrade) economic policy.* The external shift in data involves some shift in the foreign offers to trade and may be prompted by changes internal to foreign countries or by changes in trade policy abroad. Such external shifts are classified generally as (5) *changes in international demand.* Under shifts in trade policy, I shall consider mainly tariff policy,

---

[61]On the other hand, the *geometrical* applications of the H.O.S. model are innumerable. Much ingenuity has also been expended on alternative geometrical depictions. I am afraid this runs into rapidly diminishing returns, and I have deliberately refrained from entering into a survey of these geometrical techniques.

[62]Since the literature using the H.O.S. model is admirably synthesised, I shall focus largely on this, while noting the main respects in which other types of models, which have been employed, differ in assumptions and/or conclusions. A fuller survey is ruled out by limitations of space.

distinguishing between: (1) *non-discriminatory tariff change,* and (2) *discriminatory tariff change.* The literature on other forms of trade policy is either largely symmetrical with tariff analysis (as in respect of quotas and subsidies) or limited (as with state trading) so that it will be surveyed only tangentially in the course of the analysis of tariffs which dominate the analysis in the pure theory of commercial policy.

(A) *Shifts in Data (other than Trade Policy)*

(1) *Changes in demand*

Problems relating to the changes in demand in trade theory have to be carefully defined, since demand is frequently understood by trade theorists as "international demand," which is different from demand *per se.* By international demand is meant the demand for imports (and supply of exports) at some given terms of trade.[63] This demand for imports represents the excess of domestic consumption over domestic production of *importables* corresponding to the defined terms of trade. A shift in international demand is therefore to be traced to a shift in domestic consumption and/or production (which, in turn, may be autonomous or induced by policy). International demand therefore reflects, and is to be distinguished from, internal (overall) demand. Internal demand in turn reflects individual tastes and the level and distribution of purchasing power. Shifts in internal demand therefore must be distinguished again from changes in individual tastes and in the level and distribution of (earned and unearned) income.

The propositions of pure theory have very nearly sidestepped the question of the effects of changes in *internal* demand. There is no formal analysis associated with the effects of changes in a country's tastes. The changes in the internal distribution of income have been brought into the fold of economic analysis only in so far as they *result* from changes in trade policy rather than as autonomous changes

[63]The locus of these international demands is nothing but the Marshallian "offer curve" International demand is also Mill's "reciprocal demand."

whose effects are spelled out. The only striking contrast is provided by the analysis of the effects of changes in the *level* of expenditure (and its accompanying effects on demand). This is nothing but the celebrated "*transfer problem*" which concerns the analysis of the effects on the terms of trade of a transfer of expenditure from one country to another. As for changes in "international" demand, trade theory is well endowed with controversies and literature concerning the effects on the terms of trade when the foreign reciprocal demand shifts while the country's own demand for the foreign products is unchanged. In the following summary I proceed to the transfer problem, leaving shifts in international demand (which relate to changes in the external data given to the country) to be treated in a later sub-section.

The effect of a transfer on the terms of trade has been of interest because a deterioration in these terms, from the viewpoint of the transferor country, would represent a "secondary burden" supplementary to the principal burden implicit in the transfer itself. Ignoring transport costs and using the H.O.S. model (without the assumptions with respect to the factors of production and competition), the answer is immediately obvious: the terms of trade will deteriorate or improve according as $ma + m_b \lesseqgtr 1$, where m_a is the marginal propensity to spend on importables in the transferor country A and m_b in the transferee country B [11, 88, 89].[64] Since the propensity to spend on exportables, xa and xb, is here merely unity minus the propensity to spend on importables, the criterion can be rewritten in any number of alternative forms such as $m_a \lesseqgtr x_b$. Where tariffs obtain, and it is assumed that the tariff proceeds are redistributed and spent by private consumers as part of their income, the proportion of the transfer eventually turning up as expenditure on imports will be naturally smaller than m_b, since there is a

[64]It need hardly be stressed that the full-blooded H.O.S. model is not necessary for the present analysis. Only the stability conditions have to be assumed, to determine the direction of the terms of trade change purely in terms of the marginal propensities to spend on importables with respect to expenditure change.

"leakage" each time the revenue is earned from expenditure directed at imports. The criterion thus changes to whether the sum of the marginal propensities to spend on importables is greater or less than a value which is greater than unity [5, Chapter VII, p. 173]. Where transport costs are incurred, the formula must change again, except in the extreme case when the transport cost is incurred in the form of the exported good itself. Where the transport cost is incurred, at least, partially, in the form of the imported good it follows that the entire import expenditure does *not* accrue to the foreigner and, therefore, the criterion would again have to be that the sum of the marginal propensities to spend on importables be greater or less than a value greater than unity [89; 5, p. 174].[65] Mundell [11, p. I07] has extended the analysis to the multi-country case where a transfer from country i to country j will rearrange demand throughout the international economy–for commodities exported from countries other than i and j. The resulting formula does not admit of any *a priori* generalisation.[66] While these criteria are devised in a full-employment framework Johnson [5, pp. 177–83], drawing upon earlier

[65]Economists have a propensity to answer impossible questions, and they have done so in the context of the transfer problem. There has been a great deal of discussion as to whether, in the *real world,* the classical proposition that the terms of trade would turn against the transferor country still remains a *"presumption."* Fundamentally, this seems to be the wrong question to pose *until* one *has.first* investigated the empirical applicability of the analytical model used. The failure to ask this key question seems to me to vitiate the utility of the entire discussion concerning what is "plausible" as a prediction. I also wonder whether it is useful to discuss what is generally "likely" when economic analysis and empirical work can enable us, subject to errors of interpretation and estimation, to make a precise prediction whenever necessary.

[66]Johnson [5, p. 176] anticipates this conclusion in a literary analysis. He also proceeds to introduce additional commodities differently-as non-traded goods in the two countries. However, the analysis is again not presented with full algebraic treatment and it is merely stated that: "The introduction of non-traded goods does alter the criteria, since changes in demand for such goods must be classed either as changes in (virtual) demand for exportables or as changes in (virtual) demand for imports, according to whether they are more substitutable in production and consumption for one or the other. In both these cases, however, the direction of change of the commodity terms of trade is not uniquely determined by whether the transfer is undereffected or overeffected at constant prices."

work by Meade, Harberger, Metzler, and others, has synthesised and extended the analysis for a Keynesian framework where output in each country is in perfectly elastic supply at a fixed domestic-currency price level, so that output, income and employment are determined by the aggregate demand for output. The resulting criterion involves, in the most general formulation, not merely the marginal propensities to spend on imports and exportables but also now the marginal propensities to save out of both pre-transfer and transfer income. As with the full-employment case, the criterion permits the transfer again to be undereffected or over-effected at constant terms of trade.[67]

(2) *Changes in Factor Supply*

There are three ways in which changes in factor supply enter the analysis in pure theory: (i) The effect of an *autonomous* change in factor supply has been analysed. We know now, for instance, how capital accumulation or population expansion will affect the terms and volume of trade. (ii) The effect of a *shift* in a factor of production from one country to its trading partner, on the terms and volume of trade, has also been investigated. (iii) Finally, changes in factor supply *resulting* from changes in trade policy, when the supply of factors is elastic with respect to their rentals, have also been considered. These, however, are properly treated with the analysis of the effects of changes in trade policy.

[67]The transfer will be undereffected or overeffected according as

$$\left(m'_a + m'_b - \frac{m_a}{s_a} \cdot s'_a - \frac{m_b}{s_b} \cdot s'_b - 1\right) \lesseqgtr 0$$

where the transferor is country A and the transferee country B and $ma' + mb''$ is the sum of the proportions of the transfer by which expenditure on imports is altered by the financing and disposal of the transfer, m_a and m_b are the (non-transfer-income) marginal propensities to import in A and B respectively, s_a. and s_b are the marginal propensities to save (from non-transfer incomes) in A and B and sa' and sb' are the proportions of the transfer by which savings are altered [5, p. 179].

(i) *Autonomous Changes in Factor Supply.* In surveying the literature on this problem, two central difficulties arise. Firstly, there is the difficulty of distinguishing models of growth into "static" and "dynamic"; only the former belong here. Sometimes a model is presented with factors increasing at a steady rate over time, and the resulting time-paths of several variables are worked out. And yet the analysis does not really involve time in any essential way except with respect to the "disturbance" itself. Basically, what is involved is working out, for each unit of time, the effects of the factor expansion and then repeating the analysis for each other period: time merely defines the nature of the "disturbance" (*i.e.*, the increase in the factor supply) which is itself independent of the equilibrium parametric values of the preceding periods. Surely it is sensible to treat such models as "static" in nature. The second difficulty consists in separating out models that refer to increase in factor supply and those that concern technical change. Frequently the same authors, for instance Johnson [5, Chapter III], analyse both questions in the same framework. Sometimes, however, the two are not even distinguished and merely "productivity increases" defined as increases in output (attributable naturally to either cause) are discussed, as by Mundell [11], or shifts in demand and supply schedules over time are defined without explicit distinction between different causes, as by Black [59]. Where these models are discussed is inevitably arbitrary, and I have brought them in under the present sub-section.

The simplest and yet the most influential analysis of the effects of economic expansion accruing through increased factor supply is that of Johnson [5, Chapter III], who uses the H.O.S. model.[68] There is a great flood of subsequent contributions, among them by Gorden [61],

[68]Historically, the contributions occurred as a result of the interest in the causes of the dollar shortage in the post-war world. The explanation of the shortage, first propounded by Balogh [58], was in terms of the rapidly increasing productivity in the United States. Translated in terms of the H.O.S. model, with the adjustment mechanism defined in terms of the terms of trade, the explanation was inevitably formalised into a theory of the effect of growth (due to capital accumulation and technical change) on the terms of trade. The connecting link between Johnson's important contributions and the less formal writings of Balogh and others is a

which explores the model further on this issue. The analysis of the effect on the terms of trade proceeds simply by noting that the excess demand for imports (dm) at unchanged terms of *trade* would equal the difference between the change in the demand for importables (dc) and in their supply (dp).[69] If this excess demand for imports is positive, then the terms of trade will shift against the growing country provided the stability condition is satisfied. And the precise change in the terms of trade can be obtained by equating the excess demand for imports due to growth with their excess supply due to adverse terms of trade [11, 111].

Since $dm = dc - dp$, the question of the properties of dc and dp has been raised. The former involves merely a weighted sum of the individual marginal propensities to consume importables. The latter, however, has prompted interesting analytical contributions. A proposition of Rybczynski [87] states that $dp \gtrless 0$ according as importables are factor K-intensive or factor L-intensive as the supply of K increases. Where the two commodities postulated have different factor-intensities, the output of the commodity intensive in the use of a factor will decrease absolutely as the supply of the other factor rises at unchanged terms of trade.[70] A taxonomic exercise, therefore, can

---

seminal paper of Hicks [3, p. 154] which reflects all the difficulties of a pioneering contribution.

[69] In the H.O.S. model the excess demand for imports implies an equivalent excess supply of exports, and the analysis can proceed in terms of *either* good.

[70] This proposition follows immediately as follows $\frac{K}{L} \equiv \frac{Kx}{Lx} \cdot \frac{Lx}{L} + \frac{Ky}{Ly} \cdot \frac{Ly}{L}$, which states that the aggregate factor endowment ratio is a weighted sum of the factor ratios in the two activities, X and Y. If the terms of trade are kept fixed so are the factor proportions in the model used. Therefore, $\frac{Kx}{Lx}$ and $\frac{Ky}{Ly}$ are fixed. So is L. Let K now increase. The resulting increase in $\frac{K}{L}$ can be accommodated then *only* by reducing Ly and increasing Lx if X is the K-intensive activity, such that $\frac{Kx}{Lx} > \frac{Ky}{Ly}$. Thus, the output of Y, the L-intensive activity, falls when Kincreases at unchanged terms of trade [61]. Since this argument is in terms of the relative factor endowments, it is easy to generalise the argument to the case where both factors increase in supply. Thus, for instance, if both factors increase at the same rate there will be a uniform expansion of the outputs of X and Y. If K increases more rapidly the analysis implies notionally a uniform expansion of X and Y (at the rate of growth of L) plus a *reduction* in the output of Y from this expanded level (resulting from the *excess* growth of K). And so on.

be carried out, using such theorems to define the possible properties of dc and dp [5, Chapter III].

In an influential paper, written prior to the analysis discussed hitherto, Johnson [5, Chapter IV] used a model which assumed that each country consumed and exported one commodity and imported, but did not produce, the other.[71] In this model, which amounts to only a special case of the H.O.S. model, $dp = 0$, and it follows that dm must necessarily be positive unless the consumption of importables falls as output increases with factor expansion. Although it is tempting to say this is ruled out if there is no inferior good, it should be noted that although the good is not inferior in any *individual's* consumption, it *may* be for the economy in the aggregate owing to changing income distribution (associated with a changed factor supply).[72]

Three other contributions are of interest—by Mundell [11], Ramaswami [86] and Black [59]. Mundell has extended Johnson's analysis to the multi-country case, noted earlier here. The same conclusions hold as in Johnson's [5, Chapter III] analysis, provided gross complementarity among the exports of different countries is ruled out.[73]

More novel is the analysis of Ramaswami [86], who has recently attempted to distinguish between the effects of "completed" accumulation and accumulation-in-progress on the terms of trade. Characterising the analyses of Johnson and others as relating to the latter question, Ramaswami deploys altogether four models to explore the former problem. These models reduce to two basic "types". (1) One

---

[71] Johnson [5, Chapter IV) formulated his analysis in terms of exchange-rate adjustment. In the model used by him, however, it is obvious that this is tantamount to terms-of-trade adjustment. An extension to the n-country case is also available.

[72] Mundell [11], in his otherwise excellent survey, does not make this point clear and relies on the "non-inferiority" of goods to give him necessarily positive terms.

[73] It is necessarily ruled out in the two-good model, for these two goods have to be substitutes. Gross substitutability among goods is shown by Mundell to guarantee the equivalence of the two country and multi-country (-cum-multi-commodity) case.

of the two goods in Johnson's model is assumed to play a dual role–as a consumer and also as a capital good, and accumulation is conceived as a demand shift, at constant prices, from consumption to investment goods. The model is simple and can be easily put through the various paces. For instance, any investment increase means increased demand for the dual-role good. If the reduction in consumption exclusively falls on that good there is no reason to expect the terms of trade to shift. If not, adjustment is clearly necessary. (2) The other approach is to assume a *third* industry ("tools") which serves as the capital good. The analysis is a little more complex but still manageable. The relative ranking of the factor ratios in the three industries adds to the scope for interesting taxonomic analysis.

While the analyses of Johnson, Mundell and Ramaswami are in the general equilibrium framework, Black [59] has produced a model which is strictly partial-equilibrium in its approach and correspondingly of little significance.[74] Using the partial-equilibrium supply and demand schedules for commodities in a four-commodity (an export and domestic good for each country), two-country model, he introduces trend-shifts in these schedules to derive changes over time in the balance of payments and terms of trade. In contrast to the general equilibrium models, however, this approach leaves untouched the crucial question of how exactly these schedules may be expected to shift in response to accumulation (technical change, etc.).

(ii) *Transfers of Factors between Countries.* Trade theory has also examined the impact of transfers of factors of production between trading countries. The analyses fall into two classes: (1) either the movement of a factor between countries is made contingent upon the presence of an international differential in its

[74]Black describes his approach as Marshallian because his model essentially amounts to using the Marshall–Lerner devaluation analysis and introducing trend-shifts in the supply and demand schedules. The Marshallian analysis can be interpreted, of course, in a partial sense or as an unhelpful general equilibrium approach (where the elasticites are *total* elasticities). Black is interpreting the Marshallian approach in the former sense.

rental and the equilibrium condition postulates the elimination of international factor movements when international factor returns are equalised; or (2) an autonomous shift in a factor's location is analysed. The former is clearly more relevant when there is perfect freedom for factor mobility between countries; the latter is more appropriate to modern conditions where this freedom does not exist and the international migration of factors is subject to political decision-making.

Practically the only rigorous analysis in the former class is by Mundell [82], who uses the H.O.S. model. Mundell postulates a tariff imposed on a situation characterised by international equality of factor rentals. The tariff raises the rental of the factor intensively used (in the strict Samuelson sense) and thereby precipitates a movement of that factor from the other into the tariff-imposing country.[75] Ultimately, the factor prices are equalised, factor movement eliminated and commodity prices are also equalised. The tariff is redundant and can be removed without affecting the new equilibrium reached. Mundell has merely turned the factor price-equalisation theorem on its head and effectively proved a commodity price-equalisation theorem (when factor mobility is perfect but commodity mobility is not, thanks to the tariff). The terms of trade and factor prices will be identical in the new equilibrium as prior to the tariff.[76]

Of greater interest than this variation on the factor price-equalisation theorem is the analysis by Johnson [5, Chapter III] of the effects of *given* transfers of productive factors between trading countries. It represents essentially an extension of the analysis of the effect of growth on the volume and terms of trade: a transfer of factors can be analysed as a simultaneous (and equal) increase and decrease in the two countries' factor supply. Aside from the inevitable taxonomy,

[75]It is equally possible to argue that the other factor may also move in the contrary direction. In fact, multiple (indeed, an infinite number of) solutions are possible, characterised by different international distributions of factors of production.

[76]This is easy enough to see when the factor-losing country has no monopoly power in trade. When the terms of trade can vary, the result still continues to hold.

using propositions such as Rybczynski's, Johnson carefully argues that an income transfer may be associated with the factor shift. Thus, for instance, profit remittances may follow upon capital transfer. Or gifts may attend upon labour migration. The "transfer problem" analysis may thus have to be super-imposed upon the "growthand trade" analysis to get a *total* picture. Meade [9, Chapter XIX] has presented a more elaborate model, permitting international differences in production functions for each activity.[77] However, his formal analysis excludes the " transfer problem" aspects of the question.[78]

(3) *Technological Change*

Although recent writings have underlined the desirability of treating technical change integrally with capital accumulation, trade theory is cast in the neo-classical tradition which separates them out. The formal analyses of changes in technology again divide into those that treat such changes as autonomous and those which concern the transfer of technical knowledge from one trading country to another.

In the former category there are several contributions. Using the H.O.S. model, on the technological side, Johnson [5, Chapter III] has formulated the proposition that "neutral" change in an activity will decrease the output level in the other activity, at constant commodity prices.[79] This proposition can be used to define the sign of dp and the taxonomic analysis thereon is similar to that for the change in factor supply, considered in the earlier sub-section. Findlay and Grubert [62] have extended the analysis of the effects of technical change, on output-composition at constant commodity prices, to the case of biased change. For two factors, say land and labour, they

[77]This extension is of considerable significance, since the formal H.O.S. model, with the assumption of internationally identical production functions, rules out one of the central reasons why international factor migration may be *desirable.*
[78]Caves [3, Chapter V] includes several Continental and other writings on capital movements in his survey. I find it difficult, however, to extract anything both formally clear and useful from this survey.
[79]Unlike with the Rybczynski proposition, the factor prices will change although the commodity prices are held constant.

have shown that for labour-saving technical change in the labour-intensive activity there will be an absolute decrease in the output of the land-intensive activity. And that, for land-saving change in the labour-intensive activity, the fall in the output of the other activity does not necessarily follow. In general terms, there will be a fall in the output of an activity when there is technical progress in the other activity which saves on the factor used intensively in that activity.[80] Intuitively, these results are obvious. For instance, land-saving invention in the land-intensive activity has two effects: (1) the technical change, conceived *neutrally,* decreases the output of the other activity (Johnson proposition); and (2) the "notional" release of land reduces the output of the other, labour-intensive activity as well (Rybczynski proposition). The two effects thus reinforce the fall in the other activity's output. On the other hand, they oppose each other when the invention saves on the factor in which the activity is *not* intensive.[81]

Seton [90] has produced an alternative model to analyse the effects of technical change on the terms of trade. It has practically all the features of Johnson's [5, Chapter III] model, but Seton formulates his analysis in terms of concepts which underline the significance of the "weight" of the trading countries in international trade.[82] A distinguishing feature is his defining technical change exclusively as the "neutral" change discussed earlier, though Seton

[80]The definitions of "neutral," "labour-saving" and "land-saving" are in terms of technology alone. Neutral change merely amounts to multiplying the numbers on the isoquants by a scalar. Under "labour-saving" invention, at the *same* factor price-ratio, the land-labour ratio is increased; and for" land-saving" progress the land-labour ratio is decreased.

[81]Johnson [65] has ingeniously combined the analysis of technical change with a disaggregated economy assumption to trace the effects of different types of technical change on the sign of dc.

[82]Seton's analysis is lucid, but the results are quite cumbersome, largely by virtue of the novel concepts used by him and his use of proportionate rather than absolute changes. I suspect, since his propositions are consistent with those deducible from Johnson's analysis, that Seton's formulae could be reduced to forms made familiar by the other models.

does not establish any propositions concerning its effect, at constant commodity prices, on the composition of output.

Kemp's [71] is practically the only other contribution of some interest in this field. He departs from the preceding analyses in introducing Keynesian unemployment. This renders the supply curves of exports and domestic goods perfectly elastic in his four-good model (with an export and a domestic good in each of the two trading countries).[83] The results of the analysis are worked out for technological progress in both the domestic and export industries.

(4) *Changes in Non-trade Policy*

A shift in "data" can also come from a change in the (non-trade) economic policy pursued by the Government. For instance, the Government may decide to impose a tax on *importables* (instead of on imports via a tariff) in an open economy engaged in free trade. How will this affect the volume and terms of trade? Such questions have rarely been posed directly in trade theory. They have, no doubt, been raised tangentially — mostly in relation to *welfare* analysis. For instance, Meade [9, Chapters V and VI] has analysed the choice between an import duty and a consumption tax, and between an export duty and a production tax, as a means of raising revenue, the preference function being defined with respect to world advantage. These analyses indirectly involve contributions to pure theory.

Practically the only *direct* analysis of such problems, however, is due to Mundell [11], who has extended his survey of pure theory to include an original contribution on the effect of consumption and production taxes on the terms of trade (at market prices and factor cost). For instance, a consumption tax on the imported good (with the revenue redistributed as income subsidy to consumers) will always improve a country's terms of trade because its net effect is to

[83]In this respect Kemp's analysis comes close to that of Asimakopoulos [56], who has investigated the effect of a third non-traded good in a constant-cost model which is presumably otherwise analogous to the Johnson model. Kemp's analysis, however, is rigorous, whereas that of Asimakopoulos lacks in formal rigour in so far as the formal model is not fully specified.

reduce the demand for imports by the product of the compensated elasticity of demand for importables and the tax change. This proposition is intuitively obvious, since the tax can be expected normally to reduce the world demand for importables. Mundell also notes the interesting fact that tariffs and (trade) subsidies can always be simulated in their "real" effects by taxes and subsidies on commodities. Thus, for instance, a tariff on Y (or an export duty on X) is equivalent, among several other combinations, to a consumption tax on Y plus a production tax on X or a consumption tax on Y plus a production subsidy on Y.

(5) *Changes in International Demand*

Until now, the autonomous shift has been located within the trading country itself. But the problem can also be posed in terms of an *external* shift—i.e., a shift in the *foreign offer curve* (which represents a schedule of trade offers to the trading country at varying terms of trade).[84] There is indeed a considerable literature on the effect of such shifts on a trading country's terms and volume of trade. This literature was sparked off by an apparent contradiction, in the results reached by Marshall and Graham, which has now been traced to different *definitions* of a shift in the offer curve.[85]

Naturally the results will vary with the definitions chosen; and, as Kemp [70] and Oliver [84] have demonstrated by analysing the effects of three different definitions, any number of definitions may be devised as one wishes. From the viewpoint of the usefulness of the economic analysis, however, the two definitions, adopted each by Marshall and Graham, appear to be the most meaningful and have their counterpart in the standard analysis of value. Marshall's analysis defines the change in international demand in terms of a change in the price at which the given quantity (of imports) is

[84]This shift will naturally be *internal* to the foreign country itself and will reflect any or more of the four types of changes discussed earlier and/or a trade-policy change. By the same token, the analysis of this sub-section is of limited interest.
[85]In their analysis, however, the shift was in the country's *own* offer curve, *the foreign* country's offer curve remaining unchanged.

demanded; whereas Graham's definition is in terms of a change in the quantity demanded at given terms of trade. Johnson and myself [2] have argued that each of these approaches has utility in the analysis of trade problems, and hence merits retention in the repertoire of trade theorists.[86]

(B) *Shifts in trade policy*

So far I have surveyed much of the central analysis of pure theory which concerns the effects of shifts in "data" while the trade policy (usually free trade) is assumed unchanged between the two situations being compared. However, many of the principal questions in trade theory have related to the effects of a shift in the trade policy itself. This is quite natural in view of the traditional preoccupation with the choice of commercial policy. Moreover, the trade policy most frequently analysed is tariff policy.

(i) *Non-discriminatory tariff change.* Within tariff theory, further, the analysis of non-discriminatory tariff change has received a disproportionate attention. Indeed, from the viewpoint of *systematic* theoretical analysis in its positive aspects, non-discriminatory tariff change is practically the only type of tariff change to have been analysed. As with all other positive analysis of trade policy, the theory of non-discriminatory tariff changes has sprung directly out of concern with questions of trade and welfare.

The assertion of the vulgar protectionists that tariffs would increase the share of labour in the national income has, in fact,

---

[86]I may quote [2, pp. 78–9]: "Broadly speaking, Graham's approach is likely to be more convenient when... the direction of change of international equilibrium can be predicted from the effect of the change on quantity demanded at the initial price. Examples are the transfer problem and the effect of economic expansion on international trade equilibrium. Marshall's approach, on the other hand, is likely to be more convenient when the problem concerns the effects of a change in a country's commercial policy on its equilibrium prices and quantities, since the direction of change of this equilibrium can be predicted from the effect of the tariff on the quantity of imports demanded at the initial internal price, and of the corresponding reduction of the external price on the quantity of imports the foreigner would supply. Marshall himself used this technique for the analysis of tariffs and subsidies;. . ."

prompted a thorough analysis, in terms of the H.O.S. model,[87] of the entire question of the effects of non-discriminatory tariffs on commodity prices, factor prices, and the absolute and relative shares of either factor in national income. In a classic analysis Stolper and Samuelson [91] revived the controversy concerning the effect of protection on the real incomes of factors and focused on the issue which was baffling most discussants–namely, how anything definitive could be said concerning the question posed *unless* the consumption pattern of the factors was specified. In an ingenious exercise, within the framework of the H.O.S. model, the authors successfully demonstrated that conditions *could* be specified under which the impact of protection on the absolute and relative shares of factors could be definitively predicted without reference to the consumption pattern of the factors. This was accomplished via the analysis of the impact of tariffs on factor prices. Since, in the H.O.S. model, a unique relationship exists between factor and commodity prices, Stolper and Samuelson opened up, in effect, the entire modern analysis of the effects of tariffs on commodity and factor prices and on absolute and relative shares of factors in national income. Metzler [80, 81] has subsequently extended the analysis to the "paradoxical" case where a tariff *reduces* the (relative) price of the importable commodity in the tariff-imposing country. The analysis has been further extended with respect to an elastic factor supply by Kemp and Jones [72] and myself and Johnson [60], the interdependence of public and private consumption by Baldwin [57] and myself and Johnson [60], changes in income distribution by Johnson [67, 60] and the multi-country case by Mundell [11].

In the analysis the distinction between a prohibitive (*i.e.*, trade-eliminating) and a non-prohibitive tariff is of crucial importance, for two reasons: (i) with a prohibitive tariff, starting from free trade, the price of importables cannot be lowered by the imposition of the tariff (in the specified H.O.S. model), whereas it can be when the tariff is

---

[87]The assumptions concerning the factors of production are, however, not necessary to the analysis.

non-prohibitive; and (ii) a prohibitive tariff generates no revenue, whereas a non-prohibitive tariff does, creating the necessity to make some assumption about the revenue disposal. The assumption about revenue disposal is, in turn, of significance, since the results of the analysis depend upon it. The two common assumptions in tariff theory are that *either* the Government spends it directly *or* that the revenue is redistributed as an income-subsidy to the consumers, who then spend it like earned income. (The results vary unless the Government spends the revenue at internal prices in the same way as consumers do and government consumption does not alter private consumption.)

Subject to these further specifications, the H.O.S. model can be readily employed to work out a large number of formulae concerning the impact of tariff change on domestic and international terms of trade (and hence also on the absolute and relative shares in national income of each of the two classes of factors) [11, 60]. It would be tedious to record the numerous results here; besides, a fairly exhaustive survey has been provided by me elsewhere [1]. I would merely note here that the results under the strict H.O.S. model naturally get modified when any of the assumptions is changed. For instance, letting one of the factors vary in response to its rental complicates the analysis considerably [60, p. 245]. Thus, in this case, the proposition, that, when the tariff proceeds are spent by the private sector, the terms of trade will *necessarily* improve for the tariff-imposing country (which follows from the fact that, at constant terms of trade, there is an excess supply of importables measured by the product of the compensated elasticity of demand for imports and the tariff change), is no longer valid and the terms of trade can deteriorate, even though this condition is satisfied [60, p. 246].[88] Similarly, for the case of a disaggregated private sector where changes in income distribution are allowed to play a role in determining the pattern of demand, the net result of

[88]Kemp and Jones [72] have examined additionally the question of the levels of importable production and the variable factor's supply.

such disaggregation is to make the aggregate marginal propensity to spend on imports a weighted sum of these propensities for the different individuals constituting the economy [60, pp. 235–8]. The extension to the multi-country case by Mundell [11], however, does not destroy the simple elegance of the traditional conclusions, for instance, with respect to the effects on the external and internal terms of trade. Gross substitutability among the exports of different countries to the tariff-imposing country is sufficient to sustain the two-country result; further restrictions need not be imposed on the pattern of expenditure out of redistributed revenue [68]. Kemp has also re-examined the standard H.O.S. conclusions in the framework of Keynesian unemployment [3, p. 74], establishing the conditions under which Metzler's "paradoxical" result would continue to hold.[89] Of some interest is also the recent analysis by MacDougall [75, 76], which utilises the flood of empirical studies on the international price mechanism to investigate the empirical "likelihood" of Metzler's results and deduce the debatable conclusion that it is relatively small.

(ii) *Discriminatory Tariff Changes.* Discriminatory tariff changes can be distinguished according as the discrimination is between countries or between commodities. Any particular tariff may discriminate in both ways, of course, as when it is levied on a commodity which is imported only from a single foreign source.

In contrast to the analysis of non-discriminatory tariff changes, the theory of discriminatory tariff changes, in its positive aspects, is

[89](1) Under competitive conditions quotas are identical with tariffs (with redistributed revenue) and the analysis in the text is valid for them as well. Each tariff implies an equivalent quota and the other way round. Where, however, the quota system confers a domestic monopoly, the results are different. (2) Subsidies are perfectly symmetrical with the case where tariff proceeds are redistributed to the private sector. However, there is no sensible counterpart to the case where the Government spends the tariff proceeds itself [11]. (3) State trading can be easily analysed as well, for it merely turns tariff analysis on its head. Where tariff theory analyses the effect of specific tariffs (and subsidies) on the volume and terms of trade, the theory of state trading is concerned with the investigation, in effect, of the tariffs (and subsidies) which must be imposed to make a particular volume and terms of trade feasible [9]. (It may be remembered that *trade* taxes and subsidies can be reduced invariably to equivalent *production* taxes and subsidies.)

singularly lacking in formal propositions concerning the determinants of behaviour of equilibrium variables. This is to be accounted for partly by the analytical dominance of the two-good, two-country (H.O.S.) model, which rules out the possibility of discriminatory tariff changes. Partly it is also the result of the preoccupation of discriminatory tariff analysts with welfare analysis. For instance, the formal analysis of preferential tariff reduction, prompted by the post-war interest in customs unions and free-trade areas, has been almost exclusively oriented towards questions like: will a customs union increase world welfare? rather than towards problems like: how will the terms of trade of the non-member countries be affected? No doubt, welfare analysis must be founded on positive analysis. But it happens that the kind of positive analysis that is subsumed in these welfare exercises in tariff discrimination rarely has the formal neatness that is now associated with the theory of non-discriminatory tariff changes.[90]

The formal theory of customs union begins with Viner's [94] examination of the assertion that a customs union, by virtue of its being a move towards free trade, would *improve* welfare. The models employed were not fully stated, but the arguments have none the less proved seminal. Viner considered merely shifts in the given production (of a single commodity), in an essentially three-country model, from one country to another. (Where the union results in the shift of imports from the lower-cost outside country to the higher-cost partner country, he described the shift as trade-diversion. Where the preferential tariff reduction merely eliminates the inefficient, domestic industry and replaces it with imports from the member country, he named the change trade-creation.) Lipsey

[90]This is itself attributable frequently to the way in which welfare analysis has been pursued. For instance, Lipsey [121], in a brilliant paper on customs union theory, is content with demonstrating a *possibility* (that despite "trade diversion," both national and international welfare may be improved by a customs union) and does not carry the analysis through to a formal algebraic statement of the conditions under which the possibility will occur. Further again, Meade's [79] analysis is more in the nature of the demonstration of a method than a fully taxonomic and formal exercise.

[121] and Meade [79] have subsequently elaborated upon these basic concepts, stating their models more fully and introducing both the possibility of an *increase* in the volume of imports (as distinct from a mere shift in their origin) due to their cheapening domestically, as also the existence of imperfectly elastic supply curves. This has been done in the context of both a simple formalisation of Viner's (implicit) model into a two-good, three-country model [121] and a more complex version with more than two goods which admits of complementarity between imports from different sources [7, 79].

Unfortunately, all these analyses are welfare-orientated and, for reasons outlined earlier, fail to contribute, in their extant form, anything systematic and substantive to positive theory. It is only recently that Vanek [93] has directly posed the questions of positive theory in an interesting extension of the standard, Marshallian offer-curve analysis to the case of preferential tariff reductions in a two-commodity, three-country model. However, he halts his analysis short of the derivation of the conditions under which the possibilities stated by him will occur.[91] In a real sense, therefore, the question of discriminatory tariff change invites systematic and fresh analysis–in its positive aspects.[92]

4. Theorems in Dynamics

In contrast to the general richness and synthesised character of much of pure theory in its comparative statics, dynamic propositions in

[91] A fuller analysis, I am informed, has since been completed by him. An unpublished manuscript by R. A. Mundell on this subject is also reported to be in existence.

[92] Part of the difficulty in systematically analysing the customs-union problems consists in the vast number of possible cases which logically must be catalogued and analysed. For instance, even in the extremely simplified two-good, three-country model we have seven logically different possibilities (as distinct from four mentioned by Vanek [93]), catalogued in the following matrix, *presented in terms of a single commodity* which may be an export (**X**) or import (M) of, or not traded (O) by, a country and where the three countries are the home country (H) the partner country (P) and the non-member country (**N**). The categorisation is in terms of the pre-customs-union position.

international trade are comparatively few and bear no trace of any uniform design, each having been developed in virtual isolation. Dynamic trade theory, where it exists, has grown up in an essentially *ad hoc* fashion and has witnessed none of the interaction of analysis which usually accompanies the development of an area of knowledge and produces a common design, a unifying frame.

At the same time there is no dearth of interest in the dynamic aspects of trade theory, and a vast amount of non-rigorous but suggestive literature is available [3, Chapter IX]. This is supplemented by the occasional attempts of growth theorists to include international trade in their models ("for completeness," and more frequently to "show that it does not affect the validity of the approach and/or conclusions") — as, for instance, by Chakravarty [137]. I have kept away from either kind of literature — from the former because these unverified conjectures provide a fertile source for fresh theoretical analysis but themselves do not constitute it;[93] and from the latter because the trade aspects of the models are frequently the least interesting, for they are also treated as the least important.

Broadly speaking, the scant formal literature on dynamic propositions divides itself into: (1) those analyses where the inquiry concerns the effects of an *initial* change in the *trade policy,* and (2)

	H.	*P.*	*N.*
(1)	X	M	M
(2)	M	X	X
(3)	M	M	X
(4)	X	X	M
(5)	O	O	O
(6)	M	O	X
(7)	X	M	O

From the viewpoint of economic analysis, cases (1) and (2) are identical in structure; so are cases (3) and (4), so that the number of distinct cases may be considered to reduce to five. For the three-commodity model the possibilities are greater in number, and depend further on relations of substitution and complementarity between different goods.

[93]There are a few exceptions that I have made, partly to illustrate the non-rigorous character of these analyses, but mostly because they come close enough to formal analysis to merit brief comment.

those where the effects of an *initial* change in other *data* are being considered.[94]

(1) *Change in Trade Policy*

Perhaps the neatest dynamic analysis of the effects of a change in trade policy concerns that involving adaptive, mutual and sequential changes in tariffs. Starting with the imposition of an optimum tariff, levied by a country in a two-country world, the Cournot-type adjustment mechanism where each country alternatively imposes an optimum tariff leads eventually to the two possibilities demonstrated by Johnson [5, Chapter II]: (i) an eventual equilibrium where the optimum tariff of each country is the existing tariff; or (ii) each country moves into a "tariff cycle" such that the two countries oscillate between a pair of own tariffs. While the possibility of generalising the theory by changing the postulated reaction mechanism has been recognised previously, Panchmukhi [124] has recently formulated the theory of tariff retaliation in explicitly game-theoretic terms. It is highly improbable, however, that tariff retaliation can be studied profitably on the assumption that tariffs are levied, autonomously or in retaliation, to maximise the tariff-imposing country's advantage. Surely, the tariff levels *and* structure are prompted by distributional considerations (operating through pressure groups) rather than by considerations of national advantage.[95]

By contrast, the literature on the effects of changes in trade policy in the absence of retaliation is characterised by less sophistication, though greater relevance. Practically all the analyses relate to the effect of trade on the rate of growth of income–but the mechanisms postulated vary considerably, and so do the clarity and rigour that attend these contributions.

The earliest of these, and analytically impressive for its time, is the classical analysis of the effect of cheap food imports from

[94]The initial change itself may be defined to be a *continuing* one: for instance, a change in the rate of saving may be *permanent*.

[95]The question of tariff retaliation is considered at greater length in Section VI, since it has important implications for welfare analysis.

the colonies on the approach of the Stationary State. Among the clearest exponents of this theory was Mill [32], who attempted to demonstrate how, through the consequential increase in the rate of profit and hence in the accumulation of savings and capital, the approach of the Stationary State would be put off. What is not available, however, is the *precision* that we have now come to expect in theoretical writing; and unfortunately the recent mathematical formulations of the Ricardian systems (by Samuelson and Pasinetti) leave out international trade altogether, although Ricardo traced out the essence of the sequence that Mill elaborated. Other ways in which such a dynamic link between trade and growth has been established are: (i) via the effect of trade on the marginal capital–output ratio by virtue of the proposition that (free) trade increases real income [27, 132]; (ii) via the effect of trade on the distribution of income and hence on the average savings ratio [97, 99, 100]; and (iii) via the effect of trade through factor price rigidity on the level of employment, hence on real income and savings [27].[96] None of these analyses are fully rigorous. For instance, the analysts who argue via the effects on the distribution of income and hence on the average savings ratio never specify a model. And yet the sequence is clear and the models are easy to invent.[97]

---

[96]Linder [27] considers his model applicable to underdeveloped countries and uses it to turn up immiserating growth paths of output. The model is, in fact, quite symmetrical between movement from free trade to no trade and a reverse movement. For any change will bring about unemployment (due to factor-price rigidity) in the industry which should contract, and hence the contraction of real income and possible reduction in the rate of growth. The model, not being mathematically formulated, does not specify *where* the incremental output is allocated and whether the mechanism of factor allocation envisaged would be compatible with the factor-price rigidity assumption. Also, it would be pertinent to consider whether it is right to ignore the effects of change brought about by increased output: it may well be that the change implicit in trade may *offset* the change involved by growth. The analysis offered by Linder is thus not fully satisfactory.

[97]For example, a model where tractors produce tractors and com, and corn is exchanged for toys when trade opens, could easily be used to demonstrate how the possibility of trade can reduce the marginal capital–output ratio and raise the rate of growth (with given average savings ratio). For a treatment of several types

(2) *Change in Data*

The most interesting (though insufficiently formal) model, designed to analyse the effects of continuous accumulation on the trade pattern, has been presented by Bensusan-Butt [96]. He operates in a two-country, multi-commodity framework, with a simplified production technology such that each commodity has two alternative processes, one with and the other without machinery, which are known in both countries. Starting with a situation where no accumulation has previously taken place, and the cost and price structure is identical between countries, and trade is absent in consequence, Bensusan-Butt unfolds a sequence in which the steady accumulation of capital in one country leads to progressive mechanisation, and emergence as exports, of industries in the accumulating country. The resulting improvement in the other country's real income (initially through the rise of trade and subsequently through the postulated improvement in the terms of trade as the accumulation proceeds) is linked with the emergence of savings there, and the effect of this on the pattern of trade is examined.

While Bensusan-Butt's analysis examines the structure of trade, as it *evolves* sequentially, the rest of the dynamic analyses in the literature are concerned instead with the equilibrium time-paths of variables such as output, real income and terms of trade in a growing economy engaged in a *pre-defined* pattern of trade.

Srinivasan [104] has constructed an interesting two-country, three-commodity model where one country produces two goods (a consumer good and a capital good which produces all goods in the system) and the other country produces the other (consumer) good. Assuming: (1) the Paretian allocation mechanism to allocate the fully employed factors, labour and capital (good); (2) a fixed trade pattern involving the exchange of the former country's capital good with the latter country's consumer good; and (3) international lending predetermined by a linear relationship between exports and import values, Srinivasan introduces growth into the system

---

of causal links between trade and growth in a historical context, Kindleberger [101] is an excellent reference.

by letting labour grow exponentially, capital accumulate through savings and neutral technical progress characterise industries in both countries. The equilibrium time-paths of income, terms of trade and comparative factor rewards are analysed.

While in Srinivasan's model the import demand functions are ingeniously implicit in the production and trade patterns specified, Johnson [5, Chapter V] has used the more conventional approach of specifying marginal propensities to import (and spend on imports) and used them in the context of a Harrod-Domar type of flow-analysis extended to the international economy. Johnson explores, in effect, the behaviour of the equilibrium rate of growth of output and income of a country over time under the assumption of international lending and also under the more realistic postulate of exchange-rate adjustment (when the time profile of the terms of trade becomes relevant).[98]

Far more complex, and for the same reason ineffective as theory, is the analysis of Brems [98], who, using a 52-equations system (among whose novelties is trade in producers' goods), solves it to derive two L-order difference equations (where L *is* the durability, in years, of capital goods). These yield solutions which establish relations, over the time-path, between the equilibrium values of variables such as the growth rates of the two trading countries.

These analyses nearly exhaust the literature on dynamic theory—except for the "omissions" justified earlier.[99] There is little doubt that, in contrast to the comparative statics of pure theory, dynamic trade theory still calls for further, systematic analysis and synthesis.

[98]Verdoom [105] has attempted a rigorous analysis, of similar intent, but under the restrictive assumptions of: (1) fixed coefficients of production, and (2) independence of the foreign rate of growth from the rate of growth of the economy under consideration. Johnson [5, Chapter V] eliminates the former type of question altogether (because he operates with the concept of the marginal propensity to import), while his analysis is fully general on the latter question.

[99]Perhaps the only omission that I regret is that of some Japanese analyses that seem extremely interesting, though the sources I have been able to consult in English [102, 103] do not give enough formal account of these theories. I refer to the analysis of the "Marxist" economists, S. Tsuru and H. Kitamura, which links cyclical fluctuations with the *pattern* of trade [102].

5. Central Limitation: Intermediates and Capital Goods

Of greater significance is the negligible dent made so far by intermediate and capital goods in the theoretical models employed by analysts of international trade. To state this is *not* to assert that the present stock of knowledge will not survive the required change in the formulation of the models. In fact, we do know, from such little analysis as already obtains in this direction, that the survival rate tends to be quite high! More important, however, is the fact that a vast range of interesting problems, applicable to economies using intermediate and (produced) capital goods, cannot get within the range of analysis until the theorists get away from the traditional picture of primary factors and integrated processes of production (with the inevitable concomitant feature of trade in consumer goods).

The introduction of intermediates and (produced) capital goods can be accomplished in principle in either of the following alternative ways: either these enter only domestic processes but not trade or they enter trade as well. For instance, a sector producing capital goods may exist though capital goods do not enter trade. The existing theoretical analyses in trade theory exhibit the entire range of these possibilities. For example, Samuelson's [54] interest-rate equalisation model has produced but untraded capital goods. So has Ramaswami's [86] model, which analyses the effect of trade on growth. On the other hand, Srinivasan's [104] dynamic model has a capital good which is both produced and traded. As for intermediate goods, the models used by McKenzie [78, 108] and Jones [69], which explore the pattern of trade in a Ricardo-Graham framework, distinguish between the cases where intermediate goods are traded and where they are not. Vanek [55], on the other hand, uses a two-sector model where the intermediates are identical with the final goods which enter trade.

A large number of propositions continue to be valid despite the introduction of intermediates and/or capital goods in the analytical models. For instance, as Samuelson [125] and Kemp [120] have shown, the proposition that free trade is superior to no trade is valid even when intermediates exist and enter trade. Similarly, Jones [69] has shown that the pattern of efficient specialisation in the Ricardo-Graham model will continue to satisfy the bilateral comparative cost rankings postulated by Ricardo, even when intermediates enter trade. The factor price equalisation theorem again has been examined, in the light of traded intermediate goods, by Samuelson [53] and Vanek [55] without leading to any qualitative change in the traditional propositions. On the other hand, certain propositions *do* change. For instance, the *exact* pattern of specialisation in the Ricardo-Graham model naturally changes with the possibility of trade in intermediate goods [69, 78]. The effect of growth on the terms of trade again is shown by Ramaswami [86] to change qualitatively with the introduction of a (produced) capital-goods sector.[100]

Of far greater significance, however, is the fact that a whole range of interesting and important questions slip through the analyst's hands unless intermediates and (produced) capital goods are introduced into the formal models. For instance, the recent G.A.T.T. [107] discussions on the exports of "new manufactures" from the industrialising underdeveloped countries have drawn attention to the disparity between tariffs levied on unprocessed and semi-processed items (on which tariffs are relatively lower) and those on finished manufactures. It is surely interesting to examine the effects, in both positive and welfare terms, of such tariff discrimination. But the analysis just cannot get off the ground with the traditional types of analytical models![101] Let me take another important illustration.

[100]Professor Kindleberger has drawn my attention to an ingenious mimeographed paper of W. Travis which draws upon an unpublished doctoral dissertation of the author to demonstrate the drawback of the usual conclusion that tariff reduction is best carried out gradually (*i.e.*,piecemeal) to soften the impact of adjustment. Using an input–output framework, Travis shows how the adjustments in different activities demanded by different tariff changes may actually be mutually offsetting so that it may be wiser to have a simultaneous tariff reduction on many fronts than to opt for piecemeal, sequential tariff cuts. Here we have another example of the utility of having processes wing intermediates explicitly in the model, employed for analysis.

[101]We may note the related point that an apparently non-discriminatory tariff adjustment on all imports (say, 10% reduction in the tariffs on both alumina

The traditional multiplier analysis in trade theory (which has already been discussed earlier in relation to the Keynesian treatment of the transfer problem) postulates the impact of exports and/or autonomous investment on the balance of payments and the levels of domestic output and employment. But there is an extension to the concept of the *import multiplier* as well, when one considers the situation frequently experienced by economies importing raw materials, when excess capacity develops due to the shortage of foreign exchange. An extra unit of exchange (say, through foreign aid) will then increase the level of domestic output directly by a multiple which is the ratio of value added to imported inputs (the latter being the only constraint). If, however, this output enters as input into other processes lying idle for want of materials, one can easily work out (through the input–output mechanism) a whole chain of increased outputs which, on summation, yields a multiplier-measure of the increased output attributable to the incremental unit of imports. This idea has been independently formulated in various writings, by Stolper [109, 110], several Japanese economists such as Akamatsu [106] and Kojima [103], and writers on the Indian balance of payments in recent years. It demonstrates forcefully how the exclusion of intermediates from analysis would rule out from examination one of the most significant aspects of the international trade problems besetting many economies. Since imported intermediates may also lead to extra output of domestically produced capital goods which may help break other bottlenecks at a future date, or the incremental exchange may be used to import capital goods which create capacity to break bottlenecks to domestic utilisation of capacity in other sectors of use, this whole notion of the import multiplier has a further time dimension to it and equally

and aluminium) would be *de facto* discriminatory in its effects when the imports consist of both the raw material and the finished product. The effective reduction in the protective effect would be greater on the raw material. Incidentally, an analysis of the problem discussed in the text would call for some method of demarcating intermediates in a world where circularities in the Leontief flow-matrix may prevent an easy solution.

illustrates the role of produced and traded capital goods in any realistic analysis of the trade phenomena in the real world.

6. Welfare Propositions: Gains from Trade

Welfare propositions are among the oldest in pure theory. Trade theory developed in the effort to demonstrate the fallacy of the protectionist prescriptions of the Mercantilist School. Today the range of analytical questions has increased astonishingly beyond the early preoccupation with the comparison of free trade with protection. To seek design and order in this vast literature is no mean ambition.

It is useful to start with the basic proposition that the aim of policy orientated welfare economics is to provide a *ranking of policies*. This ranking may relate to *trade* policies (while the general equilibrium parameters and relationships, such as the known technology, are given). For instance, is a zero tariff (*i.e.*, free trade) superior to no trade? Is a 15% (non-discriminatory) tariff superior to a 20% tariff? Would an increase in the tariff rate be beneficial? On the other hand, the ranking may refer to policies relating to the general equilibrium *parameters and relationships*, such as the factor supply level (given the trade policy). For instance, for an open economy engaged in free trade, is migration desirable? Should the increment in capital stock be absorbed as domestic or foreign investment?[102]

[102]Although I have not done so in the text, the ranking of policies could also be classified into the ranking of *specific measures* and of *general forms of policy intervention.* Under the former, a characteristic illustration would be the ranking of two rates of tariffs. For instance, would a 5% tariff be inferior to a 3% tariff? Would a marginal reduction in the tariff rate increase welfare? Under the latter, a typical example would be the ranking of a tariff policy (without specifying a specific tariff rate) and free-trade policy. For instance, the proposition that an optimum tariff is superior to free trade is not formulated in terms of a unique tariff-rate comparison, but is rather valid in the sense that, corresponding to any income distribution chosen, there will be an optimum tariff rate which will be superior to free trade so that the utility possibility curve for an optimum tariff situation, with variable tariff rates, will lie outside (though it may touch) that for the free-trade situation.

The ranking of policies in pure theory further divides into two classes of propositions: (1) those that relate to *national* advantage; and (2) those that concern *international* advantage. Thus, for instance, the proposition that free trade is superior to no trade is sought to be established from both national and international standpoints. On the other hand, the proposition that (for a variable tariff rate) the optimum tariff is superior to free trade concerns only national advantage.

These rankings can further be classified according to the *criterion of welfare* employed. The Samuelsonian superior-for-all-income-distributions criterion has been widely used in the early development of the theory subsequent to the new welfare economics. On the other hand, it has been replaced extensively in recent years by criteria which handle the problem of income distribution in a non-purist fashion. Among them, two approaches can be distinguished, which divide mainly on the issue of the measurability of utility.

The *ordinalist* method sets up a community welfare function which *assumes* that the State adopts a policy of lump-sum transfers to fix the income-distribution at some "desired" level. The properties of this welfare function are then assumed to be parallel to those which are taken normally (with some "plausibility") to characterise individual welfare functions. It is only recently that Samuelson [126] has established the exact conditions under which "social indifference curves" will enjoy these properties—so that, in effect, the trade theorist must assume, *ipso facto,* these conditions to obtain if he uses a social-welfare function with those properties.[103]

[103] Often trade theorists omit mentioning the problem of lump-sum transfers and use community preference functions as if the community were an individual. This procedure is clearly sloppy. It is also not uncommon for some theorists to assume that the economy is composed of individuals with identical tastes and income (kept equal presumably by lump-sum transfers). This, however, is tantamount to assuming a single individual and, only in a limited, formal sense can one concede the "reduced restrictiveness" of such an assumption! It is also sometimes stated that the State "ignores the question of income distribution" and then the analyst proceeds to operate with the community indifference curves [129, p. 329]. This, however, is open to objection because: (1) the assumptions under

The ranking of trade policies can then be carried out in terms of such a community preference function, corresponding to any "desired" income distribution.

The other, alternative method of handling the problem of income distribution so as to achieve a unique ranking of policies has been that extensively used by Meade [8, 9]. He explicitly combines equity and efficiency in a single welfare function by assuming *cardinality* and the possibility of *interpersonal comparisons of welfare* (through assigned weights). This method enables the analyst to judge the change in welfare between two situations for the actual market income-distributions achieved and without having to conjure up a state of lump-sum transfers (which itself may be construed to be an advantage, from the ethical and practical viewpoints, over both the Samuelson criterion and the ordinalist method sketched earlier).[104]

---

which the community preference function would be characterised by the required properties (*e.g.*, convexity) would still have to be specified; and (2) the position implied by the statement is untenable. In what can one be "indifferent" to income distribution? The only meaning that can possibly be attributed is that the State attaches equal weight to the marginal utility of each individual-in which case the analyst ceases to be an ordinalist!

[104]Caves' [3, pp. 233–4] neat summary of Meade's method is useful. "Suppose that a change is made somewhere in the economy, such as the elimination of a monopoly position. There will be a primary gain in economic efficiency, because consumers now receive extra units of this particular product which they value above the cost to the suppliers. In addition, because of relations of substitutability and complementarity between this and other products, both in consumption and production, expenditure patterns will change throughout the economy. Spending on products with no cost-value divergence may rise; spending on other products with very large divergences may fall. Changes of this type represent secondary losses; their opposites would represent secondary gains. The process of summing these changes over the whole economic system is shown by the expression:

$$u = \sum_{i=1}^{n} \sum_{j=1}^{n} \sum_{s=1}^{e} (U_{ij} D_{ijs} - 1) \mu_j R_{js} \lambda_{ijs}$$

where the net change in utility (u) represents a summation, over all sellers, buyers, and commodities, of the unit revenue from each commodity (R) times the change in the quantity of that commodity exchanged (x), times the rate at which the marginal value to the purchaser exceeds the marginal cost to the seller ($D - 1$). Subscript s denotes a commodity, i a buyer, j a seller. In addition, distributional

Aside from the possible preferences on ethical and practical grounds, however, the shift in favour of these less-restrictive criteria has been prompted essentially by a change in the kinds of questions that economists are willing to accept from policy makers. The traditional analysis concerned itself with the ranking of specific policy measures (themselves distortionary) under otherwise "first-best" assumptions or, in ranking forms of policy intervention, compared only policies achieving fully optimal situations with those resulting in sub-optimal ones. In the former category, for instance, is the proposition that a higher tariff is inferior to a lower tariff. In the latter class the most prominent proposition has always been that an optimum tariff (which attains the first best solution) is superior to free trade (which leads to a sub-optimal solution when the country can influence its terms of trade). These rankings satisfy the Samuelson welfare criterion. Now, however, the range of policy questions has increased enormously. The policy-makers wish to know the answers to questions which inevitably involve comparing sub-optimal situations. Problems are posed such that "second-best" assumptions as also sub-optimal comparisons have to be made.[105]

---

weights appear as u_j, the weight attached to marginal income for the seller, and u_{ij}, which stands for the ratio u_i/u_j."

[105]Second-best assumptions imply that, from the entire set of assumptions that are made to demonstrate the Pareto optimality of the competitive solution, one (or more) does not obtain. Given this definition of second-best assumptions, it is useful to classify these constraints, the departures from first-best assumptions, into two categories: (1) *Behavioural* constraints; and (2) *Environmental* constraints. In the former class we can consider non-utility maximisation and non-profit maximisation by decision-making units. In the latter category we may further distinguish between (i) *State-imposed* constraints and (ii) *others.* Among the State-imposed constraints, we have the imposition of direct and indirect taxes, subsidies tariffs, restrictions of output levels, etc. The other constraints divide broadly into " *market imperfections*" (for instance, the presence of monopoly, a distortionary wage differential between sectors, divergence of the shadow rental to a factor from its actual rental, and national monopoly power in trade), " *technological characteristics*" (for instance, increasing returns to scale, and non-convexity of isoquants) and " *interdependence*" (for instance, externalities in production and in consumption).

Corresponding to the notion of second-best *assumptions* is the concept of second-best *solutions.* The difference between first-best and second-best solutions

For instance, some distortionary taxes may have to be admitted into the analysis when two tariff rates are being compared. The policy-maker is apt to say: "I cannot take off certain taxes. Given these

---

is, I suggest, best comprehended if it is founded on a distinction between those second-best assumptions that are *meaningfully* looked upon as removable (*in principle)* by intervention and those that are not. For instance, one can look upon a tax as removable and a wage differential as capable of being offset by a tax-cum-subsidy-onlabour-use, etc., so that the *standard first-best solution* (with all the first-best assumptions holding) is restorable. On the other hand, interdependence of utilities of consumers or increasing returns to scale or monopoly power in trade are not second-best assumptions which can be looked upon as capable of "elimination" so as to restore the *standard* first-best situation. With this distinction in principle, between the different types of second-best assumptions, we can define the respective first-best and second-best solutions.

In the *former* class, where the second-best constraint is removable, the first-best solution is that which would obtain if the constraint *were* removed, *i.e.* it is the standard first-best solution. The functional forms (of the optimising conditions), as also the values of the solution, will naturally be identical with those obtaining for the standard first-best solution. In the *latter* case, where the second best assumption is irremovable, the *first-best solution is that obtained by maximisation subject to the second-best assumption.* This solution may have the same functional form (of the optimising conditions) as for the solution under standard first-best assumptions. In general, the functional forms *will,* however, differ from those of the conditions for the *standard first-best solution.* Thus, for instance, where consumption extemality obtains, it would be necessary for a consumer to take into account the impact of his utility on the other consumers. Or there may be production externality, for instance, under which a producer's decision concerning the level of production may be a function of another producer's level of production. Here again, the optimising condition for producers will differ from that when no such interdependence obtains (yet the utility level reached will be identical under a policy where the State, by policy intervention, assures the fulfilment of this optimising condition under interdependence, and under the standard first-best solution when no such interdependence obtains). The second-best solution can then be defined in terms of this first-best solution not being available under the postulates made.

We thus have: (1) the *standard first-best solution* (which obtains under universally first-best assumptions); (2) the first-best solution (equivalent to the standard first-best solution) when the second-best assumption is removable in principle; (3) the second-best solution when the second-best assumption, though removable in principle, is not removable removed in practice; (4) the first-best solution (which may differ from the standard first-best solution in both functional forms of the optimising conditions and, where comparison is meaningful, in welfare level reached) when the second-best assumptions are irremovable in principle; and

taxes, will a reduction in the tariff rate be desirable?" Another familiar illustration is provided by the policymakers, who argue that

---

(5) the second-best solution when these second-best assumptions are irremovable in principle and the corresponding first-best solution cannot be obtained.

This analytical classification can be supplemented with a further set of remarks concerning the ways in which the effects of second-best assumptions are (and often, without clarity, have been) analysed.

(1) To begin with, the precise way in which the second-best solution should be delimited has to be clarified. For instance, if a country has monopoly power in trade the first-best solution would involve the imposition of an optimum tariff. Suppose that this is ruled out; then, is the second-best solution to be determined on the assumption that no tariff can be levied or on the assumption that only the optimum tariff cannot be levied? Similarly, if a wage differential cannot be eliminated entirely, are we to seek a second-best solution on the assumption that it cannot be offset in any degree or that it cannot be offset fully? There is no unique answer: it all depends on what restraints the policy-maker wishes to impose on himself. But the need for a clear definition of the problem must be underlined.

(2) Secondly, one has to distinguish between the second-best solution, which may necessitate intervention in a decentralised economy, and the *actual* solution that would prevail (under the second-best assumptions made) in the absence of intervention that is necessary to bring about the second-best solution. Thus, if a distortionary wage differential between sectors obtains, the actual solution will be different from the second-best solution [112]; the latter will call for intervention.

(3) It also follows that, starting from any actual solution, under second-best assumptions one can ask how any intervention (other than that which produces the second-best solution) will influence the level of welfare. Thus, rather than investigate what is the second-best solution, the theorist may merely interest himself in *changes* in welfare resulting from the variation in the use of one or more policy instruments when second-best assumptions obtain. Or he may even, using this method, engage in "partial optimization" and attempt to seek the optimal level of a particular policy (*e.g.*, the tariff rate) instead of seeking the optimal, second-best policy from the *entire* range of policy instruments. In trade theory it is *only* the latter two varieties of approach which have been used extensively; the question of the second-best solutions has hardly ever been posed!

This long footnote, highlighting different aspects of second-best theory, has been inserted primarily to gain a clearer grasp of the structure of many contributions to the theory of trade and welfare. I do not claim any special merits for the analytical classification proposed here over those currently available, except that it appears consistent and illuminates the logic of second-best analyses purposively. I am indebted to T. N. Srinivasan for many helpful conversations and for drawing my attention to, as also making available to me, an important unpublished paper by Otto Davis and Andrew Whinston on "Welfare Economics and the Theory of Second Best" (*Cowles Foundation Discussion Paper*, No. 146).

they cannot have universal free trade, but that a free-trade area with continuing tariffs on outside countries may be feasible. If so, would a move to a free-trade area be beneficial (to the member countries and/or the world)? Trade theorists have found that, in general, answers to such questions cannot be given, *even for particular cases* (*i.e.*, for instance, the latter question being asked in relation to a *specific* group of countries joining or opting out of a free-trade area rather than being formulated more generally so that the answer must be valid for all possible free-trade areas), unless the income distribution is specified. In general, *both* the particularising of a question (in the sense just outlined) and the choice of an income distribution are necessary to the ranking of two alternative policies. Since these questions are of interest to policy-makers, the trade theorist has naturally eschewed all Samuelsonian scruples and, in either of the two ways discussed earlier, decided to handle income distribution in a non-purist fashion so as to enable him to get along with the business of ranking the contrasted policies.

This shift towards policy-orientation of a more realistic variety has logically led to the emergence of a new trend towards the *measurement* of losses and gains from changes in policy. Partly this is a result of the shift to the non-purist welfare criteria. Meade's method, for instance, is candidly cardinal, and the sheer process of determining the direction of the welfare change from a shift in policy involves the evaluation of the magnitude of this welfare change. The measurement of losses and gains in welfare, however, has also been given great currency by ordinalists such as Johnson [132, 133], and the principal reason for this has ultimately to be found in the general demand for such measurement by those who debate policies. Policies are maintained or changed largely for non-economic reasons; and the (economic) "cost" involved is a magnitude that is commonly demanded and bandied about in discussions of public policy. Whether we like it or not, this is what the policy-makers do want; and the trade theorist, in consonance with the best traditions in the profession, has begun to meet this need in an attempt to bring economic analysis closer to fulfilling the objective that provides its ultimate *raison d' être.*[106] The result has been a definite and significant trend, in the welfare analysis of pure theory, towards measurement of welfare change. It is important enough to merit detailed analysis in Section VII.

In the present Section we will survey the qualitative propositions of welfare analysis in pure theory, utilising the analytical classifications developed so far. A full survey of the entire range of propositions is not necessary; there are endless ways in which the same theoretical principle may be applied so that a full mapping of these applications in the literature would be both tedious and exhausting. The analytical skeleton of the contributions to the analysis of welfare and trade has already been laid bare. All that needs to be done now is to survey the central analyses so that the skeleton acquires flesh.

Ranking of Policies by Samuelson Criterion: National Advantage

Among the simplest rankings by the Samuelson criterion, in relation to national advantage, is the proposition that a *higher tariff rate is inferior to a lower tariff rate.* This is valid under first-best assumptions (inclusive of the absence of national monopoly power in trade) [1]. There are clearly a very large number of such propositions that could be worked out: for instance, that a *lower trade subsidy is superior to a higher trade subsidy* (under first-best assumptions).[107]

The rankings which have traditionally held the stage in the welfare theory of trade are, however, the two celebrated propositions that: (1) *free trade is superior to no trade*; and (2) *an optimum tariff*

[106]Other interesting and important uses of the measures of gains and losses in welfare will be discussed in Section VII.

[107]These listed propositions hold because, in each case, the superior policy represents a "weakening" of the sole second-best assumption (*i.e.*, a tariff or a subsidy) in an otherwise first-best situation. Throughout the following analysis the statement that a policy is "superior" to another is to be taken to include whenever necessary the borderline case where the two produce identical welfare.

is superior to free trade (when a country has monopoly power in trade). To these Kemp [120] has recently added the proposition that (3) *restricted trade is superior to no trade,* and Ramaswami and myself [112] have argued that (4) *an optimum subsidy is superior to a tariff policy* (when there are domestic distortions).

The proposition that free trade is superior to no trade was shown by Samuelson [125], in a classic paper, to hold with standard first-best assumptions. However, its validity has subsequently been extended to the case where a country can influence its terms of trade through the exercise of monopoly power [120]. Although there have always been those who erroneously believe, and have sometimes continued to assert despite proofs to the contrary, that the proposition rests on an assumed mobility of factors of production, the proposition rests on no such postulate. Samuelson's 1939 proof [125] is clear on this issue; and Haberler [117] has subsequently provided a supporting geometrical argument which must make the truth accessible to more numerous economists. It is also necessary to note that the proposition, valid for all income distributions, holds only in the situation sense—such that, the utility possibility curve corresponding to the free-trade policy will lie uniformly outside (though it may touch) the utility possibility curve corresponding to the no-trade policy [120].[108]

The proposition that restricted trade is superior to no trade, which is also valid in the situation sense, has been shown by Kemp [120] to hold under the standard first-best assumptions (except that the country may have monopoly power in trade). By restricted trade is meant essentially trade restricted in a manner which merely brings about a divergence between foreign and domestic commodity prices. Thus, the trade may be restricted by tariffs, quotas or

[108]It is not possible to demonstrate that the actual bundle of goods obtained by adopting free trade can be redistributed so as to make at least one person better off while leaving others as well off as with the *actual bundle* in the preceding no-trade condition. This has always been understood, although some confusion has cropped up in the literature occasionally. Johnson [66, p. 259] has produced a good example, illustrative of the proposition that the redistribution of the *actual* bundle of goods so as to demonstrate the superiority of free trade over no trade may be impossible.

exchange control. It is *not* correct to infer from this proposition that *any* manner of restricted trade will be beneficial in relation to no trade: for it is easy to conceive of forms of trade, where the volume and/or value of trade is lower than under free trade and yet the net effect is to lower the country's welfare below the no-trade level. Nor should the proposition be read to mean that any trade is superior to no trade. In fact, it can be shown that (subsidy-) expanded trade may, for some income distribution, be inferior to no trade. The proposition refers exclusively, therefore, to restricted trade (of the form defined here).[109]

The third proposition in this class is the celebrated dictum that an optimum tariff is superior to free trade when a country has monopoly power in trade. This proposition was formulated, though not with modem sophistication, as early as Mill's *Principles* [32]. When a country has the ability to influence its terms of trade the marginal terms of trade diverge from the average terms of trade and a discrepancy arises, under free trade, between the domestic rate of transformation in production and the foreign rate of transformation. This divergence can be eliminated and the equality of these with the domestic rate of substitution in consumption achieved, resulting in the first-best optimum solution, when a suitable tariff rate is levied [5, Chapter II; 118]. This optimum tariff rate will naturally depend on the income distribution chosen. Hence, the proposition holds only for *variable* tariff rates, and in the situation sense. For the multi-commodity case an optimum tariff *structure* will exist, which in turn will vary with the income distribution [118].

The proposition concerning the superiority of the optimum tariff has been sought to be extended to the case where the imposition of the tariff results in retaliation. An investigation of this question requires a behavioural assumption concerning the foreigner's response (mechanism) and another with respect to the country's own method of accommodation to such response. The early

---

[109]The analysis in the text could be adapted to develop the proposition that welfare increases to a maximum as restriction decreases to free trade, then falls as trade is increasingly subsidised until welfare has fallen below the no-trade level.

assertions that, in the event of retaliation (insufficiently defined), a country could not gain from imposing an (initially, pre-retaliation) optimum tariff have subsequently been rejected as a result of the demonstration that, for any given income distribution, with a Cournottype adjustment mechanism such that each country imposes an optimum tariff while assuming the other's tariff rate as fixed, it is *possible* (though *not* necessary) that, if and when final equilibrium is achieved with no country under incentive to change the tariff rate, the country imposing the initial optimum tariff may still be better off than under free trade.[110] While this proposition is valid, it should be noted that the result of a retaliatory system depends naturally on the response mechanisms assumed. Alternative "rules of the game" can be readily imagined. For instance, the retaliation may plausibly be a function of the ability of the affected income group to coalesce into an effective pressure group—as Kindleberger's [73] historical study of the political sociology of the European tariff response to the influx of cheap American corn underlines. In this case, an integration of the protection-and-real-wages theory with the tariff-retaliation theory is called for. The easiest way in which one can demonstrate the dependence of the stated proposition on the response-mechanism assumed is to postulate a retaliatory tariff that eliminates trade (for all income distributions). Here the reversion to no trade clearly leaves the country in a position inferior to free trade, *ruling out the possibility* of an improvement over the free-trade situation.

While the preceding propositions rank *trade policies*, the final proposition considered here involves a ranking of one trade policy and another *trade policy in conjunction with a different form of policy intervention.* This proposition is that, when domestic distortions (*i.e.*, a divergence between domestic rates of transformation and

[110]Two other results are of interest: (1) the adjustment process may result in a "tariff cycle": countries may mill around the same set of tariff rates and not settle down to an equilibrium pair of tariff rates [5, pp. 42-3]; and (2) the equilibrium pair of tariff rates, where existent, will generally differ, depending on which country starts off the process.

domestic price ratios) obtain, an optimum (production) subsidy (with free trade) is superior to any tariff intervention. The former policy equates the foreign rate of transformation (F.R.T.) with the domestic rates of transformation in production (D.R.T.) and of substitution in consumption (D.R.S.), and thus turns out to be superior to a tariff policy which cannot ensure this [112].[111]

Ranking of Policies by Samuelson Criterion: International Advantage

From the viewpoint of international advantage, the proposition that *free trade is superior to any trade policy* is held to be valid [126]. The proposition holds when all the first-best assumptions obtain (though the possession of national monopoly power in trade, as long as not exercised, is permissible). The propositions that *free trade is superior to no trade, free trade is superior to expanded trade and free trade is superior to restricted trade* are only special cases of the preceding proposition.[112]

Ranking by Other Criteria: National Advantage

The bulk of the literature in the theory of trade and welfare, however, concerns the ranking of policies, which yield sub-optimal results under second-best assumptions, with the aid of non-purist criteria of welfare change. These analyses can be conveniently divided into

---

[111] I have deliberately refrained from describing the optimum subsidy policy which equates F.R.T., D.R.T. and D.R.S. as a policy which produces the first-best solution. This is because, whether it does or not, will depend on *which* second-best assumption causes this domestic distortion. Where an external economy produces such a distortion, the optimum subsidy will produce the standard first-best solution [112]. Where, however, it results from a wage differential, for instance, the optimum subsidy *cannot* produce the standard first-best solution, although it will, of course, be superior to any tariff intervention [112]. Incidentally, this also helps to illustrate the undesirability of trying to develop the theory of the second-best in terms of the violations of optimum conditions rather than in terms of the second-best assumptions themselves as proposed here.

[112] Several diagrammatic proofs of these propositions can be found in the literature. Formal mathematical proofs, however, are not easy to come by, although they could be easily devised.

those exercises that seek to evaluate the change in welfare when a trade policy is changed and those that concern the welfare change when (the trade policy remaining unchanged) some given parameter or functional relationship (*e.g.*, factor supply, known technology, etc.) shifts.

(A) *Trade policies*

The most frequent way in which the problem is posed involves a primarily negative orientation. For instance, much of the analysis in this area concerns the demonstration that, even if the income distribution is fixed at an arbitrary level, the proposition that free trade is superior to no trade will *not necessarily* hold if there are, say, domestic distortions in the economy. Meade, using his cardinal method, extends his analysis, on the other hand, to deriving the precise conditions (*e.g.*, elasticity of transformation in domestic production, the degree of distortion, etc.) under which the trade policies being compared will rank one way or the other.[113] The analysis is sometimes extended also beyond the ranking of two trade policies. For instance, instead of merely ranking a 5% tariff and zero tariff, using either the cardinal or the ordinal method, the analyst proceeds to ask what tariff rates (constituting the policy instrument available to the policy-maker) will *maximise* welfare. The optimum level at which the available policy instrument should be used is thus the aim of this analysis, which goes beyond a mere ranking of two arbitrarily chosen levels at which the policy instrument may be used.[114] While such analysis represents a process of social-utility maximisation, it should be emphasised that, except in the highly restrictive case where *all* other forms of policy intervention are excluded from the range of available policy instruments, this optimum level of the assigned

---

[113] Of course, he is concerned with the effects of *marginal* changes in policies, so that his analysis amounts to ranking, say, a given tariff and a marginally increased tariff.

[114] Since Meade's analysis is usually directed at investigating the effect on welfare of a marginal change in some tariff rate (*i.e.*, $\frac{du}{dt}$ where u is the level of social welfare and t the tariff rate), the optimum tariff level can be discovered readily by putting $\frac{du}{dt}$ equal to zero.

policy instrument will not generally represent the optimum, second-best solution under the stated, second-best assumptions (irrespective of what welfare criterion is being employed). This is really a point of some importance, since the bulk of the optimising welfare analysis in trade is constrained by the fact that it has been directed at finding the optimum level at which a *specific* trade policy instrument (*e.g.*, a tariff) should be used rather than the optimum level at which the optimum policy instrument (or combination of instruments) should be used to maximise social utility, subject to the stated assumptions, in an open economy.

The kinds of problems analysed can be divided broadly into two classes according as the second-best assumptions relate to the: (1) domestic, or the (2) foreign sector. In the former category a wide assortment of second-best assumptions has been considered: external economies; monopolies in commodity markets; infant industry arguments; factor-reward differentials between sectors of use; factor-price rigidity and increasing returns to scale. In the latter class the stage is held by the theory of discriminatory tariff reduction. These arguments are briefly discussed here, to illustrate the prefatory analysis.

(a) *External Economies.* Where the standard first-best assumptions obtain, with the exception of externalities in production, the actual market solution will be characterised by a domestic distortion (*i.e.*, a divergence between the commodity price-ratio and D.R.T.). The classic example of such externality is the dependence of honey production on the level of neighbouring apple output. The time-honoured infant-industry argument also involves externality [8].[115] Recently the theoretical interest in the coordination of investment

[115] Although the infant industry case has been classified here, it must be admitted that, formally, it has dimensions of dynamic analysis which go beyond the traditional range of external economies. Allowing for this fact, however, the case for assistance to infant industries *does* rest on an assumption of externality, as pointed out by Meade [8] and recently by Johnson [133]. For a different formal description and analysis of the infant-industry case, Haberler [117] may be consulted: his analysis, however, does not bring out the externality aspect as forcefully as needs to be.

decisions has also given us another impressive example of external economies under a regime of decentralised decision-making [97].

The resulting domestic distortions have been shown to invalidate, for instance, the proposition that free trade is (necessarily) superior to no trade [112, 117]. It is no longer possible to rank these two trade policies uniquely, either for all income distributions or (more importantly) even with any assigned income distribution for all possible cases.[116] Similarly, it can be shown that no tariff rate may exist, in any given empirical case, which will produce greater welfare than free trade [112]. The reason is obvious. Under free trade, domestic distortions imply that F.R.T.(= F.P.) = D.R.S.(= D.P.) ≠ D.R.T. (where D.P. and F.P. are the domestic and foreign price ratios respectively). On the other hand, a tariff may equate F.R.T. and D.R.T., but will disrupt the equality of F.R.T. with D.R.S. Since two sub-optimal positions are being compared, the conclusions already stated follow readily. The optimal solution for domestic distortions is clearly a production subsidy (or tax-cum-subsidy) which will

[116] As stated earlier, the ranking will depend, among other things, on the degree of divergence, the elasticity of transformation in production and so on. In this connection it is probably necessary to point out that, in the standard analysis of external economies, it is not made clear that the externality may disappear at certain levels of output of either activity. With apple blossoms and bees, where the former are already too large relative to the latter, any increase in blossoms output by diversion of resources from bees production will not be subjected to externality effects. In terms of the standard geometry (ignored throughout the text of this paper), the production possibility curve, for certain ranges of output combinations, may thus be characterised by the equality of D.R.T. and D.P. (domestic prices). If, then, free trade carries the economy's production within this range, the domestic distortions will be inapplicable and the standard, first-best solution (*i.e.*, free trade is superior to no trade) will become applicable. Thus, strictly speaking, the analysis in the text requires that the domestic distortions should be within the relevant ranges of production. This, in turn, makes very clear the crucial nature of income distribution: for, with one income distribution, an $x\%$ tariff may bring the economy within the range of domestic distortions, whereas, for another, it may not, thereby influencing the ranking of policies.

equate F.R.T., D.R.T. and D.R.S., and thereby achieve the first-best solution.[117]

(b) *Monopoly in Product Markets.* The monopoly argument is frequently taken to collapse into a simple case of domestic distortion. Hence, it is regarded as formally equivalent to the external economy argument. It follows, then, that, once again, free trade cannot be shown to be (necessarily) superior to no trade; and also that no tariff may exist, in any given case, which may yield higher welfare than free trade.

Where, however, the monopoly argument differs from the external economy case is in the fact that the degree of monopoly itself may be a function of the rate of tariff [133]. Take, for instance, the extreme case where the introduction of free trade eliminates the monopoly power and turns the domestic monopolist into a perfect competitor. In this case the proposition that free trade is superior to no trade, for instance, will still be valid. The formal identity with the external economy case therefore breaks down.

(c) *Factor-reward Differentials between Sectors.* The presence of a wage differential between sectors (for remunerating the same factor) represents a market imperfection, constituting a departure from first-best assumptions under certain circumstances.[118] Where it is distortionary, there are two immediate consequences. The rate

[117]In the light of this analysis it is possible to understand the significant qualification introduced by Haberler [4, p. 57] in his discussion of the correct prescription in the infant-industry case: "It should also be added that it is, *a priori,* probable that in many cases not a customs duty but an export bounty would be in order in as much as external economies may be realizable in the export rather than in import industries... The fact that the infant industry argument is almost exclusively employed to recommend import restrictions and practically never to justify the opposite ... shows clearly the bias of those who employ it." Of course, Haberler's case would require, as the optimal solution, an optimum (production) subsidy to the export industry. It cannot be argued, however, that if this is ruled out the trade-subsidy policy (believed guardedly by Haberler to be desirable) will necessarily produce, or will even be "likely" to produce, better results than any alternative form of trade or other intervention.

[118]A detailed discussion of the conditions under which a wage differential may be regarded as distortionary is contained in the paper by myself and V. K. Ramaswami [112]. The qualifications to which the present analysis is subject are

at which this factor and any other factor are being substituted in production in different sectors will no longer be equal. This will result in a reduction in the transformation possibilities. The production possibility curve will "shrink in." Further, at each point on the shrunk-in locus the domestic price ratio will diverge from the domestic rate of transformation (*along the shrunk-in locus*), so that we also are in a situation characterised by domestic distortions.

From these two effects, it is easy to see that: (1) free trade is not (necessarily) superior to no trade; (2) an optimum production subsidy (or taxcum-subsidy) which equates D.R.S., F.R.T. and D.R.T. (along the shrunk in transformation locus) is superior to any tariff; and (3) an optimum subsidy on labour-use, which directly offsets the wage differential, produces the standard first-best result.

(d) *Factor-price Rigidity.* Haberler [117] has sharply distinguished between factor immobility and factor-price rigidity, showing that the former leaves the welfare propositions valid under first-best conditions unaffected, whereas the latter manages to invalidate them. By arguing that factor-price rigidity in the face of commodity price-shift will lead to unemployment, Haberler has demonstrated the possibility that free trade, for any assigned income distribution and given empirical situation, may produce a deterioration in welfare in relation to no trade.[119] Haberler's analysis has recently been refined by Johnson [133], who has investigated alternative ways in which

---

also considered there. Further comments on the problem are found in Johnson [133]. Credit for pioneering the problem belongs to Hagen [118].

[119]This is illustrated by Haberler [117], for a given income distribution, as follows. Taking factor immobility as well, he shows production and consumption under no trade at S, with S.R. as the price ratio between exportables and importables. With free trade at foreign price ratio F.P., the production in importables falls to P and consumption moves to F. The result is a deterioration in welfare. Free trade, for the given income distribution, is inferior to no trade. (It has to be assumed, of course, that the factor-price rigidity is due to institutional rather than voluntary reasons.) I might refer, incidentally, to the analysis of a similar problem [97], where the wage-rate in the agricultural sector is different from the marginal value product (whereas the industrial sector pays according to the

factor-price rigidity may be defined and, in turn, combined with assumptions concerning mobility of the factors of production, to produce a varying range of propositions which confirm Haberler's results.

(e) *Increasing Returns to Scale.* When an activity in the system is subject to increasing returns to scale the locus of transformation possibilities may lose its convexity. Matthews [123] has demonstrated how, in this case, a country may be worse off under free trade than under no trade. Thus, under this second-best assumption, it is not possible to maintain that free trade is (necessarily) superior to no trade.[120]

Concavity also underlines the fact that the optimising solutions (and corresponding conditions) strictly imply only local maximisation. It can be shown that the optimum optimorum may not be reached by free trade when there is concavity over some (though not

---

marginal productivity principle), the wage-rate being "rigid" in the agricultural sector.

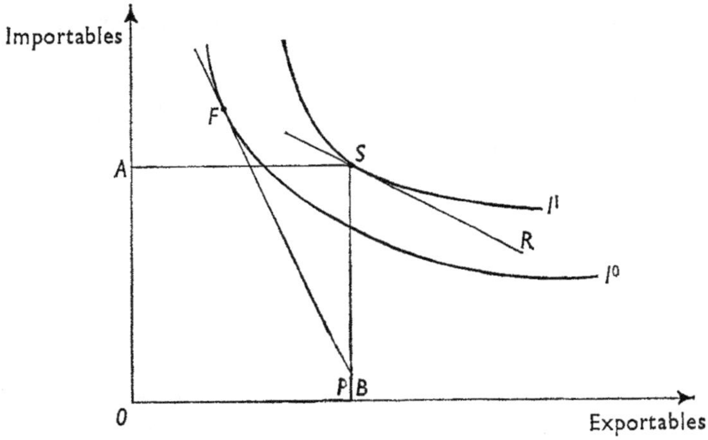

Figure 1.

[120]However, questions of stability of equilibrium arise here which have to be carefully tackled. Tinbergen [127] has constructed an ingenious example which also illustrates the point in the text. In the accompanying illustration the

the entire) range of the transformation locus, although free trade may continue to be superior to no trade.[121]

(f) *Customs Unions.* So far we have been concerned with departures from first-best assumptions on the domestic side. The welfare problem has, however, also been posed in terms of distortions arising from the presence of tariffs, subsidies and other such policies in foreign trade. Thus, for instance, a typical question has been whether, with tariffs continuing on one country, if the tariffs on another are reduced the national welfare will be increased. For any two tariff rates compared in such a situation, the ranking is subject to the income distribution chosen. Even with the income distribution chosen, no unique ranking is generally possible on an *a priori* basis.

Take, for instance, the model where the home country A can import, without having the power to affect the terms at which it can import, a commodity from either of two countries B and C. For the levels of demands relevant to the defined situation, C supplies M cheaper than B, while A is the highest-cost producer. In the initial situation, assume a tariff rate t_0 which permits C to

production associated with free trade happens to be at P (which is a stable point) and the result is welfare deterioration in relation to no trade.

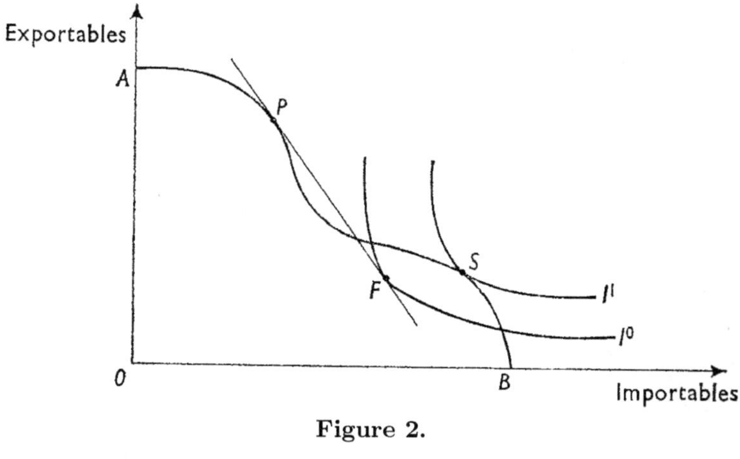

Figure 2.

[121] Thus, in the illustration, S represents the no-trade point, F and P the consumption and production points corresponding to free trade but representing

compete successfully and secure A's market. Suppose, however, that A removes the tariff on imports from B but must continue to impose it on C's exports. If this makes B's export of M to A cheaper than C's, A is shifting its source of supply to a higher-cost producer. The former situation was characterised by D.R.T. = D.R.S. ≠ F.R.T.; the latter is as well (since the most favourable rate at which A can transform its exports into imports is that determined by C's c.i.f. price in A). The choice between them cannot be made on an *a priori* basis; the choice of income distribution will also influence the ranking [7, 121]. For any given income distribution, using the ordinalist method, the ranking can naturally be worked out for any *given* empirical situation. Meade's cardinalist method would also give a unique ranking for a specific *empirical* situation.

There are many other ways in which a similar problem can be set up. One may take a case where A specialises in X and exchanges it for both Y (from B) and Z (from C). There is a uniform tariff rate on the (perfectly elastic supply of) imports of both Y and Z

only a local maximum, while F' and P' represent the equilibrium points corresponding to the optimum optimorum position under free trade.

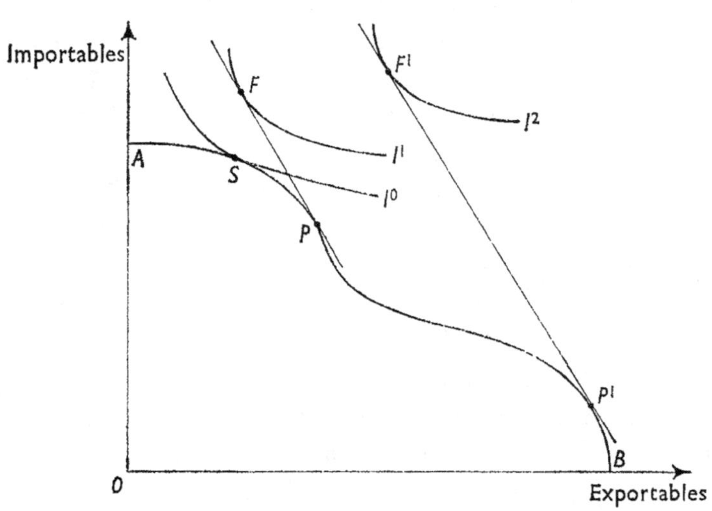

Figure 3.

into A. The actual situation, from the viewpoint of A's welfare, is characterised by

$$\left(\frac{P_y}{P_z}\right)_F = \left(\frac{P_y}{P_z}\right)_D \text{ but } \left(\frac{P_x}{P_y}\right)_F \neq \left(\frac{P_x}{P_y}\right)_D \text{ and } \left(\frac{P_x}{P_z}\right)_F \neq \left(\frac{P_x}{P_z}\right)_D$$

where the suffixes F and D refer to foreign and domestic price-ratios in A. Suppose now that the tariff on Z is abolished *while that on Y is continued.* Then the country moves into a situation where

$$\left(\frac{P_x}{P_z}\right)_F \left(\frac{P_x}{P_z}\right)_D \textit{ but } \left(\frac{P_y}{P_z}\right)_F \neq \left(\frac{P_y}{P_z}\right)_D \text{ and } \left(\frac{P_x}{P_y}\right)_F \neq \left(\frac{P_x}{P_y}\right)_D$$

The comparison is again between two sub-optimal situations in this case. No *a priori*, unique ranking is possible [7]; and the income distribution will in general influence the ranking even when a *specific* situation has been defined (with reference to the functional and parametric aspects).

(B) *Non-trade Policies*

So far only different trade policies have been compared. However, there is a considerable literature even on the effects of changes in the general equilibrium parameters and functional relationships on national welfare. Among the prominent contributions in this field are analyses of: (1) the effect of change in factor supply, and (2) the effect of technical change on welfare, when the economy is engaged in trade.

In the former category the analysis by Johnson [5, Chapter III] and myself [111] has shown how the effect of a change in factor supply on the growth of real income can be approximated, making allowance for the effect of the adjustment of the terms of trade *when the country has monopoly power in trade.* The analysis has also been extended to establish the conditions under which the growth of factor supply may actually result in the deterioration of the country's welfare through the loss of real income from worsened terms of trade outweighing the direct gain from expansion-a possibility seen independently by Edgeworth, Johnson [5, Chapter v] and myself and now widely known as the case of "immiserising growth." Basically the same analysis can be adapted to the investigation of the impact of transfers of factors of production from one country to another on each's welfare, since the only substantive difference is that the growth of factors of production is, in one case, net for the two countries, while in the latter case there is no addition to the factor supply of the two countries together but only its redistribution [5].

This analysis has also been turned around to examine the relative advantages of absorption of marginal increment in population or capital stock at home or abroad [119, 122].[122] The analysis has further been reworked in relation to the effects of shifts in technology. The results of Findlay and Grubert [62] have been used to examine the effect of different types of technical progress on national welfare, again under the second-best assumption of national monopoly power in trade [2].

Ranking by Less-restrictive Criteria: International Advantage

So far, the rankings have been concerned with national advantage. Largely owing to the nineteenth-century concern with international advantage, however, much interest still continues to be exhibited in questions of international advantage.

[122] This problem (unlike the others listed here) is of interest even under first-best assumptions for the economy. For instance, if the rental on capital abroad is higher than at home, and reflects the marginal value product, it would appear to be to private and social advantage to invest abroad. However, this is not correct, as what is socially relevant is the marginal return on the investments abroad. If the country already has invested capital abroad a fall in its rate of return through further investment will reduce the previous return, and the net benefit to the country will be *less* than the average rate of return, as Jasay [119] has noted in a valuable contribution. An important practical point may also be that the rate of return on foreign investment will always be less than the marginal-value product abroad because of corporation taxation [122]. And so on. The possibility of affecting the terms of trade differently according as home or foreign investment is chosen, which arises only under the second-best assumption of national monopoly power in trade, introduces still further theoretical questions of interest.

The great bulk of the questions have again related to the ranking of trade policies when some second-best assumption obtains. Meade [8, 9] has worked out numerous problems, investigating the optimum level of a specific trade policy under the stated second-best assumptions. There are other contributions, such as Viner's [9] and Lipsey's [121] analyses of customs unions and Ozga's [85] examination of unilateral tariff reduction by a country in a world with other tariffs. These reinforce the proposition that, in general, no *a priori* ranking of policies is possible and that the choice of income distribution can affect the ranking when second-best assumptions obtain and sub-optimal situations are being ranked.

Meade's exercises, for instance, range over many such comparisons: (1) A imports Y_1 and Y_2 from B; Y_1 and Y_2 are substitutable or complementary in A's consumption. A duty at t_2% is levied on the import of Y_2 and cannot be removed. Would a tariff on the import of Y_1 be then worthwhile and, if so, what is its optimum level? (2) A imports Y_1, which is complementary or substitutable in A's consumption with X_2, which A exports to B and on whose exports B levies an import duty. Should a tariff be imposed on the import of Y_1 into A, and if so, what is the optimum level? (3) Or there might be second-best assumptions in the domestic economy of a country. For instance, if there is a divergence in the marginal cost and value of a commodity which competes with imports, would a tariff be worthwhile, and if so, what is its optimum level?

Central Limitations of the Propositions

Regardless of the criterion of welfare change employed, the rankings considered hitherto are valid only in a static context. At least two serious limitations of these propositions spring from the admission of dynamic elements.

(1) The ranking of two tariff rates will be a function of how these two rates are reached. Starting from a current tariff rate of α%, moves to a tariff of x% and y% will, in general, rank x and y differently (for the same income distribution) than when the move takes place from an initial tariff rate of β%. In fact, even the paths

of adjustments from a single current position to each of the pairs of rates of tariffs ultimately reached may not be unique, so that, for different paths chosen, the ultimate ranking may be different. These possibilities, however, are ruled out, for instance, by the restrictive assumption of constant terms of trade (for all tariff rates) in Samuelson's 1939 proof [125] of the proposition that free trade is superior to no trade and, in Kemp's extension [120] of the proof to the case when the terms of trade will vary with the volume of trade, by the (implicit) assumption that the foreign countries' trade offers at different terms of trade are not a function of the trade policy of the country. This restrictiveness is serious in a world where policy changes, especially in international trade, are inevitably accompanied by protracted negotiations concerning the reciprocity of "benefits," and the interdependence of countries' trade policies is an impressive and irrefutable fact [107].

(2) These propositions are further limited in their reliance on one-period, static criteria. There are undoubtedly ways in which one can demonstrate that free trade is superior to no trade, for instance, in a multi-period, dynamic, welfare framework. Thus, for instance, it can be established that, for the *same* initial conditions, time profile of consumption in each period, time-horizon and the structural composition of the terminal capital stocks (*e.g.*, the ratio in which they are to be held), free trade will lead to a *greater* quantity of terminal capital stocks than no trade [1].[123] While, however, the conclusions of welfare statics can be sustained in welfare dynamics within certain frameworks, they are also refuted within others. For instance, with a *terminal* preference function (*e.g.*, the income level in the terminal period), savings ratio a function of the income distribution, and the income distribution entirely a function of the

[123]This model, from the seminal work of Dorfinan, Solow and Samuelson [113], relies on two main assumptions: (1) perfect foresight; and (2) a centralised authority whose preference function specifies the time-profile of consumption, etc.

market-imputed incomes it is possible for free trade to be *inferior* to no trade.[124]

7. Measurement Of Gains and Losses

While, in these significant respects, the welfare propositions of pure theory have continued to be limited, the static methods of welfare analysis have been strikingly extended into the field of measurement of losses and gains (as between the welfare levels reached under the ranked policies). Some of the principal factors motivating this shift have already been analysed: the impact of the shift to less purist criteria of welfare and the general demand for such measurement. To these we must add a third, interesting factor: the analytical use of such measurement in determining a "scientific tariff" [132]. This itself has its origin in the practice of computing the economic cost of given policies.

Frequently policies are pursued for a specific non-economic objective. For instance, a tariff may be imposed to achieve an assigned level of domestic production of an importable commodity. The cost of that tariff then is the cost of achieving this level of domestic production (which constitutes the non-economic objective). This notion can be extended in two profitable ways.

(1) Suppose that a tariff is the only policy instrument available. However, the non-economic objective, which consists of a *fixed-target* type of assignment (*e.g.*, achievement of a given level of import-competing production or the reduction of imports to a specific value), can be fulfilled in numerous ways. For instance, if the objective is to achieve a given reduction in the value of imports this could be achieved by tariffs on *one* or *more* of the various imported commodities. We have here, then, a problem of choosing that tariff *structure* which *minimises* the cost of achieving

[124] I am afraid, therefore, that Caves [3, p. 265] is not correct in arguing that "static welfare economics is perfectly valid in a dynamic setting for the welfare problems discussed here if the assumption is made that factors of production and commodities are perfectly mobile, that is can be re-allocated with infinite speed and zero cost."

the assigned noneconomic objective. This is a familiar problem in economic analysis, with a standard solution.

Johnson [132], in a powerful and ingenious paper, has developed this analysis, christening the minimum-cost tariff structure as "scientific" [on the (*Oxford English Dictionary*) ground that it is evolved with the aid of expert knowledge]. He uses the notion of the scientific tariff to consider the kinds of tariff structure that would be called for under a wide range of non-economic objectives such as self-sufficiency, promotion of a "way of life," increased diversification, etc., each such general non-economic objective being reduced to a suitable, operational objective, such as reduction in the value of imports and increase in the value of import-competing production.[125]

(2) But this notion of the tariff structure that minimises the cost of a fixed-target type of non-economic objective is itself restrictive. For the analysis can be meaningfully extended to the case where the policy-maker is willing to consider a whole range of variables, representing *varying degrees of fulfillment of a non-economic objective.* For instance, a policy-maker interested in reducing the value of imports may not lay down a specific value of imports as the target, but would like to choose from varying values of imports *after* ascertaining the (*minimum*) costs attached to the tariff structures that lead to these targets. The choice made would then have the usual property

[125]There are two respects, however, in which the analysis, as presented by Johnson, may be misleading. (!) He equates the marginal benefit: marginal cost ratios for tariffs on different imports, as a condition for minimum-cost tariff structure. It should be emphasised that this is only a necessary condition (which would have to be rewritten for cases involving inequalities).

(2) Secondly, he frequently talks of "measuring" a non-economic objective in terms of some observable variable: for instance, "the simplest possible measure of the benefit achieved by such a tariff (to provide national self-sufficiency and independence) in the value of imports excluded by it" [132, p. 342]. This gives the impression that Johnson is setting up an *independent* utility function to *measure* the welfare level reached (with respect to a non-economic objective) by a tariff structure: a procedure which may well be debated. What Johnson really is doing, however, is to translate vague objectives like "national self-sufficiency" into *precise* and usable objectives such as "reduction in the value of imports." And that is both necessary for the analysis to get off the ground and also a valid procedure.

(associated with maximising behaviour): any departure from the selected tariff structure would change the value of imports by an amount which, for the policymaker, is not worth the change in cost involved. The scientific tariff structure associated with this choice thus exhibits the familiar optimality property from the viewpoint of the policy-maker.[126]

An important limitation of the foregoing analysis is that it specifies a non-economic objective and considers tariffs as the only available instrument variables. While, however, this approach does yield the scientific *tariff* structure, it is possible that the same non-economic objective could have been achieved at a *smaller* cost if the range of policy instruments had been wider. An interesting paper of Corden [128] illustrates this principle tangentially. Working with a two-good model (which eliminates the question of a tariff *structure*) and the fixed-target objective of attaining a *given level* of production of the importable good, Corden has shown that, for unchangeable terms of trade, a (production) subsidy is less expensive than a tariff, whereas, for variable terms of trade, a tariff-and-subsidy measure is superior to either a tariff or a subsidy. Johnson [133], drawing on Young's earlier work, has shown, on the other hand, that, for unchangeable terms of trade, a tariff is more efficient than a subsidy when the non-economic objective is an assigned reduction in the volume of *imports* (in a two-good model). These contributions already begin to pull away in the direction of a scientific *economic* policy, as distinct from a scientific tariff (or even trade) policy.[127]

[126] Johnson [132, p. 341] refers to this question of choice among scientific tariff structures in terms of choosing the tariff "level" (which is presumably to be obtained, in his formulation, by equating the marginal benefits and costs). This may be a little misleading because in general, the scientific tariff structures for varying degrees of fulfillment of a non-economic objective may *not* be just scalar multiples of each other.

[127] Although the papers by Johnson [131, 132] and Corden [128] have been singled out in the text for their ingenious and path-breaking approach to the analysis of non-economic objectives, there are two other prior contributions which merit mention here. (1) Johnson's [129] analysis of the relationship between the tariff that would produce maximum revenue (a non-economic objective) and the optimum tariff (that equates F.R.T. with D.R.T. and D.R.S. under variable

While the measurement of gains and losses has been used *theoretically* to derive scientific tariffs, its *empirical* application has been for the more pedestrian but surer task of estimating the cost of changes in tariff policies. Among the most striking of these exercises must be reckoned Johnson's [131] attempt at measuring the gain to the United Kingdom from joining the European Common Market and Wemelsfelder's [135] study of the short-term effect of the lowering of import duties in West Germany.[128] These analyses carry the application of the welfare propositions of pure theory of trade very much further than the early, interesting attempts, most prominently that of Marris [134], at estimating the foreign rate of transformation with a view to deriving directional policy conclusions concerning tariffs.[129]

Although these exercises represent a significant, new trend in the welfare analysis of pure theory, they none the less have limitations which reflect essentially the deficiencies of the conceptual framework underlying the measurements employed.

Two different ways in which measurement has been attempted can be distinguished. They reflect, in turn, the ordinalist and cardinalist methods of (non-Samuelsonian) welfare analysis discussed in the previous section.[130]

The former, ordinalist procedure yields several alternative measures as in other applications of "surplus" theory. The theorist can

terms of trade) dates back to 1951-52. (2) Meade [9, Chapters V, VI] had also handled, in 1955, two problems which consist in the choice between a tariff and a domestic tax with a specific non-economic objective (of raising given revenue) from the viewpoint of minimising the loss in world welfare-thereby anticipating the approach in the contributions of Corden [128] and Johnson [133] towards the formulation of policy questions, not just in terms of trade policy, but in more general terms.

[128] There are other, less-impressive estimates by Verdoom and Scitovsky [7] of the gains from European integration.

[129] Marris' [134] study, while important as a pioneering empirical exercise in trade and welfare, is unpersuasive in interpretation and analysis of the statistical data.

[130] A partial-equilibrium approach to measurement has also been suggested by Gorden and Johnson [130], but is subject to well-known drawbacks that are explicitly recognised by these authors.

choose from a large number of possible measures, some of which have been analysed at length by Johnson and myself [2]. Johnson [132] happens to choose Hicks' compensating variation for his measurement.[131] Meade's method, on the other hand, yields a unique measure of the cost of a change in policy. This measure is tantamount to the Marshallian surplus measures, as is evident from the fact that his method estimates gains (losses) as the increase (decrease) in the volume of transactions in each commodity multiplied by the excess of utility derived by the buyer over the utility of that commodity to the seller, a divergence that is measured, for instance, in the case of a tax, by the rate of tax on the assumption that the price paid equals the marginal utility to the buyer and the price received the utility to the seller. Both Johnson's and Meade's measures are identical except for the differences caused by: (1) Meade's assumption of small and Johnson's of large changes,[132] and (2) Meade's Marshallian measure and Johnson's use of the compensating variation.[133]

The identity, except for the differences noted, obtains despite the different views concerning utility measurement because of the fact that, from the present viewpoint, Johnson's assumption of a well-behaved community preference function (enjoying the properties of a *single* individual's preference function) converges on Meade's *de facto* assumption of equal weights for each buyer and seller.

[131]Hence, the cost of protection, when a tariff is levied, is measured in terms of the compensation that would leave the country as well off, under the tariff, as previously under free trade.

[132]This introduces the fraction $\frac{1}{2}$ into Johnson's formulae, stemming from his having to integrate the area under the triangle for large changes. Johnson's analysis incidentally serves to refute Lipsey's contention [7] that Meade's method cannot be applied to large changes.

[133]This leads Johnson to argue in terms of the "compensated" (*i.e.*,constant-utility) indifference curve and to use a pure substitution term for changed consumption, whereas Meade does not adjust for changed utility and takes the entire change in consumption in his measure of the gain in utility to buyers. Johnson is equally more cautious in trying to adjust for rent in his measure of the production costs.

In the two respects in which the measurements diverge, Johnson's analysis clearly is an improvement. And yet, from the *operational* viewpoint, Johnson's ordinalist approach runs into an insuperable difficulty. How is the analyst to estimate the contours (albeit at the relevant points) of the hypothesised social indifference map? Meade's (theoretically less attractive) method runs into no such snags (though *other* difficulties of econometric measurement no doubt persist). Since the aim of these exercises is to measure welfare changes *in practice,* operational methods may well be judged to be superior to analytically more impressive results.

Either method, however, leaves out of reckoning, in consonance with the limitations of the conceptual static approach to welfare on which it is based, the dynamic elements in the absence of which the exercises are reduced in their usefulness. For instance, in relation to the estimates of the gains from European integration, it has frequently been noted that these estimates ignore significant considerations like the effects of competition on efficiency, on innovation, etc. They also omit the implications of improved bargaining power in negotiating tariff and other trade concessions.[134]

The most serious limitation springs from the conceptual difficulty of applying the surplus analysis when the economy is producing and/or absorbing commodities for purposes other than consumption. How, for instance, is the "consumer's surplus" on the purchase of investment goods to be estimated? To assert that this can be done as with consumer goods is to assume that the price paid for investment goods currently reflects the ultimate utility that will accrue from the production resulting from them. This assumption, however, begs a whole lot of questions which are central to the issues of dynamic welfare economics. For instance, the "correct" valuation of the investment goods will vary in general with the choice of the

[134]It should be noted, however, that the authors of the estimates are generally aware of most of these limitations.

time-horizon.[135] These issues cannot be conjured away. They are compelling when welfare comparisons are being made.

While these limitations persist, welfare analysis in pure theory has clearly reached a degree of sophistication and feasibility of useful empirical application which is impressive. These developments have brought within the fold of economic analysis many problems with direct policy relevance.

One of the major "casualties" of this progress has been the historic intellectual dominance of the "free trader." The reorientation in the view concerning the role of the analyst—the acceptance of non-economic objectives, the willingness to consider sub-optimal situations instead of strictly utopian prescriptions—has overwhelmed the profession with a new mood of judging "each case on its merits" and tailoring policies to specific objectives and situations. The few, surviving "free traders" have, in consequence, been in disarray. At the turn of the century they readily admitted the solitary, twin examples of "good" tariffs: the optimum (under national monopoly power) and the infant industry tariffs. They even proudly claimed that it was a "free trader," John Stuart Mill, who foresaw the formal arguments to support them. With the breathtaking increase in the "deviations" from the free-trade case, however, this easy "theoretical" superiority over the pragmatic protectionists has disappeared.[136] With it, the free traders, greatly reduced in number, have now taken to resting their case exclusively on "empirical," practical bases. Two varieties of arguments are frequent: (1) The unsophisticated argument is that, in practice, it is impossible to estimate the "distortions" and hence the tariff structure and level which they justify. Hence, faced with

---

[135]Moreover, the decentralisation of decision-making adds to the difficulties (*e.g.*, inconsistency and myopia in behaviour) created by imperfect foresight and necessitates a revised approach to the notions of "rational" decision making, and hence of welfare.

[136]I use the objective "pragmatic" with special emphasis. The theological protectionist is as much at fault as the theological free trader. But whereas the former has always been taken lightly, the latter has traditionally had an intellectual respectability which is now a rapidly wasting asset.

this ignorance, the economist should not advocate a move away from the free-trade situation. This contention must be rejected. Not merely does it ignore the growing trend towards estimation. It also attaches an unacceptable special weight to the situation of a zero-tariff. Indeed, even if the fact of ignorance were admitted, the most one could say was that no ranking of trade policies was possible in practice. Why should the free trader be at an advantage here? If it were contended that a departure from a given position would be incapable of positive justification, and hence free trade should be the policy, the free trader is surely worsted in the debate, since the given situation is almost always characterised by the absence of free trade. This entire approach to the validation of the prescription of free trade is thus unpersuasive. (2) A more sophisticated approach admits that distortions exist and welfare-increasing tariffs may be devised by economists. However, in practice, the way tariffs are politically engineered, they are almost always imposed so as to bring about a deterioration in welfare. This argument admits that the zero-tariff position may not be the optimal one. It merely asserts that the admissibility of tariffs will lead in practice to another sub-optimal position which is inferior. Hence the economist ought to support free trade as a political prescription.[137] It is surely difficult to accept this logic. Surely it is not demonstrable that tariffs will always be "perverse" or are "likely" to be perverse. It is equally unpersuasive to assume that politicians will readily accept the free-trade prescription when their revealed preference has continuously

[137]This argument has a long, historical tradition. It is worth quoting the famous passage of Edgeworth, arising out of Bickerdike's discussion of the case for optimum tariffs. "Thus the direct use of the theory is likely to be small. But it is to be feared that its abuse will be considerable. It affords to unscrupulous advocates of vulgar Protection a peculiarly specious pretext for introducing the thin end of the wedge. Mr. Bickerdike may be compared to a scientist who, by a new analysis, has discovered that strychnine may be administered in small doses with prospect of advantage in one or two more cases than was previously known; the result of this discovery may be to render the drug more easily procurable by those whose intention is not medicinal.... Let us admire the skill of the analyst, but label the subject of his investigation POISON" [4, p. 53].

been for *some* tariffs (though not for no trade), but that they will reject the prescription concerning the "correct" tariffs and instead settle for perverse tariffs.[138]

8. Trade Theory and Developmental Planning

While any "orthodox" survey of international economics would undoubtedly have terminated with the preceding Section, it would be singularly unfortunate if I did not address a few closing remarks to the small but important and growing literature on developmental planning (*in practice*) in its trade aspects. Happily, the subject has been brilliantly analysed in a companion Survey paper by Chenery [139] so that I can confine myself to certain ideas which have value in supplementing Chenery's account.

Broadly speaking, the classes of models that have been used to guide the choice of trade (and production) policy divide conveniently into two sets: (1) the highly simplified, decision models which usually anchor on some striking characteristic of the planned economy; and (2) more elaborate, inter-industry models. The latter, in turn, classify into models that deal with mere consistency and those that also attempt partial or fuller optimisation.

Among the class of simple, decision models, several can naturally be identified. The two most interesting, however, appear to be those that are associated with the notions of a wage-goods bottleneck and a capital-goods bottleneck. For instance, a model that postulates the availability of wage-goods (say, food) as the constraint on increased investment and growth (in an overpopulated economy with surplus labour) has prompted in practice a trade policy characterised

[138] Ethical arguments are also current. For instance, some free traders claim to be "internationalists" and object to the optimum tariff argument as purely "nationalistic" and of the "beggar-my-neighbour" variety. At the purely ethical level, of course, no argument can be refuted. In this instance, however, one can point out that free trade is optimal internationally only in the situation sense, so that the problem of income distribution does remain with the "internationalists." Moreover, the free-trade case does not take cognisance of non-economic objectives *or* dynamic welfare complications.

by imported food-grains and focuses sharply on the role of PL480 variety of foreign aid to developing countries [136]. On the other hand, a two-sector model, with two different investment and consumption goods, helps to highlight the role of developing an adequate capital-goods production base in supporting the targeted rate of investment at some future date (if the economy is faced with a shortfall in exchange earnings currently and prospectively) and hence has resulted in the utilisation of exchange to build up capacity in heavy industries [141].[139]

The central limitation of these models, however, is that they can be treacherous in ignoring *other* equally important factors: as in most economic problems, planning is necessarily a complex process. Hence, more detailed, inter-industry models which *permit* the introduction of much other information, have come to be extensively employed in framing developmental plans. Among the operational models actually used, the formulations have generally been limited in being both static and centred on just consistency [140]. Using the Leontief, static-exercise approach, the analyst takes an autonomous export vector and *either* uses the concept of an *import-structure* (involving an import-coefficients matrix analogous to the input-coefficients matrix [142]) to derive the import pattern and total corresponding to the assigned bill of goods *or* derives *imports as residuals* by taking an assigned set of production targets and setting them off against the requirements worked out from the assigned bill of goods. The former approach, using the notion of an import structure, is clearly inappropriate to a planning model which, in looking ahead, need not be tied down to an arbitrary, base-year import structure and, indeed, in doing so, rejects out of hand the important choice (available to the planner) between domestic production and imports. In this respect, the imports-as-residuals

[139]While these simple models do often serve to make an important point clear, as for instance the necessity to have a capital-goods industry, they fail in giving a clear guide line on the *magnitudes* with which the planners should work. For the latter, more detailed work, involving also other constraints in the system, will be necessary. Reliance on the former alone, therefore, may do far more harm than good. For a discussion of some of the fallacies which have actually sprung from over-reliance on such simplified modes of reasoning, the reader may refer to my paper [97].

approach, used for instance in the Indian planning framework [140], is superior.[140]

It is possible, however, to introduce explicit optimisation into these procedures, at varying levels. The most interesting innovation, from the present viewpoint, is the operational determination of the *shadow* exchange rate, as outlined by Chenery [139] in his Survey and claimed to have been used to determine the choice between imports and domestic production of commodities for Israel by him and Bruno [138] in an excellent paper which develops a useful way of framing *alternative* programmes from which the planner may make his ultimate choice. While the objectives in these exercises are to achieve partial optimisation (in limited areas of the economy) and the frameworks are essentially static, the principle of optimisation used merely reflects the basic insights of the theory of trade and welfare, and there is every prospect that further work in this area will clear the way for an operational and empirically meaningful use of trade theory in developmental planning.[141]

9. Concluding Remarks

The overwhelming impression that this survey leaves is one of an area of inquiry which has been unusually active and is witnessing the emergence of many new trends. A growing concern with empirical verification, an explicit introduction of dynamic modes of analysis,

[140] Of course, in choosing the assigned domestic production targets themselves, the planner may have *implicitly* made a choice on some sort of "optimizing" lines. More usually, however, the domestic production targets are in varying degrees "arbitrary."

[141] For instance, if there are no distortions of any sort, either internally or externally, a static (traditionalist) optimisation procedure, in a programming framework, would yield the equality of F.P. and D.P., and of F.R.T. and D.R.T. In this sense, the programming approach merely reflects the insights of trade theory. This is, after all, what one would expect, since the proposition that free trade is superior to a tariff (under standard first-best assumptions) is a statement *merely* about the relationship between F.P. and D.P., and *not* about the institutions by which this equality is brought about. The unwary reader, therefore, should note that nothing of what may have been said in favour of *free trade,* for instance, is an argument in favour of *laissez faire.*

the recognition of the importance of intermediates and capital goods, a policy orientation in welfare economics leading to interest in measurement and the attempts at the operational use of trade theory in developmental planning represent, as of today, the gravitational centres towards which the analytical interests of the profession are moving. In some of these respects trade theory is merely modernising itself, "catching up" with the advances in theory generally. But in others, as for instance in the measurement of welfare changes, trade theory is the innovator. Indeed, this is the way the subject has always grown: m a two-way flow of ideas with the general theory of value and welfare.

References*

*The references have been classified into separate groups corresponding to the Sections in the text, while the numbering is consecutive for the groups together. The correspondence between the Sections and the groups is naturally not precise. The works listed do not constitute an exhaustive bibliography; the necessary and sufficient criterion for a work to be cited is that it should have been referred to in the text.

Introduction

1. J. Bhagwati, "Some Recent Trends in the Pure Theory of International Trade," Paper presented to the Conference on *Trade in A Developing World,* held by the International Economic Association at Brissago, Switzerland, in September 1961: the volume of the Papers and Proceedings has been published by Macmillan & Co., 1963.
2. J. Bhagwati and H. G. Johnson, "Notes on some Controversies in the theory of International Trade," ECONOMIC JOURNAL, Vol. 70 (March 1960).
3. R. E. Caves, *Trade and Economic Structure* (Cambridge, Mass.: Harvard University Press, 1960).
4. G. Haberler, *A Survey of International Trade Theory,* Special papers in International Economics, No. I (International Finance Section, Department of Economics, Princeton University, 1961).
5. H. G.Johnson, *International Trade and Economic Growth,* London (George Allen and Unwin Ltd., 1958).
6. H. G. Johnson, *Money, Trade and Growth* (London: George Allen and Unwin Ltd., 1962).
7. R. G. Lipsey, "The Theory of Customs Unions: A General Survey," ECONOMIC JOURNAL, Vol. 70 (September 1960).

8. J. E. Meade, *Trade and Welfare* (*The Theory of International Economic Policy*, Vol. II) (Oxford: Oxford University Press, 1955).
9. J. E. Meade, *Mathematical Supplement (Trade and Welfare)* (Oxford: Oxford University Press, 1955).
10. J. E. Meade, *A Geometry of International Trade* (London: George Allen and Unwin Ltd., 1952).
11. R. A. Mundell, "The Pure Theory of International Trade," *American Economic Review*, Vol. 50 (March 1960).

I

12. T. Balogh, "Factor Intensities of American Foreign Trade and Technical Progress," *Review of Economics and Statistics,* Vol. 37 (November 1955).
13. B. Balassa, "An Empirical Demonstration of Classical Comparative Cost Theory," *Review of Economics and Statistics,* forthcoming.
14. J. Bhagwati, "Protection, Real Wages and Real Incomes," ECONOMIC JOURNAL, Vol. 69 (December 1959).
15. R. Bharadwaj, *Structural Basis of India's Foreign Trade* (Series in Monetary and International Economics, No. 6) (University of Bombay, 1962).
16. R. Bharadwaj, "Factor Proportions and the Structure of Indo-US Trade," *Indian Economic Journal,* Vol. 10 (October 1962).
17. J. Coppock, *International Economic Instability,* (Economic Handbook Series) (McGraw Hill Book Company Inc., 1962).
18. M. Diab, *The United States Capital Position and the Structure of the Foreign Trade* (Amsterdam: North Holland, 1956).
19. E. Heckscher, "The Effect of Foreign Trade on the Distribution of Income," *Readings in the Theory of International Trade,* Edited by H. S. Ellis and L. A. Metzler for the American Economic Association (Philadelphia: Blakiston, 1949).
20. R. Jones, "Factor Proportions and the Heckscher-Ohlin Model," *Review of Economic Studies,* Vol. 24 (1956-57).
21. I. Kravis, "Wages and Foreign Trade," *Review of Economics and Statistics,* Vol. 38 (February 1956).
22. I. Kravis, "Availability and other Influences on the Commodity Composition of Trade," *Journal of Political Economy,* Vol. 64 (April 1956).
23. S. Lebergott, "Wage Structures," *Review of Economics and Statistics,* Vol. 29 (November 1947).
24. W. Leontief, "The Use of Indifference Curves in the Analysis of Foreign Trade," *Quarterly Journal of Economics,* Vol. 47 (May 1933).
25. W. Leontief, "Domestic Production and Foreign Trade: The American Capital Position Re-examined," *Economia Internazionale,* Vol. 7 (1954).
26. W. Leontief, "Factor Proportions and the Structure of American Trade: Further Theoretical and Empirical Analysis," *Review of Economics and Statistics,* Vol. 38 (November 1956).

27. S. Linder, *An Essay on Trade and Transformation* (New York: John Wiley and Sons, 1961).
28. G. D. A. MacDougall, "British and American Exports: A Study suggested by the Theory of Comparative Costs, Part I," ECONOMIC JOURNAL, Vol. 61 (December 1951).
29. G. D. A. MacDougall, "British and American Exports: A Study Suggested by the Theory of Comparative Costs, Part II," ECONOMIC JOURNAL, Vol. 62 (September 1952).
30. G. D. A. MacDougall, M. Dawley, P. Fox and S. Pugh, "British and American Productivity, Prices and Exports: An Addendum," *Oxford Economic Papers,* Vol. 14 (October 1962).
31. M. Michaely, *Concentration in World Trade* (Contributions to Economic Analysis) (Amsterdam: North Holland Publishing Co., 1962).
32. J. S. Mill, *Principles of Political Economy,* Edited by W. J. Ashley (London: Longmans, Green and Co., 1917).
33. B. S. Minhas, "The Homohypallagic Production Function, Factor Intensity Reversals, and the Heckscher-Ohlin Theorem," *Journal of Political Economy,* Vol. 70 (April 1962).
34. B. Ohlin, *Interregional and International Trade,* Harvard Economic Studies, Vol. 39. (Cambridge, Mass.: Harvard University Press, 1933).
35. I. F. Pearce and S. F. James, "The Factor Price Equalisation Myth," *Review of Economic Studies,* Vol. 19 (1951–52).
36. R. Robinson, "Factor Problems and Comparative Advantage: Part I," *Quarterly Journal of Economics,* Vol. 70 (May 1956).
37. R. Robinson, "Factor Proportions and Comparative Advantage: Part II," *Quarterly Journal of Economics,* Vol. 70 (August 1956).
38. P. A. Samuelson, "International Trade and Equalisation of Factor Prices," ECONOMIC JOURNAL, Vol. 58 (June 1948).
39. P. A. Samuelson, "International Factor Price Equalisation Once Again," ECONOMIC JOURNAL, Vol. 59 (June 1949).
40. R. Stern, "British and American Productivity and Comparative Costs in International Trade," *Oxford Economic Papers,* Vol. 14 (October 1962).
41. W. Stolper and K. Roskamp, "Input-Output Table for East Germany with Applications to Foreign Trade," *Bulletin of the Oxford University Institute of Statistics,* Vol. 23 (November 1961).
42. M. Tatemoto and S. Ichimura, "Proportions and Foreign Trade: The Case of Japan," *Review of Economics and Statistics,* Vol. 41 (November 1959).
43. J. Vanek, "The Natural Resource Content of Foreign Trade, 1870-1955, and the Relative Abundance of Natural Resources in the United States," *Review of Economics and Statistics,* Vol. 41 (May 1959).
44. J. Viner, *Studies in the Theory of International Trade* (New York: Harper and Bros., 1937).
45. D. F. Wahl, "Capital and Labour Requirements for Canada's Foreign Trade," *Canadian Journal of Economics and Political Science,* Vol. 27 (August 1961).

II

46. R. F. Harrod, "Factor-Price Relations under Free Trade," ECONOMIC JOURNAL, Vol. 68 (June 1958).
47. H. W. Kuhn, "Factor Endowments and Factor Prices: Mathematical Appendix," *Economica,* N.S., Vol. 26 (May 1959).
48. N. Laing, "Factor Price Equalization in International Trade and Returns to Scale," *Economic Record,* Vol. 37 (September 1961).
49. L. McKenzie, "Equality of Factor Price in World Trade," *Econometrica,* Vol. 23 (July 1955).
50. J. E. Meade, "The Equalisation of Factor Prices: the Two-Good, Two-Country Three-product Case," *Metro-economica,* Vol. 2 (December 1950).
51. I. F. Pearce, "A Further Note on Factor-Commodity Price Relationships," ECONOMIC JOURNAL, Vol. 69 (December 1959).
52. S. Reiter, "Efficient International Trade and Equalisation of Prices," *International Economic Review,* Vol. 2 (January 1961).
53. P. A. Samuelson, "Prices of Factors and Goods in General Equilibrium," *Review of Economic Studies,* Vol. 21 (1953-54).
54. P.A. Samuelson, "Equalisation by Trade of the Interest Rate along with the Real Wage," *Mimeographed,* 1960.
55. J. Vanek, "Variable Factor Proportions and Inter-Industry Flows in the Theory of International Trade," *Quarterly Journal of Economics,* Vol. 77 (February 1963).

III

56. A. Asimakopulos, "A Note on Productivity Changes and the Terms of Trade," *Oxford Economic Papers,* N.S., Vol. 9 (June 1957).
57. R. E. Baldwin, "The Effects of Tariffs on International and Domestic Prices," *Quarterly Journal of Economics,* Vol. 74 (February 1960).
58. T. Balogh, "The Concept of a Dollar Shortage," *Manchester School,* Vol. 17 (May 1949).
59. J. Black, "Economic Expansion and International Trade: A Marshallian Approach," *Review of Economic Studies,* Vol. 23 (1955–56).
60. J. Bhagwati, and H. G. Johnson, "A Generalised Theory of the Effects of Tariffs on the Terms of Trade," *Oxford Economic Papers,* N.S. Vol. 13 (October 1961).
61. W. M. Corden, "Economic Expansion and International Trade: A Geometrical Approach," *Oxford Economic Papers,* N.S., Vol. 8 (June 1956).
62. R. Findlay and H. Grubert, "Factor Intensity, Technological Progress, and the Terms of Trade," *Oxford Economic Papers,* N.S. Vol. II (February 1959).
63. F. D. Graham, "The Theory of International Values," *Quarterly Journal of Economics,* Vol. 46 (August 1932).
64. H. G. Johnson," Economic Development and International Trade," *National Konomick Tidsskript* (Arganj, 1959).

65. H. G. Johnson, " Effects of changes in Comparative Costs as Influenced by Technical Change," *Malayan Economic Review,* Vol. 6 (October 1961).
66. H. G. Johnson, "International Trade, Income Distribution and the Offer Curve," *Manchester School,* Vol. 27 (September 1959).
67. H. G. Johnson, "Income Distribution, the Offer Curve and the Effects of Tariffs," *Manchester School,* Vol. 28 (September 1960).
68. H. G. Johnson, "The Pure Theory of International Trade: Comment," *American Economic Review,* Vol. 50 (September 1960).
69. R. Jones, "Comparative Advantage and the Theory of Tariffs: A Multicountry, Multi-Commodity Model," *Review of Economic Studies,* Vol. 28 (June 1961) .
70. M. C. Kemp, "The Relation between Changes in International Demand and the Terms of Trade," *Econometrica,* Vol. 24 (January 1956).
71. M. C. Kemp, "Technological Change, the Terms of Trade and Welfare," ECONOMIC JOURNAL, Vol. 65 (September 1955).
72. M. C. Kemp and R. Jones, "Variable Labour Supply and the Theory of International Trade," *Journal of Political Economy,* Vol. 70 (February 1962).
73. C. P. Kindleberger, "Group Behaviour and International Trade," *Journal of Political Economy,* Vol. 59 (February 1951).
74. A. P. Lerner, "The Symmetry between Import and Export Taxes," *Economica,* N.S. Vol. 3 (August 1936).
75. I. MacDougall, "Tariffs, Protection and the Terms of Trade," *Economic Record,* Vol. 37 (1961).
76. I. MacDougall, "A Note on Tariffs, the Terms of Trade, and the Distribution of the National Incomes," *Journal of Political Economy,* Vol. 70 (August 1962).
77. A. Marshall, *The Pure Theory of Foreign Trade* (Reprints of scarce Tracts on Political Economy) (London: London School of Economics, 1930).
78. L. McKenzie, "Specialization and Efficiency in World Production," *Review of Economic Studies,* Vol. 21 (1953–54).
79. E. Meade, *The Theory of Customs Unions* (Amsterdam: North Holland Publishing Co., 1955).
80. L. Metzler, " Tariffs, the Terms of Trade and the Distribution of National Income," *Journal of Political Economy,* Vol. 57 (February 1949).
81. L. Metzler, "Tariffs, International Demand and Domestic Prices," *Journal of Political Economy,* Vol. 57 (August 1949).
82. R. A. Mundell, "International Trade and Factor Mobility," *American Economic Review,* Vol. 47 (June 1957).
83. H. Myint, "The Classical Theory of International Trade and the Underdeveloped countries," ECONOMIC JOURNAL, Vol. 68 (June 1958).
84. F. R. Oliver, "Shifting Demand Schedules and the Terms and Volume of Trade," *Metroeconomica,* Vol. 12 (April 1960).
85. S. A. Ozga, "An Essay in the Theory of Tariffs," *Journal of Political Economy* Vol. 63 (December 1955).
86. V. K. Ramaswami, "The Effects of Accumulation on the Terms of Trade," ECONOMIC JOURNAL, Vol. 70 (September 1960).

87. T. N. Rybczynski, "Factor Endowment and Relative Commodity Prices," *Economica,* N.S., Vol. 22 (November 1955).
88. P.A. Samuelson, "The Transfer Problem and Transport Costs," ECONOMIC JOURNAL, Vol. 62 (June 1952).
89. P.A. Samuelson, "The Transfer Problem and Transport Costs," ECONOMIC JOURNAL, Vol. 62 (June 1952).
90. F. Seton, "Productivity, Trade Balance and International Structure," ECONOMIC JOURNAL, Vol. 66 (December 1956).
91. W. Stolper and P. A. Samuelson, "Protection and Real Wages," *Review of Economic Studies,* Vol. 9 (November 1941).
92. J. Vanek, "An Afterthought on the Real Cost-Opportunity Cost Dispute and some Aspects of General Equilibrium under Conditions of Variable Factor Supplies," *Review of Economic Studies,* Vol. 26 (June 1959).
93. J. Vanek, *International Trade: Theory and Economic Policy* (Illinois: Richard D. Irwin Inc., 1962).
94. J. Viner, *The Customs Union Issue* (New York: Carnegie Endowment for International Peace, 1950).
95. V. C. Walsh, "Leisure and International Trade," *Economica,* N.S. Vol. 23 (August 1956).

IV

96. D. M. Bensusan-Butt, "A Model of Trade and Accumulation," *American Economic Review,* Vol. 44 (September 1954).
97. J. Bhagwati, "The Theory of Comparative Advantage in the Context of Underdevelopment and Growth," *Pakistan Development Review,* Vol. 2 (Autumn 1962).
98. H. Brems, "The Foreign Trade Accelerator and International Transmission of Growth," *Econometrica,* Vol. 24 (July 1956).
99. F. D. Graham, "Some Aspects of Protection Further Considered," *Quarterly Journal of Economics,* Vol. 37 (February 1923).
100. A. Johnson, "Protection and the Formation of Capital," *Political Science Quarterly,* Vol. 23 (June 1908).
101. C. P. Kindleberger, "Foreign Trade and Economic Growth: Lessons from Britain and France, 1850 to 1913," *Economic History Review,* Vol. 14 (1961).
102. H. Kitamura, *International Economics* (Tokyo), March 1951.
103. K. Kojima, "A Survey of the Theories on International Economics in Japan," *Japan Science Review (Economic Sciences,* No. 1), Japan Union of Associations of Economic Sciences, 1953.
104. T. N. Srinivasan, "A Two-Country, Three-Commodity, Dynamic Model of International Trade," *Unpublished,* 1962.
105. P. J. Verdoorn, "Complementarity and Long-Range Projections," *Econometrica,* Vol. 24 (October 1956).

V

106. K. Akamatsu, "The Theory of Supply-Multiplier in Reference to the Post-War Economic Situation in Japan," *The Annals of the Hitotsubashi Academy* (October 1950).
107. G.A.T.T., *Basic Instruments and Selected Documents, Tenth Supplement* (Geneva, March 1962).
108. L. McKenzie, "On Equilibrium in Graham's Model of World Trade and Other Competitive Systems," *Econometrica,* Vol. 22 (April 1954).
109. W. Stolper, "Notes on the Dollar Shortage," *American Economic Review,* Vol. 40 (June 1950).
110. W. Stolper, "A Note on Multiplier, Flexible Exchanges and the Dollar Shortage," *Economica Internationale,* Vol. II (August 1950).

VI

111. J. Bhagwati, "Immiserizing Growth: A Geometrical Note," *Review of Economic Studies,* Vol. 25 (June 1958).
112. J. Bhagwati, and V. K. Ramaswami, "Domestic Distortions, Tariffs and the Theory of Optimum Subsidy," *Journal of Political Economy,* Vol. 71 (February 1963).
113. R. Dorfman, P. A. Samuelson and R. M. Solow, *Linear Programming and Economic Analysis* (New York: McGraw Hill, 1958).
114. M. Fleming, "The Optimal Tariff from an International Standpoint," *Review of Economics and Statistics,* Vol. 38 (February 1956).
115. W. M. Gorman, "Tariffs, Retaliation and the Elasticity of Demand for Imports," *Review of Economic Studies,* Vol. 25 (June 1958).
116. J. Graaff, "On Optimum Tariff Structures," *Review of Economic Studies,* Vol. 17 (1949–50).
117. G. Haberler, "Some Problems in the Pure Theory of International Trade," ECONOMIC JOURNAL, Vol. 60 (June 1950).
118. E. Hagen, "An Economic Justification of Protectionism," *Quarterly Journal of Economics,* Vol. 72 (November 1958).
119. A. E. Jasay, "The Choice between Home and Foreign Investment," ECONOMIC JOURNAL, Vol. 70 (March 1960).
120. M. C. Kemp, "The Gain from International Trade," ECONOMIC JOURNAL, Vol. 72 (December 1962).
121. R. G. Lipsey, "The Theory of Customs Unions: Trade Diversion and Welfare," *Economica,* N.S., Vol. 24 (February 1957).
122. G. D. A. MacDougall, "The Benefits and Costs of Private Investment from Abroad: A Theoretical Approach," *Bulletin of the Oxford University Institute of Statistics,* Vol. 22 (August 1960).
123. R. C. O. Matthews, "Reciprocal Demand and Increasing Returns," *Review of Economic Studies,* Vol. 17 (1949–50).

124. V. Panchmukhi, "A Theory for Optimum Tariff Policy," *Indian Economic Journal,* Vol. 9 (October 1961).
125. P.A. Samuelson, "The Gains from International Trade," *Canadian Journal of Economics and Political Science,* Vol. 5 (May 1939).
126. P. A. Samuelson, "The Gain from International Trade Once Again," ECONOMIC JOURNAL, Vol. 72 (December 1962).
127. J. Tinbergen, *International Economic Cooperation* (Amsterdam, 1946).

VII

128. W. M. Corden, "Tariffs, Subsidies and the Terms of Trade," *Economica,* N.S., Vol. 24 (August 1957).
129. H. G. Johnson, "Optimum Welfare and Maximum Revenue Tariffs," *Review of Economic Studies,* Vol. 19 (1951–52).
130. H. G. Johnson, "Discriminatory Tariff Reduction: A Marshallian Analysis," *Indian Journal of Economics,* Vol. 38 (July 1957).
131. H. G. Johnson, "The Gain from Freer Trade with Europe: An Estimate," *Manchester School,* Vol. 26 (September 1958).
132. H. G. Johnson, "The Cost of Protection and the Scientific Tariff," *Journal of Political Economy,* Vol. 42 (October 1960).
133. H. G. Johnson, "Optimal Trade Intervention in the Presence of Domestic Distortions," *Mimeographed,* 1963.
134. R. L. Marris, "The Purchasing Power of British Exports," *Economica,* N.S. Vol. 22 (February 1955).
135. J. Wemelsfelder, "The Short-term Effect of the Lowering of Import Duties in Germany," ECONOMIC JOURNAL, Vol. 70 (March 1960).

VIII

136. P. R. Brahmandand and C. N. Vakil, *Planning for an Expanding Economy* (Bombay: Vora & Co., 1956).
137. S. Chakravarty, *The Logic of Investment Planning* (North Holland Series) (Amsterdam: North Holland Publishing Co., 1957).
138. H. Chenery and M. Bruno, "Development Alternatives in an Open Economy: The Case of Israel," ECONOMIC JOURNAL, Vol. 72 (March 1962).
139. H. Chenery, "Comparative Advantage and Development Policy," *American Economic Review,* Vol. 51 (March 1961).
140. P. Desai, "The Development of the Indian Economy: An Exercise in Economic Planning," *Oxford Economic Papers,* Vol. 15 (October 1963).
141. P. C. Mahalanobis, "Science and National Planning," *Sankhya,* Vol. 20 (1958).
142. R. Wonnacott, *Canadian-American Dependence,* (Contributions to Economic Analysis) (Amsterdam: North Holland Publishing Co., 1961).

Chapter 4

A Survey of the Theory of International Trade: Part I, The Classical Theory*

John S. Chipman†

> I must give notice that we are now in the region of the most complicated questions which political economy affords; that the subject is one which cannot possibly be made elementary; and that a more continuous effort of attention than has yet been required, will be necessary to follow the series of deductions.
>
> —John Stuart Mill

Introduction

Economists have long been puzzled by Max Planck's famous remark to Keynes that "in early life he had thought of studying economics,

*Originally published in *Econometrica*, 33(3), pp. 477–519.

†This is the last in a series of survey articles which *Econometrica* is publishing with the support of the Rockefeller Foundation. Because of its length, this article will be published in three parts. Part 2 on the Neo-Classical Theory is scheduled to appear in the October, 1965 issue, and Part 3 on the Modem Theory in the January, 1966 issue. Research was facilitated by a grant to the author of an Auxiliary Research Award by the Social Science Research Council, as well as a grant by the National Science Foundation. Grateful acknowledgment is made to Professor Samuelson for comments on an earlier draft; he is not, of course, to be held responsible for any errors that remain. Equally absolved are M.C. Kemp and R.W. Jones, whose valuable criticisms of a later draft are greatly appreciated.

but had found it too difficult!"[1] Keynes' own interpretation of the remark was that it was not the logical structure of economic theory that had dissuaded Planck, but rather "the amalgam of logic and intuition and wide knowledge of facts, most of which are not precise, which is required for economic interpretation in its highest form."

Keynes cited Planck's remark in connection with his discussion of Marshall's work in the theory of international trade, in the *Pure Theory* (1879) and in the famous Appendix J to *Money, Credit, and Commerce* (1923), which had just appeared at that time; cf. Harrod (1951, p.137). In expressing approval of Marshall's suppression of the *Pure Theory* from publication, and of his habit of relegating mathematics to appendices, Keynes observed (with an obvious note of disparagement) that "Professor Planck could easily master the whole corpus of mathematical economics in a few days."

Even if this had been true in 1923 (which is most doubtful), it would certainly not be true today. To illustrate the point, Brouwer's fixed point theorem (1912) had not yet been proved when Marshall wrote his *Pure Theory* (1879); yet it is now known that the existence of equilibrium in Marshall's theory (when expanded to more than two commodities) cannot be established without it. Uzawa (1962) has shown, in fact, that Brouwer's fixed point theorem and the law of supply and demand are logically equivalent.

The present survey will emphasize the mathematical structure of international trade theory as it has developed up to this time. But "mathematical" must not be interpreted in the narrow sense given to the word by Keynes. Symbols must not be confused with substance; as Schumpeter acutely observed (1954, pp. 954–5), "the restatement in algebraic form of some result of non-mathematical reasoning does not constitute mathematical economics: a distinctive element enters only when the reasoning itself that produces the result is explicitly mathematical."

[1]J. M. Keynes (1924, p. 333n). (Works are referred to by author and year, sometimes by abbreviated title, and are listed alphabetically and chronologically at the end of each part of the article.)

There are two reasons for this choice of emphasis. One is that the field of international trade is particularly well provided with surveys, especially (although not exclusively) of a non-mathematical kind, and it would be pointless to try to cover ground that others have covered so well. Special mention may be made of the surveys of Edgeworth (1894), Haberler (1936), Viner (1937), Metzler (1948), Haberler (1955–61), Caves (1960), Mundell (1960), Bhagwati (1963, 1964), and Kemp (1964), as well as the encyclopaedic *History* by Schumpeter (1954).

The second reason is furnished by the opening citation. Difficult problems require adequate methods, and economists have special reason to appreciate the value of capital-intensive ones. The fact that Mill could and did use mathematical reasoning without using mathematical symbols, is a tribute to his genius, and makes his achievement all the more impressive. To try to do the same today would, like swimming the Channel, excite a certain admiration but not much respect. Appropriate mathematical tools are at last becoming available for the task; while they are not a substitute for common sense, they help remove the wasteful doctrinal controversy that has been so characteristic of the subject, paving the way for the supplanting of empirical mysticism by genuine empirical inference.

In bringing the history of thought in this field up to date, it seems appropriate not only to report on developments of the last two decades, but also to discuss some of the older writings, which fall into two categories: those which have been neglected and recently been brought to light, and those whose importance may have been overlooked and which can be better appreciated in the light of modern developments. In the first of these categories, I would include the name of Torrens, who discovered the law of comparative advantage, and of whose work we now possess the invaluable study by Robbins (1958). In the second category, I would place John Stuart Mill, as well as his predecessors Say, Ricardo, James Mill, Torrens, Malthus, and Sismondi, who — as has become evident from the publication of Sraffa's monumental edition of Ricardo's *Works and Correspondence* (1951–1955) — discovered in the course of their lively interchanges the crucial assumptions required in order to prove the existence of competitive equilibrium.

The present article deals with the theory of international values. It is divided into three parts, corresponding to the Classical, Neo-classical, and Modern theories. This division is one of convenience only, corresponding to differences in emphasis. The "classical" approach (by which I mean that of Torrens, Ricardo and Mill), while oversimplifying things on the production side, has the advantage of bringing out sharply the nature of the problem of international specialization; this early work has come back into prominence owing to the work of McKenzie and others who recognized their relationship to mathematical programming and Koopmans' activity analysis. The "neo-classical" approach (by which I mean that of Marshall, Edgeworth, Haberler, Viner, Lerner, early-Leontief, and Meade) rests in part on simplifications on both the production and consumption side, as represented by the concepts of opportunity cost and community indifference; the latter — whose status seems ambiguous in the literature, to say the least — is singled out for especial scrutiny. The "modern" approach, by which I understand the school of thought that began with Heckscher and Ohlin, but which did not really come into its own until recently with the work of Lerner and Samuelson, gives the most important role to factor endowment, and represents probably the most complex and impressive theoretical structure that has yet been developed in economic thought.

The sequel will be concerned with capital movements, the terms of trade, and the foreign exchanges; trade and economic growth; gains from trade and commercial policy; and methodological issues in econometric studies.

1. The Classical Theory

1.1. *Ricardo, Torrens, and The Law of Comparative Advantage*

The main distinguishing feature of international trade singled out by Ricardo (1817, p. 134) was the international immobility of factors of production. Factors were regarded as perfectly mobile within countries and completely immobile among countries, whereas goods were perfectly mobile within and among countries (at zero transport cost). Ricardo rather glossed over the question of the interdependence of industries, treating them as integrated, producing one output and using one primary input (labor). The latter being mobile internally, the unit cost of each good was constant, depending only on the amount of labor required to produce it.

Ricardo's exposition of the laws governing trade between two nations was extremely concise, and not entirely free from ambiguity. In his celebrated example of trade in cloth and wine between England and Portugal, he says (1817, p. 135): "England may be so circumstanced, that to produce the cloth may require the labour of 100 men for one year; and if she attempt to make the wine, it might require the labour of 120 men for the same time. England would therefore find it her interest to import wine, and to purchase it by the exportation of cloth." This is a *non sequitur,* since nothing so far has been said about Portugal; indeed, the argument could be turned around merely by redefining the units of measurement. The next passage is equally unsatisfactory, except when read in conjunction with the first: "To produce the wine in Portugal, might require only the labour of 80 men for one year, and to produce the cloth in the same country, might require the labour of 90 men for the same time. It would therefore be advantageous for her to export wine in exchange for cloth." But Ricardo saves himself in the passages that immediately follow by proceeding with a correct explanation of what was later to be called the law of comparative advantage.

Historians of economic doctrine have debated whether priority for the law of comparative advantage should go to Ricardo (1817) or to Torrens (1808, 1815); see Seligman (1903, 1911), Hollander (1910, 1911), Viner (1937, pp. 441–7), Schumpeter (1954, pp. 607–8), and Robbins (1958, pp. 18–35). The debate has centered around the question of (1) whether Torrens stated the principle first, (2) if so, whether correctly, and (3) if so, whether independently of Ricardo. It does not seem to have been recognized that Ricardo's own statement of the law is quite wanting, so much so as to cast some doubt as to whether he truly understood it; at best, his version is carelessly worded.

Seligman (1911, p. 449) based his claims for Torrens in part on the following passage from Torrens' earliest publication (1808, p. 53): "Thus, if I wish to know the extent of the advantage which arises to England, from her giving France a hundred pounds, worth of broad cloth, in exchange for a hundred pounds, worth of lace, I take the quantity of lace which England has acquired by this transaction, and compare it with the quantity which she might, at the same expense of labour and capital, have acquired by manufacturing it at home." Hollander (1911, p. 459) objected that this statement "embodies the very error against which Cairnes warned" and proceeded to cite a statement from Cairnes (1874, p. 312) that "when it is said that international trade depends on a difference in the comparative, not in the absolute, cost of producing commodities, the costs compared, it must be carefully noted, are the costs in each country of the commodities which are the subject of exchange, not the different costs of the same commodity in the exchanging countries." In other words — Cairnes seems to be saying — if among four positive quantities, the relation $a'/b' < a''/b''$ holds, this must not be confused with the relation $a'/a'' < b'/b''$; but as any high school student ought to know, the two inequalities are mathematically equivalent (see Viner (1937, pp. 438–9), who essentially spotted this same error in Cairnes). Thus Hollander's case against Torrens rested largely on this elementary error in rudimentary mathematics. But even then, he misread Torrens' statement, for what Torrens was comparing was the cost ratio in one country with the international price ratio; this made it possible for Torrens to provide a correct argument for the gains from trade, but the comparison of cost ratios (or rates of transformation) between two countries was lacking. The same kind of comparison was made by Torrens in the *External Corn Trade* (1815, pp. 221–2; 1826, p. 334): "If ... any given portion of our labour and capital can, by working up cloth, obtain from Poland a thousand quarters of wheat, while it could raise, from our own soil, only nine hundred; then ... we must increase our wealth by being, to this extent, a manufacturing, rather than an agricultural people." Seligman (1911, p. 450), who cited this passage, did not help his case by misquoting it and substituting "their own soil" for "our own soil," and perhaps it was this slip that helped deceive Hollander.

Torrens came closer to enunciating the law of comparative advantage in another passage in the *External Corn Trade* (1815, 1820, pp. 264–5; 1826, 1829, pp. 352–3), which has been cited by Leser (1881, pp. 82–3n), Seligman (1903, pp. 344–5; 1925, pp. 74–5), Viner (1937, p. 442), and Robbins (1958, p. 23). The passage in question, like the previous ones, compared the domestic rate of transformation with the international terms of exchange, but added the most important point that this would entail England's neglecting the cultivation of "tracts of her territory, though they should be equal, nay, even though they should be superior, to the lands in Poland..." This certainly expressed what is usually considered to be the essence of the law of comparative advantage, as Robbins (1958, pp. 22–3) has pointed out.

By way of contrast, Ricardo's *Essay on Profits,* which was published on the same day — February 24, 1815 — as Torrens' *External Corn Trade* (cf. Ricardo's *Works,* IV, p. 5), contains scarcely any recognition of the principle of comparative advantage. Apart from a rather vague statement (1815, p. 25) to the effect that trade leads to an "increase of the general rate of profits" and to "abundance of commodities," the closest Ricardo came at that time was in the statement (p. 32): "If ...left to ourselves ...we should gradually withdraw our capital from the cultivation of such lands, and import the produce which is at present raised upon them. The capital withdrawn would be employed in the manufacture of such commodities as would be exported in return for the corn. Such a distribution ...would be more advantageous, or it would not be adopted." But there is no very convincing explanation as to why it would be more advantageous, and hence adopted.

Torrens' *External Corn Trade* undoubtedly made an impression on Ricardo, who described the work in a letter to Malthus shortly after its appearance as "on the whole a very able performance" (*Works,* VI, p. 188). Some years later Torrens' book was described in an article which has been attributed to Ricardo's disciple McCulloch (1819, p. 56) as "one of the most valuable contributions that has of late years been made to the science of political economy" (The attribution of this article to McCulloch will be considered in greater detail in Part 2.) There can be little doubt that Ricardo was influenced by it, whether he was conscious of the indebtedness or not; nevertheless he added a great deal in his own subsequent treatment. The juxtaposition of the two sentences — if not the literal wording — implied comparison of cost ratios in two countries. And it is only in subsequent editions of Torrens' work that one finds statements such as the following one from the third edition (1826, p. 39): "while Poland can raise corn comparatively cheaper than England, or England prepare cloth comparatively cheaper than Poland, the latter ... will become an exporting, and the former an importing, country." This passage — with a subtle and significant difference of wording — had already been contained in the first two editions (1815, 1820, p. 38); the word "comparatively" was added in 1826 in both places.[2] Furthermore, Ricardo succeeded to a greater extent than Torrens in relating the principle to a larger theoretical system. Thus it would seem fair to say that both Torrens and Ricardo contributed in essential ways to the development of the law of comparative advantage; and that credit for the principal discovery should go to Torrens.[3]

[2]The second edition of the *Corn Trade* is identical with the first except for the addition of a fourth part; the first three parts appear to have been reprinted from the same plates. This would explain why the change in wording did not take place until the third edition. Similarly, the passage referred to above, quoted by Leser, Seligman, and Viner, contains a sentence (omitted in Robbins' citation) with a phrase "excess of profits" (Torrens 1815, 1820, p. 264) which detracts considerably from the worth of the statement; in the third edition (1826, p. 353) this was changed for the better to "excess of produce."

[3]It would take us too far into the sociology of knowledge to attempt to explain why it has taken so long for Torrens to gain proper recognition. The common attribution of the principle to Ricardo evidently derives its origin, at least in part, in the self-effacing modesty of Mill (1844, pp. 1–7), whose own statement of the law of comparative advantage is perhaps the first completely satisfactory one; as Schumpeter (1954, p. 529) pointed out, Mill's own achievement was "obscured by filial respect" for Ricardo. James Mill (1826, pp. 118–124) certainly played an important part in the evolution of the law. J. S. Mill pointed out (1844, p. v) that his *Essays* had been written in 1829–30, and were published in 1844 in response

Even if comparative advantage explains why trade takes place, it does not explain on what terms. Ricardo is widely regarded as having maintained that the equilibrium price ratio would settle "halfway between" the comparative cost ratios.[4] This conclusion is usually based on Ricardo's assertion (1817, p. 135): "Thus England would give the produce of the labour of 100 men, for the produce of the labour of 80," implying that the price ratio between cloth and wine would be equal to unity, which is intermediate between the cost ratios of 80/90 and 120/100. But if England should experience a 20 per cent increase in productivity in both industries, and if the two commodities continue to be measured in the same units, then "the produce of the labour of 100 men" which England will supply for the produce of Portugal's 80 will be 20 per cent higher in quantity; thus by Ricardo's own logic the price of wine will rise to 1.2 units of cloth, which corresponds to the relative cost in England. Whether or not this is a correct interpretation of Ricardo, the solution happens to correspond precisely to that which was later obtained by Mill (1852a, p. 158) on the basis of explicit assumptions about demand.

1.2. *Mill's Law of International Value*

In his remarkable essay, "On the Laws of Interchange between Nations" (1844), Mill set out to find a precise solution to the problem left open by Ricardo. It was implicit in his discussion that an intermediate price ratio would necessitate complete specialization, entailing a fixed supply of each good; the problem was then whether there would

to the writings of Torrens. The real difficulty is that Torrens' works are scarce and inaccessible, long out of print, and unavailable in most libraries. According to the records of the Library of Congress there are, among the holdings of libraries in the United States, only seven copies of the first edition of the *External Corn Trade* (1815), and six copies of the second (1820).

[4]This very concept is questionable; Viner (1937, p. 446n) defined the midpoint in terms of the arithmetic mean, an ambiguous procedure at best, since different conclusions will result depending upon which cost is in the numerator and which in the denominator. It is mathematically impossible for the reciprocal of the arithmetic mean of two distinct quantities to be equal to the arithmetic mean of their reciprocals. This difficulty would have been avoided if Viner had chosen the geometric mean.

exist a price ratio for which "the demand shall be exactly sufficient to carry off the supply" (p. 9). He recognized the possibility of "an extreme case" (p. 13) in which demand might be so rigid that no such intermediate price ratio would exist; in that case, the equilibrium price ratio would have to correspond to one of the limiting cost ratios, and there would be partial specialization in the corresponding country.[5]

Mill's mature thoughts on the theory of international trade are contained in Chapter 18 of the *Principles,* which Edgeworth (1894) described, with good reason, as the "great chapter." Edgeworth expressed himself differently, however, with regard to the supplementary Sections 6–9 which Mill added in the third (1852a) and subsequent editions. He said (1894, p. 609): "The splendid edifice of theory constructed in the first five sections is not improved by the superstructure of later date which forms the latter part of the chapter. This second story does not carry us much higher." He followed this pun by agreeing with Bastable (1903, p. 29n) that the superstructure was "laborious and confusing." Practically without exception, subsequent writers have joined the monotonous

[5]Mill had in his example assumed that demand was rigid in *one* country, and had then concluded, in the final paragraph of §1 of his essay (1844, p. 14) that "in general there will not be this extreme inequality in the degree in which the demand in the two countries varies with variations in price." This argument, though, is invalid, since the solution at an extreme (limiting) cost ratio would result equally well (in fact with greater likelihood) from rigidity of demand in *both* countries. Mill later withdrew this paragraph (by implication), since it was conspicuously omitted when the entire section was otherwise quoted in his *Principles* (1852a, Ch. 18, §2). Thus Graham (1923) misrepresented Mill when he argued that the latter ruled out the limiting solution as "an extreme and barely conceivable case"; Mill never used the expression "barely conceivable," and there does not seem to be any special reason for believing that he used the expression "an extreme case" in any sense other than the purely technical one of the extreme point of an interval. Mill was, after all, the first to point out the possibility. Evidently, differences of opinion concerning the meaning of "extremism" already existed before 1964.

chorus.[6] Schumpeter (1954, p. 608n) is almost alone in showing any appreciation and understanding of these supplementary sections.

It is time to reverse Edgeworth's judgment: for §7 of the "great chapter" contains a convincing proof (admittedly for a special case) of the existence of equilibrium; not only that, it does so in terms of what can today be recognized as an ingenious and correct solution of a problem in nonlinear programming.

Mill had already asserted the existence of equilibrium in §4 of his "great chapter" under the heading of the "Equation of International Demand," and expressed it in the words (1852a, p. 149): "The produce of a country exchanges for the produce of other countries, at such values as are required in order that the whole of her exports may exactly pay for the whole of her imports. This law of International Values is but an extension of the more general law of Value, which we called the Equation of Supply and Demand." As we might say today, Mill's law is an extension of Say's law. In §6 Mill raised the question of uniqueness; this section was criticized by Marshall (1879, pp. 15–16), Edgeworth (1894, pp. 610–12), and Metzler (1950, p. 303n), since Mill suggested that "it is conceivable that the conditions might be equally satisfied by every numerical rate which could be supposed." In Marshallian terms, this would correspond to two countries' offer curves coinciding throughout their length, giving rise to neutral equilibrium, and turning the equation of supply and demand into an identity. Subsequent writers have tended to

[6]Nicholson (1897, p. 302n) spoke of "the confusion of Mill's second statement." Viner (1937, p. 541) commented: "There has been general agreement that this additional material was unsatisfactory and unnecessary." Elliott (1950, p. 24) speaks of the "mysterious superstructure . . . which, in spite of the gentle treatment it has usually received, seems to the present writer to be very confused." And according to Metzler (1950, p. 303n): "In a long and involved argument introduced at the end of the chapter on international values in the third edition of his *Principles,* Mill attempted without success to solve the problem arising from neutral equilibrium." Finally, Mundell (1960, p. 73n) states that "John Stuart Mill recognized the possibility of multiple equilibria without reference to stability . . . , but his treatment was faulty."

interpret this as implying that Mill took this possibility seriously; but a much more plausible reading evinces Mill to be simply pointing out that "on the face of it" the equilibrium price ratio might not be determinate, and that uniqueness of equilibrium requires proof.[7] This prepares the ground for the demonstration in the subsequent section (§7), which will now be described.

Mill sets out (1852a, p. 155) to solve a special case: "As the simplest and most convenient, let us suppose that in both countries any given increase of cheapness produces an exactly proportional increase of consumption: or, in other words, that the value expended in the commodity, the cost incurred for the sake of obtaining it, is always the same, whether that cost affords a greater or a smaller quantity of the commodity." In other words, there is a unit own-elasticity of demand with respect to price, zero cross-elasticities and unit income elasticity, as well as a unit elasticity of substitution between any two goods. Such demand functions are known to be integrable, yielding a utility function of the form $U = x^\alpha y^\beta$ where x and y are the quantities of two commodities. Mill chooses the special case $\alpha = \beta$ (i.e., half of expenditure is devoted to each commodity), so without loss of generality we may take $U = xy$.

Let x', x'' be the quantities of cloth produced in Germany and England, respectively, and y', y'' the quantities of linen; let the corresponding world outputs be $x = x' + x'', y = y' + y''$.Let the production transformation sets be given by

$$\frac{x'}{a'} + \frac{y'}{b'} \leqq 1; \quad \frac{x''}{a''} + \frac{y''}{b''} \leqq 1; \tag{1.1}$$

and assume $a'/b' < a''/b''$, i.e., that Germany has a comparative advantage in linen. This inequality makes it possible to write (1.1)

[7]Metzler (1950, p. 303n) states that Mill "argued incorrectly that such neutral equilibrium would exist if each country had a unitary elasticity of demand for imports." This is incorrect. The assumption of unitary elasticity was introduced by Mill in §7 (not in §6) of his chapter, and on the contrary, Mill used it in that section to prove the uniqueness of equilibrium.

in the equivalent form[8]

$$\frac{x}{a'} + \frac{y}{b'} \leqq \frac{a}{a'}; \quad \frac{x}{a''} + \frac{y}{b''} \leqq \frac{b}{b''}, \tag{1.2}$$

where $a = a' + a'', b = b' + b''$. The problem is to maximize the quasi-concave function $U = xy$ (or equivalently, to maximize the concave positive homogeneous[9] function $V = U^{\frac{1}{2}} = x^{\frac{1}{2}}y^{\frac{1}{2}}$) subject to the linear inequalities (1.2). This is a problem in homogeneous programming (Eisenberg (1961)) — a special case of nonlinear programming (Kuhn and Tucker (1951)).

The solution, obtained in all essential respects by Mill (1852a, pp. 158–9), is as follows: Given that $a'/b' < a''/b''$, and that utility functions have the form $U = xy$ in each country, both constraints of (1.2) are effective (i.e., the equalities hold) if and only if

$$\frac{a'}{b'} \leqq \frac{a''}{b'} \leqq \frac{a''}{b''}, \tag{1.3}$$

i.e., if and only if the limiting cost ratios contain between them the ratio of England's maximum output a'' of cloth (in which she has a

[8]Derivation of (1.2) requires a little manipulation. First, if the inequalities of (1.1) are multiplied respectively by $a'$and a'',and then added, we find that

$$x + (a'/b')y' + (a''/b'')y'' \leqq a' + a'' = a$$

Now using the inequality $a'/b' < a''/b''$ we obtain

$$x + (a'/b')y' + (a'/b')y'' = x + (a'/b')y \leqq a$$

which is equivalent to the first inequality of (1.2). The second inequality of (1.2) is derived in the same way, this time multiplying the inequalities of (1.1) respectively by $b'$and b''.

[9]A real valued function $y = f(x_1, x_2, \ldots, x_n) = f(x)$ is called *quasi-concave* if, for all y_0 in its range, the set of all points $x = (x_1, x_2, \ldots, x_n)$ for which $f(x) \geqq y_0$, is convex. f is called *concave* if, for all λ A in the interval $0 \leqq \lambda \leqq 1$, $f[(1-\lambda)x + \lambda x'] \geqq (1-\lambda)f(x) + \lambda f(x')$.$f$ is called *positive homogeneous of degree* r if, for all $\lambda>0$, $f(\lambda x) = \lambda^r f(x)$, and simply *positive homogeneous* in case $r = 1$. If f is quasi-concave and positive homogeneous of degree r where $0 \leqq\leqq r1$, then f is concave. The problem of maximizing a quasi-concave function which is positive homogeneous of degree $r>0$ is obviously equivalent to the problem of maximizing an appropriate concave function which is positive homogeneous of degree 1 (the new function being the old one raised to the power 1/r).

comparative advantage) to Germany's maximum output b' of linen (in which she has a comparative advantage); furthermore this last ratio, a''/b', will be precisely the equilibrium price ratio of linen to cloth. If, instead, $a''/b'<a'/b'<a''/b''$ (i.e., England is "small"), then the equilibrium price ratio will be equal to Germany's cost ratio a'/b', so England will specialize in cloth and Germany will produce both linen and cloth; and if $a'/b'<a''/b''<a''/b'$ (i.e., England is "large"), then the equilibrium price ratio will be equal to England's cost ratio a''/b'', hence Germany will specialize in linen and England will produce both linen and cloth.

This is Mill's Law of International Value. In its astonishing simplicity, it must stand as one of the great achievements of the human intellect; and yet it has passed practically unnoticed for over a hundred years, if only because it was so advanced for its time.

Mill's law is illustrated in Figure 1, where the x-axis measures the quantity of cloth, and the y-axis the quantity of linen. Following

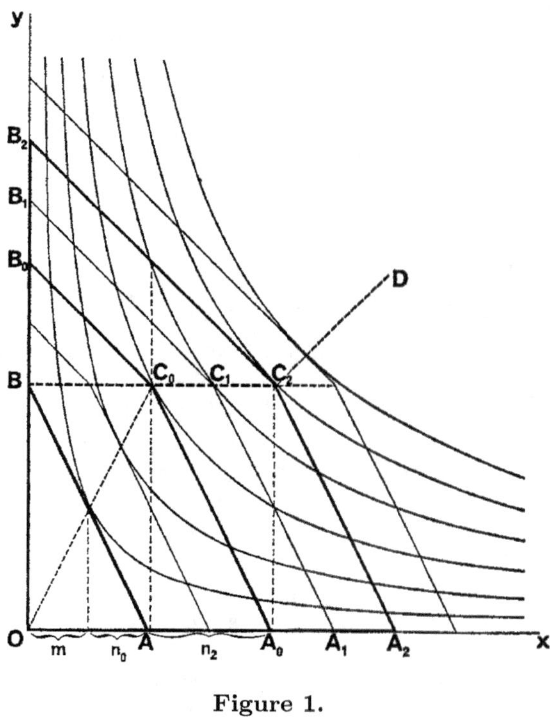

Figure 1.

Mill's illustration, we have for Germany $a' = 100 =$ its maximum output of cloth, and $b' = 200 =$ its maximum output of linen; and for England, $a'' = 100$ and $b'' = 100$ for its maximum outputs of cloth and linen. Germany's production possibility set is OAB (where OA has length a', and OB has length b'). England's production possibility set is shown displaced, at BC_0B_0 (where BC_0 has length a'', and BB_0 has length b''), its true origin being at O rather than B. Then $OA_0C_0B_0$ is the world production possibility set, which is the sum of the other two, and it is obtained geometrically by sliding BC_0B_0 down the edge BA in the manner described by Lerner (1932); such sets have been depicted by Whitin (1953, p. 523), McKenzie (1954a, p. 151), and Dorfman, Samuelson, and Solow (1958, p. 35). The indifference curve touching $B_0C_0A_0$ at C_0 is tangent to A_0C_0, whose slope is Germany's cost ratio. At the other extreme, if England's displaced production possibility set is $BC_2\,B_2$ (showing the same comparative advantage but a greater absolute advantage), the world production possibility set becomes $OA_2C_2B_2$, and the indifference curve touching $B_2C_2A_2$ at C_2 is tangent to B_2C_2 , whose slope is England's cost ratio. In the intermediate case in which England's production possibility set is given by BC_1B_1, the indifference curve touching $B_1C_1A_1$ at C_1 is tangent to neither B_1C_1 nor C_1A_1. The broken line $OC_0C_1C_2D$ is the locus of equilibrium points corresponding to all the possible absolute advantages England might have while maintaining the same comparative advantage; in the stretch OC_0 only England specializes, in the interval C_0C_2 both countries specialize, and thereafter only Germany specializes.

The meaning of the inequality (1.3) may be brought out more sharply after it is multiplied through by b'/a'' to obtain $a'/a'' \leqq 1 \leqq b'/b''$. This yields the following equivalent condition: Given that consumers in each country have utility functions of the form $U = xy$, both countries specialize if and only if

$$a' \leqq a'' \quad \text{and} \quad b'' \leqq b', \tag{1.4}$$

that is, if and only if each country has actually an absolute advantage, rather than just a comparative advantage, in the production of one of the commodities. This conclusion, which, it must be recalled, depends crucially on the assumption of unit elasticities of substitution, conflicts with a literal reading of the classical statement by James Mill (1826, p. 123): "When both countries can produce both commodities, it is not greater absolute, but greater relative, facility, that induces one of them to confine [*sic*] itself to the production of one of the commodities, and to import the other." The statements by Ricardo (1817, p. 135) and Torrens (1826, p. 39) also fail to bring out the distinction between conditions for trade and conditions for complete specialization.

Mill stated his Law of International Value in terms of the cloth previously consumed (and produced) by Germany (before trade), which, owing to the special nature of the utility function $V = x^{\frac{1}{2}}y^{\frac{1}{2}}$, would necessarily be half of its maximum output of cloth, or $m = a'/2$; and in terms of the additional cloth England can make after withdrawing from the production of linen, which likewise (given the same utility function $V = x^{\frac{1}{2}}y^{\frac{1}{2}}$) must be $n = a'' - a''/2 = a''/2$, since England will always consume exactly half of its maximum output of cloth. Writing $p = b'/a'$ and $q = b''/a''$ for the cost ratios of cloth in terms of linen, in Germany and England respectively, and multiplying (1.3) through by $b'/2$, we obtain which is the form in which the inequality was originally stated by Mill (1852a, p. 159).[10]

$$m \leqq n \leqq \frac{p}{q}m, \tag{1.5}$$

Mill's inequality can be stated in yet another way. Pareto (1909, pp. 507–11), without making reference to Mill, questioned Ricardo's assumption that the terms of trade would settle strictly in between

---

[10]Mill's statement of this inequality contains a qualification (1852a, p. 159n) to the effect that "n is always, practically speaking, confined within these limits." At first he gave an explanation of how, if $n < m$, Germany would produce both linen and cloth, since England could not provide all Germany's requirements for cloth, and "that England therefore would be able permanently to sell her ... cloth at the German cost of production." This is precisely the possibility later emphasized by Graham (1923, 1948), although Graham made no reference in his writings to this section of Mill's famous chapter. Mill went on, however, to argue that this

the two countries' comparative cost ratios. Pointing out that specialization could lead to a reduction in the world output of one of the commodities, he argued correctly that, without taking account of tastes, one could not justify the assumption that the increased world output of the other commodity would provide sufficient compensation. He went on to argue, less convincingly (pp. 508–9), that "in order that Ricardo's conclusion be certainly true," the total output of each good should be larger when there is complete specialization than would be the corresponding equilibrium output (and consumption) that would obtain in the absence of trade.

Pareto chose as an illustration the case of two individuals capable of producing bread and beads; if they should trade and specialize, this might lead to a reduction in the total output of bread, and there would be no guarantee that this would be adequately compensated for by an increase in the total output of beads. Let each person devote half of his expenditure to each commodity (as in Mill's case), and let x be the quantity of bread and y the quantity of beads. Before trade, production and consumption of bread and beads would be $x' = a'/2$ and $y' = b'/2$ for individual I and $x'' = a''/2$ and $y'' = b''/2$ for individual II; thus the total production and consumption in the absence of trade would be $x = (a' + a'')/2$ and $y = (b' + b''/2)$. Supposing II to have the comparative advantage in bread, so that $a''/b'' > a'/b'$, then complete specialization would entail $x = a''$ and $y = b'$; hence Pareto's criterion implies

$$\frac{a' + a''}{2} \leqq a''; \frac{b' + b''}{2} \leqq b', \tag{1.6}$$

"would not be the practical result," basing himself on the supposition that there would be "other commodities" in which Germany had a relative advantage, permitting England to import them and therefore supply all of Germany's needs for cloth. Here Mill changed his premises in the middle of the argument (as Edgeworth (1894, p. 613n) pointed out), so Graham could have scored a valid point against him; but he could not have done so without withdrawing his charge that Mill never considered more than two commodities. For further discussion of these points see Viner (1937, p. 449).

which is equivalent to (1.4). Thus, under Mill's assumptions, Pareto's criterion is equivalent to Mill's, and it is both necessary and sufficient for complete specialization.

But Mill's assumptions are very special; the conclusion does not even follow if the utility functions are of the form $V = x^{1-\theta}y^{\theta}$ where $0<\theta<1$ (unless $\theta = \frac{1}{2}$). This was recognized by Mill, who attempted to analyze more general cases (1852a, Ch. 18, §§8–9) but whose limited mathematical equipment precluded the derivation of any exact conditions. Pareto stated his conditions as necessary ones, but they are neither necessary nor sufficient in general. That is, even if Pareto's criterion is satisfied, if the elasticity of substitution is small enough it will still be necessary for one country to produce both commodities; and conversely, even if Pareto's criterion is not satisfied, provided the elasticity of substitution is large enough, it may still happen that equilibrium is characterized by complete specialization. Examples of both such cases are readily constructed.

Pareto's paradox, that trade with complete specialization might be incompatible with tastes, seems to be at the root of some perplexing arguments presented by Valavanis (1954); but it will be more convenient to discuss these in Part 3 (Section 3.8) of this article.

As Ricardo was alleged by Pareto and others to have done (but see Viner (1937, p. 452)), so did Taussig (1927) appear to take it for granted that the equilibrium price ratio (terms of trade) would be strictly in between the comparative cost ratios. In discussing one of the usual examples, he said (p. 24): "At any rates between, both countries would gain from an exchange." But this is not true even under Mill's assumptions. If Mill's inequality is not fulfilled, and if the relative price r of the y-good is strictly in between the comparative cost ratios, so that, for instance, $a''/b'<a'/b'<r<a''/b''<a'/b''$, then trade would necessarily lower the world production of one of the goods (the x-good); and with Millian utility functions, at least one of the countries would be worse off, and possibly both, depending on how the production was distributed. This is Pareto's paradox; it is resolved simply by Mill's law, which states that such a situation as the one just described cannot occur, that is, it cannot be a competitive equilibrium. Taussig's explanation (1927, p. 30), "The fact that [the

Americans] give up some wheat in order to get more linen proves that the rearrangement suits them better," is an argument which assumes what has to be proved, namely that there is an intermediate price ratio for which a competitive equilibrium exists. What Taussig should have said (and possibly meant to say) was that "at any *equilibrium* rates between, both countries would gain from an exchange"; and there need not be any equilibrium rates strictly in between.

Mill's law contains an important corollary, referred to by Edgeworth (1899) as "Mill's paradox," which is also illustrated in Figure 1. In Mill's words (1852a, p. 163): "the richest countries, *caeteris paribus,* gain the least by a given amount of foreign commerce: since, having a greater demand for commodities generally, they are likely to have a greater demand for foreign commodities, and thus modify the terms of interchange to their own disadvantage." In Figure 1, what today would be called a " "neutral technological change" is shown, for England, by the successive production possibility sets BB_0C_0, BB_1C_1, BB_2C_2, and the corresponding world production possibility sets OB_0 C_0A_0, $OB_1C_1A_1$, $OB_2C_2A_2$. England's terms of trade (the ratio of the price of the x-good to that of the y-good) are given by the slope of the indifference curve passing through C_0, C_1, C_2; the terms of trade stay constant along OC_0 (at Germany's cost ratio), decline along $C_0C_1C_2$ (the zone of complete specialization), and stay constant thereafter along C_2D (at England's cost ratio).

It follows that a neutral technological improvement, or general increase in productivity, results in a worsening of the developing country's terms of trade, and this for the simple reason that a market must be found for the increased relative quantity in world markets of the growing country's export goods. Thus "Mill's paradox" is not a paradox at all; rather, it is another name for the Law of Demand. It had already been anticipated by Torrens (1837, pp. 132–3) who observed that "if, in the markets of America, the demand for English goods should remain stationary, while the supply of them should be increased, then, in the American markets, a given quantity of English goods would exchange for a less quantity of American produce than before." Torrens then went on to argue that "on these obvious, and universally admitted principles of commerce, we can explain the process by which, in a commercial and manufacturing country, importing raw produce, the increase of commercial and manufacturing capital may lower the wages of the operative class." This formed the basis for his advocacy of a policy of emigration.

Mill said that the richest countries gain the least; he did not say that they lose. However, Edgeworth (1894, pp. 40–41) took up the question on the basis of Mill's earlier treatment (1852a, Ch. 18, §5) to argue that an improvement in the export industry might actually make the exporting country worse off. There ensued a controversy in which Nicholson (1897, pp. 310–11), Edgeworth (1899), and Bastable (1903, pp. 185–7) took part, and which has been discussed by Bhagwati and Johnson (1960). The phenomenon has been emphasized by Bhagwati (1958), who has called it "immiserizing growth." The question of whether a technological "improvement" can actually worsen a country's welfare is a subtle and involved one, which we cannot go into here. Suffice it to say that a worsening of the terms of trade can be expected to be more severe (1) if the improvement is confined largely to the export industry, and (2) if the elasticity of substitution between the two commodities is low, i.e., if demand is inelastic.[11]

[11] A voluminous literature on these questions has developed in recent years, and will be dis cussed in the sequel. A related phenomenon, referred to by Duncan (1938) as "Marshall's paradox," has also received considerable attention over the years; see Marshall (1923, pp. 177–80, 342–8), Graham (1932, pp. 600–2), Viner (1937, pp. 538–46), Allen (1952), Kemp (1956), and Bhagwati and Johnson (1960). Marshall's paradox consists in the statement that an increase in England's demand for German goods will result in a greater worsening of England's terms of trade if England's reciprocal demand is elastic (rather than inelastic, as just stated above in the text). As Duncan (1938, pp. 358–61) pointed out, this conclusion follows from Marshall's definition of a shift in demand as an increase in the amount of exports offered for a given amount of imports, whereas the opposite conclusion would result from Graham's (1932) definition of the shift as an increase in imports demanded for a given amount of exports. For the problem of technological change, Graham's definition is the appropriate one, Marshall's being better suited to applications in the field of commercial policy; see Bhagwati and Johnson (1960, pp. 78–9).

In conclusion, there are two quite significant features of Mill's law which are apparent in the light of modern developments. One is that it constitutes a genuine and correct proof of the existence of equilibrium, although of course Mill's mathematical limitations forced him to make very stringent assumptions. But one will not find a rigorous existence proof of any kind again until eighty years later in the work of Wald (1933–34, 1934–35). And even McKenzie's existence proof (1954a) retains all the assumptions made by Mill with the exception that the model is extended to include any number of commodities and countries; this remark is not intended in any way to detract from the importance of McKenzie's work (since, after all, the principal mathematical difficulties involved in fixed point theorems arise only in three or more dimensions, and McKenzie's methods are powerful enough to handle much more general cases), but rather to emphasize a feature of Mill's work which went unappreciated by his followers, including economists of such eminence as Edgeworth and Marshall.[12]

The second feature of Mill's law that is of particular interest today is the inequality, which establishes conditions for full or partial specialization. Considerations of this kind turn out to be of great importance for the factor price equalization theorem, as will be apparent later on in Part 3 of this article. From geometric considerations it is evident that Mill's conditions can be generalized along the following lines: the likelihood of complete specialization varies directly with (1) the elasticity of substitution between commodities, and (2) the relative equality in absolute advantages among countries.

[12]In discussing the relevant section of Mill's *Principles,* Marshall concluded (1923, pp. 354–5n) that "there is no problem to be solved at all." But this conclusion followed from an error in his diagram, which failed to talce account of the fact that each country's offer curve would, under Mill's assumptions, start off with a flat segment, and then proceed with a vertical one. This had already been spelled out by Edgeworth in a six-page footnote (1894, pp. 609–14n) which, it must be concluded, Marshall had never bothered to read! Metzler (1950, p. 303n), in the footnote already cited twice (footnotes 6 and 7 above), stated: "Marshall pointed out the error in Mill's earlier treatment of the subject." But it was Marshall who was in error, not Mill.

In order to make a case for the prevalance of partial specialization (one of the principal premises of the factor price equalization theorem), if Mill's framework is retained, one must let it rest on either (1) a low elasticity of substitution in consumption, or (2) inequality in absolute advantages, or both. It is natural to ask whether these criteria must in any way be modified or supplemented if one goes outside Mill's (and Graham's) framework. It will be seen presently that both (3) trade in intermediate products and (4) introduction of more factors of production increase the likelihood of incomplete specialization.

1.3. *Precursors of The "Superstructure": Thornton and Whewell*

There is still a certain amount of mystery surrounding Mill's supplementary sections that warrants some comment. Mill opened the new sections (1852a, Ch. 18, §§6–9) with the statement: "Thus far had the theory of international values been carried in the first and second editions of this work. But intelligent criticisms, and subsequent further investigations, have shown that the doctrine stated in the preceding pages, though correct as far as it goes, is not yet the complete theory of the subject matter." In the sixth edition (1865, p. 360), after the words "intelligent criticisms," there appears for the first time the explanation: "(chiefly those of my friend Mr. William Thornton)"; but no other changes were added. The following year Thornton (1866) published — long after the appearance of the third edition — some rather naive criticisms of the law of supply and demand, to which Mill subsequently replied (1869) in a careful and searching restatement. Thornton had evidently, in private conversation, stimulated Mill into rethinking the basic issues of the existence and uniqueness of equilibrium. None of these discussions was specifically related to international trade, however, and Mill's acknowledgment to Thornton seems like a curious afterthought — a bouquet to a close friend.

The only work of that period bearing any relation to Mill's law is that of Whewell (1856). Whewell's memoir was presented to the Cambridge Philosophical Society in 1850, and according to

Viner (1937, p. 450n), it was "printed in the same year for private circulation," though it did not appear in the Society's *Transactions* until 1856. Viner goes on to say: "Since it was primarily a criticism of Mill's doctrines, Mill may have been acquainted with it." It is scarcely conceivable that he was not, for the memoir is devoted entirely to Mill's first essay (1844) and is an honest attempt to translate Mill's argument into mathematical language. Whewell developed (pp. 130–2) the concept of "susceptibility" of demand (equal to one minus the elasticity of demand) and addressed himself to the problem of the conditions for complete specialization, given the cost conditions and demand susceptibilities in each country. He also developed (p. 146) the concept of "transferable capital," which was later contained in Mill's new sections (§7–8) and became the object of criticism on the part of Edgeworth (1894, p. 609), Bastable (1903, p. 29), and Marshall (1923, pp. 354–5). Whewell derived an inequality (p. 143) for the characterization of solutions with complete specialization; unfortunately a slip entered his argument, and his formulas are therefore valid only for certain values of the parameters.[13] From what is known concerning Mill and Whewell, the following inference seems plausible: that Mill saw Whewell's memoir and found it of considerable interest, yet did not trouble himself to go through the algebra, and may even (correctly) have suspected it of being faulty; and that if his suspicions were not enough, his deep antagonism towards Whewell would be sufficient to explain the lack of any specific acknowledgment.[14]

[13]Whewell assumed (1850, p. 143, line 3 of the text) that $x < k$ implies $tx < tk$, forgetting that this is true only if $t > 0$. Under Mill's assumptions of zero susceptibilities, Whewell's formula would give $t = -a''/a' < 0$. Had he possessed an economist's intuition, Whewell might have spotted this error after interpreting the result; except for this slip, Whewell's treatment seems to be quite valid and even ingenious, and one can only lament the fact that, having gone so far, he fell just short of deriving the correct conditions.

[14]The Rev. Dr. William Whewell was the leader of the anti-utilitarian intuitionist ("moral sense") school of ethics, and his views on these subjects aroused bitter feelings in Mill; see the latter's *Lettres Inédites à Auguste Compte,* p. 358. The very year of publication of the third edition of his *Principles,* Mill also published a blistering attack on Whewell in the *Westminster Review* (1852b) in which he

1.4. *Graham*

After Mill, the issues dealt with above receded to a great extent into the background, owing largely to the erosion of Mill's theory of value with its assumption of constant costs. The methodology of marginal analysis, with its inability to cope with corner solutions, also contributed to this de-emphasis. But the modern emphasis on the importance of inequality constraints has led to a revival of interest in the classical problems. Two post-Millian developments are especially noteworthy in their foreshadowing of modern ones: one is that of Mangoldt (1863), to be taken up in Section 1.6 below; the other is that of Graham (1923, 1932, 1948), who pursued an iconoclastic course which Haberler (1961, p. 10) has aptly described as "ultra-classical."

Graham believed that limiting price ratios were the rule, and intermediate "limbo" price ratios (1948, p. 35) the exception; he claimed with great vehemence that Mill had held the contrary view, a charge which is without foundation.[15] In spite of his protestations, his own work, much more so than that of others, is largely an elaboration of Mill's doctrines, and to some extent even a retrogression from them. It could be said of Graham what Mill already had said of Thornton (1869, p. 513): "If there is a fault to be found with him, it is one that he has in common with all those improvers of political economy by whom new and just views 'have been promulgated as contradictions of the doctrine received as fundamental, instead of being, what they almost always are, developments of them.' "

---

summarized his opinions of Whewell's work in moral philosophy in the words (p. 189): "it can scarcely be counted as any thing more than one of the thousand waves on the dead sea of commonplace." That Mill nevertheless took Whewell very seriously is evident from his *System of Logic* (especially Book III), where he discussed Whewell's epistemological writings at great length, and where he acknowledged in the Preface that this portion (pp. 185–418) of his *Logic* would not have been written but for Whewell's *History of the Inductive Sciences.* All this serves merely to establish that it is almost impossible to believe that Mill was unacquainted with Whewell's 1850 memoir.

[15]In making this assertion, I am glad to invoke the authoritative support of Viner (1937, pp. 448–9).

Graham retained Mill's assumption of constant costs, and based his conclusions on numerical examples. In one of these (1948, pp. 79–82) he assumed that commodities were consumed in fixed proportions, an assumption which practically guaranteed the extreme solution. For the most part he retained Mill's assumption of a unitary elasticity of substitution in consumption, and therefore based his claim, at least in the case of two countries and two commodities, largely on the belief that countries were of unequal size.

Graham's views rested heavily on the belief that the terms of trade were empirically stable; this belief was combined with a somewhat unusual view of human nature, according to which demand, although stable with respect to price, was highly volatile and subject to the "shifting winds of desire" (1948, p. 33); he also expressed mortification over the notion of a "naked theory of demand" (p. 37). Thus, on this premise, if limbo prices were the rule, one would observe violent fluctuations in prices, which (he said) one does not; as Metzler pointed out (1950, p. 320), from the same reasoning one would observe, on Graham's premise, violent fluctuations in output. Graham failed to appreciate the importance, pointed out by Cournot (1838, Ch. 4), of the law of large numbers and the consequent stability of aggregate demand; such stability (in the sense of low variance) has been borne out by many econometric studies (e.g., Houthakker (1957)).

Of greater interest was Graham's attempt to liberate the theory of international values from the assumption of two countries and two commodities. This had already been begun by Mill (1852a, Ch. 18, §9) and continued by Mangoldt (1863, pp. 185–224), Edgeworth (1894, pp. 630–5), and Viner (1937, pp. 459–67). The essence of Graham's doctrine lay in the idea of "linked competition" (1932), of which two examples may be mentioned: (1) There may be a third country with relative costs (between two commodities) intermediate between the relative costs of two given countries; in this case the world price ratio may coincide with the intermediate country's cost ratio, hence shifts in world demand will be reflected in reallocation of resources (labor) in the intermediate country, rather than in price movements. (2) If there are three commodities (and two countries), there may be complete specialization in two of the goods (one by each country) and production in both countries of the third good (at equal cost); again adjustments would take place via labor movements between the two industries in each country, rather than via changes in the terms of trade.

Graham's analysis suffered from dependence on numerical examples, and from the use of a confusing mathematical notation which apparently derives from Bastable (1903) and which has been perpetuated by some of his followers.[16] Most readers will find Metzler's exposition (1950) more rewarding, to which one may add the analyses of Elliott (1950), Becker (1952), and Whitin (1953), as well as the very thorough developments by McKenzie (1954a, 1954b, 1955–56). Elliott (1950, p. 23) made a valiant attempt to translate Graham's analysis into Marshallian terms, and displayed offer curves with numerous flat segments; his approach closely followed a many-commodity example considered by Marshall (1923, pp. 323–5). Elliott's construction, which is quite ingenious, is closely related to those of Mangoldt and Edgeworth; discussion of it will therefore be resumed in Section 1.6 below. Elliott concluded that numerical examples had prejudiced Graham's conclusions; McKenzie (1954b, pp. 176–7) likewise rejected Graham's presumption that "limbo" prices were improbable on a priori grounds.

1.5. *Modern Developments: McKenzie, Whitin, and Others*

It became apparent soon after the pioneering development of activity analysis and linear programming by Koopmans (1951a) and Dantzig (1951a) that these new methods were particularly appropriate for the

[16]I refer to the custom, which goes back at least to Mangoldt (1863), of using a mathematical expression such as "$20x = 30y$" to mean "20 units of commodity (x) exchange for 30 units of commodity (y)" (see, e.g., Elliott (1950, p. 23), and Whitin (1953, p. 532)). For such an equation to make any sense, either the symbols x and y must be thought of as coordinate vectors in the commodity space, and the equality sign must be thought of as denoting the relation "is exchanged for" or "has the same value as"; or else x and y must be considered as being the prices of the respective commodities.

analysis of classical models. In quick succession contributions were made to the literature by Samuelson (1952), Reiter (1953), Whitin (1953), Isard and Peck (1954), McKenzie (1954a, 1954b, 1955–56), Beckmann (1957), Dorfman, Samuelson, and Solow (1958), and Jones (1961).

Whitin (1953) considered the question of limbo prices from a geometrical point of view, taking up models with two or three countries and two or three commodities and adopting the assumption of unitary elasticity of substitution. It is a measure of Graham's influence that Whitin, though echoing Graham's cavils against Mill, was unaware of the fact that Mill had solved the problem for the case of two countries and two commodities almost exactly one hundred years before. In his mathematical appendix, Whitin formulated the problem as one in *linear* programming, which would correspond to infinite elasticity of substitution in consumption. Schumann and Todt (1957) pointed out that Whitin's algebra did not correspond to his geometry, which would instead call for the use of nonlinear programming (cf. Kuhn and Tucker (1951)).

The problem of international values was also taken up by Dorfman, Samuelson, and Solow (1958, pp. 31–45), who stated that the equilibrium solution would "almost certainly" be one of complete specialization. Again, this resulted from their use of a linear objective function, implying that both commodities were perfect substitutes.

In a significant paper, McKenzie (1954a) took up the Mill-Graham model in full generality. As has already been indicated, if the inhabitants of each country have utility functions of the Millian form $U = x_1^{\alpha 1} x_1^{\alpha 2} \ldots x_n^{\alpha n}$ (with the same parameters in all countries), the problem of equilibrium international values reduces to the problem of maximizing U subject to the appropriate linear inequalities in the nonnegative x_i's, a problem in homogeneous programming. While McKenzie adopted this assumption, his approach is more powerful and admits of much weaker assumptions about demand.[17]

[17]McKenzie stated (1954a, p. 155): "Assuming the demand functions to be continuous functions of the prices of final goods, I should conjecture that elementary proofs do not exist of this theorem unless the demand functions are

His method can be roughly described as follows: (1) corresponding to any arbitrary selection of (normalized) commodity prices (which are nonnegative and add up to unity), one can compute (from the demand functions and the zero-profit conditions of competition) the world demand for each good;[18] (2) the latter determines a ray in the commodity space and a unique intersection with the boundary of the world production possibility set; (3) the latter point on the production surface determines in turn either (a) a unique price vector — if the point is inside an (n–1)-dimensional face of the production possibility surface, or (b) a closed convex set of such vectors — if the point is in a face of lower dimension (a vertex being considered to be a 0-dimensional face). These three steps define a multi-valued mapping from the set of normalized prices into itself; this mapping has values which are closed convex sets, and it is upper semicontinuous (generalizing continuity to multi-valued mappings), so the fixed point theorem of Kakutani (1941) applies. There are difficult technical points of the proof, such as the proof of continuity and the problem of how to deal with zero prices.

---

drastically restricted." His own demand functions, being of the same form as Mill's and Graham's, are quite special; in particular, they imply identical and homothetic utility functions in every country, permitting the equilibrium problem to be translated into one in homogeneous programming. Moreover, the special form $U = \Pi_{i=1}^{\pi} x_i^{\alpha_i}$ of the utility functions, combined with the assumption of constant costs, gives rise to demand functions with linear segments, as shown by Edgeworth (1894, pp. 610–12n) and Elliott (1950, p. 23), and it is this fact that made for the simplicity of Mill's original treatment (1852a, Ch. 18, §7) and which caused Marshall (1923, p. 355n) to say that "there is no problem to be solved at all." By exploiting these simple features of the problem, an elementary (and constructive) proof of McKenzie's theorem can therefore be obtained after all.

[18]Geometrically, this corresponds to determining the supporting hyperplane to the world production possibility set, and then the point of maximum utility in this hyperplane; see the familiar diagrams in Viner (1937, p. 521), Leontief (1933, Fig. 4), and Lerner (1934, Fig. 2). It is suggestive to think of this proof in the following way: Let the "world" be thought of as an aggregate which, at any fixed prices, has determinate (not necessarily unique) net supplies and demands for all goods, vis-á-vis some imaginary outside universe; then the proof consists in establishing that there is at least one set of prices for which these net supplies and demands will all be zero. This approach shows that the international trade analogy is helpful even in establishing the possibility of autarky.

McKenzie followed this contribution with two papers (1954b, 1955–56) on the problem of efficiency in Graham models. His analysis may first of all be taken up from the standpoint of the simple two-country two-commodity case considered by Mill. Defining $u' = x'/a', v' = y'/b', u'' = x''/a'', v'' = y''/b''$, and recalling that $x = x' + x'', y = y' + y''$, the inequalities (1.1) become

$$\begin{aligned} x - a'u' - a''u'' &= 0, \\ y - b'v' - b''v'' &= 0, \\ u' + v' + \delta' &= 1, \\ u'' + v'' + \delta'' &= 1, \end{aligned} \tag{1.7}$$

where the variables $x, y, u', u'', v', v'', \delta', \delta''$ are all nonnegative, δ' and δ'' being the levels of the "disposal activities," allowing for the possibility of unemployment. The parameters a', a'', b', b'' are, of course, strictly positive, and the assumption implied by (1.7) that each country has exactly one unit of labor available is not restrictive (i.e., does not imply that the countries are of equal size or productivity), since labor need not be measured in the same units in the different countries. Thus if country I is larger (or more productive) then country II, $a'$and b' will be correspondingly higher than a'' and b''.

The system of equations (1.7) may be written in matrix notation as

$$\begin{bmatrix} -a' & 0 & -a'' & 0 & 1 & 0 & 0 & 0 \\ 0 & -b' & 0 & -b'' & 0 & 1 & 0 & 0 \\ 1 & 1 & 0 & 0 & 0 & 0 & 1 & 0 \\ 0 & 0 & 1 & 1 & 0 & 0 & 0 & 1 \end{bmatrix} \begin{bmatrix} u' \\ v' \\ u'' \\ v'' \\ x \\ y \\ \delta' \\ \delta'' \end{bmatrix} = \begin{bmatrix} 0 \\ 0 \\ 1 \\ 1 \end{bmatrix}. \tag{1.8}$$

The model is readily extended to the case of n commodities and m countries, yielding the $n + m$ equations

$$-\sum_{j=1}^{m} a_{ij}u_{ij} + x_i = 0 \qquad (i = 1, 2, 3, \ldots, n),$$
$$\sum_{i=1}^{n} u_{ij} + \delta_j = 1 \qquad (j = 1, 2, 3, \ldots, m), \tag{1.9}$$

where $\mathrm{a}_{11}, a_{12}, a_{21}, \ldots$ take the place of $a', a'', b', \ldots$ and so on.

It is well known (see Dantzig (1951a)) that if a feasible solution to (1.9) exists (that is, one with all variables $\geqq 0$), then a basic feasible solution exists (one with $n + m$ variables $\geqq 0$ and the remainder $= 0$). It is obvious, furthermore, that a feasible solution exists: e.g., there is always the trivial solution with $u_{ij} = x_i = 0$ and $\delta_j = 1$. But what is important to establish in the present case is that a nontrivial basic feasible solution exists (one with no unemployment, i.e., with all $\delta_j = 0$), and furthermore that the model shares with the transportation models of Hitchcock and Koopmans (see Koopmans (1949), Koopmans and Reiter (1951), and Dantzig (1951b)) the important property of triangularity, to be described below. Dantzig's algorithm therefore applies, and this is what underlies the graphical technique used by McKenzie (1954b); an exposition and interpretation of Dantzig's algorithm has been presented by Dorfman, Samuelson, and Solow (1958, pp. 117–21).

The existence of a nontrivial basic feasible solution can be demonstrated by a simple argument. Following McKenzie (1954b), a solution may be called a *specialization* if each country specializes in exactly one commodity (these need not be distinct); thus there are n^m possible specializations. Any specialization contains m productive activities and produces, say, $k \leqq \min\,(m, n)$ commodities; if to these we adjoin the corresponding k consumption activities, the resulting solution is clearly feasible, proving that a nontrivial basic feasible solution always exists. Moreover, the basic matrix corresponding to this solution, after suitable rearrangement of columns, is always upper triangular. For example, as one of the possible solutions of

(1.8) we have:

$$\begin{bmatrix} 1 & 0 & 0 & -a'' \\ 0 & 1 & -b' & 0 \\ 0 & 0 & 1 & 0 \\ 0 & 0 & 0 & 1 \end{bmatrix} \begin{bmatrix} x \\ y \\ v' \\ u'' \end{bmatrix} = \begin{bmatrix} 0 \\ 0 \\ 1 \\ 1 \end{bmatrix};$$

the triangularity makes it possible to solve by back substitution, obtaining $u'' = 1, v' = l, y = b'v' = b'$, and $x = a''u'' = a''$.

Not only is it true that every specialization is triangular, but furthermore, every nontrivial basic feasible solution can be shown to be representable in triangular form. The argument, while it proceeds in elementary steps, is intricate, and will not be reproduced here.[19]

In order to analyze the problem of efficient specialization, one can choose some arbitrary set of prices, and maximize the value of output; when this is done for all positive prices, one obtains the "efficient frontier." For example, in the case of three goods and two countries, with quantities x, y, z and prices p, q, r, we must maximize the linear function

$$f = px + qy + rz$$

[19]The proof derives from that of Dantzig (1951b); a good exposition of the method of proof, which lays bare the mathematical theory underlying Dantzig's method, will be found in Chapter 6 of Garvin (1960, esp. pp. 89–90). The following example will illustrate how the triangularity condition should be interpreted:

$$\begin{bmatrix} 1 & 0 & -a' & -a'' \\ 0 & -b' & 0 & 0 \\ 0 & 1 & 1 & 0 \\ 0 & 0 & 0 & 1 \end{bmatrix} \begin{bmatrix} x \\ v' \\ u' \\ u'' \end{bmatrix} = \begin{bmatrix} 0 \\ 0 \\ 1 \\ 1 \end{bmatrix}.$$

The basis here is not triangular, yet the solution is feasible, in apparent contradiction to what has just been claimed. But it is degenerate, with $v' = 0$, and can be replaced by the equivalent (also degenerate) basis

$$\begin{bmatrix} 1 & 0 & -a' & -a'' \\ 0 & 1 & 0 & 0 \\ 0 & 0 & 1 & 0 \\ 0 & 0 & 0 & 1 \end{bmatrix} \begin{bmatrix} x \\ y \\ u' \\ u'' \end{bmatrix} = \begin{bmatrix} 0 \\ 0 \\ 1 \\ 1 \end{bmatrix},$$

which is now triangular.

subject to

$$\begin{bmatrix} -a' & 0 & 0 & -a'' & 0 & 0 & 1\,0\,0\,0\,0 \\ 0 & -b' & 0 & 0 & -b'' & 0 & 0\,1\,0\,0\,0 \\ 0 & 0 & -c' & 0 & 0 & -c'' & 0\,0\,1\,0\,0 \\ 1 & 1 & 1 & 0 & 0 & 0 & 0\,0\,0\,1\,0 \\ 0 & 0 & 0 & 1 & 1 & 1 & 0\,0\,0\,0\,1 \end{bmatrix} \begin{bmatrix} u' \\ v' \\ w' \\ u'' \\ v'' \\ w'' \\ x \\ y \\ z \\ \delta' \\ \delta'' \end{bmatrix} = \begin{bmatrix} 0 \\ 0 \\ 0 \\ 1 \\ 1 \end{bmatrix}. \tag{1.10}$$

Suppose an optimal basis is given by

$$\begin{bmatrix} 1\,0\,0 & 0 & -a'' \\ 0\,1\,0 & -b' & 0 \\ 0\,0\,1 & 0 & 0 \\ 0\,0\,0 & 1 & 0 \\ 0\,0\,0 & 0 & 1 \end{bmatrix} \begin{bmatrix} x \\ y \\ z \\ v' \\ u'' \end{bmatrix} = \begin{bmatrix} 0 \\ 0 \\ 0 \\ 1 \\ 1 \end{bmatrix} - \begin{bmatrix} -a' & 0 & 0 & 0 & 0\,0 \\ 0 & 0 & -b'' & 0 & 0\,0 \\ 0 & -c' & 0 & -c'' & 0\,0 \\ 1 & 1 & 0 & 0 & 1\,0 \\ 0 & 0 & 1 & 1 & 0\,1 \end{bmatrix} \begin{bmatrix} u' \\ w' \\ v'' \\ w'' \\ \delta' \\ \delta'' \end{bmatrix},$$

where the variables on the right are set equal to 0. This has the explicit solution

$$\begin{bmatrix} x \\ y \\ z \\ v' \\ u'' \end{bmatrix} = \begin{bmatrix} a'' \\ b' \\ 0 \\ 1 \\ 1 \end{bmatrix} - \begin{bmatrix} -a' & 0 & a'' & a'' & 0 & a'' \\ b' & b' & -b'' & 0 & b' & 0 \\ 0 & -c' & 0 & -c'' & 0 & 0 \\ 1 & 1 & 0 & 0 & 1 & 0 \\ 0 & 0 & 1 & 1 & 0 & 1 \end{bmatrix} \begin{bmatrix} u' \\ w' \\ v'' \\ w'' \\ \delta' \\ \delta'' \end{bmatrix}, \tag{1.11}$$

indicating that if the variables on the right are set equal to zero then country I will specialize in (y),country II in (x),and that (z) will not be produced. Substituting these values for x, y, z in the objective function f, we obtain

$$\begin{aligned} f = pa'' + qb' - (qb' - pa')u' - (qb' - rc')w' - (pa'' - qb'')v'' \\ -(pa'' - rc'')w'' - qb's' - pa''\delta''. \end{aligned} \quad (1.12)$$

For the basis to be optimal, the coefficients of the variables on the right must be $\geqq 0$, by Dantzig's simplex criterion. Certainly $qb' > 0$ and $pa'' > 0$ by assumption, hence $\delta' = \delta'' = 0$. Now from $qb' - pa' \geqq 0$ and $pa'' - qb'' \geqq 0$ we have $a'/b' \leqq q/p \leqq a''/b''$, that is, country I has a comparative advantage in (y) and country II in (x), just as in Section 1.2 above.

In order that the z-good be produced at all, it is necessary that the above solution be *non-unique,* which entails either $qb' - rc' = 0$ or $pa'' - rc'' = 0$. Thus, if (z) is to be produced in I, then $w'>0$ and $qb' = re'$, i.e., the relative price r/q of (z) and (y) must be equal to the corresponding cost ratio b'/c' in country I. Likewise, if (z) is to be produced in II, then $w'' > 0$ and $pa'' = rc''$, i.e., the relative price r/p of (z) and (x) must be equal to the corresponding cost ratio a''/c'' in country II. This provides one of the bases for Graham's phenomenon of "linked competition."

Whitin (1953, p. 532) supported Graham's contention that "a country may import a commodity in the production of which it possesses a comparative advantage". In our notation, he assumed $a' = b' = 24, c' = 8, a'' = 16, b'' = 32, c'' = 96$, and chose as utility function $U = x^{\frac{1}{4}} y^{\frac{1}{2}} z^{\frac{1}{4}}$. He showed that country I would specialize in (x), and II in (z), and that country I would both produce and import commodity (y) "in the production of which it has a comparative advantage" (p. 533). But this conclusion depends on how one defines the term "comparative advantage." If the expression means that there exists another commodity ((z) in this case) such that, relative to that commodity, I's cost ratio $c'/b' = \frac{1}{3}$ is less than II's cost ratio $c''/b'' = 3$, then in Whitin's example one would have to say that both countries had a comparative advantage in (y) simultaneously, since with respect to (x), II's cost ratio $a''/b'' = \frac{1}{2}$ is less than I's cost ratio $a'/b' = 1$. On the other hand, if comparative advantage in a commodity is understood to mean that the cost ratio is smaller than that of other countries with respect to *every* other commodity, then in Whitin's example it could only be said that country I had a comparative advantage in (x), and country II in (z), and that neither country had a comparative advantage in (y). Thus, like many of Graham's extravagant claims, this one must be regarded as a gigantic quibble.

On the other hand, one interesting fact is brought out by Whitin's analysis, and that is that if there are more commodities than countries, and if utility functions have the form $U = x^{\alpha}y^{\beta}z^{y}$ (guaranteeing that all commodities will be produced and consumed in positive amounts), then several price ratios — a number corresponding to the excess of the number of commodities over the number of countries — will necessarily coincide with some country's cost ratios. This can be seen directly from the fact that if the values for x, y, z in (1.11) are substituted in the utility function $U = xyz$, and the nonlinear terms dropped, we obtain $U = a''b'(c'w' + c''w'')$, showing that the solution with only two commodities cannot be optimal.

When the number of countries is greater than or equal to the number of commodities (the case considered by McKenzie in his examples), there is, as McKenzie (1954b, p. 177) pointed out, no particular reason for preferring on a priori grounds an extreme price to a limbo price. In accordance with Mill's law, one has to rely on either (1) a low elasticity of substitution in consumption, or (2) inequality in absolute advantages, in order to obtain Graham's result. However, in the case in which there are more commodities than countries, the situation is this: if one or both of the above conditions holds, we can expect some price ratios to coincide with cost ratios; otherwise, we can expect that the number of commodities *produced* will be no greater than the number of countries. This is a startling result: under classical assumptions, if absolute advantages are approximately equal and elasticities of substitution relatively high, then there will be a natural tendency for the number of products to be less than or equal to the number of countries. This serves to bring out a point emphasized by Schlesinger (1933–34) and Wald (1933–34), namely that it is methodologically unsound to assume in advance that it is known how many commodities will actually be produced.

There is a further point that needs to be stressed. In the example considered above, suppose that at equilibrium prices it is optimal for country I to specialize in (y), and country II in (x); then the coefficients $qb' - pa'$ of u' and $pa'' - qb''$ of v'' in (1.12) must both be nonnegative, yielding $a'/b' \leqq q/p \leqq a''/b''$. If the third commodity is to be produced, it has already been pointed out that one of the coefficients $qb' - rc'$ of w' or $pa'' - rc''$ of w'' must be zero, hence the price r of (z) must be linked to one of the countries' cost ratios, either by $r/q = b'/c'$ or by $r/p = a''/c''$. This does not necessarily imply, however, that *both* countries will produce (z), as Graham usually assumed. It is interesting to inquire as to the conditions that will lead to this special result of Graham's: the phenomenon of *linked competition* (1932, p. 581; 1948, p. 69).

An interesting necessary condition immediately emerges. In order that (z) be produced in both countries, we must have $qb' - rc' = 0$ and $pa'' - rc'' = 0$ in (1.12), i.e., $r/q = b'/c'$ and $r/p = a''/c''$. Taking the ratio of the last two expressions, we obtain $q/p = (a''/b')(c'/c'')$. Now, it would seem a fair application of the principle of insufficient reason to suppose that both countries have exactly the same absolute advantages (for definiteness, identical production methods) in the production of (z), whence $c' = c''$and $q/p = a''/b'$. Now substituting this in the inequality $a'/b' \leqq q/p \leqq a''/b''$ obtained above, we obtain simply (1.3). Thus Mill's inequality, which (under Mill's assumptions) is necessary and sufficient for specialization in the case of two commodities, turns out to be a necessary condition for the simultaneous production in both countries of a third commodity. The very circumstances that are necessary for linked competition in the case of three commodities are likely to give rise to limbo prices in the case of two commodities; in arguing for the former and against the latter, Graham was trying to have his cake and eat it.

1.6. *Classical Treatments: Mangoldt, Edgeworth, Viner, Elliott, And Others*

Mangoldt (1863) foreshadowed much of the modern analysis in his book, which is rather a rare item,[20] known to most economists only through the exposition and development by Edgeworth (1894) which, in turn, has been further elaborated by Viner (1937).

Mangoldt's approach may best be analyzed in terms of the dual of the above linear programming problem, in which the objective function f was to be maximized subject to (1.10), the variables being constrained to be nonnegative. As shown by Dantzig and Orden (1952), this is equivalent to the dual problem of minimizing the

[20]Walras (1890, p. 320n) drew attention to the fact that Friedrich Kleinwä chter, editor of the second (posthumous) edition of Mangoldt's *Grundriss der Volkswirthschaftslehre* (1871), took it upon himself to omit the diagrams in Sections 62–7 of the text. According to Schumpeter (1954, p. 504), the second edition "leaves out the most original element in it, namely, the geometrical apparatus that Mangoldt devised for the theory of international values; but Edgeworth brought it to light again." Schumpeter also referred (p. 607) "to the first edition of Mangoldt's *Grundriss,* which appeared in 1863 and contains the relevant appendix that the editor of the posthumous second edition of 1871 thought fit to omit." Here, Schumpeter lapsed from his usual standards of scholarship and did not check the original sources. The second edition omits the diagrams (which have nothing to do with international values as such), but leaves the appendix intact. Edgeworth (1894, pp. 630–6) referred to the supply and demand curves in the first edition, but in his discussion of the appendix of Mangoldt's work, his page references were all to the second edition. Viner (1932, p. 381n) also relied on the second edition. The geometrical apparatus to which Schumpeter presumably was referring was original with Edgeworth, and bears no relation to Mangoldt's diagrams. The relevant chapter of the original 1863 edition, containing the diagrams which were removed by Kleinwächter, is now available in English translation (1962). It should perhaps be finally observed that neither one of these editions should be confused with another posthumous work by Mangoldt entitled simply *Volkswirthsehaftslehre* (1868), which is a rather ponderous treatise dealing largely with labor productivity.

objective function[21]

$$g = (\bar{p}\,\bar{q}\,\bar{r} s' s'') \begin{bmatrix} 0 \\ 0 \\ 0 \\ 1 \\ 1 \end{bmatrix} = s' + s''$$

with respect to the variables $\bar{p}, \bar{q}, \bar{r}, s', s''$ (which are unconstrained as to sign), subject to the inequalities

$$(\bar{p}\,\bar{q}\,\bar{r} s' s'') \begin{bmatrix} -a' & 0 & 0 & -a'' & 0 & 0 & 1\,0\,0\,0\,0 \\ 0 & -b' & 0 & 0 & -b'' & 0 & 0\,1\,0\,0\,0 \\ 0 & 0 & -c' & 0 & 0 & -c'' & 0\,0\,1\,0\,0 \\ 1 & 1 & 1 & 0 & 0 & 0 & 0\,0\,0\,1\,0 \\ 0 & 0 & 0 & 1 & 1 & 1 & 0\,0\,0\,0\,1 \end{bmatrix} \tag{1.13}$$
$$\geqq (0\,0\,0\,0\,0\,0\,p\,q\,r\,0\,0),$$

which become simply

$$\begin{aligned} &\bar{p}a' \leqq s', \quad \bar{p}a'' \leqq s'', \quad \bar{p} \geqq p \geqq 0, \quad s' \geqq 0, \\ &\bar{q}b' \leqq s', \quad \bar{q}b'' \leqq s'', \quad \bar{q} \geqq q \geqq 0, \quad s'' \geqq 0, \\ &\bar{r}c' \leqq s', \quad \bar{r}c' \leqq s'', \quad \bar{r} \geqq r \geqq 0, \end{aligned} \tag{1.14}$$

where use has been made of the original assumption that the prices p, q, r are nonnegative, whence the variables $\bar{p}, \bar{q}, \bar{r}, s', s''$ are, after all, constrained to be nonnegative. If all three commodities are produced (so that the levels of the consumption activities in the primal are positive), then it follows from the duality theorem of Dantzig and

[21]Dantzig and Orden state the duality theorem as follows (1952, p. 52). Let A be a given $m \times n$ matrix, b a given $m \times 1$ column vector, and c a given $1 \times n$ row vector. The primal problem is that of finding an $n \times I$ vector $x \geqq 0$ which minimizes $f = cx$ subject to $Ax = b$. The dual problem is that of finding a $1 \times m$ vector w (whose components are not restricted as to sign) that maximizes $g = wb$ subject to $wA \leqq c$. If either problem has a solution, so does the other, and min $f = \max g$. It is just a matter of notation (replacing A, b, c by their negatives) to state the primal in the form: maximize $f = cx$ subject to $Ax = b, x \geqq 0$; and its dual in the form: minimize $g = wb$ subject to $wA \geqq c$.

Orden (1952) that the inequalities $\bar{p} \geqq p, \bar{q} \geqq q, \geqq r$ will be replaced by equalities, hence the bars may be removed. Then s' and s'' may be interpreted as the resource valuations[22] in the two countries, which will be strictly positive as long as the levels δ', δ'' of the idle activities are equal to zero. The first six inequalities of (1.14) express the competitive requirements that profits be nonpositive on all productive activities (see Koopmans (1951a, p. 66)); for any productive activity carried out at a positive level, the corresponding inequality in (1.14) is replaced by an equality whence s' and s'' are determined by $s' = \max(pa', gb', rc')$ and $s'' = \max(pa'', gb'', rc'')$(see Beckmann (1957, p. 69)).

Now, Mangoldt (1863, p. 188) postulated the existence of a commodity (say the z-good) that is produced in both countries. This would imply $rc' = s'$ and $rc'' = s''$, whence $s'/c' = s''/c''$. (If $c' = c''$ this implies $s' = s''$-an example of the factor price equalization theorem.) Let the inequalities (1.14) now be written

$$\begin{aligned} p &\leqq s'/a' \equiv p', \quad & p &\leqq s''/a'' \equiv p'', \\ q &\leqq s'/b' \equiv q', \quad & q &\leqq s''/b'' \equiv q'', \\ r &\leqq s'/c' \equiv r'', \quad & r &\leqq s''/c'' \equiv r'', \end{aligned} \tag{1.15}$$

where the symbol $\equiv$ means equality by definition. Thus p', q', etc., are the costs of production of goods (x), (y), etc., in the respective countries, the "real costs" being $1/a'$, $1/b'$, etc.

Since $r = r' = r''$ by assumption, the ratio s'/s'' is determined; I shall call this ratio the factor terms of trade, as it is essentially the same as Viner's "double factoral terms of trade" (1937, p. 561). Then Mangoldt's criterion states that commodity (x) will be produced in country I or country II according as $p'<p''$ or $p'>p''$, and similarly for commodity (y). Assuming for definiteness than $p' > p''$ and $q'q''$,

[22]We might say "wage rates" here instead of "resource valuations," but this could be misleading since the units of measurement of the resource (labor) will, according to the present formulation, in general differ between countries. If comparable units had been used, and the amounts of labor had been l', l'' in the respective countries rather than 1 in both, then the objective function would have become $g = s'I' + s''l''$, and s', s'' could then be interpreted as wage rates.

we have $p'>p'' = p$ and $q''>q' = q$, since the price must be equal to the cost in the low-cost country, where the commodity is produced. The pattern of specialization for the other commodities ((x) in II, (y) in I) is determined, as are all the commodity prices.

While Mangoldt's method is ingenious, it has two drawbacks. First, it assumes that there is some commodity that is produced in both countries, and secondly (and more seriously) that it is known in advance which one. Edgeworth (1894, pp. 630–4) sought to remove these objections. The first he replaced simply by the assumption that the ratio $s'/s''$of resource valuations (the factor terms of trade) was given; he then constructed a sliding scale comprised of the logarithms of costs for both countries, the relative positions of the two scales being determined by the difference log $s'/s'' = log\ s' - log\ s''$. If, for instance, country I is to produce (y), this can only be so if $q' \leqq q''$; hence from (1.15), log q' = log s$'$+ log$(l/b') \leqq log\ s''$+log$(1/b'')$ = log q'', or log $(1/b') \leqq$ log s$''$ − log s$'$ + log(l/b'').[23]

Edgeworth fully recognized (1894, p. 633) that his slide-rule method left entirely open the question of the determination of the factor terms of trade s'/s'', which he said "depends not only on the cost of production in each country, but also on the law of demand in each country for the different commodities"; thus, "in general no conclusion ... can be drawn pending the determination of the relation on the international market between the productive powers of the two countries, the ratio which we have designated as $[s'/s'']$."

It is this gap in the argument which has been nicely filled by Elliott (1950). Quite correctly, Elliott rejected the commonly held interpretation of Marshall's "bales" as aggregates of commodities constituting a given country's exports, and took Marshall at his word (1923, p. 157) when he defined them instead as "uniform aggregate investments of her labour (of various qualities) and of her capital." In the present case, then, the "bale" is simply the quantity of labor

[23]In order to facilitate comparison, we point out that the above symbols s', s'' correspond to Edgeworth's o, o', and his symbols a, a', b', etc., correspond to $1/a'$, $1/a'', 1/b''$, etc., in the above notation. Likewise, the a_{ik}/c_i of Beckmann (1957) corresponds to $1/a_{ki}$ in (1.9) above.

employed in the production of exports, and Marshall's terms of trade are the factoral terms of trade s'/s''. Elliott proceeded (1950, p. 23) to construct each country's Marshallian offer function, on the Millian assumption of a constant proportion of each country's income being devoted to each commodity. While he did not use Edgeworth's logarithmic scale, his construction can be most easily derived by Edgeworth's method.[24] The resulting offer curves are continuous but jagged, being made up of segments of alternately infinite and zero elasticity. A construction of this kind, as Elliott pointed out, had already been outlined by Marshall (1923, pp. 323–5).

In discussing Elliott's construction, Metzler observed (1950, p. 315): "I suspect ... that the reciprocal demand technique breaks down when the number of countries exceeds two." This conjecture was cited by Whitin (1953, p. 521) in apparent approval. But there is no reason why this should be so; the individual offer functions for each country can easily be aggregated to form a global offer (or excess demand) function, as has been shown by Gale (1955, p. 159), or indeed by Metzler himself (1945, p. 280). That this should not have seemed immediately obvious is, of course, a consequence of the fact that the objects being "exchanged" are bales (units of the different countries' labor), and such exchange can only be interpreted in a formal and abstract sense; furthermore — and this is what makes the construction seem somewhat artificial — in order to construct one country's offer function, it is necessary to know not only its own production coefficients and utility function, but also the production coefficients (although not the utility functions) of the other countries. The reason for this is simple enough: data in one country are enough to determine how many of its bales it is willing to supply and how many of the various commodities it desires to purchase; the foreign production coefficients will then be needed in order to translate the demand for foreign commodities

[24]Readers of Elliott's article are advised to note that he employs Bastable's convention, referred to in footnote 16 above, of using the same symbol to designate a commodity and its price; also that there is an unfortunate misprint after equation (3) (p. 23) in which A and B have been interchanged.

into the demand for foreign bales. Thus, while Elliott's technique could be validly extended to more general cases, it would probably become quite cumbersome, and no doubt more practical methods could be found for obtaining numerical solutions. Nevertheless, no such method has yet been proposed: the algorithms suggested by McKenzie (1954b) and Dorfman, Samuelson, and Solow (1958, pp. 117–21) are suitable only for the computation of efficient (rather than equilibrium) solutions; and McKenzie's powerful existence proof (1954a) is, unfortunately, "unconstructive," and therefore of little help in solving practical cases.

Viner (1937, pp. 465–7) extended Edgeworth's method to several countries as well as several commodities. The extension is quite straightforward: an arbitrary set of values is assigned to the factor prices s', s'', s'''; this fixes the relative positions of the Edgeworth scales, from which one can at once read off the minimum cost of each commodity; its price as well as the country (or countries) where it will be produced is thereby determined. The mathematical justification for Viner's procedure is to be found in the dual of the above linear programming problem; both linear programming approaches require an arbitrary selection of prices — commodity prices in the primal and factor prices in the dual-and neither procedure by itself provides a systematic method for exploring the entire efficient surface. It was to this latter objective that McKenzie (1954b) addressed himself, with methods based on that of Koopmans (1951a) and Koopmans and Reiter (1951). McKenzie's criticism of "the error of classical ways" (1954b, p. 180) seems to suggest that there might be something invalid about Viner's method, or indeed about those of Man-goldt and Edgeworth. In fact this is not so, and the two approaches are not at all as unrelated as has been supposed. Since this has been an area of such great controversy, it will be well to try to set the record straight.

McKenzie's principal criticism (1954b, p. 180) is that "the methods of the classical economists are entirely appropriate only to the analysis of trade between two countries," and that "the deficiency of the classical methods ... is their dependence on bilateral comparison." This criticism has been reiterated by Jones (1961,

p. 163), who displayed an example involving three countries and three commodities in a pattern of specialization which he showed was inefficient despite the fact that "each country has a bilateral comparative advantage in the commodity it produces compared with any other country *and the commodity that country is assigned*" (my italics). This definition of "comparative advantage" is the same as that of Whitin already referred to, and what the example proves is that the relation so defined is not transitive. But who indeed ever claimed that it was?

It is first necessary to identify the "classical economists" who dealt with cases involving more than two commodities and two countries. Mill(1852a, Ch.18, §§4, 9) treated the question in general terms, without suggesting specific criteria; the validity of his famous dictum (1852a, pp. 143–4): "Trade among any number of countries, and in any number of commodities, must take place on the same essential principles as trade between two countries and in two commodities," must hinge on the meaning of "essential." The case of many commodities (but only two countries) was analyzed by Torrens (1827, pp. 401–7), Mangoldt (1863, Appendix II), Edgeworth (1894, pp. 630–4), Marshall (1923, Appendix H), and Haberler (1936, pp. 136–40); that of three or four commodities and two countries, and of three commodities and three countries, by Bastable (1903, pp. 36–40); that of three commodities and two countries, and of two commodities and three countries, by Taussig (1927, Ch. 9 and 10); and finally, that of several commodities and several countries, by Viner (1937, pp. 462–7).

Ohlin (1927; 1933, pp. 583–6) criticized the orthodox doctrine in terms that led Haberler (1936, p. 131) to complain: "Somebody or other is always trying to show that the Law of Comparative Cost is valid only under the simple assumptions upon which it was originally formulated." But it turns out that the only difference of opinion between Ohlin and Haberler is that the former believed he was attacking orthodoxy, whereas the latter considered himself to be defending it. The treatment by Haberler which followed, which is in accordance with Ohlin's, is similar to that of Marshall, and not essentially different from Edgeworth's. Haberler pointed out that it was just a matter of notation to rank the commodities in order of comparative advantage, as $a'/a'' > b'/b'' > c'/c'' > \ldots$, and that demand considerations would determine which intermediate commodities in the ranking would be exported or imported; the important point being that if country I exports a certain commodity, it must also export all the higher-ranking ones, and if it imports a certain commodity, it must also import all the lower-ranking ones. In this sense, "bilateral comparisons" are completely valid in the case in which there are only two countries to compare; this, McKenzie and Jones have not denied. But as Edgeworth (1894, p. 633) and Haberler (1936, p. 137) were careful to point out, and as Ohlin took pains to stress, information on comparative costs alone is not enough to determine where the dividing line will be drawn. Unfortunately, Bastable (1903, p. 36) was not so careful, and appeared to imply that comparative costs would by themselves uniquely determine the pattern of specialization.

In analyzing an example of three commodities and three countries, Bastable (1903, p. 39) obtained a correct solution,[25] and showed (p. 40) that the pattern of specialization could be changed as a result of the introduction of a third country. Nicholson (1897, p. 299) remarked that "when we bring in the fact that any one 'nation' trades not with one another [*sic*] but with many others, we have to introduce some common measure of values for the world's markets." His use of the word "money" for this common measure seems to have led later writers to question the validity of his analysis, even though

[25]Bastable's solution was correct in the sense that he obtained what will be described below as the unique efficient assignment, that is, the unique efficient specialization in which each country produces a different commodity. But he erred in implying that this was the only kind of solution possible; in his words: "From inspection it is plain that [it is] the most economical arrangement." There would be several other "economical arrangements" in which commodities were produced in more than one country and countries produced more than one commodity. The remainder of the sentence from which the above passage is quoted also contains a bad howler. Graham could have tripped Bastable up on this score, but confined himself instead (1948, Ch. IV) to the latter's treatment of the two-commodity case. Even here Graham (1948, pp. 66–7) was more concerned with Bastable's bad arithmetic than with his bad economics, and having declared that Bastable was "rather slavishly following Mill's misguided lead" (p. 64), the blame was in any case all shoved onto Mill.

he qualified it by the statement that "it may be fully admitted, as in Mill's phraseology, that 'money has little to do in the matter except to furnish a convenient mode of comparing values.'"

Taussig (1927) in his examples handled the subject from two standpoints: (1) that of the prices of the various commodities, and (2) that of the wages in the different countries; thus he considered both the primal and the dual of what can now be recognized as a linear programming problem, or indeed a nonlinear programming or equilibrium problem, since the particular solution arrived at would depend on "the play of demand." Taussig's comparisons were all with respect to prices or wages, and were therefore multilateral and not bilateral. His exposition was most lucid, and although he confined himself to numerical examples involving three commodities and two countries (Ch. 9) and two commodities and three countries (Ch. 10), he exhausted all cases.

Finally, Viner's treatment was certainly multilateral rather than bilateral, and indeed, the inefficiency of Jones' example can readily be determined by Viner's method. Jones also pointed out (1961, p. 163n) that a solution obtained by McKenzie (1954b, p. 174) was actually inefficient; Jones indicated the correct efficient specializations, and actually all three of them can be quickly read off Viner's scales. In conclusion, therefore, I have not been able to find a single example in the classical literature of the use of bilateral comparison in the analysis of multilateral trade.

1.7. *Modern Developments Resumed: Jones*

The record, it is hoped, having been set straight, let us turn to the positive results obtained by McKenzie and Jones. McKenzie (1954b, p. 171) introduced an interesting multiplicative formula which was arrived at independently and in a different way by Jones (1961, p. 165) on the basis of an ingenious use of the Hawkins-Simon theorem (1949). Jones considered the case of an equal number of commodities and countries, and sought a method for ascertaining an optimal way of assigning exactly one country to each commodity and vice versa; he called this an "$i - i$ assignment." For convenience I shall instead call such a solution simply an "assignment," reserving the term "specialization" for the broader concept of a solution in which each country produces exactly one commodity, but in which some commodities may be produced in several countries or in none at all. In the notation of equation (1.9) above, where a_{ij} is the maximum output of the ith commodity that can be produced in the jth country, suppose there is a numbering of commodities countries such that the assignment $\mathfrak{A}$ is defined by $x_i = a_{ii}, i = 1, 2, \ldots, n$. Let there be another assignment $\mathfrak{A}_\pi$ in which $x_i = a_{ij}$ and where $j = \pi(i)$, the function π being a permutation of the integers 1, 2, ..., n (Jones chooses cyclic permutations, but his analysis can be generalized). Then Jones shows that $\mathfrak{A}_\pi$ is more efficient than $\mathfrak{A}$ (in the sense that there is some way for each country i to shift its resources from commodity i to commodity $j = \pi(i)$ such that the world output of each commodity is increased) if and only if

$$\prod_{i=1}^{n} a_{i,\pi(i)} > \prod_{i=1}^{n} a_{ii}. \tag{1.16}$$

This may be called the Jones inequality; it includes as a special case the inequality $a''b'>a'b''$ (see (1.3) above), which states that if country I has a comparative advantage in commodity (y) over country II with respect to commodity (x) so that $b'/a'>b''/a''$, then the specialization $x = a'', y = b'$ is more efficient than the specialization $x = a', y = b''$ if and only if the product of the outputs is larger in the first case than in the second. Thus, Jones' criterion may be considered as a generalization of the law of comparative advantage.

Jones' inequality has a number of interesting implications, not all of which are made explicit by Jones. The first implication is that, since there is a finite number of permutations π, there is a maximum $\prod_{i=1}^{n} a_{i,\pi(i)}$; hence an efficient assignment exists. Jones took this for granted (1961, p. 164), but it is not at all obvious on the face of it; a proof based on Koopmans (1951a, p. 82) had been obtained by Beckmann (1957, p. 68). The second implication is still more remarkable, though also apparently taken for granted by Jones, who spoke of "the" optimal assignment; and that is that an optimal assignment can generally be expected to be unique, since the only exceptions would be those in which $\prod_{i=1}^{n} a_{i,\pi(i)} = \prod_{i=1}^{n} a_{ii}$ for $\pi(i) \neq i$,which can be ruled out on a priori grounds as completely improbable, except for cases such as $a_{i,\pi(i)} = a_{ii}$ for all i, in which — in any event — there would be no trade. Thus, except for degenerate cases, there is a unique efficient assignment.

Geometrically, this result states that if the number of commodities is equal to the number of countries, and the countries' production surfaces are not parallel in any direction, then the world production possibility set, which is an n-dimensional polyhedron, will have exactly one vertex in the interior of the positive orthant. If the number of countries exceeds the number of commodities, there will be several such vertices (see McKenzie (1954b, p. 174), Whitin (1953, p. 523)); whereas if the number of commodities exceeds the number of countries, there will be none (see Whitin (1953, p. 533)). The procedure to be followed in extending (1.16) to the case of unequal numbers of commodities and countries was also indicated by Jones (1961, p. 168).

1.8. *Trade in Intermediate Products*

In the course of his analysis McKenzie (1954b, p. 177) stumbled across the interesting discovery that the introduction of trade in intermediate products necessitates a fundamental alteration in the classical analysis. It is strange that this had not been noticed before, despite the fact, as McKenzie pointed out (1954b, p. 167), that the classical economists used intermediate products such as "cloth" and "linen" in their examples. Some hints of recognition that intermediate products might cause difficulties are contained in Ohlin's discussion (1933, p. 587), but Ohlin dealt only with the implications of trade in machinery (rather than goods-in-process) and therefore failed to come to grips with the main problem; or at any rate Ohlin was discussing a somewhat different problem.

Reiter (1953) and McKenzie (1954b) both pointed out that trade in intermediate products would enlarge the world production-possibility set; which should not be too surprising since, if such trade is allowed, all the possibilities previously open are still open, and more possibilities are available. What is more surprising is the effect such trade has on the determination of international values.

The principal simplification that is used in the analysis of problems in international trade is the concept of an integrated industry, using up primary factors (which are completely immobile among countries) and producing final commodities (which are perfectly mobile among countries). What is the appropriate simplification in the case of intermediate goods? In the case of some of these, such as electric power and coal, transmission and transport costs may be so high that the assumption that they are infinite may be an appropriate simplification. But in the case of petroleum, copper, cotton, wheat, etc., this is obviously not the case.

In the case of a single country, in which there is only one primary factor of production (labor), and in which joint production is excluded, the representation of each industry as an integrated industry, using up only labor and producing only a net output, is justified by Samuelson's substitution theorem (1951). This theorem was sketched by Samuelson within a neo-classical framework, was reformulated by Koopmans (1951b) in terms of his activity analysis model (1951a), generalized by Arrow (1951) and also independently developed by Georgescu-Roegen (1951); an elementary exposition was subsequently presented by Koopmans (1953). What the theorem states, essentially, is that any efficient nonnegative bill of goods (net outputs) can be sustained by only one price constellation (i.e., by one ray of prices $(kp_1, kp_2, \ldots, kp_n)$ where $k > 0$); this leads, of course, to a labor theory of value. Given this price constellation, even though many processes of production may be available to each firm or industry, only one such process will actually be used.

Geometrically (cf. Koopmans (1953, p. 104)), there will be for any one country an efficient boundary of the set of net outputs that it could produce (this includes negative net outputs, which of course would have to be matched by corresponding amounts of imports); that part of this boundary which could be achieved under autarky, i.e., that part contained in the positive orthant, will be a flat surface. When trade in intermediate products is allowed, it is no longer necessary that net outputs be positive; countries may import some of their requirements, allowing the corresponding net outputs to be negative. In the absence of international trade, the coordinate vectors which "hold up" the flat surface can be regarded as the fictitious integrated production processes; as soon as trade in intermediate products is allowed, there will be more than one possible price constellation, and it can no longer be known in advance, with respect to a given country, which of its possible production processes each of its industries will use. This was one of the points made by McKenzie (1954b, p. 179).

There is only one apparent exception to the above statement (and it is only apparent), and that is the case in which one country is so large that its prices-under-autarky rule the roost under trade; this of course is the Graham solution in which the terms of trade coincide with one of the countries' cost ratios. But even in this case, the Samuelson substitution theorem applies only to that one country, and furthermore we cannot know in advance whether a particular country's costs will dominate international prices.

One of the results of trade in intermediate products pointed out by McKenzie (1954b, 1955–56) was that his algorithm for determining efficient specializations broke down. The reason for this can be appreciated from the following example, illustrated by Figure 2. Let the production possibility set of one country be given by the shaded figure OAB, and for the other country by the (displaced) shaded figure BGF. Sliding BGF down BA to ACD, we obtain the world production-possibility set OACDFB, which intersects the axes at E and H. Now suppose the price ratio is chosen to correspond to the slope of eE (or of dD); then at this price ratio, the first country will produce at A, specializing in the x-commodity and importing the y-commodity, whereas the second country will do the opposite, producing at F (measured from B as origin). Thus world output will be determined at D, which is impossible, since it implies negative net world output of the y-commodity. Thus the world efficiency locus cannot be determined by finding the efficient solutions for each country, at any given price constellation, and then adding them up.

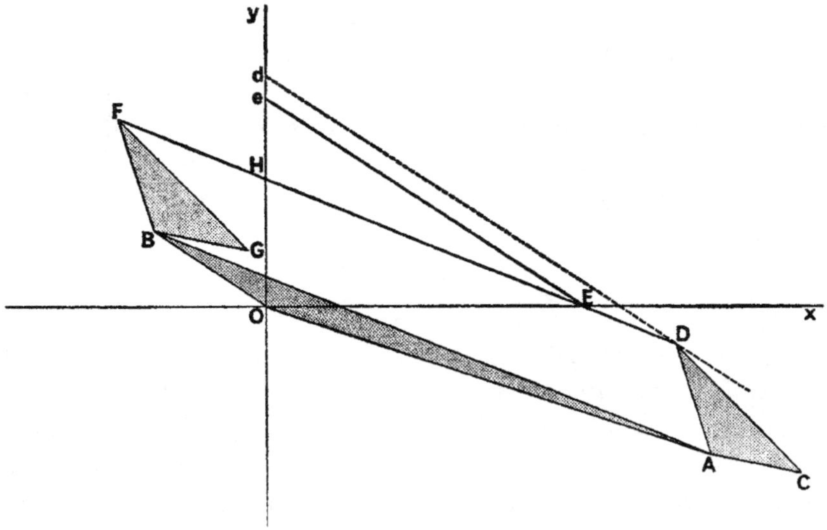

Figure 2.

The reason for the last result is obvious. Not all nonnegative price constellations can be compatible with equilibrium. To take an extreme case, suppose that in both countries the consumers regard the two commodities as perfect substitutes, so that eE and dD can be considered to be their indifference curves (we are thinking of a commodity that does duty as a consumer good as well as an industrial input, such as gasoline, for instance). Then, contrary to what one might expect, the slope eE cannot represent an equilibrium price ratio, since this would entail a solution at D, as already noted. The feasible part of the world production possibility set is just OEH, and clearly the solution must be the point E; but the only price ratio that will sustain this equilibrium is that represented by the slope FD, which is the same as that of BA. This is a case in which the first country rules the roost, its cost ratios determining the terms of trade, even though both commodities are perfect substitutes. This is an example which Graham would have greatly relished, had he considered it.

Undoubtedly the most interesting consequence of the introduction of trade in intermediate products is that which McKenzie

(1954b, pp. 177–9) and Jones (1961, pp. 166–8) have emphasized, namely the possibility of reversal in the pattern of specialization. As McKenzie notes (1954b, p. 179): "There is nothing shocking to common sense in these results. A moment's reflection will convince one that Lancashire would be unlikely to produce cotton cloth if the cotton had to be grown in England."

1.9. *Transport Costs*

"The theory of international trade," Ohlin has said (1933, p. 589), "is nothing but *internationale Standortslehre*." This is certainly a minority viewpoint (cf. Viner (1937, p. 468)). Location theory emphasizes the continuity of space, whereas international trade theory stresses its discreteness. Transport costs in international trade theory are either zero or infinite; there is nothing in between. So radical an idealization is this that it is a wonder that the theory has any bearing on reality at all. One of the devices used by Ohlin was the concept of "home market goods" (1933, p. 142), which Taussig (1927, p. 35) had introduced under the name of "domestic goods"; the concept goes back further still to Marshall (1923, pp. 354–5n) and Mill (1852a, Book III, Ch. 18, §3). These domestic commodities have infinite transport costs, but since they are substitutable in consumption and production with international commodities, an element of continuity is restored, and the resulting theory remains extremely serviceable.

Nevertheless, many attempts have been made to introduce transport costs in a more direct manner. Some of these, relevant to the models that we have been analyzing in the previous sections, will now be discussed.

One of these is the model introduced by Isard and Peck (1954). These authors acknowledged their indebtedness to Graham for many of their concepts. They considered a model of three equidistant countries, with one scarce factor called a "productive unit" (to be interpreted, perhaps, as mostly labor) and various commodities such as coal, iron ore, textiles, and steel, as well as shipping; and of these only steel and textiles were consumed by households, in fixed proportions. The principal object of interest is the shipping, of course, and for each commodity, source, and destination, a "distance input requirement" was defined; if there are n commodities and m countries, there are already nm^2 pieces of information required.

Isard and Peck found an equilibrium solution to their model, by a tentative method. Their model can actually be set up as one in activity analysis, in which commodities in different regions are considered to be different commodities; the shipping activities, as in the model of Koopmans and Reiter (1951), transform one such commodity into another. While lsard and Peck did not justify their method of solution, it can be shown to be legitimate, being closely related to the solution of the dual linear programming problem; cf. Isard (1956, pp. 208–15). This is a case in which an equilibrium problem can be transformed into a maximum problem — one in linear programming; the reason for this is that the same L-shaped indifference curves are assumed in each country, hence they can be aggregated, and community (world) indifference curves can be legitimately defined. (The same feature was at the basis of Mill's problem; these questions will be discussed in detail in Part 2.) More recently, Isard and Ostroff (1958, 1960) have greatly generalized this model, and rigorously studied its logical structure, in a treatment closely paralleling that of Arrow and Debreu (1954).

The treatment of shipping in these models does not take account of the routing of the moving equipment. In the model of Koopmans (1949) and Koopmans and Reiter (1951) this was shown to be one of the major features of the transportation problem. The movement of empty carrying capacity must presumably be accounted for in some way; even if such movement can be shown to be empirically insignificant, this could simply be a consequence of the effects of differential transport costs on the location of industry. Thus, once transportation is introduced, it is difficult not to take the whole step into location theory.

Samuelson (1952) considered the problem of equilibrium in spatially separated markets, in the case of one commodity, with given demand and supply functions in each, and given transport costs from each source to each destination. His model was based on treatments by Cournot (1838, Ch. 10) and Enke (1951) and related to earlier models discussed by Cunynghame (1903, 1904) and Barone (1908). His solution was also characterized by transforming the problem into a maximum problem; since just one commodity was involved, this could be expected on the basis of the considerations mentioned above, and it may be conjectured that his method would not extend easily to more commodities without the addition of special assumptions.

1.10. *Empirical Evidence*

In a non-experimental field such as economics, any theory or model is difficult to test, since conditions are not controlled. Before attempting to test a theory, it is wise to form some judgment as to its "robustness," that is, how small an effect small departures from assumptions will have on asserted conclusions. Therefore we cannot hope to make a thorough evaluation of empirical tests of the Millian theory until we have surveyed the entire theoretical field. Nevertheless, it will be appropriate at this stage to make some remarks concerning the impressive empirical work of MacDougall (1951, 1952, 1962), which has been followed up by Stern (1962), Balassa (1963), and others.

MacDougall (1951, p. 703) presented a diagram, drawn on a double logarithmic scale, which, in his words (p. 702), "shows the ratio of American to British output per worker in each industry — measured vertically — and the ratio of American to British exports — measured horizontally" for a large number of products in a sample of data collected in the 1930's. Noting that during this period, "American weekly wages in manufacturing were roughly double the British" (p. 697), he drew a dividing line in his chart, showing that commodities above the line had higher costs in Britain, and below the line higher costs in the United States.

Of course, this is only a slight adaptation of Edgeworth's logarithmic scale. And if no other countries were involved, what we should expect to find would be complete specialization by the United States on one side of the dividing line, and complete specialization by Britain on the other. Thus the kind of function that would be predicted by pure theory would be a step function. But what MacDougall actually found was that a linear function fitted extremely well. This curious phenomenon bears a striking resemblance to similar phenomena observed in experimental psychology, where pure theory would predict one choice or another, but in practice what is found is a smooth gradation.

This relationship held despite the fact that both countries traded more with third countries than with each other. Thus MacDougall was using bilateral comparisons in what was really a multilateral situation, as McKenzie and Jones have implied has been the practice.

Despite the logical objections that one can make, MacDougall's results seem certainly — in some sense — to be a confirmation of the Millian theory. But the theory clearly needs to be stated in more suitable form in order to fit the facts.

References*

Allen, William R.: "The Effects on Trade of Shifting Reciprocal Demand Schedules," *American Economic Review,* 42 (March 1952), 135–140.

Arrow, Kenneth J.: "Alternative Proof of the Substitution Theorem for Leontief Models in the General Case," *Activity Analysis of Production and Allocation* (edited by T. C. Koopmans). New York: John Wiley and Sons, Inc., 1951, pp. 155–164.

Arrow, Kenneth J., and Gerard Debreu: "Existence of an Equilibrium for a Competitive Economy," *Econometrica,* 22 (July 1954), 265–290.

Balassa, Bela: "An Empirical Demonstration of Classical Comparative Cost Theory," *Review of Economics and Statistics,* 45 (August 1963), 231–238.

Barone, Enrico: *Principi di Economia Politica.* Rome, 1908. Posthumous edition: *Le Opere Economiche,* Vol. II. Bologna: Nicola Zanichelli Editore, 1936.

Bastable, C. F.: *The Theory of International Trade.* Fourth Edition, revised. London: Macmillan and Co., 1903.

Becker, Gary S.: "A Note on Multi-Country Trade," *American Economic Review,* 42 (September 1952), 558–568.

*Identified in the text simply by author and year of publication, or, when convenient, by abbreviated title. When necessary, the year is followed by a letter indicating chronological order within the year. In the case of reprinted articles, page numbers in the text refer to the original source, unless specifically noted to the contrary.

Beckmann, Martin J.: "International and Interpersonal Division of Labor," *Weltwirtschaftliches Archiv,* 78 (Heft I, 1957), 67–73.

Bhagwati, Jagdish: "Immiserizing Growth: A Geometrical Note," *Review of Economic Studies,* 25 (June 1958), 201–205.

———: "Some Recent Trends in the Pure Theory of International Trade," *International Trade Theory in a Developing World* (edited by Roy Harrod assisted by Douglas Hague). London: Macmillan and Co. Ltd., 1963, pp. 1–30.

———: "The Pure Theory of International Trade," *Economic Journal,* 74 (March 1964), 1–84.

Bhagwati, Jagdish, and Harry G. Johnson: "Notes on Some Controversies in the Theory of International Trade," *Economic Journal,* 70 (March 1960), 74–93.

Brouwer, L. E. J.: "Über Abbildung von Mannigfaltigkeiten," *Mathematische Annalen,* 71 (1912), 97–115.

Cairnes, J. E.: *Some Leading Principles of Political Economy Newly Expounded.* London: Macmillan and Co., 1874.

Caves, Richard E.: *Trade and Economic Structure, Models and Methods.* Cambridge, Mass.: Harvard University Press, 1960.

Cournot, Augustin: *Recherches surles Principes Mathématiques de la Théorie des Richesses.* Paris: L. Hachette, 1838. Nouvelle édition, Paris: Marcel Rivière et Cie., 1938. English translation: *Researches into the Mathematical Principles of the Theory of Wealth.* New York: The Macmillan Co., 1897.

Cunynghame, Henry: "The Effect of Export and Import Duties on Price and Production Examined by the Graphic Method," *Economic Journal,* 13 (September 1903), 313–323.

———:*A Geometrical Political Economy.* Oxford: Clarendon Press, 1904.

Dantzig, George B. (1951a): "Maximization of a Linear Function of Variables Subject to Linear Inequalities," *Activity Analysis of Production and Allocation* (edited by T. C. Koopmans). New York: John Wiley & Sons, Inc., 1951, pp. 339–347.

——— (1951b): "Application of the Simplex Method to a Transportation Problem," *Activity Analysis of Production and Allocation* (edited by T. C. Koopmans). New York: John Wiley & Sons, Inc., 1951, pp. 359–373.

Dantzig, George b., and Alex Orden: "A Duality Theorem based on the Simplex Method," *Symposium on Linear Inequalities and Programming* held in Washington, D.C., June 14–16, 1951, Directorate of Management Analysis Service, DCS/Comptroller, Headquarters, U.S. Air Force, Reprint of Project SCOOP Manual No. 10, 1 April 1952, pp. 51–55.

Dorfman, Robert, Paul A. Samuelson, and Robert M. Solow: *Linear Programming and Economic Analysis.* New York: McGraw-Hill Book Company, Inc., 1958.

Duncan, Acheson J.: "Marshall's Paradox and the Direction of Shift in Demand," *Econometrica,* 6 (October 1938), 357–374.

Edgeworth, F. Y.: "The Theory of International Values, I, II, III," *Economic Journal,* 4 (March, September, December 1894), 35–50, 424–443, 606–638. Reprinted (with revisions and omissions) in *Papers Relating to Political Economy,* Vol. II, 3–60.

———: "On a Point in the Theory of International Trade," *Economic Journal,* 9 (March 1899), 125–128.

Eisenberg, E.: "Duality in Homogeneous Programming," *Proceedings of the American Mathematical Society,* 12 (October 1961), 783–787.

Elliott, G. A.: "The Theory of International Values," *Journal of Political Economy,* 58 (February 1950), 16–29.

Enke, Stephen: "Equilibrium among Spatially Separated Markets: Solution by Electric Analogue," *Econometrica,* 19 (January 1951), 40–47.

Gale, David: "The Law of Supply and Demand," *Mathematica Scandinavica,* 3 (1955), 155–169.

Garvin, Walter W.: *Introduction to Linear Programming.* New York: McGraw-Hill Book Company, Inc., 1960.

Georgescu-Roegen, Nicholas: "Some Properties of a Generalized Leontief Model," *Activity Analysis of Production and Allocation* (edited by T. C. Koopmans). New York: John Wiley and Sons, Inc., 1951, pp. 165–173.

Graham, Frank D.: "The Theory of International Values Re-examined," *Quarterly Journal of Economics,* 28 (November 1923), 54–86. Reprinted in *Readings in the Theory of International Trade* (edited by Howard S. Ellis and Lloyd A. Metzler). Philadelphia: The Blakiston Co., 1949, pp. 301–330.

———: "The Theory of International Values," *Quarterly Journal of Economics,* 46 (August 1932), 581–616.

———: *The Theory of International Values.* Princeton: Princeton University Press, 1948.

Haberler, Gottfried: *The Theory of International Trade, With its Applications to Commercial Policy* (translated from the German, *Die internationale Handel,* Berlin: 1933). London: William Hodge & Company, Limited, 1936.

———: *A Survey of International Trade Theory,* Special Papers in International Economics No. 1, Princeton University, 1955. Revised and enlarged edition, 1961.

Harrod, R. F.: *The Life of John Maynard Keynes.* London: Macmillan and Co. Ltd., 1951.

Hawkins, David, and Herbert A. Simon: "Note: Some Conditions of Macroeconomic Stability," *Econometrica,* 17 (July–October 1949), 245–248.

Hollander, Jacob H.: *David Ricardo, A Centenary Estimate.* Baltimore: The Johns Hopkins Press, 1910.

———: "Ricardo and Torrens," *Economic Journal,* 21 (September 1911), 455–468.

Houthakker, H. S.: "An International Comparison of Household Expenditure Patterns, Commemorating the Centenary of Engel's Law," *Econometrica,* 25 (October 1957), 532–551.

Isard, Walter: *Location and Space-Economy.* New York: Technology Press and John Wiley and Sons, 1956.

Isard, Walter, and David J. Ostroff: "Existence of a Competitive Interregional Equilibrium," *Papers and Proceedings of the Regional Science Association,* 4 (1958), 49–76.

———: "General Interregional Equilibrium," *Journal of Regional Science,* 2 (1960), 67–74.

Isard, Walter, and Merton J. Peck: "Location Theory and International and Interregional Trade Theory," *Quarterly Journal of Economics,* 68 (February 1954), 97–114.

Jones, Ronald W.: "Comparative Advantage and the Theory of Tariffs: A Multi-Country Multi-Commodity Model," *Review of Economic Studies,* 28 (June 1961), 161–175.

Kakutani, Shizuo: "A Generalization of Brouwer's Fixed Point Theorem," *Duke Mathematical Journal,* 8 (1941), 457–459.

Kemp, Murray C.: "The Relation Between Changes in International Demand and the Terms of Trade," *Econometrica,* 24 (January, 1956), 41–46.

———: *The Pure Theory of International Trade.* Englewood Cliffs, N.J.: Prentice Hall Inc., 1964.

Keynes, J. M.: "Alfred Marshall, 1842–1924," *Economic Journal,* 34 (September 1924), 311–372. Reprinted in *Memorials of Alfred Marshall* (edited by A. C. Pigou, 1925). New York: Kelley & Millman, Inc., 1956, pp.1–65; and in J. M. Keynes, *Essays in Biography.* New York: Horizon Press, Inc., 1951, pp. 125–217.

Koopmans, Tjalling C.: "Optimum Utilization of the Transportation System," *Econometrica* [Supplement], 17 (July 1949), 136–146.

——— (1951a): "Analysis of Production as an Efficient Combination of Activities," *Activity Analysis of Production and Allocation* (edited by T. C. Koopmans). New York: John Wiley & Sons, Inc., 1951, pp. 33–97.

——— (1951b): "Alternative Proof of the Substitution Theorem for Leontief Models in the Case of Three Industries," *Activity Analysis of Production and Allocation* (edited by T. C. Koopmans). New York: John Wiley and Sons, Inc., 1951, pp. 147–154.

———: "Maximization and Substitution in Linear Models of Production," *Input-Output Relations* (edited by the Netherlands Economic Institute). Leiden: H. E. Stenfert Kroese N.V., 1953, pp. 99–109.

Koopmans, Tjalling C., and Stanley Reiter: "A Model of Transportation," *Activity Analysis of Production and Allocation* (edited by T. C. Koopmans). New York: John Wiley and Sons, Inc., 1951, 222–259.

Kuhn, H. W., and A. W. Tucker: "Nonlinear Programming," *Proceedings of the Second Berkeley Symposium on Mathematical Statistics and Probability.* Berkeley: University of California Press, 1951, pp. 481–492.

Leontief, Wassily W.: "The Use of Indifference Curves in the Analysis of Foreign Trade," *Quarterly Journal of Economics,* 47 (May 1933), 493–503. Reprinted in *Readings in the Theory of International Trade* (edited by H. S. Ellis and L. A. Metzler). Philadelphia: The Blakiston Co., 1949, pp. 229–238.

Lerner, Abba P.: "The Diagrammatical Representation of Cost Conditions in International Trade," *Economica,* 12 (August 1932), 346–356. Reprinted in Lerner (1953), 85–100.

———: "The Diagrammatical Representation of Demand Conditions in International Trade," *Economica,* N.S., 1 (August 1934), 319–334. Reprinted in Lerner (1953), 101–122.

———: *Essays in Economic Analysis.* London: Macmillan and Co., Ltd., 1953.

Leser, Emanuel: *Untersuchungen zur Geschichte der Nationalökonomie.* I. Heft. Jena: Verlag von Gustav Fischer, 1881.

[McCulwch, J. R.]: "Commercial Embarrassments—Trade with France," *Edinburgh Review,* 32 (July 1819), 48–74.

MacDougall, G. D. A.: "British and American Exports: A Study Suggested by the Theory of Comparative Costs," I, II, *Economic Journal,* 61 (December 1951), 62 (September 1952), 487–521.

MacDougall, Sir Donald, Monica Dowley, Pauline Fox, and Senta Pugh: "British and American Productivity, Prices, and Exports: An Addendum," *Oxford Economic Papers,* N.S., 14 (October 1962), 297–304.

McKenzie, Lionel W. (1954a): "On Equilibrium in Graham's Model of World Trade and Other Competitive Systems," *Econometrica,* 22 (April 1954), 147–161.

——— (1954b): "Specialisation and Efficiency in World Production," *Review of Economic Studies,* 21 (June 1954), 165–180.

———: "Specialization in Production and the Production Possibility Locus," *Review of Economic Studies,* 23 (1955–56), 56–64.

Mangoldt, H. von: *Grundriss der Volkswirthschaftslehre.* Stuttgart: Verlag von J. Engelhorn, 1863. Second (posthumous) edition (revised by Friedrich Kleinwächter). Stuttgart: Verlag von Julius Maier, 1871. English translation of Book III, Chapter 3, Part 1, of the original 1863 edition, "The Exchange Ratio of Goods," *International Economic Papers,* No. 11 (edited by Alan T. Peacock, Wolfgang F. Stolper, Ralph Turvey, and Hans Liesner). London: Macmillan and Company, Limited, 1962, pp. 32–59.

———: *Volkswirthschaftslehre. Die Lehre von der Gütererzeugung, von der Vermögenserhaltung und der Vertheilung der Güter.* Stuttgart: Bibliothek der Gesammten Handelswissenschaften, Verlag von Julius Maier, 1868.

Marshall, Alfred: *The Pure Theory of Foreign Trade,* published privately, 1879. Reprinted, together with *The Pure Theory of Domestic Values.* London: London School of Economics and Political Science, 1930; third impression, 1949.

———: *Money, Credit, and Commerce.* London: Macmillan and Co., Ltd, 1923. Second printing, New York: Augustus M. Kelley, 1960.

Metzler, Lloyd A.: "Stability of Multiple Markets: The Hicks Conditions," *Econometrica,* 13, (October 1945), 277–292.

———: "The Theory of International Trade," *A Survey of Contemporary Economics* (edited by H. S. Ellis). Philadelphia: The Blakiston Company, 1948, pp. 210–254.

———: "Graham's Theory of International Values," *American Economic Review,* 40 (June, 1950), 301–322.

Mill, James: *Elements of Political Economy,* Third Edition. London: Baldwin, Cradock, and Joy, 1826. New York: Augustus M. Kelley, 1963.

Mill, John Stuart: *Essays on Some Unsettled Questions of Political Economy.* London: John W. Parker, West Strand, 1844. Reprinted by the London School of Economics and Political Science. 1948.

———: (1852a): *Principles of Political Economy with Some of their Applications to Social Philosophy,* Third Edition. London: Parker and Co., 1852. Editions: 1st (1848), 2nd (1849), 4th (1857), 5th (1862) all published by Parker & Co.; 6th (1865), 7th (1871), 8th (1878), 9th (1885) published by Longmans, Green, & Co. Page references are to Vol. II of the Fifth Edition, New York: D. Appleton and Company, 1895. Also (where noted) to the People's Edition, London: Longman, Green, Longman, Roberts, and Green, 1865.

——— (1852b): "Dr. Whewell on Moral Philosophy," *Westminster Review,* 58 (October 1852), 187–207. Reprinted in Mill's *Dissertations and Discussions,* Vol. III. New York: Henry Holt and Company, 1874, pp. 132–192.

———: "Thornton on Labour and its Claims," *Fortnightly Review,* N.S., 5 (May, June 1869), 505–518, 680–700.

———: *A System of Logic, Ratiocinative and Inductive,* People's Edition. London: Longman's, Green, and Co., 1891.

Mundell, Robert A.: "The Pure Theory of International Trade," *American Economic Review,* 50 (March 1960), 67–110.

Nicholson, J. Shield: *Principles of Political Economy,* Vol. II. New York: The Macmillan Company, 1897.

Ohlin, Bertil: "1st eine Modernisierung der Aussenhandelstheorie erforderliches?" *Weltwirtschaftliches Archiv,* 26 (1927, II), 97–115.

——— *Interregional and International Trade.* Cambridge, Mass.: Harvard University Press, 1933.

Pareto, Vilfredo: *Manuel d'Economie Politique,* translated and revised from the Italian, *Manuale di economia politica* (1906). Paris: M. Giard et E. Brière, 1909. Second French edition (identical with the 1909 edition), Paris: Marcel Giard, 1927.

Reiter, Stanley: "Trade Barriers in Activity Analysis," *Review of Economic Studies,* 20 (June 1953), 174–180.

Ricardo, David: *An Essay on The Influence of a low Price of Corn on the Profits of Stock; shewing the Inexpediency of Restrictions on Importation; with Remarks on Mr. Malthus' Two Last Publications.* London: John Murray, Albemarle Street, 1815. Reprinted in *The Works and Correspondence of David Ricardo* (edited by Piero Sraffa), Vol IV, pp. 9–41. [Page references are to the latter.)

———: *On the Principles of Political Economy, and Taxation.* London: John Murray, Albemarle Street, 1817. In *The Works and Correspondence of David Ricardo,* Vol I. (edited by Piero Sraffa). Cambridge: at the University Press, 1951. [Page references are to the latter.]

———: *The Works and Correspondence of David Ricardo,* edited by Piero Sraffa with the collaboration of M. H. Dobb. In ten volumes. Cambridge: at the University Press, 1951–1955.

Robbins, Lionel: *Robert Torrens and the Evolution of Classical Economics.* London: Macmillan and Co. Ltd., 1958.

Samuelson, Paul A.: "Abstract of a Theorem Concerning Substitutability in Open Leontief Models," *Activity Analysis of Production and Allocation* (edited by T. C. Koopmans). New York: Wiley, 1951, pp. 142–146.

———: "Spatial Price Equilibrium and Linear Programming," *American Economic Review,* 42 (June 1952), 283–303.

Schlesinger, Karl: "Über die Produktionsgleichungen der ökonomischen Wertlehre," *Ergebnisse eines mathematischen Kolloquiums,* Heft 6 (1933–1934), 10–11.

Schumann, Jochen, And Horst Todt: "Classical Theory, Graham's Theory, and Linear Programming in International Trade: Comment," *Quarterly Journal of Economics,* 71 (August 1957), 464–469.

Schumpeter, Joseph A.: *History of Economic Analysis.* New York: Oxford University Press, 1954.

Seligman, Edwin R. A.: "On Some Neglected British Economists," *Economic Journal,* 13 (September, December 1903), 335–363, 511–535. Reprinted in his *Essays in Economics.* New York: The Macmillan Company, 1925, pp. 64–121.

———: "Ricardo and Torrens," *Economic Journal,* 21 (September 1911), 448–455.

Stern, Robert M.: "British and American Productivity and Comparative Costs in International Trade," *Oxford Economic Papers,* N.S., 14 (October 1962), 275–296.

Taussig, F. W.: *International Trade.* New York: The Macmillan Company, 1927.

Thornton, William T.: "A New Theory of Supply and Demand," *Fortnightly Review,* 6 (October 1866), 420–434. Reprinted (with revisions) in *On Labour, its Wrongful Claims and Rightful Dues, its Actual Present and Possible Future.* London: Macmillan and Co., 1869, pp. 43–65.

Torrens, Robert: *The Economists Refuted.* London: S. A. and H. Oddy; and Dublin: C. La Grange, 1808. Reprinted with separate pagination in the second and third editions of R. Torrens' *The Principles and Practical Operation of Sir Robert Peel's Act of 1844 Explained and Defended.* Second edition, London: Longman, Brown, Green, Longman & Roberts, 1857; third edition, London: Longmans, 1858. [Only one copy of the original edition is known to be in existence; cf. Robbins (1958), p. 260].

———: *An Essay on the External Corn Trade.* London: J. Hatchard, 1815. Second edition, London: J. Hatchard & Son, 1820. Third, fourth, and fifth ("New") edition, London: Longman, Rees, Orme, Brown, and Green, 1826, 1827, 1829.

———: "Economical objection to extended Colonization stated and answered," in R. Torrens: *Colonization of South Australia.* London: Longman, Rees, Orme, Brown, Green, & Longman, 1835, pp. 229–249. Also in R. Torrens: *A Letter to the Right Honourable Lord John Russell, on the Ministerial Measure for Establishing Poor Laws in Ireland, and on the Auxiliary Means which it will be necessary to employ in Carrying that Measure into Effect.* London:

Longman, Rees, Orme, Brown, & Green, 1837, pp. 128–149. Again in R. Torrens: *The Budget. On Commercial and Colonial Policy.* London: Smith, Elder, and Co., 1844, 83–98. Page references are to the 1837 printing.

Uzawa, Hirofumi: "Walras' Existence Theorem and Brouwer's Fixed-Point Theorem, "*Economic Studies Quarterly,* 8 (No. 1, 1962), 59–62.

Valavanis-Vail, Stefan: "Leontief's Scarce Factor Paradox," *Journal of Political Economy,* 52 (December 1954); 523–528.

Viner, Jacob: "The Doctrine of Comparative Costs," *Weltwirtschaftliches Archiv,* 36 (1932, II), 356–414.

———: *Studies in the Theory of International Trade.* New York: Harper and Brothers Publishers, 1937.

Wald, Abraham: "Über die eindeutige positive Lösbarkeit der neuen Produktionsgleichungen," *Ergebnisse eines mathematischen Kolloquiums,* Heft 6 (1933–1934), 12–20.

———: "Über die Produktionsgleichungen der ökonomischen Wertlehre," *Ergebnisse eines mathematischen Kolloquiums,* Heft 7 (1934–1935), 1–6.

Walras, Léon: "Observations sur le principe de la théorie du prix de MM. Auspitz et Lieben," *Revue d'Economie Politique,* 4 (May-June 1890), 320–323. English translation in Léon Walras: *Elements of Pure Economics, or the Theory of Social Wealth* (translated by W. Jaffé). London: George Allen and Unwin, 1954, pp. 483–488.

Whewell, W.: "Mathematical Exposition of some Doctrines of Political Economy. Second Memoir," [Read April 15, 1850], *Transactions of the Cambridge Philosophical Society,* 9 (1856), Part I, 128–129.

Whitin, T. M.: "Classical Theory, Graham's Theory and Linear Programming in International Trade," *Quarterly Journal of Economics,* 67 (November 1953), 520–544.

Chapter 5

A Survey of the Theory of International Trade: Part II, The Neo-Classical Theory*

John S. Chipman†

1. The Neo-Classical Model

What is generally considered to be the "neo-classical" theory of international values actually consists of at least two separate strands that have been gradually woven together. One is the Marshallian apparatus of the reciprocal demand curve (or "offer curve" as it is now usually called), which is contained in Marshall's *Pure Theory* (1879), and which was privately published and not brought to light until 1930 after Marshall's death. There had, however, been an exposition with Marshall's approval by Pantaleoni (1898,

*Originally published in *Econometrica*, 33(4), pp. 685–760.

†This is the last in a series of survey articles which *Econometrica* is publishing with the support of the Rockefeller Foundation. Because of its length, this article is being published in three parts. Part 1 on the Classical Theory appeared in the July, 1965 issue and Part 3 on the Modern Theory is scheduled to appear in the January, 1966 issue. Research was facilitated by a grant to the author of an Auxiliary Research Award by the Social Science Research Council, as well as a grant by the National Science Foundation. Grateful acknowledgement is made to Professor Samuelson for comments on an earlier draft; he is not, of course, to be held responsible for any errors that remain. Equally absolved are M. C. Kemp and R. W. Jones, whose valuable criticisms of a later draft are greatly appreciated.

pp. 164–209), and later on Marshall presented his own revised version in the form of Appendix J to *Money, Credit, and Commerce* (1923). Marshall himself described this work simply as "a diagrammatic treatment of Mill's problem of international values."[1]

The other strand consists of what appears to be a spontaneous development on the part of different authors writing (in many cases) independently of one another in the early 1930's. The development may be said to have started with a paper by Haberler (1930), introducing the "production substitution curve," now usually called a transformation curve or function. This was followed by a paper presented in 1931 by Viner, reported by him later (Viner (1937, p. 521)), in which the transformation curve and "community indifference curve" (he did not use this expression) were combined in a way that is now familiar to all graduate students of international trade theory. This was followed by a classic paper by Leontief (1933) and two fundamental papers by Lerner (1932, 1934). The diagrammatic technique introduced by these writers was finally perfected by Meade (1952a), and the model was given mathematical rigor by Nikaidô (1956, 1957).

The method followed by Leontief (1933) and Lerner (1934) was that of obtaining a country's offer curve from its community indifference curves, by analogy to the corresponding derivation for the case of an individual. This derivation was already quite implicit in the work of Edgeworth (1881, pp. 104–16), who did not bother to fill in the geometrical details; these details were filled in by Pareto (1909, pp. 169–97), W. E. Johnson (1913), and Bowley (1924, pp. 5–18). Johnson's paper was, in turn, discussed at considerable length by Edgeworth (*Papers*, II, pp. 451–77).

An illustration of this kind of derivation is given in Figure 1, showing three cases corresponding to a utility function of the form

$$U = (x_1^{-\beta} + x_2^{-\beta})^{-1/\beta},$$

[1]In a letter to J. B. Clark; cf. the variorum edition of the *Principles* (1961), Vol. II, p. 10. Also, in a letter to H. Cunynghame, reproduced in A.C. Pigou, *Memorials* (1925, p. 451), he said: "As to International Trade curves: — Mine were set to a definite tune, that called by Mill. It is improbable that I shall ever publish them: but I am not certain. I am rather tired of them."

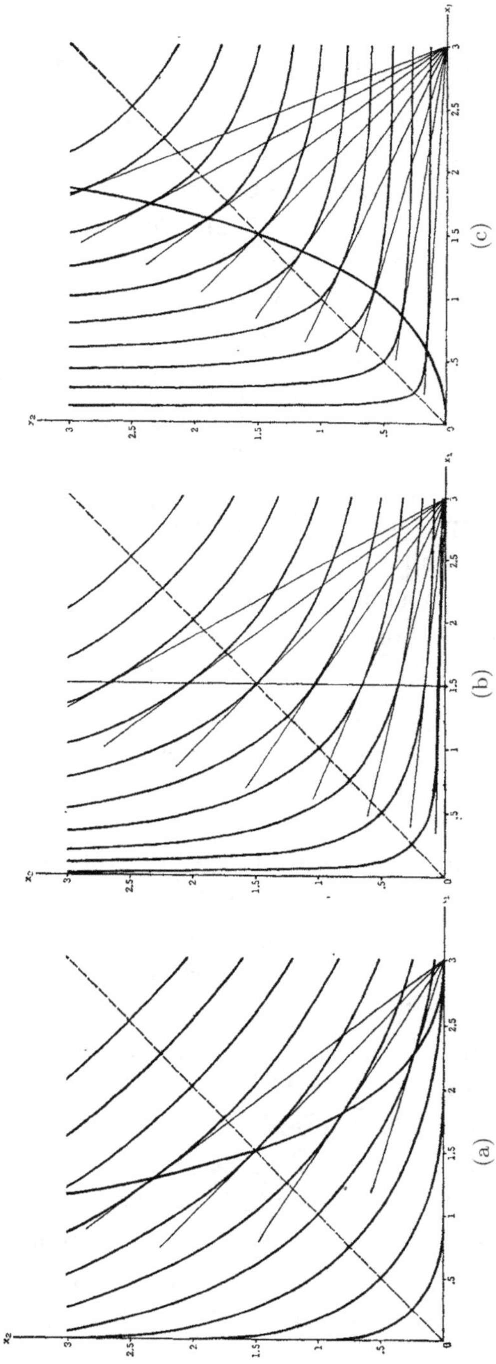

Figure 1.

which was introduced by Arrow, Chenery, Minhas, and Solow (1961). The three cases are (a) $\beta = -\frac{1}{2}$, (b) $\beta \to 0$, and (c) $\beta = 1$, the intermediate one leading to the utility function $U = x_1^{\frac{1}{2}} x_2^{\frac{1}{2}}$. The parameter β is related to the elasticity of substitution σ by the formula $\sigma = 1/(1+\beta)$, as shown by Uzawa (1962b); thus in the three cases we have (a) $\sigma = 2$, (b) $\sigma = 1$, and (c) $\sigma = \frac{1}{2}$. It is assumed that a given consumer has 3 units of commodity 1, and none of commodity 2. In Cases (a) and (c) the offer functions are parabolas (mirror images of each other), and in Case (b) a vertical straight line. The intermediate case, of course, is the Millian case, which we have already considered in detail.

This example illustrates an interesting general principle, due to Eisenberg (1961). Suppose there are two individuals, each with 3 units of commodity 1 and none of commodity 2, and suppose their utility functions correspond respectively to Case (a) and Case (c). In the aggregate, their supply of commodity 1 will be a constant, equal to three units, regardless of the price; that is, their behavior will be the same as if both of them were considered as having the intermediate utility function corresponding to Case (b). This shows that there exist cases in which it makes sense to aggregate utility functions; just what conditions make this possible is a question to be taken up again in Section 2.3 below.

Assuming for the present that the concept of a community indifference curve can be made logically acceptable, the question arises as to how best to portray production as well as consumption. This problem was solved by Meade (1952a) by means of a beautifully ingenious geometric technique, which has become a standard part of the pedagogy. In Figure 2, the set S (called the "production block") is the production possibility set, assumed to be defined independently of commodity prices; this assumes that preferences on the part of factors among different employments are invariant with respect to these prices. (A sufficient condition for this is that factors be indifferent as to employment among different occupations.) Let the vector $t = (x, y)$ represent any given trade for the country under consideration, a positive quantity signifying an import and

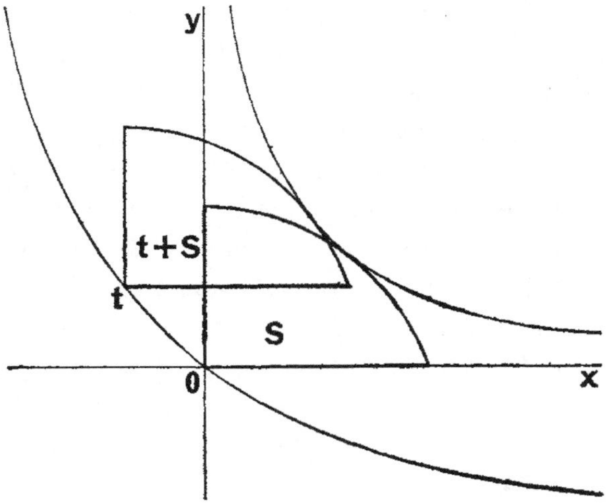

Figure 2.

a negative quantity an export; then the boundary of the set $t + S$ (which is the set of all vectors $t + s$ where $s \in S$) represents the set of all bundles available to consumers. Sliding the production block along an indifference curve, the origin t traces out Meade's "trade indifference curve"; the Marshallian offer curve is then obtained from the trade indifference curves in the usual manner.

There can be no question as to the great value which the neo-classical model, as exemplified by Meade's *Geometry* (1952a), has as a pedagogical tool. However, it is natural to inquire whether it is no more than that. It is customary for the pedagogue in international trade theory to bend over backwards in this regard, and admit that the real world is much more complex; yet he will cling to the model on the grounds of pedagogy. In spite of the disclaimers, one will actually observe that the neo-classical model has in fact other uses: generalizations are made concerning the effects of tariffs on the terms of trade, concerning the stability of a system of free exchange rates, concerning a whole host of problems, all of which depend quite crucially on at least the approximate conformity of the model to reality.

There have, of course, been attempts to set forth the neo-classical model in much more general terms. The earliest such attempt appears to be that of Pareto (1894a, 1894b, 1895), and it is rather significant that he was not able to develop the theory much beyond the counting of equations and unknowns, providing at best a loose (neither necessary nor sufficient) criterion for existence of equilibrium. This difficulty was fully appreciated by Mosak (1944, p. 179), who analyzed international trade from the most general approach, but with a view to going beyond the some-what sterile results that this approach had yielded heretofore. It is no criticism of Mosak, but simply a commentary on the nature of things, to say that he was still forced in most cases to indicate what information would be needed in order to arrive at an answer to the kind of question that is usually put for policy purposes. This is the traditional dilemma of economic theory: unless appropriate simplifications can be made, an almost impossibly large amount of information must be obtained in order that any clear conclusions can be drawn.

The difficulties were summarized by Edgeworth in a very well-known statement, which he even quoted himself (1905, p. 70):

> There is more than meets the eye in Professor Marshall's foreign trade curves. As it has been said by one who used this sort of curve [namely Edgeworth himself (1894, pp. 424–5)], a movement along a supply-and-demand curve of international trade should be considered as attended with rearrangements of internal trade; as the movement of the hand of a clock corresponds to considerable unseen movements of the machinery.

Yet Edgeworth himself displayed offer curves in his diagrams that were all derivable, as we can easily verify in retrospect, by the techniques of Leontief, Lerner, and Meade. We also know now (cf. Johnson (1959)) that there are weird-looking offer curves which are quite possible, but which could not be so derived.

Thus, bad theory can hardly be good pedagogy, and the simplified neo-classical model deserves to be evaluated on its merits.

2. The Representative Citizen

There are two quite different interpretations that might be placed on the neo-classical simplification, and it is not at all clear which is the generally received one. Let us first consider the concept, first clearly specified — within the specific context of international trade — by Pigou (1932), of the Representative Citizen. In Pigou's formulation, trade between England and Germany could be analyzed in terms of trade between a Representative Englishman and a Representative German. In Pigou's words (1932, p. 532), "each of the two countries is depicted as consisting exclusively of representative citizens, all of them exactly alike and behaving in the same way."

Pigou's concept clearly derived from Jevons (1871), who developed the notion of a "trading body" (cf. Jevons (1957, pp. 88–90)). It was implicit in his treatment (but only implicit) that trade between trading bodies could be thought of as decomposed into trade between their members; but the concept was vague enough so that it came in for considerable criticism on the part of Wicksell (1893, pp. 47–8; 1954, pp. 73–4) and Young (1912, pp. 584–5).

The Pigovian concept can be shown to be quite valid in the case of pure exchange. In this case, the "production block" becomes simply a rectangle, as indicated by Haberler (1950). While Pigou did not make reference to Edgeworth in this connection, the latter had provided a justification for such a procedure in *Mathematical Psychics* (1881, p. 35), one which has recently been elegantly spelled out and developed by Debreu and Scarf (1963, p. 241). The justification consists in the demonstration that according to Edgeworth's principle of recontract, if there are an equal number of traders on each side, identical within each group (in both their initial holdings and their tastes), then they must end up with equal final holdings. This of course is automatically assured when there is perfect competition, since the traders all have to pay the same prices (this is Jevons' Law of Indifference).

In the more general case of variable production, the situation is the same, provided constant returns to scale are assumed (cf.

Debreu and Scarf (1963, pp. 244–5)). This apparently is the situation supposed by Meade (1952a, p. 9) who assumes "that each country is made up of a set of citizens with identical tastes and factor endowments ...." These citizens must therefore be equally productive laborers, and at the same time they must be equally endowed capitalists, all with the same distribution of ownership in resources. In this case we can justify, as a conceptual device, the scaling down of the national production block in proportion to the relative size of the Representative Citizen.

The assumption that people have identical tastes is certainly not outrageous (particularly within one nation and culture), and can perhaps be justified on the grounds of biological and cultural similarity. If a rich man prefers caviar, this does not imply that his preference map is different from that of a poor man; it may simply mean that the Engel curve fans out in the direction of caviar as income increases. But this is what causes the difficulty as soon as we consider more realistic cases. If representative citizens are not equal in endowments, and if, say, we replace two of them by one who has double the endowment, then the latter citizen's indifference map must be a blown-up version of the former's; that is, the utility function has to be *homothetic.* Thus, inequality in factor endowment requires much more stringent assumptions concerning preferences.

3. Community Indifference

If the distribution of factor endowments among citizens is unequal, and if tastes (preference maps) are identical, the question arises as to what are the necessary and sufficient conditions for the existence of community indifference curves, or more exactly, what are necessary and sufficient conditions for the integrability of the collective offer function. In other words, under what conditions can it be said that a country as a whole acts "as if" it were a single "rational" unit? Contrary to a popular impression, this problem has not been completely solved, either in the affirmative or in the negative.

A sufficient condition is known; I shall call it the *strong homothety* condition. It requires that the utility functions of all citizens be not only identical but also homothetic to the origin, that is, that they be monotone transforms of positive homogeneous functions. This means that the proportions in which commodities are consumed depend only on relative commodity prices, and not on the level of income (or of utility); thus the income-consumption curves are all straight lines emanating from the origin.

From this assumption it is easy to see, upon consideration of the familiar Edgeworth box, that the locus of possible competitive equilibria, for all initial distributions of given quantities between two traders, in the straight line joining the origins. Given any quantities to be distributed between two citizens, the dimensions of the box are thereby determined, and so in turn, therefore, is the price ratio, which is invariant with respect to the initial distribution of the commodities between them. If the price ratio is to be invariant with respect to all distributions, this homothety condition is also necessary, as was pointed out by Samuelson (1956, p. 5n). It was further observed by Samuelson that this is precisely the same as the criterion which he had previously established (1952), with the use of community indifference curves, for a unilateral transfer from one country to another to have no effect on the terms of trade.

If we are to require only that price ratios are to be invariant with respect to equilibrium distributions in the *interior* of the Edgeworth box, then a weaker criterion is possible, which for convenience I shall call the *weak homothety* condition. In this case we specify the indifference curves to be homothetic not to the origin but to minus infinity (that is, to the point whose coordinates are all $-\infty$); this simply means that for every given set of prices, the income-consumption lines of different individuals must be parallel straight lines, not necessarily going through the origin.[2] This is the criterion obtained by Gorman (1953), and derived very succinctly for the case

[2]This means that for any fixed set of prices, the income-consumption lines of different individuals must be parallel to each other; it does not necessarily imply that, for any one person, the income-consumption lines are parallel for different prices. As it happens, however, in our example which follows, this is indeed the case.

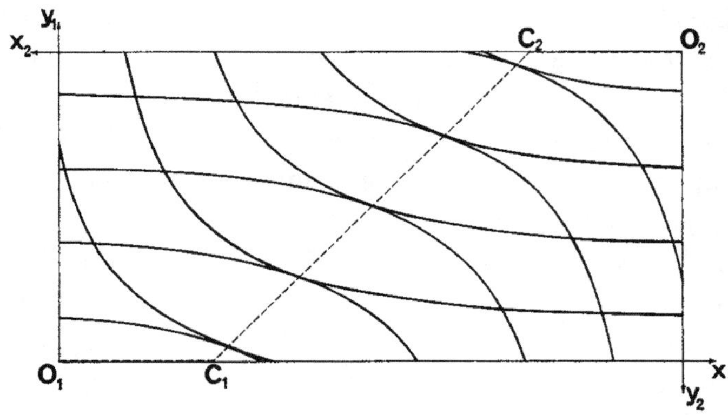

Figure 3.

of two individuals and two commodities by Samuelson (1956, p. 5n). An illustration of the Gorman conditions is given in Figure 3, where x_i and y_i are the quantities of two commodities available to the ith individual, and where the two individuals each have utility functions of the form

$$U = -e^{-x} - e^{-y}.$$

If p and q are the prices of the respective commodities, and if U is maximized subject to $px + qy =$ constant, then setting the marginal utilities proportional to the prices, we obtain

$$y - x = \log(p/q) = \log p - \log q,$$

which holds as long as x and y are nonnegative. In Figure 3, the locus of all competitive equilibria that can be reached from any initial distributions of the commodities is the broken line $O_1C_1C_2O_2$. Along the segment O_1C_1 the equilibrium price ratio corresponds to the slope of individual 2's indifference curve through any given point; along C_1C_2 it is the slope of the common tangent; and along C_2O_2, the slope of individuals indifference curve through any given point. Only if we know in advance that the initial distributions are limited in such a way that no points other than those on C_1C_2 can be reached in competitive equilibrium, will it be possible to say that the relative prices are uniquely determined.

Linear expenditure functions have a long history in mathematical economics. Gossen (1854) assumed utility functions to be quadratic, leading to linear marginal utility functions. Launhardt (1885) fully exploited these linear functions, and was evidently the first to appreciate their implications with respect to the problem of aggregation. It seems that he took linear marginal utility for granted, since no other aggregation. It seems that he took linear marginal utility for granted, since no other possibilities were considered in his work; for this, Wicksell (1893) properly took him to task. But in saying with reference to Launhardt's aggregation theorem (1885, p. 47) that "It is open to doubt whether any practical importance can be attached to it," Wicksell (1954, p. 73) was being unduly harsh; linear approximation is so generally accepted in the physical sciences that it is strange to find economists condemning it.

Allen and Bowley (1935, pp. 109–12, 135–7) considered properties of utility functions of the form

$$U = \sum_{i=1}^{n} a_i x_i + \frac{1}{2} \sum_{i=1}^{n} \sum_{i=1}^{n} a_{ij} x_i x_j,$$

and fitted the resulting linear expenditure functions (Engel curves) to budget data; some of the fits (1935, pp. 22–31) were remarkably good. Prais (1952–53) found that nonlinear functions were required for a good fit over wide ranges of income, and Houthakker (1952, 1953) raised an additional logical objection to Allen and Bowley's procedure; this was further discussed by Prais and Houthakker (1955, pp. 15–17). The objection raised by Houthakker (1952, p. 5) was that once the nonnegativity constraint is taken into account, the Engel curve for any group of commodities, or even for any single commodity, would be a broken line made up of linear segments. For instance, if in Figure 3 the price ratio is given by the slope of the tangents along C_1C_2, then the income-consumption line will be $O_1C_1C_2$; it is even possible, in the case of inferior goods, for the income-consumption line to zig-zag once across the positive quadrant.[3]

---

[3]The reader may visualize this by imagining a family of concentric ellipses, with center in the northwest quadrant, and with major axis crossing the positive

The similarity between the problem of constructing community indifference curves and Theil's formulation (1954) of the aggregation problem has been observed by Samuelson (1956, p. 5n). Theil noted two quite distinct aggregation criteria which are in a sense dual to one another. To consider a simple example, that of a linear consumption function of the form $C = a + bY$, there are two cases in which the aggregate function makes sense. One is that in which, in the m individual equations $C_i = a_i + b_i Y_i$, the micro-parameters b_i are all equal to one another; then the aggregate equation is simply Σ $\mathrm{C}_i = \Sigma a_i + b\Sigma Y_i$, where $b = b_i$ as assumed. The other case is that in which the b_i may be different, yet the incomes Y_i stay proportionate to one another, so that $Y_i = \lambda_i Y$ where $\Sigma Y_i = Y$; then the aggregate equation becomes $\Sigma C_i = \Sigma a_i + (\Sigma b_i \lambda_i)Y$, and the community acts "as if" all its members had as their marginal propensity to consume the weighted average of the micro-parameters, namely $\Sigma b_i \lambda_i$.

The second, dual, criterion also has its counterpart in the problem of constructing a community preference function. In the case of the strong homothety condition, all individuals are required to have identical and homothetic utility functions, but there is no restriction as to the distribution of resources among them. The dual situation would be that in which all individuals have the same proportionate share in total resources, but in which their utility functions, while still homothetic to the origin, are no longer required to be identical. The first criterion was what Samuelson (1956, p. 5n) called a "far-fetched but valid fifth defense of community indifference curves"; this dual one is then a sixth defense. It is perhaps equally far-fetched; that it is at any rate valid is the main result of the important paper by Eisenberg (1961).

quadrant into the southeast quadrant. Let the intersections of these ellipses with the nonnegative quadrant form the indifference curves. Then for some family of parallel budget lines, the income-consumption line will move along the x-axis to the right, then move across along a straight line to the y-axis, and then up the latter until satiety is reached.

A technique for this purpose was worked out by Houthakker (1953). However, there seem to be a number of lacunae in his method, such as the failure to take account of the possibility of local saturation (e.g., 1953, p. 61, condition 1).

Eisenberg stated the problem in the following terms: if each of m individuals has a fixed money income, and if they all have homogeneous utility functions (not necessarily identical, it must be emphasized), then their aggregate demand function is integrable, that is, it may be thought of as resulting from the maximization of some fictitious aggregate utility function,[4] subject to total expenditure being equal to total income. This formulation is not immediately applicable to the problem under consideration, but can be readily adapted to it; the relevant specialization of the theorem to the exchange model was very briefly pointed out by Eisenberg (1961, p. 337n), and is worth spelling out here in detail.

Let a_{ij} be the amount of the ith commodity initially held by the jth individual, there being n commodities and m individuals. (In the more realistic production model, we would let a_{ij} stand for the amount of the ith resource — such as labor, capital, etc. — owned by the jth individual.) Let $a_i = \sum_{j=1}^{m} a_{ij}$ be the total amount of the ith commodity, and q_j the money income of the jth individual, assumed fixed (this assumption will later be reinterpreted). Let $A = [a_{ij}]$ be the matrix of initial endowments, and $a = (a_i)$ the column vector of total holdings; let $q = (q_j)$ be the row vector of the m incomes, and $p = (p_i)$ the row vector of the n prices. Then if 1 denotes a column vector of ones, we have

$$Al = a; \quad pa = 1,$$

the second of these equations being simply a normalization of the prices (pa being the inner product of p and a). Now we show that $A = aq$ if and only if $pA = q$ for all p satisfying $pa = 1$. First, if $A = aq$, then $pA = paq = q$. Conversely, let P be an $n \times n$ nonsingular matrix whose rows all satisfy $pa = 1$. Then $Pa = \mathit{1}$, therefore $a = P^{-1}\mathit{1}$. Now if $pA = q$ for all p satisfying $pa = \mathit{1}$, then $PA = \mathit{1}q$, whence $A = P^{-1}\mathit{1}q = aq$. This proves that a necessary and

[4]Eisenberg unfortunately gave this aggregate utility function the misleading name of "social-welfare function" (1961, p.341). No welfare considerations are involved here at all, only behavior. For this important distinction, see also the remark attributed to Turvey by Meade (1952a, p. 9n).

sufficient condition for satisfying Eisenberg's criterion of constant money incomes is that $a_{ij} = a_i q_j$, whence $a_{ij}/a_{hj} = a_i/a_h$, i.e., the holdings of every single individual are proportionate to the total holdings of all individuals.

Owing to the homogeneity of utility functions, we can clearly relax (or reinterpret) the assumption that incomes are fixed. It is only necessary to assume that *relative* incomes are fixed, and this is what is guaranteed, regardless of prices, as long as each individual's initial holdings are simply scaled-down fractions of the aggregate initial holdings. The case illustrated in Figure 1 was that in which each individual held a certain quantity of one and the same commodity; then the criterion is satisfied automatically. Here, then, we have a proof of the proposition that if every member of a "trading body" possesses a certain quantity of the *same* commodity, and if their utility functions are positive homogeneous (but not necessarily identical), then the "trading body" will act *as if* it had a single utility function; Jevons is vindicated after all!

It may be conjectured that this theorem can be extended to production, provided constant returns to scale are assumed, in which case it would state that if all individuals have proportionate shares in total resources (i.e., labor and capital in proportion to aggregate labor and capital), and if they also have positive homogeneous utility functions, then a community utility function can be constructed to represent their behavior. Roughly, this means that if there are 100 equally productive workers and 50 identical machines, then each worker must own a share in half a machine; or that if a man's labor is more productive than his neighbor's, he must own correspondingly more capital. Our Representative Citizens must all be scaled-down models of Society; and conversely the State, in a very literal sense, must be Man Writ Large. But the individual utility functions need not be scaled-down replicas of the average utility function.

To summarize, we may say that if utility functions of all people are positive homogeneous, and if either (1) all people have identical tastes, or (2) all people have a distribution of resources proportionate to the aggregate distribution, then their behavior can be represented by a single utility function. Since these two conditions are independent, and each of them is sufficient, obviously neither one of them is necessary in itself. The conditions also suggest the conjecture that if the set of allowable relative incomes has dimensionality somewhere in between m and 0, then in some sense one could allow a corresponding number of degrees of freedom in the extent to which utility functions are permitted to differ from one another.

Conclusions similar to the above are also implicit in the work of Wald (1940), who had, in his work on index numbers (1939), considered the implications of linear Engel curves as suggested by Allen and Bowley. If tastes are identical and income distributions are not too unequal, so that all individuals can be regarded as being located on the same equal-sloped segments of their Engel curves (this kind of qualification is needed to take account of the important point raised by Hout-hakker), then the Engel curves can be aggregated according to Theil's first criterion. Alternatively, if individual tastes differ, but relative incomes remain unchanged, and if fluctuations in income are moderate enough so that each individual stays on the same linear segment of his Engel curve, then Theil's second criterion can be applied, and an aggregate linear Engel curve can be defined, at least over the relevant range. In either case, the question arises as to whether the preference map can be obtained from knowledge of the slope of the Engel curves; this is precisely the problem considered by Wald (1940), who solved it on the assumption of quadratic utility functions, and found necessary and sufficient conditions for integrability. Thus the essential truth of Eisenberg's theorem has actually been implicit in the economic literature ever since the publication of this important 1940 paper by Wald.

Scitovsky (1942) defined community indifference curves as loci of quantities demanded at various price ratios and a given fixed distribution of *utilities* among individuals; thus he recognized that through any point of the commodity space, there would in general pass (and cross) an infinity of aggregate indifference curves, one for each distribution of utilities compatible with that particular aggregate demand. More recently, Stolper (1950) spelt out and clarified the nature of this aggregation process; and Lerner (1932) had already employed such a procedure for aggregating transformation functions of several countries. Mathematically, what is involved is the addition of sets.

That one could in general expect that curves so constructed would cross, and that as a consequence one could not generally expect to construct an aggregate utility function, was fully appreciated by Viner (1937, pp. 521–3). Leontief (1933), who did so much to establish the concept of community indifference curves for analytical purposes, did not bring up the question of how they might be obtained from individual preferences. On the other hand, Lerner (1932, 1934) went to considerable lengths to analyze the concept, and his very interesting discussion suggests that there are still some important open questions that have not yet received the attention they deserve.

Lerner's first paper (1932) contains the following remarkable footnote:

> The consumption indifference curves in this paper are curves which show by their slope at any point the rate at which the commodities will exchange against one another when the quantities produced are those indicated by the co-ordinates of that point. It may be objected that they are not pure "indifference" curves as their shape would depend on the distribution of resources and would be affected by what is actually produced. This, however, does not matter, for although one cannot say that the community is "indifferent," in terms of absolute satisfaction, to the different points on an indifference curve, yet the *behaviour* of the community with respect to these curves is exactly comparable to that of an individual with respect to his true indifference curves. This, I think, could be demonstrated, but it is not necessary here, where all that is done, after all, is to describe equilibrium conditions.

While this expresses only a conjecture, it is noteworthy that the approach Lerner adopted was completely free from any extraneous welfare considerations.[5]

---

[5]The construction attempted in the second of two papers by Baumol (1946–47, 1949–50) cannot be regarded as successful, as was made clear by the "impossibility

In the second of his fundamental papers (1934), Lerner started out by acknowledging that "the legitimacy of the procedure still remains to be vindicated." In a foreshadowing of Samuelson's "revealed preference" theory (1947, p. 111), he then said of the community, in comparison with the individual: "It, too, can just as tautologically be said to prefer that which is acquired by the community to that which might have been acquired in its stead." The statement ceases to be a tautology, however, if the weak axiom of revealed preference is applied and it is postulated that the community must not reveal itself on another occasion to reverse its preference as between two points of equilibrium.

Such a postulate, with respect to a community, was introduced by Wald (1933–34, 1935–36, 1952), writing at the same time as Lerner. (Wald later presented an exposition of his work (1936), the mathematics of which has been simplified by Kuhn (1956b).) Wald defined demand functions with prices as dependent variables and quantities as independent variables, a procedure that was criticized by Dorfman, Samuelson, and Solow (1958, pp. 352n, 367), and quite properly so; at best, this assumed much of what was to be proved, namely uniqueness of prices. It turns out, however, that this formulation is easily rectified, which Dorfman, Samuelson, and Solow proceeded to do, but they also abandoned (p. 368) Wald's assumption that the community conformed to (what Samuelson later and independently called) the weak axiom of revealed preference.

---

theorem" of Arrow (1951b). The problem to which Baumol addressed himself was a problem in welfare economics, namely that of the construction (free of value judgments) of a social welfare function. This problem is now widely recognized as being insoluble, but it has nothing to do with the question under discussion here.

If one is willing to postulate a social welfare function with interpersonal comparisons of utility (in policy matters, this can hardly be avoided, after all), then of course that is a different matter; this was the principal subject of discussion in Samuelson's 1956 paper. A recent paper by Vanek (1964) also falls into this category. Long ago Edgeworth (1881, pp. 56–82) introduced a specific construction of this kind, based on the Fechnerian notion of just noticeable differences. There is no reason why such social welfare functions should coincide with the kind of aggregate behavior functions we are discussing in the text; in fact there is every reason to doubt it.

Morishima, although observing (1960, p. 65) that "there is no reason why the collective demand and supply functions should satisfy this axiom," adopted it in any case, and stated that "once it is assumed, we can prove that the equilibrium is unique." He relied on a theorem of Arrow and Hurwicz (1958, p. 534), which these authors have since indicated is not quite correct (1960, p. 640); nevertheless the exceptional case seems pathological enough so that we can safely say that, for practical purposes, the weak axiom of revealed preference, when applied to the community, implies uniqueness of equilibrium.[6]

Dorfman, Samuelson, and Solow (1958, p. 374) had pointed out that uniqueness would result, in the model they were considering, if the weak revealed preference axiom was assumed. And they added (pp. 374–5n): "If there are 2 or more persons, the assumption that total market demand satisfies the 'weak axiom' implies that their indifference surfaces (if they have transitive preferences) must have unitary income elasticities for all goods ..." Since unitary income elasticity is characteristic of positive homogeneous utility functions, this statement is fully in accord with Eisenberg's theorem; it is illustrated in Figure 1 above, in which individuals (a) and (c) have unitary income elasticities of demand, and in the aggregate behave as if they were both like individual (b), who conforms to the weak axiom of revealed preference.[7]

It is natural to ask how this can be reconciled with Samuelson's "impossibility theorem" (1956). The latter theorem is perfectly correct; it states that an aggregate utility function can be defined, invariant with respect to *all* redistributions of initial endowments, if and only if utility functions are identical and homothetic to the

[6]The correct theorem proved by Arrow and Hurwicz (1960) is that the weak axiom of revealed preference implies that the set of equilibria is convex. Thus, neutral equilibrium is still possible; but applying some kind of probability argument we could undoubtedly conclude that such non-isolated equilibria are totally improbable.

[7]As it happens in this example, the aggregate individual also has a unitary elasticity of substitution, but his is coincidental and not necessary to the argument.

origin. Now many, perhaps most, practical applications of international trade theory — in the fields of capital movements, commercial policy, etc. — are concerned precisely with the consequences of shifts in the distribution of wealth; in such applications, the concept of community indifference has to he used with utmost care, if at all. On the other hand, there are applications in which resource ownership and tax structure remain unchanged, so that income redistribution takes place *only via changes in factor prices;* for such cases, the requirements of the impossibility theorem are unduly severe, although its logic cannot, of course, be disputed.

As an example of the difficulties in interpretation, consider Samuelson's statement (1956, p. 3): "Logically ... it will be as hard or easy to draw up community indifference curves for the whole world as to do it for any subgroup of individuals." This statement is worth considering in detail, as it brings out many of the essential problems. If we consider methods of aggregation corresponding only to Theil's first criterion, the statement is logically correct; and of course in Figure 1 in Part 1 of this article, several world indifference curves were drawn, which was possible owing to the assumption that tastes were identical and homothetic in both countries. Now, it may be a good approximation to assume that, in the relevant range, utility functions in a rich country are identical and homothetic; and also those for a poor country, in its relevant range. But in this case, the concept of a world indifference curve would not be a valid approximation; this is a matter of practical application, rather than of strict logic.

With respect to Theil's second criterion, on the other hand, the statement quoted above is not exact. If, to take Jevons' example (1957, pp. 95–8) of two trading bodies, one of which possesses corn and the other beef, and if we assume all individuals' utility functions to be positive homogeneous, then with fixed distributions of initial endowments among individuals it is possible to define a utility function for each body, but not for the aggregate of the two. Note, however, that such utility functions for trading bodies are not invariant with respect to distribution of the one commodity among their members; a redistribution would lead to a new aggregate utility function for the trading body.

What conclusions may be drawn from this long discussion? Possibly the most fruitful approach is to find a compromise between total disaggregation on the one hand, and complete aggregation on the other. Such an approach has been followed by Johnson (1959), who has considered labor and capital as separate consuming groups, as well as separate factors; this model, which we shall discuss again in Sections 2.6 and 2.7 below, presents a most promising idealization.

4. Opportunity Cost

The concept of a production transformation curve (or substitution curve as he called it) was introduced into international trade theory by Haberler (1930). The idea was latent, but certainly not explicit, in the earlier writings of Pareto (1909) and Barone (1908). Pareto (1909, pp. 177–8) introduced the concept of a "line of indifference of obstacles," and of a tug between tastes and obstacles; but the concept seems to have been confined to individuals and firms. He did not, of course, require such a concept within his general equilibrium framework. Nevertheless in his later work Pareto (1911, Section 9, p. 601, eq. (10)) introduced a general transformation function under the heading of "liaisons of the first kind"; but no specific meaning was attached to it.

Lerner (1932) opened his early article with the puzzling statement that "in the *Weltwirtschaftliches Archiv* for July 1930 Dr. Haberler suggests that Barone's figures for the treatment of International Trade need not be restricted to conditions of constant costs ...." Haberler (1930) did not refer to Barone (1908, Ch. III) nor does it seem that he had any reason to, since Barone's curves represented simply cost ratios, and were not true transformation curves. Nevertheless, it appears from the posthumous edition of Barone's work (1936, pp. 170–3) that he had independently arrived in the years 1920–23 at the concepts of "production indifference curve" and "taste indifference curve," as well as at the famous diagram which was later to appear in Viner (1937, p. 521). Barone's production possibility sets were not convex — whether on account of occupational preference or increasing returns was not mentioned.

Another early use of these concepts was that of Young (1928, p. 540) which, he owned, "owes much to Pareto." The "curve of equal costs," as he called it, "defines the terms upon which the community can exchange one commodity for the other by merely producing less of the one and more of the other ..." He specified that convexity corresponded to diminishing returns. A "collective indifference curve" was also defined in this pioneering article, "by the condition that, at equal cost, there would be no sufficient inducement for the community to alter an annual production of x units of one commodity and y units of another in order to secure the alternative combination of the two commodities indicated by any other point on the curve"; but he had sufficient qualms to add that this was "to be taken as an expository device, not as a rigorous conception." Unlike Barone's treatment, Young's was limited to a closed economy; but Young developed the concepts a good deal further than Barone.

We need not go at any length into the rather sterile controversy over "real cost" versus "opportunity cost." It was never very clear what Viner (1937, pp. 483–493) meant by "real costs," and the theory seems to be largely a hold-over from the labor theory of value. Possibly "real costs" meant the domestic (untraded) commodities foregone in the course of producing international commodities; but if so, this was never stated. Haberler (1936, Ch. XII) set forth his doctrine in a chapter entitled "International Trade and General Equilibrium," and he later (1950, p. 224) insisted that "I never regarded the opportunity-cost theory as anything but ... a somewhat simplified general equilibrium approach," and again (1951, p. 55n) that "the opportunity cost theory is a convenient approach, a first, approximation to a general equilibrium theory, while the real cost theory is not." This is fair enough; and so is Vanek's assessment (1959b, p. 200): "The merit of Professor Viner's analysis seems to lie in his awareness of the shortcomings of the opportunity cost theory rather than in a satisfactory reinterpretation of the classical labour theory of value." One would at least like to know under what conditions the opportunity cost concept was logically unobjectionable.

If factors of production are perfectly mobile, and indifferent as between different employments, then there is no problem: there can be no ambiguity concerning the set of possible outputs since this set will not depend on market prices. But Haberler (1936, p. 183; 1950, p. 228) specifically rejected the assumption of perfect mobility. He has treated (1950) the other extreme case of perfect immobility; but in the latter case, immobile factors can be considered formally as different factors, so that according to the new definitions of "factors" we still have "perfect mobility," provided the assumption of factor price flexibility is retained (as it is by Haberler). In this other extreme case the production block (in Meade's terminology) becomes a rectangle, and international trade can be analyzed in terms of a model of pure exchange. But the production possibility set is still independent of prices. The knotty problems arise in the intermediate case in which there is partial mobility, for then the production possibility set can no longer be defined independently of prices. (Some of the conceptual difficulties that arise in this case were discussed at length by Knight (1935)). In this latter case the question arises as to whether the conclusions (especially the policy implications) drawn from the simplified neo-classical model are independent of the seemingly innocent "simplifications" introduced into the theory.

The problem of whether — and if so how — an opportunity cost locus (or general transformation function) can be defined when there are variable factor supplies is that to which Vanek (1959) has addressed himself. His procedure goes as follows. A community utility function is assumed given (he assumes that either utility functions are identical and homogeneous, or that income is optimally redistributed; since the latter course could at best tell us how the economy ought to work, rather than how it does work, I shall stick to the first alternative). This function has quantities of two commodities and two factors as arguments, the latter entering into the production of the former at constant returns to scale. *Assuming some fixed levels of consumption* of the commodities, he draws an indifference curve indicating a constant level of disutility with respect to the two factors, and then, by an ingenious use of the box-diagram technique, finds that the locus of maximum outputs of one commodity for given amounts of the other — which he calls the "production indifference curve" — will lie outside the similar curve corresponding to fixed factor supplies, and touching it at one point. The latter curve Vanek calls the "Haberlerian opportunity cost curve," though from my reading of Haberler (1936, pp. 178–9) — who pointed out that inelasticity in his production substitution curve would result from mobility being "small" — his concept seems closer to Vanek's production indifference curve.

The above analysis was based on the entirely artificial assumption that consumption levels of the two commodities were fixed. In his attempt to remove this assumption (p. 203), Vanek superimposed in the commodity space a family of consumption indifference curves and a family of the just-defined production indifference curves — forgetting that the latter were defined for a fixed amount of consumption and could therefore not be considered to be independent of the former. This oversight vitiates much of the remaining analysis.

Another approach to this problem has been pursued by Caves (1960, pp. 103–8), using an Edgeworth box-diagram technique and allowing the dimensions of the box (the factor supplies) to alter in response to changes in relative factor prices. On this basis he obtains conflicting transformation curves for fixed and variable factor supplies that cross each other. He has attributed this result to Vanek, stating (1960, p. 107–8n) that "Vanek states this conclusion and properly insists that the few writers who have contemplated the fate of the transformation with factor supplies allowed to vary have not clearly indicated this finding." I have not been able to find such a statement in Vanek's paper (1959), where instead the "production indifference curve" appears to be an envelope of transformation curves corresponding to fixed factor supplies. The latter concept is evidently the appropriate one for the case in which factors are fixed in aggregate supply, but not indifferent as between alternative occupations. In the formulation considered by Caves, on the other hand, it appears that factors are indifferent as between alternative occupations, but variable in aggregate supply. The first case can actually be reduced to the second, as Vanek suggested, by the device of enlarging the number of "factors".

The problem of variable factor supply has also been analyzed by Kemp (1964, pp. 96–107). Kemp uses the convenient approach suggested by Walsh (1956) of dealing with leisure rather than labor, so that the geometric analysis can be conducted in the space of the two commodities and leisure. There will be a three-dimensional "production block" in this space, representing production possibilities corresponding to different aggregate supplies of labor — the latter being assumed to be indifferent as between occupations. It is implicit in Kemp's analysis (1964, p. 106) that given the usual assumption of constant returns to scale, the surface of this production block is ruled (although this fact was inadvertently not indicated in Kemp's diagram (1964, p. 104)); what this means is that given any price ratio for the two commodities, the locus of points on the surface having the corresponding slope will be a set of straight line segments. In the case in which each commodity has an unambiguous "factor intensity" — this concept will be discussed in Part 3 of this article — there will be only one such line segment corresponding to each commodity price ratio. This implies that there will be exactly one supporting plane to the surface, corresponding to any given terms of trade, so that the real wage rate is unique for all quantities of labor indicated by the given line segment; this will be recognized as being simply an expression of the factor price equalization theorem. Given this wage rate as well as the commodity prices, the supply of labor is determined — assuming it to remain within the bounds just indicated, ruling out complete specialization; there will thus be a locus of equilibria on the surface of the production block, corresponding to different price ratios for the two commodities. Kemp's procedure is to project this locus onto the plane of the two commodities, thus obtaining the production possibility curve for the case of variable labor supply; it will necessarily cross the projection of the fixed-labor-supply transformation curve going through any of the equilibrium points. Thus, the transformation curves considered by Caves and Kemp are not true transformation curves in the customary sense; for the slope at any point on such a curve no longer represents the price ratio at which the corresponding commodities will be produced. Whether a transformation curve with the latter property can be defined in the case of fixed aggregate factor supplies but imperfect mobility, appears to be still an open question.

5. Determinateness of Equilibrium

The question of "determinateness" is a subtle one, about which some confusion will still be found in the literature. On the one hand, we find statements like the following one of Graham[8] (1932, p. 606):

> The "Equation of International Demand" which Mill first advanced as a solution of his problem was no solution at all. To say that "the produce of a country exchanges for the produce of other countries *at such values* as are required in order that the whole of her exports may exactly pay for the whole of her imports" is a mere truism. For, at whatever values the exports exchange for imports, the whole of the exports will exactly pay for the whole of the imports. It is hard to know how else the imports could be obtained. [Graham's, not Mill's, italics.]

On the other hand, some writers, e.g., Balogh and Streeten (1951, pp. 75–7), have appeared to suggest that there may not exist any such values equating demand and supply; at least this seems to be implied by these authors' nonintersecting curves of supply and demand for foreign exchange. Thus, seemingly the same proposition is apparently dismissed as a truism by some and vehemently challenged by others.

Still a third point of view is found, according to which it is not doubted that equilibrium may be reached, but in which it is emphasized that such an equilibrium might be socially intolerable. Such a viewpoint was expressed by Mrs. Robinson in her celebrated statement (1946–47, p. 102): "The hidden hand will always do its work, but it may work by strangulation." It is surely this third

[8]A virtually identical statement had previously been made by Knight (1924, p. 599), and Graham (1925, pp. 328–9) took issue with it at that time. More to the point is Marshall's statement (1920, p. 759): "every short clear statement of economic doctrine must be a truism, unless it be false."

consideration which is at the root of most controversies on these questions.

Let us first of all consider the prior question of determinacy (rather than optimality) of equilibrium. The above passage which Graham quoted from Mill (1848, Book III, Ch. 18, §4, p. 149) was followed by Mill's statement that "the value of a commodity always so adjusts itself as to bring the demand to the exact level of the supply." It is difficult to see what else this could be but an assertion that a solution to the equations of international demand *exists,* and moreover that such a solution will be reached (i.e., the equilibrium is *stable*). Graham, in using the words "at whatever values the exports exchange for imports ..." was therefore tacitly assuming precisely what has to be proved: that there are any such values at all. Unfortunately, Mill himself appears to have fallen into the same trap when challenged by Thornton, who furnished an example (1869, p. 49) involving indivisible commodities (horses), and hence discontinuous demand functions, in which no equilibrium price would exist which could equate demand and supply. Mill replied (1869, p. 510):

> Instead of conflicting with the law, this is the extreme case which proves the law. The law is, that the price will be that which equalises the demand with the supply; and the example proves that this only fails to be the case when there is no price that would fulfil the condition, and that even then, the same causes, still operating, keep the price at the point which will most nearly fulfil it. Is it possible to have any more complete confirmation of the law, than that in order to find a case in which the price does not conform to the law, it is necessary to find one in which there is no price that can conform to it?

If we are to interpret Mill's law as being the assertion that an equilibrium solution to the equations of international demand *exists,* then we have to conclude that the great logician has let us down, and fallen into the fallacy of *petitio principii,* a fallacy which, as Mill himself had pointed out (1891, p. 538), "is seldom resorted to, at least in express terms, by any person in his own speculations, but is committed by those who, being hard pressed by an adversary, are forced into giving reasons for an opinion of which, when they began to argue, they had not sufficiently considered the grounds."

That a thinker of Mill's stature should have committed such an elementary error in logic is rather hard to believe as long as an alternative interpretation is open. There is indeed an alternative way of interpreting Mill's law: that it states that as long as an equilibrium solution exists, then the economic system is *stable,* in the sense that *some* equilibrium price constellation will be reached. Mill did not use the terms "stable" and "unstable," but he left no doubt that the process he was discussing was a dynamic process of adjustment (1869, p. 508):

> If at the market price the demand exceeds the supply, the competition of buyers will drive up the price to the point at which there will only be purchases for as much as is offered for sale. If, on the contrary, the supply, being in excess of the demand, cannot be all disposed of at the existing price, either a part will be withdrawn to wait for a better market, or a sale will be forced by offering it at such a reduction of price as will bring forward new buyers, or tempt the old ones to increase their purchases. The law, therefore, of values, as affected by demand and supply, is that they adjust themselves so as always to bring about an *equation* between demand and supply, by the increase of the one or the diminution of the other; the movement of price being only arrested when the quantity asked for at the current price, and the quantity offered at the current price, are equal. This point of exact equilibrium may be as momentary, but is nevertheless as real, as the level of the sea. [Mill's italics.]

This was about as far as Mill could go without using mathematical analysis. As Marshall said (1879, p. 12): "His treatment of the matter is certainly inadequate: for he has failed to discover the laws which determine whether any particular position of equilibrium is stable or unstable." The real problem was not whether Mill's statement of the law of supply and demand was valid, nor whether it was tautological, but rather that the law is too complex to be adequately stated without mathematical language.

Even if equilibrium prices exist, it is not (as Graham supposed) tautological to say that "at whatever values the exports exchange for imports, the whole of the exports will exactly pay for the whole of the imports." If this be self-evident, then it is difficult to know what one should make of the vast postwar literature on "fundamental disequilibrium," "dollar shortage," and "the problem of international liquidity." As for "how else the imports could be obtained," there are many well-known methods: direct borrowing, running down of reserves, interest-induced or tax-induced capital movements, to mention only a few.

Marshall (1879, pp. 6–7) implicitly defined his offer curves in such a way that each point on a country's offer curve corresponded to a situation of balanced trade; this was later made quite explicit by Edgeworth (1925, Vol. II, p. 353n). The implication is that for any given terms of trade (equilibrium or not) facing a particular country, a "partial" equilibrium will exist ("partial" meaning really "hypothetical," that is, it need not be consistent with the corresponding hypothetical equilibrium reached by the other country or countries) at which that country's trade is balanced; this is how the offer curve is defined. The property of the offer function just described is, of course, the analogue in international trade of Walras' law; in view of its prominence in the work of Cournot (1838, Ch. 3), Mundell has described it (1960, p. 102) as "Cournot's law." Modern stability analysts such as Arrow, Block, and Hurwicz (1959, pp. 83–5) have assumed this law to hold instantaneously and identically in prices. In international trade this assumption could certainly not be made, and was certainly not made by Marshall, as is clear from the brief and somewhat satirical account which he provided (1879, p. 19n); a mathematical model of this adjustment process has been developed by Samuelson (1947, pp. 266–8).

6. Existence

The best way to appreciate the problem of "existence" of equilibrium is to consider counterexamples, that is, to study the conditions under which no equilibrium solution exists. Logic requires that all possibilities be considered, but this usually means that many of the exceptional cases will seem "pathological." A priori reasoning is, however, an unreliable guide in judging whether a particular logical possibility is pathological or not; consequently, we shall consider this logical question in a dispassionate way, leaving it to the reader to draw his own conclusions concerning its relevance to practical cases.

The first counterexample we shall take up will also be used to illustrate an important lemma introduced by Nikaidô (1956, p. 137), which provides the initial step in the existence proof. Figure 4 shows the Edgeworth box, a rectangle with origins O_1 and O_2, with the quantities x_1 and y_1 of two commodities consumed in the

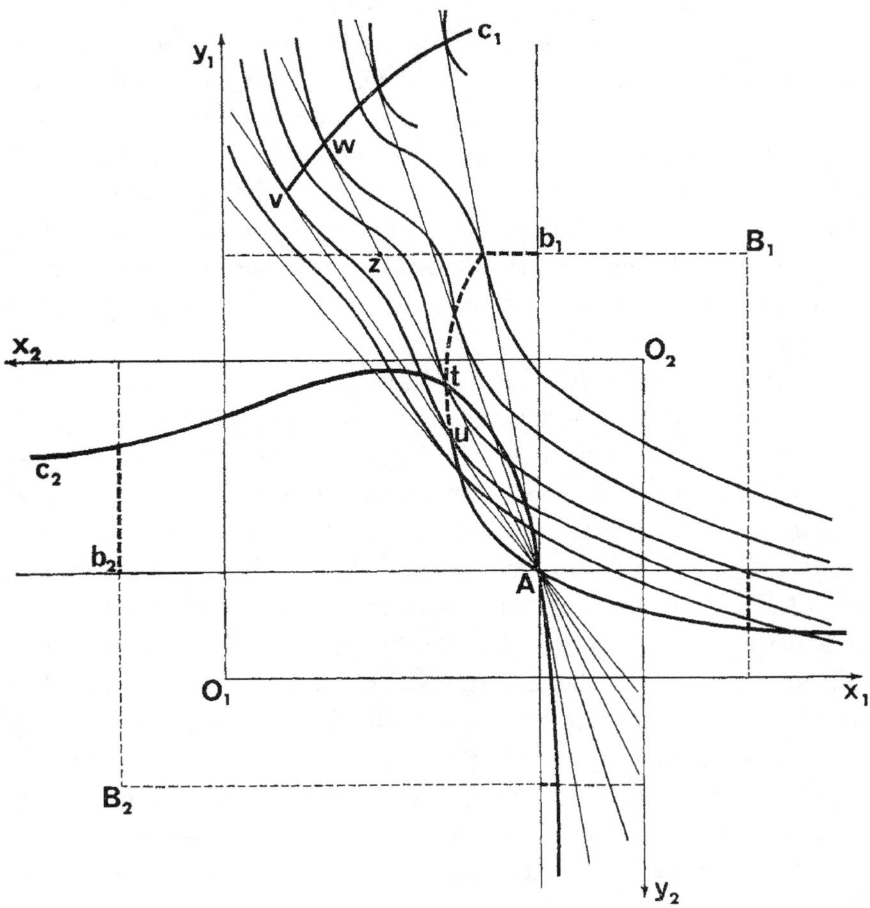

Figure 4.

first country measured to the right and upwards; the quantities x_2 and y_2 consumed in the second country are measured leftwards and downwards. The case illustrated is one of pure exchange, with initial quantities determined at the point A. The peculiar feature of the example is the non-convexity of preference in the first country; as a consequence of this, Country 1's offer curve goes from A to u, then jumps to v, and continues to w and c_1. Country 2's offer curve is the smooth curve Atc_2; since it passes through the gap in 1's offer curve, no equilibrium price ratio exists.

The non-convexity of preference gives rise to a discontinuity in the offer curve. Since the perfect divisibility of commodities is an idealization, with only a slight change this diagram could depict the kind of counterexample suggested by Thornton, which resulted from the indivisibility of commodities. Also, if the indifference curves in Figure 4 are interpreted as Meade's "trade indifference curves," their non-convexity could simply result from that of the production block, that is, could be a consequence of economies in production. But here we must be careful; the question of the proper technique to use in this case of "external economies" will have to be postponed to Section 2.8.

Now we consider Nikaidô's lemma. It will be assumed that in each country all income is spent. From the viewpoint of Country 1, the entire nonnegative quadrant $O_1x_1y_1$ may be considered as representing the set of commodity bundles from which its inhabitants will make their choices at given prices. Obviously, however, they could not conceivably obtain any bundles outside of the Edgeworth box O_1O_2. Thus we may conceive of the price system as providing, at a price ratio given, say, by the straight line Aw, the erroneous information that all the nonnegative bundles on this straight line (produced in both directions) are available; when in fact it is only the points on the corresponding segment of Aw enclosed within the Edgeworth box which are actually available. Now let B_1 represent an amount of both commodities exceeding the total amount available to *both* countries (it is measured from O_1 as origin); likewise let B_2, measured from O_2 as origin, represent a bundle exceeding the total amount available to both countries. Then Nikaidô's lemma states that given certain assumptions (continuity, monotonicity, and the convexity of preferences), equilibrium exists in the first case of unbounded choice if and only if it exists in the second case of bounded choice; that is, the problem of the existence of equilibrium remains unchanged if the choice spaces $O_1x_1y_1$ and $O_2x_2y_2$ are replaced by the rectangles O_1B_1 and O_2B_2 respectively. What Figure 4 shows is that if one of the assumptions (convexity of preference) fails, then the conclusion of Nikaidô's lemma no longer holds.

To see this, we observe that if Country 1's choices are bounded by the rectangle O_1B_1, then its offer curve becomes the continuous curve $Autb_1$. This intersects Country 2's offer curve Atb_2 at t, so an equilibrium solution exists in the bounded model but not in the unbounded one, in contradiction to the conclusion of Nikaidô's lemma.

Now let us see that Nikaidô's lemma follows from the following assumptions:[9] (1) all income is spent, and (2) if a bundle x is

[9]The assumptions used by Nikaidô (1956, p. 136) were (a) representability of preference by means of a continuous real valued utility function, (b) monotonicity of preference (i.e., if a bundle is greater than another in at least one component, and greater than or equal to the other in all the remaining components, then it is preferred), and (c) quasi-concavity (the "preferred-or-indifferent-to" sets are convex). The assumptions stipulated above follow from these, but are weaker. In particular, assumption (1) follows, as shown by Arrow and Debreu (1954, p. 272), from the assumption of insatiability (i.e., given any bundle in the set of "available" alternatives, it is always possible to find another which is preferred to it), combined with the assumption that the set of "available" alternatives is closed (it contains its boundary points). This "available" set (which we can identify with the nonnegative orthant of the commodity space) was defined by Arrow and Debreu (1954, p. 269) as the set of bundles "among which the individual could conceivably choose if there were no budgetary restraints." Thus what they really mean is "subjectively available" — available, that is, in the mind of the consumer. While this weaker assumption of closedness and insatiability is sufficient to establish Nikaidô's lemma, it is not enough to establish the existence of equilibrium; for this it has to be supplemented, as we shall see below, by some other condition, such as the assumption of monotone preferences, or the assumption that a positive amount of each good is held. Arrow and Debreu chose the latter course (as did Gale); Nikaidô (1957) chose the former.

Gale (1955, p. 156) circumvented these problems by assuming from the start that the set of available alternatives was bounded, on the grounds that "the

preferred to a bundle y, then any bundle on the segment joining x and y (other than y itself) is preferred to y. We are to prove that equilibrium exists in the unbounded case if and only if it exists in the bounded case. First, it is immediate that if an equilibrium exists in the unbounded case, then it must be in the Edgeworth box (otherwise it could certainly not be an equilibrium); hence the bundle chosen is preferred, in the case of each country, to all other bundles on the terms of trade line, and ipso facto to all other bundles on the segment of the terms of trade line within the rectangles O_1B_1 and O_2B_2; this shows that an equilibrium exists in the bounded case as well. The interesting part of the proof is therefore the converse, which states that if an equilibrium exists in the bounded case, then this will also be an equilibrium in the unbounded case. Suppose not; let t be an equilibrium in the bounded case, and suppose it is not an equilibrium in the unbounded case. This can happen only if the inhabitants of one country (say Country 1) prefer, at the price ratio determined by At, a bundle w which is outside the bounds. Therefore w is preferred to t. Let z be the point on the segment wt which is on the boundary of O_1B_1. Since the Edgeworth box $O_1\ O_2$ is strictly inside O_1B_1 by construction, we know that z cannot be in the Edgeworth box, so it cannot be a point of equilibrium; in particular, therefore, $z \neq t$. Therefore by the convexity assumption, z is preferred to t, which is a contradiction, for t could then not have been a point of equilibrium when, at the same prices, z was considered to be available.

The next counterexample to be taken up is one due essentially to Arrow (1951a, p. 528), which I shall call *Arrow's corner.* The example has also been discussed by Hurwicz (1960, p. 42), and as will be evident presently, it has quite ancient origins. Arrow introduced his example as an illustration of a Pareto optimum that could not be sustained by a competitive equilibrium; since our concern here is limited to the question of the existence of equilibrium, the

condition of boundedness is natural in view of the fixed time interval." This is a rather extraneous dynamic consideration which is not in accord with the traditional formulation in economic theory, and is at any rate made unnecessary by Nikaidd's lemma.

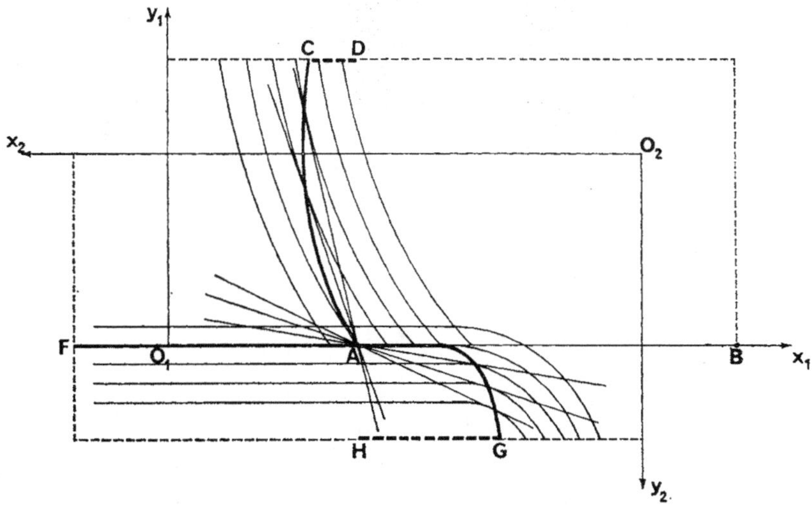

Figure 5.

example illustrated in Figure 5 is a slight modification of Arrow's, allowing for slightly weakened assumptions. The diagram shows an Edgeworth box, with the Nikaidô boundaries as in Figure 4. Three distinct peculiarities all coincide at the initial endowment point A: (1) Country 1 possesses only one of the commodities, the x-commodity, and none of the other, whereas Country 2 possesses some of each; (2) Country 2 possesses more of the x-good than it wants, and could lose some without its consumers being any worse off; (3) the inhabitants of Country 1 regard their home-produced commodity (the x-good) as a necessity, so that if its relative price falls below a critical level, they will be unwilling to trade any of it off in return for the y-commodity, whereas if their x-commodity becomes free, then they will wish to consume an unlimited amount of it (as shown by the point B). Thus Country 1's offer curve is discontinuous, consisting of DCA whenever the price of the x-good is positive, and jumping to B when the x-good becomes free. Country 2's offer curve is $FAGH$, and does not coincide with that of Country 1 at any common price ratio.

For instance, let the x-commodity be wheat, and the y-commodity be automobiles. Suppose Country 1 is a poor country that produces only wheat, and will trade it for cars only provided the latter are cheap enough. Let Country 2 be a rich country that produces both, and has an overabundance of wheat, but an insatiable demand for foreign as well as domestic cars. Then as long as the price of wheat is positive, the rich country will wish to sell its surplus wheat in return for automobiles; but since the poor country does not manufacture automobiles, the price of wheat would have to fall to zero, which, in turn, still could not be an equilibrium price, for then the poor country would demand an amount of wheat exceeding total world production.

This example has a flavor very much reminiscent of the types of objections raised against Say's law by Sismondi (1819, Vol. I, Book 4, Ch. 4) and Malthus (1820, Ch. 7), who spoke of "glutted markets." The importance of satiability in demand was well recognized by these authors. The defenders of Say's law[10] rested their case on

---

[10]There has been some dispute in the literature on the history of economic thought (see Lambert (1952, pp. 11–14; 1956, pp. 11–13)) as to whether priority for "Say's law" belongs to Say (1803, 1814) or to James Mill (1808). The relevant chapter, "Des Débouchés," of the first edition of Say's *Traité* (1803,1, pp. 152–5) expresses the idea (p. 153) that "it is not the abundance of money that improves markets, but the abundance of other products generally," and (p. 154) "once exchanges have been completed, it will be found that products have been paid for with products" (see also the *Treatise,* p. 134). But the famous dictum, "a product once created affords, *from that instant,* a market for other products to the full extent of its value," did not appear until the second edition (1814,I, p. 147; *Treatise, p* . 134). The chapter "Des Débouchés" in this edition (1814,I, pp. 143–59) was entirely rewritten, and carries over only one sentence (the second quoted above) from the original; and it contains no developments going beyond the statement contained in James Mill (1808, pp. 81–6) which had included the following passage (p. 81): "Whatever be the additional quantity of goods therefore which is at any time created in any country, an additional power of purchasing, exactly equivalent, is at the same instant created." Mill (1808, p. 76n) had referred to a passage in Say (1803, II, p. 367n) and so was undoubtedly acquainted with and influenced by this first edition. But there can be little doubt that Say's exposition in the second edition was, in turn, influenced by Mill. There is also a notable difference between the two versions: Mill (1808, p. 81) said that "the production of commodities creates, and is the one and universal cause which creates a market for the commodities *produced*" (my italics); whereas Say limited himself to claiming (1814,I, p. 147) that "a product once created affords ... a market for *other* products ... " (italics added again). Say (1803,I, pp. 153–4) had earlier presented a case in which industrious men in a primitive community would

the adjustability of production. There were two distinct arguments, however, one due to Say himself and the other put forward by Ricardo. Say (1821, p. 8) argued that "the quantity of English merchandize offered for sale in Italy and elsewhere is too great, because there is not sufficient Italian or other produce suitable to the English market." If Italy is Country 1 in Figure 5, as long as it produced a positive amount of automobiles, no matter how small, then equilibrium would exist, since the high price of cars would greatly increase Italy's effective demand for wheat. Again, in his famous chapter, *Des débouchés,* of his *Treatise* (p. 136n), Say argued: "Did Brazil produce wherewithal to purchase the English goods exported thither, those goods would not glut her market." Further: "I would not be understood to maintain in this chapter, that one product can not be raised in too great abundance, in relation to all others ; but merely that nothing is more favourable to the demand for one product, than the supply of another; that the import of English manufactures into Brazil would cease to be excessive and be rapidly absorbed, did Brazil produce on her side returns sufficiently ample; to which end it would be necessary that the legislative bodies of either country should consent, the one to free production, the other to free importation."

While Ricardo accepted Say's law, he was not impressed by this particular defense of it, and agreed with an anonymous pamphlet attacking Say's *Letters to Malthus* (1821), saying (*Works,* X, p. 410): "I am as much dissatisfied as the author with M. Say's defence of the principle which both he and I maintain to be true." In a letter to Malthus, commenting on these letters as well as on a paper he attributed to Torrens (1819), he said (*Works,* VIII, p. 22): "I think

find themselves with an unsold surplus, which would be remedied when and only when the local community increased *its* production. For the sharp and excessively doctrinaire version of the principle, priority must certainly go to Mill — doubtless a dubious distinction. At the very least James Mill deserves joint credit for "Say's law," and I can certainly not agree with Lambert's statement (1952, p. 14; 1956, p. 13) that "five years later James Mill could do no more than re-state" Say's thesis, nor with Schumpeter's assertion (1954, p. 491n) that "Say's priority is beyond the possibility of doubt."

he [Say] falls into the same error as Torrens in his article in the Edin. Rev. They both appear to think that stagnation in commerce arises from a counter set of commodities not being produced with which the commodities on sale are to be purchased, and they seem to infer that the evil will not be removed till such other commodities are in the market. But surely the true remedy is in regulating future production, — if there is a glut of one commodity produce less of that and more of another but do not let the glut continue till the purchaser chuses to produce the commodity which is more wanted."

A similar argument against the *Edinburgh Review* paper was presented by Sismondi (1820) who, in the second edition of his *Nouveaux Principes* (1827, Vol. II, p. 377n; 1953, Vol. II, p. 252n; 1957, p. 8n), attributed the article in question to McCulloch, in spite of the fact that Malthus, in a letter to Sismondi in 1820, had informed him that the author was Torrens (cf. Ricardo (*Works,* VIII, p. 376)).[11]

[11]All articles in the *Edinburgh Review* were anonymous, and the question of ascertaining the authorship of its economic articles has been summarized by Fetter (1953). Two papers attributed to McCulloch (1819, 1820) are among a long list that McCulloch subsequently prepared (cf. Fetter (1953, p. 249, note 87)). Although this list does not include the paper attributed to Torrens (1819), the paper itself contains a tell-tale reference which no one appears to have noticed (1819, p. 474): "as we explained in our former number, the transition from war to peace ..."; this is an unmistakable allusion to the paper attributed to McCulloch (1819). The second McCulloch paper (1820, p. 345) contains a similar reference to the earlier one. McCulloch coyly acknowledged authorship of the first 1819 paper in a letter to Ricardo (*Works,* VIII, p. 82), and unambiguously claimed authorship of the 1820 paper (*ibid.,* p. 190).

The attribution of "Mr. Owen's Plans ..." (1819) to Torrens is based in part on a passage in a letter from Ricardo (*Works,* VIII, p. 159) to McCulloch: "I was very much pleased with Col. Torrens essay in the last Edinb.[h] Review. I do not think there is more than one proposition in it which I should be disposed to dispute. Mr. Malthus, who passed 2 or 3 hours with me last week, was fully persuaded, till I undeceived him, that the article was written by you; he could hardly believe that Col. Torrens agreed so completely with the doctrines which both you and I have advocated." Added to this evidence is the fact that pp. 464–9 and 475–6 of the 1819 article are reproduced almost *verbatim* from a report in the *Scotsman* of a speech by Torrens (cf. Ricardo, *Works,* VIII, p. 82n); but the passage attacked by Sismondi (1820) and criticized by Ricardo

Ricardo could not have been expected to accept the argument that specialization in international trade was the source of glutted markets. The argument put forward in the Torrens (McCulloch?) paper was that "a glut is an increase in the supply of a particular class of commodities, unaccompanied by a corresponding increase in the supply of those other commodities which should serve as their equivalents" (1819, p. 471). Sismondi responded (1820; 1957, p. 14): "How are we to establish the fact that the tropical countries, where the most foodstuffs are produced with the least labour, will need English wheat in return for their sugar and spices ...?" He also ridiculed the idea that they should set about to produce these complementary commodities. He failed to note, however, that further on in the Torrens article there was an attempt to answer the question; the relevant passage, which is undoubtedly due to

---

(on pp. 470–2), as well as the reference (p. 474) to McCulloch's earlier paper, were added subsequently.

McCulloch was a notorious plagiarizer, and even the paper attributed to him (1819) contains several paraphrases of passages from Torrens' *External Corn Trade* and Ricardo's *High Price of Bullion.* Fetter (1953, p. 239) has described McCulloch's practice, exposed by "Mordecai Mullion" (John Wilson), of reproducing entire passages from his own previous publications — a practice which, to further complicate matters, Torrens engaged in himself (cf. Robbins (1958, p. viii)) — and comments: "McCulloch continued throughout his life to make liberal use of the scissors and the paste pot." There does not seem to be any special reason for supposing that he confined his scissors and paste pot to his own previous writings. Since McCulloch was the chief economic editor of the *Edinburgh Review*, it seems quite plausible that a number of passages were actually grafted on to Torrens' speech by McCulloch. Viner (1937, p. 194n) has said that "Ricardo believed that Torrens was the author of the article ... but it was more probably written by McCulloch"; Viner may well be right with respect to the particular passage which he quoted. Nevertheless there are cogent reasons for believing that the substance of the section criticized by Sismondi was actually written by Torrens. First, numerical examples of the kind used were very characteristic of Torrens, and McCulloch was known to have little patience with them; secondly, Torrens repeated the same arguments in his *Production of Wealth* (1821, pp. 372–8), and a passage (p. 378) which is obviously a reply to Malthus' criticism (1820, p. 358) of the 1819 *Edinburgh Review* article may be taken as acknowledgment of authorship of the latter on Torrens' part; finally, Torrens never abandoned the counter commodity argument, and indeed turned it around in his later work (1835) to point out its negative implications.

Torrens himself (1819, p. 473), is of considerable interest, since it must represent one of the earliest attempts to prove the existence of competitive equilibrium. He considers the question of an equilibrium of trade between a group of manufacturers and a group of cultivators, which becomes disrupted by a doubling of the productivity of the manufacturers, and he asks himself whether the farmers will be able to purchase the extra produce:

> With respect to productive cost, and therefore to exchangeable value, the double quantity of manufactured luxuries, now obtained, is exactly equal to the smaller quantity formerly obtained.... The class of cultivators, with the sacrifice of the same quantity of their unwrought luxuries, will be able to purchase and to consume a double quantity of wrought luxuries, while the class of master-manufacturers, after purchasing the same quantity of [unwrought luxuries], will be able to retain and to consume a double quantity of [wrought luxuries].

This statement contains the hidden assumption, later made explicit by Mill, that each group continues to spend the same fraction of its income on each kind of commodity, and hence behaves according to the utility function $U = xy$, where x and y are the respective quantities of wrought and unwrought luxuries. Accordingly, if manufacturers produce a of the first and cultivators produce b of the second, and if p and q are the corresponding prices, then the respective offer functions become $x_1 = a/2$ and $y_1 = pa/2q$ for the manufacturers, and $x_2 = qb/2p$ and $y_2 = b/2$ for the cultivators, corresponding to the case illustrated in Figure 1b above. Geometrically, the offer curves are perpendicular straight lines, and the equilibrium solution is $x_1 = x_2 = a/2, y_1 = y_2 = b/2$, in conformity with Torrens' example, according to which a doubling of a leads to a doubling of its consumption (x_1 and x_2) by both groups.

While this might have satisfied Ricardo, it would not have satisfied Sismondi, who favorably quoted Malthus' statement (1820, p. 358): "Another fundamental error into which the writers above-mentioned [Say, James Mill, Ricardo] and their followers appear to have fallen is, the not taking into consideration the influence of so general and important a principle in human nature, as indolence and the love of ease." (See also Malthus (1836, p. 320), Ricardo (*Works*, II, p. 313), Torrens (1821, p. 378), and Sismondi (1827, Vol. II, pp. 388–9; 1953, Vol. II, pp. 260–1; 1957, p. 13).) Malthus' statement was also a specific rebuttal to the (anonymous) Torrens article, and his point was that Torrens was assuming precisely what Malthus rejected — insatiability of demand. Ricardo never tired of expressing his belief in the insatiability of demand (e.g., *Works*, VIII, pp. 272–3), but in his reply to Malthus he granted him the premise, and nevertheless said (*Works*, II, p. 315): "Men will prefer indolence to luxuries! luxuries will not then be produced, because they cannot be produced without labour, the opposite of indolence. If not produced they cannot want a market, there can be no glut of them." This is the fundamental Ricardian answer, which was also used by Torrens (1821, pp. 378–9) and by James Mill (1826, pp. 228–45). Malthus had an answer to it, however (cf. Ricardo (*Works*, VIII, pp. 260–1)), which was that the necessary reduction in output of the over-produced good would "throw labourers out of work" and lead to general unemployment, and on this statement, he said to Ricardo, "the issue is joined between us." Even if Ricardo's position is accepted, however, his version of the classical principle takes much of the punch out of Say's law; supply creates its own demand, yes — provided, of course, that not more is supplied than will be demanded.[12]

When pressed for an explanation of glutted markets, Ricardo attributed the condition to "miscalculation" *(Works,* VIII, p. 273), and to the "prejudices and obstinacy with which men persevere in their old employments" (p. 277). James Mill's chapter (1826, pp. 228–45), while charmingly naive in its oversimplified view of reality, is a beautiful statement of the pure classical position;

[12]In the second edition of his *Traité* (1814, I, pp. 147–8), Say had protected himself by following his dogmatic pronouncement that "a product once created affords, *from that instant,* a market for other products to the full extent of its value" by the explanation: "for every product is created only to be consumed ...." But this explanation was removed from subsequent editions.

he, too, attributed gluts to "miscalculation," a procedure which comes very close to explaining a phenomenon simply by giving it a derogatory name. The argument proceeds by contradiction: it is proved, convincingly under the assumptions, that a glutted market cannot be in equilibrium; but this kind of argument could have been used just as well to prove, not that gluts cannot exist, but that equilibrium cannot exist. Torrens, on the other hand, recognized that miscalculation was in the nature of things in certain markets, and provided (1826, pp. 277–9) as clear a statement as one could wish of what is now called the "cobweb theorem," complete with empirical evidence of the com cycle during the years 1800–1825. The remedy was to extend international trade, smoothing out fluctuations (pp. 29–30) and thus lessening the effect on prices of any one country's production. A related but somewhat disappointing analysis by West (1826) appeared at the same time.

In his last work Sismondi (1824) conceded that equilibrium might eventually be reached, but stressed the difficulties of adjustment and the hardships they imposed. His emphasis on a dynamic approach makes his contribution distinctly modem in flavor. Ricardo (*Works*, IX, p. 243), who respected Sismondi and his views, should certainly have conceded as much; for it was at once the strength and weakness of his conceptual scheme that he considered all these questions in terms of states of equilibrium.

Senior (1836, p. 28) acknowledged the reality of glutted markets, and like Sismondi (1820) before him — and somewhat ruefully, it seems — specified books as the commonest example. Also (p. 29): "Everyone must recollect, when Brazil and Spanish America first became accessible, our exports of skaits, and fire-irons, and warming pans to the tropics." Thus Senior had few illusions. "Miscalculations of this kind," he added, "must obviously be of frequent occurrence; and perhaps what ought to excite our surprise is, not the extent to which they prevail, but the degree in which they are avoided." Finally, he specified the two alternative conditions for the onset of glutted markets, which we shall identify below as Conditions (3a) and (3b) for the existence of equilibrium, due respectively to Ricardo and Say: "But it appears that they can arise only from one or the other of two causes: either from the articles of wealth, with respect to which the glut exists, having been prepared for persons who do not want them, or from those persons not being provided with other articles of wealth, suited to the desires of the producers of the first-mentioned articles of wealth, to offer in exchange for them."

In his *Production of Wealth* (1821, Ch. VI, Sec. VI, pp. 339–430), Torrens had met Malthus' criticisms with an essentially "Ricardian" argument, employing elaborate numerical illustrations in what was surely the most detailed formulation of Say's law to have been attempted up to that time, and indeed, up to the time of Mill (1852). Nevertheless Torrens' views underwent a remarkable evolution in the ensuing years. Thus he was able later to say (1837, p. 139) that "there is a school of economists, who assume, that capital possesses some occult quality, or influence, by which it creates for itself the field in which it is employed, and renders demand co-extensive with the supply." After describing such economists as taking "the 'high *priori* road'" (p. 140), he forthrightly asserted (p. 143) that "in a country exporting manufactured goods, and importing raw materials, there may be a general glut of capital, and excess of production, in relation to foreign demand, which cannot be remedied by transferring capital from one branch of manufacture to another." This laid the basis for Torrens' theory of migration and colonization, which has recently attracted the attention of Thomas (1954, pp. 3–6) in the course of his extensive study of international patterns of migration (see also Kemp (1964, Ch. 9) and Robbins (1958, Ch. 6)). It is significant, however, that the evolution in Torrens' thought did not represent abandonment of his earlier *analytical* position, but on the contrary was a development to its logical conclusion of his 1819 thesis to which Ricarco had objected, that "a glut is an increase in the supply of a particular class of commodities, unaccompanied by a corresponding increase in the supply of those other commodities which should serve as their equivalents."

John Stuart Mill entered the fray under the banner of orthodoxy in his penetrating essay "Of the Influence of Consumption on Production" (1844, pp. 47–74) but, true to form, he made so many concessions to Sismondi and Malthus that his analysis can be regarded as a synthesis. The main argument was given in the rhetorical question (1844, p. 49): "To produce, implies that the producer desires to consume; why else should he give himself useless labour?" But then he admitted (p. 69) that the argument was based on a barter economy, and need not be correct in a monetary economy. In his *Principles* (1848, Book III, Ch. 14, §3, p. 108) he conceded that it was "plausible" that "those who have the means, may not have the wants, and those who have the wants may be without the means," but reiterated (p. 109) that "whoever brings additional commodities to the market, brings an additional power of purchase; we now see that he brings also an additional desire to consume; *since if he had not that desire, he would not have troubled himself to produce.*" [My italics.] Thus, with respect to Figure 5, Mill would have asked how it came to pass that Country 2 had *produced* more of the x-commodity than it needed, or if (owing to climate or technology) production had increased beyond expectations, why it should be *maintained* at that level. Even if Country 2's consumption indifference curves had the shapes indicated, showing satiability at the origin A of the offer curve $FAGH$, as long as the production block is strictly convex, Meade's trade indifference curves would have a negative slope at the origin, hence the phenomenon of Arrow's corner could not occur.[13]

Walras (1874, Lesson 7, §64) presented an example of a case in which, he claimed, there would be no solution (cf. Walras (1954,

[13]It is also tacitly assumed here, as usual, that there is "free disposal" in addition to strict convexity, so that a reduction in the output of one commodity always makes possible an increase in the output of the other commodity. This rules out the rectangular production block discussed by Haberler; see also Sohmen (1961b, p. 424). This is where the issue was drawn between Malthus and Ricardo, and Mill's argument is strictly valid only in the "long run." The importance of short-run inflexibility in the movement of resources was a prominent feature of the interesting article attributed to McCulloch (1819), who recognized that a "counter commodity" argument was needed in this case. Thus he urged, employing Torrens' slogan "commerce is an exchange of equivalents," that the remedy for the glut in English manufactures was to remove the prohibitive duties against French wines and fabrics, thus giving British exporters access to the French market.

p. 108)).[14] But consideration of his example shows that this is a play on words, for what characterizes his illustration is not the fact that there is *no solution,* but rather that there is *no trade,* which is a very different matter.[15] In fact his example possesses infinitely many solutions; that is, it admits of infinitely many price ratios compatible with the absence of trade. In such a case, obviously prices play no role. In Walras' treatment of the exchange of several commodities (1874, Lesson 11, §116), he left the impression that the problem of determinateness was just a matter of counting the number of equations and unknowns (1954, p. 162); Pareto (1911, p. 627; 1955, p. 90) gave the same impression. This objection should not be pressed too hard, however, for the conception of general equilibrium and even of the very possibility of a determinate solution were already signal accomplishments. Edgeworth (1889c, p. 504; *Papers,* II, p. 297), who must be counted among the offenders in his reliance on the counting rule, nevertheless put the problem well: "The great lesson to be learnt is this. The equations are *simultaneous,* and their solutions *determinate.* That the factors of economic equilibrium are simultaneously determined is a conception which few of the literary school have received."

[14]This example has been cited by Jaffé in his translation of Walras (1954, pp. 502–3) by way of refuting Karl Menger's reproach (cf. Wald (1933–1934, p. 20)) that "economists have merely *set up* equations, without concerning themselves with the existence and uniqueness of their solutions..." Menger's indictment was unduly harsh, and furthermore Walras recognized that uniqueness was not to be expected. Certainly Walras concerned himself with the existence problem, even though he did not obtain a rigorous proof. Nevertheless I believe Jaffé is wrong in claiming that Walras perceived the possibility of nonexistence of a solution. Things might have been different had Walras made it possible for Jaffé to insert the bracketed explanation "[from M]" instead of "[from K]" in the crucial passage (1954, p. 108).

[15]Reference may be made again to Arrow's Berkeley Symposium paper (1951a, p. 527, Figure 2). If the equilibrium in Arrow's diagram is moved to the northwest comer of the Edgeworth box, we obtain an example of what I believe Walras had in mind; in this example, each trader has a marked relative preference for his own product.

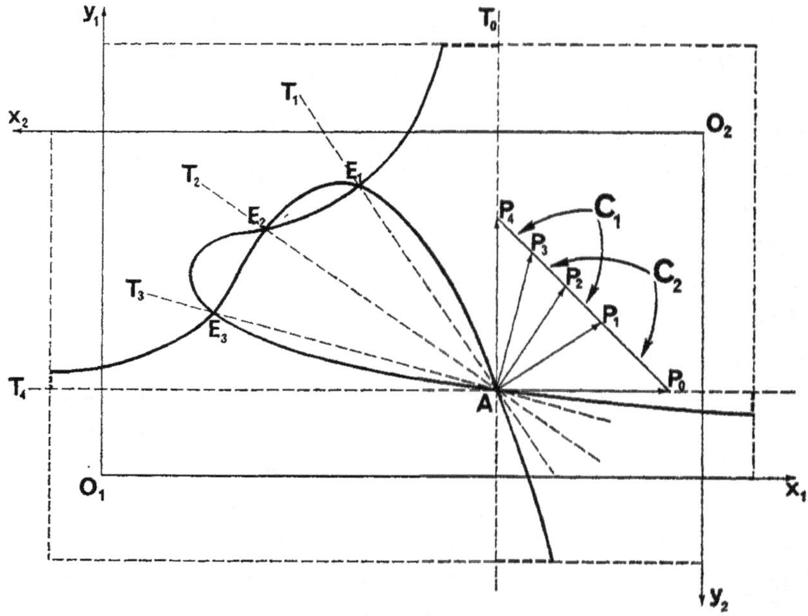

Figure 6.

Let us now proceed with the existence proof. It will be illustrated by Figure 6, which shows the familiar Marshallian offer curves for the case of two countries and two commodities, with origin at A and Edgeworth box O_1O_2, the Nikaidô bounds being shown by the dotted lines. Roughly speaking, the problem is to show, first, that under suitable assumptions the offer curves are continuous, and second, to show that this implies that they have at least one point of intersection. The diagram shows the familiar Marshallian case (1879, Figs. 4 and 8; 1923, p. 353) of multiple equilibrium with three points of intersection E_1, E_2, and E_3; Figure 6 is actually the mirror image of the kind displayed by Marshall (as well as by Edgeworth (1881, 1894) and Bowley (1924)), but corresponds to the way they were drawn by Pareto (1909, p. 192).

First, let us consider what is meant by "continuity," and what has to be assumed in order to establish it. In the case in which an offer function is single-valued (in the sense that for every price ratio, a single bundle of exports and imports is determined, as is the case in Figure 6), continuity has its usual meaning. In Figure 5, Country 1's offer curve $DCAB$ is single-valued but discontinuous, owing to the jump between A and B; Country 2's offer curve is multi-valued, since the value corresponding to a zero price for the x-commodity is not a single point but rather the entire straight segment FA of the offer curve $FAGH$; this segment is, however, a closed convex set. Finally, in Figure 4 we have an example of a multi-valued offer function — Country 1's offer curve — which has the two values u and v corresponding to the terms of trade represented by the line Auv; this set, consisting of two points u and v, is closed but not convex, since for it to be convex it would have to contain the entire segment uv.

The important properties that each country's offer function should have in order that a competitive equilibrium may exist are these: (1) the value of the function, for each set of prices, should be a closed convex set of commodity bundles; (2) this multi-valued (set valued) function should be "upper semicontinuous," meaning that if there is a convergent sequence of price constellations, and a corresponding convergent sequence of commodity bundles supplied and demanded at those prices, then the limiting commodity bundle must be one of the bundles demanded and supplied at the limiting price constellation. Thus, despite the geometric discontinuity in Figure 4 in Country 1's offer curve (the jump from u to v), the offer curve is upper semicontinuous — Gale (1955, p. 157) actually uses the term "continuous" — ; but it is not convex-valued. On the other hand the offer curve $DCAB$ in Figure 5 is (trivially) convex-valued (being single-valued), but it is not upper semicontinuous; if, corresponding to a zero price for the x-commodity, both the points A and B were values of the offer function, but not the points in between (as opposed to just the point B), then the offer function would become upper semicontinuous but it would cease to be convex-valued. It is clear, then, that the two properties of closed convex-valuedness and upper semicontinuity, taken in combination, are what correspond to the intuitive notion of continuity (or connectedness).

Now, these properties — closed convex-valuedness and upper semicontinuity — can be shown to follow from the following postulates: (1) continuity of preference,[16] (2) convexity of preference, and *either* (3a) monotonicity of preference *or* (3b) positivity of initial endowments. The usual continuous utility function with indifference curves convex to the origin (the mathematical term is "quasi-concave"; see footnote 9 in Part 1 of this article) satisfies the first two properties. Property (3a) requires that if one bundle is greater than another bundle in one component, and no smaller in the other components, then it is preferred; this is what is violated by Country 2 in Figure 5.[17] Property (3b) requires that each country have available a strictly positive amount (no matter how small) of every commodity; this is violated by Country 1 in Figure 5.

In his proof of existence, Gale (1955) postulated (1), (2), and (3b); Nikaidô in the first of his two papers (1956) postulated all four conditions, but in the second paper (1957) dropped (3b), showing that equilibrium followed from (1), (2), and (3a). Thus Gale's assumptions are in the spirit of Say, whereas Nikaidô's are in the spirit of Ricardo. In Gale's case, the procedure followed (1955, pp. 167–8) is to prove that the assumptions yield the closed convex-valuedness and upper semicontinuity of the offer functions. In Nikaidô's case (1956, pp. 140–1; 1957) the problem is a little more subtle: first, one observes that monotonicity rules out zero prices as possible equilibrium prices (since at a zero price the amount demanded by each country would be outside the Edgeworth box);

[16] A preference ordering is called *continuous* if, for all bundles $x = (x_1, x_2 \ldots, x_n)$ and $y = (y_1, y_2 \ldots, y_n)$ such that x' is preferred to y, there exist neighborhoods U of x and V of y such that x' is preferred to y' for all $x' \in U$ and all $y' \in V$(cf. Gale (1955, p. 166)). As Gale points out, this is equivalent to the apparently weaker condition that for all bundles x and y, there exist neighborhoods U' of x and V' of y such that x is preferred to y for all $x' \in U'$ and x is preferred to y' for all $y' \in V'$. The words "for all bundles x and y" are crucial to establishing this equivalence: if the conditions are stated in terms of a particular x and y only, then the first condition need not follow from the second, though the second always, of course, follows from the first.

[17] Note, however, that the Arrow-Debreu insatiability postulate is *not* violated (see footnote 9).

then one redefines the offer function, replacing a singular point such as B in Figure 5 by the limit point A (this is called the closed extension procedure, and has been exploited by Kuhn (1956b) and McKenzie (1954)). What is involved is basically very simple: if, in Figure 5, Country 2's indifference curve through A had a strictly negative slope, then the discontinuity in Country 1's offer curve would become irrelevant, and the problem would be just *as if* Country 1's offer curve were simply DCA, i.e., as if it were continuous.

From these considerations it follows that the principal remaining problem preliminary to the existence proof proper is the proof that under assumptions (1), (2), and (3b), the offer functions are closed convex-valued and upper semicontinuous. The convex-valuedness follows from the convexity of preference, by a simple argument. The difficult proof is that of continuity (cf. Gale (1955, p. 168) and Nikaidô (1956, p. 140)). The idea of the proof may be illustrated in terms of Figure 5, where Country 1's offer curve is discontinuous; as usual, the best way to understand the proof is to see why it fails when one of the assumptions is removed (in this case the assumption that Country 1 produces positive amounts of both goods). Let there be a sequence of terms of trade lines (budget lines) through A, converging to the horizontal (corresponding to a zero price of the x-commodity). It is to be shown that the bundle offered at the limiting price ratio (which we know to be B)is the limit of the sequence of bundles offered at the corresponding price ratios in the sequence (which we know, on the contrary, to be A). I shall follow Nikaidô's method, but use instead of (3a) the weaker Arrow-Debreu insatiability postulate (see footnote 9); then the chosen bundle will always be on the budget line. Choose any arbitrary bundle, say B itself, on the limiting budget line, and consider the sequence of points closest to B which are on the converging budget lines and also confined within the bounded quadrant $O_1x_1y_1$ in Figure 5 (in the present case these will become the point A itself). Now the points in the sequence of points *chosen* are, *ipso facto,* preferred or indifferent to the corresponding points (on the same budget line) in the sequence of points closest to B. Secondly, provided the initial endowments (the components of A) are strictly positive (which is what is violated in Figure 5), the sequence of points closest to B will converge to B(convexity of the space of alternatives is also needed at this point of the proof); it should perhaps be mentioned, to aid the reader of Nikaidô's paper (1956, p. 140, §4, line 20), that all these considerations are implicit in the condensed statement "we have surely $Y_n \rightarrow$Y." Thirdly, by continuity of the preference relation, the limit of the sequence of chosen points is preferred or indifferent to the Emit (B itself, as just shown) of the sequence of points closest to B. The latter conclusion is contradicted in Figure 5, owing to the fact that Country 1 produces none of the y-commodity.

Having sketched the two main preliminaries to the existence theorem — Nikaidô's lemma and the proof of closed convex-valuedness and upper semicontinuity — we now come to the existence theorem proper. First I shall trace through the procedure followed by Gale for the special case in which (as in Figure 6) the offer functions are single-valued. Gale's theorem (1955, pp. 160–161) relies on a lemma of Knaster, Kuratowski, and Mazurkiewicz (1931); this is the principal lemma from which Brouwer's fixed point theorem (1912) can be readily proved with some simple algebra (see Pontryagin (1952, pp. 57–8)). The Knaster-Kuratowski-Mazurkiewicz lemma follows, in turn, after some analysis, from an important topological result of Sperner (1928); excellent expositions of Sperner's lemma and the Knaster Kuratowski-Mazurkiewicz lemma are to be found in Aleksandrov (1956, pp. 160–163).

Now consider Figure 6. Corresponding to the terms-of-trade lines T_0, T_1, T_2, T_3, T_4, we have, perpendicular to them, the corresponding price vectors P_0, P_1, P_2, P_3, P_4, which have been normalized so that their components add up to unity. Thus the set of prices is the segment, or *simplex*, P_0P_4 (in the case of three commodities it would be a triangle, and so on). First of all we construct the aggregate offer function of all countries, or aggregate excess demand function, as it is more usually called in the literature in mathematical economics. In Figure 6 this aggregate function is not shown, but it will begin in the northwest quadrant (from A) between T_0 and T_1, then it will loop into the southeast quadrant between T_1 and T_2, make another loop in the northwest quadrant between T_2 and T_3, and stay in the southeast quadrant thereafter. Such a "floral" offer curve was depicted for the first time by H. G. Johnson (1959, p. 258). Now, on the simplex P_0P_4 we consider the set C_1 of all price vectors for which the aggregate excess demand for the first commodity (the x-commodity) is nonnegative; this is the set containing the closed segments P_1P_2 and P_3P_4. Likewise, C_2 is defined as the set of all normalized prices for which the aggregate excess demand for the second commodity (the y-commodity) is nonnegative; this consists of the closed segments P_0P_1 and P_2P_3. Now, the Knaster-Kuratowski-Mazurkiewicz lemma (K.K.M. lemma for short) states that if an (n–l)-dimensional simplex S, with vertices $V_1V_2, \ldots, V_n$, is such that there is a collection of closed sets $C_1, C_2, \ldots, C_n$, whose union is S, and such that the face spanned by any subset of vertices V_iV_j, $V_k, \ldots$, is covered by the union of the corresponding sets C$_i$, $C_j, C_k, \ldots$, then the sets $C_1, C_2, \ldots, C_n$ have a non-empty intersection. For example, let $P_4 = V_1$ and $P_0 = V_2$ in Figure 6. Then C_1 contains the vertex V_1C_2 contains the vertex V_2, and the union of C_1 and C_2 contains the simplex V_1V_2; hence there is a point common to C_1 and C_2 — in fact there are three, namely P_1, P_2, and P_3, corresponding to the equilibrium points E_1, E_2, and E_3.

Gale's existence proof therefore consists in verifying that the sets C_i, defined above, fulfil the conditions of the K.K.M. lemma. Gale extended the theorem for the case of multi-valued excess demand functions, in a proof resembling the extension by Kakutani (1941) of Brouwer's fixed point theorem (1912). Nikaidô (1956, pp. 139–40) used the Kakutani fixed point theorem directly, by the ingenious device of introducing a "price-manipulating function," which is defined as follows: given any arbitrary bundle corresponding to aggregate excess demand, choose the normalized price vector such as to maximize the value of the excess demand; then by an easy argument it is shown that this price-manipulating function and the aggregate excess demand function are simultaneously satisfied if and only if supply and demand are equal for every commodity. The price-manipulating function is also shown to be closed convex-valued and upper semicontinuous; combined with the aggregate excess demand function, it defines a multi-valued mapping from the cartesian product of the set of normalized prices and the (bounded) commodity space (both closed, bounded, convex sets — this is where Nikaidô's lemma is used) into itself. (The elements of this cartesian product are $(2n - 1)$-dimensional vectors, whose first n components correspond to quantities and whose next $n - 1$ components correspond to normalized prices.) Since this mapping has all the required properties (closed convex-valuedness and upper semicontinuity), it follows immediately from Kakutani's theorem that a fixed point exists (a set of prices and quantities satisfying both the excess demand function and the price-manipulating function simultaneously), hence equilibrium is proved.

Kuhn (1956a) followed an approach quite similar to those of Gale and Nikaidô, obtaining the results from a more powerful fixed point theorem. For a closed economy, Arrow and Debreu (1954) proved existence, likewise with extremely strong topological methods, and considered much more elaborate models involving production and shares of ownership in resources. Also for a closed economy, the existence problem has been tackled in a general form by McKenzie (1955, 1959, 1961). In most of these approaches, an aggregate excess demand function for the economy can be defined, so the methods could be adapted to the conditions of international trade without too much difficulty. We have already mentioned (in Part 1 of this article) the existence proof of Isard and Ostroff (1958, 1960) incorporating transport costs.

The earliest existence proofs in mathematical economics were those of Wald (1933–1934, 1934–1935), which have already been mentioned. A third paper by Wald (1935–1936), dealing with exchange equilibrium, was also to have appeared, but was lost;[18]

[18]This is the paper referred to in Wald's expository article (1951, pp. 380, 403), and which appeared by title only in the 8th *Ergebnisse* (1935–1936, p. 84) with the annotation: "The publication of this article, which could not be carried out in this issue owing to lack of space, will take place shortly." No further issue appeared.

I quote from a letter to me dated November 18, 1963, from Professor Oskar Morgenstern: "I saw last week Karl Menger in Chicago, and discussed with him in detail the question you raised in your letter of August 15 regarding a paper

all that remains is the statement of the problem and the proof of uniqueness contained in Wald's expository article (1936, pp. 649–59; 1951, pp. 379–91), together with examples of multiple equilibrium and of absence of equilibrium (the latter — an example with three commodities and three traders — having the same essential features as Arrow's corner). We can only conjecture what his own alternative method of proof might have been like; presumably it proceeded by induction on dimensions. The assumption leading to uniqueness (which we shall take up again in Section 2.7) was stringent; nevertheless the model was logically unobjectionable, unlike the earlier ones. Thus what we may assume to be the earliest satisfactory and mathematically rigorous proof of the existence of equilibrium was a casualty of the upheavals of those years.

7. Stability, Uniqueness, and Multiple Equilibrium

Few subjects have been so controversial as the question of stability of equilibrium in international trade. In a subject as large as this, we shall have to content ourselves with a sketch of some of the principal issues, deferring more detailed discussion to the sequel.

One point had better be clarified at the outset. Much (if not most) of the literature on stability is concerned with the question of flexible exchange rates. Now, if commodity prices are free to move, then exchange rates become redundant, as they constitute extra prices without the addition of any extra commodities. At best, then, exchange rates should be considered as proxies for other prices, some of which may in themselves be rigid; the question then becomes: which prices? In a simple model of two countries, each specializing in the production of one commodity, if the commodity prices are rigid in

by Wald. It is clear that everything that existed has been published. The paper you refer to was written but is lost. Probably Wald himself lost it when coming to this country and never bothered to rewrite it. There is no question that Wald had a proof for the exchange equilibrium, and it is a pity that we have no record of it other than the memory of the people who were associated with him at that time."

the national currencies, then the exchange rate between currencies may be identified with the terms of trade. In a many-commodity model with a single factor (labor) in each country, if factor prices (wages) are assumed fixed (in national currencies) and prices equated to minimum unit costs, then the exchange rate can be identified with the factor terms of trade (relative wages), i.e., the relative price of the Marshallian "bales." Finally, if in each country there is an untraded domestic commodity (such as housing), then the exchange rate may be considered as a proxy for the relative price of international and domestic commodities.

Obviously these three interpretations are very different. If, as I believe, it is the last that has greatest relevance to exchange rate policy, then we cannot expect analysis of the first to shed much light on it. These are two very different models. In what follows, we shall have to keep in mind these varying interpretations of the problem of international adjustment.

It is by now well recognized in the literature that the question of whether a particular position of equilibrium is stable or not depends on the process of adjustment that is specified (this was pointed out long ago by Edgeworth (1889b, 1891a)). The processes suggested by Walras (1874, Ch. 12, §125), and Marshall (1879, Ch. II) are similar but quite distinct; it has even been a debated question as to whether Walras took his own tâtonnement process seriously or merely introduced it as a method for establishing the existence of equilibrium.[19] Its chief drawback is the assumption (Walras' law)

[19]Wald (1951, p. 384) interpreted Walras' tâtonnement process as a method (but an unsuccessful one) of establishing the solvability of his equations of exchange. Actually, Walras (1954, p. 162) distinguished the two problems, since he proceeded after displaying his equations to say that "in this way, given the equations of demand, the prices are determined mathematically. It remains only to show — and this is the essential point — that the problem of exchange for which we have just given a theoretical solution is the selfsame problem that is solved empirically on the market by the mechanism of free competition." Pareto (1909, pp. 233–4) later stressed this computational feature of the market mechanism. Recently Uzawa (1960) showed how the tâtonnement process could actually be used to establish the existence of equilibrium.

that the quantities demanded and supplied at any instant satisfy, identically in prices, the budget equality of receipts and expenditures. In terms of the Marshallian diagrams, this means that the countries (satisfying "Cournot's law") must never for an instant be off their offer curves; thus only equilibrium situations could be observed, and the Walrasian tâtonnement process is a "virtual" adjustment process in which no trade takes place except at the final equilibrium. It is doubtful whether such an adjustment process has ever been observed, except possibly in highly organized commodity and security markets where, in any case, the price adjustments are virtually instantaneous.

Marshall analyzed stability in terms of points that were off the offer curves, and thus implicitly rejected Walras' law, in the sense in which this law has been stated by Lange (1942, p. 50) and applied by Arrow, Block, and Hurwicz (1959, p. 83) as an *identity* (in the prices) holding instantaneously, as opposed to a *tendency* whose absolute fulfilment is characteristic only of equilibrium states. Hahn and Negishi (1962) have introduced an adjustment process that permits modification in the distribution of the "initial endowments;" this could be considered as a device that has the effect of replacing Walras' law (although the latter is still formally satisfied in their system); the Hahn-Negishi approach therefore seems closer in spirit to the Marshallian process, that of Arrow and Hurwicz corresponding instead to the Walrasian one.

When we look closely at Marshall's description of his adjustment process (1879, p. 18), which Samuelson (1947, pp. 266–8) has faithfully translated into mathematics, we find a puzzling question which demands explanation. What adjusts in Marshall's system seems to be the production of export goods. In his analogy (p. 19n) between the offer curve and a rigid wire exerting attractions on a particle, he makes it clear that the attraction is in a horizontal direction for the home country (and vertical for the foreign), so that adjustment takes place only via each country's exports. On the face of it, this could result simply from changes in consumption, since an increase in exports can come about through a decline in domestic consumption alone (without any change in production); but then there is no reason for limiting the adjustments to the quantity of exports only, for the same considerations would lead to adjustments in imports, whether or not the latter are also manufactured at home. Marshall's adjustments must therefore be adjustments in production; but since imports do not adjust, he must implicitly assume that they are not produced at home, i.e., that specialization is complete. But in that case, what room is there left for production of exports to adjust? None, unless we assume that there is a third sector, that of domestic industry, which produces goods that do not enter into international trade. That this is what Marshall must have had in mind seems certainly to be the case, as he explained later in the following significant passage (1923, pp. 354–5n):

> Mill, however, thought to find the missing key to the otherwise insoluble problem of the "indeterminateness of the rate" in the fact that a country's imports take the place of a definite quantity of similar goods, which she used to make for herself; that the quantity of exports which she can make, is governed by the amount of her labour and capital set free from making those goods. But in this he appears to have been mistaken. The goods which a country imports, are generally different in character from those, which she would provide for herself if she had no foreign trade: and much of the capital and labour required for making her exports is almost as likely to be taken from domestic provision of goods and services which are not of a nature to be imported or exported. There is therefore no key such as Mill supposed.

Marred only by the hesitancy of the phrase "almost as likely," this evidently provides the key to Marshall's own adjustment process. An increase in exports takes place by a movement of resources out of domestic industry. But if this interpretation is correct, more problems are added than subtracted; for if production is changing in both countries, the dimensions of the Edgeworth box must be changing, as are also the shapes of the offer curves. The extreme subtlety of the Marshallian conception becomes more apparent the further one probes into it.[20]

[20]Marshall himself pointed out (1879, p. 26) that "every movement of the exchange-index entails some alteration in the shapes of the curves, and therefore in the forces which determine its succeeding movements." The reasons he gave

Walras did not present any mathematical formalization of his tâtonnement process; Marshall stopped just short of doing so in his analogy between the offer curve and a rigid wire. Thus he said (1879, p. 19n) that "if we chose to assign to these horizontal and vertical forces any particular laws, we should obtain a differential equation for the motion of the exchange index. This equation when integrated would give us the path which on this particular supposition the particle would describe. Such calculations might afford considerable scope to the ingenuity of those who devise mathematical problems, but as we shall see further on (§6) they would afford no aid to the Economist." This last sweeping statement was then explained as follows (1879, p. 25n):

> For the mathematical functions introduced into the original differential equation could not, in the present condition of our knowledge, be chosen so as to represent even approximately the economic forces that actually operate in the world. And by integrating them we should move further away from, instead of approaching nearer to the actual facts of life. For this reason, among others, the method of diagrams seems to me to be generally speaking of greater use to the Economist, than the methods of mathematical analysis. For when using the former method we have continually before us those assumptions which are justified by economic facts, and no others. Whereas the use of mathematical analysis has been found to tempt men to expend their energy on the elaboration of minute and complex hypotheses, which have indeed some distant analogy to economic conditions, but which cannot properly be said to represent in any way economic laws.

What Marshall seems to be trying to say in this passage is that "mathematical analysis" would require the specification of a *particular* functional relationship relating the speed of adjustment

---

were that familiarity with imports might change tastes. The point being made here is somewhat different: with changes in output, the offer curves defined on the basis of current output will change their shape. But Marshall's offer curves are clearly supposed to reflect long-run adjustment of production. He wrote before Edgeworth, and Edgeworth himself insisted on their subtle nature; in neglecting domestic (non-traded) production, it seems that modem interpreters of Marshall have oversimplified and perhaps even somewhat distorted Marshall's conception.

to the distance from the offer curve, whereas the "method of diagrams" makes it possible to determine the stability or instability of an equilibrium point, or the direction of movement from a given displacement, without any *specific* functional form having to be assumed. What is peculiar about the passage to a modern reader is that Marshall implied by his use of words that the "method of diagrams" was not itself a form of "mathematical analysis"; and it reflects a popular misconception about the nature of mathematical reasoning, which one still finds today: that mathematical analysis can only be brought to bear on quantitative phenomena and quantifiable relationships. On the contrary, modern stability analysis is designed to analyze the qualitative nature of the problem, and to study conditions under which the property of an equilibrium being stable or unstable is invariant with respect to a wide class of adjustment processes. Thus, Arrow, Block, and Hurwicz (1959, pp. 94–5) have been able to establish stability (for the "gross substitute" case and Walrasian adjustment process) in terms of a process that assumes only that the speeds of adjustment are continuous and sign-preserving functions of excess demand; this result has been extended to a wider class of cases by McKenzie (1960) and by Nikaidô and Uzawa (1960). The method used is the so-called "second method" of Lyapunov (1892), based on Lyapunov's theorem — recently generalized by Uzawa (1961) — that stability prevails if the distance to equilibrium (which can be measured in various ways) decreases monotonically over time. Needless to say, Marshall, writing in the 1870's, in an intellectual environment dominated by the Newtonians, could not perhaps be blamed for expressing himself as he did.

Samuelson (1941; 1942; 1947, Ch. 9, 10) appears to be the first to have explicitly formulated dynamic adjustment processes for the classical general equilibrium model in terms of systems of differential or difference equations, thus completing a development that was only implicit in the work of Hicks (1939).[21] The most important outcome

[21]Samuelson was, of course, not the first to introduce explicit dynamical models into economics; in this he was preceded by Tinbergen, Frisch, and a few others. In retrospect it seems astonishing that such a development was so long in coming.

of this development was the fundamental paper by Metzler (1945), the principal result of which was the theorem that if all commodities are gross substitutes (a concept due to Mosak (1944, p. 33)), then the Hicks conditions (that the principal minors of the Jacobian of the aggregate excess demand function should oscillate in sign) are necessary and sufficient for local stability.[22]

Thirteen years later, Hahn (1958) and Negishi (1958) independently discovered that under Metzler's assumptions of gross substitutability, the relevant Jacobian was necessarily Hicksian, and therefore equilibrium was necessarily stable (according to Metzler's criterion). Hahn used Walras' law, and Negishi made use of the homogeneity of excess demand functions; both authors relied on a theorem proved in 1912 by Frobenius (see Debreu and Herstein (1953)). Shortly afterwards, and independently of both Hahn and

[22]Metzler obtained his results on the basis of a linear approximation of the excess demand functions, a procedure which he justified (1945, p. 281n) on the grounds that (1) analysis of nonlinear systems presented great difficulties; (2) linearity could be justified empirically; and (3) "in any case, Samuelson has shown that stability of linear approximations is a necessary condition, if not a sufficient one, for stability of more complicated dynamic systems." With respect to (1), the difficulties have now been largely overcome as a result of the development initiated by Arrow and Hurwicz, who were the first to apply Lyapunov's second method to these problems. As for (2), the empirical support for linearity in prices (as opposed to linearity in income, which Metzler used as a justification) is weak indeed, and the theoretical objections are overwhelming: if all commodities (including the numéraire) are included, linearity of all excess demand functions is inconsistent with rational behavior (homogeneity of excess demand functions and satisfaction of the budget constraint); and if linearity with respect to relative prices is assumed for all commodities but the numéraire, the excess demand for the numéraire becomes highly nonlinear, introducing an artificial asymmetry.

As regards (3), Samuelson actually stated (1942, p. 16; 1947, p. 300) that "first-order stability" (stability of the approximating linear system) was *sufficient* for local stability (not necessary), which would actually be more advantageous to Metzler. However, this whole issue is academic, since under quite general conditions, first-order stability is both necessary and sufficient for local stability; this is the "fundamental stability theorem" of Poincaré (1892, Ch. 3, 4) and Lyapunov (1892, §24; 1907, pp. 291–2). For statements and proofs of this theorem, and further references, see Bellman (1953, p. 79ff.) and Coddington and Levinson (1955, pp. 314ff); see also Gantmacher (1959, Vol. II, p. 120), where an extended treatment of the Lyapunov theory will also be found.

Negishi, Arrow and Hurwicz (1958) and Arrow, Block, and Hurwicz (1959) proved two stronger results, which include those of Hahn and Negishi. The first was that under gross substitutability, equilibrium was unique (1959, Lemma 4), and the second that it was globally stable (1959, Theorem 1).

In their uniqueness proof, Arrow, Block, and Hurwicz followed that of Wald (1936, pp. 654–6; 1951, pp. 385–7), which is the reproduction of the uniqueness proof from his lost paper on exchange equilibrium (1935–1936). Wald had made the following assumptions (1951, p. 383) concerning utility functions $u = f(x_1, x_2, \ldots, x_n)$, where n is the number of commodities:

Condition 4. Marginal utility $\partial f/\partial x_i \equiv f_i$ can be factored as $f_i(x) = g(x) \cdot \phi_i(x_i)$ where $i = 1, 2, \ldots, n$ and $x = (x_1; x_2, ..., x_n)$, and where $g(x)$ is any nonvanishing function and $\phi_i(x_i)$ is continuous, nonnegative, and monotone decreasing. This is simply the old assumption of independent utilities and diminishing marginal utility.

Condition 5. For any $\lambda > 1, \phi_i(\lambda x_i)/\phi_i(x_i) > 1/\lambda$. This is a curious condition, but it is the one that, in conjunction with Condition 4, implies gross substitutability, i.e., that a rise in any price leads to a rise in the excess demand for each other commodity.[23]

What Arrow, Block, and Hurwicz observed was that only the gross substitutability resulting from Wald's conditions (together with the budget equation, which in this context really means: together with the assumption of insatiability) was needed in the proof of uniqueness. This had already been perceived by Gale (1955, p. 163),

[23]See Arrow and Hurwicz (1958, p. 546n), and Arrow, Block, and Hurwicz (1959, p. 86n, 89–90). Most of Wald's proof of uniqueness consisted, in effect, in proving gross substitutability; he showed (1951, pp. 386–7) that if $p = (p_1, p_2, \ldots, p_n)$ and $q = (q_1, q_2, \ldots, q_n)$ are two sets of prices such that $qi \geqq p_i$ for $i = 1, 2, \ldots, n$, and if $q_1 = p_1$ and $q_v > p_v$ for some $v \neq 1$, then letting $hi(p)$ denote a given individual's demand for the ith commodity at prices p, it follows that $h_1(q) > h_1(p)$. (Note the misprint in the translation of Wald (1951, p. 387) where $a''_{ij} \leqq a'_{ij}$ should be $a''_{i1} \leqq a'_{i1}$; also further up the page (also Wald (1936, p. 656)), $a_{ij}p_j \leqq a_{ij}q_j$ should read $a_{ij}p_j \leqq a_{ij}q_j$ This implies gross substitutability, which is the special case in which $p_i = q_i$ for all $i{\neq}v$,and by symmetry the argument applies for any $i \neq 1$ and $\neq v$.

who showed that uniqueness followed from a condition slightly weaker still than gross substitutability.

To illustrate Wald's Condition 5, consider a utility function of the kind introduced (as a production function) by Arrow, Chenery, Minhas, and Solow (1961), and generalized by Uzawa (1962b):

$$f(x_1, x_2, \ldots, x_n) = \left[\sum_{i=1}^{n} \alpha_i x_i^{-\beta}\right]^{-1/\beta} \quad ; \quad \beta > -1,$$

where β is related to the elasticity of substitution σ by the formula $\sigma = 1/(1+\beta) > 0$. By differentiation, it is easily verified that Wald's Condition 4 is satisfied; and that Condition 5 holds if and only if $\beta < 0$, that is, if and only if $\sigma > 1$.[24] Thus gross substitutability in this case becomes equivalent to the condition that the elasticity of substitution be greater than unity; this has already been illustrated by Figure 1.

With uniqueness proved, and local stability established (according to the method of linear approximation), it becomes a good conjecture that global stability holds, in the sense that the unique equilibrium will be approached asymptotically from any initial position. This was rigorously established by Arrow, Block, and Hurwicz (1959, Theorem 1) using Lyapunov's second method, according to which asymptotic stability prevails provided the "distance" from equilibrium decreases over time ("distance" being defined in terms of some norm — the authors used the "maximum norm," which is the largest of the excess supplies and demands of the commodities, as well as the usual "Euclidean norm," which is the square root of the sum of the squares of the excess demands).

[24]This shows that Wald was unduly apologetic when he stated (1951, p. 383) that "surely Condition 4 is not met completely in the real world. In general, there are complementary and substitutive relationships among certain goods." As the above example shows, Wald's Condition 4, even if it is unrealistic on other grounds, nevertheless allows for any degree of complementarity or substitutability. Independence of *utilities* has nothing to do with independence of *commodities* (cf. Samuelson (1947, pp. 183–4)).

In terms of his own two-country two-commodity model, this was a result which Marshall had already perceived by his "method of diagrams," though, as has been pointed out, the Marshallian adjustment process is quite different. The condition of gross substitutability was called by Marshall (1879, p. 6; 1923, p. 333) the case of "normal demand"; the uniqueness of equilibrium in this case was established in his Proposition VIII (1879, p. 11), and its stability in Proposition XIII (1879, pp. 24–5). On the face of it, it seems like a good vindication of his "method of diagrams" that Marshall was able to perceive a result (for the two-dimensional case) that the "method of mathematical analysis" employed by Metzler failed to uncover. On the other hand, neither method was capable of establishing such a result for the general case of any number of commodities and countries.

We finally come to the important problem of "global stability." First it will be necessary to define some terms. An equilibrium (or equilibrium point) is said to be locally stable if there exists a neighborhood around the equilibrium such that for any point in that neighborhood, every solution path through that point converges to the given equilibrium (see Arrow and Hurwicz (1958, p. 523)); this is a formal definition of a well understood concept. In the above definition if we insist that the condition be satisfied for all neighborhoods of the given equilibrium, it is called *globally stable*; this implies uniqueness, of course (see Arrow and Hurwicz (1958, p. 524; 1960). What we are more interested in now is the stability of a *process*[25] (see Uzawa (1961, p. 618)). An adjustment process is

[25] Arrow and Hurwicz (1958, p. 524) use the term "system." Schumpeter (1928, p. 363) introduced the useful distinction between stability of the capitalist "system" and that of the capitalist "order"; thus we can think of the economic "order" as moving from a competitive to a monopolistic regime, or *vice versa.* This kind of question is taken up by Debreu and Scarf (1963) who, following Edgeworth (1881, pp. 35–9), have shown that in a market with a large number of traders and with Edgeworth's process of recontract, the "order" converges to a competitive one as the number of traders increases indefinitely; combined with Uzawa's generalization (1962a) of Edgeworth's process (1881, 1891b), this establishes the stability of the competitive "order." But this is quite a different

(globally) stable if from any given point, every solution path through that point converges to *some* equilibrium.[26] A process is globally unstable if it is not globally stable. It is of great importance to know under what conditions the competitive economy is globally stable (in the sense of the "process" being stable); it is also interesting to inquire whether equilibrium is globally stable in the former sense, in which the process is stable and equilibrium is unique. This latter is not generally to be expected; but stability of the competitive *process* is usually believed to prevail. However, this is such a subtle and controversial question that we must examine it in detail.

The problem of global instability is the question at issue in the skirmish between Bhagwati and Johnson (1960, 1961) and Sohmen (1961a, pp. 10–11; 1961b). It is also the subject of contributions by Arrow and Hurwicz (1958), Scarf (1960), and Gale (1963). Here we have a rather glaring example of a lack of communication between non-mathematical and mathematical economists that continues to characterize much of international trade theory.

In the postwar period, much attention was paid to local stability conditions for purposes of exchange rate policy. Sohmen (1957) drew attention to the global nature of the problem, and to Marshall's treatment of it (1923, pp. 352–4), as well as to a footnote in Friedman (1953, p. 160n) containing the following passage:

> As a purely theoretical matter, there will always be some set or sets of rates that will clear the market, and, in the neighborhood of at least one of these sets of rates a rise in the rate will mean a decline in excess demand (i.e., a negative excess demand); a fall,

---

concept from the above, in which we assume that the "process" always stays within the rules of the competitive "order."

[26]Uzawa (1961) considers the more general criterion of "quasi-stability" of a process. Essentially Uzawa's concept is designed to allow for the case in which there is a possibility of neutral equilibrium, in which case the above property of local stability of a point would not hold. Since it is difficult (without introducing artificial assumptions) to rule out neutral equilibrium as an absolute impossibility (it is, after all, a limiting case of multiple separated equilibria), it is much easier mathematically to establish the quasi-stability of a process than to establish its stability.

> a rise in excess demand. Exchange rates can remain in a region in which this is not true only if they are not free to move and if some nonprice mechanism is used to ration domestic or foreign currency.

This is an assertion first of the existence of competitive equilibrium, second, of the existence of a locally stable equilibrium, and last, of global stability of the adjustment process. The validity of the above statement must hinge on what is meant by "a purely theoretical matter."

In matters of pure theory, all conclusions follow from assumptions. We have already seen cases in which, conceivably, equilibrium might not exist; in such cases, obviously the competitive process could not be stable. The question arises as to whether, under conditions that guarantee existence of equilibrium, it might still happen that equilibrium is globally unstable. We shall presently see that this is indeed a theoretical possibility, and further that there are some known sufficient conditions that rule it out. First let us consider the pure theory.

Marshall's treatment of this question is contained in his Proposition XIII (1879, pp. 24–5; 1923, pp. 352–4), where he provides a geometric argument to the effect that the offer curves have an odd number of intersections,[27] alternately stable and unstable, the

[27] There is an intriguing analogy between Marshall's proposition that the number of (isolated) equilibria is odd, and Spemer's lemma (1928), which states that if an $(n-l)$-dimensional simplex is triangulated (roughly: subdivided into sub-simplices), and if we consider a mapping of vertices of the triangulation into vertices of the original simplex, that keeps each vertex on the face of smallest dimension of the original simplex on which it is contained, then an odd number of $(n-1)$-dimensional sub-simplices of the triangulation will be mapped into the entire $(n-1)$-dimensional simplex. Zero being an even number, it follows that there is at least one.

Spemer's lemma may be intuitively understood by considering the case $n = 2$, in which we have an interval

0 1 0 0 1 1 1 0 1 1,

which is subdivided into subintervals, with end points (vertices) labelled 0 or 1 according as they are mapped into the corresponding vertices of the big interval. It is easy to verify that an odd number of subintervals are mapped into the whole

extreme-most points being stable ones (his wording was careless, since he described the origin as an unstable equilibrium, whereas it is not as a rule an equilibrium at all). Bhagwati and Johnson (1960, p. 91) objected that "the Marshallian proposition is a consequence of the way in which the curves are drawn," and proceeded to construct a counterexample in which satiability of wants and complementarity played essential roles. That such considerations are involved is evident from a theorem of Arrow and Hurwicz (1958, Theorem 6, p. 541), which puts Marshall's proposition on a rigorous basis (but in terms of the Walrasian tâtonnement process): "For two commodities ..., if the individual excess demand functions are single-valued and continuous and no individual is saturated, the system is stable." Arrow and Hurwicz left open the question of whether this theorem remains true if the number of commodities is greater than two; Scarf (1960) showed it does not, displaying examples of global instability with three commodities and three traders.

Scarf's examples were characterized by an extreme degree of complementarity, and marked differences in the preferences of the respective traders, notably a preference for one of their own commodities (all the examples, and all the Arrow-Hurwicz results, are in terms of a model of pure exchange). This was followed by a three-commodity three-trader example by Gale (1963, pp. 81–5) of global instability, in which the chief feature was the presence of Giffen's paradox. Gale's second example (pp. 85–7) is identical with an example suggested by Bhagwati and Johnson (1961, p. 428n): "It is easy to construct hypothetical examples in which only one, unstable intersection of the offer curves exists: as an illustration, suppose two countries, each of which produces a fixed quantity of a particular product and each of which consumes the two products

interval (five in the above illustration); of these, an odd number (three) retain the same orientation, and an even number (two) have the opposite orientation (cf. Pontryagin (1952, pp. 53–4)). This suggests a direct approach to the existence and stability problem that by-passes the K.K.M. lemma; it will be recalled that Spemer's lemma is the fundamental topological result used in the proof of Brouwer's fixed point theorem.

in the fixed ratio of two domestic to one imported." The utility functions for this case, as specified by Gale, are $\phi_1(x, y) = \min[x, 2y]$ for the first trader and $\phi_2(x, y) = \min[2x, y]$ for the second; the first trader starts with one unit of the x-good, and the second with one unit of the y-good. The unstable equilibrium is that in which each trader keeps two-thirds of his own product and sells the other third.

Gale was careful not to call this a case of "global instability"; he simply said that "some queer things can happen." Any slight disturbance from the unstable equilibrium sends one of the prices down to zero. What this is, is the limiting case of multiple equilibrium (as in Figure 6) in which the stable equilibria move towards the axes; the fine point in the discussion turns on whether in this limiting case there will really be "equilibrium."

This problem is best considered by examining Gale's example in conjunction with two slight variants of it. Define the subsidiary utility functions $\psi_1(x, y) = x+2y$ for the first country, and $\psi_2(x, y) = 2x + y$ for the second. In Case (1), let the utility functions be given by $\phi_1(x, y) = \min[x, 2y]$ and $\phi_2(x, y) = \min[2x, y]$ as above; then when Country 1's product (the x-good) has a zero (relative) price, only the bundles with $y = 0$ are available to it, and these all have utility $\min\,[x, 0] = 0$, whence the offer curve coincides with the horizontal. In the present example, with initial endowments $(1, 1)$, there will be an intersection of the offer curves at the point $(\frac{1}{2}, 0)$, which presumably qualifies as an equilibrium. In Case (2) let each country have a lexicographic utility function defined by $U_i(x, y) = \langle \phi_i, -\psi_i \rangle$, $i = 1, 2$, where $U_i(x, y) > U_i(x', y')$ is defined to mean that either $\phi_i(x, y) > \phi_i(x', y')$, or else $\phi_i(x, y) = \phi_i(x', y')$ and $-\psi_i(x, y) > -\psi_i(x', y')$. Then when its product is free, Country 1's demand is only $x = 0$, whereas Country 2 supplies $y = \frac{1}{2}$. Although supply exceeds demand, this still qualifies as an equilibrium in the sense of Menger (1950, pp. 99–101) and Schlesinger (1933–1934); it is in the nature of free goods to be overabundant, and if their supply is costless there would be no tendency to move away from such an equilibrium.[28] In Case (3), let the lexicographic utility functions be given by $U_i(x,y) = \langle \phi_i, \psi_i \rangle$ with the same definition as above, except that ψ_i replaces $-\psi_i$. In this case, when Country 1's product is free, it will demand an indefinitely large quantity of it, over and above its own output; thus the offer curve is discontinuous, and we have a situation of the same kind as Arrow's corner. This is technically a valid example of global instability. By symmetry, the same situation holds when Country 2's product is a free good, and the remaining equilibrium at $x_1 = y_2 = \frac{2}{3}, y_1 = x_2 = \frac{1}{3}$ is unstable.

Cases (1) and (2) provide examples of stable equilibrium, but they certainly fall in the category of cases where "the invisible hand does its work by strangulation" (cf. Balogh and Streeten (1951, p. 75)). In Case (3) the invisible hand does not even do its work; presumably any dynamic adjustment process would lead to oscillation in the neighborhood of a zero price, a situation resembling what Taussig (1921) called a "penumbra." In any event, one or other of the countries is devastated, or else convulsed. Nor would a Ricardian solution help: if Country 1's commodity is over-produced, it will continue to glut the market as long as its production is greater than half the output of Country 2's commodity; and the moment

[28] Arrow and Debreu (1954, pp. 271–2) define equilibrium by the condition that demand is greater than or equal to supply for each commodity, and that the value of excess demand for all commodities is zero (i.e., if supply exceeds demand for any commodity, then the corresponding price is equal to zero). As they acknowledge, this broader definition of equilibrium (not requiring equality between supply and demand) goes back to Schlesinger (1933–1934), and the idea goes back further to Menger (1871). According to this definition, the boundary solution discussed by Bhagwati and Johnson and by Gale is an equilibrium solution. On the other hand, Arrow and Debreu also state (1954, p. 269) that "impossible combinations of commodities, such as... the consumption of a bundle of commodities insufficient to maintain life, are regarded as excluded" from the set of available alternatives. From this point of view, the solutions in question do not qualify as equilibrium solutions, and the example becomes one of global instability. But this seems to introduce an extraneous normative consideration into a positive analysis; certainly it would come as news to the inhabitants of many a poor country to learn that starvation had now become "impossible."

its production is curtailed below half the other, the only remaining equilibrium is that in which the other country's product becomes a free good. So the Ricardian remedy works too well: it rehabilitates one country only by ruining the other country in the process. In fact both countries end up being ruined in this kind of game.

Naturally this theoretical possibility is a special limiting case, and should not be taken too seriously as providing an illustration of any real situations. It is best to consider it as a sobering reminder that pure theory admits of many strange possibilities that cannot be ruled out by a priori reasoning.

However, it will be well to clear up two points. One is the question of the proper interpretation to be attached to cases in which a commodity becomes a free good. Another is the question of the extent to which the anomalous results are dependent upon the very special assumptions made.

With respect to the first point, we may consider Figure 6 again. If Country 2 has a satiable demand for the x-commodity, its offer curve $AE_1E_2E_3$ will fall to the horizontal axis through A instead of proceeding to T_4. Likewise, if Country 1 also has a satiable demand for the x-commodity, its offer curve, coming down from T_0, may hit the horizontal axis to the left of Country 2's offer curve, instead of proceeding to A. (In this case it is reasonable to ask why the x-commodity was overproduced.) The equilibrium price of the x-commodity will be zero in this case. But this should occasion no surprise: nobody would be astonished if, upon resumption of free trade between Cuba and Guantánamo, the price of water should fall back to zero.

The situation is quite different when the zero price results from what Bhagwati and Johnson call "terminability" as opposed to "satiability." This is the case illustrated by Figures 1b and 1c, which correspond to the Arrow-Solow utility functions $\phi(x, y) = \sqrt{xy}$, and $\phi(x, y) = 1/(1/x + 1/y)$, respectively, with constant elasticities of substitution equal respectively to 1 and $\frac{1}{2}$. In fact, any utility functions with constant elasticity of substitution less than or equal to unity will yield such terminable offer functions; but it must also be emphasized that this is true if and only if there is complete specialization in the export good (a point which Bhagwati and

Johnson (1961, pp. 428–9n) failed to bring out). On the other hand, Bhagwati and Johnson (1960, pp. 90–91), following Samuelson (1948, p. 409), correctly pointed out the logical error in the argument made by Mrs. Robinson (1946–47, p. 101), that if the price of a commodity becomes high enough, the demand becomes elastic. This kind of logical error had been made long before by Bresciani-Turroni (1934, pp. 447–9), who considered an example similar to that discussed by Bhagwati and Johnson, but rejected it, at first on the logically unobjectionable grounds that such a result, "though mathematically correct, is quite absurd from an economic point of view." But he went on to argue, wrongly, that "the rise in the value of foreign currencies will not go beyond a certain limit. In fact the people of that country cannot spend more than a certain sum on foreign goods."

In the "terminability" case it is quite possible for an export price to fall to zero not because a commodity is overabundant, like water, but to a large extent because the very unfavorableness of the country's terms of trade checks its demand for both goods, allowing the foreign country to consume more of its own commodity and reduce its demand for imports still further. Thus, free goods are not necessarily a symptom of plenty; they can just as well be a symptom of poverty. It would be of no consolation to the Chileans, for example, to be told that if copper were a free goods, they could import unlimited quantities of it; it is only because there would not in such circumstances be a market for unlimited quantities of it that it is at all conceivable that it might become a free good.

Complete specialization and a high degree of complementarity characterize these cases. But it is worthy of note that this is still not enough. Suppose the indifference curves of Figure 1c are modified so that relative satiety in the import good (measured vertically) is reached; then the offer curve, instead of rising asymptotically towards the vertical from the initial endowment, will strike it. If we form an Edgeworth box with two identical countries of this kind, the interior intersection will still be stable, in spite of the high degree of complementarity. It is quite essential that each country should have a relative preference for its own product. This seems a quite arbitrary condition, difficult to justify, until we recognize that it may, in effect, be a consequence of transport costs (or tariffs).

Transport costs and other impediments to trade turned out to play an essential role in Samuelson's definitive treatment of the classical transfer problem (1954), where they were handled by the device — anticipated by Pigou (1922, p. 58) — of assuming a certain fraction of the goods to be wasted in voyage. Mundell (1957) has applied this concept to the offer curve technique, confining himself for the most part to the idealization in which each exporter absorbs (through wastage) the transport cost of his export good. It would seem far more natural to do the opposite: to assume that each country loses a certain proportion of its imports through wastage. In this way one can represent the circumstance that the relative price (to consumers) of petroleum in relation to that of automobiles is lower in Saudi Arabia than in England (rather than vice versa). We know that if utility functions are identical and homothetic, world indifference curves can be defined, and (assuming strict convexity) equilibrium is therefore unique, regardless of the degree of complementarity or specialization; also it is globally stable (cf. Scarf (1960, p. 159)). If to this simple picture we add transport costs, however, we can easily obtain multiple equilibrium, provided there is sufficient complementarity and specialization. This is readily shown by Mundell's geometric technique.[29]

The real problem is that of multiple equilibrium. And Marshall's assumptions in this regard were rather special. His Proposition VI (1879, p. 11), stating that the home offer curve cannot be cut more than once by a horizontal line, is quite arbitrary; it rules out the Giffen paradox, for instance. Even if the Giffen paradox is ruled out for individuals, Johnson has shown (1959, p. 256) how it can be

[29]This argument requires the following qualification, which has been properly urged upon me by Murray Kemp: on the face of it, we cannot be sure that it does not depend crucially on the artificial idealization used in the treatment of transport costs. The device used by Pigou, Samuelson, and Mundell leaves out of account the employment-creating and resource-using aspects of transportation; it is certainly conceivable that a more satisfactory treatment of transport costs would not give rise to multiple equilibrium.

present in the aggregate offer curve as a consequence of differences in tastes as between owners of factors of production. The even more astonishing floral offer curve Johnson displays (1959, p. 258) is derived in the same manner, by a difficult and ingenious geometric procedure. It is no less realistic a case than that displayed in Figure 1; for if two such countries join to form a common market facing a third (or if they are simply labelled "the rest of the world"), they will have an aggregate offer curve that loops around the origin.

The problem of multiple equilibrium may well be what Graham was trying to analyze with his inadequate methods. Graham stated (1932, p. 605):

> ...on the principles of the orthodox theory, any existing equilibrium must be highly unstable wherever an inelastic demand is present. A small variation in the terms of trade, arising from any cause, will evoke a further movement in those terms which will tend to carry to one or the other of the limits of the possible ratios of interchange.... In such circumstances one wonders just how such a Humpty-Dumpty as an intermediate ratio could ever have got up on the wall at all, and what could have kept him there up to the time that he eventually topples to one side or the other.

The first sentence is wrong, of course; something like transport costs must be added to give countries a relative preference (in effect) for their own products. But there is no question that in this passage Graham was using the concept of stability in the Marshallian sense of the word; the limbo price is an unstable equilibrium, and the stable equilibria are located on the flat segments of the countries' offer curves. An example of this (without reference to Graham) was displayed by Matthews (1949–50, p. 150). This is convincing and interesting; more is the pity that Graham was unable to give logical rigor to his insights.

A number of sufficient[30] conditions are known for uniqueness of equilibrium: one is gross substitutability; another is that utility

[30]Wald stated (1936, p. 657) that his Condition 5, which implies gross substitutability, is "indispensable" ("*unentbehrlich*") for uniqueness. In the English translation (1951, p. 388) this is rendered as "necessary." But it is of course

functions be homogeneous and identical. A third, the dominant diagonal condition, discussed by Newman (1959) and Arrow, Block, and Hurwicz (1959, pp. 104–6), and attributed by these authors to Hahn and Solow, is known to lead to global stability of the process; it seems, in view of the results of McKenzie (1960a) and of Gale and Nikaidô (1965) that this third criterion also leads to uniqueness.[31]

Sohmen has argued (1961a, pp. 5–11) that the Bhagwati-Johnson example is a "freak possibility," and that apart from this possibility, equilibrium will exist at positive prices (or exchange rates); in other words, he takes it as an empirically true statement that the competitive process is globally stable. He then goes on to use this to support a regime of flexible exchange rates as a policy measure.

All policy proposals reflect value judgments; the problem is to get at the root of the value judgments that are latent in these controversial issues. There are two kinds of consequences that ensue from the possibility of multiple equilibria. First there is the theoretical possibility that there may be many intersections of the offer curves, leading to a succession of stable and unstable equilibria. It is this phenomenon — and not, as is commonly supposed, the possibility of a single unstable equilibrium — to which Marshall (1923, pp. 353–4) referred when he said that "all such suggestions derive their origin from the sport of the imagination

not "necessary" in the usual mathematical sense of being implied by the conclusions and the remaining assumptions. "Indispensability" only means that the conclusion is not implied by the remaining assumptions alone; but an "indispensable" condition may be replaced by another "indispensable" one, and neither one need be "necessary."

[31]Arrow and Hurwicz (1958, p. 534) claimed that uniqueness followed from the weaker assumption that the weak axiom of revealed preference applied to the aggregate excess demand functions (in this context, to the world aggregate excess demand function). As we have already remarked, this conclusion was later weakened by Arrow and Hurwicz (1960); but quasi-stability in Uzawa's sense still holds (see Arrow, Block, and Hurwicz (1959, p. 107) and Uzawa (1961, p. 627)). Since the weak axiom is here being applied to *world* aggregate excess demand, we can safely deduce from Samuelson's (1956) impossibility theorem that, for this to hold for arbitrary resource distributions, utility functions must be identical and homothetic.

rather than the observation of facts. For they assume the total elasticity of demand of each country to be less than unity, and on the average less than one half, *throughout a large part of its schedule.* Nothing approaching to this has ever occurred in the real world: it is not inconceivable, but it is absolutely impossible" [italics added]. The consequence of such multiple equilibria would be that, given sufficiently great disturbances, price fluctuations would be very volatile. This case was discussed by Edgeworth (1894, p. 611) in his analysis of Mill's "superstructure," and it was there recognized that the case approaches the indeterminateness of neutral equilibrium. The limiting case — when the number of intersections tends to infinity — is formally equivalent to that of bilateral monopoly, whose indeterminateness was established by Edgeworth himself (1881). Since price fluctuations in commodity markets are very commonly observed, Marshall's empirical judgment certainly needs to be revised. In his later writing, Graham (1948, pp. 10–12) placed great emphasis (with reference made to von Neumann and Morgenstern (1944)) on the game-theoretic aspects of international trade with small numbers of participants, and perhaps his critics can be blamed for making an assumption — perfect competition — that Graham specifically ruled out (1948, p. 12).

"Determinateness" of equilibrium is thus closely related to uniqueness. If there is multiple equilibrium, and if disturbances are relatively large, equilibrium will become, for practical purposes, indeterminate or neutral. The condition might be called one of quasi-neutral equilibrium, or a "penumbra" in Taussig's phrase (1921, p. 397).

It is not necessary to consider such extreme cases as quasi-neutral equilibrium or "penumbra" in order to find certain weak points in the case for complete price and exchange rate flexibility. The determinacy of equilibrium, when outside disturbances are not too great, is undoubtedly a strong point in favor of such a policy; other methods may not easily avoid intermittent balance of payments crises. On the other hand if there are many equilibria, there is no particular presumption that any given one of them is best. The claim that a determinate stable equilibrium exists may therefore be beside the point. For instance, in Figure 6, it cannot be a matter of indifference to the countries concerned which of the two stable equilibria is reached. They would not have to coincide with the axes in order to be intolerable to the disadvantaged party. With respect to this kind of situation, Friedman has argued (1953, p. 160n):

> As a practical matter, the conditions necessary for any relevant range of rates to have the property that a rise increases excess demand seem to me highly unlikely to occur. But, if they should occur, it would merely mean that there might be two possible positions of equilibrium, one above, the other below, the existing controlled rate. If the higher is regarded as preferable, the implication for policy would be first to appreciate the controlled rate and then to set it free.

Preferable for whom? That is the problem. When comparing two Pareto-optimal situations, it is in the nature of things that what is preferable for one country is disadvantageous to another. Stable equilibrium under conditions of multiple equilibrium implies a certain arbitrary inequality in the world distribution of welfare. In Figure 6, if the terms of trade are in the neighborhood of T_1, corresponding to the stable equilibrium E_1, one might reasonably expect the inhabitants of Country 2 to clamor for controls, and those of Country 1 to extol the virtues of price and exchange rate flexibility; and *vice versa* if the equilibrium is at E_3. Marshall admitted as much in one of his more perceptive passages (*Industry and Trade*, 1920, p. 760).

It seems that the concept of Pareto optimality[32] has led to confusion and has sidetracked many analysts. In Figure 6, all three equilibria are Pareto optimal, and from the point of view of international distributive justice, the middle unstable one recommends itself as the fairest; this point was made by Gale (1963). Even in the extreme cases considered by Gale and by Bhagwati and Johnson, in which one or the other of the countries is ruined, the resulting equilibrium (as we decided it could be called) is Pareto optimal,

---

[32]The expression "Pareto optimal" was evidently first coined by Frisch (1953), who also distinguished between local and global Pareto optimality. In this brilliant paper Frisch subjected the concept to a forceful and highly critical analysis.

since the devastated country cannot improve its position except at the expense of the other country; indeed — within the competitive framework — except by devastating the other country. This should perhaps serve to remind us how ludicrous the criterion of Pareto optimality can be if it is used in an unthinking way. Wicksell, in his *Lectures* (1901, pp. 113–9), dealt with this question very forcibly, pointing out in later editions of this work (1934, p. 75) that as soon as multiple equilibria are admitted, the case for optimality of equilibrium breaks down, since they cannot all be the best at once. He reiterated these objections in his review (1913) of Pareto's *Manuel* (1909). Samuelson (1956) has called attention to this point once again. Recognition of the possibility of multiple equilibrium might have led to a greater clarification of the issues in the controversy between Haberler (1948) and Balogh (1949). The question is not so much whether equilibrium will be reached as whether the gains from trade can be fairly divided. This is really what the argument is all about.

8. External Economies

The classical (Ricardian) theory emphasized geographical differences as the chief source of comparative advantage, and therefore of trade. The "modern" approach begun by Heckscher and Ohlin, to be discussed in Part 3, emphasized instead the differences in factor endowments. According to both of these theories, one might expect international trade to be carried on mostly between areas that are different in respect to climate and to natural and human endowments. But it is well known that, on the contrary, most international trade is carried on between the large industrial areas that are very similar in both these respects.

In the case of Switzerland, for instance, which exports tourism and watches, both theories provide a good explanation for the tourism. Whether we say that comparatively less labor is required to produce recreational pleasure, or that Switzerland is well endowed with mountains and that recreation is a "mountain-intensive" industry, is largely a matter of taste. On the other hand, geography cannot very well explain the watches; nor does it get us very far to say that Switzerland exports watches because it is relatively well endowed with watch-makers and watch-making machinery, for this begs the question of why it is Switzerland and not some other country that should have become so endowed.

To explain such cases it is necessary to take account of economies of large-scale production. The case of Swiss watches provides as good an example as one could wish of what Marshall (1890) called "external economies"; but this term has been so misunderstood that we shall have to digress on the subject of economies as such, before discussing the part they play in international trade and specialization.

It is probably correct to say that economies of scale tend to be ignored in theoretical models not so much on empirical grounds as for the simple reason that the theoretical difficulties are considerable, and it is not generally agreed how they can be incorporated into a model of general equilibrium or whether they are at all compatible with the assumptions of perfect competition. That this is a poor reason for excluding them from consideration is evident, especially if it is true that they constitute one of the principal sources of international trade. While it is probably futile to seek for a date when economic science began, if a line is to be drawn anywhere it might be with the discovery of Adam Smith (1776) that the division of labor, combined with exchange of the products obtained from specialization, is the elemental source of the wealth of nations. It is quite clear that the division of labor stressed by Smith arose not from geographical or climatic differences, but from the economies resulting from such division, wherever the specialization might take place. Torrens (1808, pp. 14–7, 44–5) was evidently the first to make a distinction between these two sources of comparative advantage, which he called "mechanical division of labor" and "territorial division of labor." The distinction was made again by Cairnes (1874, pp. 298–302) and Haberler (1936, pp. 130–1) who tended, however, (unlike Torrens) to identify them with domestic and international trade respectively.

One of the great classical laws, well-grounded empirically in the observed tendency in the eighteenth and nineteenth centuries for manufactures to fall in price relative to foodstuffs, was that first set forth by West (1815) to the effect that agriculture was characterized by diminishing returns, and manufacturing by increasing returns. West based himself on the first chapter of Smith's *Wealth of Nations* (1776) for the idea that division of labor was more feasible in manufacturing than in agriculture; but he added the principle of diminishing returns, which had been absent from Smith. At the same time, Malthus (1815, pp. 37–9) presented a similar doctrine, later quoted *in extenso* by McCulloch (1824, p. 262), and reproduced verbatim in Malthus' *Principles* (1820, pp. 184–6; 1836, pp. 178–80); Ricardo described it as "excellent" (*Works,* II, p. 169). Malthus compared the land to machinery and observed that inferior machinery in manufacturing was replaced by superior machinery, whereas the analogous inferior "machinery" in land was not. There was a significant difference between the two theories: Malthus' doctrine was essentially an exogenous or historical law of increasing returns, whereas West's was clearly a doctrine stating that manufacturing was characterized by increasing returns to scale. West's theory may therefore be characterized as endogenous; his version of the theory is not to be found in Ricardo, but was restated by Torrens in the second edition of the *External Corn Trade* (1820, p. 407) and finally given an important role by Senior (1836, pp. 81–6). Torrens' statement (1826, p. 119) is a good one:

> But as the division of employment is limited by the extent of the market, and can be perfectly established only amongst a dense population, it follows, that in new or thinly inhabited countries, the effective powers of manufacturing industry must be extremely low. Hence, in the progress of society, the two main causes which govern the rate of profit are as antagonist muscles, modifying and balancing each other. As an increasing population compels us on the one hand to resort to inferior soils, and thus to raise the productive cost of raw produce, so it leads on the other hand to more accurate divisions of employment, and to the use of improved machinery, and thus lowers the productive cost of all wrought goods.

Marshall was later to say much the same thing (*Principles*, p. 318): "The part which nature plays in production shows a tendency to diminishing return, the part which man plays shows a tendency to increasing return."

The first fairly rigorous approach to the treatment of economies in international trade seems to be that of Marshall (1879, pp. 12–15, 26–8). Edgeworth (1889a; 1889c, note (j)) was quick to perceive the difficulties in reconciling increasing returns with competitive conditions, and claimed that a downward sloping supply curve for an industry was not compatible with stable equilibrium. It was implicit in his discussion that firms had U-shaped cost curves, and the industrial supply curves he defined had discontinuities corresponding to the entry of new firms. We should note here in passing that such discontinuities — contrary to the impression given in most contemporary textbooks — are themselves incompatible with competitive equilibrium; this was implicitly recognized by Marshall (1961, I, pp. 374–5, 458–9; II, p. 810), who noted that marginal firms were given the onus of not spoiling the market. The relevance of this to the phenomenon of glutted markets discussed by Sismondi and others in the 1820's is quite evident.

Edgeworth subsequently (*Papers*, II, pp. 305–6n) withdrew his objections to a downward-sloping supply curve, on the grounds that Marshall's introduction (1890) of the concept of external economies had made his own treatment "obsolete."[33] Accordingly, the relevant

[33]Cournot (1838, p. 102) had shown that if marginal cost was falling for any producer, "nothing would limit the production of the commodity," and as a consequence, "the effect of monopoly is not entirely extinguished, or competition is not such that the variation in the quantity delivered by each producer separately has no appreciable influence on total output and the commodity price." Marshall (*Principles*, p. 459n) took Cournot to task for proceeding "apparently without noticing" that monopoly would result from these assumptions — surely an unfair criticism (see also Marshall (1961, II, p. 521)). With reference to this passage and Edgeworth's note (j), Sraffa (1925–26, p. 304) stated (mistakenly) that "Edgeworth himself fell into an error of this kind, but later rectified it following the publication of Marshall's work, which has cleared up the question in a definitive manner and eliminated any possibility of doubt." This is a remarkable passage in the light of Sraffa's subsequent about-face.

note (j) from his earlier paper (1889c, p. 507), as well as a review (1889a) that dealt with the same problem (and where the concept of an envelope had been introduced), were excluded from the collected *Papers* (1925). Edgeworth's later treatment of the problem of external economies is to be found scattered throughout his various writings (*Papers,* I, pp. 72, 81–4; II, pp. 39–41, 88, 432–40; III, pp. 140–1). He gave generous credit (*Papers*, II, p. 88) to Cunynghame (1892) for "his path-breaking essay on the subject," although Marshall had written Edgeworth a spirited letter, immediately following the publication of Cunynghame's article, stating that he did not understand Cunynghame's "successive cost curves," and did not believe that Cunynghame understood them himself (cf. Marshall (1961, II, p. 809)). Be that as it may, they were evidently suggestive to Edgeworth, who presented his most complete treatment of the formal nature of external economies in his review of Cunynghame's book (1905).[34]

The essential idea put forward by Edgeworth (1905, pp. 66–8; *Papers*, III, pp. 140–1) was that marginal cost was a function of a particular firm's output, and also of aggregate industrial output; and that it might be rising with respect to the former and falling with respect to the latter. According to this conception, rising marginal cost curves for the individual firms would shift downwards with a rise in industrial output, leading to a falling supply curve for the industry. The same concepts were developed by Edgeworth with reference to Cunynghame's discussion of external economies (hymn books) and diseconomies (orchids) in consumption, and in this context the distinction between individual and market quantities was later adopted by Pigou (1913, p. 21). But Edgeworth noted (*Papers*, III, p. 141): "The liability of an industry to be monopolised when it obeys the law of increasing returns creates peculiar difficulty in the application of the geometrical method to supply. In order that the theory... should be extended to supply, it must be postulated

[34]A very similar treatment has been developed more recently in the interesting paper by Adams and Wheeler (1952–1953), without reference to Cunynghame and Edgeworth. See also Marshall's *Principles*, p. 463n.

that the output of each producer is small in comparison with the collective output of all his competitors...." This is the point; the individual firm must be *so* small that the entrepreneur does not take into account the influence of his output on industrial output, and therefore acts *as if* his costs were rising (as a function of his output) when actually they may be falling, or if not falling, at least rising by a smaller amount. To put the matter differently, we may distinguish between two kinds of marginal cost: those of which the entrepreneur is consciously aware as being a function of his output; and those he regards as exogenous, that is, of whose functional relationship to his own output he is, in effect, ignorant. A rise in his output may therefore be considered as leading to a movement along his own marginal cost curve, as well as to a downward shift in his and other firms' marginal cost curves. This is the Cunynghame-Edgeworth construction, and it makes possible a downward sloping industrial supply curve provided — to borrow a phrase from Keynes (1930, p. 26) who analyzed a similar situation with respect to banks — the firms "move forward in step," but — it must be added — not in concert.

To illustrate the case, an expansion in a certain industry may make possible a further division of labor, and give rise to new categories of technicians. The contribution of each individual firm to this process may be so negligible that no single entrepreneur will take into account the effect of his own scale of operations on the development of new specialized skills. This element of cost therefore plays the same parametric role as do market prices. It is curious indeed that Edgeworth, of all people, did not notice the analogy between this concept of external economies and his own limit theorem justifying the competitive price mechanism (cf. Edgeworth (1881, pp. 35–43; *Papers*, II, pp. 369–70); Debreu and Scarf (1963, pp. 240–3)). All we need to assume is that a firm's size has a small effect (negligible from its point of view) on the organization of the industry (especially the labor market), and that the firm consciously adjusts its own organization to the changed conditions of the industry.[35]

It is widely agreed that Marshall's theoretical treatment of external economies (*Principles*, esp. Book IV, Ch. XIII; Book V, Ch. XII; and Appendix H) was far from satisfactory; indeed, it seems certain that Marshall was not satisfied with it himself. In his later work (1920) he was even less precise. The concept has therefore continued to have a tenuous status, that of an inspired idea that awaits adequate formalization. Haberler (1936, pp. 206–8) presented an excellent exposition of the subject, but commented (p. 207) that external economies "are somewhat vague and indeterminate in nature"; however, it seems that it is not so much the economies, as the concept itself, which is vague and indeterminate. Marshall's only definition consists in the bare statement (*Principles*, p. 266) that external economies are those economies of scale which are "dependent on the general development of the industry." The absence of any more elaborate formal definition in Marshall's writings is so conspicuous that it must be interpreted as deliberate; Robertson used the term "evasive" (cf. Newman (1960, p. 601)). In an earlier sceptical paper Robertson (1924, p. 26), after enumerating the usual examples (including the inevitable trade journal) sighed: "we have all at some time tried to memorize and to reproduce the formidable list." In the same year, Knight (1924, p. 597) set forth his famous objection to the concept of external economies in the words: "external economies in one business unit are internal economies in some other, within the industry." Perhaps deliberately, he did not say "some

[35]Pigou (1912, pp. 172–9) set forth the principle that "the presence of increasing returns in respect of all [suppliers] together is compatible with the presence of diminishing returns in respect of the special work of each severally." This doctrine was vigorously criticized by Young (1913, p. 678n) who said: "I cannot imagine 'external economies' adequate to bring about this result." Later, however, Young (1928) accepted the idea of external economies as providing a "fruitful distinction."

other *business unit*"; if the economies are in the sector of factor suppliers, then the objection loses much of its force. Knight's paper was largely a criticism of the concept of external economies — as was Robertson's 1924 paper — as used both by Pigou (1920) and by Graham (1923). Graham based his argument for protection on an analysis which took for granted the compatibility of perfect competition and increasing returns; this very assumption is what was challenged by Knight, and as long as Knight's objection stood, Graham's entire argument — whatever other defects it had, and there were several — was vitiated by having this as its premise. In his reply to Knight, Graham (1925) failed to come to grips with the main issue; and Knight (1925) in his rejoinder fairly placed the burden of proof on those who believed that competitive conditions could be reconciled with increasing returns. In saying with respect to external economies that "I have never succeeded in picturing them in my mind," Knight (1925, p. 332) was undoubtedly expressing a feeling that was widespread but suppressed, owing to the authority of Marshall and Pigou.

Under the circumstances, the Marshallian structure seemed ready to crumble under the onslaught of Sraffa (1925–1926, 1926), the new theory of imperfect competition — in Newman's words (1960) — "rising from the ashes." It appears that Sraffa's main point was that the very concept of an industrial supply function is illegitimate, since it does not take account of the interdependence of industries; thus the supply functions of different industries are themselves interdependent. To some extent this argument anticipated the later well-known treatment by Mrs. Robinson (1941); to some extent also, however, Sraffa's objection seems to be the same as that made by von Neumann and Morgenstern (1947, p. 11) to the effect that it is improper to assume that entrepreneurs do not take into account the repercussions of their own actions when they make their decisions. To support his point of view, Sraffa invoked (1926, p. 541n) the cryptic statement by Edgeworth (1881, p. 127n) that "to treat *variables* as *constants* is the characteristic vice of the unmathematical economist." This vice was turned into a virtue by R.G.D. Allen (1932b), who objected that Edgeworth was "unable to use the method characteristic of the modern mathematical theory of value" on account of his failure adequately to comprehend "the parametric function of the market prices."[36] One could, of course, turn this argument back on Allen, as in the spirit of the theory of games, and place the burden on him (as well as on Pareto (1911)) of showing how one can justify the assumption that *entrepreneurs* — along with unmathematical economists — suppose prices to be constant, when the mathematical economist, in his wisdom, knows them to be variable. Pareto (1909, pp. 162–5) had based his justification for the assumption that consumers suppose prices to be beyond their control on the fact that there was a large number of participants in the market as well as absence of communication among them. As Debreu and Scarf demonstrated (1963), the theory of games can itself be used to justify the parametric function of prices *when the number of players approaches infinity*;[37] and this is, essentially, the main result proved by Edgeworth himself (1881). Edgeworth's whole point, in effect, was that the parametric function of prices could not be justified unless the number of participants was very large.[38]

The chief casualty of Sraffa's 1926 paper was the concept of external economies. Referring to the concept as used by Marshall (1920), he concluded (1926, p. 540) that "in so far as external economies of the kind in question exist, they are not likely to be called forth by *small* increases in production." But it is precisely

[36]Pareto (1911, pp. 601–3; 1955, pp. 67–9) was evidently the first to give a precise formulation to the concept of the parametric role of market prices; he also made the important point that general functions could play the same role, prices being the special case of constant functions. As far as I am aware, Edgeworth made no reference in any of his papers to Pareto's 1911 article. Nevertheless the idea was present in Pareto's *Manuel* (1909, pp. 564–5, 569), a work which Edgeworth knew well and much admired, and he was surely not as innocent of the concept as Allen suggested.

[37]The possibility of proving this was foreseen by von Neumann and Morgenstern (1947, pp. 13–14). As Edgeworth acknowledged (1881, p. 47) the idea goes back to Cournot (1838, Ch. 8).

[38]Marshall (1881) completely failed to appreciate this important substantive contribution of Edgeworth's, and limited himself in this strange and patronizing review largely to an attack on the use of mathematics in economics.

the *smallness* of their relative impact on any one firm which makes such economies *external*; external economies of the Marshallian kind may be defined as economies that are so widely diffused and so imperceptible in relation to an individual firm's output that they are ignored, that is, treated as negligible in the mind of the entrepreneur. This discontinuity — the treatment of something small as if it were equal to zero — is essential to the whole argument.

Pigou (1927, p. 195) attempted with only a fair degree of success to answer Sraffa's objection. He relied on a pseudo-mathematical argument concerning quantities of the "first order" and "second order," without specifying the relevant limiting process. His later paper (1928) has come to be regarded as the classic statement of the doctrine of external economies,[39] but while it was superior to the earlier one, it was still not entirely satisfactory. He correctly (1928, p. 240) stressed the importance of the assumption that "the outputs of the individual firms are small relatively to the output of the whole industry," and introduced the dichotomy used before (Edgeworth (1905), Pigou (1913)) between output of the firm and of the industry. In assuming (1928, p. 242) that "the equilibrium firm thinks of small changes in its output as involving equal and opposite changes in the output of its competitors" — an assumption he could have dispensed with had he followed the idealization of allowing the number of firms to approach infinity — Pigou came within epsilon of the definition we have been urging.

Another distinct defense of Marshallian external economies emerged at the same time. Borrowing and slightly altering some convenient terms introduced by Robertson (1957, pp. 114–23), we may call this second defense "Shovian" in contrast to the above "Pigovian" approach. Pigou believed that Marshall's representative

[39]Harrod described it in 1930 as an "important treatment" (*Essays, p.* 77). Nevertheless, in 1952 he maintained (*ibid.*, p. 176) that "increasing returns are compatible with imperfect, but not with perfect, competition."

firm was an "equilibrium firm" (1928, p. 239), whereas Shove (1928, 1930) introduced the idea, revived by Andrews (1951), of an industry that is in equilibrium although none of its constituent firms need be. This whole approach has been discussed by Newman (1960) in the light of the modern theory of stochastic processes, and the reader is referred to Newman's paper for further references too numerous to be mentioned here.

In spite of his earlier scepticism, Robertson (1930) responded to the onslaught on Marshallian economics by presenting, in the famous Symposium on Increasing Returns and the Representative Firm, an essentially Shovian defense of external economies. The Pigovian device of representing costs as a function not only of the firm's output, but also of that of the industry, left him uneasy: "one might as well argue," he said (p. 87), "that the growth in the individual bones of a baby are the result of the growth in its skeleton." Thus, in order to reconcile competition with increasing returns, he sought the solution — following Marshall (*Principles*, pp. 315ff.) — in the tendency for firms to die, like the trees in the forest. But Sraffa (1930, p. 90) made merry of the analogies to which Robertson had resorted: "at the crucial points of his argument the firms and the industry drop out of the scene, and their place is taken by the trees and the forest, the bones and the skeleton, the water-drops and the wave — indeed all the kingdoms of nature are drawn upon to contribute to the wealth of his metaphors." Sraffa might have added Edgeworth's mountaineers (*Papers*, II, p. 88), to say nothing of the beetle and the worm (*Papers*, I, p. 65). In proving that competition was incompatible with decreasing costs, Sraffa thought he had triumphed when he pointed out (p. 93): "demand price is assumed to be constant with respect to variations in the output of an individual firm in a competitive market (this is merely the definition of free competition)." No one thought to add: supply price is assumed to be rising with respect to variations in the output of an individual firm in a competitive market (this is merely the definition of external economies). If a constant demand function can be given a parametric role for the individual firm, consistent with a falling industrial demand curve for the industry, then a rising supply (marginal cost) function can play a similar role, consistent with a falling supply curve for the industry.[40]

The approach just described was adopted by Chamberlin (1933, p. 83), who assigned a parametric role to a downward sloping demand curve for a firm, on the assumption that "any adjustment in price or 'product' by a single producer spreads its influence over so many competitors that the impact felt by any one is negligible and does not lead him to any readjustment of his own situation." Recognizing that he needed such a parametric concept for the reconciliation of his system with general equilibrium, it was of no embarrassment to Chamberlin to treat costs in the same way (1933, pp. 22–3); thus he accepted the concept of external economies under pure competition and willingly incorporated them into his own system as well.

Mrs. Robinson (1933, Appendix) sought a somewhat similar resolution of the problem with her ill-fated "efficiency units" and "corrected natural units." This attempt evidently finds its roots in the curious circumstance that Pigou, in the only illustration he gave of external economies, abandoned his own assumptions without seeming to realize it. In a passage cited by Mrs. Robinson (1933, p. 338), Pigou (1928, p. 252), referred to an observation made by Sir Sydney Chapman that England's superiority to Germany in cotton production was due to the greater specialization of English firms in spinning and weaving processes, as well as in spinning of fine and coarse counts; thus "the increased specialisation of its component

[40]Viner, whose error in defining the envelope cost curve has become celebrated (1931, pp. 35–6), dealt with external economies (1931, Chart V, p. 39) by assuming each firm's average and marginal cost curves to fall vertically, so that industry output can increase only "as the result of increase in the number of producers" (p. 40). This is a case in which the baby's skeleton grows but the individual bones remain the same size. This is an arbitrary and quite unnecessary assumption. All that needs to be assumed is that the individual entrepreneur does not take *account* of the fact that increases in his output lead to a fall in his costs curves, in precisely the same way that he does not take account of the fact that increases in his output lead to a fall (but ultimately a smaller one, by assumption — this is the stability condition) in his horizontal demand curve.

firms made possible by an enlargement in an industry as a whole often involves a large reduction in costs." Since the product mix in the individual firm is variable in this example, some unspecified quantity index seems to be implied in terms of which it is possible to define a reduction in unit costs. This is essentially the problem to which Mrs. Robinson addressed herself, although the particular method she used was unsatisfactory (since the new units were defined in terms of the output) and was later retracted, a retraction which Leontief (1937, p. 346) applauded for its "commendable frankness." In the subsequent reprint of her 1941 paper, Mrs. Robinson (1952, p. 236n) castigated her earlier attempt still further by calling it "a mere aberration."

A similar dichotomy between theoretical constructions and examples furnished as illustrations is to be found in E. A. G. Robinson's study (1931), which presented many illuminating examples of vertical and lateral disintegration; in many of these, the characteristic feature is provided by economies of product specialization on the one hand, combined with diseconomies of organization on the other, leading to decreasing returns to the firm combined with increasing returns for the industry. Yet Robinson no sooner began to attempt a more formal analysis than he came, in a passage that seems to show the influence of Knight, to the wistful conclusion (1931, p. 138; 1962, p. 121): "And so we chase this will-o'-the-wisp of external economy through industry after industry, and we find it vanishing in the end or absorbed in the economies of firms or organisations below their optimum capacity" — which seems like giving up the subject. What evidently bothered Robinson, as well as Knight, was a feeling that the notion of economies which could be external to the firm but not internal to any other sector involved a fallacy, or at least an old paradox, of a whole being greater than the sum of its parts. But the same can be said for the idea that no single individual affects market prices, even though the aggregate of individuals do. As Aumann (1964) has forcefully proposed, a solution to the dilemma can be found in the idealization of a continuum of participants in the market; the only alternative solution would seem to be that of finding a satisfactory formal treatment of the processes of communication and filtering of information — an approach that was suggested by Hayek (1945) and which has been pursued by Hurwicz (1960).[41]

If Robinson is correct in holding that the form in which "economies" arise is in the greater subdivision of products, labor, and organization, then one of the conclusions towards which the above analysis leads is that, with all due respect to Leontief's (1937) methodological position, the assumption of a single-product firm, producing a homogeneous output and employing homogeneous inputs, is itself a form of implicit theorizing, since it tends to exclude external economies *a priori*; and as long as this feature of conventional theory is retained, it seems quite proper in the meantime to redress the balance by representing greater specialization — in product mixes and factor tasks — in terms of some type of construct that replaces the greater degree of specialization by greater "quantity." This is essentially what Mrs. Robinson tried to do, and this is what made it possible to represent external economies in terms of falling supply prices of factors to the *industry*, but not to the *firm.* In this way the parametric nature of external economies was displayed in terms of the already understood parametric function of prices: an increase in specialization arising out of an increase in employment in a particular industry was represented by an increase in "tasks" more than proportionate to the increase in employment; and if the cost of training is negligible and the supply curve of "labor" to the industry is rising with respect to the wage, the supply curve of "tasks" may nevertheless be falling (to the industry) in terms

[41] Hayek (1949, p. 86) described the price system as "a mechanism for communicating information." As is apparent from Hurwicz's treatment (1960), prices when considered from this standpoint play a role very similar to that of R. A. Fisher's concept of "sufficient statistics" — no more information is conveyed than is required for the problem at hand. It seems to me, however, that Hayek has somewhat overstated this aspect of the price system, as opposed to the parametric aspect: the fact that some (relevant) information is *withheld*, or even *distorted*, is sometimes just as important as the fact that some information is *conveyed.* In Lange's phrase (1937; 1938, p. 117), competition is a "game of blindman's buff"; and it is precisely this ignorance and uncertainty concerning the effects of one's own and others' actions that is relevant to the present discussion.

of the "price" of the "tasks." Such a transformation is unnecessary when it is recognized, as Pareto pointed out (1911, p. 602), that general functions — and not just constant functions — can play a parametric role; it was failure to recognize this, much more than the minor blemishes in the formulation of certain implicit constructs, that was the main defect of the "Cambridge school."

In view of the erosion that has gradually taken place in the Marshallian theory, it is perhaps not surprising that what remains is only a caricature of the original system. Thus Meade (1952b, 1955) has introduced a concept of external economies which is as remote as one could imagine from the conception that Marshall originally developed. The first kind, which Meade calls "unpaid factors" (1952b, p. 56; 1955, p. 39), is illustrated by the interaction between adjacent apple-growing and bee-keeping activities. The second kind, called "creation of atmosphere" (1952b, p. 56; 1955, p. 41), is illustrated by the beneficial effects on wheat production of the increased rainfall brought about by adjacent (?) forests for timber production. Both these examples seem so far-fetched that it is difficult to understand how an entire theory of commercial policy can be based upon them. As Scitovsky has said (1954, p. 145), "the examples of external economies given by Meade are somewhat bucolic in nature, having to do with bees, orchards, and woods. This, however, is no accident: it is not easy to find examples from industry."[42] Thus, apart from the bees and apple blossoms, it turns out that the box marked "external economies" is filled with "atmosphere," as Clapham (1922) might well have suspected all along.

---

[42]Scitovsky (1954, p. 146) also considers another concept, which he borrowed from Viner (1931, p. 39), called "pecuniary external economies," which refers to changes brought about via market prices. They arise, according to Scitovsky, "whenever the profits of one producer are affected by the actions of other producers." It would be difficult indeed to imagine a situation in which this was not the case. "Pecuniary economies" in this sense seem to be just another name for general equilibrium. The kinds of problems discussed under this head seem to be cases in which the number of participants in the market is too small for the price mechanism to work smoothly and for glutted markets to be avoided.

In Pigou's (and Edgeworth's) formulation, a firm's cost was a function of its own output and the industry's output (which includes that of the firm under consideration); in Meade's formulation, a firm's costs are a function of its own output, and of the output of the other firms. This is more than a trifling difference: for Meade's formulation leads to the discrepancies — which Pigou himself made so much of in his *Economics of Welfare* — between private and social cost, whereas the parametric formulation leads to no such divergence. This makes a great deal of difference in the conclusions to be drawn with respect to commercial policy. In the Meadian formulation, "external economies" necessarily call for some kind of permanent subsidy (cf. Meade (1955, pp. 230–4, 268)); but it is noteworthy that when Meade comes to discuss these commercial policies, he abandons his earlier bucolic and atmospheric examples and introduces "economies of conglomeration" — which seem to be none other than the Marshallian external economies.

Meade actually classifies these economies of conglomeration in his "atmospheric" category (1955, p. 258), but he does not provide a convincing explanation as to why — as in the case of timber and wheat — an increase in the size of one unit is beneficial only to other units, and does not redound at least partially to the advantage of the expanding unit. It is true that Marshall presented an argument for taxing industries subject to decreasing return and subsidizing industries subject to increasing return; but it is perfectly clear from his argument (*Principles*, pp. 470–1) that this analysis was based on principles quite different from what is now called Pareto optimality.[43]

[43]Cf. Pareto (1894b, p. 60; 1909, pp. 354, 617); "maximum ophelimity" was Pareto's name for this principle. By his own admission, Pareto (1894b, p. 58) arrived at the concept that now bears his name after criticisms of his earlier treatment had been raised by Pantaleoni and Barone. Four years earlier, Marshall (1890) called it "one interpretation" of the doctrine of "maximum satisfaction," and subsequently attributed the principle to Bastiat (*Principles*, I, p. 470; II, p. 533). But his argument for taxes and bounties was stated in terms of consumer's surplus; as usual, Marshall cannot be pinned down, but my understanding of his argument is that his tax-and-bounty scheme is justified by benefiting poor consumers at the expense of rich producers. If my interpretation is correct,

Graham (1923, pp. 202–3) used external economies as an argument for permanent protection; his position, characteristically, could hardly have been stated more emphatically: "it may be to a country's economic advantage to protect an industry which could not grow up or survive without protection and which never will be able to survive without it, an industry which has no comparative advantage when the protective duty is first levied nor ever attains one under it." Knight (1925, p. 331) forthrightly agreed that "if one can make his assumptions in regard to decreasing cost, his conclusion is correct"; he therefore rested his case on the position that competitive conditions were incompatible with decreasing costs. What I am maintaining — although a formal argument cannot be presented here — is that perfect competition is indeed compatible with decreasing cost, that the competitive equilibria that exist under these conditions — and the plural nature of such equilibria must be stressed — will accordingly be at least locally Pareto optimal. But this still does not mean that there is no argument for protection, whether temporary or permanent; permanent controls may be required in order to preserve an unstable equilibrium, or temporary controls in order to move from one stable equilibrium to another. A sketch of the argument leading to this conclusion will follow now, in the process of discussing the geometric treatment of the problem presented by Lerner (1932, 1934), Matthews (1949–50), and Meade (1952a).

In his geometric treatment, Lerner (1932) pointed out that decreasing costs would lead to nonconvexity of the production block, and in his discussions of demand conditions, concluded that there would be a discontinuity in the offer curve (1934; 1953, p. 118). It was remarked in Section 2.6 above, with respect to Figure 6, that

Marshall's pupil Pigou was completely off the track; cf. Samuelson (1947, pp. 196, 208) for a related interpretation. It should be added that Marshall presented a *distinct* argument (*Principles*, p. 472n) to the effect that owing to the possibility of multiple equilibria, one such equilibrium could be (as we would say today in the terminology of Frisch (1953)) locally but not globally Pareto optimal.

nonconvexity of the production block would lead to nonconvexity of Meade's trade indifference curves. Thus, a mechanical application of the geometrical analysis would lead one to conclude that there was a discontinuity between the points u and v in Country 1's offer curve. On the other hand, if the offer curve was defined as the locus of points of tangency between the terms of trade lines and the trade indifference curves, it would become a continuous curve, but would be "re-entrant" in Edgeworth's terminology (1894, p. 436); it is a "nice question," as he put it, as to whether this is possible. Marshall himself (1879, p. 27) had not expressed himself too clearly, and suggested that irreversible dynamic phenomena were involved. Edgeworth's conclusion was that re-entrance was not possible if economies were internal, but possible (invoking Cunynghame's successive cost curves) if they were external. On the other hand Lerner (without reference to Edgeworth) said (1953, p. 118) that "this gap is the most important part of the diagram" and concluded that decreasing costs would lead to complete specialization.

Matthews (1949–50, pp. 152–3) challenged this conclusion of Lerner's. He assumed decreasing costs to be due to external economies, which he left undefined; also, he presented a rather vague argument to the effect that there would be a divergence between private and social opportunity costs "unless external economies operate equally strongly in both industries," which he said was "most unlikely" but nevertheless assumed to hold as an "approximation." All this seems quite unnecessary in the light of the argument we have been presenting in this section. More convincingly, Matthews went on to argue that stable equilibrium would hold as long as the community indifference curves were "more sharply convex" than the production transformation curve.

Meade (1952a) took up this argument and assumed (p. 33) that taxes and subsidies were such as to remove the divergence between private and social cost. Again, this assumption does not seem necessary to the argument if external economies are defined parametrically. Apart from this, Meade argued quite convincingly (1952a, pp. 32–43) for re-entrant offer curves.

As soon as nonconvexity of the "production block" is admitted, it is no longer certain that any equilibrium exists. This, I think, is the essence of Young's thesis (1928). If we conceive of West's dichotomy between industries of increasing and of decreasing cost, and keep in mind the subtle difficulties involved in defining the production possibility set which we discussed in Section 2.4, it is evident that we can no longer even assume that the production block is bounded. It might have not only the shape indicated by Tinbergen (1945, p. 192; 1954, p. 181) and Caves (1960, p. 172), but it might even be asymptotic to the axis corresponding to the manufactured goods (assumed subject to increasing returns). As Young (1928, p. 533) observed, if division of labor is limited by the extent of the market, and if (as Adam Smith certainly implied) the extent of the market is in turn enlarged by the division of labor, it follows that "the division of labour depends in large part upon the division of labour." Young added that "this is more than mere tautology," being the source of a theory of *growth*. Thus, while Young was sceptical about external economies in 1913, his position in 1928 was that increasing returns were indeed compatible with competitive conditions, but were not compatible with competitive *equilibrium*. The geometry of this — very nearly perceived by Young (1928, pp. 540–2) — is easily seen if we consider that if the elasticity of substitution between manufactures and primary or agricultural goods is sufficiently great, and the production block extends out indefinitely along the axis of manufactured goods, then no equilibrium exists.

On the other hand, equilibrium will exist under the above conditions provided the community indifference curves are "more convex" (in a loose but obvious sense) than the transformation curve. Since increasing returns can be the source of growth, Schumpeter (1928) failed to see the distinction between a historical (exogenous) and technological (endogenous) law of increasing returns; in his later writing (1954, pp. 1047–8) he was even more rigid on this point, which seems to have been one of his few blind spots.

It has taken all this discussion to come to the conclusion that will be pointed to now: The most interesting consequence of external economies is the existence of multiple equilibria. The relevant diagram is depicted by Matthews (1949–50, p. 154), Meade (1952a, Fig. XVII), and Kemp (1964, pp. 114–7). It illustrates the case — well in accord with common sense — in which there are two stable equilibria, one in which Switzerland specializes in watches and Germany in cameras, and one in which Germany specializes in watches and Switzerland in cameras; and one unstable equilibrium in which specialization is incomplete. Matthews has argued, as Graham (1923) before him, that under these circumstances, trade might make a country worse off; this being a problem in welfare economics, I shall not attempt to discuss it here, but will simply make a few remarks about stability conditions in relation to commercial policy.

The infant-industry argument for protection can be considered as an argument for employing government action to move from one stable equilibrium to another, preferred one. In this case the tariff need only be temporary. On the other hand it would require permanent protection or controls to remain at the unstable equilibrium. As an illustration: if Canada wishes to produce all brands of automobiles, permanent protection will be required; whereas if she should specialize on one make, exporting it in return for the others, this might be accomplished by means of a temporary tariff. This was confirmed by the events of January, 1965.

These considerations, while obvious, have been slow in finding their way into formal theory. They have tended to be better appreciated by location theorists than by trade theorists.[44] Yet they were certainly recognized by Marshall, who asserted unequivocally (*Principles*, p. 671) that "England's present economic condition is the direct result of tendencies to production on a large scale." While he presented the corresponding geometrical analysis (1923, pp. 354–6), he did not much trust it, owing to the limitations of the "statical method." Accordingly, the most important conclusion of his analysis was the one that he himself failed to draw: that the presence of economies of large scale production leads to multiple

[44]Cf. Weber (1911) and Lösch (1939) where the importance of economies is recognized, although it is still not given the emphasis that one might expect. See Isard (1956) for additional references and discussion.

equilibrium, and therefore introduces an intrinsic arbitrariness into the determination of the international pattern of specialization and trade.

References

Adams, Robert W., and John T. Wheeler: "External Economies and the Supply Curve," *Review of Economic Studies*, 20 (1952–53), 24–39.

Aleksandrov, P. S.: Combinatorial Topology, Vol. I (translated from the first (1947) Russian edition). Rochester, N.Y.: Graylock Press, 1956.

Allen, R. G. D. (1932a): "The Foundations of a Mathematical Theory of Exchange," *Economica*, 12 (May, 1932), 197–226.

——— (1932b): Review of *Mathematical Psychics*, by F. Y. Edgeworth, *Economic Journal*, 42 (June, 1932), 307–309.

Allen, R. G. D., and A. L. Bowley: *Family Expenditure.* London: P. S. King and Son Ltd., 1935.

Andrews, P. W. S.: "Industrial Analysis in Economics," *Oxford Studies in the Price Mechanism* (edited by T. Wilson and P. W. S. Andrews). Oxford: Clarendon Press, 1951, pp. 139–172.

Arrow, Kenneth J. (1951a): "An Extension of the Basic Theorems of Classical Welfare Economics," in *Proceedings of the Second Berkeley Symposium on Mathematical Statistics and Probability.* Berkeley: University of California Press, 1951, pp. 507–532.

——— (1951b): *Social Choice and Individual Values.* New York: John Wiley and Sons, Inc., 1951.

Arrow, Kenneth J., H. D. Block and Leonid Hurwicz: "On the Stability of the Competitive Equilibrium, II," *Econometrica*, 27 (January, 1959), 82–109.

Arrow, K. J., H. B. Chenery, B. S. Minhas, and R. M. Solow: "Capital-Labor Substitution and Economic Efficiency," *Review of Economics and Statistics*, 43 (August, 1961), 225–250.

Arrow, Kenneth J., and Gerard Debreu: "Existence of an Equilibrium for a Competitive Economy," *Econometrica*, 22 (July, 1954), 265–290.

Arrow, Kenneth J., and Leonid Hurwicz: "On the Stability of the Competitive Equilibrium, I," *Econometrica*, 26 (October, 1958), 522–552.

———: "Some Remarks on the Equilibria of Economic Systems," *Econometrica*, 28 (July, 1960), 640–646.

Aumann, Robert J.: "Markets with a Continuum of Traders," *Econometrica*, 32 (January-April, 1964), 39–50.

Balogh, Thomas: "The Concept of a Dollar Shortage," *Manchester School of Economic and Social Studies*, 17 (May, 1949), 186–201.

Balogh, T., and P. P. Streeten: "The Inappropriateness of Simple 'Elasticity' Concepts in the Analysis of International Trade," *Bulletin of the Oxford University Institute of Statistics*, 13 (March, 1951), 65–77.

Barone, Enrico: *Principi di Economia Politica.* Rome, 1908. Posthumous edition: *Le Opere Economische*, Vol. II. Bologna: Nicola Zanichelli Editore, 1936.

Baumol, William J.: "Community Indifference," *Review of Economic Studies*, 14 (1946–47), 44–48.

———: "The Community Indifference Map: A Construction," *Review of Economic Studies*, 17 (1949–50), 189–197.

Bellman, Richard: *Stability Theory of Differential Equations.* New York: McGraw-Hill Book Company, Inc., 1953.

Bhagwati, Jagdish, and Harry G. Johnson: "Notes on Some Controversies in the Theory of International Trade," *Economic Journal*, 70 (March, 1960), 74–93.

———: "Notes on Some Controversies in the Theory of International Trade: A Rejoinder," *Economic Journal*, 71 (June, 1961), 427–430.

Bowley, A. L.: *The Mathematical Groundwork of Economics.* Oxford: Clarendon Press, 1924. Second printing, New York: Augustus M. Kelley, 1960.

Bresciani-Turroni, C.: "The 'Purchasing Power Parity' Doctrine," *L'Égypte Contemporaine*, 25 (January-February, 1934), 433–464.

Brouwer, L. E. J.: "Über Abbildung von Mannigfaltigkeiten," *Mathematische Annalen*, 71 (1912), 97–115.

Cairnes, J. E.: *Some Leading Principles of Political Economy Newly Expounded.* London: Macmillan and Co., 1874.

Caves, Richard E.: *Trade and Economic Structure, Models and Methods.* Cambridge, Mass.: Harvard University Press, 1960.

Chamberlin, Edward Hastings: *The Theory of Monopolistic Competition.* Cambridge, Mass.: Harvard University Press, 1933.

Clapham, J. H.: "Of Empty Economic Boxes," *Economic Journal*, 32 (September, 1922), 305–314.

Coddington, Earl A., and Norman Levinson: *Theory of Ordinary Differential Equations.* New York: McGraw-Hill Book Company, Inc., 1955.

Cournot, Augustin: *Recherches sur les Principes Mathématiques de la Théorie des Richesses.* Paris: L. Hachette, 1838. Nouvelle édition, Paris: Marcel Rivière et Cie., 1938. English translation: *Researches into the Mathematical Principles of the Theory of Wealth.* New York: The Macmillan Co., 1897.

Cunynghame, Henry: "Some Improvements in Simple Geometrical Methods of Treating Exchange Value, Monopoly, and Rent," *Economic Journal*, 2 (March, 1892), 35–52.

———: *A Geometrical Political Economy.* Oxford: Clarendon Press, 1904.

Debreu, Gerard, and I. N. Herstein: "Nonnegative Square Matrices," *Econometrica*, 21 (October, 1953), 597–607.

Debreu, Gerard, and Herbert Scarf: "A Limit Theorem on the Core of an Economy," *International Economic Review*, 4 (September, 1963), 235–246.

Dorfman, Robert, Paul A. Samuelson, and Robert M. Solow: *Linear Programming and Economic Analysis.* New York: McGraw-Hill Book Company, Inc., 1958.

Edgeworth, F. Y.: *Mathematical Psychics.* London: C. Kegan Paul and Co., 1881. New York: Augustus M. Kelley, undated.

——— (1889a): "The Mathematical Method in Political Economy," a review of *Untersuchungen über die Theorie des Preises* by Rudolf Auspitz and Richard Lieben, Nature, 40 (July 11, 1889), 242–244.

——— (1889b): "The Mathematical Theory of Political Economy," a review of *Éléments d'Économie Politique Pure* by Léon Walras, *Nature*, 40 (September 5, 1889), 434–436.

——— (1889c): "On the Application of Mathematics to Political Economy," the Address of the President of Section F—Economic Science and Statistics—of the British Association, *Nature*, 40 (September 19, 1889), 496–509; also, *Journal of the Royal Statistical Society*, 52 (December, 1889), 538–576. Reprinted (omitting Note J) in F. Y. Edgeworth, *Papers Relating to Political Economy* (1925), Vol. II, pp. 273–312.

——— (1891a): "La théorie mathématique de l'offre et de la demande et le coût de production," *Revue d'Économie Politique*, 5 (January, 1891), 10–28.

——— (1891b): "Osservazioni sulla teoria matematica dell' economia politica con riguardo speciale ai principi di economia di Alfredo Marshall," *Giornale degli Economisti*, Series 2, 2 (March, 1891), 233–245. "Ancora a proposito della teoria del baratto," *ibid.*, 3 (October, 1891), 316–318. Abridged English translation, "On the Determinateness of Economic Equilibrium," *Papers Relating to Political Economy*, Vol. II, 313–319.

———: "The Theory of International Values, I, II, III," *Economic Journal, 4* (March, September, December, 1894), 35–50, 424–443, 606–638. Reprinted (with revisions and omissions) in *Papers Relating to Political Economy*, Vol. II, 3–60.

———: Review of *A Geometrical Political Economy* by Henry Cunynghame, *Economic Journal*, 15 (March, 1905), 62–71. Reprinted in *Papers Relating to Political Economy*, Vol. III, pp. 136–144.

———: *Papers Relating to Political Economy*, in three volumes. London: Macmillan and Co. Ltd., 1925. Second Printing, New York: Burt Franklin, undated.

Eisenberg, E.: "Aggregation of Utility Functions," *Management Science*, 7 (July, 1961), 337–350.

Fetter, Frank Whitson: "The Authorship of Economic Articles in the *Edinburgh Review*, 1802–47," *Journal of Political Economy*, 61 (June, 1953), 232–259.

Friedman, Milton: "The Case for Flexible Exchange Rates," in Milton Friedman: *Essays in Positive Economics*. Chicago: University of Chicago Press, 1953, pp. 157–203.

Frisch, Ragnar: "On Welfare Theory and Pareto Regions," Oslo: Universitetets Scoialøkonomiske Institutt, 1953 (mimeographed). *International Economic Papers*, 9 (1959), 39–92. French translation: "La théorie de l'avantage collectif et les régions de Pareto," *Économie Appliquée*, 7 (July-September, 1954), 211–280.

Gale, David: "The Law of Supply and Demand," *Mathematica Scandinavica*, 3 (1955), 155–169.

———: "A Note on Global Instability of Competitive Equilibrium," *Naval Research Logistics Quarterly*, 10 (March, 1963), 81–87.

Gale, David, and Hukukane Nikaido^: "The Jacobian Matrix and Global Univalence of Mappings," *Mathematische Annalen*, 159 (1965), 81–93.

Gantmacher, F. R.: *The Theory of Matrices* (in two volumes). New York: Chelsea Publishing Company, 1959.

Gorman, W. M.: "Community Preference Fields," *Econometrica*, 21 (January, 1953), 63–80.

Gossen, Hermann Heinrich: *Entwickelung der Gesetze des menschlichen Verkehrs, und der daraus fiiessenden Regeln für menschliches Handeln.* Braunschweig: Druck und Verlag von Friedrich Vieweg und Sohn, 1854. Neue Ausgabe, Berlin: Verlag von R. L. Prager, 1889.

Graham, Frank D.: "Some Aspects of Protection Further Considered," *Quarterly Journal of Economics*, 37 (February, 1923), 199–227.

———: "Some Fallacies in the Interpretation of Social Cost. A Reply," *Quarterly Journal of Economics*, 39 (February, 1925), 324–330.

———: "The Theory of International Values," *Quarterly Journal of Economics*, 46 (August, 1932), 581–616.

———: *The Theory of International Values.* Princeton, N.J.: Princeton University Press, 1948.

Haberler, Gottfried: *The Theory of International Trade, with Its Applications to Commercial Policy* (translated from the German, *Die internationale Handel*, Berlin, 1933). London: William Hodge and Company, Ltd., 1936.

———: "Dollar Shortage?" in *Foreign Economic Policy for the United States* (edited by Seymour E. Harris). Cambridge, Mass.: Harvard University Press, 1948, pp. 426–445.

———: "Some Problems in the Pure Theory of International Trade," *Economic Journal*, 60 (June, 1950), 223–240.

———: "Real Cost, Money Cost and Comparative Advantage," *International Social Science Bulletin*, 3 (Spring, 1951), 54–58.

Hahn, F. H.: "Gross Substitutes and the Dynamic Stability of General Equilibrium," *Econometrica*, 26 (January, 1958) 169–170.

Hahn, Frank H., and Takashi Negishi: "A Theorem on Non-Tâtonnement Stability," *Econometrica*, 30 (July, 1962), 463–469.

Harrod, R. F.: *Economic Essays.* London: Macmillan and Co. Ltd., 1952.

Hayek, Friedrich A. von: "The Use of Knowledge in Society," *American Economic Review*, 35 (September, 1945), 519–530. Reprinted in F. A. Hayek: *Individualism and Economic Order*. London: Routledge and Kegan Paul, 1949, pp. 77–91.

Hicks, J. R.: *Value and Capital.* Oxford: Clarendon Press, pp. 1–39.

Houthakker, H. S.: "The Econometrics of Family Budgets," *Journal of the Royal Statistical Society* [A], 115 (Part I, 1952), 1–21.

———: "La forme des courbes d'Engel," *Cahiers du Séminaire d'Économétrie*, 2 (1953), 59–66.

Hurwicz, Leonid: "Optimality and Informational Efficiency in Resource Allocation Processes," in *Mathematical Methods in the Social Sciences*, 1959 (edited by K. J. Arrow, S. Karlin, and P. Suppes). Stanford, Calif.: Stanford University Press, 1960, pp. 27–46.

Isard, Walter: *Location and Space-Economy.* New York: Technology Press and John Wiley and Sons, Inc., 1956.

Isard, Walter, and David J. Ostroff: "Existence of a Competitive Interregional Equilibrium," *Papers and Proceedings of the Regional Science Association*, 4 (1958), 49–76.

———: "General Interregional Equilibrium," *Journal of Regional Science*, 2 (1960), 67–74.

Jevons, W. Stanley: *The Theory of Political Economy*, Fourth Edition. London: Macmillan and Co. Ltd., 1911. First Edition, 1871. Fifth Edition, New York: Kelley and Millman, Inc., 1957.

Johnson, Harry G.: "International Trade, Income Distribution, and the Offer Curve," *Manchester School of Economic and Social Studies*, 27 (September, 1959), 241–260.

Johnson, W. E.: "The Pure Theory of Utility Curves," *Economic Journal*, 23 (December, 1913), 483–513.

Kakutani, Shizuo: "A Generalization of Brouwer's Fixed Point Theorem," *Duke Mathematical Journal*, 8 (1941), 457–459.

Kemp, Murray C.: *The Pure Theory of International Trade.* Englewood Cliffs, N.J.: Prentice-Hall, Inc., 1964.

Keynes, John Maynard: *A Treatise on Money*, Vol. I. London: Macmillan and Co. Ltd., 1930.

Knaster, B., C. Kuratowski, and S. Mazurkiewicz: "Ein Beweis des Fixpunktsatzes für n-dimensionale Simplexe," *Fundamenta Mathematicae*, 14 (1931), 132–137.

Knight, Frank H.: "Some Fallacies in the Interpretation of Social Cost," *Quarterly Journal of Economics*, 38 (August, 1924), 582–606. Reprinted in F. H. Knight, *The Ethics of Competition and Other Essays*, New York: Augustus M. Kelley Inc., 1951, pp. 217–236. Also in *Readings in Price Theory*, Chicago: Richard D. Irwin, Inc., 1952, pp. 160–179.

———: "On Decreasing Cost and Comparative Cost. A Rejoinder," *Quarterly Journal of Economics*, 39 (February, 1925), 331–333.

———: *"Bemerkungen über Nutzen und Kosten," Zeitschrift für Nationalöko nomie*, 6 (Heft 1, 3, 1935), 28–52, 315–336. English translation: "Notes on Utility and Cost," in Frank H. Knight: *The Economic Organization.* New York: Augustus M. Kelley, Inc., 1951, pp. 122–179.

Kuhn, H. W. (1956a): "A Note on 'The Law of Supply and Demand,' " *Mathematica Scandinavica*, 4 (1956), 143–146.

——— (1956b): "On a Theorem of Wald," in *Linear Inequalities and Related Systems* (edited by H. W. Kuhn and A. W. Tucker). Princeton, N.J.: Princeton University Press, 1956, pp. 265–273.

Lambert, Paul: "La loi des débouchés avant J.-B. Say et la polémique Say-Malthus," *Revue d'Économie Politique*, 62 (January-February, 1952), 5–26. English translation: "The Law of Markets prior to J.-B. Say and the Say-Malthus Debate," *International Economic Papers*, 6 (1956), 7–22.

Lange, Oscar: "On the Economic Theory of Socialism, *Review of Economic Studies*, 4 (October 1936, February 1937), 53–71, 123–142. Reprinted in B. E. Lippincott (editor): *On the Economic Theory of Socialism*, Minneapolis: University of Minnesota Press, 1938, pp. 57–143.

———: "Say's Law: A Restatement and Criticism," *Studies in Mathematical Economics and Econometrics* (edited by Oscar Lange, Francis McIntyre, and Theodore O. Yntema). Chicago: The University of Chicago Press, 1942, pp. 49–68.

Launhardt, Wilhelm: *Mathematische Begründung der Volkswirtschaftslehre.* Leipzig: Verlag von Wilhelm Engelmann, 1885.

Leontief, Wassily W.: "The Use of Indifference Curves in the Analysis of Foreign Trade," *Quarterly Journal of Economics*, 47 (May, 1933), 493–503. Reprinted in *Readings in the Theory of International Trade* (edited by H. S. Ellis and L. A. Metzler). Philadelphia: The Blakiston Co., 1949, pp. 229–238.

———: "Implicit Theorizing: A Methodological Criticism of the Neo-Cambridge School," *Quarterly Journal of Economics*, 50 (February, 1937), 337–351. Reprinted in *Readings in Economic Analysis*, Vol. I (edited by Richard V. Clemence), Cambridge, Mass.: Addison-Wesley Press, Inc., 1950, pp. 31–45.

Lerner, Abba P.: "The Diagrammatical Representation of Cost Conditions in International Trade," *Economica*, 12 (August, 1932), 346–356. Reprinted in Lerner (1953), 85–100.

———: "The Diagrammatical Representation of Demand Conditions in International Trade," *Economica*, N. S., 1 (August, 1934), 319–334. Reprinted in Lerner (1953), 101–122.

———: *Essays in Economic Analysis.* London: Macmillan and Co. Ltd., 1953.

Lösch, August: "Eine neue Theorie des intemationalen Handels," *Weltwirtschalftliches Archiv*, 50 (September, 1939), 308–328. English translation: "A New Theory of International Trade," *International Economic Papers*, 6 (1956) 50–65.

Lyapunov, M. A.: *Obshaya zadacha ob ustoichivosti dvizheniya.* Kharkov: Kharkov Mathematical Society, 1892. French translation: "Problème général de la stabilité du mouvement," *Annales de la Faculté des Sciences de Toulouse*, Second Series, 9 (1907), 203–474. Princeton N.J.: Annals of Mathematics Studies Number 17, Princeton University Press, 1947.

[McCulloch, J. R.]: "Commercial Embarrassments—Trade with France," *Edinburgh Review*, 32 (July 1819), 48–74.

———: "Restrictions on Foreign Commerce," *Edinburgh Review*, 33 (May, 1920), 331–351.

———: "Political Economy," *Supplement to the Fourth, Fifth, and Sixth Editions of the Encyclo*paedia *Britannica*, Volume Sixth, pp. 216–278. Edinburgh: Printed for Archibald Constable and Company, 1824.

McKenzie, Lionel W.: "On Equilibrium in Graham's Model of World Trade and Other Competitive Systems," *Econometrica*, 22 (April, 1954), 147–161.

———: "Competitive Equilibrium with Dependent Consumer Preferences," *Proceedings of the Second Symposium in Linear Programming* (edited by H. A. Antosiewicz). Washington, D.C.: National Bureau of Standards, 1955, pp. 277–294.

———: "On the Existence of General Equilibrium for a Competitive Market," *Econometrica*, 27 (January, 1959), 54–71. "On the Existence of General Equilibrium: Some Corrections," *Econometrica*, 29 (April, 1961), 247–248.

——— (1960a): "Matrices with Dominant Diagonals and Economic Theory," in *Mathematical Methods in the Social Sciences*, 1959 (edited by K. J. Arrow, S. Karlin, and P. Suppes). Stanford: Stanford University Press, 1960, 47–62.

——— (1960b): "Stability of Equilibrium and the Value of Positive Excess Demand," *Econometrica*, 28 (July, 1960), 606–617.

Malthus, T. R.: *An Inquiry into the Nature and Progress of Rent, and the Principles by which it is Regulated.* London: Printed for John Murray, Albemarle Street, 1815. Baltimore: The Johns Hopkins Press, 1903.

———: *Principles of Political Economy considered with a view to their Practical Application.* London: John Murray, Albermarle Street, 1820. In *The Works and Correspondence of David Ricardo*, Vol. II (edited by Piero Sraffa with the collaboration of M. H. Dobb). Cambridge: Cambridge University Press, 1951. Second edition, London: Pickering, 1836; and New York: Augustus M. Kelley, Inc., 1951.

———: *Definitions in Political Economy.* London: John Murray, Albermarle Street, 1827. New impression, New York: Kelley and Millman, Inc., 1954.

Marshall, Alfred: *The Pure Theory of Foreign Trade*, published privately, 1879. Reprinted, together with *The Pure Theory of Domestic Values*, London: London School of Economics and Political Science, 1930; third impression, 1949.

———: Review of *Mathematical Psychics*, by F. Y. Edgeworth, *Academy*, 19 (June, 1881), 457.

———: *Principles of Economics.* London: Macmillan and Co. Ltd., 1890. Eighth edition, 1920.

Ninth (variorum) Edition in two volumes, London: Macmillan and Co. Ltd., 1961. Page references to the *Principles* are to the ninth edition (pagination of Vol. I being the same as that of the eighth edition).

——— (1920): *Industry and Trade.* London: Macmillan and Co. Ltd., 1919. Third edition, 1920.

———: *Money, Credit, and Commerce.* London: Macmillan and Co. Ltd., 1923. Second printing, New York: Augustus M. Kelley, 1960.

———: *Memorials of Alfred Marshall* (edited by A. C. Pigou). London: Macmillan and Co. Ltd., 1925. New York: Kelley and Millman, Inc., 1956.

Matthews, R. C. O.: "Reciprocal Demand and Increasing Returns," *Review of Economic Studies*, 17 (1949–50), 149–158.

Meade, J. E. (1952a). *A Geometry of International Trade.* London: George Allen and Unwin Ltd., 1952.

——— (1952b): "External Economies and Diseconomies in a Competitive Situation," *Economic Journal*, 62 (March, 1952), 54–67.

———: *The Theory of International Economic Policy*, Vol. II, *Trade and Welfare.* London: Oxford University Press, 1955.

Menger, Carl: *Grundsätze der Volkswirtschaftslehre*, Erster, allgemeiner Theil. Vienna: W. Braumüller, 1871. English translation: *Principles of Economics*, First, general part. Glencoe, Ill.: The Free Press, 1950.

Metzler, Lloyd A.: "Stability of Multiple Markets: The Hicks Conditions," *Econometrica*, 13 (October, 1945), 277–292.

Mill, James: *Commerce Defended. An anwser to the Arguments by which Mr. Spence,Mr. Cobbett,and Others,have attempted to prove that Commerce is not a Source of National Wealth.* London: Printed for C. and R. Baldwin, New Bridge Street, 1808. New York: Augustus M. Kelley, 1965.

———: *Elements of Political Economy*, Third Edition. London: Baldwin, Cradock, and Joy, 1826. New York: Augustus M. Kelley, 1963.

Mill, John Stuart: *Essays on Some Unsettled Questions of Political Economy.* London: John W. Parker, West Strand, 1844. Reprinted by the London School of Economics and Political Science, 1948.

———: *Principles of Political Economy with Some of their Applications to Social Philosophy.* London: Parker and Co., 1848. Third Edition, 1852. Page references are to Vol. II of the Fifth Edition, New York: D. Appleton and Company, 1895.

———: "Thornton on Labour and its Claims," *Fortnightly Review*, N.S., 5 (May, June 1869), 505–518, 680–700.

———: *A System of Logic, Ratiocinative and Inductive*, People's Edition. London: Longmans, Green and Co., 1891.

Morishima, Michio: "A Reconsideration of the Walras-Cassel-Leontief Model of General Equilibrium," in *Mathematical Methods in the Social Sciences, 1959* (edited by K. J. Arrow, S. Karlin, and P. Suppes). Stanford, Calif.: Stanford University Press, 1960, pp. 63–76.

Mosak, Jacob L.: *General Equilibrium Theory in International Trade.* Bloomington, Ind.: Principia Press, 1944.

Mundell, Robert A.: "Transport Costs in International Trade Theory," *Canadian Journal of Economics and Political Science*, 23 (August, 1957), 331–348.

———: "The Pure Theory of International Trade," *American Economic Review*, 50 (March, 1960), 67–110.

Negishi, Takashi: "A Note on the Stability of an Economy Where All Goods are Gross Substitutes," *Econometrica*, 26 (July, 1958), 445–447.

Neumann, John von, and Oscar Morgenstern: *Theory of Games and Economic Behavior.* Princeton: Princeton University Press, 1944. Second edition, 1947.

Newman, Peter: "Some Notes on Stability Conditions," *Review of Economic Studies*, 27 (October, 1959), 1–9.

———: "The Erosion of Marshall's Theory of Value," *Quarterly Journal of Economics*, 74 (November, 1960), 587–600. "Comment" by D. H. Robertson, ibid., 600–601.

Nikaidô, Hukukane: "On the Classical Multilateral Exchange Problem," *Metroeconomica*, 8 (August, 1956), 135–145.

———: "A Supplementary Note to 'On the Classical Multilateral Exchange Problem,"' *Metroeconomica*, 9 (December, 1957), 209–210.

Nikaidô, Hukukane, and Hirofumi Uzawa: "Stability and Non-negativity in a Walrasian Tâtonnement Process," *International Economic Review*, 1 (January, 1960), 50–59.

Pantaleoni, Maffeo: *Pure Economics*. London: Macmillan and Co. Ltd., 1898; translated (with revisions) by T. Boston Bruce, from the original Italian edition, *Manuale di Economia Pura*, 1889. Second printing, New York: Kelley and Millman, Inc., 1957.

Pareto, Vilfredo (1894a): "Teoria matematica dei cambi forestieri," *Giornale degli Economisti* [2], 8 (February, 1894), 142–173.

——— (1894b): "Il massimo di utilità dato dalla libera concorrenza," *Giornale degli Economisti* [2], 9 (July, 1894), 48–66.

———: "Teoria matematica del comercio intemazionale," *Giornale degli Economisti* [2], 10 (April, 1895), 476–498.

———: *Manuel d'Économie Politique*, translated and revised from the Italian, *Manuale di economia politica* (1906). Paris: V. Giard et E. Brière, 1909. Second French edition (identical with the 1909 edition), Paris: Marcel Giard, 1927.

———: "Économie mathématique," *Encyclopédie des sciences mathématiques*, Tome I, vol. 4, fascicule 4 (August, 1911), 591–640. English translation: "Mathematical Economics," *International Economic Papers*, No. 5, London: Macmillan and Co. Ltd., 1955, pp. 58–102.

Pigou, A. C.: *Wealth and Welfare*. London: Macmillan and Co. Ltd., 1912.

———: "The Interdependence of Different Sources of Demand and Supply in a Market," *Economic Journal*, 23 (March, 1913), 19–24.

———: *The Economics of Welfare*. London: Macmillan and Co. Ltd., 1920. Second edition, 1924. Third edition, 1929. Fourth edition, 1932.

———: "The Foreign Exchanges," *Quarterly Journal of Economics*, 37 (November, 1922), 52–74. Reprinted in A. C. Pigou: *Essays in Applied Economics*. London: P. S. King and Son Ltd., 1923, pp. 156–173.

———: "The Laws of Diminishing and Increasing Cost," *Economic Journal*, 37 (June, 1927), 188–197.

———: "An Analysis of Supply," *Economic Journal*, 38 (June, 1928), 238–257. Substantially reproduced in A. C. Pigou: *The Economics of Welfare*, third edition, London: Macmillan and Co. Ltd., 1929, Part II, Chapter XI, pp. 218–223, and Appendix III, pp. 787–800. Fourth edition, 1932, pp. 216–221, 789–802.

———: "The Effect of Reparations on the Ratio of International Interchange," *Economic Journal*, 42 (December, 1932), 532–543.

Poincaré, H.: *Les Méthodes nouvelles de la Mécanique céleste*, Vol. I. Paris: Gauthier-Villars et Fils, 1892.

Pontryagin, L. S.: *Foundations of Combinatorial Topology* (translated from the first (1947) Russian edition). Rochester, N.Y.: Graylock Press, 1952.

Prais, S. J.: "Non-Linear Estimates of the Engel Curves," *Review of Economic Studies*, 20 (1952–53), 87–104.

Prais, S. J., and H. S. Houthakker: *The Analysis of Family Budgets.* Cambridge: Cambridge University Press, 1955.

Ricardo, David: *Notes on Malthus' Principles of Political Economy* (1820) (edited with an introduction by Jacob H. Hollander and T. E. Gregory), Baltimore: The Johns Hopkins Press, 1928. In *The Works and Correspondence of David Ricardo*, Vol. II (edited by Piero Sraffa with the collaboration of M. H. Dobb), Cambridge: Cambridge University Press, 1951. Page references are to the latter.

———: *The Works and Correspondence of David Ricardo* (edited by Piero Sraffa with the collaboration of M. H. Dobb). In ten volumes. Cambridge: Cambridge University Press, 1951–1955.

Robbins, Lionel: *Robert Torrens and the Evolution of Classical Economics.* London: Macmillan and Co. Ltd., 1958.

Robertson, D. H.: "Those Empty Boxes," *Economic Journal*, 34 (March, 1924), 16–30. Reprinted in *Readings in Price Theory* (edited by George J. Stigler and Kenneth E. Boulding). Chicago: Richard D. Irwin, Inc., 1952, pp. 143–159.

———: "The Trees of the Forest," Economic Journal, 40 (March, 1930), 80–89.

———: *Lectures on Economic Principles*, Volume I. London: Staples Press Ltd., 1957.

Robinson, E. A. G.: *The Structure of Competitive Industry.* Cambridge: University Press, 1931. Revised and reset, Chicago: University of Chicago Press, 1958.

Robinson, Joan: *The Economics of Imperfect Competition.* London: Macmillan and Co. Ltd., 1933.

———: "Rising Supply Price," *Economica*, N.S., 8 (February, 1941), 1–8. Reprinted in Joan Robinson, *Collected Economic Papers*, Oxford: Basil Blackwell, 1951, pp. 35–43; and in *Readings in Price Theory* (edited by George J. Stigler and Kenneth E. Boulding), Chicago: Richard D. Irwin, Inc., 1952, pp. 233–241. Page references are to the latter.

———: "The Pure Theory of International Trade," *Review of Economic Studies*, 14 (1946–1947), 98–112. Reprinted in Joan Robinson, *Collected Economic Papers*, Oxford: Basil Blackwell, 1951, pp. 182–205.

Samuelson, Paul A.: "The Stability of Equilibrium: Linear and Nonlinear Systems," *Econometrica*, 10 (January, 1942), 1–25.

———: *Foundations of Economic Analysis.* Cambridge, Mass.: Harvard University Press, 1947.

———: "Disparity in Postwar Exchange Rates," in *Foreign Economic Policy for the United States* (edited by Seymour E. Harris). Cambridge, Mass.: Harvard University Press, 1948, pp. 397–412.

———: "The Transfer Problem and Transport Costs: The Terms of Trade when Impediments Are Absent," *Economic Journal*, 62 (June, 1952), 278–304.

———: "The Transfer Problem and Transport Costs, II: Analysis of Effects of Trade Impediments," *Economic Journal*, 64 (June, 1954), 264–289.

———: "Social Indifference Curves," *Quarterly Journal of Economics*, 70 (February, 1956), 1–22.

Say, Jean-Baptiste: *Traité d'Économie Politique*. Paris: Chez Deterville, 1803. Second edition, Paris: Chez Antoine-Augustin Renouard, 1814. Fifth edition, Paris: Chez Rapilly, 1826. English translation by C. R. Prinsep from the fourth edition (1819): *A Treatise on Political Economy, or the Production, Distribution, and Consumption of Wealth*. New American edition, Philadelphia: Grigg and Elliot, 1844. New York: Augustus M. Kelley, 1964. Page references to the Treatise are to the latter.

———: *Letters to Mr. Malthus on Several Subjects of Political Economy,and on the Cause of the* Stagnation of Commerce, translated by John Richter. London: Printed for Sherwood, Neely, and Jones, Paternoster Row, 1821.

Scarf, Herbert: "Some Examples of Global Instability of the Competitive Equilibrium," *International Economic Review*, 1 (September, 1960), 157–172.

Schlesinger, Karl: "Über die Produktionsgleichungen der ökonomischen Wertlehre," *Ergebnisse eines mathematischen Kolloquiums*, Heft 6 (1933–1934), 10–11.

Schumpeter, Joseph A.: "The Instability of Capitalism," *Economic Journal*, 38 (September, 1928), 361–386. Reprinted in *Essays of J. A. Schumpeter* (edited by Richard V. Clemence). Cambridge, Mass.: Addison-Wesley Press, Inc., 1951, pp. 47–72. Also in *Readings in Economic Analysis*, Vol. I (edited by Richard V. Clemence). Cambridge, Mass.: Addison-Wesley Press Inc., 1950, pp. 133–158.

———: *History of Economic Analysis*. New York: Oxford University Press, 1954.

Scitovszky, Tibor de: "A Reconsideration of the Theory of Tariffs," *Review of Economic Studies*, 9 (Summer, 1942), 89–110. Reprinted in *Readings in the Theory of International Trade* (edited by H. S. Ellis and L. A. Metzler). Philadelphia: The Blakiston Co., 1949, pp. 358–389.

Scitovsky, Tibor: "Two Concepts of External Economies," *Journal of Political Economy*, 62 (April, 1954), 143–151.

Senior, Nassau W.: *An Outline of the Science of Political Economy*. London: W. Clowes and Sons, 1836. New York: Augustus M. Kelley, Inc., 1951. Page references are to the latter.

Shove, G. F.: "Varying Costs and Marginal Net Products," *Economic Journal*, 38 (June, 1928), 258–266.

———: "The Representative Firm and Increasing Returns," *Economic Journal*, 40 (March, 1930), 94–116.

Sismondi, J.-C.-L. Simonde de: *Nouveaux Principes d'Économie politique, ou, de la richesse dans ses rapports avec la population*, in two volumes. First edition, Paris: Chez Delaunay, 1819. Second edition, 1827. Third edition, Geneva: Édition Jeheber, Vol. I, 1951; Vol. II, 1953.

———: "Examen de cette question: Le pouvoir de consommer s'accroît-il toujours dans la société avec le pouvoir de produire?" in *Annales de Législation et de Jurisprudence*, 1 (1820), 111–144. Reprinted in Sismondi's *Nouveaux Principles*, second edition (1827), Vol. II, pp. 373–407; third edition (1953), Vol. II, pp. 250–272. English translation: "Refutation of an Article by Robert Torrens," *International Economic Papers*, 7 (1957), 7–20.

———: "Sur la balance des consommations avec les productions," *Revue encyclopédique*, 22 (May, 1824). Reprinted in Sismondi's Nouveaux Principes, second edition (1827), Vol. II, pp. 408–458; third edition (1953), Vol. II, pp. 273–305. English translation: "On the Balance of Consumption and Production," *International Economic Papers*, 7 (1957), 20–39.

Smith, Adam: *An Inquiry into the Nature and Causes of the Wealth of Nations* (1776). London: J. M. Dent and Sons Ltd., 1933.

Sohmen, Egon: "Demand Elasticities and the Foreign-Exchange Market," *Journal of Political Economy*, 45 (October, 1957), 431–436.

——— (1961a): *Flexible Exchange Rates: Theory and Controversy.* Chicago: University of Chicago Press, 1961.

——— (1961b): "Notes on Some Controversies in the Theory of International Trade: A Comment," *Economic Journal*, 71 (June, 1961), 423–426.

Sperner, E.: "Neuer Beweis für die Invarianz der Dimensionzahl und des Gebietes," *Abhandlungen aus dem Mathematischen Seminar der Hamburgischen Universität*, 6 (1928), 265–272.

Sraffa, Piero: "Sulle relazioni fra costo e quantità prodotta," *Annali di Economia*, 2 (1925–1926), 277–328.

———: "The Laws of Returns under Competitive Conditions," *Economic Journal*, 36 (December, 1926), 535–550. Reprinted in *Readings in Economic Analysis*, Volume 2 (edited by Richard V. Clemence). Cambridge, Mass.: Addison-Wesley Press, Inc., 1950, pp. 54–69. Also in *Readings in Price Theory* (edited by George J. Stigler and Kenneth E. Boulding). Chicago: Richard D. Irwin, 1952, pp. 180–197.

———: Discussion of D. H. Robertson's "The Trees of the Forest," with rejoinder by D. H. Robertson, *Economic Journal*, 40 (March, 1930), 89–93.

Stolper, Wolfgang F.: "A Method of Constructing Community Indifference Curves," *Schweizerische Zeitschrift für Volkswirtschaft und Statistik*, 86 (April, 1950), 150–157.

Taussig, F. W.: "Is Market Price Determinate?" *Quarterly Journal of Economics*, 35 (May, 1921), 394–411. Reprinted in *Readings in Economic Analysis*, Vol. II (edited by Richard V. Clemence). Cambridge, Mass.: Addison-Wesley Press, Inc., 1950, pp. 36–53.

Theil, H.: *Linear Aggregation of Economic Relations.* Amsterdam: North-Holland Publishing Company, 1954.

Thomas, Brinley: *Migration and Economic Growth. A Study of Great Britain and the Atlantic Economy.* Cambridge: Cambridge University Press, 1954.

Thornton, William T.: "A New Theory of Supply and Demand," *Fortnightly Review*, 6 (October, 1866), 420–434. Reprinted (with revisions) in *On*

Labour, its Wrongful Claims and Rightful Dues, its Actual Present and Possible Future. London: Macmillan and Co., 1869, pp. 43–65.

Tinbergen, Jan: *International Economic Co-operation.* Amsterdam: Elsevier, 1945.

———: *International Economic Integration.* Second, completely revised, edition of *International Economic Co-operation.* Amsterdam: Elsevier, 1954.

Torrens, Robert: *The Economists Refuted; or, An Inquiry into the Nature and Extent of the Advantages derived from Trade.* London: S. A. Oddy, and C. La Grange, Dublin, 1808. In R. Torrens: *The Principles and Practical Operation of Sir Robert Peel's Act of 1844 Explained and Defended*, third edition. London: Longmans, 1858.

———: *An Essay on the External Corn Trade.* London: J. Hatchard, 1815. Second edition, London: J. Hatchard and Son, 1820. Third, fourth, and fifth ("New") editions, London: Longman, Rees, Orme, Brown, and Green, 1826, 1827, 1829.

[———]: "Mr. Owen's Plans for Relieving the National Distress," *Edinburgh Review*, 32 (October, 1819), 453–477. "On Mr. Owen's Plan, and the Causes of the Present Distress," *The Scotsman*, 3 (August 21, 1819), 265–266.

———: *An Essay on the Production of Wealth.* London: Longman, Hurst, Rees, Orme, and Brown, Paternoster Row, 1821. Italian translation: *Saggio sulla Produzione della Riechezza.* In *Biblioteca dell'Economista*, Prima Serie, Vol. XI, Turin: Unione Tipografico-Editrice Torinese, 1873.

———: "Economical objection to extended Colonization stated and answered," in R. Torrens: *Colonization of South Australia.* London: Longman, Rees, Orme, Brown, Green and Longman, 1835, pp. 229–249. Also in R. Torrens: *A Letter to the Right Honourable Lord John Rusesll, on the Ministerial Measure for Establishing Poor Laws in Ireland, and on the Auxiliary Means which it will be necessary to employ in Carrying that Measure into Effect.* London: Longman, Rees, Orme, Brown, and Green, 1837, pp. 128–149. Again in Letter IV of R. Torrens: *The Budget. On Commercial and Colonial Policy.* London: Smith, Elder, and Co., 1844, pp. 83–98. Page references are to the 1837 printing.

Uzawa, Hirofumi: "Walras' Tâtonnement in the Theory of Exchange," *Review of Economic Studies*, 27 (June, 1960), 182–194.

———: "The Stability of Dynamic Processes," *Econometrica*, 29 (October, 1961), 617–631.

——— (1962a): "On the Stability of Edgeworth's Barter Process," *International Economic Review*, 3 (May, 1962), 218–232.

——— (1962b): "Production Functions with Constant Elasticities of Substitution," *Review of Economic Studies*, 29 (October, 1962), 291–299.

Vanek, Jaroslav: "An Afterthought on the 'Real Cost—Opportunity Cost' Dispute and Some Aspects of General Equilibrium under Conditions of Variable Factor Supplies," *Review of Economic Studies*, 26 (June, 1959), 198–208.

———: "A Rehabilitation of 'Well-Behaved' Social Indifference Curves," *Review of Economic Studies*, 31 (January, 1964), 87–89.

Viner, Jacob: "Cost Curves and Supply Curves," *Zeitschrift für National ökonomie*, 3 (1931), 23–46. Reprinted in *Readings in Economic Analysis*, Volume 2 (edited by Richard V. Clemence), Cambridge, Mass.: Addison-Wesley Press Inc., 1950, pp. 8–31; with a Supplement by Professor Viner, *ibid.*, pp. 31–35. Also in *Readings in Price Theory* (edited by George J. Stigler and Kenneth E. Boulding), Chicago: Richard D. Irwin, Inc., 1952, pp. 198–232.

———: *Studies in the Theory of International Trade.* New York: Harper and Brothers Publishers, 1937.

Wald, Abraham: "Über die eindeutige positive Lösbarkeit der neuen Produktionsgleichungen," *Ergebnisse eines mathematischen Kolloquiums*, Heft 6 (1933–1934), 12–20.

———: "Über die Produktionsgleichungen der ökonomischen Wertlehre," *Ergebnisse eines mathematischen Kolloquiums*, Heft 7 (1934–1935), 1–6.

———: "Beweis für die Lösbarkeit der Tauschgleichungen der Ökonomie," reported by title in *Ergebnisse eines mathematischen Kolloquiums*, Heft 8 (1935–1936), p. 84. Original manuscript lost.

———: "Über einige Gleichungssysteme der mathematischen Ökonomie," *Zeitschrift für Nationalökonomie*, 7 (1936), 637–670. English translation: "On Some Systems of Equations of Mathematical Economics," *Econometrica*, 19 (October, 1951), 368–403.

———: "A New Formula for the Index of the Cost of Living," *Econometrica*, 7 (October, 1939), 319–331.

———: "The Approximate Determination of Indifference Surfaces by Means of Engel Curves," *Econometrica*, 8 (April, 1940), 144–175.

———: "On a Relation between Changes in Demand and Price Changes," *Econometrica*, 20 (April, 1952), 304–350.

Walras, Léon: *Éléments d'économie politique pure; ou, Théorie de la richesse sociale.* Lausanne: L. Corbaz et Cie., 1874. Second edition, 1889. Fourth edition (édition définitive), Lausanne: F. Rouge, 1926. English translation (by William Jaffé) from the fourth edition: *Elements of Pure Economics, or The Theory of Social Wealth.* London: George Allen and Unwin, 1954.

Walsh, V. C.: "Leisure and International Trade," *Economica*, N.S., 23 (August, 1956), 253–260.

Weber, Alfred: "Die Standortslehre und die Handelspolitik," *Archiv für Sozialwissenschaft und Sozialpolitik*, 32 (1911), 667–688. English translation: "Location Theory and Trade Policy," *International Economic Papers*, 8 (1958), 133–146.

West, Edward: *Essay on the Application of Capital to Land, with Observations shewing the Impolicy of any great restriction of the importation of corn,and that the Bounty of 1688 did not lower the price of it.* London: Printed for T. Underwood, 1815. Baltimore: The Johns Hopkins Press, 1903.

———: *Price of Corn and Wages of Labour.* London: John Hatchard and Son, 1826.

Wicksell, Knut: *Über Wert, Kapital und Rente.* Jena: Verlag von Gustav Fischer, 1893. English translation: *Value, Capital and Rent.* London: George Allen and Unwin Ltd., 1954.

———: *Föreläsningar i nationalekonomi,* första delen: Häft. I, *Teoretisk Nationalekonomi.* Lund: Berlingska boktryckeriet, 1901. Second edition, 1911. English translation (from the third, posthumous, edition): *Lectures on Political Economy,* Volume I. London: Routledge and Kegan Paul Ltd., 1934.

———: "Vilfredo Paretos Manuel d'économie politique," *Zeitschrift für Volkswirtschaft, Sozialpolitik und Verwaltung,* 22 (1913), 132–151. English translation: "Vilfredo Pareto's *Manuel d'économie politique,*" in Knut Wicksell: *Selected Papers on Economic Theory.* London: George Allen and Unwin Ltd., 1958, pp. 159–175.

Young, Allyn A.: "Jevons' 'Theory of Political Economy,'" *American Economic Review, 2* (September, 1912), 576–589.

———: "Pigou's Wealth and Welfare," *Quarterley Journal of Economics,* 27 (August, 1913), 672–686.

———: "Increasing Returns and Economic Progress," *Economic Journal,* 38 (December, 1928), 527–542. Reprint in *Readings in Economic Analysis,* Vol. I (edited by Richard V. Clemence). Cambridge, Mass.: Addison-Wesleys Press, Inc., 1950, pp. 117–132.

Chapter 6

A Survey of the Theory of International Trade: Part III, The Modern Theory*

John S. Chipman†

1. Historical Antecedents

The celebrated factor price equalization theorem has a curious history. Ohlin (1933) introduced to English-speaking readers an important modification to international trade theory, replacing the classical simplification, of constant costs but differing production functions among countries, with the alternative simplification of identical production functions but differing factor endowments. While many economists have remarked on the unrealism of Ohlin's simplification, an important aspect of it has not, it would seem,

*Originally published in *Econometrica*, 34(1), pp. 18–76.
†This is the last in a series of survey articles which *Econometrica* is publishing with the support of the Rockefeller Foundation. Because of its length, this article is being published in three parts. Part 1 on the Classical Theory appeared in the July, 1965 issue and Part 2 on the Neo-Classical Theory appeared in the October, 1965 issue. Research was facilitated by a grant to the author of an Auxiliary Research Award by the Social Science Research Council, as well as a grant by the National Science Foundation. Grateful acknowledgement is made to Professor Samuelson for comments on an earlier draft; he is not, of course, to be held responsible for any errors that remain. Equally absolved are M. C. Kemp and R. W. Jones, whose valuable criticisms of a later draft are greatly appreciated.

always been sufficiently appreciated. This is the fact that the classical model assumed that production relations in different countries differed in a quite arbitrary fashion; no satisfactory way had been provided for explaining how such production relations differed. In the Ohlin model, on the other hand, an element of continuity was introduced, since continuous variation of factor endowments would yield continuous (rather than arbitrary) variation in production relations. Even if differences in production relations (specifically, in transformation functions) cannot be completely explained in terms of differences in factor endowments, the Ohlin model is nevertheless susceptible to amendments that preserve meaningful relationships between different countries' production functions.

Ohlin's writings were greatly influenced by Heckscher (1919), whose work was not made available in English until 1949. Heckscher, in turn, acknowledged the influence on his thought of Wicksell (1919).[1] Ohlin asserted that there was a tendency towards factor price equalization as a result of free trade, but he tempered his argument with many qualifications, even to the point of asserting that equalization would never be complete. The partial equalization argument was taken up and made rigorous by Stolper and Samuelson (1941), and later Samuelson (1948, 1949) extended the argument to establish the case for complete equalization. Lerner (1953, p. v) relates that Samuelson's articles prompted Robbins to rediscover a seminar paper that Lerner had written in 1933 as a student, giving a rigorous demonstration of the conditions for complete equalization; this paper appeared in 1952. In the meantime Heckscher's 1919 paper was translated (in 1949), and it became evident that Heckscher himself had forthrightly stated the theorem in terms of complete equalization, and that Ohlin's many qualifications had tended to obscure the underlying logic. As Metzler (1949a, p. 4) put it, "the

[1]There were hints of an analysis in terms of factor endowments in Wicksell's thesis (1896), which appeared again in this review (1919). Nevertheless there is no trace of a concept of factor price equalization, and very little even of partial equalization, in these writings. The idea certainly appears to have been quite original with Heckscher.

theory of international trade might have been advanced considerably, in the English-speaking world at any rate, by an earlier translation of Heckscher's pioneer article." It is worth observing that Graham (1932, pp. 610–11), Iversen (1935, pp. 158–9), and Porzsolt (1945, p. 32) had also arrived at conditions under which complete equalization would occur.

The decade following Samuelson's 1949 paper was characterized by continued expositions, interpretations, controversies, and developments. Among the expositions, particular mention may be made of those of Jones (1956), Lancaster (1957a), Johnson (1957), Mookerjee (1958), and the lucid treatment by Mrs. Land (1959). Among the interpretations, the contributions of Tinbergen (1949), Meade (1950), R. Robinson (1956), Harrod (1958), Bhagwati (1959), and Ford (1963) may be mentioned. The most notable controversial exchange has been that of Pearce (1951–52, 1959), James and Pearce (1951–52), and Samuelson (1951–52). Among the important developments one must single out the definitive paper by Samuelson (1953) and the contributions by McKenzie (1955, 1962), Kuhn (1959), Nikaidô (1962), and Gale (1962); the last two contributions have since been combined in a joint article by Yale and Nikaidô (1965). The interesting mathematical treatments of certain aspects of the theory by Uzawa (1959) and Reiter (1961) must also be mentioned. We leave to the final sections the very important empirical studies of Leontief (1953, 1956, 1964), Arrow, Chenery, Minhas, and Solow (1961), and Minhas (1962, 1963). A recent survey of the literature has been made by Michaely (1964). So great have been the confusions between questions of logic and questions of interpretation and realism, that it will be more fruitful to continue the discussion along analytic rather than historical lines.

2. The Logic of the Factor Price Equalization Theorem

Central to the argument are the following assumptions: (1) all commodities are produced under constant returns to scale; (2) factors are totally inelastic in aggregate supply, as well as perfectly mobile within countries and completely immobile among countries; (3) production functions are identical among countries; (4) commodities have the same prices in all countries (i.e., there is perfect competition in world markets and absence of transport costs). Implicit in most discussions are additional assumptions about production functions, in particular the assumption that production isoquants are convex to the origin.

The mathematical structure of the factor price equalization theory rests first of all on a duality theorem proved by Shephard (1953, p. 22) and extended by Uzawa (1964). This theorem states that under the usual competitive (and concavity) assumptions, the production function (expressing output as a function of factor quantities) and cost function (expressing cost as a function of output and factor prices) are dual to one another in the sense that one can be derived from the other. That the cost function can be obtained from the production function has, of course, been very well known for a long time, and this aspect of the theory was quite fully developed by Hicks (1939) and Samuelson (1947). This part of the duality theorem is all that is required to obtain *sufficient* conditions for factor price equalization; most investigations have proceeded from this standpoint. But as always happens in a theory as it develops, interest attaches to the quest for weaker conditions, in fact the weakest possible, or *necessary,* conditions; Shephard's duality theorem is of special interest from this standpoint, since it does not depend on the assumption of homogeneity of production functions. Reiter's study (1961) appears to be the only one among the recent mathematical contributions that has approached the problem from this point of view; Reiter did not, however, avail himself of Shephard's duality theorem.

Following Samuelson (1953), let it now be assumed that there are n commodities, produced in amounts y_i $(i = 1, 2, \dots, n)$, with factors in amounts $x_{i1}, x_{i2}, \dots, x_{im}$, where $y_i = f_i(x_{i1}, x_{i2}, \dots, x_{im})$ is the production function which is homogeneous of degree 1 and concave (see Part 1, footnote 9). Let factor prices w_{i1}, $w_{i2}, \dots,$ w_{im} be given and beyond the firm's control, and let the cost $C_i = \sum_{j=1}^{m} w_{ij}x_{ij}$ be minimized subject to the production function.

Then as Samuelson (1953, p. 15) pointed out, and Shephard (1953, p. 43) rigorously proved, the minimum cost function factors into $C_i(y_i, w_{i1}, w_{i2}, \ldots, w_{im}) = y_i \cdot g_i(w_{il}, w_{i2}, \ldots, w_{im})$, where g_i is homogeneous of degree 1 (it is also concave, but this point was not rigorously established in the literature until the recent paper by Uzawa (1964)). Thus the minimum unit cost $c_i = C_i/y_i$ depends only on the factor prices, and not on output. Since this unit cost is constant, it is equal to marginal cost and therefore — under competitive conditions — to the price p_i of the product, *as long as the commodity is produced*; otherwise $c_i > p_i$ and $y_i = 0$. Now, assuming perfect mobility of factors, we have $w_{ij} = W_j$ for all j (factor prices are the same in all industries), and we have n inequalities $p_i \leqq g_i(w_1, w_2, \ldots, w_m)$.

Writing the above inequalities in vector form $p \leqq g(w)$, where $p = (p_1, p_2, \ldots, p_n)$ and $w = (w_1, w_2, \ldots, w_m)$, we have for each country the same functional relationship g (owing to identical production functions f) from factor prices w to commodity prices p, provided all goods are produced. Factor price equalization will therefore take place if (1) all n commodities are produced in each country (so that $y_i > 0$ and $C_i = p_t$), whence $p = g(w)$, and (2) the function g is (globally) invertible, so that w (in each country) is determined uniquely by p (which must be the same for all countries) according to the single-valued[2] function $w = g^{-1}(p)$. The first of these conditions is that of complete *diversification*;[3] it rules out specialization in the production of any commodity by a single country or by a proper subset of the trading countries. The second condition is that of *univalence* of the mapping $g(w)$, defining a one-to-one

[2]Of course, "single-valued" does not mean "real-valued." It means simply that the value of the function g^{-1} is a single vector of factor prices, rather than a set of vectors.

[3]The usual term is "non-specialization." But this expression is actually quite ambiguous, as Murray Kemp has pointed out to me in correspondence. When $n > 2$, there is a whole range of possibilities, between specialization in one commodity and postitive production of all commodities. Kemp has suggested "complete generalization"; "variegation" would be another possibility. But "diversification" seems a most natural expression, and so I am trying it out.

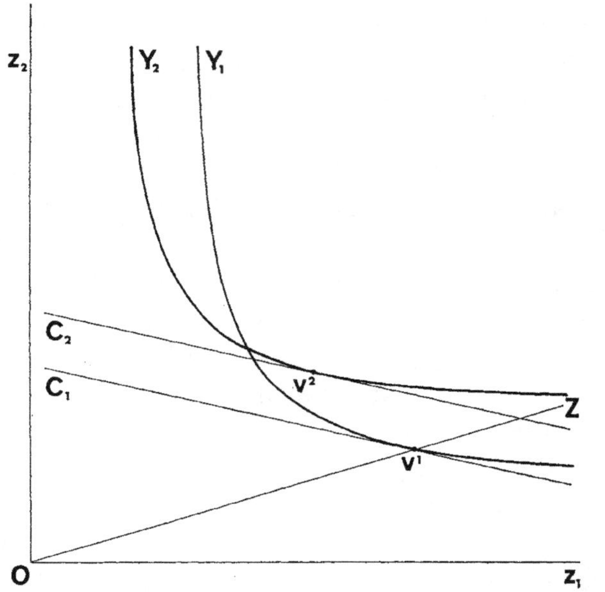

Figure 1.

correspondence between factor prices and commodity prices; this is the condition which rules out the reversal of factor intensity. It must be re-emphasized now that given the assumption that production functions are concave and positive homogeneous, these two conditions are *sufficient* for factor price equalization; they are not *necessary.* A further point should be stressed: the two conditions are *not independent,* as will be explained presently.

The argument is illustrated by Figure 1, which is essentially the diagram used by Lerner (1952). The coordinate axes measure the aggregate quantities z_1 and z_2 of two factors. Owing to the assumption of constant returns to scale the isoquants are homothetic; and once an isoquant for one commodity has been drawn, the positions of the other isoquants (corresponding to outputs of equal value of the other commodities) are determined uniquely by the relative commodity prices (this is the device employed by Mrs. Land (1959); see also Danière (1956, p. 413)). These commodity prices, in turn, may be assumed given and determined in international markets.

Assuming two factors, the diagram can be used to represent the determination of relative factor prices in each country. This may be seen as follows. By hypothesis, the isoquants Y_1 and Y_2 in Figure 1 represent the amounts of the two factors needed to produce one dollar's worth of commodity 1 and one dollar's worth of commodity 2, respectively. Now let the relative factor prices be given by the slopes of the iso-cost curves C_1 and C_2, which are tangent to Y_1 and Y_2 respectively. Owing to the assumption of perfect mobility of factors between industries, the factor prices in each industry are the same, so C_1 obviously represents a lower cost than C_2. Now if commodity 2 were to be produced (employing factors in amounts indicated by v^2), cost would have to be equal to price (owing to perfect competition) and C_2 would have to represent a dollar's worth of unit costs; but then industry 1 would make a profit by hiring factors at v^1, contrary to competitive assumptions. Competitive equilibrium — at those factor prices — must therefore be at v^1, where C_1 represents a dollar's worth of unit costs in industry 1, and C_2 exceeds a dollar's worth of unit costs in industry 2. Thus the country must specialize in the production of commodity 1. This, in turn, can be compatible with competitive equilibrium only if the country's factor endowment is given by the ray OZ passing through v^1.

Figure 2 illustrates the situation in which both commodities will be produced. It is characterized by the existence of a common tangent to two isoquants permitting production of both goods simultaneously at minimum unit cost. If the country's factor endowment is given by the factor ray OZ, then factor employments in each industry will be determined by the rays V^1 and V^2 going through the points of tangency; the required allocation of the factors is determined by completing the parallelogram at v (the point of intersection of OZ with the common tangent), resulting in combinations v^1 and v^2 of the factors employed in the respective industries.

The general rule for determining factor prices is now evident. If $y_1, y_2, \ldots, y_n$ are the amounts of n commodities measured in units of equal value, we may define the upper contour sets $X_i = \{x^i | f_i(x^i) \geq y_i\}$, where $x^i = (x_{i1}, x_{i2}, \ldots, x_{im}), i = 1, 2, \ldots, n; m$ being the number of factors. Then we form the convex hull of these

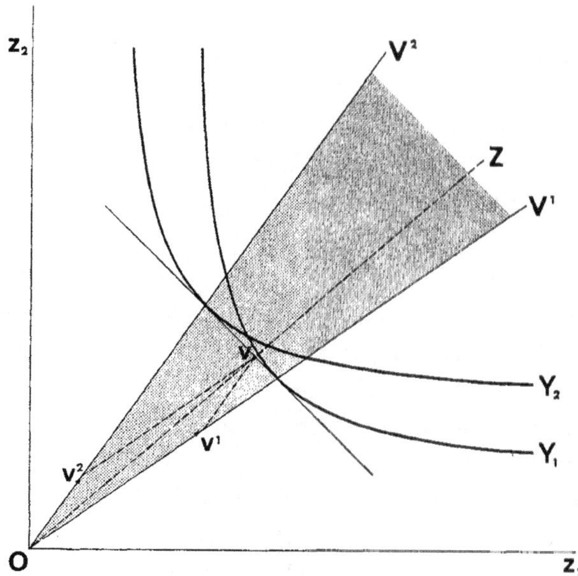

Figure 2.

sets, defined by $\{x|x = \Sigma_{i=1}^{n} \lambda_i x^i, \epsilon X_i\}$, where $\lambda_i \geqq 0$ and $\Sigma_{i=1}^{n} \lambda_i = 1$. The corresponding set in Figure 2 is composed of the areas above and to the right of the isoquents Y_1 and Y_2, as well as above and to the right of the tangent line between the two points of tangency. If the factor ray OZ is outside of the cone of diversification V^1OV^2, as in Figure 1, then the relative factor prices are determined by the slope of the isoquant intersecting the ray (the slope of C_1 tangent at v^1 in the figure); whereas if the ray of factor endowments lies inside the crucial cone as in Figure 2, then the relative factor prices will be determined by the slope of the *common* tangent as shown in the diagram. This common tangent completely determines the relative factor prices as long as the different countries' rays of factor endowments are inside the same diversification cone: *this is the essence of the factor price equalization theorem.* In the extreme case in which, for each ith commodity, a corresponding ith factor — and only that factor — was needed to produce it, then the isoquants would be L-shaped, with vertices on the respective coordinate axes; in such a case the cone of diversification would be the entire nonnegative orthant, and factor price equalization would be complete. At the other extreme, it is theoretically conceivable that all the isoquants for the various products (in Figure 2, the two isoquants) would coincide; this is the possibility first noticed by Mrs. Robinson (cf. Lerner (1953, pp. 73, 76)) and represents the limiting case in which the cone of diversification shrinks to a single ray, and there is no factor price equalization at all (unless the countries' factor endowments are the same), even though all commodities are produced. Both these limiting cases are, of course, absurd from a practical point of view, but they serve a useful pedagogical purpose in bringing out the fact that factor prices depend, in general, on factor endowments. As the factor ray swings around from horizontal to vertical position, the relative price of factor 2 falls as it becomes relatively more abundant, except when the ray traverses a cone of diversification, where it remains constant.

The question now arises as to how many such cones of complete diversification of production there may be. There could be several, or there could be none. The question of whether any such cone exists at all has been investigated by Kuhn (1959). Given that at least one such cone exists, the problem of determining under what conditions there is exactly one is, in effect, the problem that has been studied by Nikaidô (1962) and Gale (1962). These two problems will be taken up separately in Sections 3.3 and 3.4.

Let us now return to the question of the independence of the two conditions : (1) complete diversification and (2) global univalence. Figure 3 illustrates the possibility discovered by Lerner (1953, pp. 79–82), as well as by Samuelson (1949, p. 188n), that two countries with differing factor endowments could have different factor price ratios; this is the case of "factor intensity reversal." In the diagram, the isoquant Y_1Y_1 — which has a low elasticity of substitution — corresponds to commodity 1; the isoquant Y_2Y_2 corresponds to commodity 2 (for the moment, the part of the curve that branches off to Y_2^* should be ignored). There will then be two common tangents, determining two cones of diversification (A) and (B). If one country has OZ_a as its endowment ray, and the other OZ_b, then both countries will diversify, yet factor prices will be unequal.

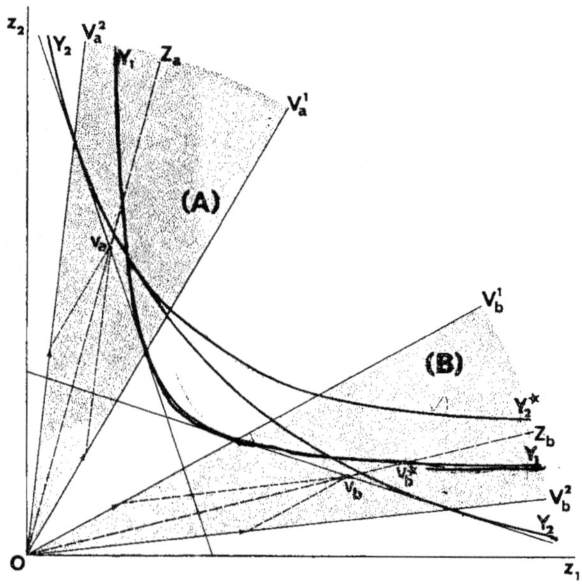

Figure 3.

(Lerner remarked that such multiple equilibria would not be stable, but evidently this was a slip, as pointed out by Pearce (1952)). Note that even though there are two diversification cones, as long as both countries have their endowment ray in the same cone, there will be factor price equalization. This was first clarified by McKenzie (1955).

Now in this example, assumption (1) is satisfied (both countries diversify), but assumption (2) is violated. If the two assumptions were independent, then it should follow that imposition of assumption (2) would bring about factor price equalization; but this is not the case. Let the isoquant for commodity 2 be altered from $\mathrm{Y}_2\mathrm{Y}_2$ to $\mathrm{Y}_2\mathrm{Y}_2^*$; then (A) becomes the only diversification cone. But this certainly does not bring about factor price equalization; if country 2's endowment ray is OZ_b, then the relative price of its factors will change from the slope of the tangent at v_b, to the slope of the isoquant at v_b^*. Factor prices in country 2 will still be unequal to those of country 1, whose endowment ray is OZ_a, and where factor prices are given by the slope of the tangent at v_a. Thus, the effect of removing factor reversal is not to bring about factor price equalization, but rather to bring about specialization, i.e., to violate the condition that every country produce a positive amount of every commodity. If both countries' factor endowments had been enclosed in the cone (A) in the first place, there would have been factor price equalization regardless of whether there was factor reversal or not, i.e., regardless of whether the production isoquant for the second commodity were Y_2Y_2 or $Y_2Y_2^*$. What the possibility of factor reversal does is to make it less likely that countries with widely differing factor endowment ratios will specialize; in spite of its theoretical interest, this does not seem very likely in practice, and Samuelson (1949) has actually described it as "pathological." Nevertheless, we shall reserve judgment on this empirical question and take it up again in connection with discussion of Minhas' work (1962, 1963).

Samuelson (1953) has stated that "without mentioning factor endowments of the country or the scale of operation of any good, we have uniquely determined its factor prices from knowledge of its commodity prices alone." While this is formally correct, although nothing is *mentioned* about relative factor endowments, a great deal is *implied* by the condition of complete diversification. This of course was recognized by Samuelson (1949) in the statement, "the answer depends upon how disparate are the initial factor endowments of the two regions — how disparate in comparison with the differences in factor intensities of the two commodities." In n dimensions it is also the case that factor price equalization will only hold for countries whose factor endowments lie within the same cone; the conditions are described by McKenzie (1955).

3. Specialization and Diversification: The Kuhn Conditions

In discussions of the factor price equalization theorem, most interest has centered on the univalence problem: *if* there exists a solution w to the system of inequalities $p \leqq g(w)$ such that $p = g(w)$, *then* under what conditions is w *uniquely* determined from knowledge of p? Under the hypothesis that a solution to $p = g(w)$ exists, a sufficient (but not necessary) condition is certainly provided by the condition that the mapping g be globally univalent. But Kuhn (1959) has — very properly — raised the point that it must be shown that a solution with $p = g(w)$ exists, i.e., that there is *some* factor endowment for which complete diversification of production is compatible with competitive equilibrium.

A whimsical illustration should serve well enough to show that a solution with complete diversification of production need not exist. Let there be two factors — labor and capital — and two commodities — men's brown shoes and green shoes. Assuming demand conditions to be such that the world price at which producers can expect to sell green shoes is very low, the corresponding isoquant, representing factor combinations required to produce a dollar's worth, will be very far out compared with that for brown shoes. Thus the isoquants will not cross anywhere, and — to nobody's surprise — green shoes will not be produced.

The postulate introduced by Kuhn to guarantee that isoquants will cross is illustrated in Figure 4. It is called the Intensity Hypothesis, and it states that there is an indexing of commodities

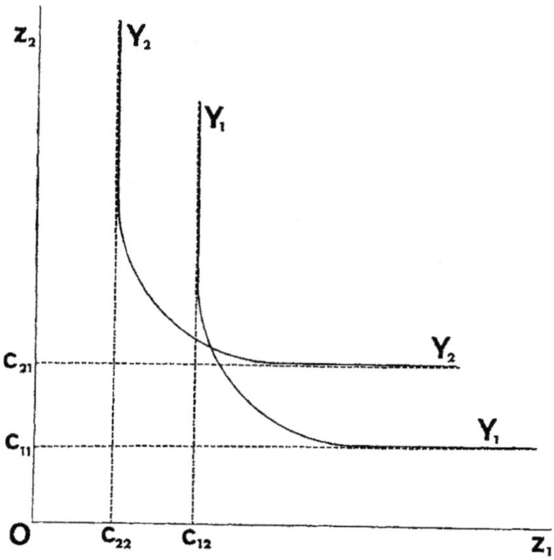

Figure 4.

and factors, associating each commodity with its intensive factor (this being just an informal interpretation), such that if $w_i = 0$ (the ith factor is free), then for some $k \neq i$ (possibly depending on the assumed values of the remaining factor prices W_j for $j \neq i$) we have $g_i(w)/p_i < g_k(w)/p_k$. Dividing each minimum unit cost $gi(w)$ by the corresponding commodity price p_i is equivalent to reckoning each commodity in units of "a dollar's worth," which was the procedure followed in interpreting the diagrams; this is necessary, of course, in order to make the magnitudes commensurate. Now, with respect to Figure 4, define $c_{i1}g_i(0, w_2)/P_i$ and $c_{i2} = g_i(w_1, 0)/p_i$, for i = 1, 2. Then the diagram shows that $c_{21} > c_{11}$, i.e., when the first factor is free ($w_1 = 0$), the second commodity is more expensive to produce than the first; likewise $c_{12} > c_{22}$, i.e., when the second factor is free ($w_2 = 0$), the first commodity is more expensive to produce than the second. And for this reason the curves cross. While this is geometrically obvious in two dimensions, it is necessary in the general case to have recourse to the Brouwer fixed point theorem.

Kuhn's ingenious proof goes as follows.[4] Assume the minimum-unit-cost functions $g_i(w)$ to be defined for semipositive w (i.e., $w \geqslant 0$, meaning that $w \geqslant 0$ and $w \neq 0$, that is, the components of w are nonnegative but not all zero), and to take on only strictly positive values (an obvious condition, not mentioned by Kuhn, but which is essential for his proof). Let the number of commodities be equal to the number of factors (a very artificial assumption, which we shall have to remove later on), and assume all n prices to be fixed and positive. (If any commodity prices were allowed to be zero, the corresponding isoquants for a dollar's worth would vanish to infinity, and this would be tantamount to reducing the number of commodities to begin with.) Then among the n minimum-unit-cost functions, choose the maximum $M(w) = \max_i g_i(w)/p_i$. (Since $g_i(w) > 0$ for all i by assumption, certainly $M(w) > 0$.) Then the

[4]Kuhn's treatment was extremely concise, and the following exposition owes much to Professor Kuhn's kindness in clearing up some obscure points in private correspondence.

formula

$$\bar{w}_i = h_i(w) = w_i + M(w) - g_i(w)/p_i \quad (i = 1, 2, \ldots, n) \qquad \text{(K)}$$

defines a mapping from the set of semipositive factor prices into itself. For convenience, let these prices be normalized so that $\Sigma_{i=1}^{n} w_i = 1$, and define $\bar{\bar{w}}_i = \bar{w}_i / \Sigma_{j=1}^{n} \bar{w}_j$. Then obviously $\Sigma_{i=1}^{n} \bar{\bar{w}}_i = 1$, so the mapping $w \to \bar{w}$ is from the (n-1)-dimensional simplex into itself, and continuous. Then from Brouwer's fixed point theorem there is a w^* such that

$$w_i^* = \dot{w}_i^* = \frac{w_i^* + M(w^*) - g_i(w^*)/p_i}{\sum_{j=1}^{n} \bar{w}_j^*} \quad (i = 1, 2, \ldots, n), \qquad \text{(B)}$$

where $w_i^* = h_i(w^*)$ from formula (K). Writing $\alpha = \Sigma_{j=1}^{n} \bar{w}_j^*$, (B) becomes $(\alpha - 1)w_i^* = M(w) - g_i(w^*)/p_i$. Now from the definition of $M, g_i(w^*)/P_i = M(w^*)$ for some i; choose such an i. Then $(\alpha - 1)w_i^* = 0$ for this i. If $w_i^* = 0$, then we would have a contradiction; $g_{i;}(w^*)/p_i$ could not have been a maximum, owing to the Intensity Hypothesis which implies that $g_k(w^*)/p_k > g_i(w^*)/p_i$ for some k. There fore $w_i^* \neq 0$ and $\alpha = 1$; but applying this to (B), we obtain $g_i(w^*)/P_i = M(w^*)$ for all i. Finally we avail ourselves of the homogeneity (of degree 1) of the minimum-unit-cost functions g_i and the fact that $M(w^*) = M > 0$, whence $g_i(w^*/M) = g_i(w^*)/M = p_i$, and putting $w = w^*/M(w^*)$ for the fixed point w^*, we have the desired solution $g(w) = p$.

However valuable Kuhn's theorem may be in itself, it leaves much to be desired from the economic as opposed to the mathematical point of view. An illustration of the limitations of the Intensity Hypothesis is shown in Figure 5, depicting a typical case of factor intensity reversal. As in the previous case, $c_{21} > c_{11}$; but this time $c_{22} > c_{12}$, that is, commodity 1 is the cheaper of the two to produce in both cases. Thus the Intensity Hypothesis is violated; nevertheless there are clearly two cones of diversification, and two solutions w to $g(w) = p$ exist. In this two-dimensional case it is evident that the Intensity Hypothesis requires the isoquants to intersect each other an odd number of times, in accordance with the peculiar feature of Sperner's lemma. This is manifestly artificial.

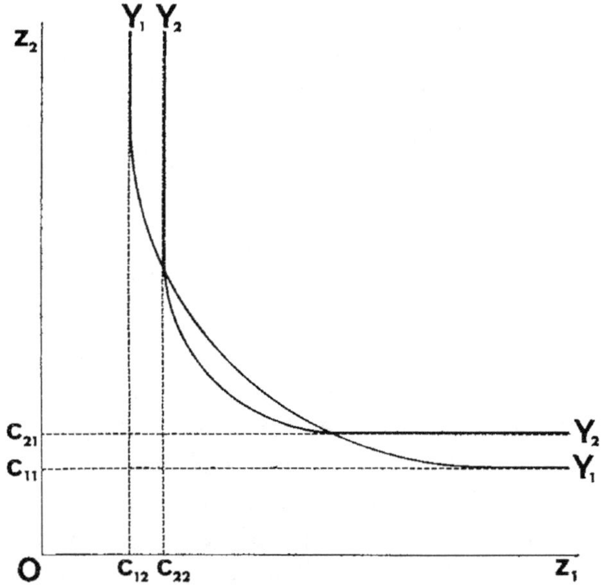

Figure 5.

There are even more serious objections that will be more readily described in connection with the analysis of production functions with constant elasticity of substitution. We shall return to these in the final section.

As a purely technical matter, it turns out that Kuhn's Intensity Hypothesis can be modified in a natural way so as to meet the objections that might be lodged against it. Let the Modified Intensity Hypothesis be stated as follows: there can be associated with each ith commodity a vector w^i of factor prices such that if $w = \sum_{j \neq i} \lambda_i w^j$ (where $\lambda_j \geqq 0$ and $\Sigma_{j=1}^{n} \lambda_j = 1$), then $g_i(w)/p_i < g_k(w)/p_k$ for some k. Kuhn's hypothesis corresponds to the special case in which the w^j are coordinate vectors, and the λ_j (the so-called barycentric coordinates of w in terms of the vertices $w^1, w^2, \ldots, w^n$) become w_j. Then one only has to make this substitution of coordinates, and the proof goes through as before.[5]

[5]The following seems to be an even simpler way of carrying out the proof, based on Gale's idea (1955) of applying directly the lemma of Knaster, Kuratowski, and

As an economic hypothesis, this modified condition is still quite awkward and hard to interpret. It comes close to assuming the conclusions. The chief difficulty is that it is misleading to regard it as an hypothesis concerning the technology, since it depends crucially on commodity prices, and hence on demand conditions. Kuhn (1959, p. 142) has described his theorem as "a rigorous demonstration of the existence of equilibrium factor prices." This is not an accurate description. Clearly there will exist equilibrium factor prices with or without the Intensity Hypothesis. The theorem should really be described as proving the existence of a combination of conceivable factor endowments for which complete diversification of production is possible under competitive conditions. Thus the problem is closely related to that of Mill's inequality, and a satisfactory solution would require examination of *international* equilibrium, with due regard to demand conditions, including especially the elasticity of substitution in consumption among the various commodities. The question essentially reduces to finding conditions under which the number of produced commodities will be at least as great as the number of employed factors.

Mazurkiewicz (1931) on closed coverings of simplexes. Define the simplex W to be the convex hull of the vertices w^i defined above, and for any we $w\epsilon W$ let its ith barycentric coordinate be denoted $\lambda_i(w)$. Define

$$S_i = \{w_| g_t(w)/p_t \geqq g_k(w)p_k \text{ for all } k\} \quad (i = 1, 2, \ldots, n);$$

then the collection $\mathfrak{S} = \{S_1, S_2, \ldots, S_n\}$ is certainly a closed covering of W. We must show that it satisfies the Knaster-Kuratowski-Mazurkiewicz condition

$$F_I \subseteq \cup_{i \epsilon I} S_i \text{ for } I \subseteq N = \{1, 2, \ldots, n\},$$

where F_I is the face of W defined by the vertices $w^i, i\epsilon I$. That is, we must show that if $\lambda_j(w) = 0$ for $j \notin I$;, then for some $i \epsilon I, g_i(w)/p_i \geq g_j(w)/p_j$ for all $j\epsilon N$. Suppose not. Let $g_i(w)/p_i = \text{Max}_j g_j(w)/p_j$ and $i \notin \mathbf{I}$; then $\lambda_i(w) = 0$, so by the Modified Intensity Hypothesis, there is a k such that $g_k(w)/p_k > g_i(w)/p_i$ which is a contradiction. It follows immediately that $\cap \mathfrak{S} \neq \emptyset$, so there is a w^* in W such that $g_i(w^*)/p_i = g_k(w^*)/p_k = \mu$, say, for all i, k. Given the obvious regularity condition that $w \geq 0$ implies $g_i(w) > 0$, we have $\mu > 0$, whence, putting $w = w^*/\mu$, we obtain (from homogeneity) $g_i(w) = g_i(w^*/\mu) = g_i(w^*)/\mu = p_i$, as desired.

4. Reversal of Factor Intensity: The Univalence Problem

The conditions under which factor prices are determined uniquely by commodity prices, when $m = n$, have been the subject of much discussion. In his 1949 paper Samuelson spelled out an assumption that was only implicit in his 1948 paper, namely that "whatever the prevailing ratio of wages to rents, the optimal proportion of labour to land is greater in clothing than in food." Using this assumption, together with diminishing marginal productivities, he used the implicit function theorem to establish that, in the two-commodity two-factor case, the function g was invertible.

The use of the implicit function theorem raised a number of questions, discussed by James and Pearce (1951–52), Samuelson (1951–52, 1953), Pearce (1959), and McKenzie (1962). Samuelson later acknowledged (1953, p. 16) that his use of this theorem had been incorrect (see also Meade (1950, p. 133n)). Though highly technical, the problem at issue is so important that it requires discussion. The inverse function theorem (cf. Apostol (1957, p. 144)) states that if $p = g(w)$ is a set of n functions $P_i = g_i(w_1, w_2, \ldots, w_n), i = 1, 2, \ldots, n$, with continuous first-order partial derivatives, and if for some set of factor prices w° the Jacobian $|\partial g_i/\partial w_j^0|$ does not vanish, then in some neighborhood of w° the function $g(w)$ is invertible (i.e., one-to-one, or locally "univalent"). If w and p are real numbers, the Jacobian is just the derivative dp/dw, and the condition $dp/dw \neq 0$ guarantees monotonicity, hence univalence. In this simple case if dp/dw holds everywhere, g is globally invertible (not just in small neighborhoods); the conjecture that this is true in general is false. Samuelson (1953, p. 16) set forth a theorem for global invertibility of differentiable functions, the main idea of which was to extend the notion of "factor intensity" to n dimensions. Nikaidô (1962) showed that his theorem was false, and presented several counterexamples.

The work of Nikaidô (1962) and Gale (1962), which was prompted by Samuelson's theorem, illustrates a point made earlier, that problems in economic theory have necessitated the development of new and neglected areas in pure mathematics. Their results have turned out to be of major importance for economic theory generally.

The principal theorem (due to Gale) is that a sufficient condition for the global univalence of a differentiable mapping $p = g(w)$, where p and w are both n−dimensional, is that the Jacobian matrix $g' = [\partial g_i/\partial w_j]$ have its principal minors all positive. This will be recognized as the same condition arrived at by Hicks (1939), Hawkins and Simon (1949), and Metzler (1950) in other connections. Some special cases of Gale's conditions are (1) that g' be positive definite and (2) that it have a positive dominant diagonal (see McKenzie (1960, p. 54)). In a proof based on Kronecker's winding number, Nikaidô has weakened the conditions, allowing the principal minors (other than the Jacobian itself) to be nonnegative. Nikaidô also showed that a modified form of Samuelson's theorem (suggested by Samuelson in correspondence with Nikaidô and Gale) was correct: the condition is that, for some ordering of both the goods and the factors, there should be positive numbers m_k and M_k such that the absolute values of the kth-order northwest principal minors of g' should be always bounded by these numbers, for $k = 1, 2, \ldots, n$.

As Kuhn (1959) noted, Samuelson's condition depends not only on the possibility of associating each commodity with a factor, but also on the ordering of the commodities (and factors). While this may seem natural in two dimensions, where "wheat" is land intensive and "watches" are labor intensive, when one passes to n dimensions, the very notion of "factor intensity" seems artificial, as Johnson (1957) has observed. Geometrically, given any two rays of factor endowments (such as OZ_a and OZ_b in Figure 3), necessarily one of them is closer to the horizontal axis and the other to the vertical; but there is no such natural association between factor rays and coordinate axes as soon as one passes to higher dimensions. There could well be a unique cone of diversification, without there being any natural way of associating its supporting rays with the coordinate axes. The concept of factor intensity is therefore more stringent than necessary for the results; this is basically what leads to the failure in higher dimensions of the Stolper-Samuelson theorem, as will be observed later on.

Kuhn himself introduced a condition for uniqueness. His sufficient condition was that for normalized factor prices w such that $\Sigma w_i = 1, \Sigma(w_i' - w_i'')(g_i(w') - g_i(w''))/p_i > 0$ for all (distinct) w' and w''; in words, that "the effect of the unit costs that move in the direction of a change in factor costs outweighs the effect of unit costs moving in the opposite direction."

Tinbergen (1949) treated the whole subject in a lucid manner; however, at the crucial point in the argument he assumed that the equations $g(w) = p$ had a unique solution. This part of the argument has been corrected by Meade (1955, p. 601). Tinbergen's argument (including the error) was repeated by Caves (1960, p. 80), who stated that uniqueness was "obvious." However, he stated that a "plausible geometric case" could be made for multiple equilibria; needless to say, algebra and geometry are not in conflict here. Laursen (1952) dealt with the problem in terms of Cobb-Douglas production functions, which are linear in logarithms; in this case, uniqueness is guaranteed automatically, as a consequence of the linearity (this will be made clearer in the final section). Uzawa (1959) took up the problem from the viewpoint of welfare economics, and also analyzed the Cobb-Douglas case in detail, concluding that factor price equalization appeared unlikely.

Reiter (1961) examined the factor price equalization theorem from a formal point of view. One of his main theorems (which relied on the incorrect Samuelson theorem, but could presumably be suitably modified) was that the conditions of constant returns to scale and identical production functions among countries were necessary as well as sufficient, as long as equalization is required to take place whenever there is complete diversification. This was proved only for the two-commodity, two-factor, two-country case, but it is undoubtedly true in general.

5. Unequal Numbers of Commodities and Factors

In the simple cases, so convenient for the classroom, in which all items (commodities, factors, and countries) come in pairs, the assumption that the number of commodities is equal to the number of factors seems innocent enough. But when the number of each is very large, the assumption of equality is patently artificial. There is no justification for such an equality to be specified in advance;

nevertheless — and this is a point worthy of note — there may well be reasons for equality of the number of *produced* commodities and *employed* factors. The theory is usually stated in terms of the number of commodities actually produced and the number of factors actually employed; but Schlesinger's objection applies, and a satisfactory formulation should leave the question of the numbers of products and of employed factors to be determined as variables of the problem.

In the case in which $n < m$ (less products than employed factors), it is generally agreed that factor price equalization will not take place. An exception to this rule would be the case in which some factors were perfect substitutes, so that full employment of resources would require the factor prices w to be confined to an n-dimensional subspace of the m-dimensional space W to which they belong. In Figure 2 this means that if there is only one commodity, factor price equalization will take place only if its isoquant is a straight line (within the convex cone defined by the two countries' endowments); in most discussions this possibility is ruled out by an implicit strict convexity assumption. This analysis suggests that it might be more fruitful to pose the problem not in terms of absolute equalization, but rather in terms of approximate equalization: if there is only one commodity, and if the elasticity of substitution between two factors in its production is very high, then there will be approximate factor price equalization; and this, surely, is all that really matters.

The case $n > m$ (more products than factors) is of greater analytic interest, and has been discussed explicitly by Samuelson (1949, 1953), Tinbergen (1949), Meade (1950, 1955), and Mrs. Land (1959); it has, however, received relatively little formal mathematical treatment. Tinbergen (1949) held that in this case factor price equalization would be less likely; Samuelson (1949) that it would be more likely; and Meade (1950) that it would be equally likely. The matter clearly calls for discussion. If the theorem is correct when there are 1000 products and 1000 factors, but no longer correct if the number of products is reduced to 999 (say, by the elimination of toothpicks) or raised to 1001 (say, by the addition of hairpins), it hardly deserves serious consideration.

Without going into all the details, we may summarize the situation in the following way. If there are more commodities than factors, and if the function $p = g(w)$ is continuous and differentiable, it must map the m-dimensional space W of factor prices into an m-dimensional manifold G in the n-dimensional space P of commodity prices, where $n > m$ (this is an old and deep topological result — the invariance of dimensionality under continuous transformations — which goes back to Brouwer); excluding the case in which there is perfect substitutability among some factors, the rank of the Jacobian matrix $g'(w)$ must be equal to m. Now, if all countries produce all commodities, prices must be equal to minimum unit costs, so the only possible equilibrium world price vectors p are those that are in G. If the Gale conditions hold for all $m \times m$ submatrices of $g'(w)$, factor prices w are uniquely determined by p and equal in all countries. Figure 6 shows a case in which the Gale conditions are violated (with a vengeance); the example is so pathological that one suspects that the univalence conditions may be considerably weakened when it is known that $n > m$ — but unfortunately, we cannot know in advance whether this will be so.

The other possibility is that of specialization. Figure 7 illustrates this case for two factors and three commodities, in the simple Leontief case of fixed technical coefficients. If country 1's factor endowment vector is in the cone AOB, and country 2's in the cone BOC, factor prices could well be different (a similar example was given by Mrs. Land (1959, p. 141)). The world production possibility frontier corresponding to this example will consist of three flat faces, one of which corresponds to the pattern of specialization indicated in Figure 7, and the other two to the cases in which the vertices of the isoquants aa, bb, cc lie respectively on a horizontal and a vertical straight line. Equilibrium solutions on the common edge of the last two faces correspond to the cases in which the vertices of the isoquants are collinear, but neither vertical nor horizontal. Thus, if we assume utility functions to be homothetic and identical among countries, we may distinguish two cases: (1) The elasticity of substitution (in consumption) is small; then the case illustrated in Figure 7 will arise when the preference for the middle commodity

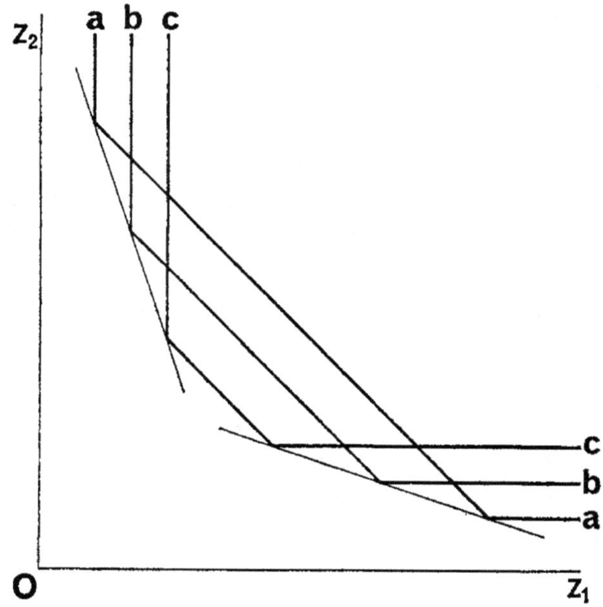

Figure 6.

b is strong relative to that for commodities a and c, whereas the cases in which the vertices of the isoquants are horizontally or vertically collinear will arise when there is a strong relative preference respectively for a or for c. (2) If the elasticity of substitution is high, an equilibrium solution becomes more likely on an edge rather than on a two-dimensional face of the production possibility frontier; then factor prices will be positive and equalized provided the preference for commodity b is sufficiently weak in comparison with that for commodities a and c.

The conclusion is now evident: it will be simplest to state it in terms of the Leontief case of fixed technical coefficients. With n commodities and m factors, each commodity determines a ray in the m-dimensional factor space; if $n > m$, there will be many convex cones (such as AOB and BOC — but not AOC) spanned by m rays, but not containing any other of the n rays. As long as all countries' factor endowments lie within any one of these cones, factor price

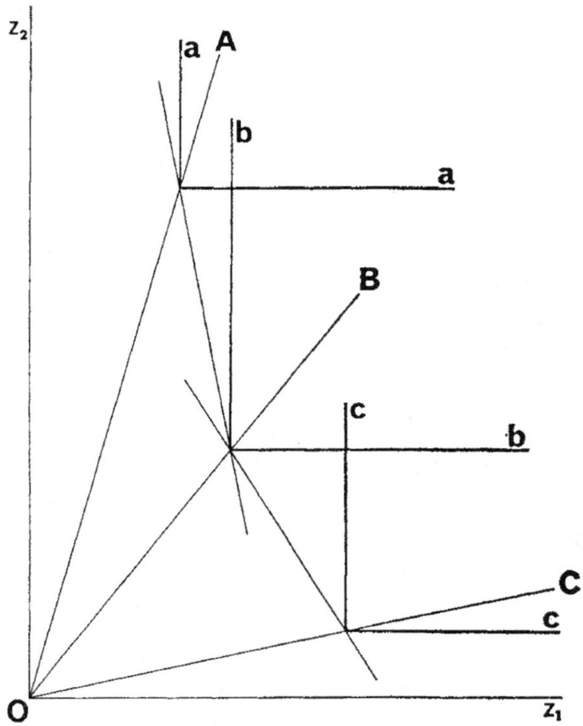

Figure 7.

equalization must prevail; the same is true for any pair of countries whose factor endowments lie within the same cone.

The question of whether adding more commodities makes factor price equalization less likely reduces to the question of whether it makes specialization more likely, as Tinbergen (1949) observed. The correct conditions were stated by Samuelson (1949, p. 192) for the two-factor case, and by Laursen (1952, p. 553) in the general case, namely that factor prices will be equalized between any pair of countries that produce simultaneously any set of m commodities, where m is the number of factors; provided univalence of g also holds, these conditions are clearly necessary and sufficient. Thus if there is a chain of countries such that any consecutive pair both produce positive amounts of the same m commodities, then factor prices will be equalized among all countries in the chain (see McKenzie (1955, p. 245)).[6]

In the Leontief case of fixed technical coefficients,[7] each commodity has an unambiguously defined factor intensity, invariant with respect to prices, which we can now define as the vector of fixed factor combinations. Thus, if the factor intensities of all commodities lie outside the convex cone enclosed by the countries' factor endowments, factor prices are necessarily equalized. But if even one commodity has a factor intensity within this cone, specialization is possible and, if it results, factor price equalization will no longer hold. A priori it seems extremely unlikely that none of the n commodities will have a factor intensity inside the cone of endowments; at least, there do not appear to be special reasons for excluding this possibility. That being the case, one can expect the possibility of specialization to be the normal outcome; nevertheless, if the elasticity of substitution in consumption is sufficiently high, there may still be complete diversification of production in some country, and therefore factor price equalization will still prevail. Tinbergen (1949) has stated, "If the number of factors is smaller than the number of products, specialization is always necessary and this no longer warrants the equality of factor prices." The phrase "always necessary" is certainly too strong, for there are two quite possible exceptions: (1) the possibility just mentioned, that the factor intensities of all products lie outside the cone of endowments, in which case specialization is actually excluded; (2) the possibility that commodities are highly substitutable in consumption, resulting

---

[6]Or, the matter can be put this way, as Kemp has suggested (in private correspondence): "It might be worth noting that if a commodity is counted as being produced if it is on the verge of being produced, the condition for FPE in all countries is that they all produce the *same* m commodities."

[7]The argument does not depend on this assumption; it merely makes it easier to express. It does, however, depend on the assumption of absence of factor intensity reversal, i.e., on the univalence of $g(w)$. A generalization of the concept of factor intensity has been furnished by R. Robinson (1956a); see also H. G. Johnson (1957).

in positive production, by a chain of countries, of all commodities whose factor intensities lie within the cone of endowments.

One of the most interesting conclusions to be drawn from this analysis is that questions of relative numbers of products and factors turn out to be very crucial; and that this result seems artificial. It does not take sufficient account of differences in elasticities of substitution, both in production and consumption. Harrod (1958) has made some very interesting observations with respect to this whole problem. "Students of imperfect competition," he observed (p. 246), "are aware of the quite genuine puzzle contained in the question — what is a commodity?" One could well add: what is a factor? In any empirical interpretation, these are subtle questions of aggregation; from Hicks' theorem (1939, pp. 312–13) it follows that *perfect* substitutability justifies such aggregation, but clearly this is, as a practical matter, one of degree. It may be that only a radical departure from conventional theory, in terms of a continuum of gradations in commodities and factors, will provide a satisfactory solution.

6. The Stolper-Samuelson Theorem

While Heckscher had stated the factor price equalization theorem in terms of complete equalization, Ohlin (1933) stated it only in terms of tendencies. Stolper and Samuelson (1941) proved a very strong theorem concerning these tendencies, namely that trade would lower the price of the "scarce"[8] factor expressed in terms of any commodity. Thus Samuelson's 1948 and 1949 papers represented the evolution of what was an outgrowth of Ohlin's more cautious statement, back full circle to Heckscher's original position. So great has been the attention given to the conditions for full equalization, that the problem originally posed by Stolper and Samuelson has

[8]I take the liberty of quoting from Professor Samuelson's comments on this description of his earlier investigation with Stolper: "There is a semantic trap here, of course. S & S did not have to decide exactly what this did *not* mean; too bad they didn't, though."

remained relatively underdeveloped. Nevertheless there have been some noteworthy contributions, among which one may mention those of Metzler (1949a, 1949b), Koo (1953), Jones (1956), Lancaster (1957b), and Bhagwati (1959).

The idea that changes in commodity prices will bring about induced shifts in resources, and corresponding changes in factor prices, is an old one, which will be found in Adam Smith (1776). It was taken up by Malthus (1814, 1815) in his two tracts on the Corn Laws, and was quite prominent also in the writings of Ricardo (1815, 1817), Torrens (1815, 1820), and McCulloch (1824). Malthus specifically posed the question in terms of the effect that a fall in the price of corn would have on the wage rate *relative* to the price of corn and other commodities. He did not obtain a clear-cut answer, but his analysis was interesting. Ricardo took the position that repeal of the Corn Laws would benefit capitalists and injure landlords, and made no bones about whose side he was on. But the absence of the concept of marginal productivity prevented any really fruitful progress in this kind of analysis.

When we come to the late nineteenth century, an analysis which came very close to anticipating the Stolper-Samuelson treatment was provided by Nicholson (1897, pp. 317–18), but the required analytical apparatus was missing. Heckscher himself specifically denied the truth of what is now called the Stolper-Samuelson theorem, in the following very interesting passage (1924, p. 49): "Finally a protective tariff which stimulates sectors which are labor-intensive would increase the demand for labor and thus increase wages.... Surely it holds here ... that it cannot be stated in advance whether *real* wages would increase, but an increase in labor's part of the total product is bound to follow."[9] Wicksell (1924, pp. 256–7) disagreed, and asserted that it was easy to construct production functions such that a tariff would raise real wages.

[9]I am much indebted to Tor Dahl for finding this passage (as well as another one to be cited further on) and providing me with a translation.

The writings of Sraffa (1925–26), Harrod (1930), and Benham (1935) also dealt with this topic, but not within the context of international trade. Nor did these authors state the essential condition of the Stolper-Samuelson theorem: that the direction in which each factor price would move would be the same relative to both of the commodity prices.[10] Mrs. Robinson (1941) also dealt with this same problem, but apologized for its lack of practical significance; this was because she dealt with a closed economy and overlooked the implications of the analysis for the theory of international trade. Her assumptions were broader than those of Stolper and Samuelson, since the problem of what could be meant by an industry of increasing returns was what lurked behind the whole issue. What none of the participants in this great debate of the 1930's took into account was that the concepts of increasing and decreasing return industries, when originally introduced and discussed by West (1815), Torrens (1820), and Senior (1836), were analyzed within the context of international trade. Even Viner, in the 1950 supplement to his 1931 paper, in which he discussed and elaborated Mrs. Robinson's analysis (1941), overlooked the fact that Stolper and Samuelson had treated the same subject during the same year.

Stolper and Samuelson were the first to introduce the Edgeworth box diagram technique into the analysis of the effect of autonomous price changes on resource allocation and factor prices. The Stolper-Samuelson argument was in terms of two commodities and two factors, and although the theorem concerning full equalization has

[10]Kemp and Jones (1962) claimed that Benham provided a "thoroughly rigorous proof of the proposition, originally put forward by Heckscher in 1919, that... a tariff will raise the real reward of one factor and lower the real reward of the other factor," and that this result was "elaborated and generalized" by Stolper and Samuelson. I have not been able to find even a statement of such a proposition in my reading of Benham, let alone a thoroughly rigorous proof. Benham spoke of the "price of agricultural land" (rather than rent — which is the relevant price) "relatively to the prices of other factors" but not relatively to commodity prices. As for Heckscher, as we have just noticed, he actually denied the proposition. Thus the Stolper-Samuelson theorem is original with Stolper and Samuelson; probably Wicksell (1924) came the closest to anticipating it.

been generalized to the case of many commodities and factors, the Stolper-Samuelson theorem has still awaited generalization. Some steps in this direction — which provided an indication that the theory might not go through as before in higher dimensions — were taken by Koo (1953), who analyzed a model with two countries, two factors, and three commodities, using an elaborate geometrical technique.

The argument of the Stolper-Samuelson theorem, as has been made clear by Bhagwati (1959), breaks into two distinct steps: (1) trade lowers the relative price of the commodity that employs the "scarce" factor relatively intensively; (2) the fall in this relative price brings about a fall in the price of the "scarce" factor relative to all commodity prices. The second step in the argument will be taken up first.

In the case of an equal number of commodities and factors, univalence of the function $p = g(w)$, where p and w are nth-order vectors and all commodities are produced, guarantees a unique relationship $w = g^{-1}(p)$ between absolute factor prices and absolute commodity prices. Assuming that a one-to-one association has been made between commodities and factors, if the ith price rises and all other commodity prices remain constant, in order that the ith price rise relative to all commodity prices, it is necessary and sufficient that it rise relative to the ith commodity price. We therefore require that $\partial(w_{i/}p_i)/\partial p_i > 0$, which is equivalent to the condition $\partial \log w_i/\partial \log p_i > 1$, that is, the elasticity of the ith factor price relative to the ith commodity price must exceed unity.

Defining $\pi = \log p$ and $\omega = \log w$, the composed function ψ may be defined by $\pi = \psi(\omega) = \log g(e^{\omega})$, whence its Jacobian matrix is $\psi'(\omega) = \hat{p}^{-1} \cdot g'(w) \cdot \hat{w}$, where $\hat{p}$ and $\hat{w}$ are diagonal matrices of commodity and factor prices. Since production functions are assumed to be homogeneous of degree 1, so are the minimum unit cost functions $g(w)$, whence by Euler's theorem each ith row sum of $\psi'(\omega)$ is equal to $\Sigma_{j=1}^{n} \partial \log g_i/\partial \log w_j = [\Sigma_{j=1}^{n}(\partial g_i/\partial w_j)w_j]/p_i = 1$. Furthermore, for the ith minimum total cost function $C_i = y_i \cdot g_i(w) = \Sigma_{j=1}^{n} w_j x_{ij}$, we have $\partial g_i/\partial w_j = \partial(C_i/y_i)/\partial w_j = (\partial C_i/\partial w_j)/y_i = x_{ij}/y_i = a_{ij}$, as has been shown by Samuelson (1953, p. 16), Shephard (1953, p. 11), and McKenzie (1959, p. 54). Thus the elements a_{ij} of the Jacobian matrix

$g'(w)$ are nonnegative, and likewise the elements $\alpha_{ij} \cdot a_{ij} - w_j/p_i$ of the Jacobian matrix $\psi'(\omega)$ are nonnegative. The latter matrix therefore has the formal properties of a stochastic matrix (of transition probabilities), since its elements are nonnegative and its row sums are equal to unity. The elasticity criterion $\partial\omega_i/\partial\pi_i > 1$ referred to above is therefore equivalent to the condition that the inverse of the Jacobian matrix $\psi'(\omega)$ have all its diagonal elements greater than unity.

For the case $n = 2$ it is always true that the inverse of a stochastic matrix (when it exists) has its diagonal elements either greater than one or less than zero; so by appropriate permutations of rows and columns (that is, by suitable association of commodities with their "intensive" factors — indeed, this provides us with a definition of "intensity"), these diagonal elements will always exceed unity. This essentially is the Stolper-Samuelson theorem. However, it no longer holds when $n > 2$, except under special conditions.

It is well known that there are conditions under which the Stolper-Samuelson theorem is valid but the Lerner-Samuelson theorem (concerning complete equalization) is not; this is the case in which complete specialization is attained before it has become possible for factor prices to be equalized. It does not appear to have been recognized, however, that the converse is also true: there are conditions under which trade can bring about complete equality of factor prices, yet it will not be so that in each country every factor price has moved in the same direction relative to each commodity price. This may easily be seen in the following example in which production functions are of the Wicksellian or "Cobb-Douglas" form (see Wick-sell (1896, p. 53)).

Let the production function for the ith commodity be $y_i = k\Pi_{j=1}^n x_{ij}^{\alpha ij}$, where $k\Pi_{j=1}^n \alpha_{ij}^{-\alpha ij}$ and $\Sigma_{j=1}^n \alpha_{ij} = 1$, $\alpha_{ij} > 0$; x_{ij} denotes the employment of the jth factor in the production of the ith commodity. The corresponding minimum unit cost function is $c_i = \Pi_{j=1}^n w_j^{\alpha ij}$, so the function $\psi(\omega)$ becomes the linear transformation $\pi = \mathrm{A}\omega$, where $\mathrm{A} = [\alpha_{ij}]$. In this case ψ (and hence g) is univalent as long as A is nonsingular, which is Joan Robinson's condition (see Lerner (1953, p. 73)). Provided all n commodities are produced, the nonvanishing of the Jacobian $|\psi'(\omega)| = |A|$ is sufficient for full equalization of factor prices in this case, even though the univalency conditions of Nikaidô, Gale, Samuelson, and McKenzie need not be realized.[11] Nevertheless, in the example

$$A^{-1} = \begin{bmatrix} .55 & .40 & .05 \\ .05 & .50 & .45 \\ .25 & .35 & .40 \end{bmatrix}^{-1} = \begin{bmatrix} .77 & -2.59 & 2.82 \\ 1.68 & 3.77 & -4.45 \\ -1.95 & -1.68 & 4.64 \end{bmatrix}$$

the elasticity of the first factor price with respect to the first commodity price is only .77, so that the consequence of a rise in the first commodity price is that the first factor price rises relative to the second and third commodity prices (which are held constant), but falls relative to the first. In the case $n = 3$ it can be shown (see Chipman (1964)) that a sufficient condition for the diagonal elements of A^{-1} to be greater than one is that the diagonal elements of A be larger than any other elements in the same column (which is much weaker than Newman's (1959) and McKenzie's (1960) diagonal dominance condition); but this does not hold for $n \geqq 4$.

If reversal of factor intensity is possible (i.e., if $g(w)$ is not univalent) then the Stolper-Samuelson theorem fails, in a certain sense, if countries' factor endowments differ sufficiently. This is where the verbal tangles come into the picture; even though two countries have identical production functions, a commodity whose production is relatively "labor intensive" in one country may be relatively "land intensive" in another; yet it may still be true that the price of a factor varies directly with and relative to the price of a certain commodity,

[11]It is worth noting that all of Nikaidô's counterexamples to Samuelson's 1953 univalence theorem violate the condition that $\psi'(\omega)$ is a stochastic matrix; since Samuelson did not take advantage of this fact in his proof, the validity of his theorem must be regarded, strictly speaking, as still an open question. Pearce (1959) actually claimed that nonvanishing of the Jacobian would be a sufficient condition for univalence, but McKenzie (1962) provided a counterexample which implicitly took account of the stochastic property of the Jacobian. Thus I would conjecture that Samuelson's theorem is still not true, and that counterexamples satisfying the "stochastic" property could still be found. The Gale-Nikaidô univalence theorems likewise take no account of this property of the Jacobian.

but which commodity this will be depends on the country's factor endowment.[12]

It is the first step of the Stolper-Samuelson argument that has attracted the profoundest scrutiny. Metzler (1949a) pointed out that if foreign reciprocal demand were inelastic, a tariff might lower the world price of the "protected" good sufficiently so that the domestic price (including the tariff) would be lower than before. In this case the effect of a tariff would be precisely the opposite of that specified by Stolper and Samuelson. Assuming that the tariff would be offset by a reduction in other taxes, Metzler showed that a fall in the domestic price of the "protected" good might be prevented if the marginal propensity to import were sufficiently high. The simplest formula (1949a, p. 18) for the conditions under which protection will raise the price of the protected good is $\eta+k > 1$, where η is the foreign elasticity of demand for imports and k is the domestic marginal propensity to import; more elaborate formulas were developed by Metzler in a later paper (1949b). Metzler's paradox has since been rediscovered by Allais (1961).

A related point has been developed by Lancaster (1957b), who has summarized his position by the statement: "Protection will raise the real wage of labour if, and only if, the country imports the labour intensive good." Lancaster's point seems to be similar to an observation of Leontief (1933) to the effect that differences in tastes can outweigh comparative costs in the determination of trade patterns; this phenomenon can also arise when tastes of owners of factors of production are the same in different countries. Even so, Lancaster appears to have assumed that protection would raise the price of the labor intensive good; in other words, he evidently overlooked the possibility of Metzler's paradox. Bhagwati (1959) provided a useful synthesis of the discussion in which he distinguished between prohibitive and nonprohibitive tariffs; he concluded that a

[12]The problem essentially is whether "factor intensity" is a local or global concept. There are many complex questions involved, which I have taken up separately (Chipman (1964)) and therefore pass over here. An exposition of some of these matters is presented in the book by Travis (1964, pp. 183–4).

tariff would raise the domestic price of the protected good in the prohibitive case, and that the outcome in the nonprohibitive case would depend on the Metzler condition $\eta + k > 1$.

7. The Problem of Interpretation; Departures from Assumptions

In view of the formidable logical complexities associated with the theory of international trade and factor prices, it is not surprising that there should have been considerable dispute concerning its interpretation in the light of what meager data are available. The objections and qualifications that have been raised against the factor-price equalization theorem can be classified into two categories: (1) those that implicitly accept the underlying assumptions, and (2) those that stress their limitations.

Those objectors who fall in the first category must of necessity rest their case on either (a) factor intensity reversal, (b) specialization, or (c) inequality among numbers of products and numbers of factors. Exception (a) has been stressed by Pearce and James (1952), Harrod (1958), and H. G. Johnson (1957). Harrod also advanced the judgment that the number of factors could be expected to exceed the number of products. Exception (c) was also taken up by Pearce (1959), who concerned himself particularly with the idea that as the number of commodities and factors becomes large, one can expect it to be less probable that all countries' factor endowments will be sufficiently close together for equalization to result; this of course leads to (b). Exception (b) was stressed by Tinbergen (1949) and Uzawa (1959), but on the whole neither (b) nor (c) has received as much attention as (a).

In view of all the possible exceptions, the discussion has taken on a taxonomic character, as is the case with most branches of international trade theory. To some extent this is necessary and desirable, since a taxonomy is, after all, nothing but a complicated mathematical function that cannot be expressed analytically and therefore has to be tabulated. The discussion has also served to bring out the important questions that need to be answered in empirical research. But the chief difficulty seems to be the problem of aggregation.

Turning to the second category of objections, the departures from assumptions that have been singled out for attention may be classified under the following heads: (A) international disparities in production functions, (B) non-constant (especially increasing) returns to scale, (C) trade in intermediate products, (D) domestic (untraded) commodities, (E) variable factor supply, and (F) international mobility of capital. There are others that could be added, but these seem to be the principal ones. In varying degrees these possibilities can be allowed for and incorporated into the general theory.

Haberler (1955) has particularly stressed (A), as has Viner (1959). Nevertheless it is implicit in much of the literature that certain types of differences in production functions and factor productivities can easily be accomodated. In particular, if differences in production functions are neutral, that is, if in one country the production function for each commodity is proportional (for any set of factor quantities) to the corresponding production function in another — a condition that Leontief (1953) called "technological parity" — the factor price equalization theorem is still valid in terms of relative factor prices, and the ratio between corresponding factor prices in different countries is determined precisely by the proportionality factor. The same consideration applies to uniform differences in the productiveness of individual factors. "Neutral" differences in production functions were very successfully exploited by Arrow, Chenery, Minhas, and Solow (1961).

Viner (1959, pp. 284–5) has gone so far as to say that differences in what he calls "productivity functions" constitute "the most important qualification of the factor-price-equalization theory," and by this expression he evidently meant differences in factor qualities. If this be so, then it must be regarded as very favorable to the principal conclusion of the Samuelson theory. If workers in one country are much poorer than those of another, it makes a great difference whether this is because the poor country is overpopulated, or whether it is because its workers are of inferior quality. The latter conclusion applies equally well in a single country with perfect factor mobility; the former obviously does not.[13]

Exception (B) has been handled by Laing (1961) in much the same way as other authors have treated (A); he allowed for external economies and assumed that production functions were homothetic, but permitted increasing returns to scale. His principal conclusion was that there would not generally be factor price equalization, which is not surprising. He did not investigate the implications of increasing returns with respect to the Stolper-Samuelson theorem; had he done so, he might have been able to establish Torrens' result (1826, pp. 163–9) that a fall in the price of corn, by inducing a movement of resources out of agriculture (subject to decreasing returns) into industry (subject to increasing returns), would raise real rent as well as real wages.

Exception (C) should, perhaps, not be called an exception. Samuelson (1953) introduced intermediate products into the analysis; it appears from his treatment that they were implicitly regarded as being internationally traded. Vanek (1963) has developed a box-diagram method for incorporating intermediate commodities. Porzsolt (1945) included an internationally traded intermediate product in his interesting analysis. McKenzie (1955) devoted considerable attention to this subject and argued that trade in intermediate products would be favorable to equalization. It does not seem that any unequivocal statement can be made, since the introduction of trade in intermediate products could bring about greater specialization.

With exception (D) we pass to an impediment to trade that works against factor price equalization. Domestic commodities were discussed by Morgan and Rees (1954) in a general way. McKenzie's analysis (1955, pp. 247–8) came straight to the point: since the factor price equalization theory rests on the mapping $p = g(w)$ between

[13]It is interesting that Senior (1830) considered low labor productivity rather than population density to be the principal explanation of low living standards in poor countries. But his treatment was ambiguous, since it was not clear to what extent the efficiency was a reflection of labor quality, and to what extent a reflection of a high ratio of capital to labor.

commodity and factor prices, where it breaks down in this case is in commodity prices not being equalized; under these circumstances one could not expect factor prices to be equalized. But McKenzie suggested that domestic commodities could be analyzed like factors, provided the demand for them was inelastic; that is, the problem becomes one of equalization of prices of domestic commodities as well as of factors. A very similar approach has been adopted by Iversen (1935, pp. 154–5), who concluded that "trade in commodities, besides equalising the prices of goods actually traded, exercises a certain equalising influence on the prices of the other goods and of the factors of production." Ohlin (1928, p. 10) went so far as to argue that capital movements would leave unchanged the relative price of "international goods" and "home market goods," basing his argument on the flexibility of resource allocation in a "progressive country." This might suggest that he believed that prices of "home market goods" would be equalized, but this was denied in his later work (1933, pp. 152–3) where, however, he argued (pp. 153–5) that trade in intermediate products, combined with a high elasticity of substitution in consumption between international and home market goods, would have an equalizing tendency on the prices of the domestic goods. McKenzie's argument was based on the analogy between domestic commodities and factors, assuming domestic commodities to be in fixed demand; but the analogy is incomplete, since fixed demand (unlike fixed supply) is, in general, incompatible with the budget constraint.

Stolper and Samuelson (1941) introduced their discussion with a reference to Taussig's statement (1927, p. 39) that "there is no such tendency to equalization" of money wages. In fairness to Taussig it must be stated that the passage comes in a chapter which is prefaced (pp. 34–5) with an emphatic assertion that "the supposition that all goods come within the range of international trade is not at all in accord with the facts." Taussig's whole argument was based on disparities in the relative prices of domestic and international commodities in different countries; thus the difference between his approach and that of Stolper and Samuelson was one of assumption rather than of analysis. And if Taussig's dictum is correct, it must be regarded as providing by far the most damaging objection that can be raised against the factor price equalization theory.

Exception (E) was analyzed by McKenzie (1955, pp. 246–7). The argument can be simply put in terms of Figure 2. If the relative price of the first commodity rises, the isoquant Y_1 will move towards the origin (relative to Y_2), and the relative price of the first factor will rise; if this brings forth a relative increase in the supply of the first factor, the ray OZ will swing to the right and might eventually depart from the diversification cone, which will swing to the left (except for the case of fixed technical coefficients). But owing to the continuous nature of the phenomenon, the possibility of factor price equalization still remains; and if factor supplies are "backward rising," the case for factor price equalization is actually strengthened.

This makes it difficult to accept the treatment by Uzawa (1959, pp. 466–8), who claimed that "complete factor price equalization will occur if and only if the initial factor endowment in all countries is the same." He based this result on the assumption that all countries had identical excess demand functions, linear with respect to all prices except the numéraire, and from this concluded that partial equalization was necessary in the sense that the Euclidean distance between two countries' factor prices (considered as points in n-dimensional space) would have to diminish. The linearity, as well as the asymmetric treatment of the numéraire, are also stringent conditions. But the greatest difficulty resides in the lack of any apparent relationship between the excess demand function and the production relations; for instance, the assumption of constant returns to scale is nowhere used and possibly ruled out. Apart from such objections, the theorem may simply state that if factor prices are equalized, then (owing to identical tastes) factor endowments will be equalized also.

Exception (F) is of great interest. Mundell (1957) has advanced the interesting argument that under conditions of factor price equalization, a tariff imposed by a labor intensive country on its capital intensive good — thus benefiting its capitalists and prejudicing its workers — will encourage capital to move in to take advantage of its higher marginal product, and the process will continue until factor prices are equalized once again, and the tariff can be removed. The substance of this argument was clearly stated long before by Heckscher (1924, p. 50): "if one considers a tariff which encourages the use of capital, and thereby increases the return on capital, the effect will be a capital inflow which will go on until the interest rate has returned to approximately its old level, and to the level which exists in other countries, but which then leaves the country with a larger amount of capital than before." Torrens (1826, pp. 156–60) had applied a similar argument (in reverse) for a capital-intensive country (England) to lower its duties (on corn) and thereby encourage a capital inflow. Lancaster (1957a) observed that the factor price equalization theorem implied that trade would continue even with perfect factor mobility; this was evidently overlooked by Burenstam Linder (1961, p. 139).

Some of these cases, among which I would count (C) and (E), seem to be fully in accord with the theory. While (A) and (B) clash with factor price equalization, they may, to a considerable degree, be fruitfully accommodated to the method of analysis. (F) turns out to be an interesting application of the theory. It would seem to me that case (D), the phenomenon of domestic, untraded commodities, is the one case that could constitute an important objection.

8. The Leontief Paradox

The celebrated "Leontief paradox" has stimulated an enormous amount of discussion; the contributions have been so numerous that it will not be possible to discuss them all in this survey. The general framework of Leontief's (1946) adaptation of his input-output model to international trade was brought to bear on the Heckscher-Ohlin theory in two important papers (1953, 1956). The latter paper also contained a new contribution to the theory of the subject, thus helping to bridge the gap between the theoretical framework of Lerner and Samuelson and the computations of Leontief's 1953 article — a gap which is largely responsible for the great volume of discussion that has appeared. Nevertheless, Leontief's theoretical treatment was based on such unnecessarily rigid assumptions concerning the nature

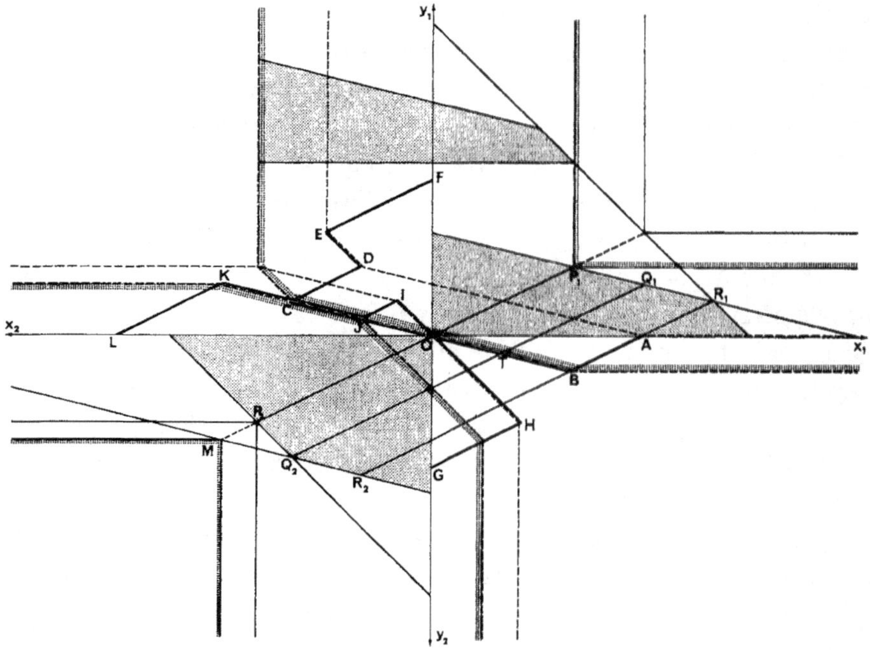

Figure 8.

of the technology and of consumer behavior that, as Hoffmeyer (1958, p. 163) has said, "Leontief has himself contributed to the confusion" over the issue.

Leontief's 1956 paper, with its assumptions of fixed proportions in both production and consumption, presents a striking contrast to his earlier 1933 contribution. The assumption of fixed technical coefficients in production, and inelastic factor supplies, leads to angular transformation functions of the kind first displayed by Koopmans (1953, p. 107); furthermore, Leontief assumed that commodities are consumed in fixed proportions, so that (since the homothety conditions are satisfied) each country has the same L-shaped community indifference curves as shown in Figure 8 (these curves are not actually shown in Leontief's chart). By an ingenious geometric device, in which the production and consumption conditions for the two countries are depicted in the positive and negative quadrants, Leontief shows that world equilibrium will be attained when the line segment P_1P_2 (whose slope is equal to the rigid proportion in which commodities must be consumed), joining points on the two countries' transformation functions, has maximum length. In Figure 8, Q_1Q_2 and R_1R_2, as well as all segments parallel to them within the parallelogram, satisfy this property. Since the corresponding pre-trade line segment has to pass through the origin, it follows that trade cannot lower the world production of any commodity (which is given by the projection of the line segment on the corresponding axis). This, of course, is a peculiar feature of the model resulting from the assumption of perfect complementarity in demand.

Figure 8 shows how Leontief's model looks when translated into the visual language of Meade's *Geometry.* The two countries' production blocks are shown by the shaded areas, and their opposite sides (such as Q_1R_1 and Q_2R_2) are parallel, indicating that production coefficients are identical in the two countries, which differ only in their factor endowment. It should be pointed out that Leontief himself (1956) specifically did not assume identical technologies; the assumption is made in this discussion simply in order to bring out the relationship between Leontief's model and the factor price equalization theory.

Using Meade's method, the angular production blocks can be slid along the L-shaped indifference curves, to obtain the dotted trade indifference curves as shown. From these, the Marshallian offer curves are derived, which look much like those of Elliott (1950). Country 1's offer curve is ABCDEF, and country 2's is GHIJKL. They intersect along the segment CJ, so that the equilibrium terms of trade are unique (contrary to an opinion of Valavanis (1958, p. 111), which was corrected by Leontief (1958, p. 121)); but although world output is unique, the individual countries' outputs are not (unless the countries' technologies are different, as Leontief himself supposed). The reflection OTB of OJC is what corresponds to Leontief's "international trade vector" (1956, p. 389 and Chart 1). Before trade, in this example, country 1 will produce and consume at P_1, and country 2 at P_2; after trade, country 1 will go on consuming at P_1; but will produce between Q_1 and R_1; whereas country 2 will increase its consumption to M and produce between Q_2 and R_2. In country 1, one of the factors (call it labor) is a free good both before and after trade; in country 2 the other factor (call it capital) is free before trade, but labor is free after trade.

Valavanis (1954) criticized Leontief's study on the grounds that "input-output models (except for rare luck) are logically incompatible with international trade." Valavanis' point (1954, p. 524) was that if all factors were fully employed before trade (which is not the case in the example just considered), in general it would be impossible for trade not to decrease the world production of some commodity; consequently, he reasoned, there would be no trade. But here he fell into the same confusion as Pareto (1909, pp. 508–9), as was pointed out in Part 1, Section 1.2. If the elasticity of substitution is high enough, there is no reason why trade should not lower the output of some commodities. Moreover, there is no reason why trade should necessarily change world output at all: trade would still be advantageous, provided countries produce commodities in different proportions.

There is one special case in which Valavanis' argument would hold, and that is the extreme case in which the following two conditions are satisfied: (1) intermediate products are not traded, and (2) commodities are perfect substitutes in consumption. Under such circumstances, we may imagine parallel indifference curves in both countries, in Figure 8, having a slope between the slopes of the lines bounding the production blocks, which represent loci of commodity outputs corresponding to full employment of labor (parallel to P_2Q_2) and capital (parallel to P_1Q_1). Under autarky, equilibrium will be at R_1 and Q_2 in the respective countries. If trade is allowed, even though some trading would be possible, it would be unnecessary; and with infinitesimal transport costs there would be no trade. In any case, equilibrium outputs would be at R_1 and Q_2, and under the assumptions, these would remain equilibrium consumptions.

But if either one of the above two assumptions is relaxed, this conclusion will no longer follow. First, let us suppose that both countries have identical homothetic utility functions, with a high but finite elasticity of substitution; and let equilibrium under autarky be at R_1 and Q_2, respectively. Then the relative price of

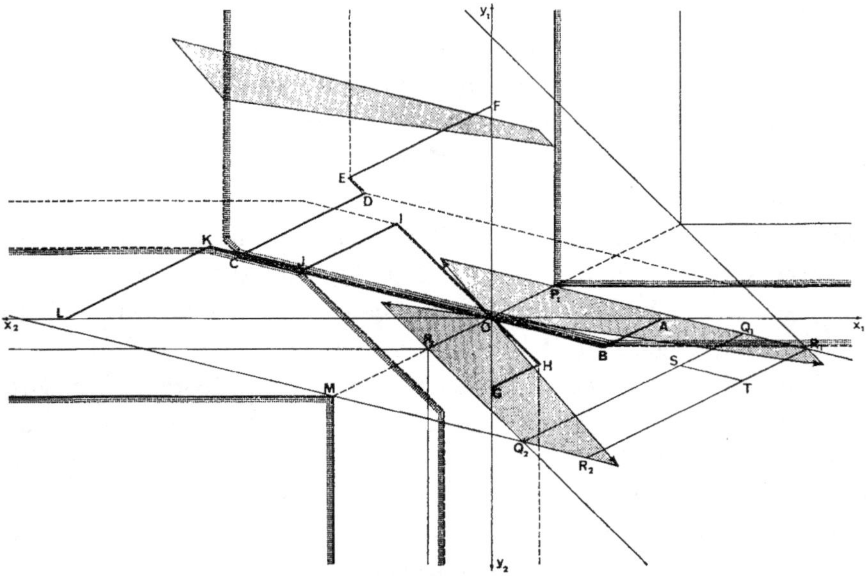

Figure 9.

the x-commodity will be higher in country 1 (where it is equal to the slope of the indifference curve through R_1) than in country 2 (where it is equal to the slope of the indifference curve through Q_2). Consequently, the international price ratio will be in between, and trade will obviously be carried out. The countries' outputs stay constant, as before, at R_1 and Q_2, so world output will remain unchanged; but this does not mean that there will be no trade! Constant total output is, after all, characteristic of models of pure exchange, and in the present instance this is exactly what the Leontief model becomes.

If, on the other hand, the assumption of perfect substitutability is imposed, but trade in intermediate products is allowed, we find that trade will, indeed, have a tendency to increase world output. This is illustrated by Figure 9, where intermediate products, when treated as inputs, are reckoned as negative commodities in the manner of Koopmans (1951). The diagram is self-explanatory, following exactly the same rules as Figure 8, incorporating Leontief's assumption of perfect complementarity in consumption, and shows that the introduction of trade in intermediate products gives rise to no new difficulties. The example has a special feature not present in the previous one, however: the vertices R_1 and Q_2 are no longer contained in the respective positive quadrants of the two countries; a similar feature was present in Figure 9. Thus, even assuming the commodities to be perfect substitutes, equilibrium under autarky would be at the intersection of P_1Q_1 with the horizontal axis, for country 1; and at the intersection of P_2Q_2 with the vertical axis for country 2. With international trade, the national net outputs will be at R_1 and Q_2, hence world output will certainly increase.

Valavanis' claim that the Leontief model is incompatible with international trade can therefore not be accepted. Both R. Robinson (1956) and Caves (1960) have pointed this out. Nevertheless, Valavanis sensed correctly that there was something very strange about the implications of input-output models for the theory of international trade; and it was this strange feature that was brought out by Leontief himself in his 1956 contribution. Leontief assumed that all commodities were perfect complements, not for illustrative purposes, but as a serious empirical hypothesis, claiming (1956, p. 390) that "for purposes of empirical analysis the restrictions imposed upon the formal properties of our system by the use of fixed consumption and production coefficients and linear equations seem to be quite appropriate."

Some consequences of such an assumption were already noticed in Section 2.7, where it was observed that perfect complementarity in consumption might lead to an equilibrium in which all countries but one were ruined. Something similar happens in the present case, namely that all factors but one become unemployed. Given Leontief's assumptions of fixed proportions in consumption, production will occur — with probability one (i.e., except out of sheer coincidence) — on an $(n-1)$-dimensional face, and consequently all factors but one will be free, with or without trade. This can be seen from Figures 8 and 9; it is only by sheerest coincidence that the ray OP_1 would pass through R_1 in Figure 8 (in Figure 9 it would be impossible). In the case of Figure 9 it was observed that with a sufficiently high elasticity of substitution, trade in intermediate products might bring about

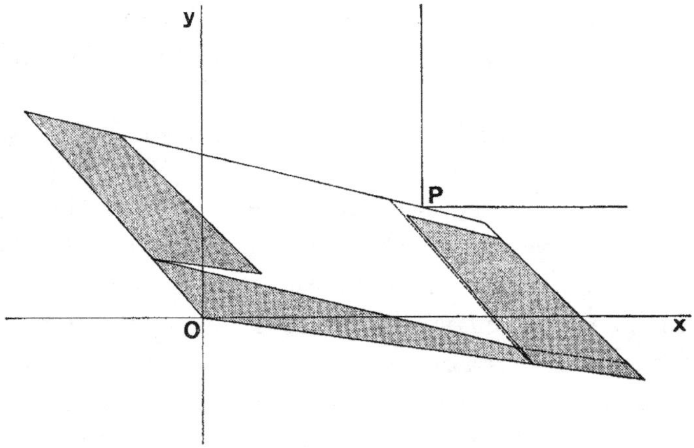

Figure 10.

full employment of both factors, which would be impossible under autarky; but this would not be so under Leontief's assumptions, according to which equilibrium outputs would be at Q_1 and Q_2, or at R_1 and R_2, or at points in between, and the terms of trade would be given by the slope of OJC, at which the offer curves intersect (coincide). (In the diagram, OST corresponds to Leontief's international trade vector.) Figure 10 shows this still more clearly; it illustrates the same example as Figure 9, using Lerner's (1932) technique of aggregating production blocks, and the aggregation of preferences is justified by the strong homothety condition. Again, it would only be by accident that the point P would coincide with the vertex of the world production possibility set. This, in effect, is simply Graham's theory all over again, generalized to take account of more than one factor.

The implications of Leontief's model for the factor price equalization theorem should now be noted. It was pointed out in Section 3.5 that when the number of commodities exceeds the number of factors, a zero elasticity of substitution in consumption implies (with probability one) that factor prices will be equalized only in the pathological case in which one of the factors is free. In order that factor prices be equalized at positive levels, a combination of the following three conditions is required: (1) a relatively high elasticity of substitution in consumption; (2) a relative preference for commodities which are extreme in their factor intensities; (3) not too disparate factor endowments.

If Leontief's 1956 analysis is pushed to its logical conclusion, one verifies that one of the factors in the foreign country (country 2) will be a free good in the absence of trade, whereas the other will be a free good after trade (as shown in Figure 8 by the movement of equilibrium output from P_2 to some position between Q_2 and R_2); and in the home country (country 1) one of the factors is free both before and after trade. In the latter case, the free factor can unambiguously be described as the abundant one, and the remaining factor as the scarce one. When more commodities are introduced, the likelihood of this pathological phenomenon diminishes, but (given Leontief's rigid demand assumptions) one will no longer have factor price equalization; a country's relatively abundant factor will then earn less at home than abroad. Leontief's paradox is the assertion that the scarce factor in the United States is capital rather than labor.[14] But an even greater paradox is the result, being a logical and inescapable consequence of Leontief's analysis: that if production functions are identical among countries, then either labor in the United States and abroad must, under such circumstances, earn zero wages; or else labor will earn less in the United States than labor of comparable quality earns abroad.

The question therefore arises as to whether Leontief's empirical findings have a meaningful interpretation, even though the underlying model does not seem consistent with common observation. Hoffmeyer (1958) and R. Robinson (1958) have adopted the view that there is such an interpretation. The relevant link between observed input-output ratios and classical theory is the important "Wong-Viner envelope theorem" sketched by Samuelson (1953, p. 19); also significant are the duality theorems of Shephard (1953), Samuelson (1958), and Uzawa (1958). Allowing for intermediate inputs, the

[14]It is most unfortunate that at a crucial point a slip entered Leontief's argument (p. 392, lines 12 and 13 of the second column); he inadvertently interchanged the words "labor" and "capital" in his discussion of the interpretation of his diagram.

Jacobian matrix of the transformation $p = g(w)$, where p is an $n \times 1$ vector of commodity prices, and w an $m \times 1$ vector of primary factor prices, is simply $g'(w) = (I - A)^{-1}B$, where A is the variable $n \times n$ matrix of input-output coefficients, and B the variable $n \times m$ matrix of factor-output coefficients;[15] the elements of $(I - A)^{-1}B$, which depend uniquely on the factor prices w (the commodity prices p being assumed given), are the ratios of factor employments in the various industries to the corresponding net outputs. Thus in the classical case, in which input-output coefficients depend on prices, it is nevertheless perfectly proper to use such input-output coefficients just as Leontief has used them. In other words, it is not necessary to assume A and B to be fixed.

Samuelson (1958) has stated the problem in terms of linear programming. Thus the condition that profits be nonpositive may be written $(I - A)^{-1}Bw \geqq p$, and the condition that resources z be not overutilized (where z is $1 \times m$) may be written $y(I - A)^{-1}B \leqq z$. The problems posed by Samuelson (1958) of determining w so as to minimize national expenditure zw subject to $(I - A)^{-1}Bw \geqq p$, and of determining y so as to maximize national product yp subject to $y(I - A)^{-1}B \leqq z$ are — in the special Leontief case in which A and B are constant — dual linear programming problems, with the solution national income $= zw = yp$.

In this special form, with input-output coefficients unresponsive to prices, linear programming theory allows of three types of solutions: (1) a "degenerate" solution with less commodities produced than the number of fully employed factors, (2) a non-unique solution with more products than fully employed factors, and (3) a unique, non-degenerate solution with equal numbers of produced goods and fully employed factors. In Figure 8 the degenerate solutions would occur at the corners of the production block where it meets the axes; the non-unique solutions would occur on either one of the faces; and the unique non-degenerate solution at the vertex R_1. Samuelson's case — on the face of it — is one in which the commodities are

[15]These matrices A and B are the transposes of the matrices used by Leontief.

perfect substitutes and the indifference curves straight lines. From this standpoint, the non-unique solutions are clearly improbable a priori in this case. At the other extreme, if $y = \lambda b$, where b is a fixed vector and λ a positive scalar, Leontief's problem (posed in the analysis of his Chart 1 (1956), but not in his mathematical appendix) is that of maximizing λ subject to $\lambda b(I - A)^{-1} \leqq z$; and the presumption here, as is obvious from the diagram, is that the solution to be expected will be on an $(n - 1)$-dimensional face.

Now, given the commodity prices, the input-output matrices A and B depend generally on factor prices; as long as these remain unknown, the problem posed by Samuelson, of maximizing yp subject to $y(I - A(w))^{-1}B(w) \leqq z$, is incomplete. As long as utility functions are identical and homothetic, this could be solved by nonlinear (homogeneous) programming. But assuming now a solution in w to be given, and posing the problem as a linear programming one with $A(w)$ and $B(w)$ evaluated for the given w, Samuelson's procedure will provide a correct solution. This provides a logically correct basis for the use of linear approximations; they are used locally, not globally. And there is no necessity to have recourse to the assumption of fixed coefficients in production and consumption. Moreover, these assumptions, giving rise to unemployment of all but one factor, seem to have distracted many economists from the positive value of Leontief's empirical investigation. Hoffmeyer (1958, p. 163) has particularly stressed this point.

In his 1953 paper, Leontief aggregated industries into 50 sectors, and factors into two groups, using data of 1947. In his 1956 paper he based himself again on the 1947 input-output matrix, but this time disaggregated into 192 sectors of commodity groups, the factors still, however, being limited to the two aggregate sectors of labor and capital.

Leontief's basic method was to determine a change Δy in the bill of goods, consisting of a proportionate reduction in exports and a proportionate reduction of "competitive imports" of equal value, compensated for by an increase in the production of import substitutes; Δy having been determined, the changes in factor requirements were computed from the formula $\Delta y(I - A)^{-1}B$. Leontief's paradoxical result was that the required capital-labor ratios would be increased, leading to the conclusion that exports were more labor intensive than imports. Leontief's own principal conclusion was that the quality of United States labor was considerably higher than that of labor abroad.

In making his calculation, Leontief classified goods such as coffee, tea, and jute as "non-competitive imports." These are commodities that are not ordinarily produced at home, and for which, consequently, there are no appropriate data in any case. These were assumed to remain constant,[16] while the "competitive imports" and exports both were hypothetically reduced. In one of his calculations, however (1956, p. 398, computation D) he enlarged this list considerably, to include among non-competitive imports most raw materials such as mineral ores, petroleum, and wood products; in this calculation, he arrived at precisely the opposite result, namely that a reduction of trade would decrease the required capital-labor ratio. This possibility had been anticipated by Diab (1956, p. 51) who argued that "a combination of capital and labor employed in the petroleum industry is more productive in Venezuela or Arabia than in the United States, and this is for the simple reason that American oil fields are less rich. Hence even if the same capital intensive technique of production is employed in both countries, the capital coefficient calculated on the basis of capital per capacity output would consequently be higher in the United States." A similar conclusion was reached by Vanek (1959).

The problem of interpreting Leontief's calculations brings to mind some acute observations made by Wicksell (1924; 1958, pp. 250–1) in his review of the 1924 Heckscher report on Swedish tariffs, which likewise contained some statistical puzzles:

---

[16]In his later calculations (1956) Leontief made allowance for the fact that a reduction in exports and competitive imports would lead to a change in the industrial demand for noncompetitive imports. But this made very little difference to the numerical results.

> Statistics are admirable when they confirm a conclusion which is plausible in itself. The empirical and rational proofs then reinforce one another. But if the statistics conflict with such a conclusion, their value is of course more dubious. The inconsistency *may* be due to incorrect theory, but it may also depend on a wrongly formulated or misinterpreted statistical observation. It is obvious that the latter alternative is more probable when the *a priori* reasons are strongest: if one fine day the sun rose at some other place or time than the one determined astronomically, we may be certain that it had nothing to do with the real sun, but was a parhelion.

That Leontief has presented us with a parhelion appears to be the prevailing view among his many critics. These may be roughly divided (with some overlap) into two groups: (1) those who question the accuracy or appropriateness of the data, and (2) those who are willing to accept the data at face value, but question their relevance or disagree with Leontief's own interpretation of them.

With respect to the data, Swerling (1954) argued that 1947 — the year for which all the input-output data were obtained — was an atypical year. This type of criticism could presumably be met only by repeating the computations for another year, and Leontief pointed out (1956, p. 396) that data for such computations were not available. Loeb (1954, p. 84) suggested that the differences in capital-labor ratios in export and competitive import industries might not be statistically significant; again, this is a very subjective matter that cannot very well be settled on the basis of computations for a single year. Leontief's basic computation (1953, p. 343; 1956, p. 392) showed that one million dollars of exports would require \$2,550,780 of capital and 182.313 man years of labor, hence a capital-labor ratio of 14,010; and that one million dollars of competitive imports would require \$3,091,339 of capital and 170.004 man years of labor, or a capital-labor ratio of 18,180. The quotient 18,180/14,010 = 1.2996 is Leontief's "index of comparative capital-labor intensity in the production of competitive import and export goods," which he denoted by α. Leontief's 1956 paper contained a misprint (p. 392), anticipated by Loeb (1954, p. 84) — in which the decimal point in the figure for man years of labor was replaced by a comma — which helped hide the fact that both these industrial groups evidently have an extraordinarily high capital-labor ratio, lending credence to Jones' (1956, pp. 8–9) conjecture that "both American exports and import-competing products [may be] produced with more capital intensive methods than abroad."

Leontief's definition of "capital" came in for some severe criticism on the part of Buchanan (1955, pp. 793–4), who described Leontief's capital coefficients as "investment requirement coefficients" which did not take account of the durability of capital. Diab (1956) made similar criticisms. These criticisms were met by Leontief in his 1956 calculations (p. 397, computation A), in which capital replacement was included in the input-output coefficients. The resulting value of his index α, (based on the same data, but in terms of a 192-sector model, rather than the aggregated 50-sector model used in 1953) was 1.1757. Unfortunately, it is not possible to tell whether this reduction was due to the adjustment for capital replacement, or to the disaggregation.

We turn now to the second class of dissenters, who have objected to Leontief's interpretation of his own data. These authors have, of course, found it necessary to supply their own alternative explanations, and the objections may be classified under the following heads: (1) perverse demand effects, (2) factor intensity reversal, and (3) Leontief's neglect of natural resources. Case (1) was made much of by Valavanis (1954), and its theoretical nature was clarified by Jones (1956); this is the possibility that a country's consumers may have a disproportionate demand for the product intensive in the country's relatively abundant factor, leading to the country importing this product and exporting the other. Such a theoretical possibility — without reference to the Heckscher-Ohlin theory — had already been pointed out by Leontief himself (1933). In the absence of specific information to the contrary, it seems reasonable, on the basis of the principle of insufficient reason, to assume that consumers in all countries have identical tastes. To allow for the anomalous case defended by Valavanis, one would then have to argue that Engel curves would fan out in the direction of capital intensive products (which — contrary to popular belief — are products such as minerals and foodstuffs, according to Leontief's calculations). Houthakker's studies (1957, 1960, 1963) suggest that there is considerable similarity in demand functions among countries, but to date there is scant evidence to support (or reject) the contention that capital intensive (and high income) countries have a disproportionate tendency to consume capital intensive goods. One might suppose that transport costs would induce a relative preference (in effect) for national products, owing to the relative price differential; but this could not explain the case in hand, for if a country imports the product intensive in its relatively abundant factor, this product will have the relatively higher price. The phenomenon must therefore be considered as a theoretical *curiosum,* and the burden of proof must surely be on those who wish to make a case for it.

The case (2) of factor intensity reversal is of much greater interest. This case was made, in effect, by Granick (1955), but apparently without his noticing its connection with the literature on factor price equalization. Jones (1956) and Brown (1957, p. 70), on the other hand, argued the case in the context of the Lemer-Samuelson theory. Within the framework of fixed technical coefficients, reversal of factor intensity is not possible; within a linear programming framework, however, it is possible to allow for great variability in methods of production used to produce a given commodity (as shown in Figure 6 above). The relevance of factor intensity reversal may be best appreciated by considering Figure 3. Let z_1 on the horizontal axis represent the quantity of labor, and z_2 on the vertical axis the quantity of capital. Suppose that the United States endowment ray OZ_a is rotated clockwise to the right side of cone (A) in such a way that it still remains within the cone; likewise, let the endowment ray OZ_b of the "rest of the world" be rotated to the right side of cone (B). Clearly, in this example, the United States is relatively more endowed with capital than the rest of the world. Nevertheless, the United States will concentrate its resources in its own labor intensive product — commodity 1 — and the rest of the world will at the same time concentrate its resources on its own labor intensive product — which in this case is commodity 2. Thus both countries may be expected to export their labor intensive products, and import their capital intensive ones. If the endowment rays were both swung to the left sides of the respective cones, both countries would be exporting their capital intensive product and importing their labor intensive one. In the remaining cases, in which both the endowment rays were either near the inside or near the outside edges of the respective cones, each country would produce a more nearly proportionate quantity of the two commodities, and there would be a smaller volume of trade. When reversal of factor intensity is present, it is therefore to be normally expected that each of the two trading countries will export the product intensive in the same factor. Thus it is not correct to infer from the fact that the United States exports its relatively labor intensive products, that the United States is relatively well endowed with labor in comparison with the rest of the world. The United States may export its labor intensive products because they are labor intensive *relative* to its factor endowment; and the export products may be relatively labor intensive precisely *because* the country is relatively well endowed with capital. This accords fully with the point cited above which was made by Jones (1956); see also Lancaster (1957a, p. 39).

A very similar analysis applies in the case in which two trading countries have different production functions. In Figure 3, let the isoquants for the United States be $\mathrm{Y}_1\mathrm{Y}_1$ and $\mathrm{Y}_2Y_2^*$; and imagine a similar branching of the curve $\mathrm{Y}_2\mathrm{Y}_2$ to a point Y_2^{**} (not shown) above and to the right of $\mathrm{Y}_1\mathrm{Y}_1$ so that the rest of the world produces according to the isoquants $\mathrm{Y}_1\mathrm{Y}_1$ and $Y_2^{**}\mathrm{Y}_2$. This merely means that — say, for reasons of climate, geography, or natural resources — commodity 1 is relatively labor intensive in the United States but relatively capital intensive abroad; and that commodity 2 is relatively capital intensive in the United States and relatively labor intensive abroad. Ellsworth (1954) evidently had this case in mind. Against this possibility Danière (1956, p. 427) argued that if such labor intensive methods were available abroad, "why are they not used in the United States?" Answer: (a) geographical differences may prevent it, and (b) even if such labor intensive methods are available in the United States, the high relative endowment of capital in the United

States, leading to a high relative cost of labor, may make the use of this method unprofitable (this is the case of factor intensity reversal).

We are now naturally led to objection (3), Leontief's neglect of natural resources. Buchanan (1955) objected very forcefully that in an ostensibly two-factor model, land should have been included under the heading of "capital" in order that any meaningful conclusions could be drawn; in other words, one can justify aggregation, but not exclusion, of factors. Brown (1957, pp. 67–8) adopted a more tolerant attitude, on the grounds that many of the factors of production under the heading of "natural resources" are unmeasurable. Leontief himself (1956, p. 395) pleaded lack of data, but also appears to have substantially conceded the force of the criticisms in the words: "The distinction between competitive and non-competitive imports can be viewed as the first step toward the extension of the empirical analysis of comparative costs to primary factors other than capital and labor." Even if countries have identical production functions, the effect of ignoring natural resources is to project isoquants onto the axes of capital and labor and, in view of the differences in natural endowments, to give rise to differences in production functions in terms of labor and capital. This brings us back to the analysis under objection (2), and if it is supposed that capital and resources are substitutes, and that both are complementary with labor, we have a ready resolution of the Leontief paradox: even though competitive imports are capital intensive in the United States, they are — according to this argument (especially that of Ellsworth (1954)) — labor intensive abroad.

Unfortunately this kind of argument is based on pure conjecture about the facts — in particular, about the technologies in foreign countries. And there are cogent reasons for questioning the conjecture: casual observation is sufficient to confirm that foreign methods of producing petroleum, copper, and other processed raw materials are just as capital intensive as those used in the United States. Indeed, a great many of the enterprises in question are owned and operated by United States corporations and may in a very real sense be regarded as an integral part of the United States economy, having little to contribute apart from tax payments to the local economies.

Information on differences in production methods in different countries is still not in a very satisfactory state, although progress has recently been made. A study by Chenery and Watanabe (1958), and one by Watanabe (1961) indicate that inter-country differences in production functions (especially in manufacturing) are not as great as might be supposed, particularly when differences in factor prices (and presumably factor qualities) are taken into account. Nevertheless these types of comparisons are beset by a special kind of difficulty: as anyone knows who has had some acquaintance with the methods used to build up input-output matrices, the data for different countries are not independent. The temptation is great to borrow pre-existing data from other countries when there is insufficient information at home. To some extent the apparent similarities in production functions for different countries may be merely a reflection of this fact.

There is also little evidence to date on differences in labor skills among countries, although the superior quality of United States labor is widely acknowledged. Leontief has cited a study by Kravis (1956), indicating that wages are higher in United States export industries than in import-competing industries, as supporting evidence; but this conflicts with Leontief's assumption of a homogeneous labor force which should, presumably, earn the same wages in each industry, and furthermore — as a consequence of his special assumptions of fixed proportions in production and consumption — earn zero wages in both. And in any case this kind of evidence has no direct bearing on international comparisons.

It has been suggested by Brown (1957, p. 71) that "the test of the relative economic scarcity of labour and capital is presumably their relative price." Plausible as this criterion sounds, it has two shortcomings: (1) if two countries have identical homogeneous production functions, and if their factor endowments lie in the same diversification cone, then the relative (and absolute) prices of labor and capital will be the same in spite of differences in their relative scarcity — this is just the factor price equalization theorem; (2) if production functions and qualities of the factors are different, then no inference can be drawn whatsoever from relative factor prices concerning relative factor scarcities. Indeed, if production functions are identical and homogeneous, up to multiplication of the inputs by suitable constants; if reversal of factor intensity is ruled out a priori; and if countries' factor endowments are assumed (a priori) to lie in the same diversification cone; *then* differences in factor prices can legitimately be used to draw inferences concerning the efficiency constants required to relate the quantities of the countries' factors. This is the inference which Leontief has drawn, namely that labor in the United States is more efficient than labor abroad, by a ratio of three to one. But the inference implicitly assumes all the conditions that have just been listed; and Leontief's procedure therefore comes perilously close to constituting the "implicit theorizing" against which he had so strongly warned in 1937.

No one can deny the fact that there are enormous differences in qualities of labor as between the United States and other countries. But first it must be noted that the relevant comparison is not, say, between workers in the United States and workers in Chile, but rather between copper miners in the United States and copper miners in Chile; the case for differences in quality or in earnings would be much more difficult to argue in the latter, more relevant, case. Secondly, it is most doubtful indeed whether superior and inferior labor can be regarded as perfect substitutes, to be compared simply by saying that United States labor is equivalent to three times as much foreign labor. Thirdly, while capital and unskilled labor are substitutes, capital and skilled labor are complements, leading to the conjecture that Leontief may have underestimated the quantity of capital required in industry in the United States. For instance, skilled workers are "produced" by educational institutions, which are presumably quite capital intensive; their productivity is aided by public health, which requires capital intensive hospital and sewage installations. It is also difficult to believe that the United States export industry makes no use of the vast highway transportation system, and yet this is what Leontief's figures show. Failure to take account of what is usually and unfortunately described as social "overhead" capital must surely cause a distinct bias in Leontief's results.[17]

How is this parhelion then to be explained? We must return to Leontief's computation D (1956, p. 398) in which the list of "non-competitive imports" was augmented to comprise all agricultural commodities other than dairy and poultry products, grains, cotton, and tobacco; all minerals other than coal, silicates, and sulphur; and pulp and primary copper. Leontief's coefficient became $\alpha = .9171$. And when 1951 data were used for the percentage composition of exports and noncompetitive imports, the result was $\alpha = .8813$ (in the 192-sector calculation in which the above listed products were not included among the non-competitive imports, the corresponding value of α was 1.0577). Thus Hoffmeyer (1958, p. 168) concluded: "If goods relying to a large extent on natural resources are excluded we find the normally expected picture that the U.S. exports capital intensive goods and imports labour intensive goods."

Hoffmeyer's conclusion is still not completely satisfactory. It has already been observed that foreign petroleum, copper, and newsprint production is highly capital intensive, probably as much so as in the United States, in relation to labor; but as Diab pointed out, more productive, and hence requiring a smaller quantity of capital in relation to output. Under such circumstances, it must be asked: Why are these raw materials produced domestically, when they could be imported at lower cost? Transport costs can provide part of the answer, but surely not all. The industries in question — including cattle raising, orange growing, petroleum and copper mining — apart

[17]Elliott (1958, p. 117) made the interesting suggestion that "a great deal of minute international division of labor may occur," and that "computations based on finer classifications give less support to the conclusion that imports are relatively capital intensive." Elliott had in mind the effect of Marshallian external economies, a consideration that Leontief (1958, p. 120) dismissed without further comment. Actually, as pointed out above, it is not possible to tell whether the reduction in Leontief's α was due to the finer subdivision or to the allowance for capital replacement.

from being natural resource industries, also can be characterized by the fact that they all enjoy in varying degrees some measure of government subsidy or protection, whether in the form of price supports, depletion allowances, tariffs, import quotas, or even embargos. That California orange growers would suffer from Mexican competition, or Texas oil producers from Venezuelan competition, these producers would themselves be the first to acknowledge. Leontief has based his entire case on the implicit assumption that the law of comparative advantage determines the existing pattern of trade. Perhaps the real significance of his factual discovery lies in the alternative inference — evidently overlooked by all the critics[18] — that restrictive policies have led to a far costlier misallocation of resources than anyone had heretofore imagined.

9. The Homohypallagic Production Function

A most important development has been the derivation and application of a new form of production function, characterized by a constant elasticity of substitution. The derivation was obtained independently by R. Solow and K. J. Arrow for two factors, and reported in a joint paper by Arrow, Chenery, Minhas, and Solow (1961, p. 226n), hereafter to be referred to as ACMS. The derivation was extended to m factors by Uzawa (1962), and further properties of the function (such as concavity) have been deduced by McFadden (1963). The ACMS paper contained a comparative study of production in the United States and Japan, reported in greater detail by Minhas (1962); a still more extensive multicountry empirical study has been undertaken by Minhas (1963).

One may distinguish between the special and general forms of the CES (constant elasticity of substitution) production function, dubbed "homohypallagic" by Minhas. The special form is $f(x) = (\sum_{i=1}^{m} \alpha_i x_i^{-\beta})^{-1/\beta}$, where $\beta > -1$ and $\beta \neq 0$, and where $\alpha_i \geqq 0$ and $\sum_{i=1}^{m} \alpha_i > 0$. As $\beta \to 0$ it is known that $f(x) \to \prod_{i=1}^{m} x_i^{\alpha'_i}$, where

[18] With the notable and recent exception of Travis (1964, p. 171), whose work unfortunately appeared too late to receive the attention it merits in this survey.

$\alpha'_i = \alpha_i / \sum_{j=1}^{m} \alpha_j$, hence clearly $\sum_{i=1}^{m} \alpha'_i = 1$.[19] Thus the Cobb-Douglas function is the limiting form as $\beta \to 0$. The elasticity of substitution is $\sigma = 1/(1+\beta)$, which is the same between any two factors. Putting $\gamma = \left(\sum_{j=1}^{m} \alpha_j\right)^{-1/\beta}$, the Arrow-Solow production function may be written in the form $f(x) = \gamma \left(\sum_{i=1}^{m} \alpha'_i x_i^{-\beta}\right)^{-1/\beta}$; the parameters α'_i, β, γ were called by ACMS the distribution parameters, the substitution parameter, and the (neutral) efficiency parameter, respectively. If γ is now held fixed in the limiting process as $\beta \to 0$, the resulting Cobb-Douglas production function becomes $f(x) \to \gamma \prod_{i=1}^{m} x_i^{\alpha'_i}$.

An illustration is given in Figure 11 of a family of CES production functions. The curves are isoquants representing factor combinations yielding a unit output according to the formula $\left(\frac{1}{2} z_1^{-\beta} + \frac{1}{2} z_2^{-\beta}\right)^{-1/\beta} = 1$. For $\beta < -1\,(\sigma < 0)$ the curvature is inappropriate, the relevant isoquants being those corresponding to $\beta > -1\,(\sigma > 0)$, for which the CES function is concave. It should be noted that for $-1 < \beta < 0\,(\infty > \sigma > 1)$, the isoquants touch the coordinate axes at a point of tangency, indicating that the commodity can be produced entirely with one factor;[20] whereas for

[19] This result is easily obtained by means of l'Hospital's rule, as follows:

$$\begin{aligned}
\lim_{\beta \to 0} \left(\sum_{i=1}^{m} \alpha_i x_i^{-\beta}\right)^{-1/\beta} &= \lim \exp\left\{(-1/\beta) \log \sum_{i=1}^{m} \alpha_i x_i^{-\beta}\right\} \\
&= \lim \exp\left\{\left(\sum_{i=1}^{m} \alpha_i x_i^{-\beta} \log x_i\right) \Big/ \left(\sum_{i=1}^{m} \alpha_i x_i^{-\beta}\right)\right\} \\
&= \exp\left\{\sum_{i=1}^{m} \alpha'_i \log x_i\right\} \\
&= \prod_{i=1}^{m} x_i^{\alpha'_i}.
\end{aligned}$$

[20] Leontief (1964, p. 345) has used this property of the CES function as a basis for questioning its adequacy as a description of industrial processes. In his words: "Except in its degenerate form when $\sigma = 0$, the CES function itself represents

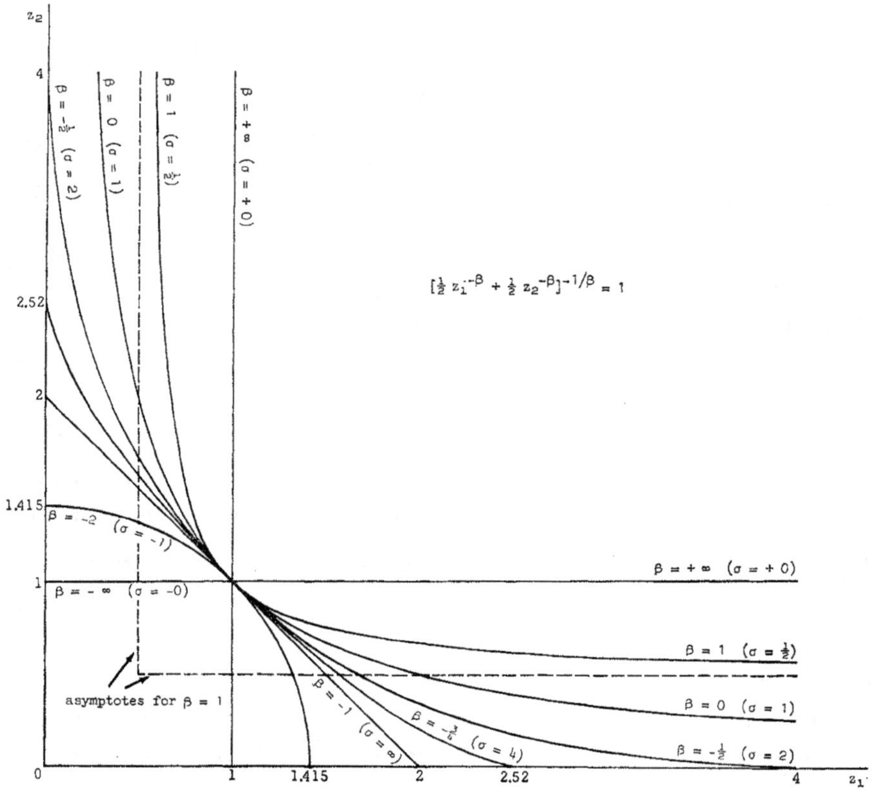

Figure 11.

$0 > \beta > \infty(1 > \sigma > 0)$ the isoquants approach asymptotes, the distance of the asymptotes from the origin increasing with β, as well as with output y.

The general form of the CES production function, derived by Uzawa (1962), is defined as follows. Let the set of integers

... a special case of homogeneous production characterized by literally unlimited substitution possibilities between factors, thus implying — when these factors are capital and labor — that any amount of finished product can be obtained with a practically negligible amount of either capital or labor provided the supply of the other factors is large enough." This is not correct; it applies only in the case $1 \leqq \sigma < \infty$, and even then (owing to the tangency) the limiting case in which only one factor would be employed would occur only when that factor was free.

$M = \{1, 2, \ldots, m\}$ be partitioned into a collection of s subsets M_j, each with m_j elements, where $\sum_{j=1}^{s} m_j = m$. The production function is defined by $y = \prod_{j=1}^{s} z_j^{\tau_j}$, where $\tau_j > 0$ and $\sum_{j=1}^{s} \tau_j = 1$, and each z_j has the special form $z_j = \left(\sum_{i \in M_j} \alpha_{ij} x_j^{-\beta_j}\right)^{-1/\beta_j}$ where $\alpha_{ij} > 0$ and $\beta_j > -1$ and $\neq 0$. Thus the elasticity of substitution is $\sigma_j = 1/(1 + \beta_j)$ between any two factors corresponding to the same subset M_j, and $= 1$ otherwise; this is the most general form of production function (Uzawa showed) such that the elasticity of substitution between any pair of factors is a constant.

Returning to the special form, suppose there are n commodities, with production functions

$$y_i = f_i(x_{i1}, x_{i2}, \ldots, x_{im}) = \left(\sum_{j=1}^{m} \alpha_{ij} x_{ij}^{-\beta_i}\right)^{1/\beta_i} \qquad (i = 1, 2, \ldots, n) \tag{1}$$

where x_{ij} is the amount of the jth factor employed in the production of the ith commodity. Let w_j be the jth factor price; then the corresponding factor demand functions are[21]

$$x_{ij} = h_{ij}(y_i; w) = y_i \alpha_{ij}^{\sigma_i} w_j^{-\sigma_i} \left(\sum_{k=1}^{m} \alpha_{ik}^{\sigma_i} w_k^{-\sigma_i}\right)^{\sigma_i/(1-\sigma_i)} \tag{2}$$

[21] As follows. The marginal productivity of the jth factor in the production of the ith commodity is $\partial f_i / \partial x_{ij} = \alpha_{ij} x_{ij}^{-(1+\beta_i)}$. Since factor prices must be proportional to marginal productivities, we have $w_j / w_k = (\alpha_{ij}/\alpha_{ik})(x_{ij}/x_{ik})^{-(1+\beta_i)}$, yielding the $m - 1$ equations $x_{ij} = x_{ik}(\alpha_{ik}/w_k)^{-\sigma_i} \cdot (\alpha_{ij}/w_j)^{\sigma_i}$, where $\sigma_i = 1/(1 + \beta_i)$. When these are substituted back into the ith production function, we obtain, as functions of the factor prices, the input-output coefficients

$$a_{ik} = x_{ik}/y_i = (\alpha_{ik}/w_k)^{\sigma_i} \left(\sum_{j=1}^{m} \alpha_{ij}^{\sigma_i} w_j^{1-\sigma_i}\right)^{\alpha_i/(1-\sigma_i)}.$$

Minimum unit costs are then obtained by computing the summations $\sum_{k=1}^{m} w_k x_{ik}/y_i$, yielding the expression (3) in the text.

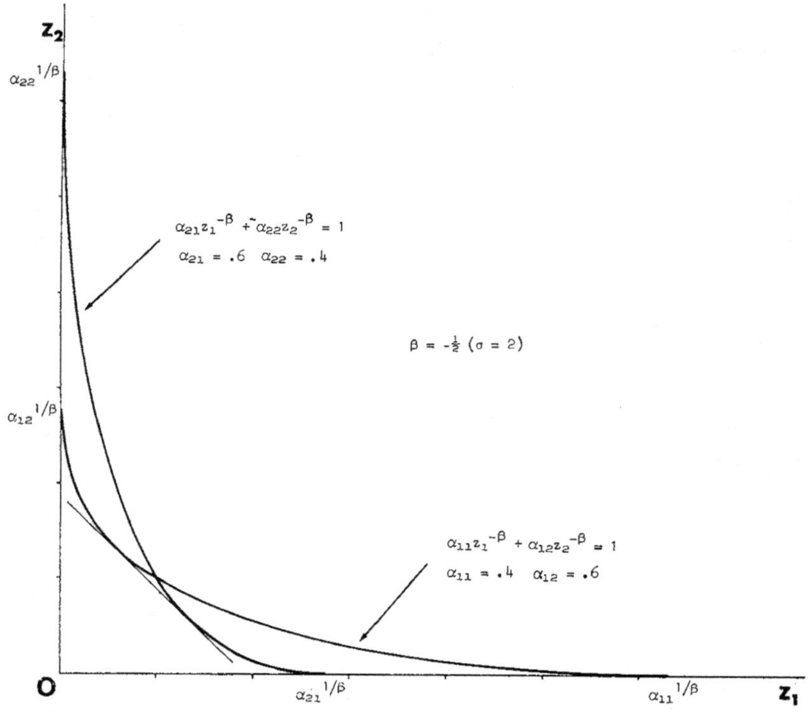

Figure 12.

for $i = 1, 2, \ldots, n$, and $j = 1, 2, \ldots, m$, and where $w = (w_1 w_2, \ldots, w_m)$, whence the minimum unit cost functions are

$$\begin{aligned} c_i &= g_i(w_1, w_2, \ldots, w_m) \\ &= \left(\sum_{j=1}^{m} \alpha_{ij}^{\sigma_i} w_j^{1-\sigma_i}\right)^{1/(1-\sigma_i)} \qquad (i = 1, 2, \ldots, n). \end{aligned} \tag{3}$$

From the assumptions of perfect competition, we have $c_i \geqq p_i$, where p_i is the ith commodity price, equality holding whenever $y_i > 0$. The problem, which was considered in Section 3.3, now arises again as to whether and under what conditions the equality will hold for at least m of the commodities.

The conditions for complete diversification of production when $m = n = 2$ are illustrated in Figures 12 and 13. Figure 12 illustrates

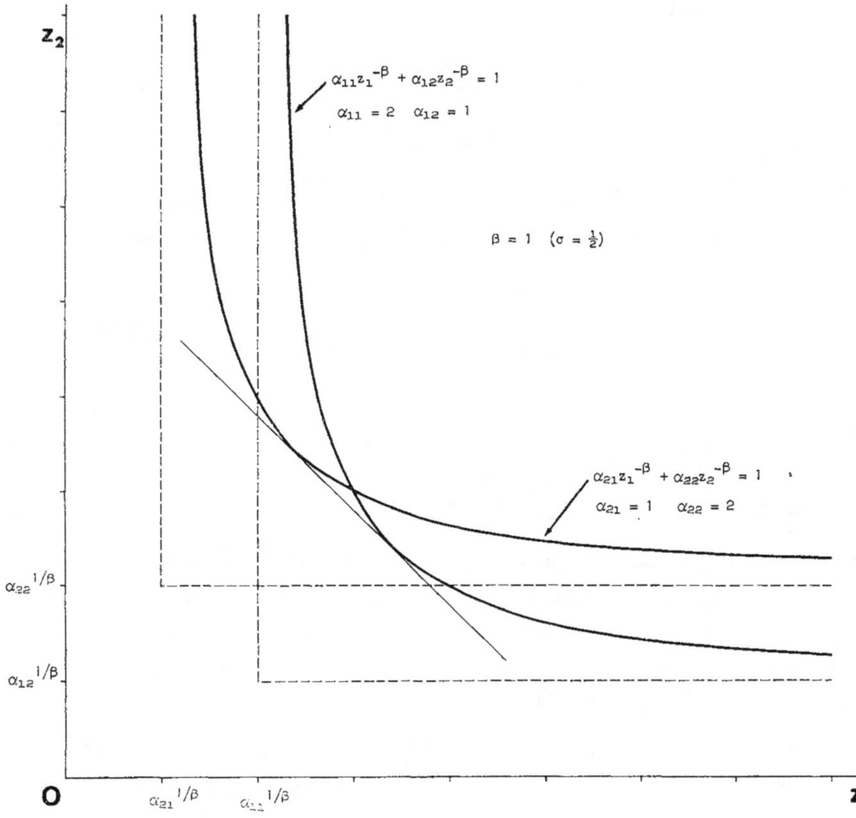

Figure 13.

the case in which $1 < \sigma < \infty$ in both industries; from (3) it is readily verified that $g_i(w) \to 0$ as $w_j \to 0$, for any j, which corresponds in Figure 12 to unit costs being zero in both industries if either one of the factor prices is equal to zero. This means that Kuhn's Intensity Hypothesis is necessarily violated for the case of CES production functions with greater than unit elasticity of substitution; nevertheless a common tangent to the isoquants certainly exists in Figure 12, so that a solution with complete diversification exists in spite of the failure of Kuhn's condition.

Figure 13 illustrates the case in which the elasticity of substitution is less than unity in both industries. For the case $m = n = 2$, we obtain from (3):

$$g_1(w_1, 0) = \alpha_{11}^{1/\beta_1} w_1; \quad g_1(0, w_2) = \alpha_{12}^{1/\beta_2} w_2;$$
$$g_2(w_1, 0) = \alpha_{21}^{1/\beta_1} w_1; \quad g_2(0, w_2) = \alpha_{22}^{1/\beta_2} w_2;$$

where use is made of the fact that $\sigma_i/(1-\sigma_i) = 1/\beta_i$, since $\sigma_i = 1/(1+\beta_i)$ by definition. Now Kuhn's Intensity Hypothesis states that

$$g_1(w_1, 0)/p_1 > g_2(w_1, 0)/p_2;$$
$$g_2(0, w_2)/p_2 > g_1(0, w_2)/p_1,$$

whence we obtain the condition

$$\frac{\alpha_{12}^{1/\beta_2}}{\alpha_{22}^{1/\beta_2}} < \frac{p_1}{p_2} < \frac{\alpha_{11}^{1/\beta_1}}{\alpha_{21}^{1/\beta_1}}, \tag{4}$$

which emphasizes the dependence of the existence condition on commodity prices. What this inequality states — as is clear from Figure 13, which illustrates the case in which $\beta_1 = \beta_2 = \beta = 1$ — is that the relative prices of the two commodities must be such that the asymptotes of the two isoquants will cross. Again, it is not difficult to see that this condition is unnecessarily strong: it is quite possible for the isoquants to cross even though their asymptotes do not. Another difficulty in the interpretation of Kuhn's Intensity Hypothesis in the present case is this: as $w_j \to 0$, $h_{ij}(y_i; w) \to \infty$ even though $w_j h_{ij} \to 0$, that is, as a factor price approaches zero, the demand for this factor will approach infinity even though its cost approaches zero. The minimum unit cost functions are therefore not economically meaningful when some factor prices are zero.

If the inequality (4) is interpreted to mean that there exist *some* relative prices for the commodities such that the asymptotes cross, then it can be written in the form

$$\begin{vmatrix} \alpha_{11}^{1/\beta_1} & \alpha_{12}^{1/\beta_2} \\ \alpha_{21}^{1/\beta_1} & \alpha_{22}^{1/\beta_2} \end{vmatrix} > 0. \tag{5}$$

In the limiting Leontief case, as $\beta_i \to +\infty$ (and $\sigma_i \to 0$) this inequality becomes necessary and sufficient; a generalization of this formula also has general validity for the case of more than two commodities and factors, as will be apparent presently.

Let us assume now that at least m commodities are produced; specifically, and without loss of generality, let us suppose that the first m out of the n commodities are produced in positive amounts, so that their prices may be equated with minimum unit costs as follows:

$$\begin{aligned} p_i &= g_i(w_1, w_2, \ldots, w_m) \\ &= \left(\sum_{j=1}^{m} \alpha_{ij}^{\sigma_i} w_j^{1-\sigma_i} \right)^{1/(1-\sigma_i)} \qquad (i = 1, 2, \ldots, m). \end{aligned} \tag{6}$$

Owing to these equations (6), the factor demand functions (2) may be simplified as follows:

$$x_{ij} = y_i \alpha_{ij}^{\sigma_i} w_j^{-\sigma_i} p_i^{\sigma_i}. \tag{7}$$

Thus the input-output coefficients (in Samuelson's (1953) notation, which — it should be recalled — are the transposes of Leontief's with subscripts interchanged) may be written as functions of the real factor prices in the form

$$a_{ij} = x_{ij}/y_i = (\alpha_{ij} p_i / w_j)^{\sigma_i}, \tag{8}$$

which states that the amount of the jth factor required to produce a unit of the ith commodity is a function of the ratio of the ith commodity price to the jth factor price, and, in particular, is independent of the remaining factor prices. It is this especially simple formula (8) which has been used, as we shall see later on, by ACMS and Minhas in order to obtain empirical estimates of the σ_i.

Equations (6) define a differentiable mapping g from the m-dimensional space W of factor prices into the n-dimensional space P of commodity prices, whose Jacobian matrix is $g'(w) = [\partial g_i/\partial w_j] = [(\alpha_{ij} p_i / w_j)^{\sigma_i}]$, which factors into the product of the diagonal matrix $[p_i^{\sigma_i}]$ and the matrix $[(\alpha_{ij}/w_j)^{\sigma_i}]$. Since $p_i^{\sigma_i} > 0$, it is clearly a necessary condition for the global univalence of the mapping g that the matrix $[(\alpha_{ij}/w_j)^{\sigma_i}]$ be nonsingular for all factor prices w_j. But this implies that $\sigma_1 = \sigma_2 = \ldots = \sigma_m$: for suppose that $\sigma_i \neq \sigma_h$; then the equations $w_j^{\sigma_i - \sigma_h} = \alpha_{ij}^{\sigma_i}/\alpha_{hj}^{\sigma_h}$ have a unique positive solution for all $j = 1, 2, \ldots, m$. If we then set $w_j = (\alpha_{ij}^{\sigma_i}/\alpha_{hj}^{\sigma_h})^{1/(\sigma_i - \sigma_h)}$ for each j, we have $(\alpha_{ij}/w_j)^{\sigma_i} = (\alpha_{hj}/w_j)^{\sigma_h}$, so the ith and hth rows of $[(\alpha_{ij}/w_j)^{\sigma_i}]$ become identical. In words, as long as two elasticities of substitution differ, there exist factor prices for which there will be reversal of factor intensity between the respective commodities; this is so because the elements $(\alpha_{ij} p_i/w_j)^{\sigma_i}$ of the Jacobian are (see equation (8)) simply the input-output coefficients $a_{ij} = x_{ij}/y_i$.

In the case of CES production functions, the nonvanishing of the Jacobian determinant $|\partial g_i/\partial w_j|$ for all factor prices w_j turns out to be a sufficient as well as a necessary condition for the global univalence of the mapping $g(w)$. For, as we have just seen, the condition implies that the elasticities of substitution σ_i are all equal to one another. Putting $\sigma_i = \sigma$ for $i = 1, 2, \ldots, m$, from the equations for minimum unit cost we have, for $\sigma \neq 1$,

$$p_i^{1-\sigma} = \sum_{j=1}^{m} \alpha_{ij}^{\sigma} w_j^{1-\sigma} \quad (i = 1, 2, \ldots, m). \tag{9}$$

These equations are linear in $p_i^{1-\sigma}$ and $w_j^{1-\sigma}$, and these terms are in one-to-one correspondence with p_i and w_j respectively. Thus the nonvanishing of the Jacobian implies that of $|\alpha_{ij}^{\sigma}|$, and owing to the linearity, this defines a one-to-one correspondence between the p_i and w_j. In the case $\sigma \to 1$ we have[22]

$$\log p_i = k_i + l_i \sum_{j=1}^{m} \alpha_{ij} \log w_j \quad (i = 1, 2, \ldots, m), \tag{10}$$

which is again linear. Thus for all $\sigma > 0$, the condition $|\alpha_{ij}^{\sigma}| \neq 0$ is necessary and sufficient for univalence of the mapping $g(w)$, provided $\sigma_i = \sigma$ for all i.

In the special case $\sigma_i = \sigma$ for all i, some particularly simple conditions for complete diversification of production can be obtained.

[22]Where $h = 1/\sum_{k=1}^{m} \alpha_{ik}, \alpha'_{ij} = l_i \alpha_{ij}$, and $k_i = -\sum_{j=1}^{m} \alpha'_{ij} \log \alpha'_{ij}$.

First, consider the special Cobb-Douglas case (10): as long as the matrix $[\alpha_{ij}]$ is nonsingular, there exists a unique solution for the log w_j, given *any* values for the log p_i; that is, there exists a unique positive solution for the factor prices w_j given any positive values for the commodity prices p_i. Thus, nonvanishing of the Jacobian is necessary and sufficient for the possibility of complete diversification in the Cobb-Douglas case, even through Kuhn's Intensity Hypothesis is necessarily violated. Secondly, in the more general case represented by equations (9), in which elasticities of substitution are equal among industries (but not necessarily equal to unity), the following can be said: a sufficient condition for the existence of a set of positive prices p_i for which the equations (9) have a positive solution in the w_j is that the matrix $[\alpha_{ij}^{\sigma}]$ should have positive principal minors. This is an immediate result of a lemma proved by Gale (1962), which was the principal lemma required for his univalence condition. One may conjecture that, as in (5), this may be generalized to the condition that $[\alpha_{ij}^{\sigma_i}]$ should have positive principal minors, in the more general case of unequal elasticities of substitution among industries.

One of the remarkable outcomes of the study of Arrow, Chenery, Minhas, and Solow is therefore the following: in the very special case of equal elasticities of substitution σ among industries, the rather mild condition $[\alpha_{ij}^{\sigma}] \neq 0$ ensures a one-to-one correspondence between factor prices and commodity prices; but if any elasticities of substitution are unequal, the correspondence is necessarily many-to-one. In particular, if elasticities of substitution are unequal, since global univalence breaks down, the Gale-Nikaidô conditions are necessarily violated; on the other hand, if elasticities of substitution are equal, the Gale-Nikaidô conditions are unnecessarily strong, the nonvanishing of the Jacobian being sufficient. Thus the Gale-Nikaidô conditions do not on the face of it appear to be entirely appropriate or relevant to the univalence aspect of the factor-price equalization problem, at least in the case of CES production functions. On the other hand, they turn out, in the case of equal elasticities of substitution among industries, to be sufficient conditions for the existence of solutions with complete diversification of production, and are therefore very relevant to this other aspect of the factor price equalization theory. It may also be shown (see Chipman (1964)) that they are closely related to the conditions required for the generalization of the Stolper-Samuelson theorem to more than two commodities and factors.

From a theoretical point of view, the ACMS study appears at first to be quite damaging to the Lerner-Samuelson factor price equalization theory, for not only does it cast doubt on one of the principal assumptions of that theory — the invariance of factor intensities — but it goes further and implies that, except under what apparently seem to be very stringent conditions (equality of elasticities of substitution among industries), the factor intensity hypothesis is necessarily violated for some factor prices. Before jumping to this conclusion, however, it is well to keep in mind that the assumption of constant elasticities of substitution is just one kind of simplification that can be introduced into the theory; that of absence of factor intensity reversal (or the "strong intensity hypothesis" — that the relative intensity of a commodity in a factor is invariant with respect to factor prices) is another.

All we can say, therefore, is that these two alternative kinds of simplification are incompatible with one another, except for the special case in which elasticities of substitution are equal among industries. When it is kept in mind that in the case of the special form of the CES function (when there are more than two factors) the elasticity of substitution must, in any industry, be the same as between any two factors, it is apparent that the assumption of constant elasticities of substitution is already quite stringent, as it introduces a rather artificial symmetry among the factors.

As long as one stays within the context of CES production functions, in order to uphold the validity of the factor price equalization theory is becomes necessary either to defend, as an empirical proposition, the equality of elasticities of substitution among industries, or else to argue that the critical values of factor prices that cause the Jacobian to vanish (and lead to reversal of factor intensities) will never be observed. The latter argument depends, in turn, on the hypothesis that relative factor endowments do not vary too greatly among countries.

In order to appreciate this, we may consider the simple case of two factors and two commodities. As long as $\alpha_{ij} > 0$, the Gale conditions simply require that the matrix

$$\begin{bmatrix} \left(\frac{\alpha_{11}}{w_1}\right)^{\sigma_1} & \left(\frac{\alpha_{12}}{w_2}\right)^{\sigma_1} \\ \left(\frac{\alpha_{21}}{w_1}\right)^{\sigma_2} & \left(\frac{\alpha_{22}}{w_2}\right)^{\sigma_2} \end{bmatrix}$$

shall have a positive determinant. This in turn implies that

$$\left(\frac{\alpha_{11}}{\alpha_{12}}\right)^{\sigma_1} \left(\frac{\alpha_{22}}{\alpha_{21}}\right)^{\sigma_2} \left(\frac{w_1}{w_2}\right)^{\sigma_2-\sigma_1} > 1.$$

This will hold provided the relative factor prices always satisfy the inequality

$$\frac{w_1}{w_2} < \left(\frac{\alpha_{11}}{\alpha_{12}}\right)^{\sigma_1/(\sigma_1-\sigma_2)} \left(\frac{\alpha_{22}}{\alpha_{21}}\right)^{\sigma_2/(\sigma_1-\sigma_2)},$$

which in turn can be reduced to the condition that in all countries the endowment of factor 2 relative to that of factor 1 must not exceed some critical ratio.

The ACMS study was devoted in large part to empirical estimation of the relevant parameters. This was done by taking advantage of the form of the input-demand functions $x_{ij} = y_i(\alpha_{ij}^{\sigma_i})(w_j/p_i)^{-\sigma_i}$ corresponding to a given rate of output y_i (see equation (8)). Putting $\tau_{ij} = \log \alpha_{ij}^{\sigma_i}$, we have

$$\log (x_{ij}/y_i) = \tau_{ij} - \sigma_i \log (w_j/p_i).$$

Treating the logarithm of the input-output ratio as the dependent variable, and that of the corresponding price ratio as the independent variable, the parameters τ_{ij} and σ_i may be estimated by the method of least squares, and from these one obtains an estimate of $\alpha_{ij} = e^{\tau_{ij}/\sigma_i}$. This is essentially the method employed by ACMS.

ACMS considered two factors of production (labor and capital), and assumed that for each industry (a large number of which were considered) the elasticity of substitution σ_i was the same in each country. Letting labor correspond to $j = 1$, x_{i1} was taken to be the amount of labor (in man years) employed in the ith industry, y_i the value added to national product by the ith industry (in thousands of U.S. dollars), and w_1/p_i the money wage rate (the total labor cost in the ith industry divided by x_{i1}) in dollars per man year. Thus the units of measurement for each commodity were chosen so as to make $p_i = 1$. Then σ_i was estimated by fitting the above equation to data on 19 countries. It should be remarked that the wage rate w_1 differed among industries, and should therefore more properly be denoted w_{i1}; these different wage rates were used in the computation, but ACMS did not remark on the fact that this amounted to tacit recognition of the failure of one of the principal assumptions of the factor price equalization theory.

The method of estimation used by ACMS and Minhas raises a number of questions. In the first place, for any industry (say the ith) each choice of factor (with observations w_j and x_{ij}) provides a different estimator for the same parameter σ_i. Still more estimators may be obtained from the equations $x_{ij}/x_{ik} = (\alpha_{ij}/\alpha_{ik})^{\sigma_i} \cdot (w_j/w_k)^{-\sigma_i}$, which in turn provide estimators for the ratios α_{ij}/α_{ik}, which will be different from the ratios of the estimators of α_{ij} and α_{ik} obtained from the previous equations. From a theoretical point of view it would certainly seem preferable to apply an iterative method to the equations $p_i^{1-\sigma_i} = \sum_{j=1}^{n} \alpha_{ij}^{\sigma_i} w_j^{1-\sigma_i}$, choosing as estimator for σ_i the value of σ_i that maximizes the multiple correlation coefficient obtained from the regression of $p_i^{1-\sigma_i}$ on the $w_j^{1-\sigma_i}$. Unfortunately, satisfactory techniques for this kind of procedure have not yet been developed.

There was, of course, an obvious reason for preferring the demand-for-labor equation to the demand-for-capital equation, which was that data on quantity of labor and on wage rates are believed to be more reliable than those for capital and interest (or rental) on capital. But the method used seems very much like pulling a rabbit out of a hat: an estimate is obtained for the elasticity of substitution between labor and capital, without employing any data whatsoever relating to capital. The other factor might just as well be given a different name, such as "land." It was on this basis that Minhas (1962, 1963) concluded that elasticities of substitution tended to be smaller than unity, and to differ from industry to industry. On the other hand Leontief (1964) performed calculations (using Minhas' (1963) data on capital) from the more symmetric formula $x_{ij}/x_{ik} = (\alpha_{ij}/\alpha_{ik})^{\alpha_i} \cdot (w_j/w_k)^{-\sigma_i}$ using both capital and labor data, but apparently used it only to obtain estimates for the term α_{ij}/α_{ik} given Minhas' estimate for σ_i. It would be interesting to see whether — as one may suspect — the estimates for σ_i obtained in this way would come closer to the value $\sigma_i = 1$, rather than the less than unit estimates that Minhas obtained in nearly all cases.

Another question relates to an ever-present bugbear — the identification problem. Since the equations fitted by ACMS are basically demand equations, the question arises as to whether factor supplies are elastic with respect to the given industries; if not, the least squares estimates of the σ_i obtained by ACMS would be subject to a downward bias, which might partly explain why most of the estimates obtained were less than one.

There is still a further feature of the estimation procedure used by ACMS and Minhas that may have biased their results. The data on value added and wage rates were converted at existing official or free exchange rates into U.S. dollars, on the basis of current values in local currencies. From (7) it follows that the relevant regression equation should have the form

$$x_{ij}/p_i y_i = \alpha_{ij}^{\sigma_i} w_j^{-\sigma_i} p_i^{\sigma_i - 1}, \tag{11}$$

whereas the regression equation actually fitted by ACMS and Minhas was of the form

$$x_{ij}/p_i y_i = \alpha_{ij}^{\sigma_i} w_j^{-\sigma_i} \tag{12}$$

This is presumably the reason why ACMS (1961, p. 227) and Minhas (1963, p. 19) made the assumptions — whose role or purpose was nowhere explained — that commodity prices did not vary systematically with wage rates, and that overvaluation or undervaluation of exchange rates likewise did not vary systematically with wage rates. Certainly these two conditions are necessary and sufficient for the legitimate use of (12) as the regression equation in place of (11); specifically, if the neglect of the variable p_i in (12) is not to cause bias in the estimation of σ_i, it must be assumed that the logarithms of p_i and w_j should have a zero correlation in the sample.

There are ample reasons, however, for supposing $\log p_i$ and $\log w_j$ to be positively correlated. According to Minhas (1963, p. 19n), "the assumption of an orthogonal relationship between local commodity prices and wage rates is far less stringent as compared with the alternative assumption that could have been made, i.e., that, ignoring transport costs, the prices of internationally traded goods are the same everywhere." (Presumably, Minhas meant to say "orthogonal relationship between deviations of logarithms of local commodity prices and of logarithms of wage rates from their sample means.") This is not so; if domestic prices of export goods are lower than their prices abroad, and if these goods are labor intensive, wage rates will be correspondingly lower (this follows from the factor price equalization theory). Similarly, any overvaluation or undervaluation of exchange rates necessarily affects prices and wages in the same direction. It is to be supposed, therefore, that logarithms of prices and logarithms of wage rates will be positively correlated in the case of labor intensive commodities, and it is readily verified that this will lead to a downward bias in the estimate of the elasticity of substitution. It is interesting to note that Minhas obtained low elasticities of substitution precisely in the highly labor intensive industries (1963, p. 20).

While the labor demand equation was sufficient to obtain estimates of σ_i and α_{i1} (w_1 being the wage rate), in order to obtain an estimate for α_{i2} it was necessary, as Leontief (1964) pointed out, to use the capital demand equation (also providing an alternative estimate of σ_i). After estimating the σ_i and the α_{i1} from the labor demand equation in each industry, ACMS inverted the equation $x_{i1}/x_{i2} = (\alpha_{i1}/\alpha_{i2})^{\sigma_i}(w_1/w_2)^{-\sigma_i}$ to get $\alpha_{i2}/\alpha_{i1} = (w_2/w_1)(x_{i2}/x_{i1})^{1/\sigma_i}$. Given the observations (one for each country) on w_2/w_1 and x_{i2}/x_{i1}, and the previously obtained estimate of σ_i (assumed the same for all countries), a series of estimates of α_{i2}/α_{i1} were obtained (one for each country as well as each industry i). Individual estimates for each country were also obtained for α_{i2} and α_{i1}, presumably in a similar fashion (not specified by ACMS). It was then desired to test whether, respectively, the parameters α_{i1}, α_{i2}, α_{i2}/α_{i1} were equal among countries. Their conclusion was that the ratio α_{i2}/α_{i1} was equal among countries, hence production functions could be written in the form $y_i = \gamma_i(\sum_{j=1}^{m} \alpha'_{ij} x_{ij}^{-\beta_i})^{-1/\beta_i}$, where (for each industry i) the β_i and $\alpha'_{ij} = \alpha_{ij}/\sum_{l=1}^{m} \alpha_{il}$ were equal among countries, but the $\gamma_i = (\sum_{l=1}^{m} \alpha_{il})^{-1/\beta_i}$ varied among countries, where (it will be recalled) $1/(1+\beta_i) = \sigma_i$. This is the "neutral efficiency hypothesis."

ACMS arrived at this conclusion in the following manner. Given the country estimates $\hat{\alpha}_{i1h}, \hat{\alpha}_{i2h}, \hat{\alpha}'_{i2h}$ (in the notation used by ACMS (1961, p. 235), these would be $\alpha_h, \beta_h, \delta_h$), where $h = 1, 2, \ldots, N$ and N is the number of countries, their coefficients of variation were compared. The latter were computed according to the formula $(\sum_{h=1}^{N} |z_h - \bar{z}|)/N\bar{z}$, where $\bar{z} = (\sum_{h=1}^{N} z_h)/N$. The coefficients of variation computed for α'_{i2} were found to be generally lower (in fact less than half as great) than those for α_{i1} and α_{i2}. This procedure seems to be fairly arbitrary, however, and does not appear to be justified by any accepted statistical methodology. If, for instance, they had computed coefficients of variation for α'_{i1} instead of α'_{i2} (in their notation, $1 - \delta$ rather than δ), they would have found them to be, on the average, almost twice as high. Those for the ratio α_{i2}/α_{i1} would have been much higher still.

The tests just described were all carried out under the hypothesis (not tested) that elasticities of substitution in the respective industries were the same among countries. Thus, interesting though it is, the neutral efficiency hypothesis must still be regarded as quite tentative. Granted the hypothesis, estimates for α'_{i1}, α'_{i2}, and γ_{ih} (a residual for each country h) were obtained in a straightforward fashion.

Given the assumption of constant α_{i2}/α_{i1} among countries (as well as constant σ_i), ACMS were able to derive alternative estimates for σ_i in the case of the United States and Japan by means of the equation $x_{i2}/x_{i1} = (\alpha_{i2}/\alpha_{i1})^{\sigma_i}(w_2/w_1)^{-\sigma_i}$, yielding the formula

$$\frac{(x_{i2}/x_{i1})_J}{(x_{i2}/x_{i1})_U} = \left[\frac{(w_1/w_2)_J}{(w_1/w_2)_U}\right]^{\sigma_i}.$$

These estimates were compared with the previous ones, and the authors (p. 239) found "a significant correlation of .55 between the two estimates." The fact that this result should be a source of satisfaction is a sobering reminder of the difficulties that still characterize econometric research. What is more to the point is that, as might have been anticipated, the estimates for σ_i obtained in this way were higher and tended to be close to unity. ACMS explained this in terms of "omission of working capital," but a much more plausible explanation would be the removal of bias occasioned by the omission of commodity prices in the regression equation (12).

The possibility of reversal of factor intensity results from the fact that the straight lines $\log(x_{i2}/x_{i1}) = \log(\alpha_{i2}/\alpha_{i1})^{\sigma_i} - \sigma_i \log(w_2/w_1)$, for $i = 1, 2, \ldots, n$, must cross one another as long as $\sigma_i \neq \sigma_h$ for $i \neq h$. This corresponds to the condition that the isoquants become tangent to one another through some endowment ray. In order that this be empirically relevant in comparisons between two countries, it is necessary to go further and ascertain whether these intersection points occur within the strip bounded by the two countries' wage-rental ratios. This was argued by Minhas (1962) to be indeed the case. But Leontief (1964) has argued quite convincingly that Minhas' conclusions no longer follow if the estimates used are those obtained from the regression of relative factor intensities on relative factor prices, and of capital-output ratios on interest. Minhas also pointed out that the strong factor intensity hypothesis implied that two countries should have the same ranking of industries by capital intensity; but he found, in performing such a comparison between the United States and Japan, that the Spearman rank correlation coefficient was not significant.

One of the most striking aspects of Minhas' (1963) results is that the estimated elasticities of substitution have values that are economically plausible and have low standard errors of estimate. In a field in which it is all too easy to obtain estimates that are far-fetched and quite inadmissible on a priori grounds, this is an impressive achievement; so impressive, in fact, that one may legitimately suspect that it is too good to be true, and that there is a simpler and more disappointing explanation for the results obtained. This is Leontief's point of view, and his argument carries a great deal of conviction. While Leontief (1953, 1956) may have overstated his case with regard to the superiority of United States labor in export industries, certainly when it comes to comparing labor in industries such as textiles and dairy products, for instance — in such diverse countries as the United States and the United Kingdom on the one hand, and India, Southern Rhodesia, and El Salvador on the other — the implicit assumption made by Minhas that labor is the same factor in all these countries cannot really be believed. And Leontief (1964) has provided a very convincing explanation as to why the estimated elasticity of substitution between labor and capital (actually, the elasticity of the output-labor ratio with respect to the wage rate) should be so close to unity: namely, that if a low wage rate is symptomatic of low efficiency, then (assuming — as Leontief implicitly seems to do — that efficient and inefficient labor are perfect substitutes, i.e., have an infinite elasticity of substitution between them) a correspondingly higher quantity of this inefficient labor will be required in order to obtain the same output.

One final point requires comment. Minhas (1963) took account of 24 commodity groups, but only two factors. Within the framework of the Samuelsonian theory, such disparity seems very unlikely; and that reversal of factor intensity should occur under such circumstances, with CES production functions, is absolutely impossible (see Figure 6 for the pathological nature of such a case). The fact that the very data used by ACMS and Minhas showed disparities in wage rates among industries surely suggests that the "labor" in the different industries cannot be the same mobile "factor." But a theory of international trade that ignores natural resources is still more extraordinary; the removal of land from the classical trichotomy appears to be an outgrowth of the postwar growth models, for which recognition of the existence of natural resources would be a positive embarrassment. Even in Leontief's researches, while the number of commodities has been increasing at an ever rapid pace, the number of factors has been making slow progress: in the second edition of the *Structure*

(1951), it was increased from zero to one; in 1953 it was raised from one to two. It is clearly time that both theorists and applied econometricians abandoned the assumption that there are only two factors of production.

References*

Allais, Maurice: "Un Paradoxe de la Théorie du Commerce International," *Money, Growth and Methodology* (edited by Hugo Hegeland). Lund: CWK Gleerup, 1961, pp. 337–350.

Apostol, Tom M.: *Mathematical Analysis.* Reading, Mass.: Addison-Wesley Publishing Company, Inc., 1957.

Arrow, K. J., H. B. Chenery, B. S. Minhas, and R. M. Solow: "Capital-Labor Substitution and Economic Efficiency," *Review of Economics and Statistics*, 43 (August 1961), 225–250.

Benham, Frederic: "Taxation and the Relative Prices of Factors of Production," *Economica*, N.S., 2 (May 1935), 198–203.

Bhagwati, Jagdish: "Protection, Real Wages and Real Income," *Economic Journal*, 69 (December 1959), 733–748.

Brown, A. J.: "Professor Leontief and the Pattern of World Trade," *Yorkshire Bulletin of Economic and Social Research*, 9 (November 1957), 63–75.

Buchanan, Norman S.: "Lines on the Leontief Paradox," *Economia Internazionale*, 8 (November 1955), 791–794.

Burenstam Linder, Staffan: *An Essay on Trade and Transformation.* Stockholm: Almqvist and Wiksell, and New York: John Wiley and Sons, 1961.

Caves, Richard E.: *Trade and Economic Structure, Models and Methods.* Cambridge, Mass.: Harvard University Press, 1960.

Chenery, Hollis B., AND TSUNEHIKO WATANABE: "International Comparisons of the Structure of Production," *Econometrica*, 26 (October 1958), 487–521.

Chipman, John S.: "Factor Price Equalization and the Stolper-Samuelson Theorem" (abstract), *Econometrica*, 32 (October 1964), 682–683.

Danirére, André: "American Trade Structure and Comparative Cost Theory," *Economia Internazionale*, 9 (August 1956), 397–437.

Diab, Muhammad Amine: *The United States Capital Position and the Structure of its Foreign Trade.* Amsterdam: North-Holland Publishing Company, 1956.

*Identified in the text simply by author and year of publication, or, when convenient, by abbreviated title. When necessary, the year is followed by a letter indicating chronological order within the year. In the case of reprinted articles, page numbers in the text refer to the original source, unless specifically noted to the contrary.

Elliott, G. A.: "The Theory of International Values," *Journal of Political Economy*, 58 (February 1950), 16–29.

———: "Factor Proportions and the Structure of American Trade: Further Theoretical and Empirical Analysis. Comment," *Review of Economics and Statistics* [Supplement], 40 (February 1958), 116–117.

Ellsworth, P. T.: "The Structure of American Foreign Trade: A New View Examined," *Review of Economics and Statistics*, 36 (August 1954), 279–285.

Ford, J. L.: "The Ohlin-Heckscher Theory of the Basis of Commodity Trade," *Economic Journal*, 73 (September 1963), 458–176.

Gale, David: "The Law of Supply and Demand," *Mathematica Scandinavica*, 3 (1955), 155–169.

———: "Univalence Theorems for Differentiable Mappings," Institute of Social and Economic Research, Osaka University, Discussion Paper No. 29, November 1962. Cited with the kind permission of the author.

Gale, David, and Hukukane Nikaidô: "The Jacobian Matrix and Global Univalence of Mappings," *Mathematische Annalen*, 159 (1965), 81–93.

Graham, Frank D.: "The Theory of International Values," *Quarterly Journal of Economics* 46 (August 1932), 581–616.

Granick, David: "The American Capital Position in Foreign Trade," *Southern Economic Journal*, 22 (October 1955), 243–248.

Haberler, Gottfried: *A Survey of International Trade Theory*, Special Papers in International Economics No. 1, Princeton University, 1955. Revised and enlarged edition, 1961.

Harrod, R. F.: "Notes on Supply," *Economic Journal*, 40 (June 1930), 232–241. Reprinted in R. F. Harrod: *Economic Essays*, London: Macmillan and Co., Limited, 1952, pp. 77–88.

———: "Factor-Price Relations Under Free Trade," *Economic Journal* 68 (June 1958), 245–255.

Hawkins, David, and Herbert A. Simon: "Note: Some Conditions of Macroeconomic Stability," *Econometrica*, 17 (July-October 1949), 245–248.

Heckscher, Eli F.: "Utrikshandelns verkan påinkomstfö rdelningen," *Ekonomist Tidskrift*, 21 (1919), Del 2, 1–32. English translation: "The Effect of Foreign Trade on the Distribution of Income," *Readings in the Theory of International Trade* (edited by H. S. Ellis and L. A. Metzler). Philadelphia: The Blakiston Co., 1949, pp. 272–300.

Heckscher, Eli F.: "Skyddstullsystemets teoretiska grander," *Betänkande angående tull-systemets verkningar i Sverige före världskriget*, Del. I, pp. 22–53. Stockholm: Statens Offentliga Utredningar, Nr. 37, 1924.

Hicks, J. R.: *Value and Capital.* Oxford: at the Clarendon Press, 1939.

Hoffmeyer, Erik: "The Leontief Paradox Critically Examined," *Manchester School of Economic and Social Studies*, 26 (May 1958), 160–179.

Houthakker, H. S.: "An International Comparison of Household Expenditure Patterns, Commemorating the Centenary of Engel's Law," *Econometrica*, 25 (October 1957), 532–551.

———: "The Influence of Prices and Incomes on Household Expenditures," *Bulletin de l'Institut International de Statistique*, 37 (2e Livraison, 1960), 9–22.

———: "Some Problems in the International Comparison of Consumption Patterns," in *L'évaluation et le rôle des besoins de biens de consommation dans les divers régimes économiques* (edited by R. Mossé). Paris: Centre National de la Recherche Scientifique, 1963, pp. 89–102.

Iversen, Carl: *Aspects of the Theory of International Capital Movements.* Copenhagen: Levin and Munksgaard, 1935.

James, S. F., and I. F. Pearce: "The Factor Price Equalisation Myth: Mathematical Appendix," *Review of Economic Studies*, 19 (1951–52), 119–120.

Johnson, Harry G.: "Factor Endowments, International Trade and Factor Prices," *Manchester School of Economic and Social Studies*, 25 (September 1957), 270–283. Reprinted in Harry G. Johnson, *International Trade and Economic Growth*, London: George Allen and Unwin Ltd., 1958, pp. 17–30.

Jones, Ronald W.: "Factor Proportions and the Heckscher-Ohlin Theorem," *Review of Economic Studies*, 24 (1956), 1–10.

Kemp, Murray C.: *The Pure Theory of International Trade.* Englewood Cliffs, N.J.: Prentice-Hall, Inc., 1964.

Kemp, Murray C., and Ronald W. Jones: "Variable Labor Supply and the Theory of International Trade," *Journal of Political Economy*, 70 (February 1962), 30–36.

Knaster, B., C. Kuratowski, and S. Mazurkiewicz: "Ein Beweis des Fixpunktsatzes für n-dimensionale Simplexe," *Fundamenta Mathematicae*, 14 (1931), 132–137.

Koo, Anthony Y. C.: "Duty and Non-Duty Imports and Income Distribution," *American Economic Review*, 43 (March 1953), 31–40.

Koopmans, Tjalling C.: "Analysis of Production as an Efficient Combination of Activities," *Activity Analysis of Production and Allocation* (edited by T. C. Koopmans). New York: John Wiley and Sons, Inc., 1951, pp. 33–97.

———: "Maximization and Substitution in Linear Models of Production," *Input-Output Relations* (edited by the Netherlands Economic Institute). Leiden, H. E. Stenfert Kroese N.V., 1953, pp. 99–109.

Kravis, Irving B.: "Wages and Foreign Trade," *Review of Economics and Statistics*, 38 (February 1956), 14–30.

Kuhn, H. W.: "Factor Endowments and Factor Prices: Mathematical Appendix," *Economica*, N. S., 26 (May 1959), 142–144.

Laing, N. F.: "Factor Price Equalisation in International Trade and Returns to Scale," *Economic Record*, 37 (September 1961), 339–351.

Lancaster, Kelvin (1957a): "The Heckscher-Ohlin Trade Model: A Geometric Treatment," *Economica*, N.S., 24 (February 1957), 19–39.

———: (1957b): "Protection and Real Wages: A Restatement, *Economic Journal*, 67 (June 1957), 199–210.

Land, A. H.: "Factor Endowments and Factor Prices," *Economica*, N.S., 26 (May 1959), 137–142.

Laursen, Svend: "Production Functions and the Theory of International Trade," *American Economic Review*, 42 (September 1952), 540–557.

Leontief, Wassily W.: "The Use of Indifference Curves in the Analysis of Foreign Trade," *Quarterly Journal of Economics*, 47 (May 1933), 493–503. Reprinted in *Readings in the Theory of International Trade* (edited by H. S. Ellis and L. A. Metzler). Philadelphia: The Blakiston Co., 1949, pp. 229–238.

———: "Implicit Theorizing: A Methodological Criticism of the Neo-Cambridge School," *Quarterly Journal of Economics*, 50 (February 1937), 337–351. Reprinted in *Readings in Economic Analysis*, Vol. I (edited by Richard V. Clemence), Cambridge, Mass.: Addison-Wesley Press Inc., 1950, pp. 31–45.

———: *The Structure of American Economy*, 1919–1939. Cambridge, Mass.: Harvard University Press, 1941. Second edition enlarged, New York: Oxford University Press, 1951.

———: "Exports, Imports, Domestic Output, and Employment," *Quarterly Journal of Economics*, 60 (February 1946), 171–193. Correction, 60 (May 1946), 469. Reprinted in Leontief (1951), pp. 163–188.

———: "Domestic Production and Foreign Trade; the American Capital Position Re-examined," *Proceedings of the American Philosophical Society*, 97 (September 1953), 332–349.

———: "Factor Proportions and the Structure of American Trade: Further Theoretical and Empirical Analysis," *Review of Economics and Statistics*, 38 (November 1956), 386–407. "Reply," *ibid.* [Supplement], 40 (February 1958), 119–122.

———: "An International Comparison of Factor Costs and Factor Use," *American Economic Review*, 54 (June 1964), 335–345.

Lerner, Abba P.: "The Diagrammatical Representation of Cost Conditions in International Trade," *Economica*, 12 (August 1932), 346–356. Reprinted in Lerner (1953), 85–100.

———: "Factor Prices and International Trade" (1933), *Económica*, N.S., 19 (February 1952), 1–15. Reprinted in Lerner (1953), 67–84.

———: *Essays in Economic Analysis.* London: Macmillan and Co. Ltd., 1953.

Loeb, Gustaaf F.: "A Estrutura do Comércio Exterior da América do Norte," *Revista Brasileira de Economia*, 8 (December 1954), 81–97.

McCulloch, J. R.: "Corn Laws and Trade," *Supplement to the Fourth, Fifth, and Sixth Editions of the Encyclopaedia Britannica*, Volume Third, pp. 342–373. Edinburgh: Printed for Archibald Constable and Company, 1824.

McFadden, Daniel: "Further Results on CES Production Functions," *Review of Economic Studies*, 30 (June 1963), 73–83.

McKenzie, Lionel W.: "Equality of Factor Prices in World Trade," *Econometrica*, 23 (July 1955), 239–257.

———: "Matrices with Dominant Diagonals and Economic Theory," *Mathematical Methods in the Social Sciences, 1959* (edited by K. J. Arrow, S. Karlin, and P. Suppes). Stanford; Stanford University Press, 1960, 47–62.

———: "Factor Price Equalization and the Jacobian Determinant," mimeographed (1962).

Malthus, T. R.: *Observations on the Effects of the Corn Laws, and of a Rise or Fall in the Price of Corn on the Agriculture and General Wealth of the Country.* London: Printed for J. Johnson and Co., 1814. Third edition, London: John Murray, Albermarle Street, 1815. Baltimore: The Johns Hopkins Press, 1932.

———: *The Grounds of an Opinion on the Policy of Restricting the Importation of Foreign Corn; Intended as An Appendix to "Observations on the Corn Laws."* London: Printed for John Murray, Albermarle Street, 1815.

Meade, J. E.: "The Equalisation of Factor Prices: The Two-Country Two-Factor Three-Product Case," *Metroeconomica*, 2 (December 1950), 129–133.

———: *A Geometry of International Trade.* London: George Allen and Unwin Ltd., 1952.

———: *The Theory of International Economic Policy*, Vol. II, *Trade and Welfare.* London: Oxford University Press, 1955.

Metzler, Lloyd A. (1949a): "Tariffs, the Terms of Trade, and the Distribution of the National Income," *Journal of Political Economy*, 57 (February 1949), 1–29.

———: (1949b): "Tariffs, International Demand, and Domestic Prices," *Journal of Political Economy*, 57 (August 1949), 345–351.

———: "A Multiple-Region Theory of Income and Trade," *Econometrica*, 18 (October 1950), 329–354.

Michaely, Michael: "Factor Proportions in International Trade: Current State of the Theory," *Kyklos*, 17 (Fasc. 4, 1964), 529–550.

Minhas, Bagicha S.: "The Homohypallagic Production Function, Factor-Intensity Reversals, and the Heckscher-Ohlin Theorem," *Journal of Political Economy*, 60 (April 1962), 138–156.

———: *An International Comparison of Factor Costs and Factor Use.* Amsterdam: North-Holland Publishing Company, 1963.

Mookerjee, Subimal: *Factor Endowments and International Trade.* Bombay: Asia Publishing House, 1958.

Morgan, E. Victor, and G. L. Rees: "Non-Traded Goods and International Factor Price Equalisation," *Economica*, N.S., 21 (November 1954), 334–339.

Mundell, R. A.: "International Trade and Factor Mobility," *American Economic Review*, 47 (June 1957), 321–335.

Newman, Peter: "Some Notes on Stability Conditions," *Review of Economic Studies*, 27 (October 1959), 1–9.

Nicholson, J. Shield: *Principles of Political Economy*, Vol. II. New York: The Macmillan Company, 1897.

Nikaidô, Hukukane: "Uniqueness of Solution of Certain Equations, I, II," Institute of Social and Economic Research, Osaka University, Discussion Papers Nos. 28, 30, November 1962. Cited with the kind permission of the author.

Ohlin, Bertil: "The Reparations Problem," *Index*, 28 (April 1928), 2–33.

———: *Interregional and International Trade.* Cambridge, Mass.: Harvard University Press, 1933.

Pareto, Vilfredo: *Manuel d'Économie Politique* (translated and revised from the Italian, *Manuale di economia politico*), Paris: V. Giard et E. Brière, 1909.

Second French edition (identical with the 1909 edition), Paris: Marcel Giard, 1927.

Pearce, I. F.: "The Factor Price Equalisation Myth," *Review of Economic Studies*, 19 (1951–52), 111–119.

———: "A Note on Mr. Lerner's Paper," *Economica*, N.S., 19 (February 1952), 16–18.

———: "A Further Note on Factor-Commodity Price Relationships," *Economic Journal*, 49 (December 1959), 725–732.

Porzsolt, L.: "Om utrikeshandelns ekonomiska verkningar," *Ekonomisk Tidskrift*, 47(March 1945), 17–33.

Reiter, Stanley: "Efficient International Trade and Equalization of Factor Prices," *International Economic Review*, 2 (January 1961), 29–64.

Ricardo, David: *An Essay on The Influence of a low Price of Corn on the Profits of Stock; shewing the Inexpediency of Restrictions on Importation: with Remarks on Mr. Malthas' Two Last Publications.* London: John Murray, Albemarle Street, 1815. Reprinted in *The Works and Correspondence of David Ricardo* (edited by Piero Sraffa), Vol. IV, pp. 9–41.

———: *On the Principles of Political Economy, and Taxation.* London: John Murray, Albemarle Street, 1817. In *The Works and Correspondence of David Ricardo* (edited by Piero Sraffa), Vol. I. Cambridge: At the University Press, 1951.

Robinson, Joan: "Rising Supply Price," *Economica*, N.S., 8 (February 1941), 1–8. Reprinted in Joan Robinson, *Collected Economic Papers*, Oxford: Basil Blackwell, 1951, pp. 35–43; and in *Readings in Price Theory* (edited by George J. Stigler and Kenneth E. Boulding), Chicago: Richard D. Irwin, Inc., 1952, pp. 233–241. Page references are to the latter.

Robinson, Romney (1956a): "Factor Proportions and Comparative Advantage: Part I," *Quarterly Journal of Economics*, 70 (May 1956), 169–192.

———: (1956b): "Factor Proportions and Comparative Advantage: Part II," *Quarterly Journal of Economics*, 70 (August 1956), 246–363.

———: "Factor Proportions and the Structure of American Trade: Further Theoretical and Empirical Analysis. Comment," *Review of Economics and Statistics* [Supplement], 40 (February 1958, 113–116.

Samuelson, Paul, A.: *Foundations of Economic Analysis.* Cambridge, Mass.: Harvard University Press, 1947.

———: "International Trade and the Equalisation of Factor Prices," *Economic Journal*, 58 (June 1948), 163–184.

———: "International Factor Price Equalisation Once Again," *Economic Journal*, 59 (June 1949), 181–197.

———: "A Comment on Factor Price Equalisation," *Review of Economic Studies*, 19 (1951–52), 121–122.

———: "Prices of Factors and Goods in General Equilibrium," *Review of Economic Studies*, 21 (1953), 1–20.

———: "Frank Knight's Theorem in Linear Programming," *Zeitschrift für Nationalökonomie*, 18 (Heft 3, 1958), 310–317.

Senior, Nassau W.: *Three Lectures on the Cost of Obtaining Money.* London: John Murray, Albemarle-Street, 1830.

———: *An Outline of the Science of Political Economy.* London: W. Clowes and Sons, 1836. New York: Augustus M. Kelley, Inc., 1951. Page references are to the latter.

Shephard, Ronald W.: *Cost and Production Functions.* Princeton: Princeton University Press, 1953.

Smith, Adam: *An Inquiry into Nature and Causes of the Wealth of Nations* (1776). London: J. M. Dent and Sons Ltd., 1933.

Sraffa, Piero: "Sulle relazioni fra costo e quantità prodotta," *Annali di Economia,* 2 (1925–1926), 277–328.

Stolper, Wolfgang F., and Paul A. Samuelson: "Protection and Real Wages," *Review of Economic Studies,* 9 (November 1941), 58–73. Reprinted in *Readings in the Theory of International Trade,* (edited by H. S. Ellis and L. A. Metzler). Philadelphia: The Blakiston Company, 1949, pp. 333–357.

Swerling, Boris C.: "Capital Shortage and Labor Surplus in the United States?" *Review of Economics and Statistics,* 36 (August 1954), 286–289.

Taussig, F. W.: *International Trade.* New York: The Macmillan Company, 1927.

Tinbergen, Jan: "The Equalisation of Factor Prices between Free-Trade Areas," *Metroeconomica,* 1 (July 1949), 39–7. Reprinted in Jan Tinbergen: *Selected Papers.* Amsterdam: North-Holland Publishing Company, 1959, pp. 112–123.

Torrens, Robert: *An Essay on the External Corn Trade.* London: J.Hatchard, 1815. Second edition, London: J. Hatchard and Son, 1820. Third, fourth, and fifth ("New") edition, London: Longman, Rees, Orme, Brown, and Green, 1826, 1827, 1829.

Travis, William Penfield: *The Theory of Trade and Protection.* Cambridge, Mass.: Harvard University Press, 1964.

Uzawa, Hirofumi: "A Note on the Menger-Wieser Theory of Imputation," *Zeitschrift für Nationalökonomie,* 18 (Heft 3, 1958), 318–334.

———: "Prices of the Factors of Production in International Trade," *Econometrica,* 27 (July 1959), 448–468.

———: "Production Functions with Constant Elasticities of Substitution," *Review of Economic Studies,* 29 (October 1962), 291–299.

———: "Duality Principles in the Theory of Cost and Production," *International Economic Review,* 5 (May 1964), 216–220.

Valavanis-Vail, Stefan: "Leontief's Scarce Factor Paradox," *Journal of Political Economy,* 52 (December 1954), 523–528.

Valavanis, Stefan: "Factor Proportions and the Structure of American Trade: Comment," *Review of Economics and Statistics* [Supplement], 40 (February 1958), 111–119.

Vanek, Jaroslav: "The Natural Resource Content of Foreign Trade, 1870–1955, and the Relative Abundance of Natural Resources in the United States," *Review of Economics and Statistics,* 41 (May 1959), 146–153.

———: "Variable Factor Proportions and Inter-Industry Flows in the Theory of International Trade," *Quarterly Journal of Economics*, 77 (February 1963), 129–142.

Viner, Jacob: "Cost Curves and Supply Carves," Zeitschrift für Nationalökonomie, 3 (1931), 23–46. Reprinted in *Readings in Economic Analysis*, Volume 2 (edited by Richard V. Clemence), Cambridge, Mass.: Addison-Wesley Press Inc., 1950, pp. 8–31; with a Supplement by Professor Viner, *ibid.*, pp. 31–35. Also in *Readings in Price Theory* (edited by George J. Stigler and Kenneth E. Boulding), Chicago: Richard D. Irwin, Inc., 1952, pp. 198–232.

———: "Relative Abundance of the Factors and International Trade," *Ekonomi, Politik, Samhälle.* Stockholm: Bokförlaget folk och samhälle, 1959, pp. 279–293.

Watanabe, Tsunehiko: "A Test of the Constancy of Input-Output Coefficients among Countries," *International Economic Review*, 2 (September 1961), 340–350.

West, Edward: *Essay on the Application of Capital to Land, with Observations shewing the Impolicy of any great restriction of the importation of corn, and that the Bounty of 1688 did not lower the price of it.* London: Printed for T. Underwood, 1815. Baltimore: The Johns Hopkins Press, 1903.

Wicksell, Knut: *Finanztheoretische Untersuchungen, nebst Darstellung und Kritik des Steuerwesens Schwedens.* Jena: Verlag von Gustav Fischer, 1896.

———: "Svenska Produktionsproblem," a review of *Svenska produktionsproblem*, by Eli F. Heckscher. *Forum*, 6 (January 1919), 16–17, 29–31.

———: "Tullskydd och frihandel," *Ekonomisk Tidskrift*, 26 (Heft 9–10, 1924), 149–164. English translation: "Protection and Free Trade," in Knut Wickseil: *Selected Papers on Economic Theory.* London: George Allen and Unwin Ltd., 1958, pp. 250–266.

Chapter 7

Factor Market Distortions, Production, and Trade: A Survey*

Stephen P. Magee†

1. Introduction

The traditional interest of economists in monopoly power and other distortions in product markets is shifting toward the problem of distortions and differentials in factor markets. The purpose of this paper is to review a portion of the existing literature in this area and provide some minor extensions, with special emphasis on the implications for international trade. General studies which include at

*Originally published in *Oxford Economic Papers*, 25(1), pp. 1–43.

†This paper is a revision of Chapter 1 of the author's Ph.D. dissertation [100]. He is indebted to the three members of his dissertation committee, Jagdish Bhagwati, Charles Kindleberger, and Paul Samuelson; to Robert E. Baldwin, Charles Metcalf, J. David Richardson, and other participants in the International Trade Workshop at the University of Wisconsin (where the paper was presented, Feb. 1972); and to John Burton, Richard Caves, Robert Flanagan, Horst Herberg, Ronald Jones, Murray Kemp, Nan Magee, Carlos Rodriquez, and especially W. M. Corden for discussions, suggestions, and comments. He is grateful to the Woodrow Wilson National Fellowship Foundation, the Institute of International Studies, University of California, Berkeley, the National Science Foundation, and the Graduate School of Business, University of Chicago, for research support. Naturally, no survey is comprehensive: no doubt, some very important articles have been missed. Papers which came to my attention after the references were numbered have been included in footnotes.

least brief discussions of the problem of factor market imperfections have been written by Bhagwati [16], Caves [31], Corden [34], Johnson [77], Linder [96], Myint [116], Taussig [149], and Viner [158]. We do not consider here issues in the current controversy over the theory of capital (see Harcourt's survey [61]).

Several theoretical papers on the subject should be mentioned. Four early works are by Cairnes [30], Manoilesco [104], Ohlin [118], and Viner [156]. While Stolper and Samuelson [146] do not deal with distortions *per se*, their study of factor rewards in general equilibrium provides an important analytical tool in this area. In the 1950s Eckaus [39], Haberler [52], Hagen [54], and Lewis [95] wrote on the subject while Bhagwati and Ramaswami [20], Bhagwati, Ramaswami, and Srinivasan [21], Fishlow and David [42], Johnson [77], Johnson [78], Johnson and Mieszkowski [80], and the present author [100] studied the problem in the 1960s. Since 1969 no fewer than thirty-six theoretical and empirical papers have appeared or are in draft form. One of the most interesting early papers in the group is the qualitative study written by Ohlin [118] in 1931, in which he reviews Manoilesco's book [104]; it is interesting because it arrives at several of the conclusions which have been developed mathematically by the modern writers. A comprehensive modern treatment of the welfare effects is by Bhagwati [19], who has formulated a general theory encompassing the three causes and four possible types of economic distortions (factor distortions being only one of the four).

Several taxonomies have been suggested for classifying the causes and types of factor market imperfections. Bhagwati [19] cited three *causes* of differentials in his welfare paper: endogenous (due to some market imperfection under *laissez-faire*), and either autonomous or instrumental policy imposed differentials.

Following an earlier paper by Bhagwati [17], we can expand the traditional definition of a differential to incorporate two types. First, factor prices may be the same in all industries but there may exist a differential between real factor rewards and their marginal products in one or more industries. Second, real factor rewards may equal their respective marginal products in each industry but there may be a differential between the price of an identical factor in different industries. This expanded definition of a differential will thus incorporate more than one of the various inequalities which may arise in the factor market equilibrium conditions.

The word 'differential' is used here as a positive or purely descriptive term while 'distortion' denotes that a differential has certain normative or welfare implications (see Bhagwati and Ramaswami [20]). In the present context, a distortion can always be attributed to a differential of one sort or another, but not every differential implies that a distortion exists. Thus, a differential is a necessary but not a sufficient condition for a distortion.

For example, many studies have found factor price differentials which do not necessarily indicate distortion. The differentials may be caused by differences in

1. age and experience among workers in [1], [55], [59], [76], [91], [112];
2. education and skill reflecting a return on human capital in [1], [3], [20], [55], [59], [73], [75], [76], [83], [91], [112], [118], [123], [128], [136];
3. regional differentials due to moving costs or other factors in [1], [20], [25], [49], [58], [59], [105], [140], [162];
4. factor preference or disutility associated with particular industries or regions in [1], [42], [52], [68], [77], [118], [156], [157];
5. risk aversion in [41]; and
6. regional differences due to geographic concentration of low wage-low skill industries in [47], [58].

On the other hand, an even larger number of differentials have been cited as sources of welfare distortion. The causes of these differentials include:

1. imperfect knowledge in [39], [42];
2. the rural-urban dichotomy in [54];
3. racism in [13], [27], [119], [150], [162];
4. monopoly power through unionism in [2], [20], [33], [78], [80], [94], [99], [110], [118], [125], [133], [136], [141], [151], [154];

5. monopoly power by one or both factors coupled with market power by producers in product markets (bilateral monopoly) in [2], [7], [26], [60], [61], [72], [130], [133], [137];
6. the maintenance and spread of union wage increases by 'pattern setting' in [98], [137];
7. seniority based on age or education which does not reflect economic superiority in [1], [76], [91], [162];
8. differences between the export- and import-competing sector's access to foreign capital in [36], or differences in ocean freight rates charged to the two sectors in [106];
9. discrimination against women or children in [17], [76], [91], [162];
10. collusion across industries by a factor which acts as a discriminating monopolist, charging different prices in each industry because of differing elasticities of derived demand for the factor in [133];
11. disguised unemployment in agriculture relative to manufacturing in [20], [78], [95];
12. differential factor taxation or subsidy in [76], [77], [91], [111], [132];
13. factory legislation, social regulation, or policy control for 'prestige-cum-humanitarian' or other normative reasons in [20], [22], [39];
14. movements in union/non-union differentials in the business cycle in [120], [125], [151]; and
15. limited mobility with differential product growth in [54], [78], [104].

In Bhagwati's terminology [19], the first eleven types are caused by endogenous forces while (12) and (13) are policy imposed; all thirteen are distortionary in a static context, while (14) and (15) involve both a distortion and comparative statics, raising the possibility of immiserizing growth. Further, in dynamic systems, differentials may be observed during the adjustment process between two equilibrium points. This problem will be discussed later.

Differentials, regardless of their cause, have two major effects: the first is on the economic *structure* while the second is on *welfare.* The structural effects are independent of whether the differential is distortionary. Bhagwati has suggested the following classification of the structural effects of a differential:

(i) the *output* effects,
(ii) the *shrinkage* of the production possibilities curve due to operation off the efficiency locus in capital-labour space,
(iii) *non-tangency,* i.e. non-equivalence of the marginal rates of transformation and substitution in product space,
(iv) *convexity,* i.e. the possibility that the production possibilities curve becomes convex to the origin because of the differential,
(v) the *factor market* effects, including possible reversal of the product factor intensities, and
(vi) the *trade* effects.

For convenience, these effects will be referred to in the text only by the word which is italicized. The welfare and policy implications of a differential, on the other hand, depend on whether it is distortionary or not. In most of the cases to be considered, we shall assume that the differential causes a distortion in order to pursue the welfare question. While one-factor models are considered, most of the analysis pertains to two-factor models where we make the traditional assumptions of two factors in fixed total supply and immobile internationally, two goods, perfect competition in both product and factor markets, increasing opportunity costs between the two products, constant returns to scale in production, and no externalities. The assumption of perfect factor markets where prices are flexible and the factors are perfectly mobile between industries will be relaxed in what follows.

In Section II, factor price rigidity and factor immobility are considered. Because the bulk of the recent literature deals with factor price differentials, the next three sections are devoted to them: Section III is an introduction and examination of the one-factor model, Section IV considers the structural effects in two-factor models, and Section V deals with the welfare effects. Section VI is a brief review of empirical work and Section VII contains some concluding remarks.

2. Factor Price Rigidity and Immobility

A. Factor price rigidity

Haberler [52] and Johnson [77] have discussed the introduction of trade into an autarkic economy which is initially Pareto optimal. In addition to trade, they added the condition that factor prices must remain rigid at their original level. This rigidity may be caused by a combination of institutional forces such as minimum wage legislation, governmental regulation or control, labour unions, or other forces. In the new equilibrium, production of the import-competing good must cease, given the assumption of constant returns to scale. Since all of the intensive factors in the import-competing sector cannot be absorbed by the expansion of the export industry, some of it will be unemployed in the new equilibrium. The Stolper–Samuelson [146] analogue is that trade expansion has hurt a portion of the import-competing industry's intensive factor via unemployment rather than through adverse price changes.

This result can be illustrated geometrically in Fig. 1. Line L_0 (whose slope is P_x/P_y)[1] represents relative product prices in autarky: production and consumption occur at P_0. The introduction of trade increases P_x/P_y to L_2, moving production to P_2 and consumption to C_2 when no distortions are present. However, with factor price rigidity, the new production point cannot be at P_2 but must occur between P_3 and C. The precise point depends on which good is the numeraire because of the index number problem. Haberler and Johnson conclude that free trade may actually reduce welfare in this situation. Bardhan [8], Batra and Pattanaik [10], and Kemp [85] have questioned the allocation of the net welfare effects of two exogenous changes (the introduction of trade and the introduction of the distortion via rigid prices) to one of the changes alone, i.e. trade. We know that the introduction of trade alone cannot decrease

[1]Throughout this paper I shall ignore signs when referring to slopes of curves, demand elasticities, and elasticities of substitution. Thus, an increase in the slope of L_0, for example, means a greater absolute slope rather than a greater algebraic slope.

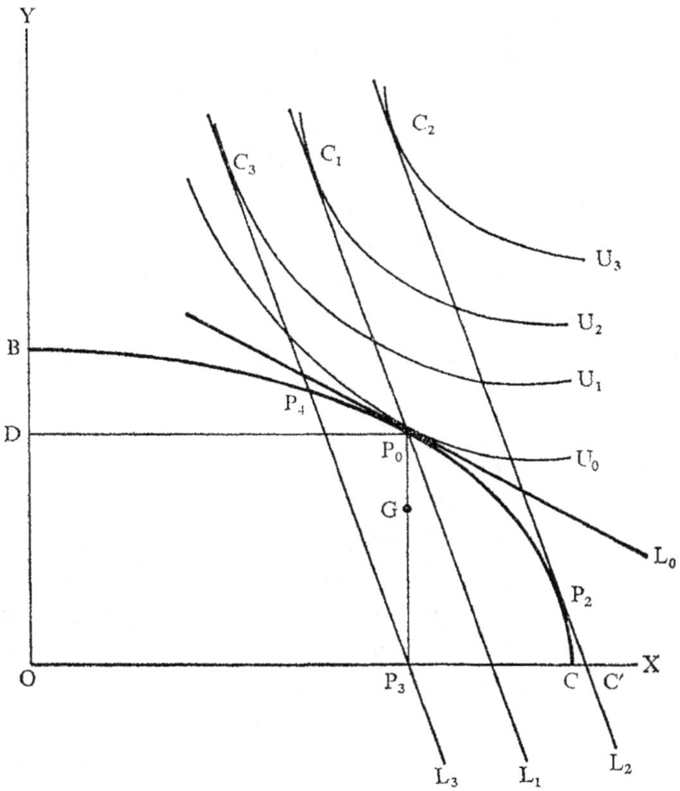

Figure 1.

welfare and the introduction of a distortion alone must reduce it. The effects of these two actions should be separated. Of course, no distortion is implied if factor prices are rigid because the supply of a factor is perfectly elastic at a given price (for the economy as a whole, this is precluded by our assumption of a fixed total supply of each factor).

Eckaus [39] and others have discussed the case where fixed coefficients in the production of both goods coupled with certain product price ratios imply a zero price for one of the factors of production, such as labour. Societal constraints which require a non-zero wage impose a differential between the actual wage (which may be the same in all industries) and the shadow wage (which equals zero for the economy as a whole). Bhagwati [17] has used the Samuelson factor price equalization diagram to illustrate the unemployment effects of such a divergence between the actual and shadow wage in the more general case of a labour-surplus economy where the production functions permit smooth substitutibility. To remedy this distortion, he recommends a tax-cum-subsidy on factor use in all sectors as the first-best policy; next in order of preference would be a tax-cum-subsidy policy on the domestic production of importables or a tariff on imports.

Policy remedies aimed at factor use are also first-best in Lewis's case [95] where wages are identical in all industries but they are above the marginal product of labour in one sector — agriculture. Both shrinkage and non-tangency along the transformation curve contribute to the decline in welfare which accompanies this case.

Harris and Todaro [62] have considered theoretically a more recent problem plaguing less developed countries: i.e. continued rural to urban migration in spite of positive marginal products in agriculture and substantial urban unemployment. They find that such behaviour is rational, given urban minimum wage levels above agricultural earnings, government hiring and wage subsidies, and that migration responds to urban-rural differences in *expected* earnings. Empirically, the correlation between regions of high unemployment and high wages has been observed by Hall [57] in the United States and Bryce [28] in Panama.

B. Factor immobility

We consider next the case where factor prices are flexible but the factors are immobile between industries. Cairnes [30] explored this possibility in a *one*-factor model with his famous theory of 'non-competing groups' of labour. He felt that all workers could be classified into four skill categories [30, pp. 72–3] within which there was perfect substitutibility but between which there was none. An analytical solution to this problem is to divide labour into four new factors and redefine the production functions (see [31], [42], and [118]). Ohlin [119], however, felt that in the long run the different qualities of labour are not necessarily separable since high wages in skilled groups induce entry from lower-skilled categories.

On the other hand, we can also assume that there are inter-industry barriers to labour mobility even though labour is of identical quality in both industries in a one-factor, two-good model. By assuming that the economy is Pareto optimal in autarky and that factors will not move out of their autarky positions when trade is introduced, then with trade, we observe perfect factor immobility, and no change in the production of either good. Furthermore, the Ricardian pattern of trade follows: the country exports the good whose world price exceeds the autarky price. The differential between wages in the two industries after trade, reflecting the failure of factors to move, causes the non-tangency between the new price line and the old transformation curve. Welfare improves with trade in spite of the immobility. However, it would improve still further if labour became mobile and the system were permitted to specialize in the export product. Viner [156, p. 124] gave an intuitive argument for the price and wage effects of trade in 1932: '[In this case], trade between the two countries will result only in changes in the relative prices of the two commodities, [and] in relative wages in the two occupations. . . . '

The problem of factor immobility in *two*-factor models with international trade has been investigated by Haberler [52] and Johnson [77]. For simplicity, both assume that the country faces given terms of trade in world markets. They then compare a country before and after trade to see if it is possible for the country to gain from trade when its domestic factors are completely immobile between industries. In Fig. 1, the country produces and consumes at the Pareto optimal point P_0 in autarky. If domestic factors were perfectly mobile, we find as before that the introduction of trade increases the price ratio P_x/P_y from L_0 to the international terms of trade denoted by line L_2, production moves to P_2 and consumption to C_2 in the Pareto optimal equilibrium. The gain from trade is illustrated by movement from community indifference curve U_0 to U_3.

However, if factors are completely immobile, it is still possible to gain from trade. If the increase in P_x/P_y from L_0 to L_1 is accompanied by flexible factor prices, then we remain at point P_0

in Fig. 1 and the gain from trade is from U_0 to U_2. Johnson [77, pp. 13–14] notes that the total gain from trade (U_0 to U_3) can be broken into two parts: the 'consumption or exchange' gain (U_0 to U_2) and the 'production or specialization' gain (U_2 to U_3). Thus, Haberler and Johnson showed, in effect, that the distortion introduced via factor immobility merely eliminates the production gain; the consumption gain remains when factor prices are flexible. The methodological criticism noted earlier ([8], [10], [85]), applies here as well. The gain from trade is actually from U_0 to U_3; however, the introduction of the distortion via immobility results in a loss from U_3 back to U_2. Thus, the effect of both the exogenous changes is the movement from U_0 to U_2.

We note the following structural effects in this case. First, both Haberler and Johnson showed that the transformation curve in Fig. 1 shrinks to $DP_0\ P_3$, so that shrinkage affects all points on the transformation curve except the actual equilibrium point P_0.

Second, we know that the prices of both factors in the export industry (X) increase in proportion to the change in relative commodity prices when trade is introduced. This can be shown by letting P_x, P_y and w_x, w_y, r_x, r_y denote commodity and factor prices in X and Y and X_k, X_l and Y_k, Y_l denote the marginal productivities of capital and labour in X and Y. We assume that the traditional first order conditions hold in pretrade equilibrium before the rigidity is introduced:

$$\frac{P_x}{P_y} \cdot \frac{X_l}{Y_l} = \frac{w_x}{w_y} \tag{1}$$

$$\frac{P_x}{P_y} \cdot \frac{X_k}{Y_k} = \frac{r_x}{r_y}. \tag{2}$$

With perfect competition, the right-hand side of both equations equals one, so that the system corresponds to P_0 in Fig. 1 where L_0 is tangent to BP_0C. With factors immobile, the average physical productivities of the products can be treated as if they are constant. Thus, if P_x/P_y increases 20 per cent when trade is introduced, then w_x/w_y and r_x/r_y must increase by 20 per cent, so that in the new equilibrium $w_x = 1 \cdot 2w_y$ and $r_x = 1 \cdot 2r_y$.

This can be viewed in another way. From the zero profit condition we can write

$$\frac{P_x}{P_y} = \left[\frac{Y}{X}\right] \cdot \left[\frac{w_x L_x + r_x K_x}{w_y L_y + r_y K_y}\right]. \tag{3}$$

By assumption, Y, X, L_x, K_x, L_y, and K_y all remain constant after trade is introduced so that a 20 per cent increase in P_x/P_y implies a 20 per cent increase in the ratio of X to Y's relative factor rewards (the second bracket on the right-hand side of (3)). We get the Cairnesian result that the return to these industry-specific factors are determined exclusively by changes in demand (the supply of the factors is perfectly 'inelastic'). The Stolper–Samuelson [146] analogue would go something like this: increased relative export prices with immobile factors benefit all factors in the export industry proportionately, instead of just the intensive factor; as a result, a constant multiplicative differential is introduced in the price of X's factors relative to the price of identical factor services in Y.

Thus, the structural effects are formally similar to those in the one-factor case: an identical differential is paid for both factors in the export industry; the factor market equilibrium point, by definition, remains constant; there is no shrinkage of the transformation curve at the equilibrium point; the pattern of trade corresponds to the Heckscher–Ohlin theorem (if it would have without immobility); and the non-tangency issue is irrelevant since the marginal rate of transformation is indeterminate at the corner of the transformation curve $DP_0\ P_3$ at P_0 (although there is non-tangency between the new price line and the slope of the old transformation curve BP_0C). The case of factor immobility is important empirically: it is relevant, for example, to the problem of the 'dual economy' discussed in much of the economic development literature.

Finally, following Johnson [77], we can combine factor *immobility* and factor price *rigidity* in four ways to yield the following results when trade is introduced (all are illustrated in Fig. 1). We assume that trade causes P_x/P_y to increase.

(i) If both factors are immobile and both factor prices rigid in terms of X, production of Y ceases and both of its factors are completely unemployed while production of X remains constant at point P_3.

(ii) If both factors are immobile and the price of only one of them is rigid, then production of Y will not cease completely so that production will occur at some point such as G along the line P_0P_3.

(iii) If one factor is mobile with a rigid price and the other is immobile but with a flexible price, the system will arrive at a point to the right of P_0P_3 and not above point G.

(iv) If one factor is mobile with a flexible price and the other is immobile with a rigid price, the system will arrive at a point somewhere to the right of the line P_0P_3.

These cases are also considered at some length in Batra and Pattanaik [10]. In all of the cases where factor prices are rigid, the results depend on whether the rigid factor price is measured in terms of X, Y, or some constant utility combination of the two.

Jones [82], however, finds that the restricted entry form of factor market distortion does not result in non-tangency between the product price ratio and the transformation curve and the latter does not become convex while factor price differentials usually do generate non-tangency. One difficulty with the differential model is that it may be difficult to maintain factor price differentials over long periods of time without restricted entry.

Hemming and Corden [65] have examined optimal policy alternatives in cases where output changes result in unemployment, the latter being necessary for labour movement. This work has been extended by Ramaswami [127] and Corden [35]. In another context, Ramaswami [126] examines policy-induced international factor immobility. In considering optimal restrictions on factor movements, he finds that optimal taxation of the immigration of the scarce factor is superior to optimal restriction of the emigration of the abundant factor. This was extended by Webb [159] to the case where two governments negotiate such taxation in a bilateral monopoly situation.

3. An Introduction To Factor Price Differentials

A. Types of differentials

The most widely discussed cause of factor market distortions is the case where factors are relatively mobile and their prices flexible and yet a differential exists in the price of a factor in different industries. As mentioned earlier, this case is not always clearly distinguishable from the case where immobility exists. For example, labour unions frequently exploit their monopoly power by a combination of price setting and restricted entry, the latter being a special form of immobility.

Differentials may be observed in static or comparative static systems and in systems in the dynamic adjustment process between two equilibria. We noted early in the paper a number of causes of non-dynamic differentials. We will discuss briefly the *dynamic* variety. They are harder to classify as distortions since the size of the differential depends on the time period chosen, the speed of convergence (assuming stability), the size of the initial shock, and how recent the system was jolted by some parametric shift. The dynamic differential is another case of partial factor mobility where adjustment to change is not instantaneous. A non-explosive cobweb model with lagged supply and demand reactions generates an observable differential if the period of observation is small or no differential if it is sufficiently long. Hagen's [54] use of more rapid demand expansion for manufactures than for agriculture to generate a factor distortion has been criticized by Kenen [88], Koo [91], Fishlow and David [42], and Bhagwati and Ramaswami [20] as 'illegitimately superimposing a dynamic argument upon a comparative statics framework' [20, p. 48]. Johansen [75] has a dynamic model which explains interindustry wage differentials in terms of different productivity growth.

Recent papers, following Inada [74] and Uekawa [152], have explored growth models in which one factor (Herberg [68]) or all factors (Herberg and Kemp [70]) are imperfectly mobile. This allows generation of endogenous differentials, which disappear in the steady state. The empirical question of growth with regional income differentials has been analysed by Fukuchi and Nobukuni [48] for Japan and others.

In less formal models, one can imagine both 'demand-pull differentials' and 'cost-push differentials', generated by sectoral shifts in either the demand for or supply of particular factors (with the other curve being less than perfectly elastic). Regardless of the initial cause, the disparity in prices will not remain as a permanent differential unless some economic or non-economic force acts to maintain it. Schlesinger [137], for example, has attributed union success to its alteration of the labour supply function; consequently, 'excessive' wage demands would classify unionization as a cost-push differential. But the union differential may not be maintained indefinitely without restricted entry since free entry would erode the differential. On the other hand, discrimination by race, sex, or age might be introduced through a demand-pull differential in favour of certain segments of the labour force, which is maintained on largely non-economic grounds. These assumptions of restricted entry or non-economic forces are not required to justify differentials caused by factor taxation which differs by sector, since after tax returns are everywhere equal.

In short, one should examine very carefully the way in which a differential is introduced, whether it is narrowing through the traditional dynamic adjustment process and if not, what assumptions are required to maintain it. More systematic analyses should be done on the *policy* implications of the time dimension, such as the present discounted costs of dynamic endogenous differentials and the stability properties of tax-cum-subsidy policies designed to close endogenous differentials more rapidly.

We turn now from differentials caused by dynamic forces to static models, in which differentials are exogenous to the system. In the next section we shall examine static differentials in one-factor models.

B. Differentials in one-factor models

The earliest works on factor price differentials dealt primarily with the Ricardian case of only one factor — labour. See, for example,

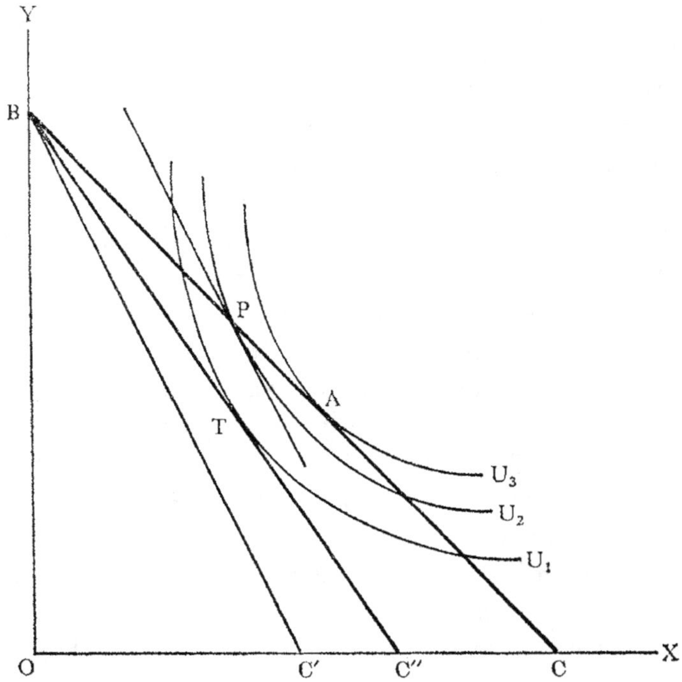

Figure 2.

the discussions in Cairnes [30], Taussig [149], Ohlin [118], Viner [156], and Hagen [54]. Hagen [54, pp. 504–5] has the best discussion of the one-factor, two-good model. We have reproduced one of his diagrams in Fig. 2. The transformation curve BC is linear because of the one-factor constant returns assumption. With no distortion, the economy will produce and consume at A in autarky. If we introduce a differential such that wages in X are double those in Y, the new domestic price ratio P_x/P_y will equal the slope of BC', which is twice as steep as BC. This can be formalized as follows. Using the fixed coefficient production functions $X = aL_x$ and $Y = bL_y$, profit maximization yields the non-specialized first order conditions $P_x = w_x/a$ and $P_y = w_y/b$ where w_x and w_y are the wages in X and Y. Thus,

$$\frac{P_x}{P_y} = \frac{w_x}{w_y} \cdot \frac{b}{a}.$$

Without distortion, $w_x/w_y = 1$, but when we double (w_x/w_y), then P_x/P_y doubles. Thus, the original price ratio along BC in Fig. 2 is $[b/a]$ while the slope of a price line such as BC' is $2[b/a]$.

In the absence of trade, the economy will produce and consume at P when the distortion is present. At that point, the marginal rate of substitution, which equals the price ratio corresponding to the slope of BC', does not equal the marginal rate of transformation (the slope of BC). If the country initiates trade and faces fixed international terms of trade, slope BC'', which lies between the slopes of BC and BC', the country will specialize in Y, export Y, and consume at T, which in this case is inferior to both P and A. Hagen was using this analysis to show that protectionism can be superior to free trade, i.e. that the utility level at P with a prohibitive tariff and factor distortion is superior to the free trade level at T.

Notice also that the pattern of trade depends on the size and direction of the differential. If the distorted domestic price ratio had been less than the international terms of trade (slope BC''), then the country would have specialized in X rather than Y. Using the formula developed above, we can say, in general, that if $[P_x/P_y]_I$ denotes the international terms of trade,

$$\left[\frac{P_x}{P_y}\right]_I \gtrless \frac{w_x}{w_y} \cdot \frac{b}{a} \text{ implies specialization in } \begin{Bmatrix} X \\ Y \end{Bmatrix}.$$

Clearly, w_x/w_y can be manipulated by the differential to cause specialization either way. In summary, the differential reduces output of the industry paying the differential, causes non-tangency in autarky, and can reverse the pattern of trade.

Models with one factor and more than two products were discussed by Cairnes [30] in his controversy with the classicists. Cairnes argued that if labour is divided into non-competing groups with each group aligned with a specific product, wage differentials will be determined exclusively by the demand for each product. Marshall and Taussig [149, pp. 53–4] criticized Cairnes for ignoring the long-run supply response of labour (reproduction would increase within each non-competing group whenever its wages rose above the subsistence level). Taussig [149, p. 57] went so far as to argue that international trade 'is not likely to modify the alignment of grades [of labour] within a country', although that alignment could certainly affect international trade, as in his cases of pre-World War I German chemical exports and United States iron and steel exports. Taussig showed that the classical explanation of the pattern of trade still holds if the structure of relative wage distortions is the same between countries.

Samuelson [135] and others have discussed comparative advantage in a one-factor, many-good model without wage distortion; an explanation of the pattern of trade in this one-factor model *with* wage distortion can be developed by borrowing the Mangoldt–Edgeworth technique discussed by Viner [158, pp. 458–62]. We shall consider only two countries. The technique is general enough to consider cases where both the level and structure of wages differ by country but we are interested here only in the structural aspects (this is oversimplifying since the levels of wages are determined partly by the reciprocal demand of the two countries for each other's products). We noted earlier that the cost of good i in a one-factor model (where a_i represents the constant output–labour ratio and w_i represents that wage paid by industry i) can be written

$$P_i = w_i/a_i \quad i = 1, \ldots, 5. \tag{4}$$

Assume initially that there are no factor price distortions so that w_i is the same for all five industries. We can plot the logarithms of $P_1, \ldots, P_5$ for country I from a fixed point 0 in Fig. 3*a* on the left side of the line. Similarly, the logarithms of the prices, $P_1, \ldots, P_5$ for country II, measured from the same point $0'$, are plotted on the right side of the line in Fig. 3*a*. If the wage levels in country II are greater (less) than those in I, $0'$ will lie above (below) 0. We have ruled this out by assumption. We can now determine which products will be exported by each country. Since the costs of goods 1, 2, and 3 are lower and 4, 5, higher in country II in Fig. 3*a*, then country II exports the former and country I the latter.

The Mangoldt–Edgeworth diagram can be used to show that when wage differentials are introduced, it is possible to obtain almost any pattern of trade. For example, if the relative wages of goods 1,

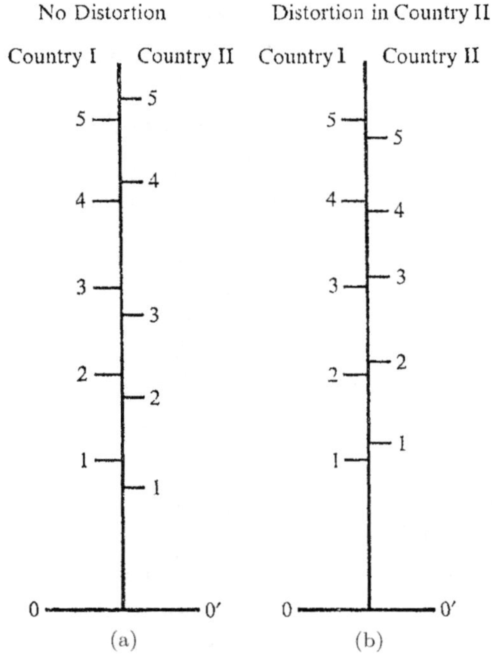

Figure 3.

2, and 3 are increased and those of 4 and 5 fall in country II with the introduction of the differentials, then the pattern of trade can be reversed as in Fig. 3*b*. The same analysis can be performed using equation (4). This approach also illustrates Taussig's point that if the wage distortions are the same between countries, the pattern of trade is unaffected.

4. Differentials in Two-factor Models: The Structural Effects

A. Preliminary remarks, shrinkage, and non-tangency

Two important theoretical articles in the past decade on the structural effects of factor price differentials were published by Harberger [60] and Johnson [78]. Harberger's paper was concerned exclusively with the incidence of the U.S. corporate income-tax, and was followed by Mieszkowski [111]. After some delay, Johnson's paper stimulated an avalanche of research on the mathematical properties of general equilibrium models in which factor price differentials are present. At least six theoretical papers were written independently which explored factor price differentials and their effects on various properties of an economic system: Bhagwati and Srinivasan [23], Herberg and Kemp [69], Johnson and Mieszkowski [80], Lloyd [97], Magee [100], and Mundlak [115]. While each paper was concerned with slightly different problems, there was virtual unanimity on results where identical problems were considered. These papers elicited others by Batra and Pattanaik [11], Herberg, Kemp, and Magee [71], and Jones [82], among others. In this subsection, we shall explore the shrinkage and non-tangency issues.

First, we shall examine the problem of shrinkage of the production possibility curve and its non-tangency with the product price line. We noted earlier that factor-price differentials in two-factor models may place the system below its optimum transformation curve in product space (the *shrinkage* effect) if the factor market equilibrium is not on the efficiency locus in the Edgeworth–Bowley box.[2] Point A in Figs. 4*a* and 4*b* indicates no distortion while point D may indicate, for example, that X is paying a relatively higher price for capital than Y. Point D is on a transformation curve BDC in Fig. 4*b* which is inferior to the optimum curve BAC. If output of Y is held constant at Y_m in Fig. 4*a* (equal to OM in Fig. 4*b*), removal of the distortion (allowing product prices to change appropriately) implies movement from point D to E (in Fig. 4*a*), which increases output of X from X_d to X_e (or from MD to ME in Fig. 4*b*). Extending this argument to every point along the outer transformation curve, we can show that for any degree of distortion, the distortion curve BDC lies everywhere inside BAC, except at the two specialization points B and C. Eckaus [39, p. 373] has called the outer curve the 'technical transformation curve' and those inside of it 'market transformation curves' since they are generated by factor market distortions. We

[2]Jorge Marquez has shown that the shrinkage phenomenon is a second order effect starting from no distortion.

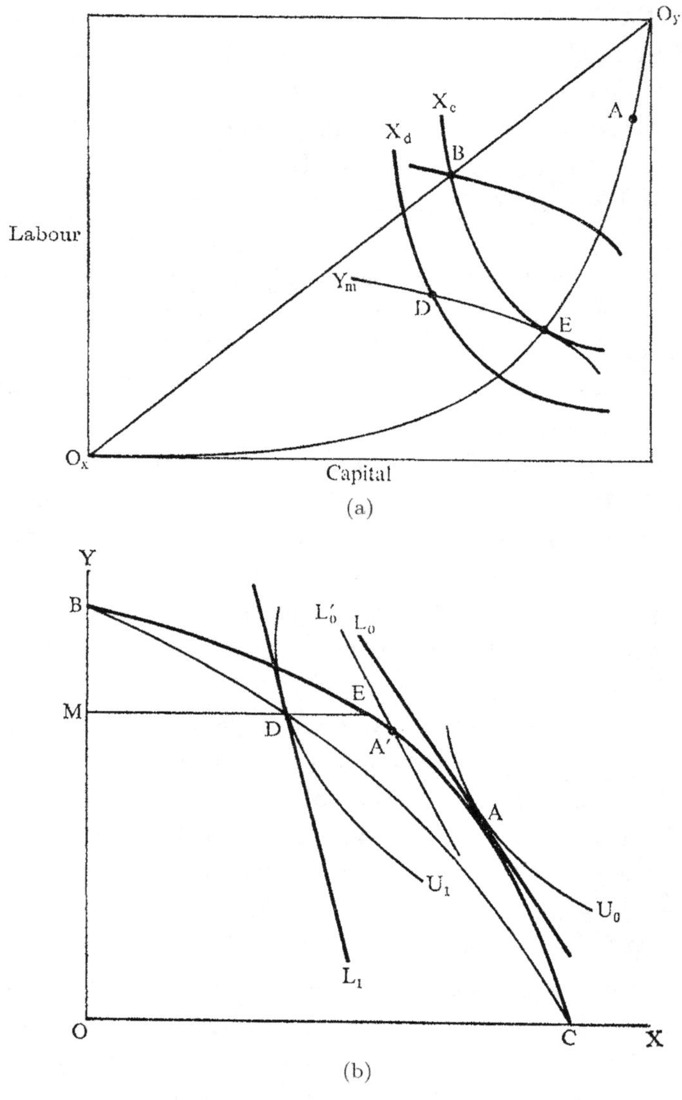

Figure 4.

shall follow Fishlow and David [42] and others calling in them simply 'outer' and 'inner' transformation curves.

Factor price differentials can break the equivalence of the marginal technical rates of substitution between factors and the marginal rates of substitution and transformation between products. Next, we shall examine when this does and does not occur. Again, we consider the two-good, two-factor model discussed in equations (1) and (2). We can rewrite the first-order conditions for profit maximization as follows:

$$P_x X_l = w_x \tag{5}$$

$$P_y Y_l = w_y \tag{6}$$

$$P_x X_k = r_x \tag{7}$$

$$P_y Y_k = r_y. \tag{8}$$

A distortion occurs whenever a differential exists such that $w_x \neq w_y$ or $r_x \neq r_y$. Following Hagen [54, pp. 507–8], we can take the total derivative of the production functions for both goods, replace the marginal productivities with their equilibrium values from equations (5) to (8), use the endowment constraints and write

$$-\frac{dY}{dX} = \frac{P_x}{P_y} \cdot \left[\frac{r_y \mathrm{d}k_x + w_y \mathrm{d}L_x}{r_x \mathrm{d}k_x + w_x \mathrm{d}L_x}\right]. \tag{9}$$

The marginal rate of transformation (*MRT*) and the marginal rate of substitution (*MRS*) differ if the bracketed term in (9), which we shall call 'the non-tangency factor', differs from one.

If the cost of both factors is identical in each industry, equations (5) to (8) yield

$$\frac{X_l}{Y_l} = \frac{X_k}{Y_k} \tag{10}$$

and the bracketed term in (9) equals one so that the system is Pareto optimal and no distortion exists. Thus, we get a factor market *distortion* and *shrinkage* if the equality in (10), is broken, and *non-tangency* if the non-tangency factor in (9) differs from one. We shall examine three possibilities:

first, non-tangency but no shrinkage;
second, shrinkage but no non-tangency; and
third, both shrinkage and non-tangency.

First, consider non-tangency but no shrinkage. If industry (X) faces an identical differential $t(>1)$ for both factors, there is no distortion in the factor markets since from equations (5) to (8),

$$\frac{X_k}{X_l} = \frac{tY_k}{tY_l} \tag{11}$$

and the differentials cancel. Since we remain on the efficiency locus in the Edgeworth–Bowley box, we also remain on the outer transformation curve BAC in $X - Y$ space. The product markets are distorted, however, since from equation (9),

$$MRT = \frac{1}{t} MRS. \tag{12}$$

Thus, we have violated the marginal equivalences in product space so that price line L_0' will intersect BAC at a point such as A' from above in Fig. 4*b*, with the non-tangency factor less than one. This case is similar to that of pure monopoly.

Second, we consider shrinkage but no non-tangency. If industry X pays a higher price for $K2(t = r_x/r_y > 1)$ but a lower price for $L2(s = w_x/w_y < 1)$, then the factor market is distorted since

$$\frac{X_k}{X_1} = \frac{t}{s} \cdot \frac{Y_k}{Y_1} \tag{13}$$

with $(t/s) > 1$. The empirical possibility of this case in less developed countries has been considered by Myint [117], among others. The product market equivalences may or may not be distorted, however, since the $MRT \gtrless MRS$ depending on whether the net effect of s and t causes the non-tangency factor in (9) to be $\gtrless 1$. In the special case where the non-tangency factor equals one, we have an example in which the marginal factor equivalences are broken but the marginal product equivalences are not. Thus, the price line would be tangent to the inner transformation curve at the production equilibrium point.

Third, we consider both shrinkage and non-tangency. This includes all situations in the second case, just considered, in which the non-tangency factor does not equal one. It also includes situations in which only one of the two-factor markets is distorted. If industry X has to pay a higher price for one of its factors, such as capital

($r_x > r_y$), the system moves above the efficiency locus to a point such as D in Fig. 4*a* so that

$$\frac{X_k}{X_1} = t\left[\frac{Y_k}{Y_1}\right] \tag{14}$$

where $t = (r_x/r_y) > 1$. The marginal technical rates of factor substitution now differ by t. Similarly, from (9) we know that the non-tangency factor is less than one so that $MRS > MRT$; i.e. the relative market price of X is greater than its opportunity cost because of the higher factor market costs to X induced by the differential. The slope of the price line $L_1 = MRS$ is greater than MRT, the slope of the inner transformation curve BDC at D in Fig. 4*b*. Thus, when there is only one differential paid by one industry, the marginal equivalences are broken in both the factor and product markets. Since much of the existing literature deals with this case of the single differential, we shall now explore it in some depth.

B. The factor market and supply response

We start the discussion with the factor market, since important results for the entire system depend upon certain features of the factor market. Assume that products X and Y are produced by linearly homogeneous production functions and that the capital–labour ratios in each industry are denoted by k_x and k_y. We assume in the absence of distortion that product X is capital intensive. The distortion is introduced by assuming that the capital market incorporates a factor price differential t, defined by

$$r_x = tr_y \tag{15}$$

while the labour market does not ($w_x = w_y$). Following Johnson [78], we know from equation (14) that if $t > 1$ (< 1), we are above (below) the non-distorted efficiency locus $O_x\ EO_y$ in Fig. 4*a*, since the left-hand side of equation (14) is the slope of the X isoquant and the bracketed term on the right-hand side is the slope of the Y isoquant. Any locus of points along which t is constant and unequal to 1 is called a 'distorted efficiency locus' (equilibrium product prices, P_x/P_y, vary along this line). Corresponding to every distorted efficiency locus, there is an 'inner' or shrunken production possibility curve in the output space. Any sequence of equilibrium points along which relative product prices are fixed while t varies is called a 'distortion equilibrium locus'.

Once we leave the special case where $t = 1$, we must distinguish two types of factor intensities: those in the physical sense and those in the value sense (see Jones [82]). Let *PH* represent the 'physical' definition of relative factor intensity, i.e. the difference in the capital–labour ratios in the two industries:

$$PH \equiv k_x - k_y. \tag{16}$$

Similarly, let *VA* represent the 'value' definition of relative factor intensity, i.e. the difference in the shares of capital relative to labour in the two industries:

$$VA \equiv \frac{r_x K_x}{w_x L_x} - \frac{r_y K_y}{w_y L_y} \equiv (r/w)_x k_x - (r/w)_y k_y. \tag{17}$$

In the absence of distortion (when $t = 1$), both *PH* and *VA* always have the same sign, so that along the non-distorted efficiency locus in the Edgeworth–Bowley box, the physical factor intensities and the value factor intensities of the products always correspond.

Johnson [78] has noted that if an industry pays a differential for its physically intensive factor, the *physical* factor intensities of the products can reverse. If production isoquants are homothetic, the differential t must exceed the ratio of the slopes of the X to the Y isoquants along the diagonal in the Edgeworth–Bowley box (e.g. the relative slopes at point R in Fig. 5). We shall denote by sets I and II non-specialized factor market equilibria for which the physical factor intensities are not reversed or are reversed, respectively. In Fig. 5, set I corresponds to non-specialized points below the diagonal and set II to non-specialized points above the diagonal. Magee [101] showed that it is impossible to move from set I to set II by merely changing the differential. Herberg, Kemp, and Magee [71] extended this, proving that the set of relative product prices giving non-specialized equilibrium below the diagonal in the Edgeworth–Bowley box and the set of relative product prices giving equilibrium above

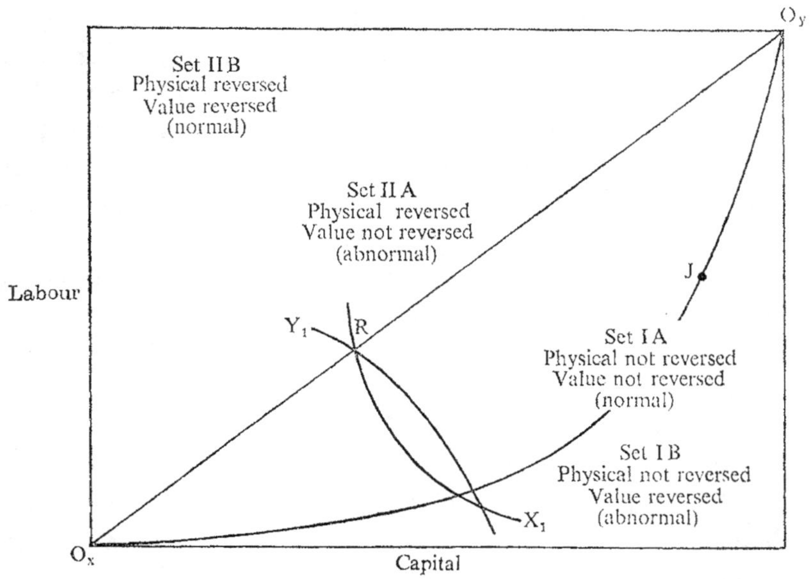

Figure 5.

the diagonal are mutually exclusive. Geometrically it is clear that the sets of t's corresponding to non-reversal in set I in Fig. 5 does not overlap with the t's in set II ([71], [78], [80], [101], and [115]). All of the values of t and P_x/P_y in Set II exceed the values of t and P_x/P_y in set I in Fig. 5 [71].[3] In order to cross the diagonal and remain non-specialized, *both* the differential and relative product prices must change.

We turn now to the effect of differentials on the relative *value* factor intensities. Bhagwati and Srinivasan [23], Herberg and Kemp [69], Jones [82], Lloyd [97], Magee [101], and Mundlak [115] have all shown that factor price differentials can reverse relative value factor intensities. We shall denote by sets A and B non-specialized factor market equilibria for which the original value factor intensities are not reversed or are reversed, respectively. For many production functions, it is possible for the value factor intensities to reverse on both sides of

---

[3]Intuitively, as t increases the X industry is penalized as it moves toward Set II; to remain non-specialized, P_x/P_y must be raised to offset the higher t.

the diagonal, so that we get the configuration shown in Fig. 5. One comment which relates Fig. 5 to factor markets in general is that all non-specialized points between the non-distorted efficiency locus $O_x\ JO_y$ and the diagonal $O_x\ RO_y$, both inclusive, are members of set A [101]. Otherwise, the regions denoting sets A and B are purely stylized — they are shown only to denote logical possibilities and not a particular concatenation of factor market equilibria.

The importance of the physical value distinction for the entire system (not just factor markets) is explored by Jones [82]. His argument runs as follows. Physical factor proportions link changes in the real variables of the model, the community's outputs, and factor endowments. The value ranking given by distributive shares serves to link the financial variables, the prices of outputs, and rental for the service of inputs. The relationship between changes in physical variables (e.g. outputs) and financial variables (e.g. output prices) depend crucially on whether physical and value rankings of factor proportions correspond. The uses of the words 'financial' and 'real' do not imply the existence of any monetary assets in the model, but rather the distinction between relative price and share variables on the one hand and quantity variables on the other. The two definitions of factor intensity correspond (do not correspond) if PH and VA in equations (16) and (17) have the same (opposite) sign.

For example, many of the recent papers ([11], [23], [69], [71], [82], [97], [101], and [115]) find that an increase in $P = P_x/P_y$ (with the differential held constant) increases the supply of X if the physical and value intensities correspond and reduces X if they do not. Consequently, the supply response of outputs to changes in P is *normal* if, and only if, neither the physical nor the value intensities are reversed (set IA in Fig. 5), or both the physical and value intensities are reversed (set IIB) and *abnormal* if, and only if, relative factor intensities have reversed in the physical sense only (set IIA) or relative factor intensities have reversed in the value sense only (set IB). Thus, the supply of a product is positively related to relative product prices in the normal cases; supply is perfectly elastic with respect to prices whenever the physical or the value factor intensities of the products are identical;[4] and supply is negatively related to prices in the abnormal cases.

The response of outputs to changes in the differential (with product prices constant) is the same (see [11], [71], [82], [101], and [115]). An increase in a differential paid by an industry on either factor reduces output (the normal case) if the physical and value factor intensities correspond and increases output if they do not (the abnormal case).

Now that the output effects have been mentioned, we return to a more detailed analysis of factor market behaviour. Until very recently, writers in this area were either not aware of or failed to pursue the perverse possibilities posed by non-correspondence of the physical and value factor intensities (Harberger [60], Johnson [78], Johnson and Mieszkowski [80], Mieszkowski [111]). Consequently, their contributions cover half of the logical possibilities — those in which the response of the system to changes in either relative product prices on the differential is normal.

Since all of the points along the non-distorted efficiency locus $O_x AO_y$ in Fig. 6 are in the *normal* set IA, let us consider the effects of the introduction of a capital differential in industry X starting from point A, such that t increases from $t = 1$ to $t > 1$ (see [80] and [101]). First, if we hold output of X constant, there is a 'substitution' effect away from capital in industry X, indicated by movement from A to E. The substitution effect causes the capital–labour ratio to decline in X and rise in Y. The curve O_xEO_y is a distorted efficiency locus, along which the ratio of the X to the Y isoquants equals the new value of the differential t. The system cannot remain at E, however, since negative profits exist in the X industry; thus, there is an 'output' effect, which causes a reduction in the production of X. Consequently, the new factor market equilibrium must be below E on the distorted efficiency locus O_xEO_y. The output effect causes

[4]The reason is that the derivatives of outputs with respect to relative prices have zeros in their denominators when either *PH* or *VA* equal zero.

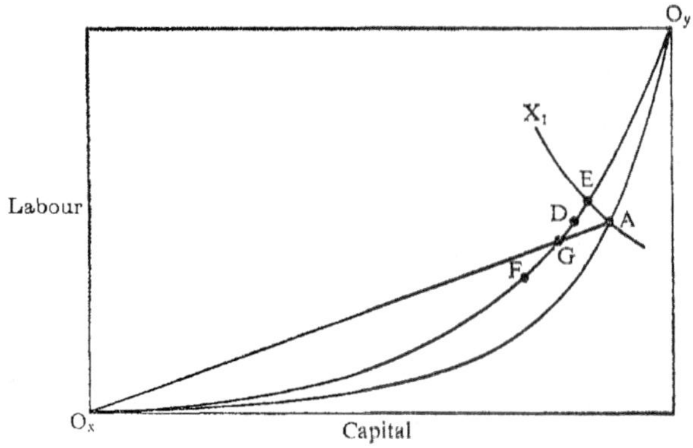

Figure 6.

the capital–labour ratios to increase in both X and Y (starting from point E). In terms of the effect on the capital–labour ratio in the industry paying the differential, the substitution and output effects work in opposite directions when the differential is increased on the industry's intensive factor and in the same direction when it is increased on the non-intensive factor.

An important question is whether the new factor market equilibrium is above or below point G on the distorted efficiency locus. Jones [82] and Magee [100] and [101] have shown that if relative product prices are unchanged from their value at point A (e.g. if the country does not possess monopoly power in trade), the new equilibrium with the increase in t must always be below point G, at a point such as F. Thus, whenever an industry must pay a differential on its intensive factor, such as capital, with product prices fixed, *the output effect always dominates the substitution effect.* Capital–labour ratios rise in both industries and by the homogeneity postulate, capital is *worse* off in both industries. The implications for labour unions or any factor with market power are clear: if product prices are relatively fixed, they should introduce differentials in sectors of the economy in which they are the non-intensive factor [101]. A related result is Johnson's [79] examination of minimum wage laws. He finds that if they are applied to only one sector, labour may be better off in all sectors. On the other hand, a minimum wage law applied to all sectors will result in unemployment.

If product prices are not fixed we get a third effect, called the 'price' effect. The increase in the price of the product paying the increased differential will mitigate part of the adverse output effect so that the new equilibrium will be above F on the distorted efficiency locus. If the new equilibrium is below G, the previous factor welfare results still hold; if it is above G, then capital is better off in industry X and worse off in Y. The actual location of the new point depends upon demand (see Harberger [60], Johnson and Mieszkowski [80], and Mieszkowski [111] for discussion of this point).

Returning to the situation in which output prices are fixed, and considering all cases, we can say that an increase in a differential causes a decrease (increase) in the relative price of the factor if it is the physically intensive (non-intensive) factor in the industry paying the increased differential when the physical and the value factor intensities correspond.[5] This leads to an increase (reduction) in the physical proportions of that factor used in both industries. The same statement holds for a decrease in the relative price of a commodity with any fixed differential. This implies that if we continue to define factor intensities in a physical sense, then the Stolper–Samuelson theorem holds in the normal case, but is reversed in the abnormal case ([11] and [101]). If, however, factor intensities are defined in the value sense, the Stolper–Samuelson theorem holds in all cases [71]. This follows Jones's [82] dictum that the value ranking given by distributive shares serves as a link between all financial variables (product prices and factor prices).

A useful theorem relating the factor market to the product market is that if both capital–labour ratios move in the same direction, then output responses are unambiguously determined; since k_x and k_y move in the same direction, the knowledge of dk_i/dt or $dk_i/\mathrm{d}P$ is sufficient to determine $\mathrm{d}X/\mathrm{d}t$, $\mathrm{d}Y/\mathrm{d}t$, $\mathrm{d}X/\mathrm{d}P$, and $\mathrm{d}Y/\mathrm{d}P$, and the latter need not be calculated ([100] and [101]). This

[5]The opposite holds when the factor intensities do not correspond.

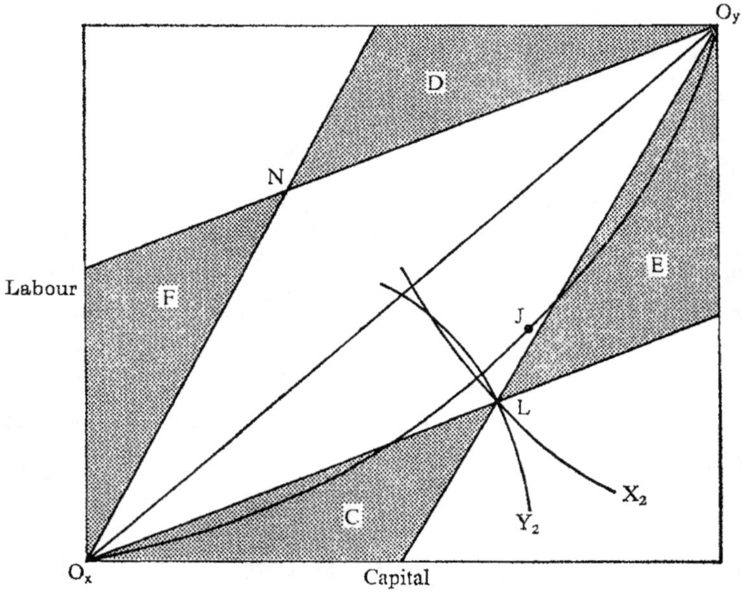

Figure 7.

is illustrated in Fig. 7. Starting from point L (where neither type of reversal has occurred), an increase in the differential which X must pay for capital (regardless of whether $t > 1$ or $t < 1$ initially) increases k_x and k_y so that the new equilibrium must be in shaded area C. Clearly, output of X falls and Y increases. If the physical but not the value factor intensities of the products are reversed so that we start from point N, an increase in the capital differential paid by X results in a perverse result, namely, an increase in X and decrease in Y as the factor market equilibrium moves from N into area D.

With regard to factor supplies, we know that an exogenous increase in a country's endowment of a factor with distortion leads to a relative increase in the production of the good using that factor intensely in the physical sense. Consequently, so long as we define factor intensities in the physical sense, Rybczynski's theorem holds without modification, regardless of the degree of factor market distortion and regardless of whether the distortion has reversed the value factor intensities of the product ([82] and [101]).

C. Physical and value factor intensity reversals

It is of some interest to know what characteristics of the production functions are associated with physical and value factor intensity reversals. The value of t required to cross the diagonal and give physical reversal diminishes as the product elasticities of factor substitution increase in size and as the non-distorted factor intensities of the products become more similar. It is more difficult to generalize about value factor intensity reversals.[6] They are impossible with Cobb–Douglas production functions since the relative shares going to capital and labour are invariant to changes in either prices or the differential (Herberg and Kemp [69]).

If the physical factor intensities have not been reversed, value factor intensity reversals are possible only if an industry pays a differential on its non-intensive factor, which places the factor market equilibrium in the area on the side of the non-distorted efficiency locus opposite the diagonal in the Edgeworth–Bowley box ([82], [101], and [115]). Thus, value reversals are impossible if $t > 1$ in set I. In general, if t is held constant and P_x/P_y varies, the value factor intensities never reverse if S_x and S_y are constant and equal, reverse once if the elasticities of factor substitution, S_x and S_y, are constant and different, and may reverse more than once in all other cases [71]. It is also true that for any given value of k_y (along which $(r/w)_y$ is constant by the homogeneity assumption), the value intensities never reverse if $S_x = 1$, reverse once if S_x is constant but unequal to one and may reverse more than once in all other cases [71].

Geometrically, the Samuelson–Johnson factor price equalization diagram can be used to extend these results (see [100] and [101] for the application of this diagram to factor price differentials). Specifically, even in the case where an industry pays a differential on its non-intensive factor in set I ($t < 1$ or below the non-distorted efficiency locus $O_x\ JO_y$ in the Edgeworth–Bowley box in Fig. 5), it is impossible for the value factor intensities to reverse if $S_x \leq 1$ and $S_y \geq 1$. The argument proceeds as follows. Since the country does not

[6] i.e. as the isoquants get flatter and their tangencies get closer to the diagonal.

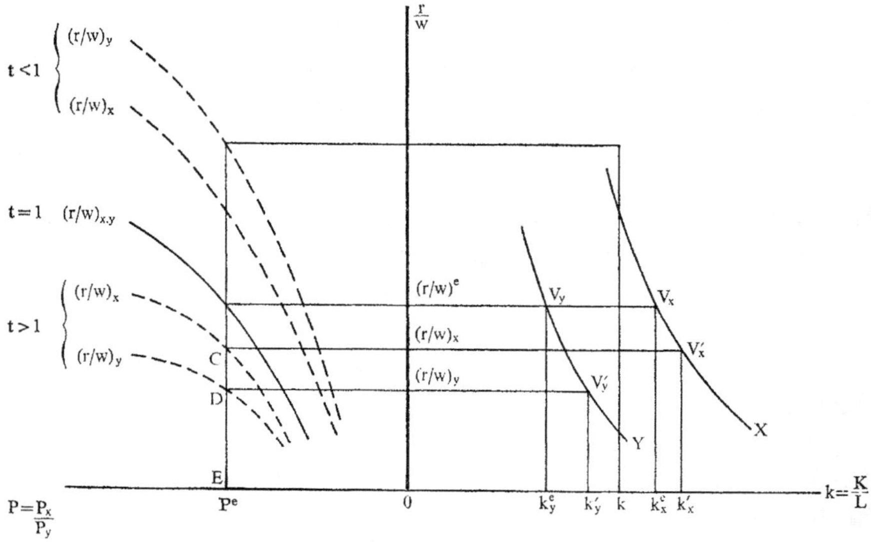

Figure 8.

possess monopoly power in trade, it faces a fixed world equilibrium product price ratio, P^e. The areas under the X and Y curves in the right-hand side of Fig. 8 equal the ratio of the capital to labour factor shares in each industry, rK/wL. The elasticities of factor substitution in the two industries, i.e. the percentage change in K/L for a given percentage change in r/w, are equal to the elasticities of the X and Y curves.

Observe that in the absence of distortion ($t = 1$), the physical and the value factor intensities of the two products must coincide. From equation (16) the difference in physical factor intensities at $(r/w)^e$ is

$$PH \equiv 0k_x^e - 0k_y^e > 0$$

while the difference in the value factor intensities from equation (17) is the difference in the areas under the X and Y curves, or

$$VA \equiv \text{area } 0V_x - \text{area } 0V_y \equiv \text{area } k_y^e V_x > 0.$$

If t increases to some value greater than one, the unique link between product prices and factor prices in the left-hand side of the diagram is broken: we now have a separate $(r/w)_i$ curve for each industry i.

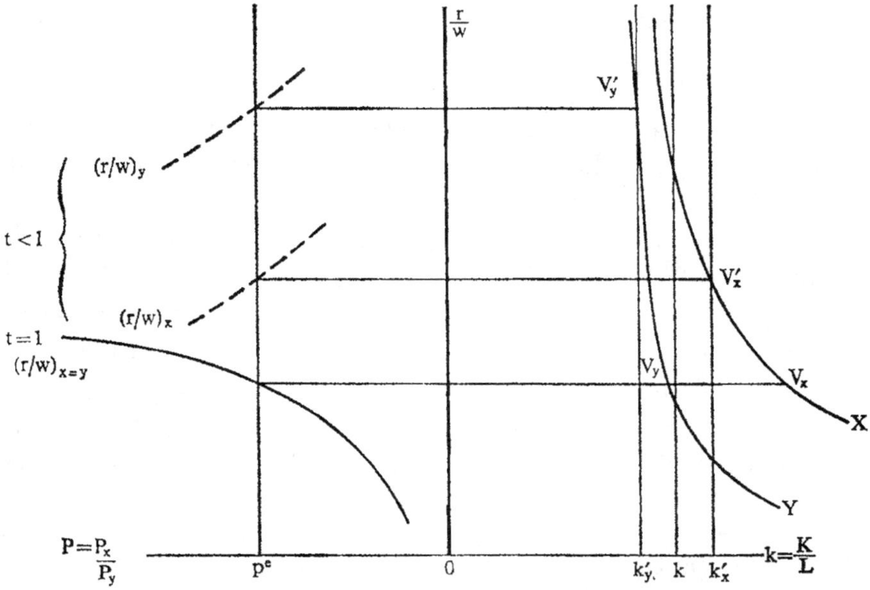

Figure 9.

We saw earlier that at fixed commodity prices, the relative return to capital must fall in both industries. Thus, the two new curves lie below the old $t = 1$ curve and the ratio of the height of the X to Y curve must equal the new differential ($t = CE/DE$). When the value and the physical factor intensities correspond (do not correspond), the curves are positively (negatively) sloped. Whether capital increases or decreases its share of the value of output in each industry when t changes depends on the elasticities of factor substitution, $S_i(i = X, Y)$. If $S_i < 1$, the share of capital in industry i falls as the area under the curve declines. If $S_i > 1$, the share of capital increases.

If industry Y, where capital is the non-intensive factor, is forced to pay a differential for capital ($t < 1$), these results are just reversed: capital is better (worse) off in both industries and increases (decreases) its share of industry i's output if $S_i < 1 (> 1)$. If t decreases sufficiently, we get the case shown in Fig. 9 where the value but not the physical factor intensities of the products have been reversed, sinces

$$VA_{t<1} \equiv \text{area } 0V_x'\text{–area } 0V_y' < 0.$$

The dashed lines $(r/w)_i$ for $t < 1$ must be negatively sloped since the relationship $(r/w)_i = f_i(P_x/P_y)$ has the property $f_i' > 0$ without reversal and $f_i' < 0$ with reversal, as mentioned earlier.

In general, starting from any point in set IA, reducing t moves points V_x and V_y up the X and Y curves in the right-hand side of Fig. 8 [101]. Geometrically, it is clear that *VA* will not change signs as t is decreased if the area under the X curve is constant or increases while the area under the Y curve is constant or decreases, i.e. $S_x \leq 1$ and $S_y \geq 1$, which is what we set out to establish on page 24. Notice that the elasticities of substitution in this case do not need to be constant.

D. The shape of the transformation curve

We have noted the possibility of perverse supply response to relative product price changes. A related area which has drawn attention is the question of the shape of the transformation curve with differentials. The problem has been examined by [20], [23], [42], [69], [78], [82], and [97], to name a few. While this is of enormous theoretical importance, it is of little empirical importance. In Mundlak's [115, p. 531] words, 'The examination of the convexity of the transformation curve is of little interest. What matters . . . is the relationships between [outputs] and [prices].' Ironically, this statement is true because of the extensive examinations of Bhagwati and Srinivasan [23], Herberg and Kemp [69], and Lloyd [97] into the convexity question. Independently, they discovered the important result that normal and perverse output responses to price changes are not necessarily related to the concavity or convexity (from below) of the transformation curve. Thus, normal output response is possible along convex portions and perverse response along concave portions of the transformation curve. Jones [82] has extended the discussion, showing how the 'wedge' (i.e. the gap or the non-tangency factor between the price line and the distorted transformation curve) varies along the curve.

Many propositions have been derived linking the shape of the transformation curve to the factor market and production functions. We shall mention three:

1. If a differential paid to the *intensive* factor (so measured in the absence of distortion) in an industry is large enough, it can cause the physical factor intensities to reverse. Before reversal, the transformation curve lies outside a chord joining its end points; at the reversal value, the transformation curve coincides with the chord; after reversal, the transformation curve lies inside the chord (Johnson [78]).
2. In the Cobb–Douglas case, a differential paid by an industry on its *intensive* factor (above O_xJO_y in Fig. 5) will be accompanied by a concave transformation curve with normal output response to price changes before physical reversal, and a convex transformation curve with perverse output response after physical reversal (Johnson [78] and Herberg and Kemp [69]).
3. If, in the Cobb–Douglas case, a differential is paid by an industry on its *non-intensive* factor (below O_xJO_y in Fig. 5), then all output-price relationships are normal, regardless of the concavity or convexity of the transformation curve; in fact, the transformation curve may be uniformly convex or uniformly concave or partly concave and partly convex, but it cannot change its curvature more than twice (Herberg and Kemp [69]).

E. International trade and factor movements

The Samuelson–Johnson diagram in Fig. 8 illustrates the impossibility of international factor price equalization with differentials. If the home factor market has a differential, t, while the foreign market does not, then $(r/w)_i$ at home exceeds (is less than) r/w abroad when $t < 1 (> 1)$, even with product prices equalized ([100] and [101]). Foreign factor prices are read off of the $t = 1$ curve in the left half of Fig. 8. The possibility of value intensity reversals raises the even more interesting point made by Bhagwati and Srinivasan [23] that multiple equilibria are possible with differentials so that even if both product prices *and* differentials are identical in two countries, factor price equalization may not occur if one country is at one non-specialized equilibrium point and the other country at another.

The effects of distortions on the pattern of trade in two-factor models are the same as those developed earlier for one-factor models: trade can go either way so that the Heckscher–Ohlin model appears to break down. Cases of perverse trade specialization have been mentioned either explicitly or implicitly by Bhagwati and Ramaswami [20], Caves [31], Haberler [52], Hagen [54], Johnson [77], Lewis [95], Magee [100] and [101], and Ohlin [118] among others.

Following [101], consider a country without monopoly power in trade in which the two-factor intensities correspond (Batra and Pattanaik [11] extend [101] to permit variable international terms of trade). If the *export* industry pays a differential, both exports and imports decline toward zero, trade becomes small relative to national income, and a reversal of the pattern of trade is possible. With the export differential, the price of the physically abundant factor in the country falls in both industries below its price in foreign markets (even with free trade and internationally equalized product prices) so that the abundant factor in the distorted home market will wish to emigrate. If permitted, this will speed up the trade reversal process, leading to eventual production specialization in what was formerly the imported product.

On the other hand, if the *import-competing* industry pays a differential, both imports and exports increase, strengthening the original pattern of trade, and trade becomes larger relative to national income. The price of the physically abundant factor in the country rises in both industries above its price abroad, resulting in a paradoxical flow of factors from regions where they are already scarce to the country where they are relatively abundant. This moves the country toward production specialization in the initial export product. Next, assume that capital is mobile internationally but labour is not and there are greater interindustry barriers to capital flows domestically than there are internationally. If the *import-competing* industry pays a differential on capital, its non-intensive factor, and tries to offset this disadvantage by having the government impose a tariff on imports, then it is possible to have capital cross-flows, i.e. capital leaving the export industry and going abroad while foreign capital is being attracted into the import-competing industry.

If we denote by sets I and II whether the original pattern of trade has or has not been reversed, the Edgeworth–Bowley box may be divisible into as many as eight distinct regions [102]. Regardless of the definition of factor intensity used, four of these yield apparent empirical support for the Heckscher–Ohlin theorem (the observed relative factor intensity of the exported good corresponds to the relative factor abundance of the country) while the other four give Leontief-type results.

We have already noted that in the normal case, an increase in the differential paid by an industry on either of its factors may raise the relative price of its product ([11], [82], and [101]). If the increase occurs in the export sector, the country's terms of trade will improve and if it occurs in the import-competing sector, they will deteriorate, given appropriate stability assumptions. Batra and Pattanaik [11] and Jones [82] note that a reversal of only one of the factor intensities can lead to the opposite result, namely, an increased export differential being associated with a decrease in the terms of trade.

Finally, a word on stability in the static models ([68] and [70] consider stability in dynamic contexts). Jones [82] notes that in the abnormal cases where the physical and value factor intensities do not correspond, changes in the differential, t, or the capital–labour factor endowment, k, elicit price responses which reinforce rather than moderate the initial change, so that the conditions required for stability 'are apt to be rather stringent' and that in the abnormal case, high values for S_x and S_y endanger stability rather than encourage it, contrary to the normal case.

5. Differentials: The Welfare Effects

The welfare consequences of factor price differentials in both one- and two-factor models have elicited a lot of interest. Manoilesco

[104] started one debate in 1931 with his observation that Eastern European countries were being hurt by trade with Western Europe because free trade was forcing them to specialize in slow growth and low productivity agricultural pursuits while Western Europe benefited from specialization in manufactured products, where productivity was higher. The differentials in the marginal productivities in the two sectors convinced him that protection of the manufacturing industries in less developed countries would be superior to free trade. This theme was formalized for both one- and two-factor models by Hagen [54]. At least three propositions can be made on this issue.

First, protection may or may not be superior to free trade with factor price differentials. This traditional second-best argument has been made by a number of authors ([20], [52], and [77], among others).

Second, from a welfare point of view, protectionism is not the optimal policy response to differentials. This proposition has had an interesting history of independent rediscovery over a thirty-year period. The proposition was made by Ohlin [118] in 1931, restated by Meade [109] and Hagen [55] in the 1950s and rediscovered by Bhagwati and Ramaswami [20] in 1963. The optimal policy is factor taxation or subsidy. To quote Ohlin: 'A cash bonus corresponding to the extra labour costs would bring the situation closer to a more normal one, than a system of duties can do' [118, p. 44]. Further, Ohlin noted that if the differential is caused by factor immobility, then duties will just increase the differential, whereas the rational policy is 'to increase the labour mobility and do away with the watertight labour compartment' [118, p. 44].

Third, policies can be ranked in terms of their efficacy in offsetting differentials. Bhagwati [19] ranks these policies as follows.

1. First-best: factor tax-cum-subsidy;
2. Second-best: production tax-cum-subsidy;

3. Third-best: tariff (trade subsidy);
4. Consumption tax-cum-subsidy will not help.

A paper dealing with second-best policy intervention involving distortions without trade has been written by Fishlow and David [42].

In response to a paper by Kemp and Negishi [86], Bhagwati, Ramaswami, and Srinivasan [21] have written an extremely interesting paper in which they derive an equation, now quite in vogue, which yields some interesting results (this paper is a predecessor of [19]). Following [20], they consider the equality of the domestic rate of substitution (DRS), the domestic rate of transformation (DRT) and the foreign rate of transformation (FRT). They find that if only two out of three of these are equal under *laissez-faire,* then there is some policy which will raise welfare, even though the equality of the first two variables is broken thereby. If all three of these variables are unequal, there is no feasible policy which will raise welfare.

Bhagwati [19], following the theory of the second-best, states that reduction of a differential with other distortions in the system may not increase welfare, while reduction of a differential with no other distortion in the system necessarily increases welfare. Bhagwati, Batra, and Pattanaik [11] and Foster and Sonnenschein [45] note that the second proposition is contingent upon the existence of a single equilibrium point. Batra and Pattanaik show that an increased differential lowers real income, and hence welfare, in the normal cases and increases income and welfare in the abnormal cases with product prices fixed. Thus, a decrease in one distortion, even with no other distortions present, does not necessarily mean an improvement in welfare (this is another consequence of distortion-induced reversals of the value factor intensities of the products which make multiple equilibria possible).

In another paper, Batra and Pattanaik [9] find that a *decrease* in a country's terms of trade may lead to an *increase* in welfare if factor markets are distorted. This may have a bearing on the debate over the secular deterioration of the terms of trade of the less developed countries since their factor markets are notoriously imperfect.[7] Empirical work should be undertaken to investigate the importance of this point. Finally, Kemp and Negishi [87] examine welfare with distortions in a model with many products and factors and variable returns to scale.

6. Empirical Studies

This section will review briefly some empirical work on factor price differentials. This discussion is included as a supplement to the theoretical review, and for that reason is not an exhaustive treatment. In Section I we reviewed several causes for both distortionary and non-distortionary differentials. Excellent examples of the latter are given in Mincer's survey [112]. The econometric, methodological, and measurement problems associated with measuring differentials have been investigated by Bahral [6], Hall [57], Hanna and Denison [58], Hart [63], Johansen [75], and Perlman [124]. An outstanding paper with good coverage of the pre-1962 literature has been written by Reder [129]. The studies by Clark [32, Ch. 10] and Bellerby [14] are examples of some of the applied work in the area. In this section we will consider four topics: immobility, union power, the corporate income-tax, and factor distortions with trade.

The reluctance of factors to move in response to higher real incomes may involve a quantum effect: they will not move to the higher income area or industry until the differential passes a certain threshold [118]. This inertia was demonstrated by Lester [93], who found in his survey of forty-eight labour market areas that the high-wage to low-wage ratio for identical jobs in the same community sometimes averaged 1.5. Meyers [110, p. 94] noted that 'there is a good bit of evidence to show that differences between job and no job are more effective in inducing movement of labour

[7]This argument was extended to the immiserizing growth case in R. Batra and G. W. Scully, 'The theory of wage differentials: welfare and immiserizing growth', *Journal of International Economics*, 1 (May 1971), pp. 241–7.

than differences in wages'. Stafford [145] observes that unionization probably reduces geographical mobility (although Parker and Burton [122] were not able to attribute a pre-war to post-war decline in U.S. mobility to unionization). Two interesting studies on migration have attempted to calculate the wage differential required to induce migration ([144] and [155]). Sjaastad [144] finds in the U.S. that 'the typical migrant would be indifferent between two destinations, one of which was 146 miles more distant than the other, if the average annual labour earnings were $106 higher (1947–9 dollars) in the more distant one'. Vanderkamp [155] makes similar calculations for Canada, finding somewhat smaller income–distance trade-offs. Benham, Maurizi, and Reder [15], in a study of the mobility of physicians and dentists in the United States, found that the latter are much more impeded geographically than the former because of state licensing requirements.

Marshall's work on the determinants of union power has been reviewed by Allen [2]. These determinants include an inelastic demand for the product's output, technological necessity, a low proportion of total costs attributable to labour (i.e. a capital-intensive unionized sector) and inelastic supplies of the co-operating factors. A large body of empirical work has been done on union/non-union wage differentials in the United States, where roughly a fourth of the labour force is unionized [94, p. 5]. Many of the earlier studies on unionization are discussed in Lewis [94], which is the standard reference work up to 1963. Several of these studies are summarized chronologically in Table 1. Roughly nine estimated that unions raise union over non-union wages, three concurred but with qualifications depending on the phase of the business cycle, five felt unions had little or no effect, and Douglas [37] found that the union/non-union wage ratio was less than one and declining in the early twentieth century.

One of the most interesting results is that unions improve their position *vis-à-vis* non-union labour in troughs but are hurt at peaks of the business cycle (see [94], [125], and [147]). Thus, in addition to utilizing idle resources, high levels of employment also work to reduce distortions in labour pricing caused by contractual rigidity in union

Table 1. A survey of the effects of unionism on wages in the U.S.

	Author	Date of study	Scope of study	Conclusions
1.	Douglas [37]	1930	Real wages in U.S., 1890–1926	In 1920, the ratio of union/non-union wages was far below the level in 1890–9; ratio began to rise in early 1920s.
2.	Friedman [46]	1951	Comment on post-war inflation	The effect of unions on wages exaggerated; not over 10–20% of labour force affected by unions.
3.	Sultan [147]	1954	Measured ratio of share of union/non-union (1929 = 100) between 1929 and 1951	Unions showed relative improvement in 1931–4, 1934–8, 1941–9 and declined in 1929–31, 1939–40, 1949–51.
4.	Locks [98]	1955	Investigated Cleveland, Ohio, labour market, 1945–50	Found greater tendency for pattern-bargaining among union than non-unionized plants.
5.	Ulman [153]	1955	Comment on Friedman [46]	Unions may be able to affect the structure of wages without affecting the level of wages.
6.	Eisemann [40]	1956	Inter-industry wage changes 1939–47	Does not find that unions affected wage increases significantly over this period.
7.	Maher [103]	1956	Used BLS data for 7 industries in 1950 cross-section study	Found no significant differences in union and non-union wages.
8.	Simler [143]	1961	Data: 1899–1954	Found little relationship between labour's share in manufacturing industries and unionism.
9.	Lurie [99]	1961	Data for transit industry for selected years, 1920–48	Union over non-union returns: 1920s 15–20%, early 1930s 20–25%, late 1930s 5–10%, 1940s below 18%.
10.	Ozanne [120]	1962	Occupational differentials for McCormick Works (1858–1959)	Prosperity widens and depression narrows occupational differentials.

(*Continued*)

Table 1. (*Continued*)

	Author	Date of study	Scope of study	Conclusions
11.	Lewis [94]	1963	Unionism since the 1920s in the U.S.	Union/non-union differentials highest in depressions and lowest at peaks of economic activity. Union over non-union returns: 1932–3 over 25% 1947–8 less than 5%.
12.	Segal [141]	1964	Case studies	Unions are more successful with industries servicing local markets than those in national markets and with concentrated rather than competitive industries.
13.	Weiss [161]	1966	Compared union and non-union private wage and salary income for 1959 reported in the 1/1000 sample of the 1960 Census	The union/non-union differential largely evaporates after personal characteristics of the labour force are considered.
14.	Stafford [145]	1968	Used portions of 1966 Survey of Consumer Finances gathered by the Survey Research Center, University of Michigan, to modify Weiss [161]	The union/non-union differential is 26% for operatives, 18% for clerical and sales workers and 0% (not statistically significant) for skilled labour (professionals, non-self-employed managers, etc.), even after personal characteristics of the labour force are considered.
15.	Clover [33]	1968	Used BLS data of 31 surveys of earnings in 23 manufacturing industries, 1960–5	Union wages exceeded non-union wages by 18% although the differential narrowed some-what over the period.

(*Continued*)

Table 1. (*Continued*)

	Author	Date of study	Scope of study	Conclusions
16.	Pierson [125]	1968	Combines quarterly data for U.S. manufacturing (1953–66) into two groups: union and non-union	Average annual wage changes: union, 3.62% non-union, 2.97%, with higher profit rates in union strength closely tied to adaptability to cost-of-living changes. Union strength has less impact in periods of low unemployment.
17.	Throop [151]	1968	Cross-section data for 1950 and 1960 for 2-digit manufacturing and 7 other industries	Estimates that the union/non-union wage differential increased 12.7% points 1950–60, after allowing for skill-level changes, city size, and labour supply.
18.	Ashenfelter [4]	1971	Used 1967 Survey of Economic Opportunity data for U.S. urban males (8,123 white and 3,897 black) to investigate union effects on wage discrimination	The union/non-union wage differential is 9.7% for white males and 20.5% for black males. Craft unions are more discriminatory than industrial unions. Black/white male wages were 3.4% higher in 1967 than they would have been in the absence of unionism.

wages. Fishlow and David [42, p. 534] argued, following Hagen [54], that the microeconomic 'direction of [a] differential will, in general, be determined by demand conditions'. To this sectoral effect we can add that they are also affected by changes in *aggregate* demand.

It is of some interest to compare the proportion of workers which are unionized by country. Table 2 is reproduced from Utsumi [154] and shows that the lowest percentage of the group is in the United States while the highest is in the United Kingdom and West Germany.

Table 2. Unionization by countries.

Country	Degree of unionization	Year of measurement
1. United States	27–31%	1953
2. Japan	38.9%	1955
3. France	40.0%	1950
4. West Germany	44.2%	1953
5. United Kingdom	44.6%	1953

Source: Utsumi [154].

This section will not systematically review studies dealing with differentials in the returns to capital. Risk aversion is the most frequently mentioned cause (see, for example, Fisher's paper [41]). In an early study, Bain [7] found that average post-tax profit rates were 12.1 per cent in concentrated industries and 6.9 per cent in all other industries. It is not clear what portion of these monopoly–oligopoly profits reflect differential returns to capital. Segal [141] and others have tried to establish a relationship between factor price differentials and industries which have product market power. Schwartzman [139] was unable to establish a relationship between monopoly and either high or low wages. On the other hand, Weiss [161] found relatively higher wages in concentrated industries, but noted that this was due to the economic superiority of labour in these industries (higher productivity, embodied human capital, etc.).

There is a body of rather controversial literature dealing with the incidence of the U.S. corporate income-tax. If it were a tax on pure profits, there should be no attempted shifting through price, output, or factor market effects. Hall [56] was unable to find evidence of shifting in either the product or factor markets while Harberger [60] found that capital bears between 112 and 120 per cent of the tax burden, so that it distorts the factor market for capital between the corporate and non-corporate sectors. The question is a complicated one, however, and the variance in the two results just cited is symptomatic of the lack of consensus in this area.

Finally, a number of studies have related differentials to international trade. A good general discussion of labour and trade is provided by Mitchell [113]. Kravis [92] found that U.S. wages in 1947 in the leading export industries were $1.46 while they were only $1.23 in import-competing industries. Keesing [84] found that United States exports are skilled-labour intensive while import-competing products use relatively large amounts of unskilled labour in their production, which helps explain Kravis's earlier result (see also Mitchell [114]). Bourque [25] shows that import-competing industries locate primarily in the South, where skill levels are lower than the national average. Salant [132] has discussed trade and the corporate income-tax while Marx [106] has discovered that differentials penalize U.S. exporters relative to importers in the purchase of non-primary inputs such as ocean freight. Several studies have examined inter-country wage differences: Mitchell [114] and Papola and Bharadwaj [121], to name two.

To date, I know of no empirical work which explores the theoretical question of physical and value factor intensity reversals discussed in the previous sections. This is certainly an important and fruitful area for future research.

7. Concluding Remarks

One is struck, in doing a survey, at the cyclical repetition of economic discoveries. For its time, probably the most outstanding work out of the 162 papers surveyed is the book review written by Ohlin [118] in 1931. It is purely qualitative but it arrives at many of the modern results of the structural and welfare effects of differentials in the normal case. The following quote from Ohlin [118] brilliantly anticipates the recent theoretical work on unionization: the adverse output effects in the unionized industry and expansion of the non-unionized industry ([11], [23], [69], [71], [82], [97], [100], [101], and [115]), the decline in real income and welfare attributable to the differential ([9], [11], [19], [20], [21], [42], [52], [54], [77], [86], and [109]), the dependence of the reallocation of labour on the elasticity of demand for the final product, which is particularly high for internationally traded goods ([37], [60], [82], [100], [101], [111]), the dependence of the effects on the product factor intensities ([11], [23],

[60], [69], [71], [78], [80], [82], [97], [100], [101], [111]), and the welfare superiority of factor subsidies to import duties ([8], [9], [10], [11], [19], [20], [21], [52], [77], and [109]):

> The high wage industry, where the marginal productivity of labour is relatively great, is kept back, while the low wage industry develops more than it would have done under conditions of uniform wage rates. The national income in terms of goods and services is reduced. It depends upon the circumstances in each particular case, whether this influence on the distribution of labour between various industries is great or not. Generally, a forcing up of wages in an industry will have greater influence the more elastic is the demand for its products. For this reason the pursuance of such a policy in export industries will reduce the number of workers there employed much more than its practice in home market industries. If the wages paid to workers in the trade union makes up only a small part of the commodity price [i.e., capital intensive] the decline in sales and, thus, the shift in production is likely to be small . . . [For welfare purposes] a cash bonus corresponding to the extra labour costs would bring the situation more close to a 'normal' one, than a system of duties can do. [118, pp. 39–40, 44.]

Obviously, book reviews today are just not what they used to be.

University of Chicago

References

1. Adams, F. G., 'The size of individual incomes: socioeconomic variables and chance variation', *Review of Economics and Statistics,* 40 (Nov. 1958), pp. 390–8.
2. Allen, Bruce T., 'Market concentration and wage increases, U.S. manufacturing, 1947–1964', *Industrial and Labor Relations Review,* 21 (Apr. 1968), pp. 353–66.
3. Altman, Stuart H., and Fisher, Anthony C., 'Marginal product of labor, wages and disequilibrium: comment', *Review of Economics and Statistics,* 51 (Nov. 1969), pp. 485–6.
4. Ashenfelter, Orley, 'Racial discrimination and trade unionism', *Journal of Political Economy,* 80 (May, 1972).
5. Auerbach, Robert, 'The effects of price supports on output and factor prices in agriculture', *Journal of Political Economy,* 78 (Nov./Dec. 1970), pp. 1355–61.

6. BahraL, Uri, 'Wage differentials and specification bias in estimates of relative labor prices', *Review of Economics and Statistics,* 44 (Nov. 1962), pp. 473–81.
7. Bain, J. S., 'Relation of profit rate to industry concentration: American manufacturing, 1936–1940', *Quarterly Journal of Economics,* 65 (Aug. 1951), pp. 293–324.
8. Bardhan, P. K., 'Factor market disequilibrium and the theory of protection', *Oxford Economic Papers,* 16 (Nov. 1964), pp. 375–88.
9. Batra, R., and Pattanaik, P. K., 'Domestic distortions and the gains from trade', *Economic Journal,* 80 (Sept. 1970), pp. 638–49.
10. ——— 'Factor market imperfections and gains from trade', *Oxford Economic Papers,* 23 (July 1971), pp. 182–8.
11. ——— 'Factor market imperfections, the terms of trade and welfare', *American Economic Review,* 61 (Dec. 1971), pp. 946–55.
12. Behman, Sara, 'Wage changes, institutions and relative factor prices in manufacturing', *Review of Economics and Statistics,* 51 (Aug. 1969), pp. 227–38.
13. Bell, Duran, 'Occupational discrimination as a source of income differences: lessons of the 1960's', *American Economic Review,* 62 (May, 1972), pp. 363–72.
14. Bellerby, J. R., in association with G. R. Allen and others, *Agriculture and Industry Relative Income.* London: Macmillan, 1956.
15. Benham, Lee; Maurizi, Alex, and Reder, Melvin W., 'Migration, location and remuneration of medical personnel: physicians and dentists', *Review of Economics and Statistics,* 50 (Aug. 1968), pp. 332–47 (reprinted in [29]).
16. Bhagwati, Jagdish, 'The pure theory of international trade: a survey', *Economic Journal,* 74 (Mar. 1964), pp. 1–84.
17. ——— *The Theory and Practice of Commercial Policy,* Frank Graham Memorial Lecture (1967), Special Papers in International Economics No. 8, Princeton University, 1968.
18. ——— 'Distortions and immiserizing growth: a generalization', *Review of Economic Studies,* 35 (Oct. 1968), pp. 481–5.
19. ——— 'The generalized theory of distortions and welfare', in J. Bhagwati, R. Jones, R. Mundell, and J. Vanek, eds., *Trade, Balance of Payments and Growth,* Papers in International Economics in Honour of Charles P. Kindleberger. Amsterdam: North Holland, 1971.
20. ——— and Ramaswami, V. K., 'Domestic distortions, tariffs and the theory of optimum subsidy', *Journal of Political Economy,* 71 (Feb. 1963), pp. 44–50.
21. ——— and Srinivasan, T. N., 'Domestic distortions, tariffs and the theory of optimum subsidy: some further results', *Journal of Political Economy,* 77 (Sept. 1969), pp. 1005–10.
22. ——— and Srinivasan, T. N., 'Optimal policy intervention to achieve non-economic objectives', *Review of Economic Studies,* 36 (Jan. 1969), pp. 27–38.

23. Bhagwati, Jagdish and Srinivasan, T. N., 'The theory of wage differentials: production response and factor price equalization', *Journal of International Economics*, 1 (Feb. 1971), pp. 19–35.
24. Black, J., 'Foreign trade and real wages', *Economic Journal*, 79 (Mar. 1969), pp. 184–5.
25. Bourque, P. J., 'Geographic earnings differentials and foreign trade', *Review of Economics and Statistics*, 40 (May 1958), pp. 177–9.
26. Bronfenbrenner, M., 'Wages in excess of marginal revenue product', *Southern Economic Journal*, 16 (Jan. 1950), pp. 297–309.
27. ——— 'Potential monopsony in labor markets', *Industrial and Labor Relations Review*, 9 (July 1956), pp. 577–88.
28. Bryce, Herrington, J., 'Regional labor earnings differentials in a small developing country: the Republic of Panama', *Journal of Regional Science*, 9 (Dec. 1969), pp. 405–15.
29. Burton, John F., jr.; Benham, Lee K.; Vaughn, William M. III, and Flanagan, Robert J., *Readings in Labor Market Analysis*. New York: Holt, Rinehart and Winston, 1971.
30. Cairnes, J. E., *Some Leadinq Principles of Political Economy*. London: Macmillan, 1874.
31. Caves, Richard, *Trade and Economic Structure*. Cambridge, Mass.: Harvard University Press, 1960, pp. 58–68.
32. Clark, Colin, *The Conditions of Economic Progress*. London: Macmillan, 1957.
33. Clover, Vernon T., 'Compensation in union and nonunion plants, 1960–1965', *Industrial and Labor Relations Review*, 21 (Jan. 1968), pp. 226–33.
34. Corden, W. M., *Recent Developments in the Theory of International Trade*. International Finance Section, Department of Economics, Princeton University, 1965.
35. ——— 'Wage rigidity and the balance of payments: a third-best argument for tariffs?', mimeographed, 1971.
36. Despres, E., and Kindleberger, C. P., 'The mechanism for adjustment in international payments———the lessons of postwar experience', *American Economic Review*, 42 (May 1952), pp. 332–44.
37. Douglas, P. H., *Real Wages in the United States, 1890–1926*. Houghton–Mifflin, 1930.
38. Eagley, R. V., 'Market power as an intervening mechanism in Phillips curve analysis', *Economica, New Series*, 32 (Feb. 1965), pp. 48–64.
39. Eckaus, R. S., 'The factor proportions problem in underdeveloped areas', in A. N. Agarwala and S. P. Singh, eds., *The Economics of Underdevelopment*. New York: Oxford University Press, 1963, pp. 348–78. Reprinted from the *American Economic Review*, 45 (Sept. 1955), pp. 539–65.
40. Eisemann, D. M., 'Inter-industry wage changes, 1939–1947', *Review of Economics and Statistics*, 38 (Nov. 1956), pp. 445–8.
41. Fisher, L., 'Determinants of risk premiums on corporate bonds', *Journal of Political Economy*, 67 (June 1959), pp. 217–37.

42. Fishlow, Albert, and David, Paul A., 'Optimal resource allocation in an imperfect market setting', *Journal of Political Economy,* 69 (Dec. 1961), pp. 529–46.
43. Fogel, W. A., 'Job rate ranges: a theoretical and empirical analysis', *Industrial and Labor Relations Review,* 17 (July 1964), pp. 584–97.
44. Forchheimer, Karl, 'The role of relative wage differences in international trade', *Quarterly Journal of Economics,* 62 (Nov. 1947), pp. 1–30.
45. Foster, Edward, and Sonnenschein, Hugo, 'Price distortion and economic welfare', *Econometrica,* 38 (Mar. 1970), pp. 281–97.
46. Friedman, Milton, 'Some comments on the significance of labor unions for economic policy', in David M. Wright, ed., *The Impact of the Union.* New York: Harcourt Brace, 1951, pp. 204–34.
47. Fuchs, Victor R., and Perlman, Richard, 'Recent trends in Southern wage differentials', *Review of Economics and Statistics,* 42 (Aug. 1960), pp. 292–300.
48. Fukuchi, Takao, and Nobukuni, Makoto, 'An econometric analysis of national growth and regional income equality', *International Economic Review,* 11 (Feb. 1970), pp. 84–100.
49. Gallaway, Lowell, 'The North–South wage differential', *Review of Economics and Statistics,* 45 (Aug. 1963), pp. 264–72.
50. Garbarino, Joseph, 'A theory of interindustry wage structure variation', *Quarterly Journal of Economics,* 64 (May 1950), pp. 282–305.
51. Haberler, Gottfried, *The Theory of International Trade.* New York: Macmillan, 1937.
52. ——— 'Some problems in the pure theory of international trade', *Economic Journal,* 60 (June 1950), pp. 223–40.
53. ——— 'Real cost, money cost and comparative advantage', *International Social Science Bulletin,* 3 (Spring, 1951), pp. 54–8.
54. Hagen, Everett E., 'An economic justification of protectionism', *Quarterly Journal of Economics,* 72 (Nov. 1958), pp. 496–514.
55. ——— 'Reply', *Quarterly Journal of Economics,* 75 (Feb. 1961), pp. 145–51.
56. Hall, Challis A., 'Direct shifting of the corporation income tax in manufacturing', *American Economic Review,* 54 (May 1964), pp. 258–71.
57. Hall, Robert E., 'Why is the unemployment rate so high at full employment?', *Brookings Papers on Economic Activity* (No. 3, 1970), pp. 369–410.
58. Hanna, Frank A. (and E. F. Denison's comment), 'Analysis of interstate income differentials: theory and practice', in Conference on Research in Income and Wealth, *Regional Income* ('Studies in Income and Wealth', Vol. 21). Princeton, N.J.: Princeton University Press (for the National Bureau of Economic Research), 1957, pp. 113–79.
59. Hanoch, Giora, 'An economic analysis of earnings and schooling', *Journal of Human Resources,* 2 (No. 3, 1967), pp. 310–29.
60. Harberger, Arnold C., 'The incidence of the corporation income tax', *Journal of Political Economy,* 70 (June, 1962), pp. 215–40.

61. Harcourt, G. C., 'Some Cambridge controversies in the theory of capital', *Journal of Economic Literature,* 7 (June 1969), pp. 369–405.
62. Harris, J. R., and Todaro, M. P., 'Migration, unemployment and development: a two-sector analysis', *American Economic Review,* 60 (Mar. 1970), pp. 126–42.
63. Hart, P. E., 'Statistical measures of concentration vs. concentration ratios', *Review of Economics and Statistics,* 43 (Feb. 1961), pp. 85–6.
64. Heckscher, Eli, 'The effect of foreign trade on the distribution of income', *Ekonomisk Tidskrift,* 21 (1919), pp. 497–512. Reprinted in H. S. Ellis and L. A. Metzler, eds., *Readings in the Theory of International Trade.* Homewood, Ill.: Richard D. Irwin, 1949, pp. 272–300.
65. Hemming, M. F. W., and Corden, W. M., 'Import restriction as an instrument of balance of payments policy', *Economic Journal,* 68 (Sept. 1958), pp. 483–510.
66. Henderson, A., 'The restriction of foreign trade', *Manchester School of Economics and Social Studies,* 17 (Jan. 1949), pp. 12–35.
67. Henderson, John P., 'An intercity comparison of differentials in earnings and the city worker's cost of living', *Review of Economic Statistics,* 37 (Nov. 1955), pp. 407–11.
68. Herberg, Horst, 'On a two-sector model with non-shiftable capital and labour-market imperfections', *Zeitschrift für die gesamte Staatswissenschaft,* 128 (Apr. 1972), pp. 10–21.
69. Herberg, Horst, and Kemp, Murray C., 'Factor market distortions, the shape of the locus of competitive outputs and the relation between product prices and equilibrium outputs', in J. Bhagwati, R. Jones, R. Mundell, and J. Vanek, eds., *Trade, Balance of Payments and Growth,* Papers in International Economics in Honour of Charles P. Kindleberger. Amsterdam: North Holland, 1971.
70. ——— 'Growth and factor market "imperfections"', mimeographed, 1971.
71. ——— and Magee, Stephen P., 'Factor market distortions, the reversal of relative factor intensities, and the relation between product prices and equilibrium outputs ', *Economic Record,* 47 (Dec. 1971), pp. 518–30.
72. Hieser, R. O., 'Wage determination with bilateral monopoly in the labour market: a theoretical treatment', *Economic Record,* 46 (Mar. 1970), pp. 55–72.
73. Holmes, R. A., and Munro, J. M., 'Regional nonfarm income differences in Canada: an econometric study', *Journal of Regional Science,* 10 (Apr. 1970), pp. 65–74.
74. Inada, K., 'Investment in fixed capital and the stability of growth equilibrium', *Review of Economic Studies,* 33 (Jan. 1966), pp. 19–30.
75. Johansen, Leif, 'A note on the theory of interindustrial wage differentials', *Review of Economic Studies,* 25 (Feb. 1958), pp. 109–13.
76. Johnson, D. G., 'Labor mobility and agricultural adjustment', in E. O. Heady, H. G. Diesslin, H. R. Jensen, and G. L. Johnson, eds., *Agricultural Adjustment Problems in a Growing Economy.* Ames, Iowa: Iowa State College Press, 1958.

77. Johnson, Harry G., 'Optimal trade intervention in the presence of domestic distortions', in Baldwin, *et al., Trade, Growth and the Balance of Payments.* Amsterdam: North Holland, 1965, pp. 3–34.
78. ——— 'Factor market distortions and the shape of the transformation curve', *Econometrica,* 34 (July 1966), pp. 686–98.
79. ——— 'Minimum wage laws: a general equilibrium analysis', *Canadian Journal of Economics,* 2 (Nov. 1969), pp. 599–604.
80. ——— and Mieszkowski, Peter, 'The effects of unionization on the distribution of income: a general equilibrium approach', *Quarterly Journal of Economics,* 84 (Nov. 1970), pp. 539–61.
81. Jones, Ronald W., 'The structure of simple general equilibrium models', *Journal of Political Economy,* 73 (Dec. 1965), pp. 557–72
82. ——— 'Distortions in factor markets and the general equilibrium model of production', *Journal of Political Economy,* 79 (May/June 1971), pp. 437–59.
83. Kafka, A., 'A new argument for protectionism?', *Quarterly Journal of Economics,* 76 (Feb. 1962), pp. 163–6.
84. Keesing, Donald, 'Labor skills and comparative advantage', *American Economic Review,* 56 (May 1966), pp. 249–58.
85. Kemp, Murray C., 'Some issues in the analysis of trade gains', *Oxford Economic Papers,* 20 (July 1968), pp. 149–61.
86. ——— and Negishi, T., 'Domestic distortions, tariffs and the theory of optimum subsidy', *Journal of Political Economy,* 77 (Nov. 1969), pp. 1011–13.
87. ——— 'Variable returns to scale commodity taxes, factor market distortions and their implications for trade gains', *Swedish Journal of Economics,* 72 (June 1970), pp. 1–11.
88. Kenen, P. B., 'Development, mobility and the case for tariffs: a dissenting note', *Kyklos,* 16 (Fasc. 2, 1963), pp. 321–4.
89. Kindleberger, Charles P., *International Economics,* 1st ed., Homewood, Ill.: Richard D. Irwin, 1953.
90. ——— *The Terms of Trade: A European Case Study.* Cambridge, Mass.: M.I.T. Press, 1956.
91. Koo, A. Y. C., 'An economic justification for protectionism: comment', *Quarterly Journal of Economics,* 75 (Feb. 1961), pp. 133–44.
92. Kravis, Irving B., 'Wages and foreign trade', *Review of Economics and Statistics,* 38 (Feb. 1956), pp. 14–30.
93. Lester, Richard A., 'A range theory of wage differentials', *Industrial and Labor Relations Review,* 5 (July 1952), pp. 483–500.
94. Lewis, H. G., *Unionism and Relative Wages in the United States.* Chicago: University of Chicago Press, 1963.
95. Lewis, W. Arthur, 'Economic development with unlimited supplies of labour', in A. N. Agarwala and S. P. Singh, eds., *The Economics of Under-development.* New York: Oxford University Press, 1963, pp. 400–49. Reprinted from *The Manchester School,* 22 (May 1954), pp. 139–91.

96. Linder, Staffan Burenstam, *An Essay on Trade and Transformation.* New York: John Wiley and Sons, 1961, pp. 76–8.
97. Lloyd, P. J., 'The shape of the transformation curve with and without factor market distortions', *Australian Economic Papers,* 9 (June 1970), pp. 52–61.
98. Locks, Mitchell O., 'The influence of pattern-bargaining on manufacturing wages in the Cleveland, Ohio, labor market, 1945–1950', *Review of Economics and Statistics,* 37 (Feb. 1955), pp. 70–6.
99. Lurie, Melvin, 'The effect of unionization on wages in the transit industry', *Journal of Political Economy,* 69 (Dec. 1961), pp. 558–72.
100. Magee, Stephen P., 'Factor market distortions and the pure theory of international trade', unpublished Ph.D. dissertation, Massachusetts Institute of Technology, May 1969.
101. ——— 'Factor market distortions, production, distribution and the pure theory of international trade', *Quarterly Journal of Economics,* 75 (Nov. 1971), pp. 623–43 (a revision of Chapters 2 and 3 of [100]).
102. ——— 'Factor market distortions and empirical tests of the Heckscher–Ohlin theorem', Working Paper No. 11 (Nov. 1971), Studies in International Business and Economics, Institute of International Studies, University of California, Berkeley (a revision of Chapter 4 of [100]).
103. Maher, J. E., 'Union, nonunion wage differentials', *American Economic Review,* 46 (June 1956), pp. 336–52.
104. Manoilesco, Mihail, *The Theory of Protection and International Trade.* London: P. S. King and Son, Ltd., 1931.
105. Mansfield, Edwin, 'Wage differentials in the cotton textile industry, 1933–1952', *Review of Economics and Statistics,* 37 (Feb. 1955), pp. 77–82.
106. Marx, Daniel, 'Regulation of international liner shipping and "freedom of the seas" ', *Journal of Industrial Economics,* 16 (Nov. 1967), pp. 46–62.
107. McGuire, Timothy W., and Rapping, Leonard A., 'The supply of labor and manufacturing wage determination in the United States: an empirical examination', *International Economic Review,* 11 (June 1970), pp. 258–68.
108. McLean, A. A., 'Selective employment tax: impact on prices and the balance of payments', *Scottish Journal of Political Economy,* 17 (Feb. 1970), pp. 1–17.
109. Meade, J. E., *Trade and Welfare.* London: Oxford University Press, 1955.
110. Meyers, F., 'Price theory and union monopoly: reply', *Industrial and Labor Relations Review,* 13 (Oct. 1959), pp. 94–5.
111. Mieszkowski, P. M., 'On the theory of tax incidence', *Journal of Political Economy,* 75 (June 1967), pp. 250–62.
112. Mincer, Jacob, 'The distribution of labor incomes: a survey with special reference to the human capital approach', *Journal of Economic Literature,* 8 (Mar. 1970), pp. 1–26.
113. Mitchell, Daniel J. B., *Essays on Labor and International Trade.* University of California at Los Angeles: Institute of Industrial Relations, 1970.
114. Mitchell, Edward J., 'Explaining the international pattern of labor productivity and wages: a production model with two labor inputs', *Review of Economics and Statistics,* 50 (Nov. 1968), pp. 461–9.

115. Mundlak, Yair, 'Further implications of distortion in the factor market', *Econometrica,* 38 (May 1970), pp. 517–32.
116. Myint, H., 'Protection and economic development', in R. Harrod and D. C. Hague, eds., *International Trade Theory in a Developing World.* London: Macmillan, 1963.
117. ——— *The Economics of Developing Countries.* London: Hutchinson University Library, 1967.
118. Ohlin, Bertil, 'Protection and non-competing groups', *Weltwirtschaftliches Archiv,* 33 (Heft 1, 1931), pp. 30–45.
119. ——— *Interregional and International Trade.* Cambridge, Mass.: Harvard University Press, 1933.
120. Ozanne, Robert, 'A century of occupational differentials in manufacturing', *Review of Economics and Statistics,* 44 (Aug. 1962), pp. 292–9.
121. Papola, T. S., and Bharadwaj, V. P., 'Dynamics of industrial wage structure: an inter-country analysis', *Economic Journal,* 80 (Mar. 1970), pp. 72–90.
122. Parker, John E., and Burton, John F., 'Volunteer labor mobility in the U.S. manufacturing sector', in Gerald G. Somers, ed., *Proceedings of the Twentieth Annual Winter Meeting.* Industrial Relations Research Association, 1968, pp. 61–70 (reprinted in [29]).
123. Peitchinis, S. G., 'Occupational wage differentials in Canada, 1939–1965', *Australian Economic Papers,* 8 (June 1969), pp. 20–40.
124. Perlman, R., 'A note on the measurement of real wage differentials', *Review of Economics and Statistics,* 41 (May 1959), pp. 192–5.
125. Pierson, Gail, 'The effect of union strength on the U.S. "Phillips Curve" ', *American Economic Review,* 58 (June 1968), pp. 456–67.
126. Ramaswami, V. K., 'International factor movement and the national advantage', *Economica,* 35 (Aug. 1968), pp. 305–27.
127. ——— 'Welfare maximization when domestic factor movement entails external diseconomies', *Journal of Political Economy,* 78 (Sept./Oct. 1970), pp. 1061–8.
128. Reder, Melvin W., 'The theory of occupational wage differentials ', *American Economic Review,* 45 (Dec. 1955), pp. 833–52.
129. ——— 'Wage differentials: theory and measurement', in *Aspects of Labor Economics.* New York: National Bureau of Economic Research, 1962, pp. 257–99 (reprinted in [29]).
130. Robinson, Joan, *The Economics of Imperfect Competition.* London: Macmillan, 1934.
131. Ross, A. M., and Goldner, W., 'Forces affecting the interindustry wage structure', *Quarterly Journal of Economics,* 64 (May 1950), pp. 254–81.
132. Salant, Walter S., 'The balance of payments deficit and the tax structure', *Review of Economics and Statistics,* 46 (May 1964), pp. 131–8.
133. Samuelson, M. C., 'The Australian case for protection re-examined', *Quarterly Journal of Economics,* 54 (Nov. 1939), pp. 143–9.
134. Samuelson, P. A., *Foundations of Economic Analysis.* Cambridge, Mass.: Harvard University Press, 1947, Chapter VIII.

135. ——— 'Theoretical notes on trade problems', *Review of Economics and Statistics,* 46 (May 1964), pp. 145–54.
136. Sawhney, P. K., 'Inter-industry wage differentials in India', *Indian Economic Journal,* 17 (Aug./Sept. 1969), pp. 28–56.
137. Schlesinger, J. R., 'Market structure, union power and inflation', *Southern Economic Journal,* 24 (Jan. 1958), pp. 296–312.
138. Schwartzman, David, 'The effect of monopoly on price', *Journal of Political Economy,* 67 (Aug. 1959), pp. 352–62.
139. ——— 'Monopoly and wages', *Canadian Journal of Economics and Political Science,* 26 (Aug. 1960), pp. 428–38.
140. Segal, M., 'Regional wage differences in manufacturing in the postwar period', *Review of Economics and Statistics,* 43 (May 1961), pp. 148–55.
141. ——— 'The relation between union wage impact and market structure', *Quarterly Journal of Economics,* 78 (Feb. 1964), pp. 96–114.
142. Shepherd, William G., 'Trends of concentration in American manufacturing industries, 1947–1958', *Review of Economics and Statistics,* 46 (May 1964), pp. 200–12.
143. Simler, N. J., 'Unionism and labor's share in manufacturing industries', *Review of Economics and Statistics,* 43 (Nov. 1961), pp. 369–78.
144. Sjaastad, Larry A., 'The costs and returns of human migration', *Journal of Political Economy,* 70 (Oct. 1962, supplement), pp. 80–93 (reprinted in [29]).
145. Stafford, Frank, 'Concentration and labor earnings: comment', *American Economic Review,* 58 (Mar. 1968), pp. 174–81.
146. Stolper, W., and Samuelson, P. A., 'Protection and real wages', *The Review of Economic Studies,* 9 (Nov. 1941), pp. 58–73.
147. Sultan, Paul E., 'Unionism and wage-income ratios: 1929–1951', *Review of Economics and Statistics,* 36 (Feb. 1954), pp. 67–73.
148. Tarshis, Lorie, 'Factor inputs and international price comparisons', in M. Abramovitz, *et al.,* eds., *The Allocation of Economic Resources.* Stanford, Calif.: Stanford University Press, 1959, pp. 236–44.
149. Taussig, F., *International Trade.* New York: Macmillan, 1927, pp. 43–60.
150. Taylor, David P., 'Discrimination and occupational wage differences in the market for unskilled labor', *Industrial and Labor Relations Review,* 21 (Apr. 1968), pp. 375–90 (reprinted in [29]).
151. Throop, A. W., 'The union-nonunion wage differential and cost-push inflation', *American Economic Review,* 58 (Mar. 1968), pp. 79–99.
152. Uekawa, Y., 'On a two-sector growth model with non-shiftable capital', mimeographed, 1970 (forthcoming in the *International Economic Review).*
153. Ulman, L., 'Marshall and Friedman on union strength', *Review of Economics and Statistics,* 37 (Nov. 1955), pp. 384–401 (reprinted in [29]).
154. Utsumi, Y., 'Rigidity of wage rate and the interfirm wage differentials', *Osaka Economic Papers,* 6 (Feb. 1958), pp. 39–58.
155. Vanderkamp, John, 'Migration flows, their determinants and the effects of return migration', *Journal of Political Economy,* 79 (Sept./Oct. 1971), pp. 1012–31.

156. Viner, Jacob, 'The theory of protection and international trade: a review', *Journal of Political Economy,* 40 (Feb. 1932), pp. 121–5.
157. ——— *International Trade and Economic Development.* Oxford: Oxford University Press, 1953.
158. ——— *Studies in the Theory of International Trade.* London: George Allen and Unwin, reprinted, 1964, pp. 453–62, 493–500.
159. Webb, L. Roy, 'International factor movement and the national advantage: a comment', *Economica,* 37 (Feb. 1970), pp. 81–4.
160. Weinstein, P. A., 'Featherbedding: a theoretical analysis', *Journal of Political Economy,* 68 (Aug. 1960), pp. 379–87.
161. Weiss, Leonard, 'Concentration and labor earnings', *American Economic Review,* 56 (Mar. 1966), pp. 96–117 (reprinted in [29]).
162. Wolfson, R. J., 'An econometric investigation of regional differentials in American agricultural wages', *Econometrica,* 26 (Apr. 1958), pp. 225–57.

Chapter 8

National and International Returns to Scale in the Modern Theory of International Trade*

Wilfred J. Ethier†

For over a quarter century, the Heckscher-Ohlin-Samuelson (H-O-S) trade model has thoroughly dominated work in the pure theory of international trade. Indeed this model is often identified as "the" modern theory of trade. But this dominance has always been rendered uneasy by a widespread suspicion that the salient facts of modern commerce are inconsistent with the theoretical structure. Two broad areas of suspicion may be identified.

The first, concerned with whether actual trade patterns and factor endowments are related as predicted by the theory, consists of the Leontief Paradox and the huge volume of work it stimulated. My interpretation of this literature is that the factor-endowments theory of trade fares reasonably well, but that its two-factor, two-commodity

*Originally published in *The American Economic Review*, 72(3), pp. 389–405.

†Professor of economics, University of Pennsylvania. The research for this paper was supported by the National Science Foundation under grant no. SES-7925614. I have benefited from seminars at the universities of Pennsylvania, Western Ontario, and Wisconsin, and Northwestern University. Richard Caves also supplied useful comments and suggestions.

version is essentially an inadequate description of reality. I have on other occasions investigated the consequences of many goods and factors, and do not wish to do so now. This paper will accordingly confine itself to a factor-endowments model with two primary factors and two final goods.

The second (by no means unrelated) area of suspicion centers on the stylized fact that the largest and fastest growing component of world trade since World War II has been the exchange of manufactures between the industrialized economies. By contrast, the H-O-S model, and neoclassical theory generally, sees little basis for trade between similar economies. Two manifestations of this point may be found in the empirical literature. The first, of relevance to international monetary problems, concerns departures from purchasing-power parity among the industrial countries even for fairly disaggregated indices of traded goods (see Irving Kravis and Richard Lipsey). The second, a central concern of this paper, involves intraindustry trade.

Although two-way trade had long been observed, it first became of major concern when economists investigated the consequences of economic integration in Europe (see, for example, P. J. Verdoorn; Bela Balassa, 1966) and noted a tendency, not towards increased specialization, but rather for all countries to simultaneously increase exports of most categories of manufactures. Indeed in some cases specialization actually declined. Subsequent work divorced the phenomenon of intraindustry trade from economic integration, and exposed the pervasive expansion of such trade between all industrial countries and across most manufacturing sectors, irrespective of tariff barriers or their changes (Helmut Hesse; Herbert Grubel and Peter Lloyd, 1975; Emilio Pagoulatos and Robert Sorenson; and Richard Caves), furthermore this expansion does not appear to be a matter of transition between equilibria[1] (Caves).

[1]See Gary Hufbauer and John Chilas for a contrasting argument that intra-industry trade is due to the GATT method of tariff reduction and to transitory responses with quasi-fixed factors of production. Joseph M. Finger also offers some contrasting evidence.

The most natural explanations of intraindustry trade, advanced by Gottfried Haberler (p. 34) long ago, are product heterogeneity within aggregates and border trade (and its seasonal analog). But accumulated empirical work (for example, Hesse; Grubel and Lloyd, 1975; and Caves) strongly suggests that these explanations are inadequate.[2] Attention has accordingly shifted to product differentiation and economies of scale (in theory the two go together, as scale economies supply the limitation to the degree of differentiation).[3]

International trade theory does contain a sizable literature on increasing returns to scale (see, for example, R. C. O. Matthews; James Meade; and Murray Kemp, 1969), but this literature would not appear to offer much that is relevant to the phenomenon at issue. Indeed it has not on balance had great influence on trade theory generally. This is no doubt largely because increasing returns establish a strong presumption for complete specialization, multiple equilibria, and indeterminacy, conclusions that both vitiate the standard comparative statics methodology of trade theory and that also bear questionable relevance to the facts of contemporary trade. Furthermore, this theory has generally assumed that the economies of scale were external to the firm and appropriate at an aggregate level, assumptions that preclude much relevance to intraindustry trade. Empirical work has likewise encountered difficulty in coming to grips with scale economies, although many researchers have argued their importance (for example, Balassa, 1961, 1967; Donald J. Daly *et al.*, Nicholas Owen, and Caves), and some have found relevance to intraindustry trade.

---

[2]Grubel and Lloyd (1975), for example, found significant Australian intraindustry trade even at the seven-digit level. I do not mean to suggest that such trade indicates a violation of commodity arbitrage and could not be made to disappear completely in the face of relentless disaggregation. Indeed the theory to follow will make use of product differentiation. Rather the point is that intraindustry trade appears significant even with sufficient disaggregation to remove relative cost differences between sectors as a likely determinant of such trade, so that the traditional theory, while not necessarily contradicted, fails to offer an explanation.

[3]Theoretical discussions of intraindustry trade can be found in Grubel; H. Peter Gray; Grubel and Lloyd (1975); and Robert Davies.

Recently I pointed out (1979a) that scale economies resulting from an increased division of labor rather than from, say, an increased plant size, depended at an aggregate level upon the size of the world market rather than upon geographical concentration of the industry, as supposed in the traditional theory. Such "international" returns to scale were shown to be free of the presumption of indeterminacy and multiple equilibria[4] characteristic of "national" returns to scale, to imply a theory of intraindustry trade in intermediate goods, and generally to lead to conclusions much more in accord with the stylized facts of modern trade.

The purpose of this paper is to argue that, in the context of international returns, the factor-endowments theory is consistent with, and indeed helps to explain, the stylized facts discussed above. In order to do this I shall construct a simple but detailed model yielding international returns to scale, and employ this model to systematically explore the relations between such international returns, the traditional national returns to scale, and the modern (or factor endowments) theory of international trade. I have four broad messages. 1) International returns depend in an essential way on an interaction between the two types of scale economies, which is also an interaction of internal and external (to the firm) economies. 2) The basic theorems of the factor-endowments theory are essentially robust in the presence of such scale economies, in contrast to the conclusions of the traditional literature.[5] Nevertheless there are some important modifications. 3) Intraindustry trade, like interindustry trade, has a factor-endowments basis. However, such trade is basically *complementary* to international factor mobility. 4) Although the existence of internal-scale economies and product differentiation are essential to the theory, the degree of such phenomena need not be an essential determinant of the degree of intraindustry trade.

[4]International scale economies actually "bury" these problems rather than eliminate them, as will become clear below.

[5]In this respect the present paper complements recent work establishing the general validity of the basic H-O-S propositions. See Kemp (1976); Ronald Jones and José Scheinkman; my 1974, 1979b articles; Winston Chang, *et al.*

Recently Paul Krugman (1979, 1981); Avinash Dixit and Viktor Norman; Elhanen Helpman; and Colin Lawrence and Pablo Spiller have extended to an international context the Avinash Dixit-Joseph Stiglitz formalization of Chamberlinian monopolistic competition; and Kelvin Lancaster has also applied to international trade his product-characteristics approach to consumption theory. These authors are concerned with the same stylized facts that my earlier paper (1979a) had been, and they reach some broadly analogous conclusions, although from entirely different theoretical starting points. The present paper is not concerned with the differentiated consumer goods that are their subject. However I do hope to treat the differentiated producer goods central to my own theory in such a way as to bring out the parallels between the approaches of these other authors and my earlier work on intraindustry trade (I cannot resist the temptation to point out that producers' goods are in fact much more prominent in trade than are consumers' goods).

1. National and International Scale Economies

A. Production

Capital and labor combine to produce wheat (W) and manufactures (M). Wheat is produced subject to constant returns to scale via a smooth production function of the familiar sort. Manufactures, on the other hand, are potentially subject to increasing returns to scale, and I suppose that the production function for M is separable in the sense that I can write $M = km$, where k is an index of scale economies and m an index of the scale of operations; m can be thought of as produced via a familiar smooth production function. Thus the endowment of capital and labor determines a transformation curve:

$$W = T(m). \tag{1}$$

The possibility of returns to scale in manufacturing arises, first, from exploitation of the division of labor, as in the hoary examples of Adam Smith's pin factory and the Swiss watch industry. Finished manufactures are costlessly assembled from intermediate manufactured components.[6] The number n of components that are actually produced will be endogenously determined, and, I assume, only a fraction of a large number of potentially producible intermediate goods.[7] I am not interested in issues which depend upon distinctions between potential intermediate goods, so I assume that they are all producible from capital and labor via identical production functions, and that all produced components contribute in totally symmetric fashion to the finished manufactures. Under these assumptions, all components which are actually produced will be produced in equal amounts, and I denote the output of each such component by x, so that the total number of produced components of all types is nx. Assume that the output of finished manufactures is given by

$$M = n^{\alpha-1}(nx) \tag{2}$$

for some parameter $\alpha > 1$. It will be convenient to adopt the following specific form of the production function (2), where x_i denotes the quantity of the ith component and β is a parameter, $1 > \beta > 0$.

$$M = n^{\alpha}\left[\sum_{i=1}^{n}\left(\frac{x_i^{\beta}}{n}\right)\right]^{1/\beta}. \tag{2'}$$

With all the x_i, equal to a common x, as will be the case in equilibrium, (2′) reduces to (2). A higher value of β indicates that components can be more easily substituted for each other in the assembly of finished manufactures. Thus lower values of β correspond to greater "product differentiation" within the manufacturing sector. (Note the analogy to the ways in which Dixit-Stiglitz; Krugman, 1979, 1981; Dixit-Norman; and Helpman measure the utility obtained from a bundle of differentiated consumer goods.)

---

[6]One could instead interpret the intermediate goods as successive stages, Austrian fashion, or alternatively, allow some of the components to be assembly services, so that assembly is not costless. Either interpretation would leave the balance of this paper unscathed.

[7]I ignore the difficulty of interpreting nonintegral values of n.

The gains from an increased division of labor would mandate the production of an infinitesimal amount of an infinite number of separate components if that were possible. I assume that indivisibilities in the production of components prevents this[8] (the division of labor is limited by the extent of the market). If the scale variable m is interpreted as an index of the number of bundles of factors devoted to manufacturing production, suppose that the number of such bundles required to produce x units of any component is $ax+b$, for some $a, b > 0$. Then

$$m = n(ax+b). \tag{3}$$

The technology of the model is formally summarized by equations (1), (2) (or (2′)), and (3), with the usual H-O-S model behind the transformation curve $T(m)$.

Note that there are two distinct sources of increasing returns to scale. The individual component production functions, $ax + b$, display what Balassa (1967, ch. 5) refers to as "economies of scale in the traditional sense," and which I term "national" returns. These involve considerations of minimal plant size and the like, and they require total production x to be geographically concentrated. I assume that these economies are internalized by firms, and I shall examine equilibria in which the total output of each produced component is provided by a single firm in a single location. (I shall sometimes refer casually to b in equation (3) as "fixed costs," but I will not assume that b is variable in the long run.)

The finished-manufactures production function (2), or (2′), displays constant returns to scale for a given value of n. But an expansion of the manufacturing sector arising from an increased number of components (a rise in n with constant x) displays increasing returns, since M rises in greater proportion than nx. These economies reflect not an increased plant size but rather a greater division of labor; they are what Balassa (1967, ch. 5) refers to as "horizontal specialization" or "vertical specialization," and were the subject of my earlier paper

[8]This assumption was implicit in my earlier paper (1979a) and explicit in Dixit-Stiglitz and in Krugman (1979).

(1979a), where they were called "international" returns to scale. Economies of this sort depend upon the size of the market for finished manufactures, and they do not require that all manufacturing output be concentrated at a single place. I assume that these economies are external to the individual firm. Components are assembled into finished manufactures by many competitive firms, each of which takes n as a parameter and consequently views itself as subject to constant returns to scale.

B. Autarkic equilibrium

Consider a closed economy with the above technology. An individual producer of finished manufactures uses components, subject to (2′), with n as a parameter. If q_0 and q denote the prices, in terms of wheat, of some pair of produced components with outputs x_0 and x, then cost minimization by producers of M, subject to (2′), requires

$$x_0 = x(q/q_0)^{1/1-\beta}. \tag{4}$$

If n is sufficiently large so that the producer of each component acts as though his behavior does not influence that of other component producers, condition (4) is the demand curve faced by the producer of x_0, for given q and x. This curve has an elasticity of $1/(1-\beta)$. The component-producer purchases the services of primary factors in competitive markets and therefore has a cost function given by $-T'(m)[ax_0 + b]$, where $T'(m)$ is exogenous to the individual firm. This firm will therefore equate marginal revenue and marginal cost, and maximize its profit, by charging the price

$$q_0 = -T'(m)a/\beta. \tag{5}$$

Because of the symmetry assumption, q_0 is the price of each component that is actually produced. The profit of each component-producing firm is $q_0x_0 + T'(m)[ax_0 + b]$. These profits will be driven to zero in equilibrium by the entry and exit of firms, that is, by variations in n, as each component is produced by only one firm.

Thus, from equation (5),

$$x_0 = b\beta/a(1-\beta). \tag{6}$$

Finally, the number n of components is given by equation (3), for any given m and for $x = x_0$.

$$n = (1-\beta)m/b. \tag{7}$$

Equations (5), (6), and (7) now imply the value of k for $M = km$:

$$k = ([(1-\beta)/b]^{\alpha-1}\beta/\alpha)m^{\alpha-1}. \tag{8}$$

The relative supply price P_s of M in terms of wheat is given by $P_S M = q_0 nx$, or $P_s \mathrm{n}^\alpha x = q_0 nx$, or $P_s = n^{1-\alpha} q_0$. Thus substitution yields the supply curve of M:

$$P_s = -T'(m)/k. \tag{9}$$

The supply curve is illustrated in Figure 1. The term M_0 denotes the value of M when $T = 0$, and the curve P_s shows for each value of M the minimum price at which that quantity would be

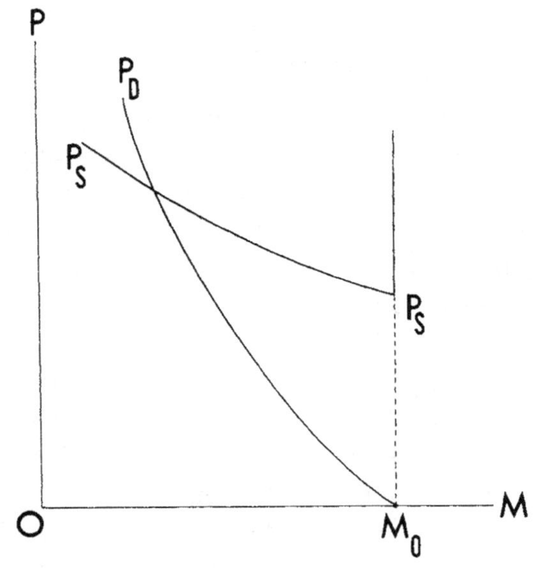

Figure 1.

supplied (i.e., expression (9)). Note from (6) that x is independent of m. Thus a reallocation of resources from W to M involves an expansion of M production by an increase in n. The manufacturing sector thus displays increasing returns to scale, allowing a negatively sloped supply curve, as illustrated.

The picture of autarkic equilibrium is completed by a description of the demand for final goods. I assume that a constant fraction γ of income is always spent on manufactures. Each output combination M and W determines a demand price P_D that will clear commodity markets: $P_D M = \gamma[W + P_D M]$. Thus the demand curve can be written as

$$P_D = [\gamma/(1-\gamma)]T(m)/km. \tag{10}$$

The demand curve has a negative slope, as illustrated in Figure 1, and it is easy to show that equations (9) and (10) imply that the demand curve intersects the supply curve from above. Thus in autarky the economy possesses a unique equilibrium which features production of both final goods.

C. International equilibrium

Consider next free international trade between two economies—of the sort just described—identical in all respects other than factor endowments. Let m and m^* denote the scale of manufacturing operations at home and abroad (variables pertaining to the foreign country will be distinguished by an asterisk). In free-trade equilibrium the total output of each component will be concentrated in a single country. Thus, if m and m^* are both positive, the two countries produce distinct collections of components. Equation (4) continues to represent the demand curve faced by each component producer (in either country), and the same argument as before establishes that (6) gives the output of each component actually produced somewhere. Then, if n_H and n_F denote the number of components produced at home and abroad, respectively, it follows as before that $n_H = (1-\beta)m/b$ and $n_F = (1-\beta)m^*/b$ so that $n = n_H + n_F$ is given by

$$n = (1 - \beta)(m + m^*)/b, \tag{11}$$

and so, from (2), the world output of finished manufactures is

$$M + M^* = (\beta/\alpha) \times [(1 - \beta)/b]^{\alpha-1}(m + m*)^{\alpha}. \tag{12}$$

What determines m, m^* and the relative prices? To answer this question I use the allocation-curve technique[9] developed in my 1979a and forthcoming articles. For any m and m^*, the world demand price of finished manufactures in terms of wheat is given by

$$\begin{aligned} P_D &= \frac{\gamma}{1-\gamma}\frac{T(m) + S(m^*)}{M + M^*} \\ &= \frac{\gamma}{1-\gamma}\frac{a}{\beta}\left(\frac{b}{1-\beta}\right)^{\alpha-1}\frac{T(m) + S(m^*)}{(m + m^*)^{\alpha}} \end{aligned} \tag{13}$$

where $S(m^*) = W^*$ denotes the foreign transformation curve. The home supply price P_S^H must be given by

$$P_S^H = -[(1 - \beta)(m + m^*)/b]^{1-\alpha}T'(m)a/\beta. \tag{14}$$

Home-country equilibrium requires $P_D = P_S^H$, or, from equations (13) and (14),

$$\gamma[T(m) + S(m^*)] + (1 - \gamma)(m + m^*)T'(m) = 0. \tag{15}$$

Equation (15) defines the "home allocation curve": the collection of m and m^* for which the home country is in equilibrium in the international economy. This relation is depicted as the HH' curve in each panel of Figure 2. It is easily shown that the curve has a negative slope, that $P_D < P_S^H$ above the curve, and that $P_D > P_S^H$ below. In Figure 2, m_0 and m_0^* denote the manufacturing scales if the home and foreign economies, respectively, specialize to manufactures, so the world is confined to the rectangle $0m_0Em_0^*$ in each panel, and that part of the graph of (15) lying outside this rectangle is irrelevant

[9]The remainder of this section is rather terse as it closely follows my 1979a article, to which the reader is referred for more detail.

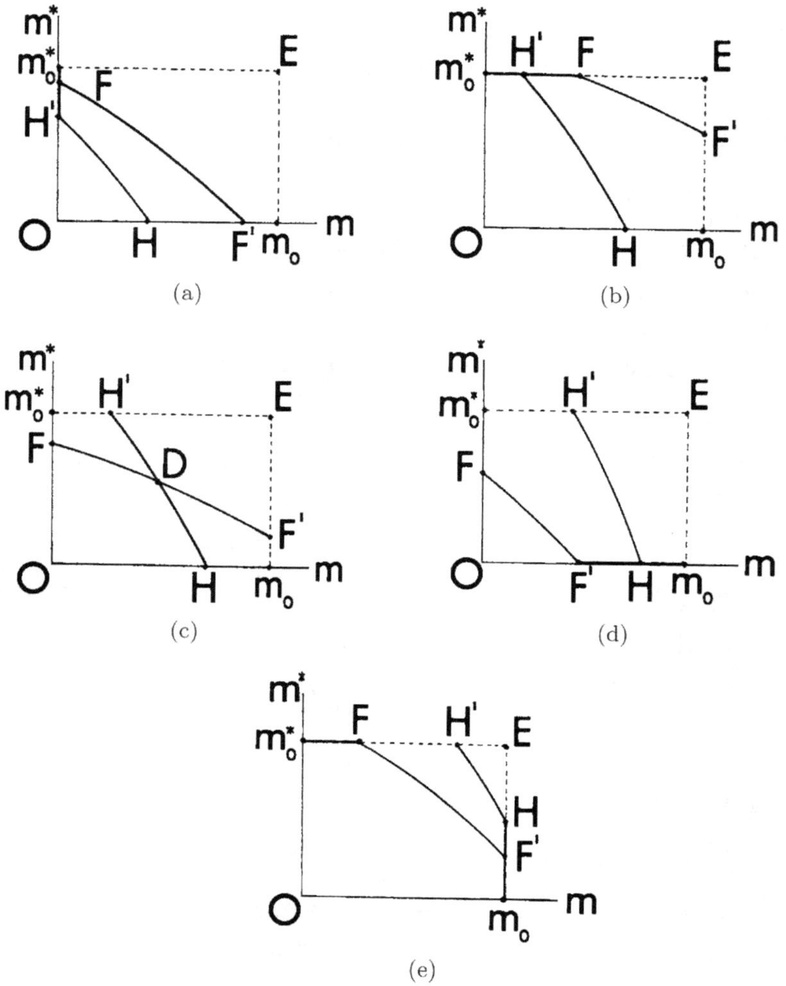

Figure 2.

(it is easy to see that the graph of (15) cannot be completely excluded from the rectangle). If the home economy specializes, equilibrium is consistent with an excess of the relative demand price of the produced good over its relative supply price. Thus the home allocation curve also contains any part of $0m_0^*$ that lies above the intersection of $H'H$ with the vertical axis, and also any part of m_0E below its intersection with $H'H$.

Similarly, the foreign allocation curve, showing the m and m^* for which $P_D = P_S^H$, the foreign relative supply price, is given by

$$\gamma[T(m) + S(m^*)] + (1-\gamma)(m+m^*)S'(m^*) = 0. \tag{16}$$

The graph of (16) is shown as FF' in each panel of Figure (2). As illustrated, FF' must decline less steeply than $H'H$, reflecting the fact that each country's supply price is relatively more sensitive than the world demand price to that country's allocation of resources compared to the foreign allocation. Any part of m_0^*E lying below FF' and any part of $0m_0$ above FF' also constitute part of the foreign allocation curve.

International equilibrium requires each country to be individually in equilibrium in the world economy and is therefore determined by the intersection of the two allocation curves. Figure 2 depicts the five qualitatively distinct possibilities; equilibrium is shown by points F, H', D, H, and F' in panels (a)-(e), respectively (in addition there are the two boundary cases, featuring complete specialization in both countries, between cases (a) and (b) and between (d) and (e)). Evidently each case yields a unique international equilibrium.

The equilibrium values of m and m^* determine the relative price of finished manufactures in terms of wheat from equation (13) (or (14)). Then n is given by (11) and x by (6). The price of each component is as indicated by (5), or, if the home economy specializes to wheat, by the foreign analog.

Note that equation (12) can also be written $M+M^* = k(m+m^*)$ where $k = (\beta/a) \cdot [(1-\beta)/b]^{\alpha-1}(m+m^*)^{\alpha-1}$, thereby emphasizing that the extent of external scale economies depends on the size of the world market alone. If M and M^* denote the quantities of finished manufactures to which the respective countries obtain effective title as a result of their manufacturing activity (i.e., the most finished manufactures each country could consume without offering any wheat in exchange), then,

$$M = km; M^* = km^*. \tag{17}$$

Note that M and M^* need not equal the quantities of finished manufactures actually assembled in each country. With assembly costless it can be divided in any way between the two countries. (If one of the components were an assembly process, $M + M^*$ would be all assembled in the country where that process happened to be located.)

2. The Modern Theory

Armed with a complete description of international equilibrium, this section inquires into the fate of the four central propositions supplied by the H-O-S model.[10] Henceforth manufacturing is assumed relatively capital intensive and wheat relatively labor intensive. Since inherent properties of the two factors do not figure in this paper, this pattern of factor intensities is in a formal sense only a definition. But the definition is not arbitrary: one intuitively associates a greater division of labor with significant use of capital. This could be introduced by letting manufacturing production explicitly take time, adding a positive interest rate, and allowing components to be producers' goods generally. It is straightforward to extend the main results of this paper to such a context by using the techniques in my article (1979b), provided attention is restricted to steady states.

A. Factor-price equalization

Suppose that both countries operate both sectors, so that equilibrium is as in Figure 2(c). Then equations (15) and (16) hold, implying that $T'(m) = S'(m^*)$. Likewise, T' and S' are necessarily unequal if one or both countries specializes completely.[11] Now, with the assumption of identical technology, equality of T' and S' implies that domestically produced components sell at the same price as all foreign-produced components, from (14) and its foreign counterpart. Since T and S are generated by conventional H-O-S technologies, the standard factor-price equalization argument can now be employed to yield.

---

[10]For a discussion of the basic H-O-S propositions see, for example, Caves and Ronald Jones.

[11]Except, of course, for the borderline case of "incipient diversification" in one country.

Proposition 1. *Factor-Price Equalization. If both countries operate both sectors, and are not separated by a factor-intensity reversal, free trade implies factor-price equalization. A separating reversal, or (nonincipient) specialization in either country, precludes such equalization.*

B. The Rybczynski theorem

Note, first, that if domestic factor endowments are altered and $T'(m)$ is kept unchanged, the standard Rybczynski argument applies exactly: an increase in capital will cause a more than proportionate rise in m and a fall in W.

The next step is to relate the change in m to the production of individual components and finished manufactures. Expression (5) implies that constancy of $T'(m)$ is equivalent to constancy of the relative prices of components in terms of wheat. Then (6) implies that endowment changes cause *no* changes in the outputs of those components that are produced both before and after, while (7) reveals that the *number* of produced components varies in proportion to m. Thus:

Proposition 2. *Rybczynski. At constant relative component prices, an increase in the capital stock will absolutely reduce the production of wheat, have no effect on the outputs of all components initially produced, and increase the number of produced components in greater proportion than the rise in the capital stock itself.*

Several features of this Rybczynski theorem deserve emphasis. First, despite the pervasive presence of economies of scale, the standard results are completely preserved at the interindustry level: changes in endowments produce magnified changes in the outputs of wheat and aggregate manufactures. Because all produced components sell at the same price and have equal outputs, aggregate component production can be measured by nx which changes proportionally to n since the adjustment of manufacturing output occurs through variations in the *number* of components rather than in the *outputs* of individual components.

Second, at a disaggregated level, endowment changes produce magnified changes in the outputs of wheat and of those components which change status (and thereby experience infinite proportional output changes). The (zero) proportional output changes of the other components will be weighted averages of proportional endowment changes if and only if the latter are in opposite directions.

Note, third, that the present version of the Rybczynski theorem places no restrictions on the relative price of finished manufactures. Nor does it make any claims about the effective output M of these final goods. This is because international economies of scale influence the production of final manufactures independently of the internal, national, economies associated with the production of individual components. The extent of the former depends upon patterns of production in both countries. Thus, in order to describe the effects of endowment changes in one country on that country's (effective) output of finished manufactures, the behavior of the rest of the world must be considered.

With relative component prices held fixed, m^* will be unchanged. Now equation (17) implies that the proportional change in Mequals that in m plus that in k. With m^* constant, the proportional change in k equals that in m multiplied by $[(\alpha - 1)m/(m + m^*)]$. This is straightforward: an increase in m takes the form of an increased number of components and thereby raises M both directly and indirectly through the scale economies made possible by the increased division of labor. The latter *scale effect* depends upon the rate $\alpha - 1$ at which scale economies are realized, plus the extent to which an increase in m constitutes an increase in world manufacturing $m+m^*$. In any event, M changes in the same direction as m and in even greater proportion, so that the effect of economies of scale is to simply accentuate the standard results.

With constant component prices, changes in the scale of manufacturing activity must change the relative price of finished manufactures. Equation (14) reveals that this price falls in the proportion $(\alpha - 1)[m/(m + m^*)]\hat{m}$, where I use a circumflex to denote proportional change. This is the same scale effect as above, entering in for the same reason. The relative price of finished manufactures falls in the proportion that k rises; thus the *value* of finished manufactures, in terms of either wheat or components, rises in the same proportion as aggregate component output. This is a reflection of the external character of the relevant scale economies.

Proposition 3. *At constant relative component prices, an increase in capital increases the output of finished manufactures relative to that of components (and therefore to the capital stock), and also reduces the price of finished manufactures, so that the value of the output of finished manufactures rises in the same proportion as that of aggregate components.*

It is natural to wonder how the Rybczynski theorem is affected when the relative price of finished manufactures in terms of wheat is held constant. The exercise is not in fact very interesting because of the international interdependence. For example, equation (14) reveals that any increase in m brought about by endowment changes must be accompanied by an increase in T' sufficient to leave $(m+m^*)^{1-\alpha}T'$ unchanged. Thus the relative price of components in terms of wheat rises, and the factor prices and techniques must change as well. Furthermore, if the rest of the world is not specialized to wheat, the equilibrium condition of equal component prices requires foreign changes in factor prices and techniques.

C. The Stolper-Samuelson theorem

Expression (5) implies that the wheat price of components is linked to factor prices in essentially the same way as are commodity prices in the standard H-O-S model. Then the usual argument establishes the following:

$$\hat{P}_C = \theta_{km}\hat{r} + \theta_{Lm}\hat{w}; \tag{18}$$

$$\hat{P}_W = \theta_{kW}\hat{r} + \theta_{LW}\hat{w}. \tag{19}$$

In these equations P_C, P_W, r, and w denote the nominal prices of industrial components, wheat, capital and labor, respectively (so that $q = P_C/P_W$). The θ_{kW} and θ_{LW} denote capital's and labor's distributive shares in the wheat industry and analogously for θ_{km}

and θ_{Lm} in the components industry. The following is immediate from (18) and (19).

Proposition 4. *An increase in the price of wheat relative to the price of all components will raise the wage relative to the prices of both wheat and components and will reduce the rent relative to the prices of both wheat and components.*

Industrial components are intermediate goods, and only wheat and finished manufactures are consumed. Thus Proposition 4 says nothing about real factor rewards and so fails to come to grips with the essence of the Stolper-Samuelson Theorem. The price P_M of finished manufactures is related to that of components by $P_M = n^{1-\alpha}P_C$, so that

$$\hat{P}_M = \hat{P}_C - (\alpha - 1)\hat{n}. \tag{20}$$

Now $\hat{n} = \hat{m}[m/(m+m^*)]$, and $\hat{m}$ can be related to $\hat{P}_M - \hat{P}_W$ by differentiation of (14) to obtain

$$(\hat{P}_m - \hat{P}_W) = \left[m\frac{T''}{T'} - (\alpha - 1)\frac{m}{m+m^*}\right]\hat{m}. \tag{21}$$

Substitution into (20) gives

$$(\hat{P}_M - \hat{P}_C) = Z(\hat{P}_M - \hat{P}_W) \tag{22}$$

where the elasticity of the *intraindustry* price structure P_M/P_C with respect to the *interindustry* price structure P_M/P_W is $Z = 1/(1 - [mT''/T']/[(\alpha-1)m/(m+m^*)])$.

Note first that, although Z may be of either sign, it can never fall between zero and unity. Thus variations in the intra-industry price structure are never damped versions of variations in the interindustry structure. This reflects the role of scale economies. A change in relative prices involves a reallocation of resources. If resources move into manufacturing, that is, if $\hat{m} > 0$, this will be associated with an increase in P_C/P_W to a degree dependent upon the curvature of the transformation curve. Since the cost of components contributes towards the cost of manufactures, this will also tend to be associated with a rise in P_M/P_W. This effect is simply the familiar H-O-S phenomenon, and I accordingly call it the *intersectoral price effect* of $\hat{m}$; it is reflected in the first term in the brackets in (21).

The variation in m will involve a variation in n rather than x, so individual firms will not experience internal scale economies. But the expansion of world manufacturing will induce external scale economies, and this *scale effect* will tend to reduce the cost of finished manufactures and will therefore work against the intersectoral effect. This scale effect, reflected in the second term in brackets in (21), is the same elasticity of k with respect to m encountered above. If the intersectoral effect dominates, P_M/P_W will therefore change in the same direction as, but to a lessor extent than, P_C/P_W, whereas a dominant scale effect[12] means that a rise in P_C/P_W actually reduces P_M/P_W.

Proposition 5. *If the scale effect dominates the intersectoral effect* ($Z > 0$), *changes in the intrasectoral price structure* P_M/P_C *are magnifications of changes in the intersectoral structure* P_M/P_W. *If the intersectoral effect dominates the scale effect* ($Z < 0$), *the two relative prices always change in opposite directions.*

We are now in a position to relate factor rewards to final-goods prices. Substituting equation (22) into (18) and (19) gives

$$\hat{P}_M = \theta_{kW}\left[\frac{(\theta_{km}/\theta_{kW}) - Z}{1 - Z}\right]\hat{r} + \theta_{LW}\left[\frac{(\theta_{Lm}/\theta_{LW}) - Z}{1 - Z}\right]\hat{w} \tag{23}$$

$$\hat{P}_W = \theta_{kW}\hat{r} + \theta_{LW}\hat{w}. \tag{19}$$

Note first that (19) is not affected, so that the proportional change in the price of wheat is still a weighted average of those in the two factor rewards. Second, the coefficients of $\hat{w}$ and $\hat{r}$ in (23) sum to unity, as in (18). With labor designated intensive to wheat, $\theta_{Lm} < \theta_{LW}$, so that the exclusion of Z from between zero

[12] These conclusions can perhaps be made clearer by rewriting equation (22) as $(\hat{P}_C - \hat{P}_W) = (1 - Z)(\hat{P}_M - \hat{P}_W)$ and noting that Z cannot fall between zero and unity.

and unity renders the coefficients of $\hat{w}$ in (23) positive. Thus that of $\hat{r}$ is less than unity. This is all that can be said without restrictions on technology.

If $Z < 0$, the coefficient of $\hat{r}$ in (23) is positive, so that $\hat{P}_M$ is a weighted average of $\hat{r}$ and $\hat{w}$. Furthermore, the coefficient of $\hat{r}$ in (23) exceeds that of $\hat{r}$ in (19), and the usual Stolper-Samuelson argument follows. If, on the other hand, $Z > 0$, then in fact $Z > 1$, so the coefficient of $\hat{r}$ in (23) is less than that in (19) and the standard results can not possibly hold.

Proposition 6. *Stolper-Samuelson. An increase in the price of manufactures relative to wheat raises the rent and lowers the wage relative to both final-goods prices, if and only if the intersectoral effect dominates the scale effect.*

The reason for this result is straightforward. A dominant intersectoral effect ensures that a change in P_M/P_W produces a larger change, in the same direction, in P_C/P_W, to which Proposition 4 can be applied to yield the standard result. A dominant scale effect precludes this result by causing P_C/P_W to change in the opposite direction. Note that Propositions 5 and 6 together give a very simple test for the validity of the Stolper-Samuelson theorem: The intrasectoral price structure P_M/P_C and the intersectoral structure P_M/P_W should always change in opposite directions.

If Z exceeds unity it may or may not also exceed θ_{km}/θ_{kW}. If the scale effect is sufficiently dominant so that Z does exceed this latter term, the coefficient of $\hat{r}$ in equation (23) is again positive and $\hat{P}_M$ is a weighted average of $\hat{w}$ and $\hat{r}$. But the coefficient of $\hat{r}$ in (23) is less than that of $\hat{r}$ in (19). Thus the standard Stolper-Samuelson argument applies, but with the role of the factor-intensity pattern reversed, so that an "anti-Stolper-Samuelson" result follows.

Proposition 7. *An increase in the price of manufactures relative to wheat raises the wage and reduces the rent relative to both final-good* *prices, if and only if the scale effect dominates the intersectoral effect sufficiently so that* $Z > \theta_{km}/\theta_{kW}$.

Finally, if Z lies between unity and θ_{km}/θ_{kW}, the coefficient of $\hat{r}$ in (23) is negative, and that of $\hat{w}$ in (23) exceeds that of $\hat{w}$ in (19). Thus any change in P_M/P_W causes w to rise relative to one final-good price and fall relative to the other, but the rental still behaves as above.

Proposition 8. *The relative price of manufactures and the real income of capital vary in the same or opposite directions according as the intersectoral and intrasectoral price structures vary in identical or opposite directions.*

Note that a large scale effect tends to destroy the duality between the Stolper-Samuelson and Rybczynski theorems, since it works to reverse the former while leaving the latter unscathed.[13]

D. The Heckscher-Ohlin theorem

Suppose that both countries produce both goods in international equilibrium, as in Figure 2(c). Then $T'(m) = S'(m^*)$, and Proposition 3 implies that the output ratio M/W is higher in the country endowed with the higher capital-labor ratio. Since the two countries consume the two final goods in equal proportions, each country is a net exporter of the sector intensive to its relatively abundant factor.

Next suppose that at least one country specializes completely. As illustrated in Figure 2, the home allocation curve is steeper than the foreign and, in this case, must lie either wholly outside or wholly inside the foreign. In the former case (Figure 2, panels (d) and (e)) the home country is a wheat importer and in the latter case (Figure 2, panels (a) and (b)) a wheat exporter. What distinguishes the two cases?

[13]See Krugman (1981) for an interesting alternative treatment of income distribution in a model featuring relative factor-endowment differences and intraindustry trade in differentiated consumer goods.

At point F', m and m^* satisfy equation (16). In the home country, from equations (13) and (14),

$$P_D - P_S^H = \frac{a}{\beta}\left(\frac{b}{1-\beta}\right)^{\alpha-1}(m+m^*)^{1-\alpha} \times \left[\frac{\gamma}{1-\gamma}\frac{T+S}{m+m^*} + T'\right].$$

Substitution of (16) into this expression reveals that, at F', $P_D - P_S^H$ has the same sign as $[T'(m) - S'(m^*)]$. Now, if F' falls in the interval $0m_0$, $m^* = 0$ and $0 < m \leq m_0$, whereas $0 \leq m^* < m_0^*$ and $m = m_0$ if F' lies in the interval m_0E. In either case, $T' - S'$ is necessarily negative if the foreign country is relatively capital abundant, provided that the two countries are not separated by a factor-intensity reversal. Then $P_D < P_S^H$ at F, which implies that F' lies above the home allocation curve. A similar argument applied to F reveals that the home allocation curve necessarily lies above the foreign when the home country is relatively capital abundant. Panels (a) and (b) of Figure accordingly illustrate home relative labor abundance, and panels (d) and (e) illustrate home capital abundance.

Proposition 9. *Heckscher-Ohlin. In international equilibrium, each country necessarily exports the good intensive in its relatively abundant factor, if the two countries are not separated by a factor-intensity reversal.*

The quantity version of the Heckscher-Ohlin theorem remains intact. Clearly the price version cannot similarly escape unscathed: the scale effect can alter the relation between commodity and factor prices. Also, Section I showed that relative autarkic commodity prices depend upon national size as well as relative endowments. Since only the latter determine trade patterns, these patterns need not reflect autarkic price differences.

But in spite of all this, the price version does have a role to play, a role that depends on a distinction between intraindustry trade and interindustry trade. Basically, the pattern of free *interindustry* trade (the net exchange of manufactures for wheat) will correspond to what the pattern of relative factor prices in the two countries would be in the absence of such trade but with free *intraindustry* trade (the exchange of components). The latter in effect isolates the influence of internationally decreasing costs.

To see this, consider a *quasi-autarkic equilibrium* in which the two countries freely exchange industrial components, but in which there is no trade in wheat. That is, the home economy consumes $W = T(m)$ and $M = km$, where $k = \beta[(m+m^*)(1-\beta)/b]^{\alpha-1}/a$, and analogously abroad. Such an equilibrium is as described in Section I.B. for each country, except that the two economies are linked by a common value of k dependent upon $m + m^*$. The equilibrium values of m and m^* are the solution to

$$\gamma T(m) - (1-\gamma)T'(m)(m+m^*) = 0$$
$$\gamma S(m^*) + (1-\gamma)S'(m^*)(m+m^*) = 0.$$

In such an equilibrium, the home relative demand and supply prices are given by equations (10) and (9), and analogously abroad. If relative demand prices happen to be equal in the two countries, (10) implies $T(m)/m = S(m^*)/m^*$, since in quasi-autarkic equilibrium the countries share common values of k and n. Thus $T'(m)/m$ exceeds or falls short of $S'(m^*)/m^*$ according as the home country is relatively capital or labor abundant (in a physical sense). Or, in view of (9), the home relative supply price is less or greater than the foreign according as the home economy is relatively capital abundant or not. For demand price to equal supply price in each country, it is consequently necessary that the quasi-autarkic equilibrium relative price of manufactures be less in the relatively capital-abundant country. Proposition 9 then implies that the free-trade exchange of wheat for manufactures is accurately predicted by comparative quasi-autarkic relative commodity prices.

Since in quasi autarky the two countries have distinct relative prices but common values of n and k, the logic of Proposition 6 can be employed to compare the two national equilibria in the absence of a scale effect. This gives the present form of the price version of the Heckscher-Ohlin Theorem.

Proposition 10. *Quasi-Autarky Theorem. In the absence of a separating factor-intensity reversal, each country in free trade is a net exporter of the sector relatively intensive in that factor with the lower relative quasi-autarkic price in that country.*

Note that the quasi-autarky theorem applies to a world such as that envisioned by Gary Hufbauer and John Chilas, who stress that trade between industrial countries is largely intraindustry and involves much less interindustry specialization than does interregional trade within the United States. They see this as due in large part to the pattern of tariff reductions made since the war.

3. The Factor-Endowments Basis of Intraindustry Trade

The previous sections have established the continued relevance to *interindustry* trade of the basic Heckscher-Ohlin idea that trade is a substitute for international factor mobility. The present environment, for example, does no violence to the factor-price-equalization theorem.

The purpose of this section is to establish that *intraindustry* trade likewise has a factor-endowments basis, but that such trade is *complementary* to international factor mobility. Thus a similarity of factor endowments between nations tends to promote such trade as it limits the scope for interindustrial exchange. This property is emerging as a central feature of models with intraindustry trade. The result was first deduced in my article (1979a) and subsequently appeared in the quite distinct work based on differentiated consumer goods.

A. The complementarity theorem

Recall the assumption that finished manufactures are costlessly assembled from bundles of all components. The above analysis established that if both countries produce manufactures, they specialize to distinct collections of components.

It will prove convenient, and consistent with both the balance of this paper and most empirical work, to measure intraindustry trade as what it would be if finished manufactures were assumed to be costlessly assembled where consumed, and if no component entered trade more than once, so that international trade in manufactures therefore consisted entirely of the shipment of components from their country of manufacture to where they are combined with other components and consumed. Then the home country's import M_C and export X_C of manufactures (components) must be

$$M_C = n_F x g, \quad X_C = n_H x(1-g);$$

where g equals domestic national income as a fraction of world income (i.e., $(PM+W)/[P(M+M^*)+W+W^*]$). I shall use the relative index[14] employed by Hesse, Grubel and Lloyd, Caves and others: $\rho = 1 - |X_C - M_C|/(X_C + M_C)$. Then substitution yields

$$\begin{aligned} \rho = 2gn_F/[(1-g)n_H + gn_F] \quad &\text{if } n_H \geq gn, \\ 2(1-g)n_H/[(1-g)n_H + gn_F] \quad &\text{if } n_H \leq gn. \end{aligned} \tag{24}$$

Higher values of ρ indicate relatively more intraindustry trade; $\rho = 1$ if all manufacturing trade is intraindustry and $\rho = 0$ if it is all interindustry.

The complementarity between intraindustry trade and factor movements should now be apparent. Let h and h^* denote the capital-labor endowment ratios at home and abroad, and designate the home country as the capital abundant one, so that $h > h^*$. Suppose that the two countries freely trade, with neither country specialized and with factor prices equalized. Suppose now that the factors are slightly "traded" between the two countries so as to reduce $h - h^*$ while leaving each country's income unchanged at the unchanged factor prices and commodity prices. Then n_H falls, n_F rises by the same amount, and g is unchanged. Now, since the home economy is relatively capital abundant, its share of the world output of components (n_H/n) must exceed its share of world income, g. Thus ρ equals the top expression in (24), which directly reveals that a relative-endowment-equalizing trade of factors must raise ρ.

[14] Alternative measures are discussed in Grubel and Lloyd (1971).

Proposition 11. *Complementarity Theorem. If both countries initially produce both goods, and if there are no separating factor-intensity reversals, a small relative-endowment-equalizing trade of primary factors will increase* ρ.

The basic complementarity property becomes most apparent upon the comparison of extreme cases. If the two countries' endowments differ sufficiently so that one country specializes to wheat there is no intraindustry trade and all trade is interindustrial. If, on the other hand, $K = K^*$ and $L = L^*$, there is no basis at all for interindustry trade (each country will be self-sufficient in wheat), but intraindustry trade will be maximized since the two countries will produce distinct collections of an equal number of components.

B. Technological structure and intraindustry trade

While the Complementarity Theorem establishes that intraindustry trade is sensitive to factor endowments, it is nonetheless clear that the existence of such trade is due to the assumptions about the technology of manufacturing production. Attention thus naturally focuses on the sensitivity of my measure of intraindustry trade to the technological parameters: a, b, and β.

Note, first, that these parameters do not influence the basic allocation of resources which, by Proposition 9, is determined as described by the modern theory of international trade. The intersection of the allocation curves determines m and m^*, and these curves are invariant with respect to all three parameters. Attention therefore focuses on equations (6) and (7).

Consider the relative measure ρ. Changes in the technological parameters will not change g, because they produce offsetting changes on the volume and the relative price of finished manufactures, from (12) and (14). Substitution of (7) into the top line of (24) gives $\rho = 2gm^*/[(1-g)m + gm^*]$. This immediately yields

Proposition 12. *The relative index of intraindustry trade is invariant with respect to the degree of product differentiation and the levels of fixed and marginal costs.*

An increase in marginal costs, by reducing x with n_H and n_F constant, lowers both types of trade in proportion. An increase in product differentiation also reduces interindustry trade *pari-passu* with intraindustry trade. This is surprising: with the existence of intraindustry trade dependent upon product differentiation, one might expect more differentiation to increase such trade. But the explanation is simple. From (7) the number of components does rise, but (6) reveals that the output of each falls in even greater proportion, because of fixed costs.

In sum, the technological parameters play a knife-edge role: their existence is crucial for the present theory, but changes in their values have few effects, or sometimes counterintuitive effects, upon intraindustry trade. Empirical investigations have so far produced mixed results (see Pagoulatos and Sorenson; Caves; and references cited therein).

C. Multilateral trade

A brief consideration of this paper's implications for multilateral trade further illustrates the above discussion and also brings out some features that can not arise at all in the two-country framework, but that reflect the stylized facts of modern trade.

The model used thus far is retained, except that many countries of the sort described above are allowed. Suppose that no factor-intensity reversal is displayed by the common technology. Let h_m and h_W denote the capital-labor ratios in the two sectors in countries which diversify production at the existing prices. Denote by h' the capital labor ratio having the property that any country with an endowment $h > h'$ necessarily imports wheat, and any country with an endowment $h < h'$ necessarily exports wheat.[15] Assume $h_m > h' > h_W$. The various possibilities an individual country could experience are indicated in Table 1.

The concerns of the Complementarity Theorem are best brought out in Cases II, III, and IV where similarities of endowments

[15]If all countries diversify in production, h' equals the world capital-labor ratio.

Table 1. Possibilities in Multilateral Trade.

Case	Endowment	Production	Intraindustry Trade	Interindustry Trade
I	$h \geq h_m$	specialized to m	with all other I, II, III, IV countries	imports W from IV and V
II	$h_m > h \geq h'$	diversified	with all other I, II, III,IV countries	imports some W from IV and V
III	$h = h'$	diversified	with all other I, II, III, IV countries	none
IV	$h' > h > h_W$	diversified	with all other I, II, III, IV countries	exports some W to I and II
V	$h_W \geq h$	specialized to W	none	exports W to I and II

(to each other and to the world as a whole) foster intraindustry trade while limiting interindustry trade. Cases I and V, on the other hand, illustrate behavior that can not arise in a two-country context. Countries in Case I engage in extensive intraindustry trade with the rest of the world (including other Case I countries), by virtue of their specialization to manufacturing, despite the fact that their endowments are quite different from that of the rest of the world as a whole. Countries in Case V, because they specialize to wheat, engage in no intraindustry trade at all with each other (or with anyone else), no matter how closely the factor endowments of these countries resemble each other. The relevance of all this to the stylized facts of contemporary trade should be clear.

4. Conclusion

This paper has developed a simple model of the interaction of national scale economies—internal to individual firms—with international returns to scale—external to firms— and with the modern, factor-endowments, theory of international trade. The result furnishes a detailed microeconomic backdrop to my earlier paper (1979a). In addition two conclusions emerge.

First, as formalized in the Complementarity Theorem, intraindustry trade in manufactures is complementary to international factor movements. Although the existence of such trade depends upon product differentiation and scale economies, these features play a knife-edge role and thereby leave the determination of the level of intraindustry trade largely to relative factor endowments. Second, the basic propositions of the modern theory of international trade remain, on the whole, essentially valid in the presence of scale economies, although some significant modifications do arise.

The second conclusion contrasts rather strongly with the traditional increasing-returns literature—thoroughly preoccupied with national returns to scale. The present treatment also gives national returns a prominent place. The indeterminacy and multiple equilibria characteristic of the standard analysis are still present (because national returns are still present), in terms of the location of production of individual components. But the sharp difference in my conclusions follows from the fact that, when national and international economies are allowed to interact, disturbances to equilibrium typically take the form of changes in the number of production units rather than in their size, so that the concerns of the traditional theory do not arise. Of course it is possible to chip away at this conclusion by relaxing some of my assumptions, especially those that components are symmetric and that internal scale economies arise solely from fixed costs. These assumptions reflect in simple form my views of what is relatively important, but they cannot be literally accurate.

My earlier paper (1979a) argued that international increasing returns to scale are significant in the modern world economy. The present paper suggests that the conclusions of the earlier need not be altered even if national scale economies are also widespread and important. The resulting theory appears empirically relevant, with respect to both the stylized facts cited at the beginning of this article and also to recent studies—see Caves, and Rudolf Loertscher and Frank Wolter.

References

Balassa, Bela, *The Theory of Economic Integration,* Homewood: Irwin, 1961.

———, "Tariff Reduction and Trade in Manufactures among the Industrial Countries," *American Economic Review,* June 1966, *56,* 466–73.

———, *Trade Liberalization among Industrial Countries,* New York: McGraw-Hill, 1967.

Caves, Richard, "Intra-Industry Trade and Market Structure in the Industrial Countries," *Oxford Economic Papers,* March 1981, *33,* 203–33.

——— and Jones, Ronald W., *World Trade and Payments,* 2nd ed., Boston: Little Brown, 1977.

Chang, Winston, Ethier, Wilfred J., and Kemp, Murray C., "The Theorems of International Trade with Joint Production," *Journal of International Economics,* August 1980, *10,* 377–94.

Daly, Donald J., Key, B. A., and Spence, E. J., *Scale and Specialization in Canadian Manufacturing,* Staff Study No. 21, Economic Council of Canada, 1968.

Davies, Robert, "Two-Way International Trade: A Comment," *Weltwirtschaftliches Archiv,* 1977, No. 1, *113,* 179–81.

Dixit, Avinash, K. and Norman, Viktor, *Theory of International Trade,* Cambridge: Cambridge University Press, 1980.

——— and Stiglitz, Joseph, "Monopolistic Competition and Optimum Product Diversity," *American Economic Review,* June 1977, *67,* 297–308.

Ethier, Wilfred J., "Some of the Theorems of International Trade With Many Goods and Factors," *Journal of International Economics,* May 1974, *4,* 199–206.

———, (1979a) "Internationally Decreasing Costs and World Trade," *Journal of International Economics,* February 1979, *9,* 1–24.

———, (1979b) "The Theorems of International Trade in Time-Phased Economies," *Journal of International Economics,* May 1979, *9,* 225–38.

———, "Decreasing Costs in International Trade and Frank Graham's Argument for Protection," *Econometrica,* forthcoming.

Finger, Joseph M., "Trade Overlap and Intra-Industry Trade," *Economic Inquiry,* December 1975, *13,* 581–89.

Gray, H. Peter, "Two-Way International Trade in Manufactures: A Theoretical Underpinning," *Weltwirtschaftliches Archiv,* 1973, No. 1, *109,* 19–29.

Grubel, Herbert G., "The Theory of Intra-Industry Trade," in I. A. McDougall and R. H. Snape, eds., *Studies in International Economics,* Amsterdam: North-Holland, 1970.

——— and Lloyd, Peter J., "The Empirical Measurement of Intra-Industry Trade," *Economic Record,* December 1971, *47,* 494–517.

——— and ———, *Intra-Industry Trade: The Theory and Measurement of International Trade in Differentiated Products,* London: Macmillan, 1975.

Haberler, Gottfried, *The Theory of International Trade, with its Applications to Commercial Policy,* London: W. Hodge, 1936.

Helpman, Elhanen, "International Trade in the Presence of Product Differentiation, Economies of Scale and Monopolistic Competition," *Journal of International Economics,* August 1981, *11,* 305–40.

Hesse, Helmut, "Hypotheses for the Explanation of Trade Between Industrial Countries, 1953–1970," in H. Giersch ed., *The International Division of Labour: Problems and Perspectives,* Tubingen: J. C. B. Mohr, 1974.

Hufbauer, Gary C. and Chilas, John C., "Specialization by Industrial Countries: Extent and Consequences," in H. Giersch, ed., *The International Division of Labour: Problems and Perspectives,* Tubingen: J. C. B. Mohr, 1974.

Jones, Ronald and Scheinkman, José A., "The Relevance of the Two-Sector Production Model in Trade Theory," *Journal of Political Economy,* October 1977, *85,* 909–36.

Kemp, Murray C., *The Pure Theory of International Trade and Investment,* Englewood Cliffs: Prentice-Hall, 1969.

——, *Three Topics in the Theory of International Trade,* Amsterdam: North-Holland, 1976.

Kravis, Irving B. and Lipsey, Richard E., "Price Behavior in the Light of Balance of Payments Theories," *Journal of International Economics,* May 1978, *8,* 193–246.

Krugman, Paul, "Increasing Returns, Monopolistic Competition, and International Trade," *Journal of International Economics,* November 1979, *9,* 469–80.

———, "Intraindustry Specialization and the Gains from Trade," *Journal of Political Economy,* October 1981, *89,* 959–73.

Lancaster, Kelvin, "Intra-Industry Trade under Perfect Monopolistic Competition," *Journal of International Economies,* May 1980, *10,* 151–76.

Lawrence, Colin and Spiller, Pablo, "Product Diversity, Economies of Scale and International Trade," mimeo., 1980.

Loertscher, Rudolf and Wolter, Frank, "Determinants of Intra-Industry Trade," *Weltwirtschaftliches Archiv,* 1980, *116,* 280–93.

Matthews, R. C. O., " Reciprocal Demand and Increasing Returns," *Review of Economic Studies,* 1950, No. 2, *17,* 149–58.

Meade, James E., *A Geometry of International Trade,* London: George Allen and Unwin, 1952.

Owen, Nicholas, "Scale Economies in the EEC," *European Economic Review,* February 1976, *7,* 143–63.

Pagoulatos, Emilio and Sorenson, Robert, "Two-Way International Trade: An Econometric Analysis," *Weltwirtschaftliches Archiv,* 1975, No. 3, *111,* 454–65.

Verdoom, P. J., "The Intra-Block Trade of Benelux," in E. A. G. Robinson, ed., *Economic Consequences of the Size of Nations,* London: Macmillan, 1960.

Chapter 9

The Structure of Foreign Trade*

Elhanan Helpman†

World merchandise exports amounted to \$5.3 trillion in 1997 and exports of commercial services amounted to \$1.3 trillion. These are unprecedented volumes that have expanded much faster than income in the postwar period. Figure 1 presents long-term trends in the real volumes of merchandise trade and output. While trade grew at an annual rate of 2.6 percent during this period, output grew at only 1.5 percent. More than half of the volume of merchandise trade flows amongst developed countries and less than 15 percent flows amongst developing countries. The rest, about one third, represents North-South trade between developed and developing countries.

What explains these large volumes of trade? Why do some countries export computers while others export footwear? Can exports of airplanes be explained in the same way as exports of paper products? Questions of this type have been examined for many years. In attempting to answer them, economists have developed an elaborate analytical apparatus that has been greatly enriched in the

*Originally published in *The Journal of Economic Perspectives*, 13(2), pp. 121–144.

†*Elhanan Helpman is Professor of Economics, Harvard University, Cambridge, Massachusetts, and Tel Aviv University, Tel Aviv, Israel, and Fellow of the Canadian Institute for Advanced Research, Toronto, Ontario.*

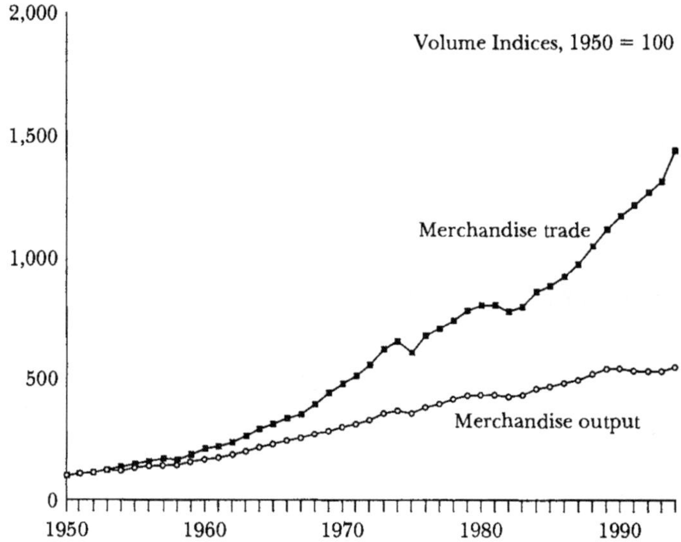

Figure 1. Long-term Trends of World Merchandise Trade and Output, 1950–1994.

Source: WTO, Trends and Statistics 1995.

last two decades. They have used the insights from trade theory to examine ever richer data sets in order to discover systematic patterns of trade flows and to evaluate how well available theories match these data. Nevertheless, although we do have today better answers to some of these questions than our predecessors had 40 years ago, the evolving structure of world trade defies simple explanations. I describe in this paper what we know about foreign trade and in what ways our understanding has improved as a result of the last 20 years of research.

The paper is in five parts. In the next Section I briefly review early insights: David Ricardo's theory of comparative advantage and a simplified version of the Heckscher-Ohlin theory. In the following Section I discuss and evaluate further developments of the Heckscher-Ohlin approach during the 1960s, 1970s and 1980s. While the first two decades provided mostly theoretical insights, major empirical innovations appeared in the 1980s. The third part of the paper is devoted to a discussion of the most recent developments on this front. Next, in part four, comes a discussion and evaluation of research based on economies of scale and product differentiation. This work was done mostly in the 1980s and 1990s. An emphasis on the interplay between theoretical and empirical research characterizes the entire presentation. Conclusions are provided in the closing section.

Early Insights

David Ricardo's theory of comparative advantage, developed at the beginning of the 19th century, has played a major role in modern thinking about trade. Ricardian trade models assume that only labor is used to produce goods and services, with a given fixed coefficient between labor and output of a particular product in each country. The theory predicts that a country will export products in which it has a comparative advantage; that is, products where its labor productivity is high relative to its labor productivity in other products. The simple Ricardo model remains useful for thinking about a host of issues, such as the effects of technological progress on patterns of specialization and the distribution of gains from trade.

However, there are hardly any empirical studies of trade flows that build strictly on Ricardo's insights. A few appeared in the 1950s and '60s (McDougall, 1951, 1952; Stern, 1962), but it quickly became apparent that such models are of limited use in employing data to analyze the overall structure of foreign trade. The main difficulty is that Ricardo's theory is mute on a key ingredient: what causes labor productivity to differ across countries?[1] Differences in the use of capital comprise an important source of variation in labor productivity. Capital-rich countries are able to allocate more capital

[1]Eaton and Kortum (1997) provide the first study of a Ricardian model that contains an explanation of labor productivity based on a country's technology level. Using extreme value distributions for labor productivity they derive an equation for bilateral trade flows. They estimate this equation for a sample of OECD countries, using cumulative investment in R&D and the number of scientists and engineers as proxies for technology levels. The fit appears to be good.

per worker to all economic activities than capital-poor countries, but they may do so to a different degree in various lines of business. This raises the question: what determines the allocation of capital to industries and thereby labor productivity? But once the role of capital is taken seriously, it may be best to abandon the exclusive focus on labor productivity and think about what determines trade flows amongst countries that have additional inputs besides labor.

Eli Heckscher (1919) and Bertil Ohlin (1924) provided a framework for thinking about trade in this situation. They emphasized the roles of labor, capital and land in agriculture and industry, trying to explain how their availability shapes a country's pattern of specialization and trade. Paul Samuelson and his followers elaborated a two-factor two-sector version that became the cornerstone of modern trade theory (Samuelson, 1948; Jones, 1956-57, 1965). Samuelson's version is crisp and elegant. By focusing on labor and capital as inputs and on export- and import-competing sectors, it cuts to the heart of the matter. The model was widely adopted as the workhorse of the profession. According to the two-factor, two-sector version of the Heckscher-Ohlin theory, a country should export the product that is relatively intensive in using the factor with which the country is relatively well- endowed. Thinking about labor and capital as the two inputs, it means that a capital-rich country — a country that has more capital per worker than its trade partners — should export the capital-intensive product.

The argument can be made in two parts. First, if factor prices are not equalized, then the rental rate on capital relative to the wage rate is lower in the capital-rich country.[2] As a result, it uses in all product lines more capital per worker than the capital-poor country. But, as shown by Lerner (1952), under these circumstances the capital-rich country has a cost advantage in the capital-intensive products, which it ends up exporting. This implies that its exports are more capital-intensive than its imports. That is, if we were to calculate how much

[2]Capital accumulation in conjunction with international (financial) capital mobility tend to reduce divergent rental rates on capital. Nevertheless, differences can persist for long periods of time.

capital and labor are embodied in the country's exports and how much capital and labor are embodied in its imports, we should find that for the capital-rich country the ratio of capital to labor is larger in exports than in imports. Second, if factor prices are equalized, then the capital-rich and capital-poor countries use the same ratios of capital to labor to produce identical products. But because the capital-rich country has a disproportionately large amount of capital relative to labor, it ends up producing a disproportionately large amount of capital-intensive products. Otherwise it cannot maintain full employment of labor and capital. It then follows that with a similar composition of demand (that results, for example, from identical homothetic preferences in all countries), the capital-rich country exports capital-intensive products in this case too. So we find again that in the capital-rich country the ratio of capital to labor embodied in exports is larger than the ratio of capital to labor embodied in imports.

There are two concepts of trade in this theory: trade in goods and trade in factor content. Trade in goods is standard; wheat and airplanes are goods, and they can be imported or exported. Trade in factor content is different. It refers to the inputs that are embodied in exports or imports. For example, if a unit of imported wheat is produced with half a unit of land, three units of labor and five units of water, then the factor content of the imported wheat is half a unit of land, three units of labor and five units of water. Using this approach one can calculate the factor content of exports, the factor content of imports, and the factor content of net exports, which is the difference between the two.

Leontief (1954) put the prediction that a capital-rich country should export capital-intensive products to a test. He calculated labor-output and capital-output ratios for various sectors of the U.S. economy, and then — with the aid of these coefficients — calculated how much labor and capital are embodied in exports and how much in imports. Surprisingly, Leontief found that in 1947 the capital-labor ratio embodied in imports exceeded the ratio embodied in exports by 60 percent! The surprise emanated from the fact that after the war, the United States was considered to be the most capital-rich country in the world and the Heckscher-Ohlin theory predicts for such a country a higher capital intensity of exports than imports. His finding became known as the "Leontief paradox."

There were attempts to examine additional data sets, but while the paradox is less pronounced in later data sets, it does not disappear. Leontief proposed his own resolution for the paradox. He had used the assumption that the U.S. input-output coefficients also apply to imports, which is the case when foreign suppliers use the same techniques of production as domestic producers. When countries have access to the same technologies and factor prices are equalized, this assumption is justified. But, pointed out Leontief, if a U.S. worker is much more productive than a foreign worker, then the U.S. should export relatively labor-intensive products. Why would, however, U.S. workers be so much more productive, especially after controlling for capital availability? This explanation seems to resolve one paradox by introducing another.

Further Developments: 1960s, 1970s and 1980s

The two-factor two-sector version of the Heckscher-Ohlin theory was extended in the 1960s and '70s; Ethier (1984) offers a review of the literature at this time. These studies had a variety of purposes, but what is central for this paper is the fact that from these studies grew a surprisingly simple theoretical specification, in which two types of relationships could provide the underpinning for an analysis of the generalized Heckscher-Ohlin theory.

The first set of relationships involves production. Let a_{ij} represent the quantity of input i used in the manufacturing of one unit of output j. I ignore intermediate inputs. Therefore these coefficients describe primary inputs only, which would include various types of capital, such as machines and structures; various types of labor, such as high school dropouts and college graduates; and various types of land, such as pasture and arable land. Cost-minimizing manufacturers choose these coefficients from the available technology, taking factor prices as given. As a result, these coefficients depend in a particular country on its technology and factor rewards.

In the simplest version of this model, the technology is taken to be the same everywhere and factor prices are assumed to be equalized across countries.[3] In this case, the same coefficients are used in all countries. Then, if an economy fully employs its resources, we can derive a factor-market clearing condition. (If a resource is not fully employed, replace its quantity with the actually employed value.) Let V_i^k represent the quantity of input i in country k. Similarly, let X_j^k represent the output of good j in country k. Then full employment of resources implies

$$\sum_j a_{ij} X_j^k = V_i^k$$

for all inputs i and all countries k.

The second set of relationships comes from consumption. Preferences are assumed to be the same in all countries and homothetic; that is, a ray drawn from the origin of an indifference map will intersect all indifference surfaces at points with the same slopes. These assumptions are strong ones. They imply that the composition of consumption (the share of spending going to a product) is the same everywhere. Namely, if we denote by s^k the share of country k in consumption, then consumption of good j in country k is given by

$$C_j^k = s^k \overline{X_j}$$

for all goods j and all countries k, where $\overline{X_j} = \Sigma_k X_j^k$ is aggregate world output of good j. When trade is balanced, the share s^k equals country k's share in world income.

These two sets of fundamental relationships imply empirical specifications. Each country's production of any good is determined by its primary factor endowments, while each country's consumption of goods is determined by overall spending.[4] Exports will be those

[3]Factor prices are not the same in all countries, not even in the OECD countries. But as O'Rourke and Williamson (1999) demonstrate, trade and migration are powerful forces that lead to convergence of factor prices. See Williamson (1998) for a review.

[4]Uniqueness of the production structure requires additional assumptions, such as the equality of the number of inputs and outputs.

products where the country produces more than it consumes, and imports will be those products where the country produces less than it consumes. The model allows countries to run trade deficits or surpluses. The model implies a linear set of relationships between net exports and factor endowments. Each relationship, for petroleum products, forest products, machinery or chemical products, can be estimated from cross-country data. We do not need data on production coefficients or technology, because these are assumed to be the same in all countries. We do need data on net exports, which are readily available, and data on factor endowments, which are not readily available — at least not in comparable form.

Ed Leamer has done more than anybody else to promote a research agenda centered on the construction of such data sets. For example, Leamer (1984) started a new line of empirical research by estimating this linear relationship using a newly constructed data set. The simple linear specification performs very well in explaining actual patterns of trade on a cross section of 60 countries in his data set, for both 1958 and 1975. Examples of the type of effects that were estimated include the availability of oil raising net exports of petroleum products, but also reducing net exports of machinery in 1975; and the abundance of literate, non-professional workers raising exports of labor-intensive manufactures, such as apparel and footwear. Leamer's estimation maintains the assumption of linearity, which works well for most sectors. In some sectors, however, such as chemicals, the data favor a non-linear specification.

While estimates of this type are interesting, they do not provide a test of the generalized Heckscher-Ohlin theory. The reason is that the theory predicts a relationship between endowments and trade mediated by *technology*. To test it therefore requires independent information about all three objects: technology, endowments, trade.

Two concepts of trade have surfaced so far: trade in goods and trade in factor content. The former is a natural focus of trade theory, and was examined by Leamer. The latter was examined by Leontief. Leontief's procedure can be generalized by constructing measures of the factor content of net exports, as suggested by Vanek (1968). With identical technology coefficients in all countries, this procedure is straightforward. Just convert net exports of goods into the factor content of net exports, by multiplying the quantity of net exports of each good with the input coefficient a_{ij} and summing over all goods, using the common technology matrix. What Vanek has shown, is that under the model's assumptions this measure of *factor content* should equal the economy's measure of *factor abundance*. The latter is constructed as follows. Begin with the total factor content of production, which equals the economy's factor endowment, and then subtract out the factor content that goes into domestic consumption, where consumption of each input is proportional to the country's share of world spending. The result will be a measure of factor abundance. On net, inputs that are relatively abundant are exported while those that are relatively scarce are imported. Vanek's key equation is

$$F_i^k = V_i^k - s^k \overline{V}_i$$

for all inputs i and all countries k, where F_i^k is the factor content of net exports of input i in country k and $\bar{V}_i = \Sigma_k V_i^k$ is the aggregate endowment of input i in the world economy.

Vanek's (1968) equation was used by Leamer (1980) to point out a shortcoming of Leontief s procedure: whenever there are more than two inputs, that is, more than just labor and capital, a comparison of the ratio of the embodied quantities of just two of them in imports and exports does not provide the relevant metric for rejecting the theory. This may sound like a possible neat resolution of the Leontief paradox. It is not. As pointed out by Brecher and Chaudhri (1982), the fact that the United States was a net exporter of labor services has an implication for consumption per worker; that is, U.S. consumption per worker should fall short of world consumption per worker, which is not born out by the data.

Bowen, Leamer and Sveikauskas (1987), who were the first to use independent information about endowments, technology and trade, performed two types of tests on Vanek's (1968) key equation. They used the U.S. technology matrix to calculate the factor content of net exports F_i^k for all countries. Their tests involved comparing these measures of factor content with the measures of factor abundance

$\bar{V}_i^k - s^k \bar{V}_i$. They were done with data for 12 inputs and 27 countries (for 1967). One test compared the signs of the two calculations — that is, whether a factor that was predicted to be exported by the factor abundance measure was also exported by the factor content measure (and similarly for imports) — and found disagreement one-third of the time. Another test compared the rank order of the inputs in the calculated measures of the factor content of net exports with the measures of factor abundance and found disagreement about half the time. This appears to be bad news for the expanded Heckscher-Ohlin theory. But how bad the news is hard to gauge, because in this exercise the theory is not tested against a well-specified alternative. For this reason it is also possible to take a more positive attitude and to argue that the theory explains a reasonably large fraction of the variation — across factors and countries — of the factor content of net trade flows.

Recent Advances

Although Bowen, Leamer and Sveikauskas (1987) pointed out difficulties with the Vanek equation, they did not investigate whether the data deviate systematically from the theoretical predictions. This important task was undertaken by Trefler (1995). He compiled a new data set, for 33 countries, that disaggregates endowments into nine inputs. The countries in the sample accounted for three-quarters of world exports and nearly 80 percent of world income in 1983. Again, Trefler first calculated the factor content of net exports, using the U.S. technology matrix for all countries, and then compared them to the factor abundance measures. Vanek's (1968) theoretical prediction is that the two measures should have a correlation of 1. Trefler found instead a correlation of .28.[5] A sign test of the Bowen, Leamer and Sveikauskas (1987) type was successful in only about one-half of

[5]All the reported calculations use normalized data, which is obtained from the original data by dividing every input by the standard deviation across countries of the difference

$$F_i^k = \left(V_i^k - S^k \overline{V_i}\right)$$

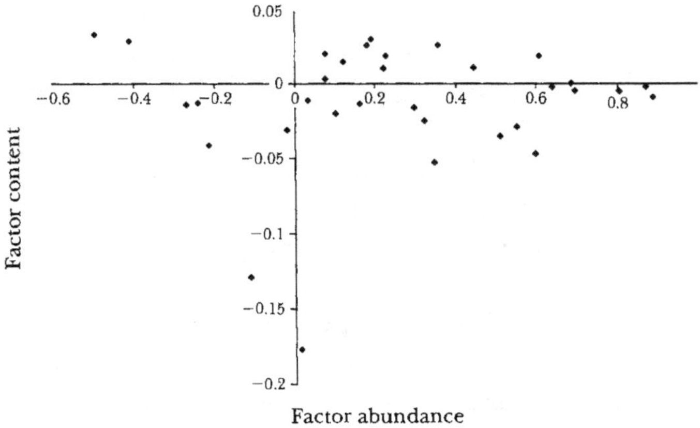

Figure 2. Factor Abundance and Factor Content Measures: Capital data. *Source*: Trefler (1995). Every observation has been divided by the quantity of the input in the country.

the cases. It therefore appears that Trefler's data fits the expanded Heckscher-Ohlin theory as well or as badly as Bowen, Leamer and Sveikauskas's data does.

Trefler (1995) showed clearly in what ways these data deviate from the theoretical predictions. First, the measures of the factor content of net exports are compressed towards zero relative to the factor abundance measures. That is, even in cases in which both variables have the same sign, the former is much smaller in absolute value than the latter. This compression is striking. It is not unusual in these data for the absolute value of the factor abundance measure to be 10 to 50 times higher than the absolute value of the factor content of trade, as one can see in Figure 2, which presents these measures for capital (every point represents a country). Second, whenever a poor country exports an input on net, it exports less than predicted by its factor abundance measure. And whenever it imports an input on net, it imports more than predicted by its factor abundance measure. For rich countries the opposite is true. If one takes the factor content

and by the measure of country size $(s^k)^{1/2}$. Here relative country size is measured by its share in aggregate GDP.

measure of net exports derived from trade flows and then subtracts from it the factor abundance measure, derived by subtracting the factor content of domestic consumption from the domestic factor endowment, that difference has a correlation of .87 with per capita GDP. Third, poor countries tend to be abundant in more factors than rich countries, in the sense that they have more inputs for which the domestic endowment exceeds the quantity of the factor embodied in domestic consumption. Indeed, the correlation between the factor abundance measure and per capita GDP is −.89.[6]

This characterization is of lasting value. It gives us a better understanding of the ways in which the data do not match the theory. It provides a clear theoretical challenge: How should the model be modified to better fit the data?

Trefler also followed up on the earlier suggestion of Leontief that perhaps these differences could be explained by differences in productivity across inputs and countries. Suppose, as suggested by Leontief, that inputs are not equally productive in all countries. If U.S. labor is, for example, two times as productive as labor in Italy, then 1000 hours of U.S. labor services are equivalent to 2000 hours of labor services in Italy. Taking one country as the benchmark, we can then convert the endowment of all other countries into equivalent units of the benchmark country. It is then possible to use Trefler's data to calculate what the productivity differences would have to be between countries so that a modified Vanek equation would hold exactly.[7] Using this approach, Trefler (1993) first calculated labor

[6]These results cannot be explained by trade imbalances, which are much too small for this purpose.

[7]Taking one country as the benchmark, we can convert the endowment V_i^k of country k into $\pi_i^k V_i^k$ equivalent units of the benchmark country, where π_i^k is the productivity of input i in country k relative to the same input in the benchmark country. Under these circumstances Vanek's equation in the text becomes

$$F_i^k = \pi_i^k V_i^k - s^k \sum_l \pi_i^l V_i^l$$

for all k and i, where the factor content of net exports F_i^k is calculated using the benchmark country's technology.

and capital productivity coefficients for a set of countries relative to the United States, and he then compared them with the wage rate and the return to capital in these countries relative to the United States. According to the theory, if there is factor price equalization, then in a cross-country comparison the relative rewards should equal the relative productivity parameters. Indeed, Trefler found the relative factor rewards to be highly correlated with the calculated relative productivity parameters.

In a later paper, Trefler (1995) took several alternative approaches to estimating productivity parameters. In one approach, he assumed that the productivity parameters are country-specific but not factor-specific; that is, if U.S. labor is two times as productive as Italian labor, so is U.S. capital and land. Thus, each country's productivity is represented by a common productivity advantage in all lines of business, and this advantage can be thought of as a Hicks-neutral technical difference. Trefler's second observation — namely, that poor countries appear to export too little of their abundant factors while rich countries export too much — suggests that Hicks-neutral productivity differences can help explain these data. Trefler's second approach was to divide countries into two sets, developed and developing, so that the factor-specific productivity parameters are the same in each group of countries, but differ across the two groups. Of these two choices, Trefler concluded that the Hicks-neutral specification performs better.[8]

To better account for the "missing trade" — that is, the finding that the factor content of net exports as measured from trade statistics is so much smaller than the difference between total factor endowments and factors that are embodied in domestic consumption — Trefler also introduced a home bias in demand. He found that this bias, together with the Hicks-neutral productivity differences, provides the best explanation of the data. I find the use of a home bias in demand unappealing. There is plenty of

[8]Bowen, Leamer and Sveikauskas (1987) also examined productivity differences. Unfortunately, due to a programming error their results are not correct.

independent evidence that technologies differ across countries (for example, Harrigan, 1997). There is no such evidence for demand patterns, except for biases that are related to income levels.

Trefler uncovered patterns in the gaps between the Heckscher-Ohlin theory and the actual data on factor content and factor abundance. Apparently, technological differences between countries help to explain these gaps. The work by Davis, Weinstein, Bradford and Shimpo (1997) supports this emphasis. These authors set out to evaluate the two fundamental relationships discussed earlier in this paper: the production relationship in which sectoral output levels are used to calculate aggregate demands for inputs which are then required to equal factor endowments; and the consumption relationship that consumption vectors in different countries are proportional to each other.

They evaluated the production relationship in a cross-section of countries and a cross-section of Japanese regions, using Japan's technology matrix in all cases. They used output data to calculate the demand for inputs. According to the theory, this vector of input demands should match the vector of factor endowments. To examine how close these two vectors are to each other they performed on them rank order tests of the type introduced by Bowen, Leamer and Sveikauskas (1987).

They found that the match is not good in the international data, but is remarkably accurate in the Japanese regions. One plausible interpretation of this finding is that techniques of production are very similar across Japanese regions but differ significantly across countries. The failure of the common technology model to work in the international data can emanate either from lack of factor price equalization (which we know to be true from data on wages) or from differences in technological opportunities (which we also know to be the case). At the moment there are no estimates of how much of the failure is attributable to each of these potential causes.[9]

[9]Impediments to trade can cause differences in factor prices. But such impediments have declined systematically over time. And regional wage differentials persist for long periods of time within countries.

In looking at the consumption relationship, Davis, Weinstein, Bradford and Shimpo (1997) considered how accurately the structure of consumption can be captured by a model which posits that the share of consumption going to different goods is the same in all areas. In one exercise, they tested whether regional "absorption" (consumption plus investment) vectors in Japan are proportional to the aggregate Japanese absorption vector, concluding that they are. Next they tested whether the Japanese absorption vectors are proportional to world production, concluding that they are.

Since both the fundamental production and consumption relationships seem to hold well for the regions of Japan, Davis, Weinstein, Bradford and Shimpo (1997) went on to test a Vanek-style (1968) relationship with Japanese data, comparing a measure of the factor content of net exports with a measure of factor abundance. What they found was that even though the fundamental underlying production and consumption relationships hold across regions of Japan, the Vanek relationship does not fit the Japanese data well. As in Trefler's data set, this case too exhibits "missing trade;" namely, the computed factor content of net exports is much smaller in absolute value than what is predicted by factor abundance (that is, by the total factors subtracting out factors used for domestic consumption). For example, while net exports of noncollege labor services amount to 3.6 percent of this factor endowment, the factor abundance calculation predicts imports of 31 percent of this factor endowment — a large deviation indeed.

How can these different findings be reconciled? Davis, Weinstein, Bradford and Shimpo (1997) propose a partial resolution. The test just described used Japanese production coefficients, assumed to be the same for all countries. If one instead recognizes that other countries may use different production coefficients, it is possible to obtain a modified Vanek equation in which the world's aggregate factor endowment is replaced with the inputs that would have been used if every country were to use Japan's technology matrix. With this modification in place the puzzle of the "missing trade" is reduced, although not eliminated.

It is clearly possible to use a Heckscher-Ohlin modeling approach to explain the trade data if one allows arbitrary differences in techniques of production across countries. But this answer is not useful; after all, any and every pattern of factor content can be explained with arbitrary differences in techniques of production. The challenge is to use key features of countries to explain the reason for differences in techniques of production, and in turn, to have these differences better explain the trade data.

One possible approach is to look at models where the differences in techniques of production come about because factor prices are not equalized across countries. To give an example, consider a world of two countries, two inputs and two outputs, in which differences in factor composition are wide enough that there is no factor price equalization. Let the factors be capital and labor, let the products be food and clothing, and let clothing be capital-intensive. The technologies are the same in both countries. However, since country A has a high capital-labor ratio and therefore a relatively low rental rate on capital, it employs more capital and less labor than country B would employ in the same line of business. Suppose also that due to the extreme differences in factor endowments, country A manufactures only clothing and B produces only food. It can be shown that under these circumstances the capital-rich country A exports on net less capital services than predicted by Vanek's factor abundance measure and imports on net less labor services than predicted by this measure (Helpman, 1998b). A similar conclusion is obtained from an analysis of the labor-rich country. To see why, note that using the factor coefficients from country A introduces no bias in the calculation of the factor content of A's *exports.* But it biases the calculation of the factor content of A's *imports,* because foreign manufacturers use different input-output coefficients — they use less capital and more labor per unit output. Therefore the use of A's coefficients overstates the amount of capital and understates the amount of labor embodied in its imports. As a result *net* exports of capital services are understated and so are *net* imports of labor services. This is why differences in techniques of production that result from factor price differences help to explain the phenomenon of "missing trade."

But how much "missing trade" can be explained by cross-country variations in factor rewards? At the moment there is no clear answer to this question. Davis and Weinstein (1998a) have recently shown that, indeed, countries with more capital per worker use more capital-intensive techniques than countries with less capital per worker. And moreover, adjustments of technology matrixes for such differences in factor endowments help to explain the factor content of net exports. However, Hicks-neutral differences in technology are also required for a good fit, and such productivity differences remain extremely important even after accounting for differences in factor composition.[10]

Things do not look so bleak when attention is focused on the pattern of specialization in domestic production rather than trade. Reeve (1998) estimated a relationship between outputs and inputs for a sample of 20 OECD countries, using data on 15 sectors and five types of inputs: capital, three grades of labor and arable land. He found that cross-country variations in factor endowments explain over 40 percent of the variation in output levels. If one allows for cross-country differences in Hicks-neutral productivity levels — that is, the productivity of a factor is country-specific but does not vary across inputs in a country — the fit improves significantly and an additional 7 percent of the variation in output levels is explained. In decomposing output changes from 1970 to 1985, Reeve finds

[10]The problem of missing trade appears to be much too severe to be explained with moderate differences between countries. For example, using a regression approach to look at Trefler's (1993) data set of 33 countries, Gabaix (1997) estimated the affects of factor endowments on the factor content of net exports. He allows factor-specific productivity levels to differ across countries, but assumes that they are proportional to factor rewards. Under these circumstances the model predicts a coefficient of 1 on the factor-augmented endowment measures. Gabaix finds instead coefficients close to zero. In addition he shows that Trefler's (1993) calculation of cross-country differences in productivity of inputs is insensitive to the factor content of net exports, in the sense that virtually identical numbers are obtained when the factor content of net exports is assumed to be zero.

that shifts in factor endowments and the techniques of production explain over 80 percent of the changes in the sectoral output levels. Interestingly, changing factor endowments contributes about twice as much as changing techniques of production.

This suggests that as imperfect as the theory is, some of its components fare well empirically. My conclusion from the evidence is that to close the gap between the theory and the data, we need to model more carefully the cross-country differences in techniques of production that are driven by both technological differences and differences in factor rewards. This view is strengthened by Hakura's (1997) findings, as well as by Davis and Weinstein (1998a). Using data for five of the original European Union countries, she first confirms the Bowen, Leamer and Sveikauskas (1987) finding that a Vanek-style (1968) comparison of the factor content of net exports with a factor abundance calculation has the correct sign pattern in only about one-half of the observations. But this fraction rises to 70–80 percent when each country's techniques of production are used instead of a common technology matrix. This fraction rises even further when allowance is made for non-traded intermediate inputs. Evidently, allowing for differences in techniques of production can dramatically improve the fit of factor content equations. Now economists need to identify the forces that induce countries to choose different techniques of production.

Economies of Scale and Product Differentiation

Concurrent with the refinement of the Heckscher-Ohlin trade theory and the development of its empirical implications for the factor content of net trade flows, a new trade theory that emphasizes economies of scale and product differentiation emerged in the 1980s. Helpman (1984) offers a review of the literature on trade with economies of scale and Krugman (1995) reviews the literature on trade with differentiated products and monopolistic competition. At the early stages of its development, the new theory seemed to threaten the Heckscher-Ohlin orthodoxy. But it became clear that these new explanations of trade were actually complementary to the explanations provided by factor endowments. This called for an integrative view of foreign trade that would allow for an interplay between economies of scale, product differentiation, and factor proportions. Helpman and Krugman (1985) developed such an approach, making allowance for sectors that differ in their sources of scale economies, in conduct, and in market structure.

Much of this research was originally motivated by the observation that large volumes of trade flow between countries with similar factor proportions and that significant trade overlap exists within industries, which seemed to imply that a considerable portion of trade was not being driven by factor endowment differences. These facts have not changed. In 1996, the 15 countries of the European Union exported (and imported) a little over $2 trillion worth of merchandise, and about 65 percent of this trade was within the EU. Europe's imports from Japan alone exceeded its imports from *all* of Africa and were more than twice as high as its imports from *all* of the Middle East (WTO, 1997, Table A10). Evidently, the EU countries trade with countries that are similar to themselves more than they trade with the very different economies of Africa and the Middle East. More broadly, the industrial countries trade with each other much more than they trade with less developed countries.

Measures of trade overlap within industries have remained high. These measures consider imports and exports within each industry, evaluate how much overlap there is in every sector, and provide a summary statistic of the share of total trade that consists of such overlaps.[11] To construct such an index for bilateral trade between two countries k and l, take the minimum of the bilateral import volumes; for example, if in one industry country k imports $20 billion from l and country l imports $30 billion from k, choose the $20 billion. Add these volumes up. Divide by the sum over all industries of all bilateral imports. Multiply by two, to adjust for the fact that the numerator refers to imports of only one country, while the denominator refers

[11] According to the Heckscher-Ohlin theory such overlaps should not exist. Davis (1995) has proposed, however, that small differences in individual product-related technologies can produce such overlaps even in a Heckscher-Ohlin framework.

to imports of both countries. By construction, this index is between zero and one with higher values representing more trade overlap. To take a couple of examples, the share of intra-industry trade in the United Kingdom was 53.2 percent in 1970, and then increased to 74.4 percent in 1980 and 84.6 percent in 1990. In Germany, it increased from 55.8 percent in 1970 to 56.6 percent in 1980 and 72.2 percent in 1990 (OECD, 1996, Table 1.8). These two countries represent a general trend of rising shares of intra-industry trade. Declines in this index are rare, but it happened in Norway as a result of the oil boom. Shares of intra-industry trade are especially high in some sectors. In pharmaceuticals, for example, intra-industry trade accounted for 98 percent of trade in finished products in the United States in 1991, 70 percent in France and 32 percent in Japan. In the same year, intra-industry trade accounted for 70 percent of trade in intermediate pharmaceutical products in the United States, 82 percent in France and 64 percent in Japan (OECD, 1996, Table 2.12).

Helpman and Krugman (1995) have shown that economies of scale, product differentiation, and various forms of conduct are compatible with factor price equalization and, as a consequence, with Vanek-type equations for the factor content of trade. For this reason the empirical evidence that I reviewed so far is also relevant for the richer theory developed in the 1980s. Grossman and Helpman (1991) show conditions under which the Vanek-type equations also remain valid in economies that invest in research and development.

Although factor price equalization and the employment of identical techniques of production in all countries can take place with economies of scale, their presence makes this less likely. Scale economies drive countries to specialize in different products, which enhances the incentives for foreign trade. For this reason, they help to explain large trade volumes between similar countries. At the same time, economies of scale make it more likely that countries will employ different techniques of production. This is especially so when there are dynamic economies of scale, be they driven by learning-by-doing or investment in research and development, in which case some companies have access to technologies that are not available to rivals.[12] Since the empirical evidence does not appear to be consistent with the use of identical techniques of production worldwide, or even within groups of relatively homogeneous countries, the study of country-specific technological developments becomes important for understanding international trade.

Intra-Industry Trade

The first comprehensive study of the extent of trade overlap was done by Grubel and Lloyd (1975). They devised the index of intra-industry trade described a moment ago, and showed that the index was high in many countries. Even before the theory of intra-industry trade was properly developed, Loertscher and Wolter (1980) had established some patterns about trade overlap. In particular, they found that the share of intra-industry trade is high when the trading partners are highly developed and at a similar level of development, and when the trading partners are large and do not differ too much in size.

To explain extensive intra-industry trade, sectors with product differentiation were introduced into the theory. Many products are differentiated by brand, from simple goods such as breakfast cereal, toothpaste or clothing, to sophisticated ones such as cars, computers or magnetic resonance imaging machines. Many producer goods are differentiated in some way as well, including capital goods such as drilling machines and intermediate inputs such as microprocessors. The theory applies to all such goods. It starts by noting that product differentiation typically involves economies of scale. A brand has to be developed, such as a lightweight laptop, or it has to be designed, such as a dress fashion. In either case, the company that develops the product gains some monopoly power, because the market does not provide a perfect substitute for its unique brand. Moreover,

[12]Such advantages exist at least temporarily, as is evident from a variety of technological races in the electronics and pharmaceutical industries. See Grossman and Helpman (1995) for a review of the literature on the links between trade and technology.

companies are driven to differentiate their creations from the brands of rivals.

Economies of scale limit the range of products that are profitably supported by the market; the smaller the economies of scale, the more brands become available. With international trade, countries specialize in different brands. When every country demands a wide spectrum of varieties, international trade leads naturally to trade overlap: brand-specific economies of scale lead to intra-industry trade. Although empirical researchers have sought an association between the degree of economies of scale in a sector and the extent of its intra-industry trade, the theory does not appear to imply such a relationship. What matters is that economies of scale exist, not their size.

According to the theory, the share of intra-industry trade is larger between countries that are similar both in composition of factor endowments and in size. Helpman (1987) examined the empirical validity of these results. He used the absolute difference in GDP per capita to capture the composition of factor endowments and the size of each country's GDP to capture the size variables. For a sample of 14 industrial countries he estimated such a relationship to assess how well these variables predicted the share of intra-industry trade in bilateral trade flows between nations. He found that the partial correlations had the predicted signs for most of the years between 1970 and 1981; that is, the extent of trade overlap was larger the more similar were the countries' income per capita, the smaller was the larger country and the larger was the smaller country.

However, this relationship may not be robust. In Helpman's (1987) results, the magnitude of the findings appears to weaken over time. Moreover, Hummels and Levinsohn (1995) both confirm Helpman's findings and call them into question. They find that Helpman's results continue to hold, for example, if instead of using income per capita to capture factor differences, one uses income per worker or absolute differences in capital-labor and land-labor ratios. But when they inserted country-pair dummy variables into the specification, it appeared that most of the variation in the share of intra-industry trade could be explained by country-pair dummies.

That is, unspecified characteristics of country pairs explain more than the variables emphasized by the theory! This finding raises an obvious need to broaden the theory to arrive at a better empirical specification.

Volume of Trade

Economies of scale and product differentiation strengthen the tendency to specialize, and in turn, specialization encourages a greater volume of international trade. To see how trade volumes are determined by specialization, consider an extreme case in which every country is completely specialized in a subset of products, each country has the same homothetic preferences for consuming goods, and trade is balanced, so that spending levels on each good are proportional to GDP levels (as in the fundamental consumption relationship given earlier). This relationship implies that a given percentage increase in the GDP of a country will raise its volume of trade (exports plus imports) with any other country by the same percentage amount; it is called a "gravity equation."[13] Gravity equations go back to Tinbergen (1962); Linnemann (1966) provided a comprehensive analysis. Typical specifications estimate the effects of income on trade, controlling for the distance between the trade partners. Distance has a negative effect on the volume of trade.

Equations of this form — aggregated in various ways — have been estimated time and again, providing a good fit to many data sets. Helpman (1987) used it to calculate the volume of trade amongst 14 industrial countries as a fraction of their aggregate income. According to the theory, this fraction is larger the more similar are the countries'

[13]Assuming that all countries have the same homothetic preferences and that there is complete specialization implies that country k imports from l the fraction s^k of l's output. The volume of trade (imports plus exports) between these two countries therefore equals $Q^{k,l} = s^k Y^l + s^l Y^k$, where Y^k is the GDP level of country k. If, in addition, spending levels are proportional to GDP levels, $s^k = Y^k/Y$ and $Q^{k,l} = 2Y^k Y^l/Y$, where Y is the world's GDP.

income levels as measured by a similarity index $1 - \Sigma_k (s^k)^2$.[14] To see how this works as an income similarity index, take the case of two countries. In this case the index is very close to zero whenever one country is much bigger than the other, since s^k is close to zero for the small country and close to one for the large country. When the two countries are equal in size $s^k = 1/2$ for each, and the similarity index obtains the value ½, which is the largest possible value in the presence of two countries. Helpman found that between 1956 and 1981, this index increased and the fraction of income traded within the group increased as well. This co-movement is consistent with models of product differentiation in which specialization in production is driven by brand proliferation.

A reexamination of Helpman's (1987) evidence with a focus on *bilateral* trade flows was performed by Hummels and Levinsohn (1995). They confirmed Helpman's finding for a group of industrial countries. But they also applied the same approach to a group of mixed countries — some developed, others less developed — arguing that if product differentiation is the main reason for the good fit, the equation should not perform well in the mixed sample, since trade between different economies should presumably be based more on factor differences and less on trade in similar differentiated products. Although their main equation did not fit the mixed sample as well as it did the homogeneous sample, it was remarkably good nevertheless. They concluded that the evidence does not lend support to the view

[14]To derive this similarity index recall from the previous footnote that country k's imports from country l are $s^k Y^l$, where s^k is the share of country k in world spending and Y^l represents income of country l. It follows that k's imports from all other countries equals $s^k(Y - Y^k)$, where Y stands for world income. Next note that assuming that spending is proportional to income implies $s^k = Y^k/Y$. Therefore, the total volume of world trade is given by

$$\sum_k s^k(Y - Y^k) = \sum_k \frac{Y^k}{Y}(Y - Y^k) = Y\left[1 - \sum_k (s^k)^2\right]$$

This implies that the volume of trade equals the fraction $1 - \Sigma_k (s^k)^2$ of world income.

that product differentiation is the key to why the volume of trade seems to increase with similarity in size of the trading economies.

Evenett and Keller (1998) developed an alternate estimation procedure that sheds more direct light on whether product differentiation or differences in factor endowments might explain the empirical relationships between the volume of trade and the size distribution of countries. Using a mixed sample of countries (similar to Hummels and Levinsohn), Evenett and Keller divided the observations of country pairs into those that have less than 5 percent of intra-industry trade and those that have more, and they assumed that country pairs in the first sample trade homogeneous products. They then investigated whether the data favors a specification in which differences in factor proportions between the countries in the first sample are large enough to lead to specialization in this group, which would justify a gravity equation (that is, a link between the volume of trade and the size of countries) despite the lack of product differentiation, but failed to find evidence in favor of this hypothesis.[15] They also divided the remaining countries into five classes that differed in the degree of intra-industry trade. They tested whether the gravity equation provides a better approximation to the data for countries with a higher share of intra-industry trade, and found that it does. This finding favors the view that product differentiation is at the core of the relationship between the volume of trade and the size distribution of countries.

As mentioned earlier, developed economies trade mostly with each other rather than with less developed countries, and trade within the group of less developed countries is only a small fraction of total world trade (about 15 percent). To see how product

[15]Deardorff (1998) made the argument that a gravity equation can be derived from a generalized Heckscher-Ohlin model with large differences in factor composition that lead to specialization in production. Although this is a theoretical possibility, the Evenett-Keller evidence suggests that it has little empirical content. Deardorff's alternative derivation of the gravity equation for economies with homogenous products, which is based on random divisions of imports across the exporting countries, is not even appealing on theoretical grounds. I agree with Grossman's (1998) position on this point.

differentiation helps to account for these facts, consider a world that consists of developed countries (the North) and less developed countries (the South). All countries in the North are the same size and have the same factor endowments; the same is true of countries in the South. However, the composition of factor endowments differs between the North and the South. In some sectors, there is product differentiation, in others products are homogeneous. Now suppose that due to differences in factor composition the North specializes in differentiated products while the South specializes in homogeneous products. Since all the developing countries are the same size, and producing the same homogenous products, the countries of the South do not trade with each other. However, each South country imports a fixed fraction of output from each North country. The North countries all import some fixed fraction of output from every country in the North and the same fraction from the South region.

Now, for concreteness, suppose that there are 20 countries in the North, each one accounting for 4 percent of world output. The North accounts therefore for 80 percent of the world's output and it is four times as large as the South. In this setting, trade among the North economies will be a large proportion of world trade, because the North economies are larger to begin with, and they specialize. With these reasonable sizes of economies the volume of trade among the developed countries in the North is about twice as large as their trade with the South.[16] This is a simple calibration, close to the mark. In the data, this ratio is about 1.6.

Of course, assuming no trade at all between economies in the South is an extreme condition. Surely, some internal trade does exist in the South, since factor proportions are not the same in every country. But this extreme formulation helps to make the main point. Generally there will be less intra-group trade in the South the

[16]It is shown in Helpman (1998b) that under these assumptions the ratio of North-North to North- South trade equals $s^N(n^N-1)/2(1-s^Nn^N)$, where s^N is the relative size of a country in the North and η^N is the number of countries in the North. Using $s^N = .04$ and $\eta^N = 20$, therefore implies a ratio of 1.9.

more the South specializes in homogeneous products and the less its countries differ in factor compositions.

A Heckscher-Ohlin approach assuming homogenous products can also be used to explain such volumes of North-North and North-South trade, without any need for product differentiation, by incorporating any necessary differences in techniques of production across goods and sectors as well as suitable cross-country differences in factor endowments. Davis (1997) gives an example. However, while I find such arguments to be an interesting intellectual exercise, they are of little practical value. Explaining the observed trade patterns with only homogeneous products requires too much fine tuning of the technology to be convincing. The broad structure of world trade is more naturally explained with the aid of product differentiation than without it.

To conclude, the available evidence supports the view that economies of scale with product differentiation are valuable components in the explanation of trade flows. However, it still leaves room for factor endowments to play a role.

Economies of Scale

Modern trade theory places significant weight on economies of scale and product differentiation in explaining the structure of foreign trade. Its usefulness has been gauged by a variety of implications that help to interpret various facts, and by the fit of some of its implications in various data sets. However, this research provides no direct evidence on the extent of economies of scale. In fact, most of the implications that have been examined do not depend on the *degree* of economies of scale, just on their existence. Although this is good enough for many purposes, for a variety of welfare-related questions it is important to have a sense of the size of economies of scale. Some micro production studies find economies of scale in single-country data sets. But such studies cannot provide comparable estimates of economies of scale at the sectoral level and may, therefore, underestimate the size of scale effects because, as suggested by Marshall, economies of scale at the sector level can emanate from the interaction of firms and factor markets within an industry.

Antweiler and Trefler (1997) have developed a methodology for estimating returns to scale at the sectoral level from international data. They constructed a data set for 71 countries, with 37 industries and 11 factors, spanning a period from 1972 to 1992. The key theoretical observation that enables them to estimate the degree of economies of scale is that a variant of the Vanek (1968) equation, which has been mentioned a number of times already, also holds in the presence of economies of scale. The Vanek relationship, of course, is to look first at the factor content of net exports, calculated by applying factor production coefficients to import and export data, and then to compare that result to the difference between total factors in an economy and factors used in domestic consumption. In the Antweiler and Trefler variant of the Vanek approach, the factor content of exports and imports is calculated separately for each and every trade partner, which allows all countries to use different techniques of production.

One way to specify the difference in techniques of production is to allow differences in factor productivity levels across countries, as in Trefler (1993). An alternative approach, however, is to attribute cross-country variations in productivity levels to differences in scale. As a result of scale economies, the use of inputs per unit output declines (on average) as output expands. Assuming that the productivity parameters are proportional to factor rewards, then scale economies are the only remaining source of cross-country variations in productivity levels. By parameterizing the effects of scale economies, one can therefore estimate the suitable coefficients from such modified Vanek equations. The results show that productivity is indeed higher the higher the level of output; costs fall by about 0.15 to 0.20 percent when output rises by 1 percent. These estimates are larger than those often obtained from micro studies on economies of scale. Moreover, these estimates have low standard errors. The estimates imply further that output expansion leads to shifts in the techniques of production that raise the demand for skilled relative to unskilled workers.

Some other estimates of economies of scale across national economies are becoming available, as well. Harrigan (1999) uses estimates of production functions for a sample of OECD countries to assess whether economies of scale at the sectoral level or Hicks-neutral differences in the technological efficiency of countries better explain cross-country variations in sectoral levels of total factor productivity. The results are mixed. Differences in total factor productivity are large, and economies of scale do not explain them adequately. Neutral technological differences provide a somewhat better fit. Since one does not exclude the other, it would be interesting to allow for both scale economies and technological differences, but Harrigan's data does not allow estimating this decomposition accurately.

Yet another inquiry into economies of scale based on international data is provided by Davis and Weinstein (1998b). Their point of departure is Krugman's (1980) home-market effect. Krugman introduced transport costs for varieties of a differentiated product that are produced with economies of scale in a two-country model with one input (labor) and two sectors, one differentiated and the other homogeneous. In this sort of environment, where production functions are the same in both countries, the pattern of specialization is undetermined in the absence of transport costs. But with transport costs, the size of local demand determines the profitability of manufacturing differentiated products. The larger country, with its greater demand, supports the development of a disproportionate number of brands and therefore exports them on net. The important role of the size effect is here in demand, not supply.

More generally, in economies where transport costs are important and the size of the home market matters, shifts in the aggregate demand for a country's products will have a disproportionately large effect on its output of products with economies of scale. In pure Heckscher-Ohlin-type economies (no economies of scale and no product differentiation) with no transport costs, such effects are nil, while in Heckscher-Ohlin-type economies with transport costs they are less than proportional. It is therefore possible to discriminate between these alternative models by estimating the effects of aggregate demand on the output of various products.

To estimate the demand for goods in a particular sector of a country, Davis and Weinstein (1998b) first estimate how trade flows are affected by the size of the economy as compared to its trading partners, accounting for distances between countries. Their sample consists of 22 OECD countries and 25 sectors. As is typical for such equations, the trade volume declines with distance. Using these estimates they then construct relative demand levels for every industry and estimate the effect of this demand for the country's products, which emanates from all countries including the home country, on the local supply. Pooling over industries, they find that a 1 percent increase in demand raises local output by 1.6 percent, which provides evidence in favor of scale effects. Performing the same estimation for every industry separately they obtain less accurate estimates. Nevertheless, in 11 out of the 25 sectors the coefficients are significantly larger than one, supporting the presence of economies of scale. Davis and Weinstein (1997) estimated a similar model on regional data from Japan, and also found scale effects in a number of sectors.

Conclusions

Some researchers have argued that the modern theory of international trade with economies of scale and product differentiation is not needed to explain key features of world trade — such as the existence of intra-industry trade, the connection between the growth in economies and the growth of trade volumes, or the difference between North-North and North-South trade volumes. Researchers in this tradition strive to convince us that there is no need to incorporate economies of scale or product differentiation into trade theory, since for any given pattern we can find a structure of a traditional Heckscher-Ohlin model with homogenous goods that also produces it. This is, of course, a legitimate and intellectually interesting debate. But in my view, product differentiation is so prevalent that it is hard to see why it is even necessary to justify its presence in economic models. If anything, it should be necessary to justify the use of models with homogeneous products only. Just think about the products we consume: food, clothing, furniture, home appliances, sports equipment, cars — almost anything — they all are differentiated products. The same can be said about intermediate inputs and capital goods, as well as about a host of services, such as banking, insurance, or travel. Whenever product differentiation helps to explain certain phenomena, it is only natural to embrace this assumption, rather than to insist on the construction of models with homogenous products that also explain them.

All this being said, the ultimate test is in the direct and indirect evidence. There is plenty of direct evidence, from observation and otherwise, that product differentiation is prevalent. But this does not imply necessarily that the available models of international trade with product differentiation provide a good explanation of the data. It is fair to say that none of the existing models does a great job explaining the data. But adding product differentiation does improve the fit between theory and data. Moreover, since the inherent richness of the models with product differentiation has not yet been much explored, such models carry the potential of providing even better explanations.

We now have a rich theory of international trade that emphasizes economies of scale, product differentiation and differences in factor composition as key determinants of the structure of world trade. In combination, these factors explain significant parts of specialization patterns, volumes of trade, factor content of trade, and the broad patterns of trade across regions.

But despite the research effort in the last 20 years, these explanations are still incomplete. This is partly the result of the fact that the nature of world trade is changing rapidly. Technological change has modified the patterns of specialization, reduced trading costs and encouraged larger trade volumes; new countries have joined the trading system; and multinational corporations have spread their nets more widely than ever before. In the new economy there is plenty of manmade comparative advantage and product cycles, which are occasionally short-lived. We need a more technologically-oriented trade theory and more emphasis on dynamics to understand these developments. Such theories have been elaborated in the 1990s and they will undoubtedly affect future empirical research.

■ *This is an extended and elaborated version of the Bemhard-Harms Prize lecture, delivered at the Kiel Institute for World Economics in June 1998. The original lecture was published in Helpman (1998a). Most technical details are missing from this presentation. Many of them can be found in my working paper, Helpman (1998b), which also contains more information about recent studies. Many thanks to Don Davis, Bradford De Long, Gene Grossman, Ed Learner, Jim Levinsohn, Alan Krueger, Timothy Taylor, Manuel Trajtenberg and Dan Trefler for comments on an earlier draft, to Jaiho Chung for research assistance, to Jane Trahan for editorial assistance, and to the National Science Foundation for financial support.*

References

Antweiler, W. and D. Trefler. 1997. "Increasing Returns and All That: A View from Trade," mimeo.

Bowen, H. P., E. E. Leamer, and L. Sveikauskas. 1987. "Multicountry, Multifactor Tests of the Factor Abundance Theory." *American Economic Review.* December, 77:5, pp. 791–809.

Brecher, R. A. and E. V. Chaudhri. 1995. "The Leontief Paradox Continued." *Journal of Political Economy.* August, 90:4, pp. 820–23.

Davis, D. R. 1995. "Intra-Industry Trade: A Heckscher-Ohlin-Ricardo Approach." *Journal of International Economics.* November 39:3-4, pp. 201–26.

Davis, D. R. 1997. "Critical Evidence on Comparative Advantage? North-North Trade in a Multilateral World." *Journal of Political Economy.*

Davis, D. R. and D. E. Weinstein. 1997. "Economic Geography and Regional Production Structure: An Empirical Investigation," mimeo. Forthcoming in the *European Economic Review.*

Davis, D. R. and D. E. Weinstein. 1998a. "An Account of Global Factor Trade." NBER Working Paper 6785.

Davis, D. R. and D. E. Weinstein. 1998b. "Market Access, Economic Geography and Comparative Advantage: An Empirical Assessment," mimeo.

Davis, D. R., D. E. Weinstein, S. C. Bradford, and K. Shimpo. 1997. "Using International and Japanese Regional Data to Determine When the Factor Abundance Theory of Trade Works." *American Economic Review.* June, 87:3, pp. 421–46.

Deardorff, A. V. 1998. "Determinants of Bilateral Trade: Does Gravity Work in a Neoclassical World?" In *The Regionalization of the World Economy.* Frankel, J. A. ed. Chicago: The University of Chicago Press.

Eaton, J. and S. Kortum. 1997. "Technology and Bilateral Trade." NBER Working Paper No. 6253.

Ethier, W. J. 1984. "Higher Dimensional Issues in Trade Theory," in *Handbook of International Economics.* Jones, R. W. and P. Kenen, eds. Amsterdam: North Holland.

Evenett, S. J. and Keller, W. 1998. "On Theories Explaining the Success of the Gravity Equation," mimeo.

Gabaix, X. 1997. "The Factor Content of Trade: A Rejection of the Heckscher-Ohlin-Leontief Hypothesis," mimeo.

Grossman, G. M. 1998. "Comment," in *The Regionalization of the World Economy.* Frankel, J. A., ed. Chicago: The University of Chicago Press.

Grossman, G. M. and E. Helpman. 1991. *Innovation and Growth in the Global Economy.* Cambridge, MA: The MIT Press.

Grossman, G. M. and E. Helpman. 1995. "Technology and Trade," in *Handbook of International Economics, Vol. 3.* Grossman, G. M. and K. Rogoff, eds. Amsterdam: North Holland.

Grubel, H. and P. Lloyd. 1975. *Intra-Industry Trade: The Theory and Measurement of International Trade in Differentiated Products.* London: Macmillan.

Hakura, D. 1997. "A Test of the General Validity of the Heckscher-Ohlin Theorem for Trade in the European Community," mimeo.

Harrigan, J. 1997. "Technology, Factor Supplies, and International Specialization: Estimating the Neoclassical Model." *American Economic Review.* September, 87:4, pp. 475–94.

Harrigan, J. 1999 (forthcoming). "Estimation of Cross-Country Differences in Industry Production Functions." *Journal of International Economics.*

Heckscher, E. F. 1919. "The Effect of Foreign Trade on the Distribution of Income." *Economisk Tidskrift.* In *Heckscher-Ohlin Trade Theory.* Heckscher, E. F. and B. Ohlin. Cambridge, MA: The MIT Press, 1991 (translated, edited and introduced by Harry Flam and M. June Flanders).

Helpman, E. 1984. "Increasing Returns, Imperfect Markets, and Trade Theory," in *Handbook of International Economics, Vol. I.* Jones, R. W. and P. Kenen, eds. Amsterdam: North Holland.

Helpman, E. 1987. "Imperfect Competition and International Trade: Evidence from Fourteen Industrial Countries." *Journal of the Japanese and International Economies.* 1:1, pp. 62–81.

Helpman, E. 1998a. "Explaining the Structure of Foreign Trade: Where Do We Stand?" *Weltwirtschaftliches Archiv.* 143:4, pp. 576–89.

Helpman, E. 1998b. "The Structure of Foreign Trade." NBER Working Paper No. 6752.

Helpman, E. and P. R. Krugman. 1985. *Market Structure and Foreign Trade.* Cambridge, MA: The MIT Press.

Hummels, D. and J. Levinsohn. 1995. "Monopolistic Competition and International Trade: Reconsidering the Evidence." *Quarterly Journal of Economics.* August, 110:3, pp. 799–836.

Jones, R. W. 1956-57. "Factor Proportions and the Heckscher-Ohlin Theorem." *Review of Economic Studies.* 24:1, pp. 1–10.

Jones, R. W. 1965. "The Structure of Simple General Equilibrium Models." *Journal of Political Economy.* 73:6, pp. 557–72.

Krugman, P. R. 1980. "Scale Economies, Product Differentiation, and the Pattern of Trade." *American Economic Review.* December, 70:5, pp. 950–59.

Krugman, P. R. 1995. "Increasing Returns, Imperfect Competition and the Positive Theory of International Trade," in *Handbook of International Economics, Vol. 3.* Grossman, G. and K. Rogoff, eds. Amsterdam: North Holland.

Learner, E. E. 1980. "The Leontief Paradox, Reconsidered." *Journal of Political Economy.* June, 88:3, pp. 495–503.

Leamer, E. E. 1984. *Sources of International Comparative Advantage.* Cambridge, MA, and London: The MIT Press.

Leontief, W. W. 1954. "Domestic Production and Foreign Trade: The American Capital Position Re-examined." *Economica Intemazionale.* February, 7, pp. 9–36.

Lerner, A. 1952. "Factor Prices and International Trade." *Economica.* February, 19, pp. 1–15.

Linnemann, H. 1966. *An Econometric Study of International Trade Flows.* Amsterdam: North Holland.

Loertscher, R. and F. Wolter. 1980. "Determinants of Intra-Industry Trade: Among Countries and Across Countries." *Weltwirtschaftliches Archiv.* 116:2, pp. 280–93.

McDougall, G. D. A. 1951. "British and American Exports: A Study Suggested by the Theory of Comparative Costs, Part I." *Economic Journal.* December, 61, pp. 697–724.

McDougall, G. D. A. 1952. "British and American Exports: A Study Suggested by the Theory of Comparative Costs, Part II." *Economic Journal.* September, 62, pp. 487–521.

OECD. 1996. *Globalization of Industry.* Paris.

Ohlin, B. 1924. "The Theory of Trade," in *Heckscher-Ohlin Trade Theory.* Heckscher, E.F. and B. Ohlin. Cambridge, MA: The MIT Press, 1991 (translated, edited and introduced by Harry Flam and M. June Flanders).

O'Rourke, K. and J. G. Williamson. 1999 (forthcoming). *Globalization and History: The Evolution of a 19th Century Atlantic Economy.* Cambridge, MA: The MIT Press.

Reeve, T. A. 1998. *Essays in International Trade,* Ph.D. dissertation, Harvard University.

Samuelson, P. A. 1948. "International Trade and the Equalization of Factor Prices." *Economic Journal.* June, 58, pp. 163–84.

Stern, R. M. 1962. "British and American Productivity and Comparative Costs in International Trade." *Oxford Economic Papers.*

Tinbergen, J. 1962. *Shaping the World Economy: Suggestions for an International Economic Policy.* New York: Twentieth Century Fund.

Trefler, D. 1993. "International Factor Price Differences: Leontief was Right!" *Journal of Political Economy.* December, 101:6, pp. 961–87.

Trefler, D. 1995. "The Case of the Missing Trade and Other Mysteries." *American Economic Review.* December, 85:5, pp. 1029–46.
Vanek, J. 1968. "Factor Proportions Theory: The N-factor Case." *Kyklos.* 21, 749–54.
Williamson, J. G. 1998. "Globalization, Labor Markets and Policy Backlash in the Past." *Journal of Economic Perspectives.* Fall, 12:4, pp. 51–72.
WTO. 1997. *Annual Report 1997, Vol. II,* France.

Chapter 10

Of Hype and Hyperbolas: Introducing the New Economic Geography*

J. Peter Neary†

1. Introduction

New economic geography has come of age. Launched by Paul Krugman in a 1991 *JPE* paper, extended in a series of articles by Krugman, Masahisa Fujita, Tony Venables and a growing band of associates, recently institutionalized with the appearance of a new journal, it has now been comprehensively synthesized between hard

*Originally published in *Journal of Economic Literature*, 39(2), pp. 535–561. Masahisa Fujita, Paul Krugman, and Anthony J. Venables (1999): *The Spatial Economy: Cities, Regions, and International Trade.* Cambridge Mass.: MIT Press, pp. xiii + 367. ISBN 0-262-06204-6.

†University College Dublin and CEPR. Some of the ideas below were presented at a seminar in Leuven and at conferences in Bergen, Geneva, and Royaumont. I am very grateful to participants on these occasions and to Mary Amiti, Richard Baldwin, Frédéric Robert-Nicoud, Gianmarco Ottaviano, Jacques Thisse, Tony Venables, the editor and two anonymous referees for comments. This paper was written while I was visiting the Laboratoire d'Econometrie of the Ecole Polytechnique, Paris, and it forms part of the Globalisation Programme of the Centre for Economic Performance at LSE, funded by the UK ESRC.

covers[1] in *The Spatial Economy* by Fujita, Krugman, and Venables (henceforward "FKV").

Such rapid progress would make anyone dizzy, and at times the authors risk getting carried away with their heady prose style. They find the predictions of one model so plausible that they call it "History of the World, Part I" (p. 253); they describe the pattern of world industrialization implied by another as "a story of breathtaking scope" (p. 277); and on his website Krugman expresses the hope that economic geography will one day become as important a field as international trade. This sort of hype, even if tongue-in-cheek, is not to everyone's taste, especially when the results rely on special functional forms and all too often can only be derived by numerical methods. What next, the unconvinced reader may be tempted to ask. The tee-shirt? The movie?

In this paper I argue that, despite the hype, there is interesting work here which deserves to be better known. The key contribution of the new economic geography is a framework in which standard building blocks of mainstream economics (especially rational decision making and simple general equilibrium models) are used to model the trade-off between dispersal and agglomeration, or centrifugal and centripetal forces. The approach thus gives a choice-theoretic basis for a "propensity to agglomerate"—only a propensity, since agglomeration is a possible outcome but not an inevitable one.

I begin with exposition. In Section 2, I try to show that the basic new economic geography model is much simpler than most presentations suggest. I use a simple diagram to illustrate how the model works, and give a self-contained algebraic derivation of the main results (with technical details in appendices). But that in turn suggests that for some purposes the model may be too simple. In Section 4, I argue that it is, and try to disentangle which lessons are wedded to the special functional forms typically used and which

[1]The first issue of the *Journal of Economic Geography,* published by Oxford University Press, and with an editorial board representing both "old" and "new" approaches, appeared in January 2001. Ottaviano and Diego Puga (1998) and Fujita and Thisse (2000) provide overviews of the field.

are of more generality. In between, Section 3 highlights some of the novel insights that come from applying the model to topics in regional economics, urban economics, and international trade. In Section 5, I discuss how much is new in the new economic geography, and finally, in Section 6, I comment on policy implications and empirical tests.

2. The Core of the Core-Periphery Model

Like so much recent work in a variety of fields, the underlying model in most of the new economic geography is one of Chamberlinian monopolistic competition, parameterized using the symmetric constant-elasticity-of-substitution utility function of Avinash Dixit and Joseph Stiglitz (1977). As the authors disarmingly admit, the book "sometimes looks as if it should be entitled *Games You Can Play with CES Functions*"! But these are not everyone's idea of games. The authors have made a huge effort to expound the model clearly, but even they cannot prevent the calculations from degenerating at times into a near-impenetrable soup of CES algebra. All the more reason then to try and present the main ideas in a simple diagram. In this section, I first illustrate equilibrium in a closed economy, and then extend it to take account of transport costs, factor mobility, and intermediate inputs.

2.1. *Equilibrium à la Chamberlin-Dixit-Stiglitz*

Start with a closed economy, or, more in the spirit of the book, a world in which all economic activity is concentrated at a single point. There are two sectors. Agriculture is perfectly competitive and produces a homogeneous good under constant returns to scale. Manufacturing is monopolistically competitive and produces many varieties under increasing returns to scale. Each sector uses a single factor specific to it: farmers in agriculture, workers in manufacturing. Aggregate utility is a Cobb–Douglas function of agricultural output A and of a CES sub-utility function M derived from consuming manufactures:

$$U = M^{\mu} A^{1-\mu}, \quad M^{\frac{\sigma-1}{\sigma}} = \sum_{i}^{n} m_i^{\frac{\sigma-1}{\sigma}} \tag{1}$$

where m_i is the amount of each variety of the manufactured good demanded and σ (which must exceed one) is the elasticity of substitution between varieties.[2] From (1), μ is the share of nominal income Y spent on manufactures. This in turn is allocated between individual varieties according to demand functions which are log-linear in own price p_i and in total spending on manufactures μY, both deflated by a manufacturing price index P:[3]

$$m_i = \mu \left(\frac{P_i}{P}\right)^{-\sigma} \frac{Y}{P} \text{ where : } p1 - \sigma = \sum_{j}^{n} p_j^{1-\sigma} \tag{2}$$

Turn next to manufacturing firms. Because the manufacturing sub-utility function embodies a preference for diversity, and there are increasing returns to scale, each firm produces a distinct variety. Hence the number of firms, n, is also the number of varieties consumed, and firm output q_i equals the demand for that variety m_i. The typical firm therefore faces the demand function 2. However, a key feature of the Dixit–Stiglitz approach is that firms ignore the effects of their actions on income Y and on the industry price index P. Hence the demand curve perceived by the typical firm is not 2 but rather:

$$q = \phi p^{-\sigma} \text{ where : } \phi = \mu Y P^{\sigma-1} \tag{3}$$

with the intercept ϕ assumed to be taken as given by the firm. Since all firms are identical, the subscript i can be suppressed. Marginal

---

[2]I follow FKV's notation for the most part, though with some simplifications. Here I assume a finite number of firms, which makes the equations a bit neater at the cost of some hand-waving: I need to assume that the number of firms is sufficiently large that the integer constraint is not binding. This seems reasonable, and is standard in the literature, though see some intriguing speculative comments on the role of integer constraints on page 223.

[3]P is the unit expenditure function dual to the sub-utility function M. Note that it is defined in terms of *negative* exponents (since σ must exceed one): a frequent source of confusion.

revenue $(d(pq)/dq)$ is then easily shown to be:

$$MR = \frac{\sigma - 1}{\sigma} p \tag{4}$$

Equations (3) and (4) define two constant-elasticity curves in $\{p,q\}$ space, labelled D and MR respectively in Figure 1. (Ignore the numbered arrows in the figure for now.)

The cost structure of a typical firm is even simpler. Workers are hired at a given wage w, fixed costs are Fw and variable costs per unit output are cw. Hence total costs are:

$$C = (F + cq)w \tag{5}$$

This implies a horizontal marginal cost curve at the level cw, and an average cost curve which is a rectangular hyperbola with respect to the vertical axis and the marginal cost curve. These curves are also illustrated in Figure 1, labelled MC and AC respectively.

Equilibrium for the firm exhibits Chamberlin's tangency condition, as Figure 1 shows. Moreover, the special functional forms imply very simple expressions for equilibrium price and output. From profit maximization, marginal revenue equals marginal cost:

$$\frac{\sigma - 1}{\sigma} p = cw \tag{6}$$

So the price-marginal-cost mark-up depends only on σ; while free entry drives profits to zero: $\pi = pq - (F + cq)w = 0$, which simplifies, using (6), to give the level of output:

$$q = (\sigma - 1)\frac{F}{c} \tag{7}$$

So the equilibrium output of each firm is totally independent of developments outside the industry: it depends only on the cost parameters F and c and on the elasticity of substitution σ. Changes in any other parameters or variables (including income Y and the

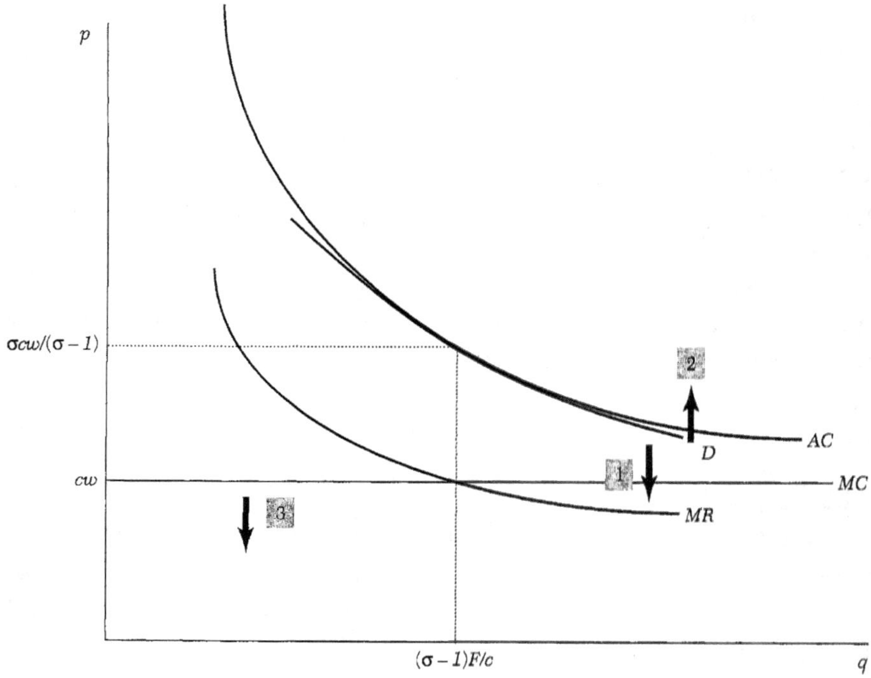

Figure 1. Chamberlin-Dixit-Stiglitz Equilibrium and Effects of Entry by a New Firm.

wage rate w) lead to adjustments in industry output via changes in the number of firms only.[4]

2.2. *Transport Costs and the Home-Market Effect*

So far, I have interpreted the model as a closed economy. However, everything said until now applies also to a multi-regional or multi-national economy, provided we make the strong assumptions (not shocking to trade theorists, though possibly so to others) of identical tastes, identical technology, and no barriers to goods trade. Of these

[4]This adjustment mechanism can be written $\dot{n} = f(\pi), f(0) = 0,\ f' > 0$. To test for local stability, totally differentiate π in the neighborhood of equilibrium: $d\pi = (pq/\sigma)\hat{q}$, where $\hat{q} \equiv dq/q$. Hence profits are monotonic in demand. When Y and w are given, q (and hence π) is decreasing in n from 3, so equilibrium is stable. Matters are different when Y and w are endogenous, as in Section 2.3.

three assumptions the first and second are maintained throughout the book. The next step is to relax the third by introducing transport costs, modelled using the so-called "iceberg" assumption, that a constant fraction of output is lost in transportation. This seemingly innocuous change takes us from a world with equalized factor prices, whether under Ricardian (one-factor) assumptions as in Krugman (1979), or Heckscher–Ohlin (two-factor) assumptions as in Dixit and Victor Norman (1980, Section 9.3), and Elhanan Helpman and Krugman (1985); and transports us to a world with international differences in goods and factor prices as in Krugman (1980).

So, switch to two countries, labelled "1" and "2" respectively. (In the relevant sections of the book they are called "regions"; more on this in Section 4.) Assume that the cost of transporting a unit of manufactures in either direction is $T - 1$ times the producer price (which is also the price paid by consumers in the country of production); this amounts to assuming that, for every T units shipped, only one unit arrives. Agricultural goods by contrast incur no transport costs. (I return to this assumption in Section 4.) How much of the preceding model must be changed? Perhaps surprisingly, the answer is that, apart from adding country subscripts to utility, wages and so on, only two equations need to be altered. First, the demand function 3 facing a typical firm located in country 1 must be extended to incorporate exports. A little manipulation gives:[5]

$$q_1 = \phi_1 p_1^{-\sigma} \quad \text{where}: \quad \phi_1 = \mu[Y_1 P_1^{\sigma-1} + Y_2 P_2^{\sigma-1} T^{1-\sigma}] \tag{8}$$

Total demand depends positively on the industry price index (P_1 and P_2) and on the level of manufacturing expenditure (μY_1 and μY_2) in both markets, and negatively on the level of trade costs T. Note, however, that firms are oblivious to all these complications: the

[5]Since each firm produces a distinct variety, the demand which a typical country-1 firm faces in market s is identical to 2: $q_{1s} = \mu(p_{1s}/P_s)^{-\sigma} Y_s/P_s$, though with the proviso that p_{1s} equals the price paid by *consumers* in market s. This matters for exports, since $p_{12} = p_1$T(where p_1 is the producer or mill price). In addition, this demand function gives the level of export *sales,* whereas we must gross up by transport costs to get export *shipments:* so total demand equals $q_1 = q_{11} + Tq_{12}$. Combining these expressions gives (8).

perceived demand function is identical to 3. Herein lies the simplicity of iceberg transport costs. CES preferences yield log-linear demand functions. Adding log-linear transport costs changes the level but not the elasticity of the perceived demand functions.

The second equation that must be changed is that for the price index. In a closed-economy equilibrium, with all varieties selling for the same price, 2 simplifies to $P^{1-\sigma} = np^{1-\sigma}$. Matters are more complicated with two countries and transport costs, because the consumer prices of goods from different countries are not the same: the n_1 domestic varieties cost p_1, while the n_2 imported varieties cost p_2T. Hence the price index becomes:

$$P_1^{1-\sigma} = n_1 p_1^{1-\sigma} + n_2(p_2T)^{1-\sigma} \tag{9}$$

Since every firm sells in both markets, the price index is decreasing in the number of firms in both markets (because greater variety benefits consumers) and is increasing in trade costs.

Equations (8) and (9), with the corresponding equations for country 2, define a sub-system that, for given demands Y_1 and Y_2 and given wages w_1 and w_2 (so from 6 prices are also given), determines the size of the manufacturing sector in both countries, n_1 and n_2, and the price indices P_1 and P_2. Inspecting the equations shows they share an important feature: provided transport costs are strictly positive ($T > 1$), the left-hand sides are more responsive to home than to foreign variables. This asymmetry has two useful implications, which are most easily seen by linearizing the model around the symmetric equilibrium (where $Y_1 = Y_2$, $n_1 = n_2$, etc.) and considering a small increase in the size of country 1 (so country subscripts can be dropped: $\hat{Y} = \hat{Y}_1 = -\hat{Y}_2$, $\hat{n} = \hat{n}_1 = -\hat{n}_2$, etc., where a circumflex denotes a proportional rate of change). Differentiating first equation (9) gives:

$$\hat{P} = -\frac{Z}{\sigma - 1}\hat{n} + Z\hat{p}, \quad \text{where}: \quad Z \equiv \frac{1 - T^{1-\sigma}}{1 + T^{1-\sigma}} \tag{10}$$

Here Z is an index of transport costs, which ranges from zero to one. With wages and hence p fixed, equation (10) gives what FKV call the "price index effect": because imports incur transport costs but home-produced varieties do not, the cost of living is lower the larger the market. Next, differentiating (8) gives:

$$\hat{q} = Z[\hat{Y} + (\sigma - 1)\hat{P}] - \sigma\hat{p} \tag{11}$$

If firm output and the price of each individual variety are fixed, an increase in demand can only be accommodated by a fall in the industry price index. From (10), this in turn requires an increase in the number of varieties: eliminating $\hat{P}$ from (10) and (11) gives:

$$\hat{n} = \frac{1}{Z}\hat{Y} \tag{12}$$

This gives what Krugman (1980) calls the "home-market effect": the country with higher demand has (since $Z < 1$) a proportionately larger share of manufacturing.

2.3. *Migration and Agglomeration*

The home-market effect is of independent interest since it predicts that countries with a larger home market tend to export manufactures.[6] This can be given a core-periphery interpretation, as in Krugman and Venables (1990): larger countries have a disproportionately larger share of manufacturing. However, by itself the home-market effect is only a prelude to a complete theory of economic geography. It assumes rather than explains international differences in incomes, since as yet there is no force pushing toward agglomeration in the model. Two such forces are considered in the book, international labor mobility (following Krugman 1991) and intermediate inputs (pioneered by Venables 1996 and developed by Krugman and Venables 1995). In this subsection, I concentrate on the former.

Assume therefore that the farmers who produce agricultural goods are country- as well as sector-specific, with equal numbers in each country. Hence (with no agricultural transport costs) the wage and the price of agricultural output can be set equal to

[6]The effect has also been shown to hold in some though not all other models. See Head, Mayer, and Ries (1999).

unity everywhere. By contrast, the workers employed in manufacturing move internationally in response to differences in real wages (ω_s in country s, equal to nominal wages w_s deflated by the consumer price index P_s^{μ}). Note that the relevant price index is the local one: workers consume only in the country where they are employed.

We are finally ready to address the central theoretical question in the new economic geography: when will the equilibrium exhibit diversification, with manufacturing produced in both countries, and when will it exhibit agglomeration in one country, or a "coreperiphery" pattern? These are actually two distinct questions, since it turns out that equilibrium is not unique for all parameter values. To answer them, consider in turn the local stability of diversified and agglomerated equilibria. Assume that workers migrate rapidly between countries in response to differences in real wages and that manufacturing firms enter or leave the industry sluggishly in response to profits or losses.[7]

[7]A digression on dynamics. Following Krugman (1991), FKV test equilibria for stability by asking how migration by a single worker affects relative real wages. If they end up higher in the host country, then further migration is encouraged and the initial equilibrium is unstable. This heuristic argument is equivalent to testing for local stability a dynamic adjustment mechanism, whereby migration is driven by the real-wage ratio. Two comments are in order. First, this adjustment mechanism assumes that firms are always in equilibrium; i.e., that entry and exit of firms occurs infinitely faster than migration. Reversing these assumptions, as in Puga (1999), does not affect the stability conclusions. I follow Puga's approach here since it can be more easily related to Figure 1 and since (unlike FKV's approach) it applies with minimal modifications to the intermediate-goods model of Section 2.4. Second, both these dynamic adjustment mechanisms are myopic: migrating workers or newly entering firms consider only current returns (relative real wages or relative profits) in making their decisions. FKV justify such non-rational expectations by appealing, rather unsatisfactorily, to the "replicator dynamics" of evolutionary game theory. (See pp. 7–8 and p. 77, footnote 2: "our model can, if one likes, be regarded as an evolutionary game.") I prefer a more robust defense. Just as in the comparison between Neary (1978) and Michael Mussa (1978), replacing *ad hoc* with forward-looking dynamics leads to greater elegance and a more satisfactory basis for normative analysis. However, it makes no difference to positive comparative-statics predictions. This has been demonstrated formally for the internationally mobile labor variant of the core-periphery model by Richard Baldwin (1999b).

Take first the case where the world economy is in a symmetric diversified equilibrium, and go through the following thought experiment. Assume that a single new manufacturing firm enters in country 1 (and, for symmetry, a single firm exits in country 2) and ask how this affects the incentives for further entry or exit. If profits in country 1 (which are initially zero) fall relative to country 2, the diversified equilibrium is stable: the new firm is encouraged to exit and the initial equilibrium is restored. However, if relative profits in country 1 rise, the initial equilibrium is unstable. More firms are encouraged to enter and the world economy moves towards an equilibrium with agglomeration: more than half of world manufacturing locates in country 1.

There are three effects of entry, indicated by the numbered arrows in Figure 1. The first arises from the price-index effect: an extra firm lowers the industry price index, which reduces the demand facing each existing firm. In Figure 1, the demand and marginal revenue curves shift downward, as indicated by the arrow numbered "1." This competition effect reduces profits and so encourages stability of the diversified equilibrium. By contrast, the two other effects raise profits and so encourage instability and a tendency towards agglomeration.

The second effect is a *demand* or *backward* linkage. An extra firm raises the demand for labor in country 1. This puts incipient upward pressure on local wages, which encourages foreign workers to migrate. The new workers in turn raise demand for local varieties. The demand and marginal revenue curves shift upwards in Figure 1, as indicated by the arrow numbered "2," and this tends to *raise* profitability.

It is easy to see which of these two effects dominates, if we assume provisionally that nominal wages do not change. From (10) and (11), the stabilizing competition effect depends on Z: when transport costs are higher, a real-location of firms has a greater impact in lowering the price level and raising competition in the expanding country. As for the demand linkage, consider the effects of entry on country 1's labor market. Supply is L, and demand is $n(F + cq)$, so from (7) the labor-market equilibrium condition is:

$$L = n\sigma F \tag{13}$$

(Once again, country subscripts can be dropped since we are linearizing around a symmetric equilibrium: whatever goes up in country 1 must come down in country 2.) If equilibrium is to be maintained, entry of new firms must be matched by an equi-proportionate increase in the labor force. To see how this affects demand, consider its effect on national income. With the number of farmers fixed and their wage constant by choice of numeraire, the proportional change in national income equals the changes in the manufacturing wage and labor force, times the share of the sector in GNP, μ:[8]

$$\hat{Y} = \mu(\hat{w} + \hat{L}) \tag{14}$$

Hence, with w fixed, the magnitude of the demand linkage depends on μ. Returning to 11, the demand linkage dominates the competition effect at the initial wage, so entry by a new firm raises the demand facing all existing firms, if and only if μ is greater than Z. When this condition holds the initial diversified equilibrium is unstable: agglomeration is more likely when the share of manufacturing in national income is high and when transport costs are low.

However, this condition ($\mu < Z$) underestimates the pressure towards agglomeration, because migration is driven by differentials in *real* rather than nominal wages. As we have seen, entry by a new firm lowers the price index in country 1. But this induces a third effect, since it reduces the cost of living for workers and so tends to raise real wages in country 1. The resulting migration restores international equality of real wages, which means that the nominal wage must fall. The result is a *cost* or *forward* linkage which shifts the average and marginal cost curves downwards in Figure 1, as indicated by the arrow numbered "3," and so *raises* profitability further.

[8]Since the initial equilibrium is symmetric, there is no inter-industry trade. Hence the share of manufacturing in each country's GNP equals its share in consumption, μ. Note that this has nothing to do with choice of units. Following Krugman (1991), FKV choose units such that the world labor force equals μ and the world supply of farmers equals $1 - \mu$. But this is not needed to prove any of the results that follow, and I find it distracting. I comment on other choices of units in Section 4.

Deriving a necessary and sufficient condition for stability of the diversified equilibrium requires combining the three effects explicitly, and is best left to the appendix. However, it is fairly easy to see how stability is affected by changes in the three key parameters, T, μ, and σ. Higher transport costs T always encourage stability. For sufficiently high T, imports are so expensive that home production is always profitable;[9] while for sufficiently low T, diversification is always unstable since the countries are *ex ante* identical (neither has a comparative advantage). Somewhere in between is a threshold level of trade costs T^B, the "break" point, at which the diversified equilibrium is on the brink of instability. (Such a threshold must exist provided there is some incentive for agglomeration, which means, provided μ is strictly positive.) A convenient way to summarize the results is to consider how T^B varies with the other parameters. As shown in the appendix:

Proposition 1. *T^B is increasing in μ and decreasing in σ.*

The threshold value T^B must be increasing in μ since both potentially destabilizing effects are more important the greater is μ. First, the greater the share of manufactures in national income, the greater the demand linkage whereby entry by a new firm induces migration which raises demand and hence encourages further entry (in older times this would have been called a "bootstraps" effect) hence the larger the range of trade costs at which diversification is not an equilibrium. Second, the greater the budget share of manufactures, the greater is the cost linkage whereby entry by a new firm lowers the cost of living and so encourages further migration and entry. Finally, the threshold value of T is negatively related to σ, the elasticity of substitution in

[9] Actually, this is an assumption rather than an intrinsic property of the model. When Z equals one, the numerator of equation (22) in the appendix equals $-(\sigma - 1 - \sigma\mu)(1-\mu)$. Hence, if $\sigma - 1 < \sigma\mu$, the diversified equilibrium is unstable even when Z is one (transport costs are infinite, so the economies are closed). It makes sense to rule out this possibility, where the propensity to agglomerate is always one. So we assume that the preference for diversity and/or the budget share of manufactures are sufficiently low to ensure that $\sigma - 1 > \sigma\mu$. FKV call this the "no-black-hole" condition.

demand. Higher σ means that consumers view different varieties as closer substitutes. Such a reduced preference for diversity leads to an equilibrium with fewer varieties and a higher output of each. (Recall equation 7.) As a result, both countries are more likely to hold on to some production at low trade costs.

Transport costs lower than the break level T^B are sufficient for the existence of an agglomerated equilibrium. Are they necessary? To show that the answer is "no," consider a different thought experiment. Assume that the world economy initially exhibits a core-periphery pattern and ask whether there are incentives for a firm to deviate from it. Assuming (arbitrarily) that manufacturing is agglomerated in country 1, can a firm earn positive profits by entering in country 2?

We can answer this question heuristically by referring again to Figure 1, this time with all three arrows *reversed.* Assume that the initial equilibrium illustrated is that in the core (country 1) and ask what are the incentives for a potential firm to enter in the periphery. The first incentive is that it faces less competition from country-1 firms in serving country-2 consumers. Hence the demand and marginal revenue curves are higher (represented by the arrow numbered "1" in reverse). On the other hand, a periphery firm has worse market access to consumers in the core: this demand linkage is represented by the arrow numbered "2" in reverse. Finally, because the periphery has fewer firms to begin with, the bulk of manufactures consumed there must be imported, incurring transport costs. The cost of living is therefore higher in the periphery, so, to induce workers to migrate, a new firm in the periphery must pay higher nominal wages. This cost linkage is represented by the arrow numbered "3" in reverse.

In the light of this intuitive discussion it is not surprising that there is once again a threshold level of trade costs, T^S, the "sustain" point, at which agglomeration ceases to be an equilibrium. This new threshold has the same relationship to the underlying parameters as T^B, and for similar reasons:

Proposition 2. *T^S is increasing in μ and decreasing in σ.*

Finally, a key result is that the two thresholds can be unambiguously ranked:

Proposition 3. *T^S is higher than T^B provided only that μ is strictly positive.*

There is always some range of trade costs at which half the world's manufacturing firms are content to locate in each country but a single firm on its own has no incentive to exit in the core or enter in the periphery. The appendix proves the result and shows that it is driven by the cost linkage: if workers cared only about nominal wages, perhaps because they consumed only in their home country, the break and sustain thresholds would coincide.[10]

In the light of propositions 1 to 3, Figure 2 illustrates how the number and types of equilibria vary with the level of trade costs T. (FKV call this diagram evocatively a "tomahawk bifurcation.") The vertical axis measures λ, the share of the world manufacturing labor force located in country 1; solid and dotted lines denote stable and unstable equilibria respectively. Recall that the countries are *ex ante* identical, so at every level of trade costs there exists a symmetric diversified equilibrium. However, from proposition 1, it is unstable for trade costs below T^B. Similarly, from proposition 2, the core-periphery equilibrium cannot be sustained for trade costs above T^S. At or below T^S, there are *two* stable core-periphery configurations: manufacturing may agglomerate in either country. Finally, from proposition 3, there are three stable equilibria between T^B and T^S, one diversified and two agglomerated.[11] It is this gap between T^B and T^S which opens up the possibilities of multiple equilibria and hysteresis that are the distinctive predictions of the economic geography literature and which are highlighted in the book.

---

[10]Hence international capital mobility, at least as normally modelled in trade theory, with capital reallocating internationally in response to differences in *nominal* rentals, would not give the same richness of results: T^B and T^S would coincide. See Baldwin (1999a).

[11]Could there be other stable equilibria? The inherent symmetry of the model makes it unlikely, but no analytic proof is provided in the book, so we have to rely on simulation results to be sure.

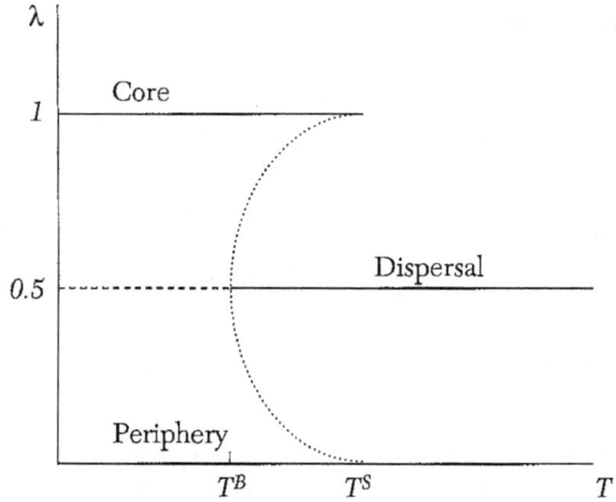

Figure 2. Agglomerated and Dispersed Equilibria as a Function of Trade Costs.

Within the range where $T^B < T < T^S$, *both* agglomeration and diversification are possible equilibria, so history and policy have a potential role in influencing which equilibrium prevails.

Now we are ready to apply the model. For example, falls in trade costs from initially high levels will lead to catastrophic agglomeration once T^B is reached; subsequent reversals of the trend in trade costs (as long as they remain below T^S) will not restore the diversified equilibrium; and whichever country is lucky enough to first acquire the manufacturing agglomeration will hold on to its initial advantage indefinitely. Complicating the model by adding other exogenous variables clearly opens the door to many more such "stories of breathtaking scope," or, if you prefer, interesting comparative-statics applications.

2.4. *Intermediate Inputs and Agglomeration*

We have seen that models that exhibit a propensity to agglomerate require increasing returns and transport costs. But we have also seen that these features are not enough: some mechanism that actually brings about agglomeration is also needed. So far, international labor mobility has been the mechanism assumed. An alternative route is to allow for inter-industry linkages. The potential importance of intermediate inputs in models of monopolistic competition, and the relative ease of incorporating them into the Dixit–Stiglitz model, have been clear since Wilfred Ethier (1982). It turns out that they provide another channel for agglomeration and lead to an analysis that is almost identical to that of labor mobility.

Assume that labor is now permanently country-specific, though it is used in both agriculture and industry. Manufacturing also uses an intermediate good, which is a CES aggregate of the output of all manufacturing firms (both domestic and foreign). For convenience, assume this aggregate has the same elasticity of substitution as the manufacturing sub-utility function M, so the price index for intermediates facing producers in country 1 is just P_1 (given as before by 9). Intermediates are then combined with labor to form a Cobb–Douglas composite input, with unit cost W_1 and intermediate cost share α:

$$W_1 = w_1^{1-\alpha} P_1^{\alpha} \tag{15}$$

Hence, production costs depend positively on the local price index P_1.

The second way in which the model is altered is that the demand for each variety comes not only from consumers but also from firms. So, for example, the demand from country-1 consumers μY_1 which appears in every demand function must be replaced by total country-1 expenditure on manufactures E_1, given by:

$$E_1 = \mu Y_1 + \alpha n_1 p_1 q_1 \tag{16}$$

Local consumers spend μY_1 as before; in addition the n_1 local firms spend a fraction α of their revenue $p_1 q_1$ on intermediates.

It is now straightforward to write down the full model. The cost of the composite input W_1 replaces the wage rate in the pricing equation 6; but otherwise the equations for individual firms derived in Section 2.1 are unchanged. And total country s expenditure, E_s, replaces consumer expenditure μY_s in the demand function 8 (and in the corresponding demand function facing firms in country 2); but otherwise the equilibrium equations derived in Section 2.2 are unchanged. (In particular, the price index equation 9 still holds.) The model can then be solved in exactly the same way as in Section 2.3. Matters are particularly simple if we make the further assumption that the agricultural wage rate is always fixed. (The consequences of relaxing this are considered in Section 3.) This in turn fixes the manufacturing wage and gives the model a partial equilibrium flavor, but the pay-off is considerable. FKV show that the results are very similar to those of the model with internationally mobile labor. In particular, the expressions for the break and sustain levels of transport costs are identical to (23) and (29), except that α, the cost share of intermediate goods, replaces μ, the budget share of manufactures. This is because, as equations (15) and (16) show, it is now α that determines the magnitude of the cost and demand linkages. Hence, the analysis of the model (whether diagrammatically or algebraically) proceeds essentially as in the internationally mobile labor case.

3. Extending the Model

Almost every chapter of the book relies on the basic model just outlined. From among many interesting extensions, let me highlight three.

Generalizing the model to many locations might seem impossible without resort to simulation. However, the authors succeed in deriving a local analytic result for a multi-location extension by borrowing a result from theoretical biology due to the mathematician Alan Turing. Assume a circular world in which a continuum of locations, each identical to one of the two countries in the last section, is spread evenly around the circumference. (FKV call this the "racetrack" economy.) Start from a uniform distribution of manufacturing (the "flat earth" equilibrium). Whether this symmetric equilibrium is broken depends on the stability of a dynamic labor-adjustment mechanism similar to that used to calculate the threshold T^B above. Turing's result can now be invoked to derive an analytic expression for the (algebraically) largest eigenvalue of the linearized dynamic system. If this is positive, the symmetric equilibrium will be broken and the economy will move towards a pattern of agglomeration. The agglomerated locations will be spread evenly around the circle in a pattern which can be represented by a sine curve, and the Turing result allows their frequency to be calculated. It turns out that exactly the same forces that apply at the two-country level determine this frequency: agglomerated equilibria will be fewer and located more sparsely around the circle the lower are transport costs, the higher the share of spending on manufacturing, and the lower the elasticity of substitution in demand. This shows that the forces found to be crucial in the two-country case apply much more generally.

A second extension retains the assumption of a continuum of locations but assumes that they are spread along an infinite line rather than around the circumference of a circle. Now, population and hence economic activity are not spread evenly along the line. Rather the population is initially large enough to support only a single location for manufacturing (which naturally can be called a "city"). A final difference is that the only variable factor, labor, is equally suited to both manufacturing and agriculture. Hence both sectors must pay the same wage in equilibrium. All this makes the set-up identical to that commonly used in formal models of urban economics. Now add a manufacturing sector such as that of Section 2 potentially active at each point, and ask how the equilibrium pattern of manufacturing location changes as the population grows. It turns out that the details can only by solved by simulation, but they can be expressed in terms of a neat technical trick. This calculates a "market potential function" which gives as a function of distance from the city the *virtual* manufacturing wage at each location (i.e., the wage at which production there just breaks even) relative to the current equilibrium wage. This curve is always downward-sloping in the neighborhood of an existing city: increasing returns plus transport costs mean that every city casts a "shadow" within which it is not profitable for other manufacturing to locate. But it need not be monotonically decreasing and may hit unity at other locations, in which case manufacturing (and so cities) will be established there. Simulations show that, as population grows, the initially monocentric city system gives rise to increasing numbers of cities which emerge to produce for the hinterland. Finally, the model is extended to allow for many industries, differing in terms of their substitution elasticities and transport costs, following Fujita,

Krugman, and Tomoya Mori (1999). Again, simulations show that the extended model implies a hierarchy of cities: a central city in which all industries are located, and an evolving series of subsidiary cities which attract "lower-order" industries (meaning those with higher transport costs and/or higher elasticities of substitution). This pattern of urban growth mimics real-world developments, and provides a theoretical rationale for a hierarchical or "central place" urban system of the kind described by location theorists such as Walter Christaller (1933) and August Lösch (1940).

A third extension takes the intermediate goods variant of the basic model and extends it to full general equilibrium by allowing wages to be endogenously determined (for example, by diminishing returns to labor in agriculture, because land is in scarce supply). Analytic results for this case are not available, but simulations reveal a common feature, independent of the details of different models. As before, industry is dispersed and wages are equalized internationally at high transport costs, and falls in transport costs lead to agglomeration. The new feature is that agglomeration drives up wages in the core country, which introduces a disincentive for industry to locate there. As transport costs fall further, this disincentive comes to dominate, so industry once again becomes dispersed and (when transport costs reach zero) wages are equalized internationally. This suggests a general phenomenon: there is likely to be a U-shaped relationship between the level of manufacturing transport costs and the propensity to agglomerate. Clearly many factors other than rises in agricultural wages (such as housing as in Helpman 1997) can cause diseconomies of agglomeration and so lead to dispersal of manufacturing and convergence of per capita incomes in what Krugman and Venables (1995) call the "globalization" phase of the world economy.

Following Puga and Venables (1996), this model is then extended to allow for many countries and industries, and to consider the effects of exogenous growth (uniform increases in the efficiency of all factors) rather than exogenous falls in transport costs. Simulations of the resulting pattern of industrialization show that manufacturing gradually spreads to other countries, with industries that are more labor-intensive and have weaker inter-industry linkages leading the way (since they benefit more from lower wages in countries that have not yet industrialized and benefit less from agglomeration in the initial core country).

4. Limitations of the Model

Models are unrealistic by definition. Simplifying assumptions are a virtue when the goal is to illustrate possibilities that previously could not be shown to hold. However, when it comes to applying a model to other questions, the assumptions may not be so helpful. In this section, I argue that the model used throughout the book has a number of special features that make it less suitable for addressing some issues. In particular, I want to single out the ways it treats increasing returns, firms' strategies, transport costs and, finally, space itself.

Increasing returns are intrinsic to the model, of course, and the cost function 5 is probably the most natural way of specifying such a technology in a simple tractable way. A quirk of the Dixit–Stiglitz model, however, is that standard measures of the degree of returns to scale turn out to depend not on the cost parameters F and c but rather on the elasticity of substitution. Though σ starts as a taste parameter, it ends up as an index of returns to scale. There is nothing wrong with this in principle, but it raises issues in interpreting the results and also highlights the shadowy role played by individual firms in the model.

Figure 3 illustrates how different values of σ affect the equilibrium. Consider first the case where σ is high. As an assumption this can be expressed in various equivalent ways: different varieties are closer substitutes; products are less differentiated; there is less preference for diversity. As a consequence, equilibrium is at a point such as A. From (7), firm output is relatively high, so fewer varieties are produced with higher output of each. From (6), price is close to marginal cost, so the demand and marginal revenue curves are flat and close together. By contrast, if σ is low, equilibrium is at a point such as B. Now there is a greater preference for diversity,

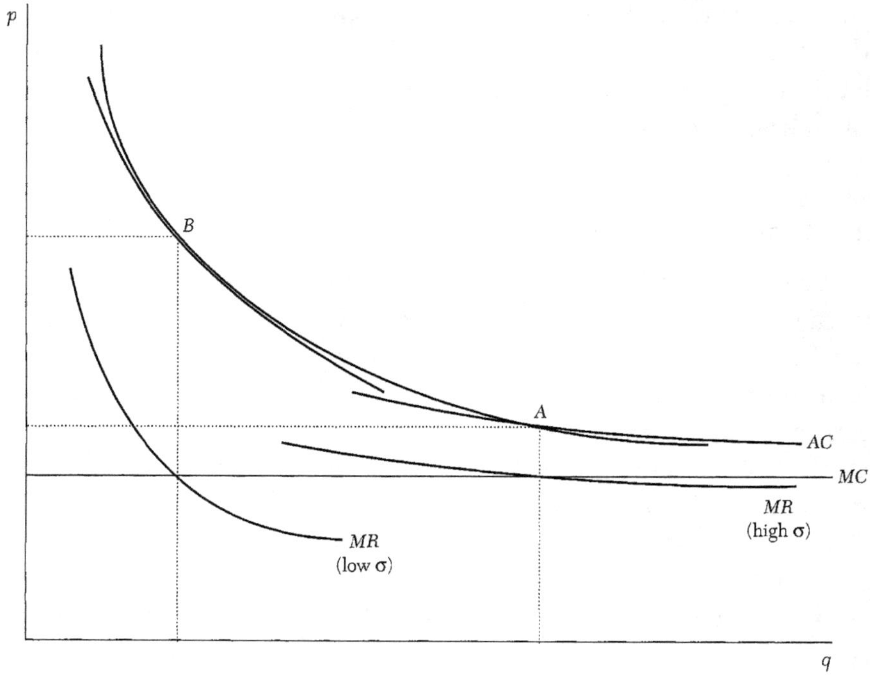

Figure 3. Effects of Changes in the Elasticity of Substitution.

so more varieties are produced with less output of each. To cover the fixed costs of shorter production runs, the price-marginal-cost margin must be high, with the demand and marginal revenue curves relatively convex and far apart.

Since the only underlying difference between the two cases is the value of σ, it can be interpreted as "an inverse index of equilibrium economies of scale" (Krugman 1991, p. 490). (In equilibrium, $\sigma/(\sigma-1)$ equals the ratio of the composite factor's marginal product to its average product, or one over the output elasticity of total costs.) But this terminology risks suggesting to the unwary that the theory of the firm embodied in the model is richer than in fact it is. It is not that industries with a higher value of σ have access to a different technology, rather that the pattern of demand encourages them to produce at a different scale. Better surely to say that returns to scale are more exploited at A than at B.

All of this is obscured by a particular normalization used for much of the book. Units are chosen to set the fixed and marginal cost parameters F and c equal to μ/σ and $(\sigma - 1)/\sigma$ respectively. This is harmless for local analysis, and may help in deriving analytical expressions for the break and sustain levels of transport costs, equations (23) and (29). (Though as I have shown in Section 2, it can be dispensed with.) But in non-local comparisons it seems both unnecessary and undesirable. Unnecessary since one of the points of simulations is surely to avoid reducing the dimensionality of the parameter space. Undesirable because the effects of greater substitutability in demand (a rise in σ) cannot be distinguished from the effects of a higher ratio of variable to fixed costs. Changes in one are exactly offset by changes in the other such that (from 7) both firm output q and the unit input requirement $F + cq$ are always equal to μ. This in turn can lead to questionable interpretations. For example, bakery shops are given as an illustration of a high-σ industry (p. 193). Figure 3 shows that this makes little sense in the absence of normalization.

This discussion reflects a worrying fact: like the traditional competitive model, the Dixit–Stiglitz model has almost nothing to say about individual firms. Except for the fact that it incorporates increasing returns, the new economic geography has industrial organization underpinnings which are very rudimentary. In particular, the assumption of free entry—a perfectly elastic supply of firms at all locations—allows almost no role for strategic interactions between firms.[12] As a result, while costs may be fixed they are never sunk, so firms, industries, and even cities are always free to move. Footloose cities seem particularly odd. They might make sense in a long-run model, but even then not in the context of a growing economy with

[12]There is only one mention of strategic behavior in the book: a brief reference (on page 52) to Alasdair Smith and Venables (1988), who show that an increase in market size has a pro-competitive effect if firms adopt either Cournot or Bertrand conjectures, so enhancing the home-market effect. This is an interesting point, but like Pierre-Philippe Combes (1997), it allows only for *postentry, one-shot,* strategic behavior. When oligopolistic firm conjectures are combined with free entry and exit, it is the latter that drives most of the results.

given technology such as that explored in Part 3 of the book. The authors note (p. 213) that introducing urban infrastructure would avoid the problem but that begs the question of exactly how to model it other than in an ad hoc way.

Completely footloose firms also sit oddly with the discussion of the emergence of industrial clusters or a "manufacturing base" in chapter 16, since the logic of the model is that such clusters are themselves footloose. At a superficial level the model is of course prejudiced in favor of a manufacturing base. The prior existence of other firms at one location lowers the costs of entry for a new firm there. Yet this feature alone does not seem to capture many of the issues that arise in discussions of industrial policy. Hysteresis or lock-in arises only from pecuniary (market-mediated) externalities in the new economic geography, not from technological externalities or local public goods (such as R&D spillovers). Further, the myopic Chamberlinian firms used throughout the book cannot engage in industrial strategies to shore up their position. They cannot make strategic commitments to create artificial barriers to entry, nor vertically integrate to internalize the externalities arising from the combination of intermediate inputs with increasing returns. And of course out-sourcing or cross-border horizontal mergers in response to changes in trade policy, technology, or market size are not allowed. The absence of these considerations makes the model less relevant to current debates on industrial location than it at first appears.

Transport costs are intrinsic to the model: if they are low enough, there are no barriers to agglomeration (though congestion effects may make it unprofitable); if they are high enough, there can be no departure from diversification. Such elementary insights should be robust to alternative specifications of transportation technology. But as we have seen, the detailed results in the book rely on the assumption of "iceberg" transport costs, usually attributed to Paul Samuelson. This amounts to assuming that the technology used to transport a good is identical to that used to produce it. This works for icebergs; also for grain if the main cost of transporting it is the grain consumed on the way by the horses pulling the wagon. (FKV note on p. 59 that von Thünen gave this example in 1826, so anticipating Samuelson by well over a century.) But it is obviously a very special case. An older literature in trade theory tried to model the transportation sector explicitly in a Heckscher–Ohlin framework, treating it just like any other industry, with an endogenous capital-labor ratio. (See Rodney Falvey 1976 for example.) That approach never led to simple or easily summarizable results, and is now largely forgotten. Perhaps it is due a revival. Even more important, in a field that emphasizes the importance of increasing returns, would be to allow for fixed costs in transportation. Of all industries, it seems to be characterized by very high ratios of fixed to variable costs, which is presumably why it is typically either publicly owned or highly concentrated. This is particularly important if transport costs are interpreted broadly to include the communications and other costs associated with trade, which are likely to exhibit network externalities. (See Richard Harris 1995.) Overall, the models in this book make interesting predictions about the effects of exogenous changes in per-unit transport costs. However, they are not well suited to examining positive questions such as the links between transportation, technology, and agglomeration (will what Danny Quah 1997 has called the increasing "weightlessness" of GNP facilitate backyard capitalism?) or normative questions such as the optimal level of provision of transport infrastructure.

A final point about transport costs is that, as noted earlier, the basic model assumes that they apply only to manufactures, and that agricultural goods (which really means goods produced under constant returns) are transported freely. Donald Davis (1998) criticizes this on two counts. He makes the empirical point that real-world transport costs appear to be at least as high for the latter, and he shows theoretically (in the model of Section 2.2 above) that this neutralizes the home-market effect. Chapter 7 of the book derives similar results (without referring to Davis) but gives them a totally different spin. Whereas Davis concludes that there is "no compelling argument ... that market size will matter for industrial structure, ..." FKV note that a reduction of agricultural transport costs may trigger agglomeration. So, relatively low agricultural transport costs are either a necessary and implausible condition for agglomeration, or a source of yet more "stories of breathtaking scope": take your pick.

Geography is about space, and as the authors note (p. 325), a strength of the book is that it integrates the continuous approach to space of location theory with the discrete approach of trade theory. However, they never mention an offsetting drawback: space is almost always one-dimensional, whether along a line or (as in the "racetrack" economy) around a circle. (The sole exception is an interesting digression in chapter 13 showing how forks in a valley are natural locations for agglomeration). Perhaps it will prove possible to extend the Dixit–Stiglitz approach to a two-dimensional plain, though the complexities involved (such as the overlapping circular "shadows" cast by competing cities) suggest that the results may be long on trigonometry and short on elegance. Even if this can be done, the worry will remain that omitting strategic considerations misses much of importance. Strategic location issues in two dimensions are unresolved, but no references are given to the extensive literature on this topic. (Fujita and Thisse 1996 is a recent overview.)

Apart from dimensionality, it is also necessary to specify the spatial unit of analysis. The book deals in turn with regions, cities, and countries, but there is nothing intrinsic to the models that conclusively identifies these units. In particular, FKV assert, with little discussion, that the distinction between regions and countries coincides with the difference between factor mobility and intermediate inputs as the trigger for agglomeration. Ultimately, this is an empirical judgement and it is easy to think of counterexamples. (Labor mobility from some small to large European countries is considerable; and surely Silicon Valley, if it fits the new economic geography paradigm at all, reflects a regional concentration of intermediate supply rather than of migration-induced final demand for computer hardware and software?) More generally, the new economic geography, with its emphasis on pecuniary externalities, faces competition in the market for ideas from alternative theories at both ends of the spatial spectrum. At the local level, pure externalities such as knowledge spillovers may well prove to be the determining force behind most agglomerations. Krugman (1991) could dismiss technological externalities as a satisfactory basis for modelling spatial agglomeration with the quip "How far does a technological spillover spill?" But subsequent empirical work by David Audretsch and Maryann Feldman (1996), among others, has shown that their geographic reach can be measured, and that they are typically very localized. As for the national level, it is not obvious that agglomeration effects are nearly so crucial there. It is possible for example to give a factor-endowments-based explanation for the pattern of East Asian development, which is at least as plausible as Puga and Venables's agglomeration story. (See Jaime Ventura 1997.) And, as I note in Neary (1999), calibration studies tend to find that the extent of intermediate input usage is not sufficient to yield strong agglomeration effects at the national level. Only further theoretical and empirical work will tell at what level of spatial analysis, if any, the forces emphasized in this book are the dominant influences on agglomeration and economic development.

5. Old versus New Economic Geography?

"With friends like this, who needs enemies?" the authors may wonder if they have read this far. But in fact the new economic geography has real enemies out there; or, more prosaically, reputable academic critics who question the whole research program rather than just the details of its implementation. In particular, economic geographers of a more traditional kind, typically based in geography rather than economics departments, have not taken kindly to the self-proclaimed arrival of a new paradigm. Ron Martin (1999) summarizes their objections and concludes that what he calls the 'new geographical economics' "represents a case of mistaken identity: it is not that new, and it most certainly is not geography." No doubt this hostility is partly induced by Krugman's prose style: guaranteed to influence people but not necessarily to win friends, not at least from the ranks of those wedded to different approaches. But there are genuine issues at stake. Is this just a turf war, or have economists taken a bridge too far?

Martin's central objection to the new economic geography is that its mathematical formalism leads it to neglect "real places."

Economic geographers of whom he approves avoid abstract theory, and focus instead on the contingency and particularity of real communities going about "the ordinary business of life." This methodological position reflects the "movement away from logical positivism" that took place in geography in the late 1970s. Though not averse to theory in general, even to economic theory provided it is "heterodox," economic geographers prefer to build explanations "'from below', often relying upon close dialogue with individual agents and organisations, and linking this 'local' knowledge with wider, larger stylized facts and conceptual frameworks."

Economists call these case studies, and regularly bemoan the fact that not enough get done. But the key issue is whether such studies can ever be "theory-free." Most economists would argue not, and would follow FKV in preferring an explicit model to inform (though not blindly predetermine) a case study rather than letting the facts speak for themselves. It is ironic that Krugman should be the target of such criticism, since he has shown unusual sympathy with heterodox traditions. In the same book (Krugman 1995) where he takes "old" economic geography to task, he also argues that increased formalism in economics as a whole held back progress in development and spatial economics, since pre-Dixit-Stiglitz no clean way of modelling imperfect competition was available. This may seem like trying to have it both ways, but it reflects the attitude of most working economists to what FKV call (p. 79) "aggressively unrealistic" models. They are, as the Roman poet Propertius said of his lover, difficult to live with, impossible to live without.

As for the "new" in "new economic geography," FKV make explicit their intellectual debt to location theory and regional science.[13] But they also make a persuasive case that they have extended their insights significantly by giving them behavioral underpinnings. It is one thing to make assertions about processes of cumulative causation leading to agglomeration, or to describe urban systems as

[13]Mention could also be made of Hesham Abdel-Rahman (1988), who used the Dixit–Stiglitz specification to explain agglomeration at the city level, and with Ping Wang (Abdel-Rahman and Wang 1995) developed a model of a core-periphery urban system.

central-place hierarchies. It is quite another to explain such patterns as the outcome of decentralized self-interested behavior.

Given mainstream economists' impatience with methodology, it is a fair bet that debates between old and new economic geographers will have little influence on the direction of future economic research. The genie is out of the bottle, and FKV are sure to inspire further theoretical developments.[14] Such work is important, but probably hard empirical work is even more so if nonbelievers are to be persuaded that the new approach represents a promising way forward. And, on a more hopeful note, perhaps there is potential common ground in the process of empirical implementation, scope for integrating the theoretical insights of the new economic geography with the detailed contingent knowledge of the old.

6. From Theory to ... What? Empirical and Policy Applications

FKV do not present any empirical work of their own.[15] Nor do they discuss the policy implications of the new economic geography at length. But it is in these areas that the ultimate usefulness of the field will most likely be determined.

As far as empirics are concerned, the increasing availability of large data sets has encouraged a recent explosion of studies showing

[14]Interesting recent contributions not already mentioned include Gianmarco Ottaviano, Taka-toshi Tabuchi, and Jacques-François Thisse (1999), who develop an agglomeration model with linear rather than Dixit–Stiglitz preferences: they find that the basic insights remain intact, though incorporating transport costs enriches the model's outcomes; and Baldwin (1999a) and Philippe Martin and Ottaviano (1999), who embed economic geography in explicit growth models.

[15]The only empirical chapter in the book is a digression on the sizes of cities and the difficulties of accounting for the empirical regularity known as "Zipf's Law" or the "rank-size rule": to a remarkably close approximation, data on city size tend to show that the rth largest city has $1/r$ of the total population. This pattern is not exhibited by the simulations of the authors' model discussed in Section 3 above, although Xavier Gabaix (1999) has shown that it can be explained by assuming that both the growth rate and the variance of the growth rate of a city's population are independent of city size.

the relevance of location to many economic phenomena.[16] Among many examples, see the work of Audretsch and Feldman on local R&D spillovers mentioned above; John Gallup and Jeffrey Sachs (1998) who show the influence on living standards of geographical features such as latitude and length of coastline; and the revival of interest in the "gravity equation" which emphasizes the role of distance in explaining trade patterns. (See Alan Deardorff 1998 for a discussion of its theoretical underpinnings and further references.) While these studies have developed independently of the new economic geography, there is also a small but growing body of empirical work that builds directly on it. Most of the papers are unpublished, so a full evaluation is premature. Nevertheless some patterns can be identified.

One group of papers takes seriously the injunction of Edward Learner and James Levinsohn (1995): "estimate do not test." Stephen Redding and Venables (2000) use cross-section data on 103 countries to estimate the intermediate-goods model of Section 2.4, with incomes and firm numbers exogenous. They use the estimated coefficients from a gravity equation for trade flows to construct measures of demand and cost linkages;[17] these in turn are used to explain cross-country variations in incomes and in manufacturing wages and prices. Remarkably, they find that demand and cost linkages alone explain up to 70 percent of the cross-country variation in per capita income and up to 50 percent of the variation in manufacturing wages. Gordon Hanson (1998) uses Helpman's (1997) variant of the mobile-labor model of Section 2.3 to estimate the determinants of ten-year changes in wages from 1970 to 1990 in all

[16] This is not to mention the many empirical studies of regional growth and convergence. At the risk of descending into semantics, I am inclined to agree with Martin (1999) that these do not constitute economic geography proper (either old or new) since for the most part they merely take regions as units of analysis without specifically considering issues of relative location (such as transport costs, market access, etc.).

[17] This empirical technique, discussed further below, seems to originate with Learner (1997).

3,075 counties of the continental United States. Including distance-weighted measures of housing stock and wages in adjacent states, as the theory suggests, improves the fit over an ad hoc specification (which only includes distance-weighted incomes). The estimated equation explains over 20 percent of the variation in the dependent variable and yields parameter estimates that are reasonably consistent with theory. Finally, whereas the other two papers use distance to proxy for transport costs, Pierre-Philippe Combes and Miren Lafourcade (2000) use a very detailed data set on actual transport costs in mainland France. They estimate a specification based on a model similar to FKV's to explain employment patterns in 64 sectors (including services as well as manufacturing) across 341 employment areas and find that, when allowance is made for intermediate inputs, transport costs have a significant impact on specialization patterns in nearly all sectors.

These papers show the usefulness of the economic geography model in guiding empirical work. However, they do not test the model against plausible alternatives, and the specifications they estimate are not necessarily inconsistent with other perspectives. A different set of papers attempts to discriminate between economic geography and alternative theories. Sukkoo Kim (1995) uses a long data set (from 1860 to 1987) on U.S. manufacturing employment to measure trends in regional specialization and industrial localization. He argues that the evidence is inconsistent with an important role for external economies, since industry localization patterns are negatively correlated with characteristics associated with external economies. In particular, high-tech sectors are less localized. Kim does not discuss the distinction between technological and pecuniary externalities, but his findings are also inconsistent with the latter provided we interpret high-tech sectors in the economic geography framework as sectors with higher shares of intermediate inputs and higher "equilibrium economies of scale," which the model predicts should be more agglomerated. By contrast, Kim finds that average plant size (his proxy for scale economies) explains industry localization patterns over time (recall that the new economic geography model relies on increasing returns but has nothing to say about firm or plant size); while raw material intensity (his proxy for Heckscher–Ohlin endowment effects) explains localization patterns across industries.

More encouraging results for the economic geography model come from a series of papers by Donald Davis and David Weinstein. They focus on the home-market effect, which as we have seen is a key building block of the model, though not sufficient for it. They note that this effect does not arise in models where trade is determined by comparative advantage. In such models, a positive shock to home demand for a good only affects home production if it raises price; but the price increase calls forth extra imports and so dampens the effect of demand on home production. By contrast, equation (12) shows that in a monopolistically competitive model with transport costs, a positive shock to home demand has a magnified effect on home production. This difference suggests a test that can discriminate between the two sets of models. In a first application to OECD data, Davis and Weinstein (1996), they found no evidence for home-market effects: above-average home demand for a sector was typically associated with a less-than-proportional excess of local production above the world average. However, in subsequent work, Davis and Weinstein (1998) interpret "home" demand more broadly: as in Redding and Venables, they use the estimated coefficients from a gravity equation for trade flows to measure *effective* home demand (including demand from trading partners, inversely weighted by distance). This time the home-market effect shows up as important for between one-half and two-thirds of manufacturing output (with comparative advantage determining trade patterns for the remainder). These results complement their finding in Davis and Weinstein (1999) that home-market effects are important in explaining the structure of production across Japanese regions.

To summarize, the overall thrust of these papers is support for Krugman (1980) from Davis and Weinstein, but rejection of Krugman (1991) by Kim. But much more work needs to be done. In particular, I am not aware of any cross-industry tests of the model's predictions about the effects of the "three T's": tastes, technology, and transport costs (all potentially measurable variables). As we saw in Section 2, agglomeration is more likely in industries with higher demand (both final and intermediate), greater product diversity, and lower transport costs. Further work is needed to refine these implications and to devise plausible tests of them against real rather than straw alternatives. If the theory fails to find support from this process of empirical testing, it will not fade away but it will be much less persuasive. Of course, falsifiability at least in principle is a strength rather than a weakness of the model. The ultimate defense of the new economic geography is one that FKV themselves might prefer not to make: it could be wrong.

With the empirical verdict not yet in, is it too early to draw policy conclusions? The field's potential to throw light on policy is undoubtedly part of its appeal. This is especially true in Europe, where the development of the theory has coincided with debates on the effects of moves to deepen European union through greater economic and monetary integration, and to widen it through enlargement. Fears that these developments may deindustrialize the periphery have so far proved groundless: in the immediate aftermath of the January 1999 launch of European monetary union, the fastest-growing countries in the European Union have been small (the Netherlands), peripheral (Spain), or both (Finland and Ireland). Nevertheless, it is clear that Europe is at a different stage of economic-geographical evolution than the United States. Kim (1995) shows that U.S. interregional specialization reached its peak during the interwar years but (as of 1987) has fallen continuously and substantially since. By contrast, Karen Helene Midelfart-Knarvik, Henry Overman, and Venables (2000) show that international specialization in the EU increased from 1980-83 to 1994-97. In the light of this relevance to topical issues, it is hardly surprising that the new economic geography has stimulated more academic interest in Europe than in the United States, as a comparison of the recent CEPR and NBER trade programs shows. Moreover, the approach has already been used fruitfully as a background to policy discussions, as in Pontus Braunerhjelm, Riccardo Faini, Victor Norman, Frances Ruane, and Paul Seabright (2000). But using the models to evaluate policy options explicitly is surely premature.

The key problem is that the policy implications of the basic core-periphery model are just too stark to be true. The model turns Sartre's "Hell is other people" on its head: agglomeration is unambiguously good for you. Because the cost of living is lower in the core, it is always better to live there than in the periphery, with the level of utility in a diversified economy lying in between. Even when congestion costs are added to the model, utility is always at least as great in the core as in the periphery and is usually higher. Faced with multiple equilibria which have a clear welfare ranking, it is tempting to suggest a role for government in "picking equilibria." This in turn may encourage a new sub-field of "strategic location policy," perhaps drawing on fifteen years' work on strategic trade policy, which, as James Brander (1995) and Neary and Dermot Leahy (2000) argue, has produced much interesting theory but no simple robust rules to guide policy making. All these are temptations to be resisted, since they take too literally the neat structure of the model, and ignore the econometric difficulties in estimating the nonlinear, non-monotonic relations it predicts. In any case, greater industrial specialization, even if it takes the form of more agglomeration, is not the same as deindustrialization once we allow for many sectors. And, of course, the neglect of strategic issues which I discussed in Section 4 is particularly relevant in this context. No harm then that FKV are mostly neutral on the applicability of the models to policy (except for some tentative interventionist thoughts in the chapter on industrial clustering).

7. Conclusion

In this paper, I have taken the appearance of FKV's book as an opportunity to review the "new" economic geography. It is not the only approach to location and agglomeration economists have taken. Many authors such as Brian Arthur (1986) and Robert Lucas (1988) have theorized about the role of regions and cities in economic development. But no other body of work does quite the same thing as the new economic geography: explain agglomeration in a theoretical framework that is tractable, has solid micro foundations, and makes testable empirical predictions. So, to paraphrase Robert Solow (1962), everyone should read this book, or at least encourage their students to do so!

Remember though that Solow's remark was made about the two-sector growth model, as emblematic of the 1960s as mini-skirts or the Beatles, though not as long-lasting. Will the new economic geography prove more durable? I suspect that it will, though maybe not as a distinct field. Instead, I am tempted to suggest that it will survive as "merely" another simple general equilibrium model, supplementing the trade theorist's tool kit; to quote Solow again, another "general equilibrium model of matchbox size" (since even a continuum of identical matchboxes arranged symmetrically around a circle is, well, just a matchbox).[18] Saying this risks sounding disparaging (and falls short of the authors' ambitions). But it is high praise in my view.

The new economic geography is firmly in the tradition of trade theory in at least two respects. First, it follows Ohlin in viewing interregional and international trade as different manifestations of the same influences. National boundaries are often coterminous with some economic forces, such as public policies, language, and institutions. But most influences on trade and industrial patterns operate similarly in large regions and small countries, and so the study of them should use the same analytic tools. Ohlin's view was not ignored—there are many examples of trade models applied to regional issues—but as long as trade theory remained tied to the competitive paradigm, its relevance was questionable. (Though, as Krugman 1999 notes, Ohlin himself gave an important role to increasing returns as a determinant of trade patterns.) In stressing the relevance to regional issues of models derived from trade theory, Krugman has not so much created a new subfield as extended the applicability of an old one.

[18]Those who remember the lessons of Ronald Jones (1965) will have noted how the exposition in Section 2 is simplified by using standard techniques for analyzing simple general equilibrium models: logarithmic differentiation, a focus on factor-market equilibrium conditions, etc.

Second, both the strengths and weaknesses of the new economic geography reflect the fact that it follows the tradition of focusing on a single cause of trade and location: technology in Ricardo, factor endowments in Heckscher–Ohlin, monopolistic competition in Krugman (1979), or oligopolistic competition in Brander (1981). Models such as these, which strip away the superfluous to focus on a single feature, are essential for understanding the world. Adding pecuniary externalities to the list and working out their implications is a significant achievement. But no one monocausal model can hope to capture the complexities of any applied problem, certainly not a model where space is one-dimensional, firms are identical and infinitesimal, and every function in sight is either constant-elasticity or a rectangular hyperbola. So, hold on the tee-shirt, skip the movie, but do read this book, possibly the best on interregional and international trade and location since Ohlin.

Appendix: Proofs of Propositions[21]

Proof of Proposition 1: Totally differentiating the model at the symmetric equilibrium gives six equations in eight variables, $\hat{q}, \hat{Y}, \hat{P}, \hat{p}, \hat{n}, \hat{w}, \hat{L}$ and $\hat{\omega}$. Equation 10 gives the change in the home price index, and equation 11 gives the change in demand facing an individual home firm. Firms always maximize profits, so from (6) prices and wages move together:

$$\hat{p} = \hat{\omega} \tag{17}$$

The full-employment condition (13) implies that the labor force and the number of firms in the home country must always move together:

$$\hat{L} = \hat{n} \tag{18}$$

From the definition of the real wage ω:

$$\hat{\omega} = \hat{w} - \mu\hat{P} \tag{19}$$

Finally, equation (14) gives the change in GNP.

[21]Propositions 1 and 2 first appear in Krugman and Venables (1995) and Krugman (1991) respectively; propositions 3 and 4 appear to be new.

As noted in footnote 9, two alternative approaches can be taken to testing whether the symmetric equilibrium is stable. FKV assume that firms are always in equilibrium whereas migration takes time. In my notation, they set $\hat{q}$ equal to zero (since output is always at its equilibrium value, given by 7), take $\hat{L}$ as exogenous, and solve for $\hat{\omega}/\hat{L}$. Here, following Puga (1999), I assume instead that workers are always in equilibrium whereas entry and exit take time. Hence, I set $\hat{\omega}$ equal to zero (migration ensures that the real wage is the same in both countries) take $\hat{n}$ as exogenous, and solve for $\hat{q}/\hat{n}$. (From footnote 6, changes in profits are monotonic in changes in q). Both approaches yield the same stability condition.

To solve for $\hat{q}/\hat{n}$, first use (10) and (14) to eliminate $\hat{P}$ and $\hat{Y}$ from (11), and then use (17) and (18) to replace $\hat{p}$ and $\hat{L}$ by $\hat{w}$ and $\hat{n}$ respectively. This yields:

$$\hat{q} = (\mu - Z)Z\hat{n} - [\sigma - \{\mu + (\sigma - 1)Z\}Z]\hat{w} \tag{20}$$

The first term on the right-hand side gives the first result quoted in the text: with equal nominal wages in the two countries ($\hat{w} = 0$), equilibrium is stable if and only if μ is less than Z. Next, to impose equality of *real* wages, I need to solve for the change in the price index from (10), setting $\hat{p} = \hat{w} = \mu\hat{P}$ (using (19) with $\hat{w}$ equal to zero):

$$\hat{P} = -\frac{Z}{(\sigma - 1)(1 - \mu Z)}\hat{n} \tag{21}$$

Note in passing that the coefficient of $\hat{w}$ in (20) is negative and that $\hat{P}$ itself is negative from (21).

(This is just the price index effect with real rather than nominal wages fixed.) These results confirm the assertion made in the text: the condition $\mu > Z$ underestimates the pressure toward agglomeration, since the symmetric equilibrium can be unstable even when the condition is not met. To find the full stability condition, substitute from (21) into (20) (once again setting $\hat{w}$ equal to $\mu\hat{P}$):

$$\hat{q} = \frac{(2\sigma - 1)\mu - \{\sigma(1 + \mu^2) - 1\}Z}{(\sigma - 1)(1 - \mu Z)}Z\hat{n} \tag{22}$$

The denominator is positive since $\sigma > l > \mu, Z$. Hence the threshold value of Z is that which sets the numerator equal to zero. Using the definition of Z from (10), we can solve in turn for the threshold value of T:

$$T^B(\mu_+, \sigma_-) = \left[\frac{\{\sigma(1+\mu)-1\}(1+\mu)}{\{\sigma(1-\mu)-1\}(1-\mu)}\right]^{\frac{1}{\sigma-1}}. \tag{23}$$

The proposition follows by differentiating this expression with respect to μ and σ.

Proof of Proposition 2: Consider the initial agglomerated equilibrium. Since μ is the fraction of world income spent on manufactures, national income in country 1, Y_1, equals its agricultural output X_A plus world manufacturing output $\mu(Y_1 + Y_2)$. By contrast, country 2 has no manufacturing, so its income Y_2 is simply X_A. Combining these equations gives:

$$Y_2 = \frac{1-\mu}{1+\mu} Y_1 \tag{24}$$

Income is lower in the periphery, because there are no manufacturing workers there. Next, from equation (9) for the manufacturing price index, with n_2 initially zero:

$$P_2 = P_1 T \tag{25}$$

Manufacturing prices are higher in the periphery because all manufactures must be imported.

Now, consider whether there are incentives for firms to exit in the core and enter in the periphery. This will be profitable if a typical firm can sell more in the periphery than in the core. Assume to begin with that migration equalizes nominal wages. Then relative demands depend on the ratio of the demand intercepts. That in the core is given by (8), which simplifies, using (24) and (25), to:

$$\phi_1 = \frac{2\mu}{1+\mu} Y_1 P_1^{\sigma-1} \tag{26}$$

As for the demand intercept in the periphery, it is given by an equation symmetric to (8):

$$\phi_2 = \mu[Y_1 P_1^{\sigma-1} T^{1-\alpha} + Y_2 P_2^{\sigma-1}] \tag{27}$$

Using (24), (25), and (26), potential demand in the periphery relative to the core is:

$$\phi_2 = H\phi_1 \text{ where} : H \equiv \frac{1+\mu}{2} T^{1-\sigma} + \frac{1-\mu}{2} T^{\sigma-1} \tag{28}$$

Because of transport costs, a periphery firm is at a disadvantage ($T^{1-\sigma} < 1$) in serving the larger market, but has an advantage ($T^{1-\sigma} > 1$) in serving the smaller local market. The balance of advantage is ambiguous and depends on whether H is greater or less than one.

Finally, just as in the earlier discussion of the stability of the diversified equilibrium, migration equalizes *real* not nominal wages. This places potential periphery firms at a further disadvantage, since they must charge higher prices to cover the higher nominal wages needed to compensate workers for the higher cost of living: $p_2/p_1 = w_2/w_1 = \omega_2 P/\omega_1 P = T^{\mu}$ (from (25)). Hence, the full expression for relative demands, which must equal one when deviation from the agglomerated equilibrium is just profitable, is:

$$\frac{q_2}{q_1} = \frac{\phi_2 p_2^{-\sigma}}{\phi_1 p_1^{-\sigma}} = H\left(\frac{p_2}{p_1}\right)^{-\sigma} = HT^{-\sigma\mu} = 1 \tag{29}$$

Since $T^{-\sigma\mu}$ is less than one, the level of trade costs sufficient to equalize nominal wages (i.e., just sufficient to set H equal to one) overestimates the incentives to deviate from the agglomerated equilibrium: at that level, real wages in the periphery are still lower than in the core. To equalize real wages requires a higher level of trade costs, defined by setting the left-hand side of (29) equal to one.

Equation (29) is trivially satisfied for $T = 1$: with no transport costs, firms are indifferent between locations. At $T = 1$ the left-hand side is decreasing in T, so q_2/q_1 must fall below one, but it must rise above it for high T (provided the "no-black-hole" condition is met). The second value of T at which (29) is satisfied defines a new threshold, T^S, at which agglomeration is just on the margin of being an equilibrium. The proposition is proved by totally differentiating (29) and evaluating in the neighborhood of T^S.

Proof of Proposition 3:[22] Direct comparison of the two thresholds T^B and T^S is not promising, since (29) only defines the latter implicitly. Instead, consider the left-hand side of (29), which gives the incentive to deviate from the agglomerated equilibrium, and evaluate it at the break threshold T^B. This defines a function h of μ:

$$h(\mu) \equiv H[T^B(\mu)] \cdot [T^B(\mu)]^{-\sigma\mu} \tag{30}$$

By inspection, $h(0) = 1$: if there is no demand for manufactures, there is no propensity to agglomerate at any level of transport costs, so the break and sustain thresholds coincide. The proposition is proved by showing that, if there is any finite demand for manufactures (i.e., for any value of μ in the interior of the admissible region: $\mu \in (0, (\sigma - 1)/\sigma)$), there is no incentive to deviate from the agglomerated equilibrium (i.e., $h(\mu) < 1$), when $T = T^B$.

Begin with the first derivative of ln$h$ (writing H^B as shorthand for $H[T^B(\mu)]$):

$$\frac{d\ln h}{d\mu} = \frac{d\ln H^B}{d\mu} - \sigma\ln T^B - \sigma\mu\frac{d\ln T^B}{d\mu} \tag{31}$$

This is zero at $\mu = 0$ (obvious for the second and third terms; refer to (34) below for the first). To eliminate the term in $\ln T^B$, proceed to the second derivative:

$$\frac{d^2\ln h}{d\mu^2} = \frac{d^2\ln H^B}{d\mu^2} - 2\sigma\frac{d\ln T^B}{d\mu} - \sigma\mu\frac{d^2\ln T^B}{d\mu^2} \tag{32}$$

[22]Many thanks to Frédéric Robert-Nicoud for spotting an error in my first proof and for pointing me in the direction of this one.

Evaluating this requires explicit expressions for $\ln T^B$ and its derivatives:

$$\begin{aligned}
(\sigma - 1)\ln T^B &= \ln\alpha - \ln\beta + \ln(1+\mu) - \ln(1-\mu) \geq 0 \\
(\sigma - 1)\frac{d\ln T^B}{d\mu} &= \frac{\sigma}{\alpha} + \frac{\sigma}{\beta} + \frac{1}{1+\mu} + \frac{1}{1-\mu} > 0 \\
(\sigma - 1)\frac{d^2\ln T^B}{d\mu^2} &= -\frac{\sigma^2}{\alpha^2} + \frac{\sigma^2}{\beta^2} - \frac{1}{(1+\mu)^2} + \frac{1}{(1-\mu)^2} > 0
\end{aligned} \tag{33}$$

where $\alpha \equiv \sigma - 1 + \sigma\mu > 0$ and $\beta \equiv \sigma - 1 - \sigma\mu > 0$ (the latter is the no-black-hole condition). I also need explicit expressions for $\ln H^B$ and its derivatives:

$$\begin{aligned}
\ln H^B &= \ln\eta - \ln\alpha - \ln\beta \geq 0 \\
\frac{d\ln H^B}{d\mu} &= \frac{2\sigma(3\sigma-2)\mu}{\eta} - \frac{\sigma}{\alpha} + \frac{\sigma}{\beta} \geq 0 \\
\frac{d^2\ln H^B}{d\mu^2} &= \frac{2\sigma(3\sigma-2)}{\eta^2}[(\sigma-1)^2 + \sigma(3\sigma-2)\mu^2] + \frac{\sigma^2}{\alpha^2} + \frac{\sigma^2}{\beta^2}
\end{aligned} \tag{34}$$

where: $\eta \equiv (\sigma-1)^2 + \sigma(3\sigma-2)\mu^2 > 0$. Substituting into 32 and collecting terms gives:

$$\begin{aligned}
\frac{d^2\ln h}{d\mu^2} = &\frac{2\sigma(\sigma-1)^2(3\sigma-2)}{\eta^2} - \frac{2\sigma^2(3\sigma-2)^2\mu^2}{\eta^2} - \frac{2\sigma^2}{\alpha\beta} \\
&-\frac{4\sigma}{\sigma-1}\frac{1}{(1-\mu^2)^2}
\end{aligned} \tag{35}$$

This is zero at $\mu = 0$ and approaches minus infinity as μ approaches the black-hole threshold ($\beta = 0$); its second term is zero at $\mu = 0$ and negative otherwise; and each of the other three terms is decreasing in μ.[23] Hence (35) is negative throughout the admissible region. To sum up, h equals unity and is stationary in μ at $\mu = 0$, and it is concave in μ throughout. It follows that $h(\mu) < 1$ for $\mu > 0$. Hence, at the

[23]This follows since η is increasing in μ and $\alpha\beta = (\sigma-1)^2 - \sigma^2\mu^2$ is decreasing in μ.

break threshold of transport costs, there is no incentive to deviate from the agglomerated equilibrium, so $T^B < T^S$, as required.

To show that the cost linkage is crucial for proposition 3, consider two new thresholds, $T^{B'}$ and $T^{S'}$, defined respectively as the break and sustain levels of trade costs that equalize *nominal* rather than real wages between countries. Then: *Proposition 4:* $T^{B'}$ equals $T^{S'}$, and both are less than T^B and T^S, provided $\mu > 0$.

Proof of Proposition 4: From the discussion following (14), $T^{B'}$ is defined by the condition $Z = \mu$. Substituting for Z from (10) gives: $(T^{B'})^{\sigma-1} = (1+\mu)/(1-\mu)$. As for $T^{S'}$, it is evident from (28) that it is defined by the condition $H = 1$, or $(1+\mu)T^{1-\sigma} + (1-\mu)T^{\sigma-1} = 2$. This is a quadratic in $T^{\sigma-1}$. Solving, and ignoring the trivial root $T = 1$, gives $(T^{S'})^{\sigma-1} = (1+\mu)/(1-\mu)$. This proves that $T^{B'} = T^{S'}$. But we have already seen that (provided μ is strictly positive) the level of trade costs just sufficient to yield equal nominal wages *under*estimates the incentives to deviate from the symmetric equilibrium, so $T^{B'} < T^B$; while it *over*estimates the incentives to deviate from the agglomerated equilibrium, so $T^{S'} < T^S$.

References

Abdel-Rahman, Hesham M. 1988. "Product Differentiation, Monopolistic Competition, and City Size," *Reg. Sci. Urban Econ.* 18:1, pp. 69–86.

Abdel-Rahman, Hesham M. and Ping Wang. 1988. "Toward a General Equilibrium Theory of a Core-Periphery System of Cities," *Reg. Sci. Urban Econ.* 25:4, pp. 529–46.

Arthur, W. Brian. 1986. "Industry Location Patterns and the Importance of History," in *Increasing Returns and Path Dependence in the Economy.* W. Brian Arthur, ed. Michigan U. Press, pp. 49–68.

Audretsch, David B. and Maryann P. Feldman. 1996. "R&D Spillovers and the Geography of Innovation and Production," *Amer. Econ. Rev.* 86:3, pp. 630–40.

Baldwin, Richard E. 1999a. "Agglomeration and Endogenous Capital," *Eur. Econ. Rev.* 43:2, pp. 253–80.

———. 1999b. "The Core-Periphery Model with Forward-Looking Expectations," CEPR Discussion Paper 2085.

Brakman, Steven; Harry Garretsen and Charles van Marrewijk. 2001. *An Introduction to Geographical Economics.* Cambridge: Cambridge U. Press, forthcoming.

Brander, James A. 1981. "Intra-Industry Trade in Identical Commodities," *J. Int. Econ.* 11:1, pp. 1–14.

———. 1995. "Strategic Trade Policy," in *Handbook of International Economics, Vol. 3.* Gene M. Grossman and Kenneth Rogoff, eds. Amsterdam: North-Holland, pp. 1395–455.

Braunerhjelm, Pontus; Riccardo Faini, Victor Norman, Frances Ruane and Paul Seabright. 2000. *Integration and the Regions of Europe: How the Right Policies Can Prevent Polarization.* London: CEPR.

Christaller, Walter. 1933. *Central Places of Southern Germany.* Jena, Germany: Fischer. (English translation, London: Prentice Hall, 1966.)

Combes, Pierre-Philippe. 1997. "Industrial Agglomeration under Cournot Competition," *Ann. Econ. Statist.* 45, pp. 161–82.

Combes, Pierre-Philippe and Miren Lafourcade. 2000. "Transportation Costs and Regional Employment Inequalities: Evidence from France, 1993," mimeo, CERAS.

Davis, Donald R. 1998. "The Home Market, Trade and Industrial Structure," *Amer. Econ. Rev.* 88:5, pp. 1264–76.

Davis, Donald R. and David E. Weinstein. 1996. "Does Economic Geography Matter for International Specialization?" NBER Working Paper 5706.

———. 1998. "Market Access, Economic Geography and Comparative Advantage: An Empirical Assessment," NBER Working Paper 6787.

———. 1999. "Economic Geography and Regional Production Structure: An Empirical Investigation," *Eur. Econ. Rev.* 43:2, pp. 379–407.

Deardorff, Alan V. 1998. "Determinants of Bilateral Trade: Does Gravity Work in a Neoclassical World?" in *The Regionalization of the World Economy.* Jeffrey A. Frankel, ed. Chicago: U. Chicago Press, pp. 7–22.

Dixit, Avinash K. and Victor Norman. 1980. *Theory of International Trade: A Dual, General Equilibrium Approach.* London: Cambridge U. Press.

Dixit, Avinash K. and Joseph E. Stiglitz. 1977. "Monopolistic Competition and Optimum Product Diversity," *Amer. Econ. Rev.* 67:3, pp. 297–308.

Ethier, Wilfred J. 1982. "National and International Returns to Scale in the Theory of International Trade," *Amer. Econ. Rev.* 72:3, pp. 389–405.

Falvey, Rodney E. 1976. "Transport Costs in the Pure Theory of International Trade," *Econ. J.* 86:343, pp. 536–50.

Fujita, Masahisa; Paul Krugman and Tomoya Mori. 1999. "On the Evolution of Hierarchical Urban Systems," *Eur. Econ. Rev.* 43:2, pp. 209–51.

Fujita, Masahisa and Jacques-François Thisse. 1996. "Economics of Agglomeration," *J. Japanese Int. Econ.* 10:4, pp. 339–78.

———. 2000. "Agglomeration and Market Interaction," presented to the World Congress of the Econometric Society, Seattle.

Gabaix, Xavier. 1999. "Zipf's Law for Cities: An Explanation," *Quart. J. Econ.* 114, pp. 739–67.

Gallup, John Luke and Jeffrey D. Sachs with Andrew D. Mellinger. 1998. "Geography and Economic Development," in *Annual World Bank Conference on Development Economics.* Boris Pleskovic and Joseph E. Stiglitz, eds. Washington DC: World Bank, pp. 127–78.

Hanson, Gordon H. 1998. "Market Potential, Increasing Returns, and Geographic Concentration," NBER Working Paper 6429.

Harris, Richard. 1995. "Trade and Communication Costs," *Can. J. Econ.* 28, pp. 46–75.

Head, K.; T. Mayer and J. Ries. 1999. "On the Pervasiveness of Home Market Effects," mimeo, U. British Columbia.

Helpman, Elhanan. 1997. "The Size of Regions," in *Topics in Public Economics: Theoretical and Applied Analysis.* David Pines, Efraim Sadka and Itzhak Zilcha, eds. Cambridge: Cambridge U. Press.

Helpman, Elhanan and Paul R. Krugman. 1985. *Market Structure and Foreign Trade.* Cambridge, MA: MIT Press.

Jones, Ronald W. 1965. "The Structure of Simple General Equilibrium Models," *J. Polit. Econ.* 73, pp. 557–72.

Kim, Sukkoo. 1995. "Expansion of Markets and the Geographic Distribution of Economic Activities: The Trends in U.S. Regional Manufacturing Structure, 1860–1987," *Quart. J. Econ.* 110:4, pp. 881–908.

Krugman, Paul R. 1979. "Increasing Returns, Monopolistic Competition and International Trade," *J. Int. Econ.* 9:4, pp. 469–79.

———. 1980. "Scale Economies, Product Differentiation and the Pattern of Trade," *Amer. Econ. Rev.* 70, pp. 950–59.

———. 1991. "Increasing Returns and Economic Geography," *J. Polit. Econ.* 99:3, pp. 483–99.

———. 1995. *Development, Geography and Economic Theory.* Cambridge, MA: MIT Press.

———. 1999. "Was It All in Ohlin?" at http://web.mit.edu/krugman/www/ohlin.html.

Krugman, Paul R. and Anthony J. Venables. 1990. "Integration and the Competitiveness of Peripheral Industry," in *Unity with Diversity in the European Community.* Christopher Bliss and Jorge Braga de Macedo, eds. Cambridge: Cambridge U. Press, pp. 56–75.

———. 1995. "Globalization and the Inequality of Nations," *Quart. J. Econ.* 110:4, pp. 857–80.

Leamer, Edward E. 1997. "Access to Western Markets and Eastern Effort," in *Lessons from the Economic Transition: Central and Eastern Europe in the 1990s.* Salvatore Zecchini, ed. Dordrecht: Kluwer Academic, pp. 503–26.

Leamer, Edward E. and James Levinsohn. 1995. "International Trade Theory: The Evidence," in *Handbook of International Economics, Vol. 3.* Gene M. Grossman and Kenneth Rogoff, eds. Amsterdam: North-Holland, pp. 1339–94.

Lösch, August. 1940. *The Economics of Location,* Jena, Germany: Fischer. (English translation, New Haven: Yale U. Press, 1954.)

Lucas, Robert E., Jr. 1988. "On the Mechanics of Economic Development," *J. Mon. Econ.* 22:1, pp. 3–42.

Martin, Philippe P. and Gianmarco I. P. Ottaviano. 1999. "Growing Locations: Industry Location in a Model of Endogenous Growth," *Eur. Econ. Rev.* 43:2, pp. 281–302.

Martin, Ron. 1999, "The New 'Geographical Turn' in Economics: Some Critical Reflections," *Cambridge J. Econ.* 23:1, pp. 65–91.

Midelfart-Knarvik, Karen Helene; Henry G. Overman and Anthony J. Venables. 2000. "Comparative Advantage and Economic Geography: Estimating the Location of Production in the EU," mimeo, LSE.

Mussa, Michael. 1978. "Dynamic Adjustment in the Heckscher-Ohlin-Samuelson Model," *J. Polit. Econ.* 86, pp. 775–92.

Neary, J. Peter. 1978. "Dynamic Stability and the Theory of Factor-Market Distortions," *Amer. Econ. Rev.* 68:4, pp. 671–82.

———. 1999. "Discussion" of "Economic Policy and the Manufacturing Base: Hysteresis in Location" (by Anthony J. Venables), in *Dynamic Issues in Commercial Policy Analysis.* Richard E. Baldwin and Joseph F. Francois, eds. Cambridge: Cambridge U. Press, pp. 196–201.

Neary, J. Peter and Dermot Leahy. 2000. "Strategic Trade and Industrial Policy Towards Dynamic Oligopolies," *Econ. J.* 110:463, pp. 484–508.

Ohlin, Bertil. 1933. *Interregional and International Trade.* Cambridge, MA: Harvard U. Press.

Ottaviano, Gianmarco and Diego Puga. 1998. "Agglomeration in the Global Economy: A Survey of the 'New Economic Geography'," *World Econ.* 21, pp. 707–31.

Ottaviano, Gianmarco; Takatoshi Tabuchi and Jacques-François Thisse. 2000. "Agglomeration and Trade Revisited," mimeo, CORE, U. Catholique de Louvain.

Puga, Diego. 1999. "The Rise and Fall of Regional Inequalities," *Eur. Econ. Rev.* 43:2, pp. 303–34.

Puga, Diego and Anthony J. Venables. 1996. "The Spread of Industry: Spatial Agglomeration and Economic Development," *J. Japanese Int. Econ.* 10:4, pp. 440–64.

Quah, Danny T. 1997. "Increasingly Weightless Economies," *Bank Engl. Quart. Bull.* 37, pp. 49–56.

Redding, Stephen and Anthony J. Venables. 2000. "Economic Geography and International Inequality," mimeo, LSE.

Smith, Alasdair and Anthony J. Venables. 1988. "Completing the Internal Market in the European Union: Some Industry Simulations," *Eur. Econ. Rev.* 32:7, pp. 1501–25.

Solow, Robert M. 1962. "Comment" on "On a Two-Sector Model of Economic Growth" (by Hirofumi Uzawa), *Rev. Econ. Stud.* 29, pp. 255–57.

Venables, Anthony J. 1996. "Equilibrium Locations of Vertically Linked Industries," *Int. Econ. Rev.* 37:2, pp. 341–59.

———. 1999. "Economic Policy and the Manufacturing Base: Hysteresis in Location," in *Dynamic. Issues in Commercial Policy Analysis.* Richard E. Baldwin and Joseph F. Francois, eds. Cambridge: Cambridge U. Press, pp. 177–95.

Ventura, Jaume. 1997. "Growth and Interdependence," *Quart. J. Econ.* 112:1, pp. 57–84.

Chapter 11

Growth and International Trade: A Heckscher–Ohlin Approach

Jean-Pierre Laffargue

Department of Economics, University of Paris 1
jean-pierre.laffargue@orange.fr

We combine in a unified model the Ramsey exogenous and the Rebelo endogenous growth models with the Heckscher–Ohlin trade one. We show that openness to trade induces the (conditional) equalization of factor prices across countries, but is insufficient to cause the convergence of their outputs and stocks of capital per capita: A poor country may (under conditions) grow faster than the rich ones, but it permanently remains poorer. However, openness to trade *plus* a high preference for the future (higher than in the rich countries contrarily to what was assumed for the previous result) allows a poor country to grow fast and eventually to catch up with the rich ones. This result can explain the fast development of Eastern Asia since the 1960s or 1980s.

1. Introduction

The two basic growth models, the Ramsey neoclassical and the Rebelo AK ones, were developed for a closed economy.[1] We remind that the first model assumes an exogenous long-run growth rate (more precisely that the efficiency of labor grows at exogenous rate). It concludes that capital and consumption per capita converge

[1]See Benassy (2011) for an introduction to these models.

to a balanced growth path, which depends on technological and preference parameters, but not on the initial state of the economy. Hence, as soon as we correct for differences in these parameters, poor and rich countries' outputs per capita converge to the same balanced growth path. This implies that on the transitional path, poor countries grow faster than rich countries. On the other hand, the long run growth rate of the AK model is endogenous that is depends on the technological and preference parameters. Hence, if we still correct for differences in parameters, poor and rich countries will grow at the same rate. However, the level of the balanced growth path of the output per capita of a country will depend on its initial stock of capital, which is usually called a hysteresis property. Consequently, poor countries have permanently lower output (consumption and capital) per capita than rich countries.

A series of empirical studies (see Barro, 1991, for a pioneering article and Barro and Sala-i-Martin, 2004, Chapter 12, for an extensive review) conclude that poor countries grow faster than rich ones (after the introduction in the regressions of variables controlling for differences in technological and preference parameters of the theoretical models). This 'conditional' convergence result is consistent with the Ramsey model. The AK model has no transitional path: the economy immediately settles on its balanced growth path. However, a very natural extension due to Jones and Manuelli (1991, see also Barro, 2004, Chapter 4) introduces such a transitional path along which poor countries grow faster than rich ones. Hence, endogenous growth models can be made consistent with actual but incomplete convergence.

In these times of globalization, it can appear strange to investigate growth in a closed economy framework. Hence, the previous models have been extended in three directions by assuming: (1) factor international mobility (capital or labor); (2) knowledge spillover; (3) trade in commodities. This chapter deals with the third extension. To include trade in a growth model we need to consider at least two tradable goods, two countries and a reason for them to trade. We adopt in this paper the Heckscher–Ohlin approach that is trade originates because of differences in factor abundance across countries.[2]

The Heckscher–Ohlin model of two countries, two goods and two factors, which is static, establishes two results, which are important for the dynamic analysis:

- The conditional factor price equalization theorem: the costs of capital and labor (measured in efficiency units) are the same in the two countries, if each of them produces the two goods that is if their factor endowments are in the cone of diversification.
- Then, the relative prices of the two goods and the two factors, the factor inputs needed for one unit of production of each good and the bounds of the diversification cone only depend on the ratio between the world endowments of capital and labor.

To obtain a dynamic version of the Heckscher–Ohlin model we assume that investment combines the two goods in the same ratio as consumption, that the efficiency of labor increases at constant rate, the same in both sectors and countries and we introduce an intertemporal utility function of the consumers, which is the same in both countries. A consequence of the conditional factor price equalization theorem is that the model can be solved recursively. First, we can aggregate the two countries in a one sector world growth model. According to the values of the parameters this model is a neoclassical Ramsey exogenous growth model, or a Jones and Manuelli endogenous growth model, or an endogenous contractionary model.

Then, after having solved the world model, we can compute the solution of the model of a country. This model has a hysteresis property, which means that it has infinity of steady states and the one it converges to is determined by the value of its initial stock of capital. If the world economy follows a path determined by a Ramsey exogenous growth model, all countries have the same exogenous

[2]An alternative approach is the Ricardian one, where trade is driven by technological comparative advantage (see Acemoglu, 2009, Chapter 19, for an introduction).

growth rate in the long run. Depending on conditions on parameters and the initial stocks of capital, the poorer country can grow at faster (or lower) rate than the richer country, for some time or permanently. But it remains permanently poorer. Of course, in the absence of trade, the two countries converge to the same steady state. However, in spite of this catching up of the poorer country, simulations show that free trade improves the intertemporal welfare of both countries.

If the world economy follows a path determined by an endogenous growth model, all countries have the same endogenous growth rate in the long run. However, we have the same hysteresis result, and if a poor country may permanently grow faster than a rich one, it will not catch up on it.

Hence, we establish that openness to trade induces the equalization of factor costs across countries, but is insufficient to imply the convergence of the outputs per capita of poor and rich countries to a common value. However, the first property remains valid if a poor country is small and discounts the future at low rate that is saves and invests much. In this case openness to trade keeps the return on capital steady instead of decreasing. Consequently, the dynamics of the economy of a poor and open country is determined by an AK endogenous growth model and not an exogenous growth model as if it were closed to international trade. The excess of its growth rate over its exogenous part increases with its preference for the future (its discount factor). Free trade and high savings and investment generate high growth, a theoretical result consistent with the fast development we can observe in Eastern Asia since the 1960s or 1980s.

An originality of this paper is having technology and preferences fully specified as CES functions. The usual presentation of the Heckscher–Ohlin model is done with general functions only constrained by sign or limit conditions on them and their first two derivatives. Growth models are most often presented in semi-parametric form. We believe that the loss in generality implied by our choice is more than compensated by allowing obtaining global results that depend on structural parameters and exogenous variables. We will also see that the CES specification enables our model to encompass the Ramsey and the Jones and Manuelli ones.

Our model is written in discrete time. We think that this helps to present it in more intuitive terms and to derive its mathematical properties more easily than if it were written in continuous time. Finally, our two choices allow to easily running simulations (we will quote important references that extensively use simulations).

Sections 2 and 3 present the static Heckscher–Ohlin model: First the partial equilibrium of a country facing exogenous international prices, then the general equilibrium of the two countries, which determines these prices. Section 4 introduces a dynamic extension of the Heckscher–Ohlin model and analyzes, first the properties of the world model and then the properties of the model of a country. Section 5 presents two important extensions of the model. Section 6 introduces complementary references. Section 7 concludes.

2. A Partial Equilibrium Model of Production and Trade

We consider an economy with two countries denoted N and S (for North and South), which produce two goods A and B, with two factor inputs K and L (for capital and labor). Assuming more than two countries would change nothing to the results of this and the other sections, but the assumption that there are as many goods as factors is essential. The endowments in factors of the two countries, respectively K_N, K_S and L_N, L_S, are fixed and we allow no movements of factors across borders. The production functions of the sectors, which produce the two goods in country i ($i = N, S$) are CES:

$$X_{Ai} = \left[\alpha_A K_{Ai}^b + \beta_A \left(\pi_i L_{Ai}\right)^b\right]^{1/b} \tag{1a}$$

$$X_{Bi} = \left[\alpha_B K_{Bi}^b + \beta_B \left(\pi_i L_{Bi}\right)^b\right]^{1/b} \tag{1b}$$

with $\alpha_A, \beta_A, \alpha_B, \beta_B \geq 0$ and $b < 1$ and nonzero.

X_{Ai} and X_{Bi} are the outputs of goods A and B in country i, produced using the inputs of capital and labor $K_{Ai}, K_{Bi}, L_{Ai}, L_{Bi}$. The technologies are the same in the two countries, but for the labor efficiency term π_i, which is higher in North than in South and the same in both sectors. The elasticity of substitution between the two factors, $\sigma = 1/(1-b)$, is also the same in the two sectors.

We define the *efficiency labor* inputs in the two sectors by: $L'_{Ai} = \pi_i L_{Ai}$ and $L'_{Bi} = \pi_i L_{Bi}$. Then, the production functions expressed with these new variables are the same in the two countries. Capital and labor are fully mobile between sectors:

$$K_{Ai} + K_{Bi} = K_i \tag{2a}$$

$$L'_{Ai} + L'_{Bi} = L'_i \equiv \pi_i L_i \tag{2b}$$

The two goods are freely traded without transport costs between the two countries and so they have the same prices, P_A and P_B, in both of them. We assume in this section that these world prices are exogenously fixed and we focus the analysis on the equilibrium in country i. The costs of capital and efficiency labor are denoted r_i and w'_i (the cost of labor is: $w_i = \pi_i w'_i$).[3] They are endogenous variables of the model. We assume that factor markets operate under perfect competition. As the production functions are homogenous of degree one in their inputs (that is production operates under constant return to scale), each firm in a given sector minimizes its unit cost. Consider sector A for instance, and define the factor inputs needed for one unit of production as: $a_{KAi} = K_{Ai}/X_{Ai}$ and $a_{LAi} = L'_{Ai}/X_{Ai}$. These two variables are the solution of the program: $c_{Ai}(r_i, w'_i) = \min_{a_{Ki}, a_{Li}>0}\{r_i a_{Ki} + w'_i a_{Li} | 1 = \alpha_A a^b_{KAi} + \beta_A a^b_{LAi}\}$, where $c_{Ai}(r_i, w'_i)$ is the unit-cost function of sector A in country i. We easily deduce from the first order conditions of the program:

$$a_{KAi} = \frac{(\alpha_A/r_i)^{1/(1-b)}}{\left[\alpha_A(\alpha_A/r_i)^{b/(1-b)} + \beta_A(\beta_A/w'_i)^{b/(1-b)}\right]^{1/b}} \tag{3a}$$

$$a_{LAi} = \frac{(\beta_A/w'_i)^{1/(1-b)}}{\left[\alpha_A(\alpha_A/r_i)^{b/(1-b)} + \beta_A(\beta_A/w'_i)^{b/(1-b)}\right]^{1/b}} \tag{3b}$$

[3]We indifferently use the terms cost of capital and return on capital or cost of labor, wage rate and return on labor.

Then, the expression of the unit-cost function is:

$$c_A\left(r_i, w_i'\right) = \left[\alpha_A\left(\alpha_A/r_i\right)^{b/(1-b)} + \beta_A\left(\beta_A/w_i'\right)^{b/(1-b)}\right]^{-(1-b)/b} \qquad (4)$$

We note that this function is the same in the two countries, as the production functions are also the same. We obtain similar expressions for sector B.

Now, we introduce the important assumption that goods A and B respectively are capital intensive and labor intensive *for all values of* r_i/w_i'. This means that the ratio of the capital to labor necessary to produce one unit of output is higher in sector A than in sector B, *whatever the factor costs ratio*. This latter requirement is called the *absence of factor intensity reversal*. Hence, we have[4]: $\frac{a_{KAi}}{a_{LAi}} = \left(\frac{\alpha_A}{r_i}\frac{w_i^i}{\beta_A}\right)^{1/(1-b)} > \frac{a_{KBi}}{a_{LBi}} = \left(\frac{\alpha_B}{r_i}\frac{w_i^i}{\beta_B}\right)^{1/(1-b)}$, or

$$\alpha_A\beta_B - \alpha_B\beta_A > 0 \qquad (5)$$

Under free competition on the good markets and with constant return to scale, the profit of each firm must be zero. Hence, *if both goods are produced* in country i, we have:

$$P_A = c_A\left(r_i, w_i'\right) \quad \text{and} \quad P_B = c_B\left(r_i, w_i'\right) \qquad (6)$$

These two equations implicitly define the equilibrium values of the factor costs w_i' and r_i in function of the prices of the two goods. More precisely, with Equation (4) they can be rewritten as:

$$1/P_A^{b/(1-b)} = \alpha_A^{1/(1-b)}/r_i^{b/(1-b)} + \beta_A^{1/(1-b)}/w_i'^{b/(1-b)} \qquad (7a)$$

$$1/P_B^{b/(1-b)} = \alpha_B^{1/(1-b)}/r_i^{b/(1-b)} + \beta_B^{1/(1-b)}/w_i'^{b/(1-b)} \qquad (7b)$$

---

[4]If the elasticity of substitution between factors was not the same in the two sectors, the absence of factor intensity reversal could not be satisfied.

The solution of this system of two equations in $r_i^{b/(1-b)}$ and $w_i'^{b/(1-b)}$ is:

$$\left(\frac{r_i}{P_A}\right)^{b/(1-b)} = \frac{\Delta}{\beta_A^{1/(1-b)}\left[(\beta_B/\beta_A)^{1/(1-b)} - (P_A/P_B)^{b/(1-b)}\right]} \tag{8a}$$

$$\left(\frac{w_i'}{P_A}\right)^{b/(1-b)} = \frac{\Delta}{\alpha_A^{1/(1-b)}\left[-(\alpha_B/\alpha_A)^{1/(1-b)} + (P_A/P_B)^{b/(1-b)}\right]} \tag{8b}$$

with $\Delta = (\alpha_A\beta_B)^{1/(1-b)} - (\alpha_B\beta_A)^{1/(1-b)} > 0$, by condition (5).

This solution is admissible that is $r_i^{b/(1-b)}$ and $w_i'^{b/(1-b)}$ are positive if:

$$\left(\frac{\alpha_B}{\alpha_A}\right)^{1/(1-b)} < \left(\frac{P_A}{P_B}\right)^{b/(1-b)} < \left(\frac{\beta_B}{\beta_A}\right)^{1/(1-b)} \tag{9}$$

We will establish in the general equilibrium model of Section 3 that this condition is satisfied.

Finally, from Equations (3a), (3b), (8a) and (8b) we obtain the expressions of the factor inputs needed for one unit of production in function of the prices of goods and factors:

$$\begin{aligned} a_{KAi} &= (\alpha_A P_A/r_i)^{1/(1-b)}, \quad a_{LAi} = \left(\beta_A P_A/w_i'\right)^{1/(1-b)}, \\ a_{KBi} &= (\alpha_B P_B/r_i)^{1/(1-b)}, \quad a_{LBi} = \left(\beta_B P_B/w_i'\right)^{1/(1-b)} \end{aligned} \tag{10}$$

Hence, we have established that *if each country produces the two goods*, they share the same costs of factors r and w', which only depend on the world prices of goods and on technology parameters. This important result, called the *factor price equalization theorem*, is due to Samuelson (1949). Then, the factor inputs needed for one unit of production, a_{KA}, a_{LA}, a_{KB} and a_{LB}, are also the same in both countries. However, it is the efficiency labor cost, which is the same in North and South; labor cost itself is higher in North: $w_N = \pi_N w' > \pi_S w' = w_S$. This latter property is called the *conditional factor price equalization theorem*, which means that the costs of labor equalize after correcting of differences in labor efficiency.

Assume small changes in the price of the two goods, such that the relative price of the good intensive in capital increases: $\frac{dP_A}{P_A} - \frac{dP_B}{P_B} > 0$. From the differentiation of Equations (8a) and (8b) we obtain:

$$\frac{dr}{r} = \frac{(P_A/P_B)^{b/(1-b)}}{(\beta_B/\beta_A)^{1/(1-b)} - (P_A/P_B)^{b/(1-b)}} \left(\frac{dP_A}{P_A} - \frac{dP_B}{P_B} \right) + \frac{dP_A}{P_A} > \frac{dP_A}{P_A} > \frac{dP_B}{P_B} \tag{11a}$$

$$\frac{dw'}{w'} = \frac{-(\alpha_B/\alpha_A)^{1/(1-b)}}{-(\alpha_B/\alpha_A)^{1/(1-b)} + (P_A/P_B)^{b/(1-b)}} \left(\frac{dP_A}{P_A} - \frac{dP_B}{P_B} \right) + \frac{dP_B}{P_B} < \frac{dP_B}{P_B} < \frac{dP_A}{P_A} \tag{11b}$$

We can see that the return on capital increases by more than the price of each good and that the wage rate (of efficiency labor) decreases by more than the price of each good. This is the *Stolper–Samuelson Theorem* (1941), which expresses that an increase in the relative price of a good will raise the real return of the factor used intensively in that good, and reduce the real return to the other factor.

We still have to write the equilibrium of the market of each factor:

$$a_{KA}X_{Ai} + a_{KB}X_{Bi} = K_i \tag{12a}$$

$$a_{LA}X_{Ai} + a_{LB}X_{Bi} = L'_i \tag{12b}$$

We solve this system of two equations in the outputs of country i and get:

$$X_{Ai} = \left(a_{LB}K_i - a_{KB}L'_i\right)/\Delta' \tag{13a}$$

$$X_{Bi} = \left(-a_{LA}K_i + a_{KA}L'_i\right)/\Delta' \tag{13b}$$

with: $\Delta' = a_{KA}a_{LB} - a_{KB}a_{LA} = \Delta[P_AP_B/(rw')]^{1/(1-b)} > 0$ because of Equations (10) and condition (5).

Assume that the two factor endowments K_i and L'_i change *without affecting the prices of the two goods* and consequently the factor prices and the factor inputs needed for one unit of production. Then, we deduce from Equations (13a) and (13b) the *Rybczynski*

Theorem (1955): An increase in a factor endowment will increase the output of the sector using it intensively and decrease the output of the other sector.[5]

Eventually, the solutions (13a) and (13b) are admissible if $X_{Ai}, X_{Bi} > 0$ (remember that we have assumed that both goods are produced in each country). Then, we must have:

$$\frac{a_{KB}}{a_{LB}} < \frac{K_i}{L_i'} < \frac{a_{KA}}{a_{LA}} \tag{14a}$$

These inequalities define the *cone of diversification* to which the endowment vector (K_i, L_i) must belong. This condition can be rewritten in the terms of the good prices (with Equations (5), (8a) and (8b)):

$$\left(\frac{\alpha_B}{\beta_B}\right)^{1/(1-b)} \frac{1}{F\left(P_A/P_B\right)} < \frac{K_i}{L_i'} < \left(\frac{\alpha_A}{\beta_A}\right)^{1/(1-b)} \frac{1}{F\left(P_A/P_B\right)} \tag{14b}$$

with:

$$\left(\frac{r}{w'}\right)^{1/(1-b)} = F\left(P_A/P_B\right)$$

$$\equiv \left[(\alpha_A/\beta_A)^{1/(1-b)} \frac{-(\alpha_B/\alpha_A)^{1/(1-b)} + (P_A/P_B)^{b/(1-b)}}{(\beta_B/\beta_A)^{1/(1-b)} - (P_A/P_B)^{b/(1-b)}}\right]^{1/b}$$

3. A General Equilibrium Model of Trade: The Heckscher–Ohlin Model

Instead of assuming that the prices of the two goods are exogenous, and limiting the model to its production and supply side, we

[5]From equations (8a) on one side and (13a) and (10) on the other side we deduce:

$$\frac{\partial r}{\partial P_A} = \left(\frac{r}{P_A}\right)^{1/(1-b)} \frac{\beta_B^{1/(1-b)}}{\Delta} = \frac{\partial X_{Ai}}{\partial K_i}$$

Hence, the Stolper-Samuelson derivatives are equal to the Rybczynsky derivatives. Samuelson (1953–1954) called this result the "reciprocity relations".

introduce consumers and a demand side and compute the equilibrium prices. The consumers of country i have the utility function:

$$U_i = \left(C_{Ai}^b + C_{Bi}^b\right)^{1/b} \tag{15}$$

where C_{Ai} and C_{Bi} are their consumption of each good.[6]

We assume that preferences are the same in both countries. In order to obtain an analytical expression of the equilibrium prices, we also assume that the elasticity of substitution is the same for the utility and the production functions, that is: $\sigma = 1/(1-b)$.

We assume in this section that the factor endowment of each country is inside the cone of diversification and so that the conditional factor price equalization theorem is valid. Then, we can compute the *world equilibrium*. For that we sum Equations (13a) and (13b) across countries and obtain the expressions of the world outputs in function of the world factor endowment:

$$X_A = \left(a_{LB}K - a_{KB}L'\right)/\Delta' \tag{16a}$$

$$X_B = \left(-a_{LA}K + a_{KA}L'\right)/\Delta' \tag{16b}$$

With Equations (10) and (14b) we obtain the following expression of the world outputs ratio:

$$\frac{X_A}{X_B} = \left(\frac{\beta_B P_B}{\beta_A P_A}\right)^{1/(1-b)} \frac{F\left(P_A/P_B\right)K/L' - \left(\alpha_B/\beta_B\right)^{1/(1-b)}}{-F\left(P_A/P_B\right)K/L' + \left(\alpha_A/\beta_A\right)^{1/(1-b)}} \tag{17}$$

Consumers minimize their consumption cost necessary to reach a given level of utility: $\min_{C_A,C_B>0}\ \{P_A C_A + P_B C_B | U = (C_A^b + C_B^b)^{1/b}\}$. We deduce from the first-order conditions of this program the ratio of the consumption of both goods (which is the same for all consumers, independently of their incomes, because preferences are

[6]Introducing weights different from one in this CES function would not be more general, because we could redefine the units of measurement of the goods to obtain unit weights.

homothetic):

$$C_A/C_B = (P_B/P_A)^{1/(1-b)} \tag{18}$$

In the general equilibrium the world production and consumption of each good are the same. Hence, we have: $X_A/X_B = C_A/C_B$, or:

$$\left(\frac{\beta_B}{\beta_A}\right)^{1/(1-b)} \frac{F(P_A/P_B)K/L' - (\alpha_B/\beta_B)^{1/(1-b)}}{-F(P_A/P_B)K/L' + (\alpha_A/\beta_A)^{1/(1-b)}} = 1 \tag{19}$$

We deduce from this equation the value of $F(P_A/P_B)$:

$$F(P_A/P_B) = \lambda L'/(\mu K), \text{with } \lambda = \alpha_A^{1/(1-b)} + \alpha_B^{1/(1-b)}$$
$$\text{and } \mu = \beta_A^{1/(1-b)} + \beta_B^{1/(1-b)} \tag{20}$$

From the expression of $F(P_A/P_B)$ in Equation (14b) we obtain the value of the ratio of the prices of goods A and B:

$$\frac{P_A}{P_B} = \left[\frac{\alpha_B^{1/(1-b)}(K/\lambda)^b + \beta_B^{1/(1-b)}(L'/\mu)^b}{\alpha_A^{1/(1-b)}(K/\lambda)^b + \beta_A^{1/(1-b)}(L'/\mu)^b}\right]^{(1-b)/b} \tag{21}$$

When the ratio between the world capital and the world labor K/L' increases from zero to infinity, the ratio between the prices of the good intensive in capital and the good intensive in labor decreases, from $(\beta_B/\beta_A)^{1/b}$ to $(\alpha_B/\alpha_A)^{1/b}$ if $b > 0$, or from $(\alpha_B/\alpha_A)^{1/b}$ to $(\beta_B/\beta_A)^{1/b}$ if $b < 0$. In both cases the condition (9) assumed in the previous section is satisfied.[7]

Hence, we have established that the values of the relative prices of the two goods and the two factors, P_A/P_B and r/w', and of the factor inputs needed for one unit of production, a_{KA}, a_{LA}, a_{KB} and a_{LB}, only depend on the ratio between the world endowments of capital and labor K/L'.

[7]Ventura (1997) makes the extreme assumption that: $\beta_A = \alpha_B = 0$, which means that good A only uses capital and good B only uses labor in their production. Then, when the ratio of capital to labor endowments increases from zero to infinity, the relative price of good A in term of good B decreases from infinity to zero.

Now, we can turn to the equilibrium of country i. Its production of both goods is given by Equations (13a) and (13b). Its share in the world consumption of each good is the same as its share in world income: $s_i = \frac{P_A X_{Ai} + P_B X_{Bi}}{P_A X_A + P_B X_B}$. We have:

$$C_{Ai} = s_i C_A = s_i X_A = s_i \left(a_{LB} K - a_{KB} L'\right) / \Delta' \qquad (22a)$$

$$C_{Bi} = s_i C_B = s_i X_B = s_i \left(-a_{LA} K + a_{KA} L'\right) / \Delta' \qquad (22b)$$

We deduce from Equations (10), (13a), (13b), (14b) and (20): $s_i = \frac{HK_i + L'_i}{HK + L'}$, with $H = \frac{P_A a_{LB} - P_B a_{LA}}{-P_A a_{KB} + P_B a_{KA}} = (\frac{\lambda L'}{\mu K})^{1-b}$. Hence:

$$s_i = \frac{\left[\lambda L' / \left(\mu K\right)\right]^{1-b} K_i + L'_i}{\left[\lambda L' / \left(\mu K\right)\right]^{1-b} K + L'} \qquad (23)$$

The exports of good A by country i are: $X_{Ai} - C_{Ai} = \frac{a_{LB}(K_i - s_i K) - a_{KB}(L'_i - s_i L')}{\Delta'}$ that is:

$$X_{Ai} - C_{Ai} = \frac{a_{KB}\left[\lambda L'/(\mu K)\right]^{1-b} + a_{LB}}{K\left[\lambda L'/(\mu K)\right]^{1-b} + L'} \frac{L' L'_i}{\Delta'} \left(\frac{K_i}{L'_i} - \frac{K}{L'}\right) \qquad (24)$$

We deduce from the balance of trade identity the expression of the exports of good B by the same country: $X_{Bi} - C_{Bi} = -(P_A/P_B)(X_{Ai} - C_{Ai})$.

If $i = N$, that is if country i is the North, its capital/labor endowment ratio is higher than in the South and so than the world ratio: $K_N/L'_N > K/L'$. Hence, North exports good A (which is capital intensive) and imports good B (which is labor intensive). We have established the *Heckscher–Ohlin Theorem*: A country exports the good that uses its abundant factor intensively.

Finally, we have assumed in this section that the factor endowment of each country belongs to the cone of diversification.

From Equations (14b) and (20) this condition becomes[8]:

$$\frac{(\beta_A/\beta_B)^{1/(1-b)}+1}{(\alpha_A/\alpha_B)^{1/(1-b)}+1}\frac{K}{L'} < \frac{K_i}{L_i'} < \frac{(\beta_B/\beta_A)^{1/(1-b)}+1}{(\alpha_B/\alpha_A)^{1/(1-b)}+1}\frac{K}{L'} \tag{25}$$

4. A General Equilibrium Growth Model

In this section, we introduce and analyze a dynamic extension of the Heckscher–Ohlin model. In the first subsection we present the different elements of this extension and note that the dynamic model is block recursive, as in the static case. In Section 4.2, we analyze the world model, which is the first block. The second block, the model of country i, is analyzed in Sections 4.3, 4.4 and 4.5.

4.1. *A Dynamic Extension of the Heckscher–Ohlin Model*

We extend the model of the previous section by adding four ingredients.

1. First, we introduce time in the form of a sequence of periods: $t = 0, 1, 2, \ldots$ Period zero is the current period, the future is perfectly foresighted by the agents and all variables are indexed by their period.
2. The output of each good can be consumed, but it also can be used to increase the stock of capital. More precisely, consumers still consume both goods in the ratio given by Equation (18). Enterprises also invest in both goods and we assume that *they combine them in the same ratio.* These assumptions are usually presented in the following way. There exist firms, which combine the 'intermediary' goods A and B and produce a 'final' good

[8]If we assume that $\beta_A = \alpha_B = 0$ that is that good A only uses capital and good B only uses labor for their production, like Ventura (1997), we obtain: $0 < K_i/L_i' < \infty$, or $K_i L_i' > 0$. The diversification cone becomes the open positive orthant in plane(K, L').

according to the CES function (identical to Equation 15):

$$Y_t = \left(X_{At}^b + X_{Bt}^b\right)^{1/b} \tag{26}$$

The final good is the numeraire whose price is one. These firms operate under perfect competition and maximize their profit: $Y_t - P_{At}X_{At} - P_{Bt}X_{Bt}$. The first-order condition of their program gives the composition of the final good (which is identical to Equation (18) and the same in both countries):

$$X_{At}/X_{Bt} = (P_{Bt}/P_{At})^{1/(1-b)} \tag{27}$$

The zero-profit condition for the firms producing the final good is:

$$P_{At}^{-b/(1-b)} + P_{Bt}^{-b/(1-b)} = 1 \tag{28}$$

The world output of final good is allocated between the domestic consumption C_{it} and the investment I_{it} of both countries:

$$Y_t = C_{Nt} + C_{St} + I_{Nt} + I_{St} \tag{29}$$

The dynamics of capital in country i is given by the accounting equation:

$$K_{i,t+1} = I_{it} + (1-\delta)\,K_{it}, \quad \text{with } 0 \le \delta \le 1 \tag{30}$$

where δ is the capital depreciation rate and K_{it} the stock of capital at the beginning of period t, available for production during the period.[9]

3. Population remains the same over time in each country (assuming a constant expansion rate of population, $n > 1$, the same in each country, would add nothing substantial to the analysis).

[9] Of course, in the 'real world' the combination of the two 'intermediary' goods into a 'final' good is directly made by the consumers and firms when they consume or invest. The firms producing the final good are just fictions, practical for exposing the model. There is no restriction in assuming that there is no international trade in this good and that its production takes place in the country, which consumes it or uses it for investment.

The consumers in country i maximize their intertemporal utility function:

$$U_i = \sum_{t=0}^{\infty} \beta^t C_{it}^{1-\theta} / (1-\theta), \text{ with } 0 < \beta < 1, \theta > 0 \tag{31}$$

with the discount factor β and inverse of the intertemporal elasticity of substitution θ the same in both countries.

From the consumers intertemporal optimization we obtain the Euler equation:

$$C_{i,t+1} = [\beta (1 + r_{i,t+1} - \delta)]^{1/\theta} C_{it} \tag{32}$$

We add the transversality condition of the consumers program, which is that the present value of their future capital tends to zero when time increases indefinitely:

$$\lim_{t\to\infty} \frac{K_{it}}{\prod_{\tau=1}^{t} (1 + r_{i\tau} - \delta)} = \lim_{t\to\infty} \beta^t K_{it} (C_{it}/C_{i0})^{-\theta} = 0 \tag{33}$$

4. The efficiency of labor in all countries increases at the same expansion rate $g \geq 1 : \pi_{it} = \pi_i g^t$. That means that we allow only labor-augmenting technological progress, as in the neoclassical growth model.

   Labor and the wage rate measured in efficiency units are still defined by: $L'_i = \pi_i L_i$ and $w'_{it} = w_{it}/\pi_i$. It will be practical, as the efficiency of labor has a trend, to redefine production, consumption, investment and capital in *intensive form* by the formulae: $x_{Ait} = X_{Ait}/g^t$, $x_{Bit} = X_{Bit}/g^t$, $c_{it} = C_{it}/g^t$, $i_{it} = I_{it}/g^t$ and $k_{it} = K_{it}/g^t$. The equations of the model can easily be rewritten in the new variables. For instance, the production function of good A in country i (Equation (1a)) becomes: $x_{Ait} = [\alpha_A k^b_{Ait} + \beta_A L'^b_{Ai}]^{1/b}$. The capital accumulation identity (30) becomes: $gk_{i,t+1} = i_{it} + (1-\delta)k_{it}$. The intertemporal utility of the consumers of country i (31) becomes: $U_i = \sum_{t=0}^{\infty} (\beta g^{1-\theta})^t c_{it}^{1-\theta}/(1-\theta)$, with the assumption $\beta g^{1-\theta} < 1$ so that the series converges if c_{it} is bounded. The Euler equation (32) becomes: $c_{i,t+1} = [\beta g^{-\theta}(1 +$

$r_{i,t+1} - \delta)]^{1/\theta} c_{it}$ and the transversality condition (33) becomes: $\lim_{t\to\infty} \frac{k_{it}}{\prod_{\tau=1}^{t}[(1+r_{i\tau}-\delta)/g]} = \lim_{t\to\infty} (\beta g^{1-\theta})^t k_{it}(c_{it}/c_{i0})^{-\theta} = 0$.

We will assume in the rest of the section that the factor endowment of each country in each period is inside the cone of diversification (given by Equation (25)) and so that the conditional factor price equalization theorem is valid: $r_{it} = r_t$ and $w'_{it} = w'_t$. Consequently, the factor inputs needed for one unit of production: $a_{KAit} = k_{Ait}/x_{Ait}$, etc., are the same in both countries. Then, the model can be solved recursively: first, the world model, which aggregates the outputs, consumption, investment and capital of the two countries, then the model of country i.

4.2. *The World Model*

Proposition 1, which is proven in the appendix, gives the equations of the world model.

Proposition 1. *The world model, which determines the dynamics of the world output of final good, capital, investment and consumption, is:*

$$\max \sum_{t=0}^{\infty} \left(\beta g^{1-\theta}\right)^t c_t^{1-\theta} / (1-\theta) \tag{34}$$

$$g k_{t+1} = i_t + (1-\delta) k_t \tag{35}$$

$$c_t + i_t = y_t = \left[\lambda (k_t/\lambda)^b + \mu (L'/\mu)^b\right]^{1/b} \tag{36}$$

The solution of this program is given by the Euler equation and the transversality condition:

$$c_{t+1} = \left[\beta g^{-\theta} (1 + r_{t+1} - \delta)\right]^{1/\theta} c_t \tag{37}$$

$$\lim_{t\to\infty} \left(\beta g^{1-\theta}\right)^t k_t (c_t/c_0)^{-\theta} = 0 \tag{38}$$

Moreover, the expressions of the factor costs are given by:

$$
\begin{aligned}
r_t &= \partial y_t/\partial k_t = \left\{\lambda + \mu\left[\left(L'/\mu\right)/\left(k_t/\lambda\right)\right]^b\right\}^{(1-b)/b}, \\
w'_t &= \partial y_t/\partial L' = \left\{\lambda\left[\left(k_t/\lambda\right)/\left(L'/\mu\right)\right]^b + \mu\right\}^{(1-b)/b}
\end{aligned} \tag{39}
$$

from which we deduce the factor-price frontier $(r_t^{b/(1-b)} - \lambda)(w_t'^{b/(1-b)} - \mu) = \lambda\mu$.

The outputs and prices of the intermediary goods are:

$$
\begin{aligned}
x_{Jt} &= \left[\alpha_J^{1/(1-b)}\left(k_t/\lambda\right)^b + \beta_J^{1/(1-b)}\left(L'/\mu\right)^b\right]^{1/b}, \\
P_{Jt}^{b/(1-b)} &= \frac{\lambda\left(k_t/\lambda\right)^b + \mu\left(L'/\mu\right)^b}{\alpha_J^{1/(1-b)}\left(k_t/\lambda\right)^b + \beta_J^{1/(1-b)}\left(L'/\mu\right)^b}, J = A, B
\end{aligned} \tag{40}
$$

The three following propositions give the solution of the dynamic system (35) to (38) under three configurations of the parameters, when the initial stock of world capital k_0 is given. They show that the CES specification that we have retained is rich enough to encompass the neo-classical exogenous growth model of Ramsey, the extension by Jones and Manuelli (1991) of the AK endogenous growth model of Rebelo and a sustained contractionary model. The proofs are given in the appendix.

Proposition 2. *If*

$$
\begin{aligned}
&b > 0 \text{ and } 1/(\beta g^{-\theta}) - 1 + \delta > \lambda^{(1-b)/b}, \text{ or } b < 0 \\
&\text{and } 1/(\beta g^{-\theta}) - 1 + \delta < \lambda^{(1-b)/b}
\end{aligned} \tag{41}
$$

the world economy converges to a steady state where:

$$
\begin{aligned}
&r^* = 1/\left(\beta g^{-\theta}\right) - 1 + \delta, k^* = \lambda\frac{L'}{\mu}\left[\frac{\mu}{r^{*b/(1-b)} - \lambda}\right]^{1/b}, \\
&i^* = (g + \delta)\, k^*
\end{aligned} \tag{42}
$$

$$
y^* = \left[\lambda\left(k^*/\lambda\right)^b + \mu\left(L'/\mu\right)^b\right]^{1/b}, \quad c^* = y^* - i^* \tag{43}
$$

The dynamics of the world stock of capital in the neighborhood of the steady state is given by:

$$k_{t+1} - k^* = \Lambda_1 (k_t - k^*) \tag{44}$$

where Λ_1 *is the root smaller than one of the second degree polynomial:*

$$P(\Lambda) \equiv (1-\Lambda)\left[\frac{1+r^*-\delta-a_{12}}{g} - \Lambda\right] + \frac{a_{12}}{g}, \quad \text{with}$$
$$a_{12} = -\frac{1-b}{\theta}\frac{r^{*b/(1-b)}-\lambda}{r^{*b/(1-b)}}\frac{r^*}{1+r^*-\delta}\frac{c^*}{k^*} \tag{45}$$

Under condition (41) the world model is identical to the neoclassical Ramsey growth model[10].

Proposition 3. *If*

$$b > 0 \text{ and } 1/(\beta g^{-\theta}) - 1 + \delta < \lambda^{(1-b)/b} \tag{46}$$

the world economy model (in intensive variables) exhibits sustained growth. The expansion rate of capital, production and consumption tends to $G = [\beta g^{-\theta}(1+\lambda^{(1-b)/b} - \delta)]^{1/\theta} > 1$ *when time increases indefinitely. The detrended capital stock* $k_t/G^t = K_t/(gG)^t$ *tends to a fixed value, which depends on the initial stock of capital* k_0 *(hence the model presents a hysteresis property*[11]*).*

Under condition (46) the world model is identical to the CES version of the Jones and Manuelli endogenous growth model (1990, see also Barro and Sala-i-Martin, 2004, Chapter 4).

[10]The usual presentation of the Ramsey model assumes a general production function, which satisfies the Inada's conditions. Under these conditions, which are not satisfied by the CES function (except in the limit case when $b = 0$), there is no need for permissive conditions like (41) and the cases presented in the two following propositions do not arise.

[11]We must add in this proposition and the next the condition: $\beta(gG)^{1-\theta} < 1$, to satisfy the transversality condition.

Proposition 4. *If*

$$b < 0 \text{ and } 1/(\beta g^{-\theta}) - 1 + \delta > \lambda^{(1-b)/b} \tag{47}$$

the world economy variables (in their intensive form) contract at the asymptotic rate: $G = [\beta g^{-\theta}(1 + \lambda^{(1-b)/b} - \delta)]^{1/\theta} < 1$. *If* $gG < 1$, *capital and production in their original form tend to zero when time increases indefinitely. If* $gG > 1$, *the economy grows at the asymptotic rate* gG. *The detrended capital stock* $k_t/G^t = K_t/(gG)^t$ *tends to a fixed value, which depends on the initial stock of capital* k_0 *(hence we still have a hysteresis property).*

This proposition is quite similar to the previous one, except that it substitutes endogenous growth by endogenous contraction.[12]

4.3. *The Equations of the Model of Country i*

The equations of the model of country i in period t are:

- The expression of the production of the two intermediary goods, given by Equations (13a) and (13b):

$$x_{Ait} = \left(a_{LBt}k_{it} - a_{KBt}L_i'\right)/\Delta_t' \tag{48a}$$

$$x_{Bit} = \left(-a_{LAt}k_{it} + a_{KAt}L_i'\right)/\Delta_t' \tag{48b}$$

- The equality between the production of final good and the sum of consumption and investment (which implies the equilibrium of the balance of trade):

$$y_{it} \equiv P_{At}x_{Ait} + P_{Bt}x_{Bit} = c_{it} + i_{it} \tag{49}$$

---

[12]Ventura (1997) considers a model similar to ours, but with the simplifying assumptions: $\beta_A = \alpha_B = 0$ (good A is produced out of capital and good B is produced out of labor) and $\theta = 1$. He obtains our Propositions 2 and 3 in his setting. Acemoglu (2009, Chapter 19) makes the same simplifying assumptions. But instead of aggregating the two intermediary goods with a CES production function (which does not satisfy Inada's conditions) he uses an unspecified function, which satisfies these conditions. Then, Proposition 2 is always valid, without a restrictive condition like (41).

- The Euler equation (32):

$$c_{i,t+1} = [\beta g^{-\theta} (1 + r_{t+1} - \delta)]^{1/\theta} c_{it} \tag{50}$$

- The accounting identity, which determines the capital at the end of the period, given by Equation (30):

$$g k_{i,t+1} = i_{it} + (1 - \delta) k_{it} \tag{51}$$

and the transversality condition (33).

Hence, we have five equations, which determine the value in period t of five variables, $x_{Ait}, x_{Bit}, c_{it}, i_{it}, k_{i,t+1}$, in function of the stock of capital at the beginning of the period, k_{it}, and of the consumption of the next period $c_{i,t+1}$. The values of the variables non-indexed by i were computed by the world model. The values of the five same variables for the other country can be computed as the difference between their world and country i values.

The model is linear, and (using $y_{it} = r_t k_{it} + w_t' L_i'$) can be rewritten in the following state-space form:

$$\begin{pmatrix} c_{i,t+1} \\ k_{i,t+1} \end{pmatrix} = \begin{pmatrix} a_{11t} & 0 \\ -1/g & a_{22t} \end{pmatrix} \begin{pmatrix} c_{it} \\ k_{it} \end{pmatrix} + \begin{pmatrix} 0 \\ d_{2t} \end{pmatrix} \tag{52}$$

with: $a_{11t} = \left[\beta g^{-\theta}(1 + r_{t+1} - \delta)\right]^{1/\theta}$, $a_{22t} = (1 + r_t - \delta)/g$ and $d_{2t} = w_t' L_i'/g$

4.4. *The Solution of the Model of Country i When the World Model is of the Neo-classical Exogenous Growth Kind*

Assume that condition (41) is satisfied that is that we are in the case of Proposition 2 where the world dynamics is given by the neo-classical exogenous growth model of Ramsey. We compute the path followed by the variables of country i in the specific case when the sum of the initial stock of capital of the two countries is equal to the steady state of the world stock of capital: $k_{N0} + k_{S0} = k^*$. Then, all the world variables are and remain in their steady state and consequently the model of country i becomes:

$$\begin{pmatrix} c_{i,t+1} \\ k_{i,t+1} \end{pmatrix} = \begin{pmatrix} 1 & 0 \\ -1/g & (1+r^* - \delta)/g \end{pmatrix} \begin{pmatrix} c_{it} \\ k_{it} \end{pmatrix} + \begin{pmatrix} 0 \\ w'^* L_i'/g \end{pmatrix} \quad (53)$$

with the initial condition $k_{i0} > 0$ given. Of course the initial value of the capital stock has to be smaller than the world capital: $k_{i0} < k^*$, and such that the endowment of the two countries are in the diversification cone (Equation (25)).

The model has an infinity of steady states, which satisfy the equation: $[r^* - \delta - (g-1)]k_i^* + w^* L_i' = c_i^*$ and can be parameterized by k_i^*.

The first equation of the dynamic system is: $c_{i,t+1} = c_{it} = c^*$. From the second equation we deduce: $k_{i,t+1} - k_i^* = [(1+r^* - \delta)/g](k_{it} - k_i^*) = [(1+r^* - \delta)/g]^{t+1}(k_{i0} - k_i^*)$. We get from Equation (42): $(1 + r^* - \delta)/g = 1/(\beta g^{1-\theta}) > 1$. Then, the only steady state value of the stock of capital such that $k_{i,t+1}$ converges to it when time increases indefinitely is: $k_i^* = k_{i0}$. Hence, the stock of capital of country i remains permanently stuck at its initial value: $k_{it} = k_i^* = k_{i0}$.[13]

Of course, we could have set the initial value of the stock of capital in the other country such that the world economy is not in its steady state but just converges to it. Then, the dynamics of the model of country i becomes less trivial. This dynamics is investigated by Ventura (1997) and Bajona and Kehoe (2010). For instance, Bajona and Kehoe establish conditions on the parameters of the model and the initial stock of world capital such that the difference in the output per worker (measured in efficiency units) between country i and the world, $\frac{|y_{it}/L_i' - y_t/L'|}{y_t/L'}$, permanently decreases or increases over time. They call these two cases *convergence*[14] and *divergence*, although, in

[13]We could also proceed as in the proofs of Propositions 2 and 3: The system has an eigenvalue equal to one and the other, $(1+r^* - \delta)/g$, is larger than one. Then, the Blanchard and Kahn's condition is satisfied and there exists a unique solution path of the model, which converges to a steady state, which is determined by the initial stock of capital (hysteresis property).

[14]Convergence means that poor countries grow faster than rich ones. This agrees with the empirical conclusion quoted in the introduction that, after controlling

the first case the outputs per worker of country i and of the world do not converge to the same value.

In summary, we have established that the North and the South will converge to different steady states. We have described a case where the low initial capital endowment of the South perpetuates over time. Bajona and Kehoe establish sufficient conditions under which the poverty of the South decrease, or increase over time. But even in the most favorable case the South cannot catch up with the North.[15] The intuitive reason for this result is that trade in good allows for factor price equalization across countries with different aggregate capital-labor ratios. But the convergence of factor costs is insufficient to induce the convergence of the capital–labor ratio.

These no-convergence results cease being valid if international trade becomes impossible. Then, the model of each country is a Ramsey growth model and its variables (deflated by the quantity of labor measured in efficiency units) converge to the same steady state. Moreover, we can apply to each country Equation (44) of Proposition 2 that the dynamics of the stock of capital in the neighborhood of the steady state is given by: $k_{i,t+1} - k_i^* = \Lambda_1 \left(k_{it} - k_i^*\right)$, with $0 < \Lambda_1 < 1$. Then, we deduce that the growth rate of the stock of capital is: $\frac{k_{i,t+1}-k_{it}}{k_{it}} = (1-\Lambda_1)(\frac{k_i^*}{k_{it}} - 1)$, and decreases with k_{it}. Hence, capital grows at higher rate in a poor than in a rich country. The intuitive reason for this result is that as accumulation proceeds, the marginal product of capital falls, making further capital accumulation less productive. We can quote Bajona and Kehoe (2010): "In many environments where income levels converge over time if the countries are closed, they diverge if the countries are open. This is because favorable changes in the terms of trade for poor countries reduce their incentive to accumulate capital".

for differences in parameters, poor countries tend to grow faster than the rich ones.

[15]This result was first established (to our knowledge) by Chen (1992). Atkeson and Kehoe (2000) focus on the case when the South is small and has an initial endowment outside the diversification cone. Then, it only produces the labor-intensive good B, its endowment converges to a point on the lower boundary of the diversification cone and there it continues to being specialized in the production of good B.

4.5. *The Solution of the Model of Country i When the World Model is of the Endogenous Growth Kind*

Now, we consider the case when condition (46) is satisfied that is when Proposition 3 applies and the world economy (in intensive variables) grows at an expansion rate, which tends to: $G = [\beta g^{-\theta}(1 + \lambda^{(1-b)/b} - \delta)]^{1/\theta} > 1$. We redefine the consumption and the capital of country i, c_{it} and k_{it}, by dividing them by G^t. Then, we have the proposition whose proof is given in the appendix:

Proposition 5. *If time increases indefinitely, the consumption and capital of country i tend to one of the infinity of steady states defined by:* $0 < k_i^* < k^*, c_i^* = (1 + \lambda^{(1-b)/b} - \delta - gG)k_i^*$, *and selected by the initial value of the capital stock,* k_{i0}.

Hence, we still have a property of hysteresis and non-convergence. Bajona and Kehoe establish that in many circumstances the difference in the outputs per worker between country i and the world, $\frac{|y_{it}/L_i' - y_t/L'|}{y_t/L'}$, permanently *decreases* over time. These authors call this property *convergence* although this difference does not tend to zero.

It would be repetitive to analyze the third case of endogenous contraction of the world economy when condition (48) is satisfied, but we can easily see that we still have an hysteresis property for the consumption and capital of country i deflated by the contraction trend.

We have assumed in the whole section that both countries are inside the cone of diversification. This assumption is not innocent. For instance, Bajona and Kehoe (2010) show that in some circumstances even if all countries start in the cone of diversification, some necessarily will leave it in the future.[16]

[16]These authors obtain sufficient conditions under which factor price equalization in a given period ensures factor price equalization in all future periods. Unfortunately, these conditions do not cover many cases for which the only solution is to simulate the model.

5. Extensions

In the first subsection we assume that the South has a higher preference for the future and a much smaller size than the North; we establish that free trade allows South to grow faster than North. In the second subsection we introduce a third intermediary good, which gives rise to a new growth regime, where capital cost is higher in the South and labor cost is higher in the North. Although this regime is only transitory, it can last for a long period of time.

5.1. *Eastern Asia Openness and High Growth*

The results of the previous section could give the impression that international trade prevents poor countries from catching-up with the rich ones. As catching-up is possible in the absence of international trade, the message looks as recommending poor countries to close their borders and adopt a policy of self-centered growth if they want to develop.[17] Here, we will strongly qualify this interpretation by showing that openness, although being by itself insufficient, is an essential element of a strategy of fast growth.

We assume that the South is very small in comparison to the North and so that its effects on the dynamics of the world model are negligible and that this dynamics is practically the same as for the North model. We assume that condition (41) is satisfied for the North and so that we are in the case of Proposition 2, with the world dynamics determined by a neo-classical exogenous growth model. We also assume that the North and the world economy are in their steady state equilibrium and that the discount factor is higher in the South: $\beta_S > \beta_N$, that is that the South has higher preference for the

[17]The fact that autarky, at the difference of free trade, allows for the convergence of the South to the North economy does not mean that it also raises the intertemporal welfare of the South. Cunat and Maffezoli's simulations (2004) reach the opposite conclusion that the welfares of the South and the North are higher under free trade (see Section 5.2). We already knew from the first welfare theorem, and factor-price equalization that hold in all periods under free trade, that the free trade equilibrium, but not the autarky one, is Pareto optimal.

future.[18] Then, the state-space form of the model of the South is:

$$\begin{pmatrix} c_{S,t+1} \\ k_{S,t+1} \end{pmatrix} = \begin{pmatrix} (\beta_S/\beta_N)^{1/\theta} & 0 \\ -1/g & (1+r^*-\delta)/g \end{pmatrix} \begin{pmatrix} c_{St} \\ k_{St} \end{pmatrix} + \begin{pmatrix} 0 \\ w'^* L'_S/g \end{pmatrix} \tag{54}$$

with k_{S0} given, the condition of transversality (33): $\lim_{t\to\infty}(\beta_S g^{1-\theta})^t$ $k_{St}(c_{St}/c_{S0})^{-\theta} = 0$ and $\beta_N g^{1-\theta} < \beta_S g^{1-\theta} < 1$.

This dynamic system has no steady state. However, define: $G = (\beta_S/\beta_N)^{1/\theta} > 1$, $c'_{St} = c_{St}/G^t$ and $k'_{St} = [k_{St} + w'^* L'_S/(1+r^*-\delta-g)]/G^t$. The model rewritten with these new variables becomes:

$$\begin{pmatrix} c'_{S,t+1} \\ k'_{S,t+1} \end{pmatrix} = \begin{pmatrix} 1 & 0 \\ -1/(gG) & (1+r^*-\delta)/(gG) \end{pmatrix} \begin{pmatrix} c'_{St} \\ k'_{St} \end{pmatrix} \tag{55}$$

with $k'_{S0} = k_{S0} + w'^* L'_S/(1+r^*-\delta-g)$ given, $\lim_{t\to\infty}[\beta_S(gG)^{1-\theta}]^t$ $k'_{St}(c'_{St}/c'_{S0})^{-\theta} = 0$.

We proceed as in Section 4.4. The model with its new variables has an infinity of steady states, which satisfy the equation: $[r^* - \delta - (gG-1)]k'^*_S = c'^*_S$ and can be parameterized by k'^*_S. The first equation of the dynamic system is: $c'_{S,t+1} = c'_{St} = c'^*_S$. From the second equation we deduce: $k'_{S,t+1} - k'^*_S = \frac{1+r^*-\delta}{gG}(k'_{St} - k'^*_S) = \left(\frac{1+r^*-\delta}{gG}\right)^{t+1}(k'_{S0} - k'^*_S)$. With Equation (42) we get: $\frac{1+r^*-\delta}{gG} = \frac{1}{\beta_N g^{1-\theta}(\beta_S/\beta_N)^{1/\theta}}$. We make the supplementary assumption that the discount factor of the South is not too high: $\beta_S/\beta_N < 1/(\beta_N g^{1-\theta})^\theta$. Then, we have: $(1+r^*-\delta)/(gG) > 1$, and we deduce that the only steady state value of the stock of capital such that $k'_{S,t+1}$ converges to it when time increases indefinitely is: $k'^*_S = k'_{S0}$. Hence, we have established that the economy of the South (with its variables

[18]The discrepancy between β_S and β_N is a way of modeling an active government policy of investment support (through subsidies, preferential access to cheap credit, etc.). Such a policy can be justified by assuming that the government is more far-sighted than its people, takes into account the welfare of future generations, etc. A good illustration of our assumption is the Republics of Korea from 1962, when it was poor and started a policy of fast growth based on high investment and exports. See the excellent book by Studwell (2013).

expressed in intensive form) instantaneously settles on a balanced growth path: $c_{St} = c_{S0}G^t$, $k_{St} + \frac{w'^*L'_S}{1+r^*-\delta-g} = \left(k_{S0} + \frac{w'^*L'_S}{1+r^*-\delta-g}\right)G^t$, $c_{S0} = (1+r^*-\delta-g)\left(k_{S0} + \frac{w'^*L'_S}{1+r^*-\delta-g}\right)$. The expansion growth rate G increases with the discount factor in the South's preferences β_S that is with its taste for the future.

We can have a good and intuitive understanding of this result in the Ventura's case, when good A only uses capital and good B only uses labor in its production. Strong investment in the South increases its supply of good A. But as this supply is a small share of world supply, its price, which is proportional to the return on capital, does not decrease. If the South could not export its higher supply of good A and had to absorb it locally, its price and the return on capital would decrease, which would progressively ruin the growth effect of the South's low discount of the future. In our more general case, an application of the Rybczynski theorem shows that higher investment in the South still induces a higher production of good A, but also a lower production of good B. The South's imports of the former good (which is capital intensive, e.g. manufacturing) decrease over time. In this model, economic growth leads to structural transformation and not to capital deepening (Ventura, 1997). The conclusion of this subsection is that a poor country can grow at fast rate if it opens to international trade and adopts a policy of encouragement to investment and exports.

5.2. *Incomplete Specialization and Partial Factor Price Equalization*

In the previous section we compared the case of free trade where each country produced the two goods, to the case of autarky. Cunat and Maffezzoli (2004) analyze an important intermediary case. Their model, like the Ventura (1997) one, assumes that a first (intermediary) good is produced out of capital and a second good is produced out of labor. But it adds a third good whose production requires capital and labor. The concept of diversification cone is easily extended to the one of *factor price equalization set*: If the factor endowments of both countries are inside this set, each country produces the three goods and shares the same factor prices with its partner. Otherwise, if these endowments are outside this set, we obtain a new regime where North specializes in the production of the capital intensive and mixed goods, and South in the production of the latter and the labor intensive good. Then, the two countries trade with each other, but the cost of capital is higher in the South and the cost of labor is higher in the North.

We saw in Section 3 and 4 that under free trade and factor price equalization, the factor costs are determined by the *world* factor endowment; under autarky the factor costs in each country are determined by *its own* factor endowment. In the new regime introduced by Cunat and Maffezzoli, the factor costs in each country are determined by the factor endowments of *both countries*.

Cunat and Maffezzoli assume that the world economy is in the situation of our Proposition 2: its dynamics is given by a neoclassical Ramsey exogenous growth model. Their most important result is that if the initial endowments of North and South sufficiently differ (are outside the factor price equalization set), their respective growths will occur in the new regime for a long period of time. At the end of this period, growth enters a regime similar to the one described in Section 4.4, where factor prices equalize between countries. Hence, the solution of the model of the two authors has still the hysteresis property that the capital and consumption per capita of the South converge to lower values than in the North. However, even if there is no catching up, the South grows faster than the North when they are in the new regime.

6. More Reading

Chapters 1–3 of Feenstra (2004) give an excellent presentation of the Heckscher–Ohlin model and its extensions. They differ from our Sections 2 and 3 by making as general as possible assumptions on technology and preferences instead of using parametric specifications of the production and utility functions. Feenstra discusses what happens to the main results in the presence of factor intensity reversal, or if the factor endowment of a country is outside the cone of diversification. He also extends the results to the case where the number of goods or factor inputs is larger than two. When, these numbers are still the same, the factor-price equalization theorem generalizes well. The Stolper–Samuelson and the Rybczynski theorems continue to hold, though not quite as strong as in the two-by-two case. If the number of factors is higher than the number of goods, factor-price equalization does not hold. It continues to hold if there are more goods than factors, if the factor endowments do not differ too much across countries (more precisely if they belong to a factor price equalization set, which generalizes the concept of diversification cone, as in Section 5.2),but in this case the amounts of production occurring in each country is indeterminate.

A brief and clear reference for the Ramsey and Rebelo AK models can be found in (Benassy, 2011). For more advanced material the reader can refer to (Acemoglu, 2009) or to (Barro and Sala-i-Martin, 2004).

The infinity of steady states and the property of hysteresis rest on the assumption that the interest rate (that is the return on capital minus its depreciation rate) in each country is determined in the long run by parameters that have the same value in both of them (see Equation (4.2)). Baxter (1992) notes that interest rates also depend on the domestic taxation regime and that distortionary taxes can create a wedge between those prevailing in the two nations. In this case, we cannot have factor price equalization and one of the two countries, at least, specializes in the production of a unique good. Then, the steady state of each economy is unique and independent of initial conditions. An important conclusion of this author is that a small change in taxes may induce a radical change in specialization. Another way of getting rid of the infinity of steady states is to assume that the production functions of the two countries differ by Hicks-neutral factors (Brecher, Chen and Choudhri, 2002). However, in this case factor price equalization does not hold and the Hecksher-Ohlin theorem is not valid anymore. A last way of obtaining a unique and stable steady state is to introduce an adjustment cost in capital accumulation and allow trade in domestic and foreign securities (Ono and Shabata, 2005).

Ventura (1997) was the first to make the assumption, which greatly simplifies the analysis, that investment and consumption combine the intermediary goods in the same proportion (or are made of the same final good). Older papers and some more recent ones (Bardhan, 1965, Oniki and Uzawa, 1965, Stiglitz, 1970, Smith, 1984, Baxter, 1992, Chen, 1992, Deardroff, 2001, Brecher, Chen and Choudhri, 2002, Ono and Shibata, 2005) make the different assumption, usual in closed economy neoclassical two-sector growth models, that investment is entirely made of one of the two goods and consumption is made of the other. These models are more difficult to analyze and may exhibit complicated dynamics (for instance the model of Chen, 1992, may display in some circumstances a two-period limit cycle).

Bardhan (1965), Oniki and Uzawa (1965) and Smith (1984) assume an exogenous and constant saving rate instead of deducing its value from the consumer intertemporal preferences. They find that the capital per capita of each country converges to the same steady state and so that international trade vanishes in the long run. Hence, they obtain the same conditional convergence as in the Ramsey (or Solow) growth model of a closed economy. This result contrasts with ours of an infinity of steady states (each corresponding to a different saving rate), and the selection of the one to which the economy converges by the value of the initial stock of capital (the hysteresis property). Then, there is still international trade in the long run. Deardoff (2001) and Ventura (2004) use an overlapping generation framework in which savings are a fixed proportion of wages. They also find that the economy of each country converges to a unique steady state, or to one of a small number of possible steady states,[19] instead of the infinity that we obtain with our intertemporal preferences modelling.

---

[19]If the number of stable steady states is larger than one, these models give a theoretical explanation of the existence of clubs convergence, where poor countries converge to a low steady state while rich countries converge to a high one, identified by many empirical studies. Countries, which converge to different steady states, continue to trade in the long run.

Chatterjee and Shukayev (2012) show that, when hit by country-specific productivity shocks, the stock of capital of a small open economy converges to the same invariant distribution, with support including the entire diversification cone, independently of initial conditions. Hence, the long-run average income of this economy is also independent of its initial conditions and the hysteresis property is no more valid. These authors also establish by a series of simulations that the bigger the amplitude of the shocks, the faster the convergence. They obtain again the property of hysteresis when the shock amplitude tends to zero, but also if the productivity shocks are common to the two countries. Hence, uncertainty is not sufficient to get rid of this property.

7. Conclusion

We have presented a dynamic extension of the Heckscher–Ohlin model to investigate the interaction between international trade and growth. Our model encompasses the Ramsey exogenous and the AK endogenous growth approach.

Our main result is that a poor country may grow faster than the rich ones, but remains permanently poorer. However, this conclusion is reached under the assumption of the same preferences for the future for all nations. If this preference is higher in the poor country, it can grow at faster rate and eventually become itself rich. This result is consistent with the fast development of Eastern Asia since the 1960s or 1980s.

Appendix

Proof of Proposition 1

The first equations of the model are:

- The expression of the price ratio of the intermediary goods, given by Equation (21):

$$\left(\frac{P_{At}}{P_{Bt}}\right)^{b/(1-b)} = \frac{\alpha_B^{1/(1-b)}\left(k_t/\lambda\right)^b + \beta_B^{1/(1-b)}\left(L'/\mu\right)^b}{\alpha_A^{1/(1-b)}\left(k_t/\lambda\right)^b + \beta_A^{1/(1-b)}\left(L'/\mu\right)^b} \tag{A.1}$$

- Equation (28), which norms the price of these goods:

$$P_{At}^{-b/(1-b)} + P_{Bt}^{-b/(1-b)} = 1 \tag{A.2}$$

- The expression of the factor prices given by Equations (8a) and (8b):

$$\left(\frac{r_t}{P_{At}}\right)^{b/(1-b)} = \frac{\Delta}{\beta_B^{1/(1-b)} - \beta_A^{1/(1-b)} \left(P_{At}/P_{Bt}\right)^{b/(1-b)}} \tag{A.3}$$

$$\left(\frac{w_t'}{P_{At}}\right)^{b/(1-b)} = \frac{\Delta}{-\alpha_B^{1/(1-b)} + \alpha_A^{1/(1-b)} \left(P_{At}/P_{Bt}\right)^{b/(1-b)}} \tag{A.4}$$

We easily deduce:

$$\left(\frac{r_t}{P_{At}}\right)^{b/(1-b)} = \alpha_A^{b/(1-b)} + \beta_A^{b/(1-b)} \left(\frac{\lambda L'}{\mu k_t}\right)^b,$$

$$\left(\frac{r_t}{P_{Bt}}\right)^{b/(1-b)} = \alpha_B^{b/(1-b)} + \beta_B^{b/(1-b)} \left(\frac{\lambda L'}{\mu k_t}\right)^b,$$

$$\left(\frac{w_t'}{P_{At}}\right)^{b/(1-b)} = \frac{\alpha_A^{b/(1-b)} + \beta_A^{b/(1-b)} [\lambda L'/(\mu k_t)]^b}{[\lambda L'/(\mu k_t)]^b},$$

$$\left(\frac{w_t'}{P_{Bt}}\right)^{b/(1-b)} = \frac{\alpha_B^{b/(1-b)} + \beta_B^{b/(1-b)} [\lambda L'/(\mu k_t)]^b}{[\lambda L'/(\mu k_t)]^b}.$$

Finally, we obtain Equations (39).

Other equations are:

- The expression of the factor inputs needed for one unit of production, given by Equations (10):

$$a_{KAt} = \left(\alpha_A P_{At}/r_t\right)^{1/(1-b)}, \quad a_{LAt} = \left(\beta_A P_{At}/w_t'\right)^{1/(1-b)},$$

$$a_{KBt} = \left(\alpha_B P_{Bt}/r_t\right)^{1/(1-b)}, \quad a_{LBt} = \left(\beta_B P_{Bt}/w_t'\right)^{1/(1-b)}$$

(A.5–A.8)

- The expression of the world production of the two intermediary goods, given by Equations (16a) and (16b):

$$x_{At} = \left(a_{LBt}k_t - a_{KBt}L'\right)/\Delta'_t = \left[\left(\beta_B r_t/P_{At}\right)^{1/(1-b)} k_t - \left(\alpha_B w'_t/P_{At}\right)^{1/(1-b)} L'\right]/\Delta \tag{A.9}$$

$$x_{Bt} = \left(-a_{LAt}k_t + a_{KAt}L'\right)/\Delta'_t = \left[-\left(\beta_A r_t/P_{Bt}\right)^{1/(1-b)} k_t + \left(\alpha_A w'_t/P_{Bt}\right)^{1/(1-b)} L'\right]/\Delta \tag{A.10}$$

We easily deduce Equations (40).
Another equation is the expression of the production of final good given by Equation (26):

$$y_t = \left(x_{At}^b + x_{Bt}^b\right)^{1/b} \tag{A.11}$$

We easily deduce Equation (36).
The last equations are:

- The accounting identities that determine the investment of the period and the capital at the beginning of the next period, which are Equations (29) and (30) and from which we deduce Equations (35).
- As the consumers share the same preferences (Equation (31)), they maximize their intertemporal welfare given by Equation (34). We obtain the Euler equation and the transversality conditions of the consumer program (37) and (38) (consistent with Equations (32) and (33)). □

Proof of Proposition 2

We begin by computing the steady state of the dynamic system and establish under which condition it exists. First, from Equation (37) we obtain the value of the return on capital (42). Then, from Equation (39) we obtain the stock of capital (Equation (42)). This equation has a solution if $r^{*b/(1-b)} > \lambda$, which gives condition (41). The other equations are direct applications of Equations (35) and (36).

Then, we compute the linear approximation of the model in the neighborhood of its steady state and obtain:

$$\begin{pmatrix} dc'_{t+1} \\ dk_{t+1} \end{pmatrix} = \begin{pmatrix} 1 & a_{12} \\ -1/g & a_{22}/g \end{pmatrix} \begin{pmatrix} dc'_t \\ dk_t \end{pmatrix} \tag{A.12}$$

with

$$\begin{aligned} c'_t &= c_t/[\beta g^{-\theta}(1+r_t-\delta)]^{1/\theta}, \\ a_{12} &= -\frac{1-b}{\theta}\frac{r^{*b/(1-b)}-\lambda}{r^{*b/(1-b)}}\frac{r^*}{1+r^*-\delta}\frac{c^*}{k^*}, \\ a_{22} &= 1+r^*-\delta-a_{12}, \\ dk_0 &= k_0-k^* \end{aligned}$$

given.

The dynamic system determines the world equilibrium in period t (the values of dc'_t and dk_{t+1}) in function of the value of the predetermined variable, which is the stock of capital at the beginning of the period dk_t, and the value of the anticipated variable that is the discounted consumption in the following period dc'_{t+1}. We define a solution of the model as a path of its variables, which satisfies its equations for a given initial value of the predetermined variable dk_0 and which tends to satisfy the equations determining the steady state when time increases indefinitely. It is a standard result of the theory of growth that a path, which does not satisfy this requirement, violates the transversality condition. Blanchard and Kanh (1980) established (under some regularity conditions that are satisfied here) that a necessary and sufficient condition for the existence and uniqueness of a solution is that the number of eigenvalues of modulus less than or equal to one of the linear approximation of the model is equal to the number of its predetermined variables. Then, the number of eigenvalues of modulus larger than one is equal to the number of anticipated variables (see Laffargue, 2004 for technical complements).

The eigenvalues of the system are the roots of the second degree polynomial $P(\Lambda)$ defined by Equation (45). We have: $P(0) = (1 + r^* - \delta)/g > 0$ and $P(1) = a_{12}/g < 0$. Hence, the two eigenvalues are real and positive. One Λ_1 is smaller than one and the other Λ_2 is larger than one. The Blanchard and Kanh's conditions are satisfied and the model determines a unique path for its endogenous variables in the neighborhood of its steady state. Finally, we can easily prove that $dk_{t+1} = \Lambda_1 dk_t$. □

Proof of Proposition 3

k_t increases indefinitely with t. Hence, r_t decreases to $\lambda^{(1-b)/b} > 1/(\beta g^{-\theta}) - 1 + \delta$. The expansion rate of consumption $c_{t+1}/c_t = [\beta g^{-\theta}(1 + r_{t+1} - \delta)]^{1/\theta}$ decreases and tends to $G = [\beta g^{-\theta}(1 + \lambda^{(1-b)/b} - \delta)]^{1/\theta} > 1$. We define the new intensive variables by dividing the former ones, c_t, k_t, i_t, y_t, by G^t. There will be no ambiguity by keeping the same notation for them. The model becomes (after the elimination of i_t and y_t):

$$gGk_{t+1} = -c_t + \left[\lambda\left(k_t/\lambda\right)^b + \mu\left(L'G^{-t}/\mu\right)^b\right]^{1/b} + (1-\delta)\, k_t \tag{A.13}$$

$$c_{t+1} = \left[\beta\,(gG)^{-\theta}\left(1 + r_{t+1} - \delta\right)\right]^{1/\theta} c_t \tag{A.14}$$

$$r_t = \left\{\lambda + \mu\left[\left(L'G^{-t}/\mu\right)/\left(k_t/\lambda\right)\right]^b\right\}^{(1-b)/b} \tag{A.15}$$

$$\lim_{t\to\infty} \left[\beta\,(gG)^{1-\theta}\right]^t k_t\,(c_t/c_0)^{-\theta} = 0 \tag{A.16}$$

We set $\tau = 1/t$. Then, the steady state of the model is given by: $\tau = 0$, $r^* = \lambda^{(1-b)/b}$, $c^* = \lambda^{1/b}(k^*/\lambda)^b - (gG - 1 + \delta)\, k^*$. Hence, there are an infinity of steady states, parameterized by the stock of capital $0 < k^* < \bar{k}$, where $\bar{k}$ is the positive root of the right-hand side of the last equation.

We compute the linear approximation of the model in the neighborhood of a steady state and obtain $dr_t = 0$ and:

$$\begin{pmatrix} dc_{t+1} \\ dk_{t+1} \end{pmatrix} = \begin{pmatrix} 1 & 0 \\ -1/(gG) & \left(1 + \lambda^{(1-b)/b} - \delta\right)/(gG) \end{pmatrix} \begin{pmatrix} dc_t \\ dk_t \end{pmatrix} \tag{A.17}$$

The model has one anticipated variable, c_t, and one predetermined variable, k_t. It has one eigenvalue equal to one. The other eigenvalue is: $\frac{1+\lambda^{(1-b)/b}-\delta}{gG} = \frac{1}{\beta(gG)^{1-\theta}} > 1$. The Blanchard and Kahn's conditions are satisfied. Hence, there exists a unique solution path of the model, which is selected by the initial stock of capital. □

Proof of Proposition 4

k_t decreases indefinitely with t. Hence, r_t increases to $\lambda^{(1-b)/b} < 1/(\beta g^{-\theta}) - 1 + \delta$. The expansion rate of consumption $c_{t+1}/c_t = [\beta g^{-\theta}(1+r_{t+1}-\delta)]^{1/\theta}$ increases and tends to $G = [\beta g^{-\theta}(1+\lambda^{(1-b)/b} - \delta)]^{1/\theta} < 1$. Hence, capital, production, investment and consumption, in their intensive form, tend to zero. They will tend to zero in their original form if $gG < 1$. If $gG > 1 > G$, they will asymptotically grow at rate gG in their original form.

We make the same change of variables as in the proof of Proposition 3 and follow the same analysis. Then, we obtain the same hysteresis result. □

Proof of Proposition 5

The model of country i (Equation (52)) can be rewritten:

$$\begin{pmatrix} c_{i,t+1} \\ k_{i,t+1} \end{pmatrix} = \begin{pmatrix} \left[\beta\,(gG)^{-\theta}\,(1+r_{t+1}-\delta)\right]^{1/\theta} & 0 \\ -1/\,(gG) & (1+r_t-\delta)\,/\,(gG) \end{pmatrix} \times \begin{pmatrix} c_{it} \\ k_{it} \end{pmatrix} + \begin{pmatrix} 0 \\ w'_t L'_i/\,(gG) \end{pmatrix} \tag{A.18}$$

We deduce from Equations (39): $\frac{w'_t L'_i}{G^t} = [\lambda(\frac{k_t}{\lambda}\frac{\mu}{L'}\frac{1}{G^{bt/(1-b)}})^b + \frac{\mu}{G^{bt/(1-b)}}]^{(1-b)/b} L'_i$ and $r_t = [\lambda + \mu(\frac{L'}{\mu}\frac{\lambda}{k_t}\frac{1}{G^t})^b]^{(1-b)/b}$. When t increases indefinitely, the model has an infinity of steady states, given in the proposition. In the neighborhood of one of them we have: $d(w'_t L'_i/G^t) = 0$ and $dr_t = (1-b)\lambda^{(1-b)/b} dk_t/k^*$. The linear approximation of the model in this neighborhood is:

$$\begin{pmatrix} dc_{i,t+1} \\ dk_{i,t+1} \end{pmatrix} = \begin{pmatrix} 1 & 0 \\ -\frac{1}{gG} & \frac{1+\lambda^{(1-b)/b}-\delta}{gG} \end{pmatrix} \begin{pmatrix} dc_{it} \\ dk_{it} \end{pmatrix} + \begin{pmatrix} \frac{(1-b)\lambda^{(1-b)/b}}{\theta(1+\lambda^{(1-b)/b}-\delta)} c_i^* \frac{dk_t}{k^*} \\ 0 \end{pmatrix} \tag{A.19}$$

with dk_{i0} given.

This dynamic system has one predetermined variable dk_{it} and one anticipated variable dc_{it}. It has one eigenvalue equal to one and the other equal to $\frac{1+\lambda^{(1-b)/b}-\delta}{gG} = \frac{1}{\beta(gG)^{1-\theta}} > 1$. The Blanchard and Kahn's condition are satisfied and the steady state is selected by the initial condition. □

Acknowledgment

We thank the participants of the Ninth IEFS China Annual Conference, July 26–28, 2017, UIBE, Beijing, for helpful comments and suggestions.

References

Acemoglu, D. (2009). *Introduction to Modern Economic Growth.* Princeton, NJ: Princeton University Press.

Atkeson, A. and Kehoe, P.J. (2000). Paths of development for early- and late-bloomers in a dynamic Heckscher–Ohlin model, Federal Reserve Bank of Minneapolis, Research Department Staff Report 256.

Bajona, C. and Kehoe, T.J. (2010). Trade, growth, and convergence in a dynamic Heckscher–Ohlin model, *Review of Economic Dynamics*, 13, 487–513.

Bardhan, P.K. (1965). Equilibrium growth in the international economics, *Quarterly Journal of Economics*, 49, 455–64.

Barro, R.J. (1991). Economic growth in a cross section of countries, *Quarterly Journal of Economics*, 106, 407–443.

Barro, R.J. and Sala-i-Martin, X. (2004). *Economic Growth*, 2nd Ed. Cambridge, MA: The MIT Press.

Baxter, M. (1992). Fiscal policy, specialization, and trade in the two-sector model: The return of Ricardo? *Journal of Political Economy*, 100, 713–744.

Bénassy, J.P. (2011). *Macroeconomic Theory.* Oxford: Oxford University Press.

Blanchard, O. and Kahn, C.M. (1980). The solution of linear difference models under rational expectations, *Econometrica*, 48, 1305–1313.

Brecher, R.A., Chen, Z. and Choudhri, E.U. (2002). Absolute and comparative advantage reconsidered: The pattern of international trade with optimal saving, *Review of International Economics*, 10, 645–656.

Chatterjee, P. and Shukayev, M. (2012). A stochastic dynamic model of trade and growth: Convergence and diversification, *Journal of Economic Dynamics and Control*, 36(3), 416–432.

Chen, Z. (1992). Long-run equilibria in a dynamic Heckscher–Ohlin model. *Canadian Journal of Economics*, 25, 923–943.

Cunat, A. and Maffezzoli, M. (2004). Neoclassical growth and commodity trade, *Review of Economic Dynamics*, 7, 707–736.

Deardoff, A.V. (2001). Rich and poor countries in neoclassical trade and growth, *The Economic Journal*, 111(470), 277–294.

Feenstra, R.C. (2004). *Advanced International Trade: Theory and Evidence,* Princeton, NJ: Princeton University Press.

Jones, L.E. and Manuelli, R.E. (1990). A convex model of equilibrium growth: Theory and policy implications, *Journal of Political Economy,* 98(5), 1008–1038.

Laffargue, J.P. (2004). A sufficient condition for the existence and the uniqueness of a solution in macroeconomic models with perfect foresight, *Journal of Economic Dynamics and Control,* 28, 1955–1975.

Oniki, H. and Uzawa, H. (1965). Patterns of trade and investment in a dynamic model of international trade, *Review of Economic Studies,* 32, 15–38.

Ono, Y. and Shibata, A. (2005). Fiscal spending, relative-price dynamics, and welfare in a world economy, *Review of International Economics,* 13(2), 216–236.

Rybczynski, T.N. (1955). Factor endowments and relative commodity prices, *Economica,* 22, 336–341.

Samuelson, P.A. (1949). International factor-price equalization once again, *Economic Journal,* 59, 181–197.

Samuelson, P.A. (1953–54). The price of goods and factors in general equilibrium, *Review of Economic Studies,* 21, 1–20.

Smith, A. (1984). Capital theory and trade theory, in *Handbook of International Economics,* Vol. 1, P.B. Kenen, and R.W. Jones (eds.). Amsterdam: Elsevier, pp. 289–324.

Stiglitz, J.E. (1970). Factor price equalization in a dynamic economy, *Journal of Political Economy,* 78, 456–488.

Stolper, W.F. and Samuelson, P.A. (1941). Protection and real wages, *Review of Economic Studies,* 9, 58–73.

Studwell, J. (2013). *How Asia Works. Success and Failure in the World's Most Dynamic Region.* NY: Grove Press.

Ventura, J. (1997). Growth and interdependence, *Quarterly Journal of Economics,* 112, 57–84.

Ventura, J. (2005). A global view of economic growth, in *Handbook of Economic Growth,* P. Aghion, and Durlauf, S. (eds.). North Holland, Amsterdam: Elsevier, pp. 1419–1497.

Chapter 12

Trade and Economic Growth: The Case of China

Tan Li*,‡ and Larry D Qiu†,§

**School of International Business,*
Southwestern University of Finance and Economics, China
†Faculty of Business and Economics,
The University of Hong Kong, Pok Fu Lam, Hong Kong
‡litan@swufe.edu.cn
§larryqiu@hku.hk

This chapter presents China's foreign trade performance since its economic reform and opening-up in 1978. Moreover, the current chapter reviews the literature on the effects of trade on economic growth in general and that on China in particular. Data from 1978 to 2015 in China show the strong correlation between trade and economic growth. To determine the causal effect, we compare a few coastal provinces (representing considerably open regions) with inland provinces (representing less open regions). We also perform a simple regression using data from all provinces. Evidence suggests that the increase in the export-to-GDP ratio leads to substantially high growth in terms of GDP per capita.

1. Introduction

China has undergone an unprecedented economic transformation since 1978, when it began its reform and opening-up. Prior to this reform, China was one of the poorest countries in the world, with its real GDP per capita a mere fortieth of that of the US level. With an average annual growth rate exceeding 8% thereafter,

China's real GDP per capita increased to USD 6500 (at 2010 constant price) in 2015, which is approximately one-eighth of the US level.[1] Meanwhile, China has also been rapidly integrating into the global economic system. Prior to 1980, China was a negligible player in the global market but eventually developed as the world's largest exporter of goods and commodities in 2009. China's share in world merchandise export surpassed 10% in 2010 and reached 14.2% in 2015. In addition, China is the second largest country in terms of merchandise import, comprising 10.3% of world import in 2015. Along with this impressive performance in terms of trade and economic growth, China's trade policy has undergone considerable changes. In particular, China has continuously lowered its tariff and nontariff barriers prior to and after its entry into the World Trade Organization (WTO). Consequently, China's trading rights have been completely liberalized, import quotas have been eliminated, and strong disciplines have been imposed on state trading enterprises and subsidies. Thus, China is an ideal field of investigation on the correlation between trade and economic growth.

We ask two questions in this chapter: Does trade boom promote economic growth in China? If yes, to what extent does trade contribute to economic growth? The answers to these two questions are significant for an improved understanding of the Chinese economic "miracle." Moreover, such answers are crucial for many other developing countries that endeavor to follow China's pattern to accelerate their economic development via trade liberalization.

2. Literature Review

2.1. *Literature on Trade and Economic Growth*

Trade and its relation to economic growth has been a central topic in the endogenous growth literature. New growth theories suggest that trade policies affect long-term economic growth through its influence on technological change. Grossman and Helpman (1992)

[1]Data are taken from the World Bank's World Development Indicator, and real GDP per capita is based on 2010 constant US dollar.

summarized that trade protection will promote economic growth if it encourages investment in research-intensive industries for countries with comparative advantage in these industries.

Causal observations and systematic empirical exercises suggest that countries with considerably open-oriented trade grow more rapidly than countries with substantially protectionist trade stance. The empirical literature on trade and economic development has two strands. One focuses on the relationship between *trade volume* and economic growth, whereas the other emphasizes on the effects of *trade policy* on economic growth. These two lines of literature have subtle differences. Rodriguez and Rodrik (2000) noted that the trade volume literature asks "Does international trade raise the growth rate of income?", whereas the trade policy literature asks "Do countries with low barriers to international trade grow rapidly?" Trade volumes are definitely related to trade policies. However, trade volumes are also determined by other forces, such as reduction in transport costs, shifts in world demand, and geographic factors. Therefore, their effects on economic development are not expected to be quantitatively the same.

The common difficulty in both lines of literature is the endogeneity issue. For example, consider a cross-national regression of income per capita on the ratio of trade to GDP. Such regression generally presents a moderate positive relation. However, the positive coefficient does not necessarily reflect the causal effect of trade on income because trade ratio (or trade volume) is endogenous. A similar logic applies to the trade policy literature, where most studies use import tariff rates or coverage ratio for nontariff barriers to measure the restrictiveness of a country's trade policy. Anderson and Neary (1992) developed a "trade restrictiveness index," which theoretically incorporates the effects of tariff and nontariff barriers. However, the use of trade restrictiveness measures does not alleviate the endogeneity problem. The reason is that tariff and nontariff barriers are also endogenous and may be correlated with other domestic policies that also affect economic growth.

Frankel and Romer (1999) recognized the aforementioned situation and used the geographical component of trade volumes as an instrument to identify the effects of trade on income levels. These authors determined a quantitatively larger effect of trade on income than the ordinary least squares (OLS) estimation method. Their results imply that the estimation bias in the OLS estimation does not overshadow the positive and robust effects of trade on income.

Overall, numerous studies empirically test the relation between trade policy or trade volume and economic growth. Harrison (1996) presented one of the early studies along this line, in which she used numerous indexes for trade openness and trade volume. Although the correlation between trade openness measures is not consistently strong, they are generally determined to have a positive effect on income levels. Yanikkaya (2003) followed Harrison (1996) and empirically tested the relationship between trade openness and income using cross-country data (including those on China). He used various measures for trade openness and determined that most measures are positively associated with economic growth. However, trade tariffs are found to be positively associated with growth, which is lacking in the study of Harrison (1996). Chang *et al.* (2009) further studied how the growth effect of trade openness differs under different policies. They built a model, in which gains from trade depend on the degree of labor market flexibility. They also presented a cross-country, panel data evidence that serves as proxies of educational investment, financial development, inflation stabilization, public infrastructure, and other reforms that affect the growth effects of trade openness.

Although early studies focus on answering whether trade influences economic growth at the aggregate level, researchers have recently developed interests to determine the channels through which trade may affect income. The endogenous growth models assert that the ultimate source of economic development originates from productivity growth. Given the increasing availability of micro-level data on firms and plants, the recent empirical literature endeavors to analyze the effects of trade liberalization on firm productivity. Pavcnik (2002), Amiti and Konings (2007), De Loecker (2007), and Topalova and Khandelwal (2011) provided confirming evidence of tariff reduction on firm productivity by using data from Chile, Indonesia, Slovenia, and India, respectively.

2.2. *Literature on Trade and Economic Growth in China*

Although China has been included in most cross-national studies, this country is also the exclusive subject of many studies. Previous studies rely on national aggregate data. Liu *et al.* (2002) used the quarterly data from 1981 to 1997 to analyze the relationship among China's export, foreign direct investment (FDI), and economic growth. These researchers applied the vector autoregression method and determined that export and economic growth are mutually reinforced. However, most studies in this line of literature address the issue by maximizing the extensive variation of trade and economic development across provinces and, over time, in China. Chen and Feng (2000) used provincial data from 1978 to 1989 and determined that international trade is positively associated with GDP growth. Yao (2006) also adopted panel data that cover 28 provinces over the period 1978–2000. He determined that export and FDI have positive effects on economic growth at the provincial level.

Regarding China's trade liberalization, Yu (2015) constructed a firm-specific tariff rate and analyzed the effects of tariff reduction on the productivity of Chinese firms. The OLS regressions show that an average of 10% tariff reduction will increase the productivity of a firm by 2% to 6%. Concerned with the potential endogeneity of tariff cuts: the author also conducted an instrumental variable estimation and obtained robust results. Liu and Qiu (2016) determined that tariff reductions in intermediate input imports in China actually reduce the incentive of Chinese firms to innovate as measured by their patent applications.

Industrial linkage may lead to positive or negative externality on firm productivity that results from trade liberalization. Bas and Causa (2013) considered the productivity effect of the regulation of upstream sectors on downstream manufacturing firms. The types of upstream regulation include input trade policy, product market regulation in nonmanufacturing sectors, and financial market reform. The preceding authors used the ORBIS data of Chinese manufacturing enterprises from 2001 to 2008. They constructed input trade policy indicators from the weighted average of tariffs on intermediate goods at the three-digit industry level for 50 manufacturing industries from 2003 to 2008. Econometric results show that these upstream policies have improved firm-level productivity. In particular, the input tariff cuts and deregulation of upstream sectors lead to considerably large productivity gains for downstream firms with close proximity to industrial technology frontiers. By contrast, financial reforms result in substantial productivity increase for firms that are distant from industry frontiers.

3. Facts on Trade and Economic Growth in China

This section describes the overall trade and income development in China, as well as presents a few stylized facts.

3.1. *Trade Performance of China*

The Chinese economy has been integrating into the world since 1979. The export and import rates of China have increased rapidly, particularly after Deng Xiaoping's southern tour in 1992.

Figure 1 and Table 1 show the trade performance of China at the macro level. The following observations are presented. First, China achieves high trade growth in terms of import and export, with the annual growth rate at over 20% in most of the years. Second, China maintains a high degree of openness, which is measured using trade-to-GDP ratio. For many years, China's trade-to-GDP ratio is over 40%, whereas export-to-GDP ratio is above 20%, which is extremely high for a large economy. Third, although the absolute value of export and import continued to increase, the trade-to-GDP and export-to-GDP ratios reached their peak in 2006. Lastly, China has experienced an overall trade surplus since 1990, and the size of the surplus has increased rapidly.

We observe that the merchandise export China as a share of global export has increased from approximately 1% prior to the opening-up of the economy to 14.2% in 2015. The share of China's

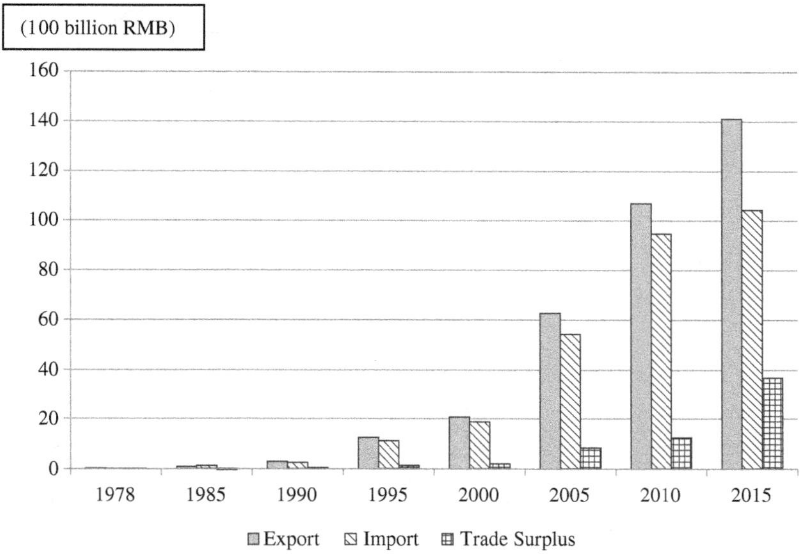

Figure 1. China's Trade Performance 1978–2015.

Source: *Chinese Statistical Yearbook*, various years.

Table 1. Openness of Chinese Economy.

	(%)									
	1978	1985	1990	1995	2000	2001	2002	2003	2004	2005
Trade/GDP	9.65	22.71	29.78	38.66	39.58	38.47	42.70	51.89	59.76	63.22
Export/GDP	4.56	8.89	15.99	20.48	20.80	20.09	22.39	26.72	30.71	33.88
	2006	2007	2008	2009	2010	2011	2012	2013	2014	2015
Trade/GDP	65.17	62.78	57.29	44.19	50.24	49.97	47.00	43.37	41.03	35.63
Export/GDP	35.87	35.20	31.97	24.06	26.65	26.05	24.90	23.04	22.34	20.49

Source: Trade and GDP data are from *Chinese Statistical Yearbook*, various years, and calculated by the authors.

merchandise import experienced a similar and steady increasing pattern. China's share of world import reached its peak at 10.6% in 2013 and slightly reverted to 10.3% two years thereafter. Moreover, China replaced Germany as the largest exporter in the world merchandise trade in 2009 and overtook the US as the leading trader

Table 2. China's Shares in World Merchandise Trade.

Year	China's export share in world (%)	China's import share in world (%)
1948	0.9	0.6
1953	1.2	1.6
1963	1.3	0.9
1973	1.0	0.9
1983	1.2	1.1
1993	2.5	2.7
2003	5.9	5.4
2006	8.2	6.5
2007	8.9	6.8
2008	9.1	7.0
2009	9.9	8.1
2010	10.6	9.3
2011	10.7	9.7
2012	11.4	10.0
2013	12.1	10.6
2014	12.7	10.5
2015	14.2	10.3

Source: WTO *World/International Trade Statistics*, various years.

in 2013. Since then, China has maintained its rank as the world's largest exporter of merchandise. China's merchandise import ranked second at the end of 2015. Table 2 summarizes the statistics of China's share in the world merchandise trade.

Figure 2 shows that capital goods take the largest share of China's import and export. Consumer goods and raw materials are the second largest product groups of China's export and import, respectively. This situation indicates that China is the world's production factory, that is, it imports materials and intermediate goods, turns them thereafter to consumption goods, and eventually exports them. This structure or pattern, which is called processing trade in China, has been maintained for many years. As domestic demand increases and China's labor cost increases, the emphasis will eventually shift in the future. Table 3 presents the distribution of Chinese exports on a considerably detailed classification of products.

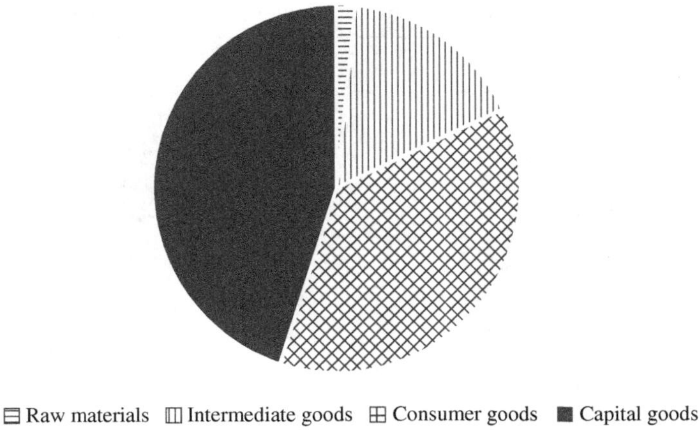

(a) **Exports**

(b) **Imports**

Figure 2. Components of Chinese Exports and Imports in 2015.

Source: *World Bank*, http://wits.worldbank.org/CountryProfile/en/Country/CHN/Year/2015/Summary.

Mechanical and electrical products are the leading products of Chinese exports, half of which are high-tech products in 2012.

The geographical configuration of China's trade has also been evolving. Table 4 presents China's top 10 exporting markets in 2001 and 2015. The five largest exporting markets have not changed in the

Table 3. Product Composite of Chinese Export in 2012.

Product	Export share (%)
Animal products	0.76
Chemicals	4.61
Food products	1.34
Footwear	2.87
Fuels	1.51
Hides and skins	1.55
Mechanical and electrical products	42.09
High tech products	21.28
Metals	7.28
Minerals	0.19
Miscellaneous	10.09
Plastic or rubber	3.79
Stone and glass	4.16
Textiles and clothing	12.01
Transportation	5.29
Vegetable	0.89
Wood	1.58

Source: HSBC China Trade Forecast 2014.

Table 4. China's Top 10 Export Partners.

	2001 (%)		2015 (%)
USA	20.43	USA	18.00
Hong Kong	17.49	Hong Kong	14.65
Japan	16.89	Japan	5.96
South Korea	4.70	South Korea	4.45
Germany	3.66	Germany	3.03
Netherlands	2.74	Vietnam	2.91
United Kingdom	2.55	United Kingdom	2.61
Singapore	2.18	Netherlands	2.61
Taipei	1.88	India	2.55
Italy	1.50	Singapore	2.33

Source: Bilateral trade data are from UN Comtrade data, and calculated by the authors.

Table 5. China's Top 10 Import Partners.

	2001 (%)		2015 (%)
Japan	17.57	South Korea	10.38
Taipei	11.22	USA	8.95
USA	10.76	Taipei	8.62
South Korea	9.60	Japan	8.51
Germany	5.65	Germany	5.21
Hong Kong	3.87	Australia	4.39
Russia	3.27	Malaysia	3.17
Malaysia	2.55	Brazil	2.64
Australia	2.23	Switzerland	2.45
Singapore	2.11	Thailand	2.21

Source: Bilateral trade data are from UN Comtrade data, and calculated by the authors.

entire period. However, considerable analysis will reveal that developing countries have consumed a larger percentage of Chinese export than before. In fact, non-organization for economic co-operation and development (OECD) countries have taken over OECD countries as China's primary export markets in 2012. Moreover, the share of non-OECD countries is expected to increase steadily in the future. The declining importance of the Japanese market for Chinese export is apparent; Japan's share of Chinese export decreased from 16.89% in 2001 to 5.96% in 2015. Although Vietnam's economy is relatively small, its share of Chinese export (2.91%) shows increasing economic ties between the two countries. Table 5 reports the top 10 importing countries of China in 2001 and 2015. China's neighboring countries, namely, Japan and South Korea, as well as the US, Germany, and Chinese Taipei, remain the top five importing partners. China also increases imports from emerging markets, such as Brazil and Thailand. Tables 4 and 5 show a few common features. China's export and import partners have been substantially diversified in the past 15 years, as illustrated by the decline of the shares of the leading trading partners.

Processing trade and foreign-invested enterprises (FIEs) have overshadowed others in the 1990s and 2000s. Figure 3 shows the

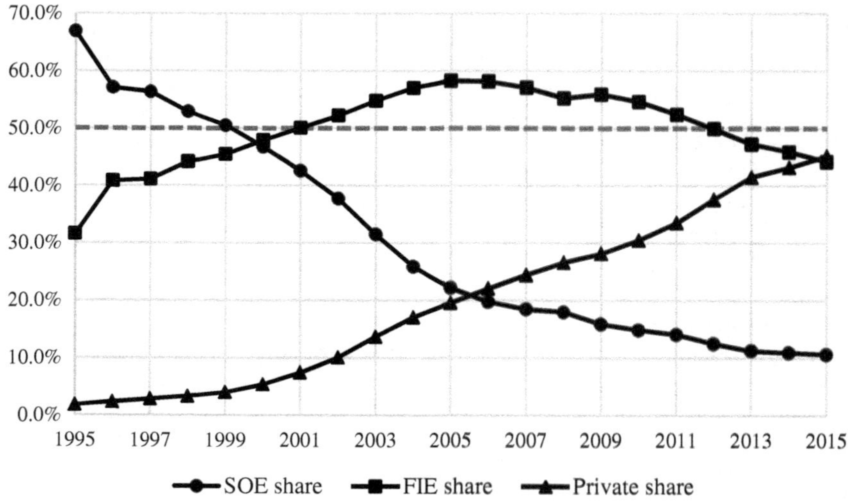

Figure 3. Ownership of Exporting Firms in China (1995–2015).

Source: Trade report by the Ministry of Commerce of China, various years.

evolution of export shares of state-owned enterprises (SOEs), FIEs, and private firms from 1994 to 2014. SOEs had dominated export activities until the end of 1990s. FIEs have replaced SOEs as the main exporting engines since the beginning of the 2000s. The prevalence of the FIE export during the 2000s is consistent with the proliferation of processing trade. Figure 4 describes the changes of processing and ordinary trades in China. The underlying reason for the co-movement is that FIEs in China engaged disproportionally more in processing trade than in ordinary trade.

The private sector in China's export started as an insignificant player but has experienced steady growth in the entire period. Domestic firms (i.e. SOEs and private firms) have overtaken FIEs as the dominant exporters from China since 2012. In 2015, private firms alone have even taken the leading role in Chinese exporting. The development of indigenous firms in China has resulted in the increase in the share of ordinary trade since 2010.

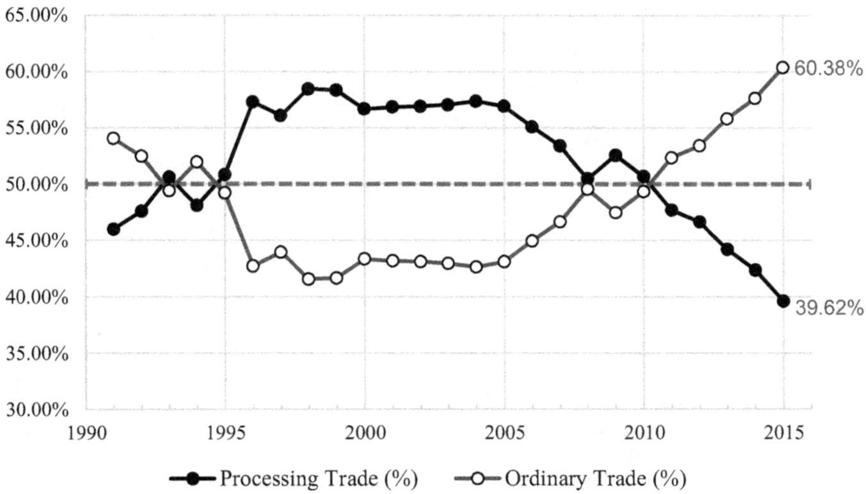

Figure 4. Processing Trade vs. Ordinary Trade in China (1990–2015).

Source: Trade report by the Ministry of Commerce of China, various years.

3.2. *Economic Growth in China and the Role of Trade*

China was a poor country in terms of living standard from the 1960s to the 1980s. The Chinese economy emerged when the country started its economic reform and adopted the opening-up policy in 1978. After 30 years of rapid growth, China has become the second largest economy in the world (after the US) and has entered the upper–middle income country list in terms of average income. Using the US as a benchmark, the GDP per capita of China converted using the current exchange rate (adjusted for inflation) in 1990 was only one-fiftieth of the level of the US. The rapid growth of the Chinese economy in the past three decades has successfully narrowed the gap. China's GDP per capita in 2015 is one-eighth of that of the US. The converted GDP by purchasing power parity (PPP) provides a similar scenario. The gap between the average income in China and that in the US will be considerably small if gauged using the PPP measures.

Table 6. GDP per capita of China and United States (1960–2015).

	China		United States	
	GDP per capita (constant 2010 US$)	GDP per capita, PPP	GDP per capita (constant 2010 US$)	GDP per capita, PPP
1960	192		17037	
1970	228		23310	
1980	348		28734	
1985	539		32307	
1990	731	987	36312	23954
1995	1228	1869	38678	28782
2000	1772	2933	45056	36450
2005	2738	5093	48756	44308
2010	4561	9333	48374	48374
2015	6497	14450	51638	56116

Source: *World Bank World Development Indicator.*

China's GDP per capita converted by PPP relative to the US level was approximately 1:25 in 1990 and converged to 1:4 in 2015. Table 6 presents the comparison of average income between China and the US.

We can observe the correlation between trade and economic development by combining the figures of trade and economic growth (see Figure 5). Moreover, Figure 5 shows the co-movement of the real GDP per capita and the significance of trade on an annual basis. Real per capita GDP is shown on the left axis. The right axes of Figures 5(a) and 5(b) show the trade-to-GDP and export-to-GDP ratios, respectively. Both panels present a similar pattern. Prior to 1978, the real GDP per capita vacillated below USD 300 (at 2010 constant price). During this pre-reform period, China's total trade barely exceeded 10% of the GDP, and the export rate did not increase above 5% of the GDP. After 1978, the export rate increased rapidly, particularly after 1990. After China's entry into WTO in 2001, the export-to-GDP ratio increased from 20% to its peak of 37% in 2006. The trade-to-GDP ratio follows a similar pattern as the export-to-GDP ratio. However, the level of trade-to-GDP ratio is nearly twice as large as the export-to-GDP ratio. Even during the

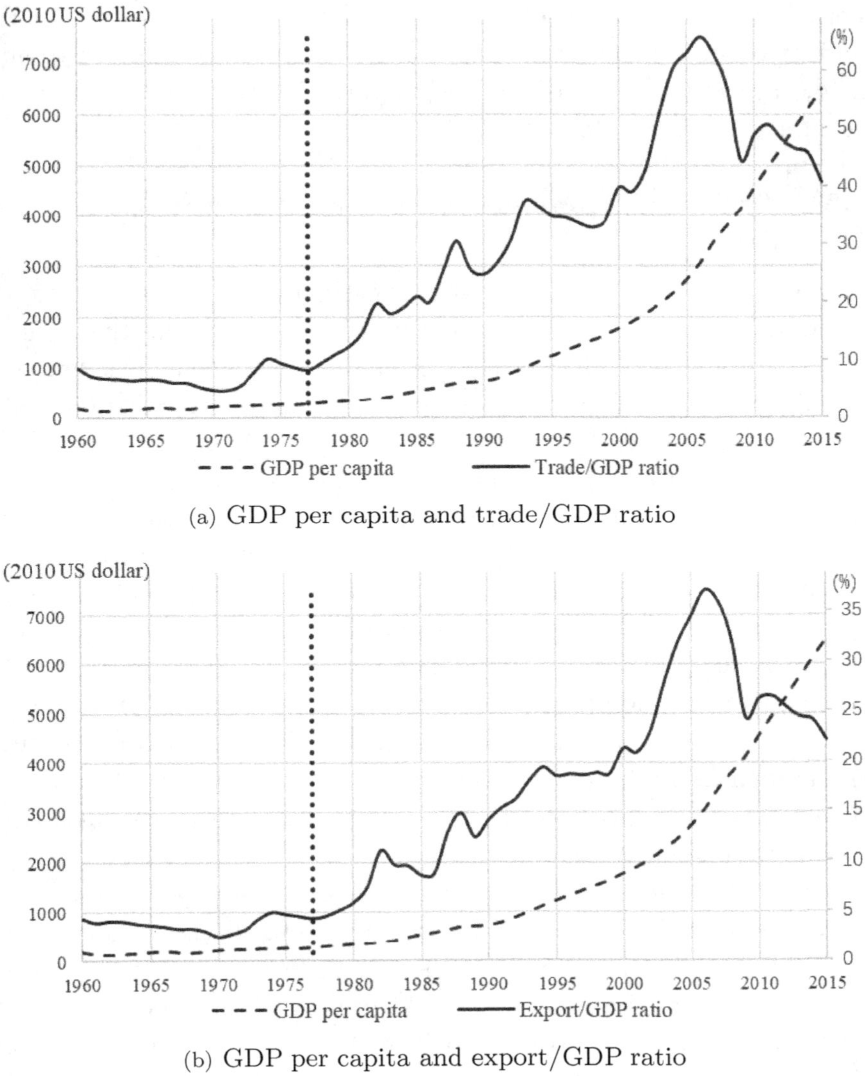

(a) GDP per capita and trade/GDP ratio

(b) GDP per capita and export/GDP ratio

Figure 5. GDP per capita and Trade Dependence in China.

Source: GDP per capita, trade and export data are from *Chinese Statistical Yearbook*, various years, and calculated by the authors.

period after the recent global financial crisis, China's trade-to-GDP and export-to-GDP ratios still maintained at approximately 45% and 25%, respectively. These two basic figures indicate that trade and economic growth go together in China.

3.3. *Trade and Economic Growth in Different Provinces*

Although the aggregate statistics of trade and income suggest a possible positive trade effect on growth in China, the result using national level data suffers from the endogeneity problem as highlighted in the literature. The use of trade and income data at the regional level can facilitate the mitigation of the problem. This situation is particularly true because different regions in China have diverse trade exposures and income disparities. Meanwhile, tariff and nontariff trade policies are decided by the central government; thus, trade policy is uniform in China.[2] These two features provide us with an ideal subject for studying the effect of trade on economic growth.

Many anecdotal stories support our conjecture that trade boom promotes economic growth. Coastal provinces, such as Guangdong and Fujian, grew faster than the country average and were substantially open in trade as well. Newspaper articles in the 1990s often related the rapid growth of the average income in the coastal areas to their abundant trade opportunities.

Table 7 provides a statistical comparison. We selected two coastal provinces with high trade exposure to the world (i.e. Guangdong and Fujian) and two inland provinces with low trade exposure (i.e. Heilongjiang and Shanxi). At the beginning of the opening-up in 1978, the low trade exposure provinces have higher average income than the coastal provinces. GDP per capita in Heilongjiang was 564, which is considerably higher than that in Guangdong (370) and Fujian (273). GDP per capita in Shanxi was 365, which is similar to that in Guangdong and higher than that in Fujian. The economic growth ever since has been substantial in the coastal areas.

[2]Except for a few trade facilitation policies in special economic zones.

Table 7. Income and Trade Exposure for Selected Provinces in China.

	High Trade Exposure Region				Low Trade Exposure Region		
Year	GDP per capita (Current RMB)	Trade/GDP ratio (%)	Export/GDP ratio (%)	Year	GDP per capita (Current RMB)	Trade/GDP ratio (%)	Export/GDP ratio (%)
A. Guangdong				*C. Heilongjiang*			
1978	370	60.29	52.61	1978	564	1.81	1.81
1985	1026	65.21	35.80	1985	1062	10.06	8.14
1990	2480	188.12	98.78	1990	2028	14.68	10.67
1995	8130	122.67	67.25	1995	5465	8.28	4.05
2000	12700	111.84	60.61	2000	8294	6.71	3.22
2005	24600	132.83	74.48	2005	14467	12.19	7.74
2010	44700	119.41	68.46	2010	27076	17.22	10.80
2014	63500	111.18	67.12	2014	39226	18.11	7.91
B. Fujian				*D. Shanxi*			
1978	273	21.36	20.04	1978	365	0.56	0.56
1985	741	31.46	19.45	1985	838	10.89	7.26
1990	1788	58.04	32.76	1990	1528	5.32	4.29
1995	6526	48.27	26.42	1995	3569	8.81	7.33
2000	11194	39.47	24.17	2000	5722	6.70	4.70
2005	18646	58.00	37.30	2005	12647	9.18	5.84
2010	40025	51.67	34.20	2010	26283	9.57	3.58
2014	63472	51.65	32.01	2014	35064	8.91	4.91

Source: Data are taken from *Chinese Statistical Yearbook*, and calculated by the authors.

Guangdong and Fujian had surpassed the threshold of USD 10,000 in GDP per capita in the late 1990s. In 2000, the average income in Heilongjiang and Shanxi was approximately two-thirds and one-half, respectively, of Guangdong's level. The rapid economic development in Guangdong and other coastal areas in the past four decades is closely related to the flourishing trade activities in the once neglected southern areas of China. Guangdong has attracted a large-scale processing trade in the early period of the opening-up, partially due to its proximity to Hong Kong, kinship, and network. The trade-to-GDP ratio in Guangdong has been above 100% since the late 1980s, and the export-to-GDP ratio has been approximately half of the trade/GDP ratio. Fujian, which is located in the northeast of Guangdong, has experienced a similar economic growth pattern as Guangdong province. GDP per capita in Fujian increased from RMB 273 in 1978 to RMB 11,000 in 2000, and further increased to RMB 63,000 in 2014. Trade exposure has been higher in Fujian than in all inland provinces, although not as outstanding as in Guangdong.

Panels C and D of Table 7 show the growth path for the two selected inland provinces, namely, Heilongjiang and Shanxi, respectively. The trade-to-GDP ratio has never exceeded 20% in Heilongjiang and was barely above 10% in Shanxi only in 1985. Economic growth was also considerably slow in these two provinces. GDP per capita in the inland provinces began at a high income level in 1978 but has lagged behind the coastal areas since 1990.

The distinction of economic growth path between other coastal and inland provinces provides a similar story: extensive trade activities are associated with substantially high economic growth and income level. Although the impact of trade on the local economy may not be as substantial as the case in Guangdong province, the statistics of each province indicate a positive relation between trade growth and economic development.

4. Simple Regression Analysis

The preceding section briefly analyzed the relation between trade growth and economic growth in China at the country level, as well as illustrated the regional difference based on a few representative provinces. This section provides a few econometric evidence on the extent by which trade contributes to economic growth in China. Accordingly, we explore the extensive variation in trade and economic development across 31 provinces from 1978 to 2012. Moreover, we use the following general production function, with GDP as a function of physical capital, human capital, arable land, trade, and technology:

$$Y_{it} = A_{it}F(K_{it}, Pop_{it}, H_{it}, N_{it}, Trade_{it}), \tag{1}$$

where Y is the GDP, K is the physical capital, Pop is the size of the labor force, H is the total human capital, N is the natural resource, *Trade* is the proxy for trade policy or trade outcome, and subscripts i and t are the province and time (year), respectively.

We obtain the function of GDP per capita by dividing the total production function by the population (or labor force):

$$y_{it} = A_{it}f(k_{it}, h_{it}, n_{it}, Trade_{it}), \tag{2}$$

where y is the GDP per capita, k is the physical capital per capita, h is the measured average human capital, and n is the natural resource per capita.

Thereafter, we run a simple regression in Equation (2) to decompose the components of the GDP per capita. We use fixed asset investment as proxy for physical capital. Average schooling year in each province is used to measure the average human capital. Arable land size per capita is used to proxy for natural resources. Trade-to-GDP ratio is our trade outcome measure.

Our data source is China's *Statistical Yearbook*, where we extract all the provincial data from 1978 to 2015. Given that our interest lies on the effects of trade on long-term economic growth, we follow the literature by using the five-year average of GDP per capita as our dependent variable. Accordingly, the five-year average is also taken as our independent variable. Thus, we have seven complete timespans from 1978 to 2012.

Table 8 presents the regression results. All variables are in log value. Column (1) presents the regression of the GDP per capita on trade share, fixed asset per capita, and land per capita for 31

Table 8. Cross-province Income and Trade in China: 1978–2012.

Ln(GDP per capita)	(1)	(2)
Ln(tradeshare)	0.0399***	0.1744***
	(0.0126)	(0.0216)
Ln(fixasspc)	0.6968***	0.6052***
	(0.0262)	(0.0429)
Ln(landpc)	−0.0829***	−0.0180
	(0.0084)	(0.0142)
Ln(edupc)		0.5750***
		(0.1213)
Constant	3.1650***	2.1936***
	(0.1110)	(0.3308)
Observations	217	93
R-squared	0.9879	0.9717
Year FE	Yes	Yes

Note: Our dependent variable is the log of GDP per capita averaging at five-year intervals. Independent variables include Ln(tradeshare), log of trade-to-GDP ratio; Ln(fixasspc), log of per capita fixed asset; Ln(landpc), arable land divided by population; and Ln(edupc), average schooling years. Thirty-one provinces in Mainland China are included. The seven timespans are 1978–1982, 1983–1987, 1988–1992, 1993–1997, 1998–2002, 2003–2007, and 2008–2012. Standard errors in parentheses. *** for $p < 0.01$.

provinces and seven timespans. Column (2) further controls for the average education level. However, the sample size decreases from 217 to 93 because the education data are only available for all provinces after 1997. In spite of the sample size difference, these two columns provide similar results. Physical capital and human capital are determined to be positively associated with per capita GDP. Land per capita is negatively related to the average income level although not statistically significant in the last column. Moreover, provinces with high trade-to-GDP ratios also have high income levels. This last result suggests that trade development is beneficial to economic development at the regional level. Our full regression in column (2) indicates that the contribution of trade growth to economic growth is approximately one-third of the magnitude of either physical capital or human capital.

5. Concluding Remarks

This chapter presents a scenario of the performance of China's foreign trade since its economic reform and opening-up in 1978. Moreover, the current chapter reviews the literature on the effects of trade on economic growth in general and that on China in particular. Using data from 1978 to 2015 in China, we can show the strong correlation between trade growth and economic growth. To determine the causal effect, we compare a few coastal provinces (representing more open regions) and inland provinces (representing less open regions). We also run a simple regression using data from all provinces. Evidence suggests that the increase in the export-to-GDP ratio leads to substantially high growth in GDP per capita.

Although the literature on trade and economic development focuses on the income level, we should be cautious in interpreting the existing results. Our results, which are similar to those in numerous other reports, show that trade promotes average income but it has nothing to do with the effect on income inequality. The basic trade model (i.e. particularly the Heckscher–Ohlin model) informs us that when a labor-abundant country, such as China, opens for trade, labor would be better off, whereas capital owners would be worse off. However, empirical studies have yet to succeed in finding the supporting evidence for the theoretical prediction. Han *et al.* (2012) used the data of the Chinese Urban Household Survey from 1988 to 2008 and found that regions that are substantially exposed to trade liberalization experienced large changes in wage inequality. This result is in contrast with the prediction from the HO model. In their analysis, the aforementioned researchers maximized two events related to trade liberalization, Deng Xiaoping's 1992 South tour and China's entry into WTO in 2001. They also have shown that the return to education has increased after trade liberalization, particularly China's entry into WTO. Mah (2013) discovered a similar result, that is, trade liberalization has led to a substantially high income inequality in China. Gender wage inequality has also been studied by a few researchers. Chen *et al.* (2013) used the 2004 census data to study globalization and gender wage inequality in China. They found that foreign and exporting firms employ numerous female workers, and foreign and export orientation reduces gender wage gap within the same region and industry. Gender wage discrimination is observed only among private non-exporting firms.

The channels through which trade may influence economic growth have yet to be studied thoroughly. Economic theories have suggested at least three channels, namely, imported inputs, market access (increasing return to scale), and innovation. Accordingly, additional studies in identifying the precise channels are necessary.

We should also note that GDP growth does not necessarily mean welfare improvement. Trade boom may affect welfare through other non-monetary channels. The trade effect on an individual's education choice, health, and subjective happiness is a significant topic that can be explored in the future.

References

Amiti, M. and Jozef, K. (2007). Trade liberalization, intermediate inputs, and productivity: Evidence from Indonesia. *The American Economic Review,* 97(5), 1611–1638.

Anderson, J.E. and Peter, J.N. (1992). Trade reform with quotas, partial rent retention, and tariffs. *Econometrica: Journal of the Econometric Society,* 57–76.

Bas, M. and Orsetta, C. (2013). Trade and product market policies in upstream sectors and productivity in downstream sectors: Firm-level evidence from China. *Journal of Comparative Economics,* 41(3), 843–862.

Chang, R., Linda, K. and Norman, V.L. (2009). Openness can be good for growth: The role of policy complementarities. *Journal of Development Economics,* 90(1), 33–49.

Chen, B. and Yi, F. (2000). Determinants of economic growth in China: Private enterprise, education, and openness. *China Economic Review,* 11(1), 1–15.

Chen, Z., Ying, G., Huiwen, L. and Chi, W. (2013). Globalization and gender wage inequality in China. *World Development,* 44, 256–266.

De Loecker, J. (2007). Do exports generate higher productivity? Evidence from Slovenia. *Journal of International Economics,* 73(1), 69–98.

Frankel, J.A. and David, R. (1999). Does trade cause growth? *American Economic Review,* 379–399.

Grossman, G.M. and Elhanan, H. (1993). *Innovation and Growth in the Global Economy.* Cambridge, Massachusetts: MIT Press.

Han, J., Runjuan, L. and Junsen, Z. (2012). Globalization and wage inequality: Evidence from urban China. *Journal of International Economics,* 87(2), 288–297.

Harrison, A. (1996). Openness and growth: A time-series, cross-country analysis for developing countries. *Journal of Development Economics,* 48(2), 419–447.

Liu, X., Peter, B. and Paul, J.N.S. (2002). Relationships between economic growth, foreign direct investment and trade: Evidence from China. *Applied Economics,* 34(11), 1433–1440.

Liu, Q. and Larry, D.Q. (2016). Intermediate input imports and innovation: Evidence from Chinese firms. *Journal of International Economics,* 3, 166–183.

Mah, J.S. (2013). Globalization, decentralization and income inequality: The case of China. *Economic Modelling,* 31, 653–658.

Pavcnik, N. (2002). Trade liberalization, exit, and productivity improvements: Evidence from Chilean plants. *The Review of Economic Studies,* 69(1), 245–276.

Rodriguez, F. and Dani, R. (2000). Trade policy and economic growth: A skeptic's guide to the cross-national evidence. *NBER Macroeconomics Annual,* 15, 261–325.

Topalova, P. and Amit, K. (2011). Trade liberalization and firm productivity: The case of India. *Review of Economics and Statistics,* 93(3), 995–1009.

Yanikkaya, H. (2003). Trade openness and economic growth: A cross-country empirical investigation. *Journal of Development Economics,* 72(1), 57–89.

Yao, S. (2006). On economic growth, FDI and exports in China. *Applied Economics,* 38(3), 339–351.

Yu, M. (2015). Processing trade, tariff reductions and firm productivity: Evidence from Chinese firms. *The Economic Journal,* 125(585), 943–988.

Chapter 13

Strategic Delegation of Strategic Trade Policy

Vijay Mohan

vijay.mohan@outlook.com

This survey revisits the issue of welfare-maximizing taxes versus revenue-maximizing taxes when governments can delegate strategic trade policy to a policymaker, such as the bureaucracy. The connection between this strand of the literature on strategic trade policy and the earlier industrial organization literature on strategic managerial delegation within a firm is highlighted.

1. Introduction

Strategic trade policy refers to government policy that influences the strategic interaction of firms competing in oligopolistic international markets (Brander, 1995). Strategic interdependence between firms represents a distortion, and provides a rationale for interventionist policies in international trade. As such, strategic trade policy is linked to the broader idea of second-best policy in the presence of distortions (Bhagwati, 1971). The focus of strategic trade policy is 'profit-shifting': capturing a larger share of the economic rents available in an international oligopolistic industry by altering the strategic interaction in favor of the domestic firm.

Early and influential analyses of strategic trade policy were couched in the 'third market' export framework, where two firms located in two countries (operating under two separate governments) compete for consumers in a third market. Brander and Spencer (1985) show that strategic trade policy optimally involves the use of subsidies when firms engage in Cournot competition. Eaton and Grossman (1986), on the other hand, suggest that optimal interventionist policy takes the form of an export tax when firms engage in Bertrand competition. The nature of government intervention is sensitive, therefore, to the nature of competition between firms.[1] When deriving these optimal policies, both papers assume that the objective of government intervention is to improve a nation's welfare. With some exceptions, the assumption that governments are benevolent welfare maximizers has been retained in much of the literature on strategic trade policy, which has grown exponentially since these early contributions.

Welfare maximization, however, is not the only objective open to governments. An alternative that presents itself is tax revenue maximization.[2] Following Brennan and Buchanan (1980), it has become common in the tax literature to refer to governments that pursue the objective of tax revenue maximization as Leviathans. One of the early results in trade theory based on competitive markets and a two country framework (comprising one exporter and one importer) was that the welfare-maximizing export tax is lower than the revenue-maximizing tax, but that the former yields a higher level of welfare (Johnson 1950–1951; Tower, 1977).[3] In the framework without strategic interaction, therefore, Leviathans set higher taxes and collect higher revenues, but welfare-maximizing governments achieve higher welfare.

[1]This represents a significant problem for the practical implementation of strategic trade policy, since it requires that governments know the nature of competition in each industry that it intervenes in. Miller and Pazgal (2005) show that when strategic managerial delegation is added to the third market export model, the optimal trade policy is invariant to changes in the mode of competition, as long as owners can exert sufficient control over managers.

[2]Governments may also set policy to pursue non-economic objectives such as self-sufficiency, national security and so on (Bhagwati and Srinivasan, 1969), or cater to political and lobbying interests.

[3]Though these arguments were couched in terms of tariffs rather than export taxes, the results are parallel.

In this survey we examine a subset of the third country export literature that focuses on the relative merits of welfare-maximizing taxes versus revenue-maximizing taxes in the presence of strategic interaction between firms. In the third market setting with price competition a paradox emerges[4]: while revenue-maximizing taxes continue to be higher than welfare-maximizing taxes, the welfare of countries may also be higher in the former case than the latter (Panagariya and Schiff, 1994). Leviathans can, in fact, achieve higher welfare than benevolent welfare-maximizing governments once we move away from the competitive setting to allow for strategic interaction and price competition. Essentially, with Bertrand competition the taxes that governments set are strategic complements, and the aggressive tax competition when governments engage in welfare maximization lowers welfare in both countries. Tax revenue maximization tempers this aggressiveness, which can potentially improve welfare for both countries.

The possibility of revenue-maximizing taxes leading to higher welfare than welfare-maximizing ones gives rise to a new issue: can a welfare-maximizing government pursue the objective of revenue maximization if that raises welfare? There is clearly a problem here: since a welfare-maximizing government has the objective of maximizing welfare by definition, maximizing tax revenues is not a credible strategy. The question now becomes whether a welfare-maximizing government can commit credibly to setting taxes that maximize revenues.

This question has a close parallel in industrial organization theory. Economic theory assumes that firms maximize profits; however, other objectives such as sales revenue or market share maximization are possible. This multiplicity of objectives becomes especially relevant when one recognizes that firms have a hierarchy where owners of the firm hire managers to implement day-to-day pricing and output decisions. A series of papers by Vickers (1985), Fershtman and Judd (1987), and Sklivas (1987) provided seminal contributions

[4]We also assume that goods are substitutes.

to the idea of strategic managerial delegation in an oligopoly: A profit-maximizing owner may find it advantageous to provide her firm's manager with contractual incentives for pursuing objectives other than profit maximization. This beneficially manipulates her manager's behavior and, consequently, the strategic responses of the owners and managers of rival firms. One of the results to emerge is that when goods are substitutes and firms engage in Bertrand competition, owners can realize higher profits than profit-maximizing behavior entails. This is achieved by providing their managers with incentives for pursuing an objective different than pure profit maximization, essentially by penalizing the manager for input expenditures. Delegation of decisions to managers, therefore, serves as a form of commitment for profit-maximizing owners to pursue other objectives.[5]

The implication of this for strategic trade policy is immediate. If governments can delegate tax-setting responsibility to policymakers such as bureaucrats,[6] by manipulating bureaucratic incentives, governments can commit to maximizing tax revenues rather than maximizing welfare, thereby realizing a higher level of welfare than by directly setting welfare-maximizing taxes. To put this slightly differently, delegation allows welfare-maximizing governments to mimic the behavior of Leviathans when this is strategically beneficial.

Our survey of the role of delegation in strategic trade policy is organized as follows. In Section 2, we summarize the contributions of Vickers (1985), Fershtman and Judd (1987), and Sklivas (1987). In doing so, Section 2 analyzes the structure of the strategic managerial delegation problem in both Cournot and Bertrand settings. This lays the foundation for an examination in Section 3 of the impact of delegation on strategic trade policy. While some papers in the literature have analyzed strategic policy delegation within a Cournot framework (Trandel and Skeath, 1996; Collie, 1997), our focus is on

[5]The intellectual foundations behind the possibility that delegating decisions to other agents can make certain actions credible is described in Schelling (1960).

[6]For a review of the political science perspective of the delegation to bureaucracy, see Huber and Shipan (2011).

the Bertrand case (Clarke and Collie, 2008), since this yields the possibility that welfare may be higher with tax revenue maximization. One of the problems with the differentiated duopoly model used by Clarke and Collie (2008) is the existence of a multiplicity of possible outcomes, depending on the degree of product substitutability. In Section 4, we review a Hotelling model of strategic policy delegation (Mohan and Hazari, 2012) that achieves a unique equilibrium where providing incentives for tax revenue maximization is the dominant strategy for governments. Moreover, the welfare achieved in this equilibrium exceeds the welfare achieved when both governments engage in welfare maximization. In Section 5, we outline extensions and other issues related to strategic delegation in trade theory including the impact of network externalities (Hoernig, 2012; Ghosh and Pal, 2017) and the effect of firm level managerial delegation in trade policy (Das, 1997). Section 6 provides concluding comments.

2. The Antecedents: Strategic Managerial Delegation in a Firm

2.1. *The Model Set-up*

Consider a duopoly with two firms, F_1 and F_2, each of which has an owner and a manager. An owner of a firm has the objective of profit maximization. In order to achieve this objective each owner can employ a manager, who is delegated the task of setting output (in Cournot competition) or prices (in Bertrand competition). The model comprises two stages. In the first stage, the owner offers a contract to a manager. Given this contract, in the second stage, the manager sets output or price based on the incentives provided in the contract. Once all decisions have been taken, the output is sold to consumers and profits are realized, which accrue to the owners. Managers are then paid according to the terms of the contract.

To model consumer behavior and demand we assume the existence of a representative consumer with quasilinear preferences:

$$U = m + \alpha(x_1 + x_2) - \frac{1}{2}(x_1^2 + 2\beta x_1 x_2 + x_2^2) \tag{1}$$

where m represents the output of a numeraire good; x_i represents the output produced by F_i sold at a price p_i, $\forall i \in \{1, 2\}$.[7] The parameter β captures the relationship between x_1 and x_2. In this survey, we assume that $\beta \in (0, 1)$, which implies that the two products are substitutes.[8]

Equation (1) yields linear demand and inverse demand curves, $\forall i, j \in \{1, 2\}, i \neq j$:

$$p_i = \alpha - x_i - \beta x_j \tag{2}$$

$$x_i = \frac{1}{(1-\beta^2)}[\alpha(1-\beta) - p_i + \beta p_j] \tag{3}$$

We assume that the marginal costs are constant and equal to c for both firms.[9] Based on (2) and (3), owners maximize profits, $\forall i \in \{1, 2\}$:

$$\pi_i = p_i x_i - c x_i \tag{4}$$

While the owner of firm F_i maximizes profits, she delegates price and output decisions to a manager Mi who is provided with incentives to make her decisions based on a performance measure, μ_i, which depends on some linear combination of profits (π_i) and sales revenues

---

[7]In what follows, the subscript i refers to an arbitrary firm, and the subscript j refers to the other firm.

[8]Allowing the feasible range to extent to the interval $\beta \in (-1, 0)$ allows for the two products to be complements as well. As Singh and Vives (1984) show, in this framework, Cournot (Bertrand) competition with substitutes is the dual of Bertrand (Cournot) competition with complements. As such, we need to compute outcomes for only one case, either substitutes or complements. The results for the other case correspond through duality. Moreover, we have excluded the endpoints $\beta = 0$ (the two products are independent) and $\beta = 1$ (the two are perfect substitutes). Not allowing $\beta = 1$ ensures product differentiation. While this is not crucial when we consider quantity (Cournot) competition, it is required in the scenarios with price (Bertrand) competition in order to allow price to exceed marginal cost.

[9]While not necessary for all the scenarios considered in the survey, we place the restriction that $0 < c < \frac{\alpha}{1-\beta}$ to ensure that trade in the market occurs and that demands are positive in the model.

(r_i)[10]:

$$\mu_i = \lambda_i \pi_i + (1 - \lambda_i) r_i = r_i - c\lambda_i x_i \tag{5}$$

We assume that the manager's compensation is an increasing and linear function of μ_i. The manager, therefore, chooses x_i or p_i (depending on whether we consider a Cournot or Bertrand game) to maximize μ_i. Equation (5) indicates that an owner's choice of λ_i affects the weight her manager places on the cost of production. In the case where $\lambda_i = 1$, $\mu_i = \pi_i$ and the manager has incentives to maximize profits; on the other hand, when $\lambda_i = 0$, $\mu_i = r_i$ and the manager has incentives to maximize sales revenues. The owner chooses λ_i to maximizes profits, and we place no restriction on the magnitude that λ_i can take. The logic of the delegation process can be summarized as a two-stage game:

Stage 1: Owners select λ_i (non-cooperatively) to maximize π_i
Stage 2: Managers select x_i or p_i (non-cooperatively) to maximize μ_i

We assume that each manager knows the incentive contract in place for the other manager (that is, λ_j is known to M_i), so that information between managers is symmetric at Stage 2. We solve the game using backward induction.

2.2. *Cournot Competition*

With Cournot competition, at Stage 2 the managers choose output to maximize:

$$\mu_i = (\alpha - x_i - \beta x_j) x_i - c\lambda_i x_i \tag{6}$$

---

[10]This is not the only type of managerial incentive scheme analyzed in the literature. An alternative incentive scheme involves a relative performance measure such as $m_i = \pi_i + v_i \pi_j$, so that the incentives of the manager is conditioned by the relative profits of the two firms. See Miller and Pazgal (2005), for example, where this incentive scheme used in the context of strategic trade policy.

The first order conditions yield the reaction functions, $\forall i, j \in \{1, 2\}$, $i \neq j$:

$$x_i = \frac{1}{2}(\alpha - c\lambda_i - \beta x_j) \tag{7}$$

As expected, given that $\beta \in (0, 1)$, the reaction functions are downward sloping in the Cournot setting, and the managers view outputs as strategic substitutes. More interestingly, Equation (7) shows that a decrease in the choice of λ_i by the owner of F_i causes her manager's reaction function to shift rightward, which indicates more aggressive behavior by the manager in terms of setting the output.

Solving Equation (7) for the optimal Stage 2 outputs and prices as a function of λ_i and λ_j, we get, $\forall i, j \in \{1, 2\}$:

$$x_i(\lambda_i, \lambda_j) = \frac{1}{(4 - \beta^2)}[\alpha(2 - \beta) - 2c\lambda_i + \beta c\lambda_j] \tag{8}$$

$$p_i(\lambda_i, \lambda_j) = x_i(\lambda_i, \lambda_j) + c\lambda_i \tag{9}$$

The Stage 2 output chosen by M_i depends, therefore, not only on the incentives provided by the owner of F_i, but also on in incentives provided to M_j by the owner of F_j. If we set $\lambda_1 = \lambda_2 = 1$ in Equation (8), we get the standard profit-maximizing Cournot solution with $x_1(\lambda_1 = 1, \lambda_2 = 1) = x_2(\lambda_1 = 1, \lambda_2 = 1) = \frac{\alpha - c}{2+\beta} = x^C$. This outcome is represented by point C in Figure 1, and the reaction functions by R_i^C.

Now consider the Stage 1 owner's problem. Based on Equations (8) and (9), each owner selects λ_i to maximize profits:

$$\pi_i(\lambda_i, \lambda_j) = x_i[x_i - c(1 - \lambda_i)] \tag{10}$$

Here, x_i is given by Equation (8).

The reaction function derived from (10) is:

$$\lambda_i = \frac{1}{4c(2 - \beta^2)}[2c(4 - \beta^2) - \beta^2\alpha(2 - \beta) - \beta^3 c\lambda_j] \tag{11}$$

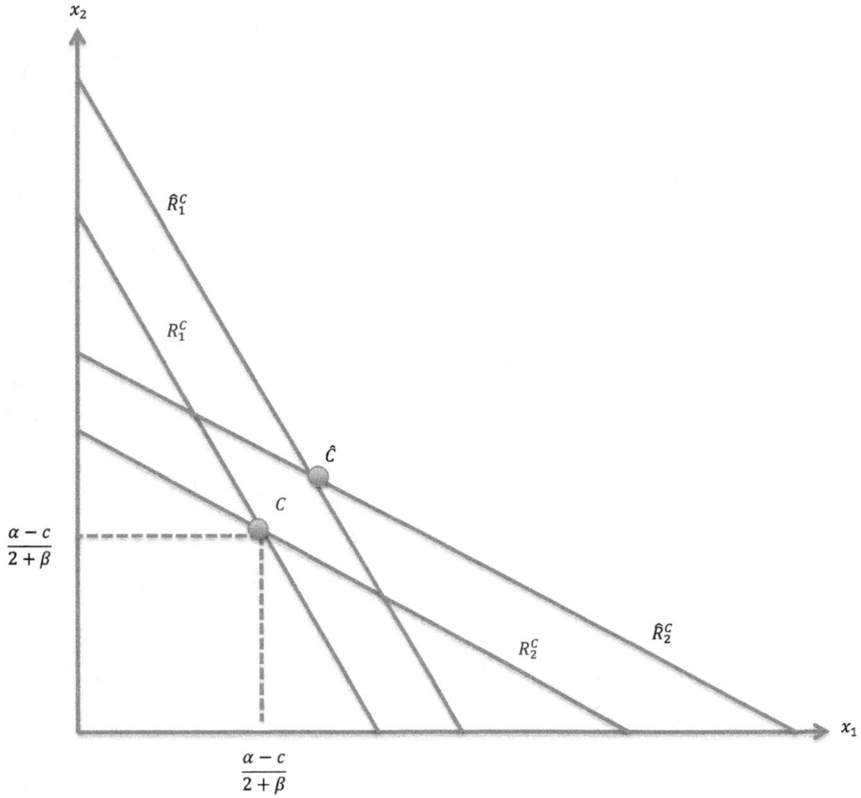

Figure 1.

Equation (11) implies that with Cournot competition, λ_i and λ_j are strategic substitutes. We can also see straight away that the traditional Cournot equilibrium represented by point C in Figure 1 cannot be an equilibrium in this extended delegation game. Suppose we fix $\lambda_2 = 1$ and, consequently, manager M_2's reaction function by R_2^C in Figure 1. Substituting $\lambda_2 = 1$ in Equation (11), it is evident that the best response for the owner of F_1 is to set $\lambda_1 < 1$. Equation (7) indicates that this results in M_1's reaction function shifting rightwards from its position at R_1^C (and slide along R_2^C), which induces M_1 to behave more aggressively and expand output. If both owners can move away from profit maximization, the equilibrium is represented by $\hat{C}$ in Figure 1.[11] Solving the equations represented by (11),[12] the equilibrium choices of the owners are:

$$\hat{\lambda}_1^C = \hat{\lambda}_2^C = \hat{\lambda}^C = \frac{2c(2+\beta) - \beta^2\alpha}{2c(2+\beta) - \beta^2 c} < 1 \tag{12}$$

From (8), the equilibrium output with managerial delegation is:

$$\hat{x}^C = \frac{\alpha - c}{(2+\beta-\frac{\beta^2}{2})} > \frac{\alpha - c}{2+\beta} = x^C \tag{13}$$

The output is higher with managerial delegation than the traditional Cournot equilibrium, as is shown in Figure 1. Finally, substituting the value of $\hat{\lambda}^C$ in Equation (10):

$$\hat{\pi}^C = \frac{2(2-\beta^2)(\alpha-c)^2}{(2(2+\beta)-\beta^2)^2} < \frac{(\alpha-c)^2}{(2+\beta)^2} = \pi^C \tag{14}$$

These results are summarized below.

Proposition 1 (Vickers, 1984; Fershtman and Judd, 1987; Sklivas, 1987). *With quantity competition and strategic managerial delegation:*

(a) *Even though owners are profit-maximizers, they set incentives for managers that put some weight on sales revenue as well. In other words, the equilibrium share to profits in the managerial incentive structure satisfies* $\hat{\lambda}^C < 1$.
(b) *Output levels satisfy* $\hat{x}^C > x^C$. *So, managers set output more aggressively than the levels implied by traditional Cournot profit-maximizing behavior.*
(c) *Profit levels satisfy* $\hat{\pi}^C < \pi^C$, *which implies that profits are lower with managerial delegation than that obtained when both owners maximize profits.*

---

[11] In what follows, we use the superscript '^' to represent the delegation equilibrium.

[12] This symmetric equilibrium can be calculated by setting $\lambda_i = \lambda_j = \hat{\lambda}^C$ in Equation (11).

2.3. *Bertrand Competition*

Consider now the situation when managers compete in price space. Other than that, we retain the same modeling assumptions and procedure as Section 2.2. At Stage 2, a manager's optimization problem is to maximize:

$$\mu_i = \frac{1}{(1-\beta^2)}[\alpha(1-\beta) - p_i + \beta p_j](p_i - c\lambda_i) \tag{15}$$

The reaction functions obtained from the first order conditions are:

$$p_i = \frac{1}{2}[\alpha(1-\beta) + \beta p_j + c\lambda_i] \tag{16}$$

Equation (16) indicates that an increase in λ_i will induce manager M_i to raise price and, consequently, behave less aggressively. Solving (16) for the Stage 2 equilibrium, we obtain the optimal prices, output and profit:

$$p_i(\lambda_i, \lambda_j) = \frac{1}{(4-\beta^2)}[\alpha(1-\beta)(2+\beta) + 2c\lambda_i + \beta c\lambda_j] \tag{17}$$

$$x_i(\lambda_i, \lambda_j) = \frac{1}{(1-\beta^2)(4-\beta^2)} \times [\alpha(1-\beta)(2+\beta) - c\lambda_i(2-\beta^2) + \beta c\lambda_j] \tag{18}$$

$$\pi_i(\lambda_i, \lambda_j) = \frac{1}{(1-\beta^2)}[p_i(\lambda_i, \lambda_j) - c][p_i(\lambda_i, \lambda_j) - c\lambda_i] \tag{19}$$

In the traditional differentiated Bertrand game with profit-maximizing price setting, $\lambda_1 = \lambda_2 = 1$, which implies that $p_1(\lambda_1 = 1, \lambda_2 = 1) = p_2(\lambda_1 = 1, \lambda_2 = 1) = \frac{\alpha(1-\beta)+c}{2-\beta} = p^B$. This equilibrium is shown in Figure 2 labeled by the point B, which is the point of intersection of the reaction functions labeled R_i^B. From Equation (19), we see that in this case the profits of the two firms are:

$$\pi^B = \frac{(1-\beta)^2}{(2-\beta)^2(1-\beta^2)}(\alpha - c)^2 \tag{20}$$

At Stage 1, the owner of F_i selects λ_i to maximize profits in Equation (19), from which we obtain the reaction functions:

$$\lambda_i = \frac{\alpha\beta^2(1-\beta)(2+\beta)+c(2-\beta^2)(4-\beta^2)}{4c(2-\beta^2)} + \frac{\beta^3}{4(2-\beta^2)}\lambda_j \quad (21)$$

Equation (21) indicates that with Bertrand competition λ_i and λ_j are strategic complements (in contrast to their being strategic substitutes with Cournot competition, as shown in Equation (11)). As with Cournot competition, the profit-maximizing prices at point B in Figure 2 does not represent an equilibrium of the delegation game. Specifically, setting $\lambda_j = 1$ in Equation (21), the best response for

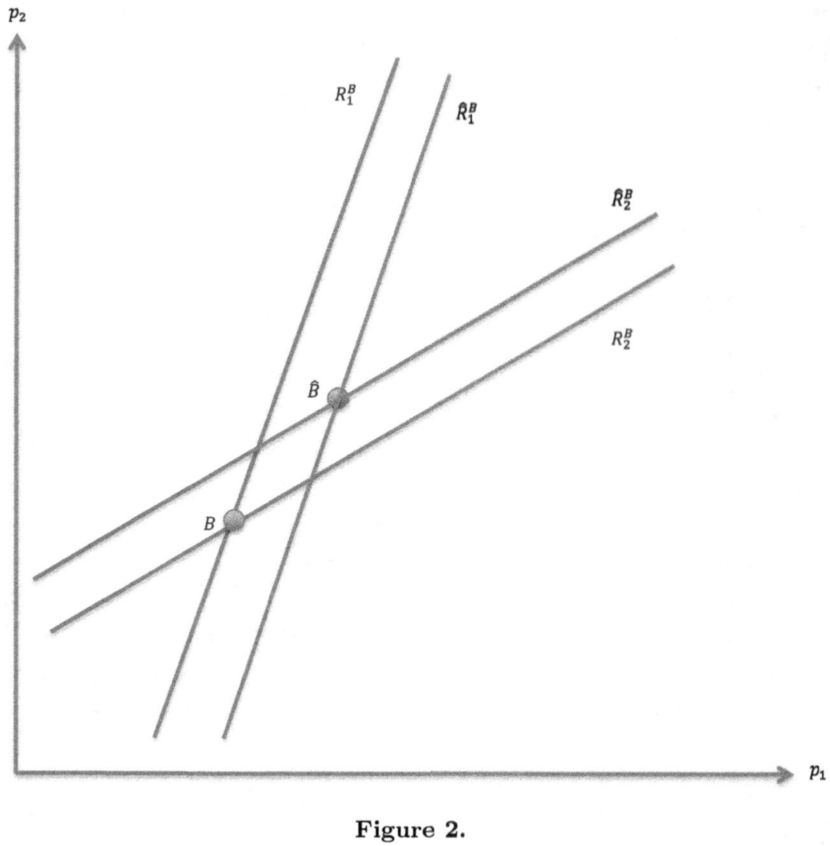

Figure 2.

the owner of F_i is to set $\lambda_i > 1$, which then shifts the reaction function of M_i rightwards and raises prices set by both managers (since prices are strategic complements). From Equation (20), the equilibrium involves both owners setting:

$$\hat{\lambda}_1^B = \hat{\lambda}_2^B = \hat{\lambda}^B = \frac{\alpha\beta^2(1-\beta)(2+\beta) + c(2-\beta^2)(4-\beta^2)}{c(8-4\beta^2-\beta^3)} > 1 \quad (22)$$

In the Bertrand case, therefore, an owner has the incentive to overweight profits, since this raises the weight the manager attaches to costs, and forces the manager to adopt a less aggressive pricing strategy.

Plugging the value of $\hat{\lambda}^B$ in Equation (19), we obtain:

$$\begin{aligned}\hat{\pi}^B &= \frac{(1-\beta)^2}{(2-\beta)^2(1-\beta^2)}\left[(\alpha-c)^2 + \frac{c(\hat{\lambda}^B-1)(\alpha-c\hat{\lambda}^B)}{(1-\beta)}\right] \\ &> \frac{(1-\beta)^2}{(2-\beta)^2(1-\beta^2)}(\alpha-c)^2 = \pi^B \end{aligned} \quad (23)$$

Equation (23) indicates that, paradoxically, owners obtain higher profits by providing their managers incentives that are not geared towards profit-maximization. Unlike the traditional Cournot model where quantities are strategic substitutes, in the Bertrand model with strategic complementarities, profit maximization results in aggressive price reductions that reduce profits. By setting $\hat{\lambda}^B > 1$ when delegating price-setting decisions to a manager, the owner credibly commits to moving away from profit maximization and reducing the aggressiveness with which prices are set strategically. This results in higher profits.

Proposition 2 (Vickers, 1984; Fershtman and Judd, 1987; Sklivas, 1987). *With price competition and strategic managerial delegation:*

(a) *Even though owners are profit-maximizers, they set incentives for managers that overweight profits. In other words, the equilibrium share to profits in the managerial incentive structure satisfies* $\hat{\lambda}^B > 1$.

(b) *Prices satisfy* $\hat{p}^B > p^B$. *So, managers set prices less aggressively than the levels implied by traditional Bertrand profit-maximizing behavior in a differentiated oligopoly.*

(c) *Profit levels satisfy* $\hat{\pi}^B > \pi^B$, *which implies that profits are higher with managerial delegation than that obtained when both owners maximize profits.*

Indeed, it is the presence of this paradoxical result in part (c) above that has resulted in a number of papers in the trade literature (which are reviewed in Section 3 below) exploring its consequences for strategic trade policy. Given that this result occurs with strategic complementarities (as with the Bertrand model described here), and not strategic substitutability (as with the Cournot model), we focus predominantly on the former in the subsequent analysis.

3. Strategic Trade Policy with Price Competition and Delegation

In this section, we examine the implications of delegation in strategic trade theory by extending the third market export model with price competition to allow for delegation.[13] Following Eaton and Grossman (1986), we know that the optimal policy in this case involves export taxes.

3.1. *The Model with Price Competition*

Consider two firms F_1 and F_2 located in two separate countries (Country 1 and Country 2) competing for exports to a third market. Demand in the third market is characterized by Equations (1)–(3). We assume that firms compete in prices to maximize profits. Firm

[13]For an examination of the outcomes under Cournot competition and development of ideas parallel to Section 2.2 in the strategic trade setting, see Collie (1997) and Trandel and Skeath (1996).

F_i sells output x_i to the third market at price p_i, and has a constant marginal cost of production c.[14]

Each country has a government ($G_i, i \in \{1, 2\}$) that has the objective of welfare maximization, which it achieves through its export tax policy.[15] In the third country export model the total surplus or welfare for each country is defined to be the sum of its firm's profits and the tax revenues collected by its government. The consumer surplus resulting from a firm's output is ignored, as the product is consumed by citizens of a third country. For a given tax rate t_i in Country i, the profit of firm F_i, $\forall i \in \{1, 2\}$, is:

$$\Pi_i = p_i x_i - c x_i - t_i x_i \tag{24}$$

The tax revenue collected by G_i is:

$$R_i = t_i x_i \tag{25}$$

The total surplus for Country i, which equals welfare in this type of modeling, is given by:

$$W_i = R_i + \Pi_i = p_i x_i - c x_i \tag{26}$$

While each government has the objective of welfare maximization it can delegate tax setting to a policymaker, such as a bureaucrat, whose incentives may depend on some combination of welfare and tax revenue collected.[16] We use the notation M_1 and M_2 to denote the bureaucrat in Country 1 and Country 2, respectively. As with

[14]The assumption that both firms have identical marginal cost of c is not innocuous. In general, when costs differ, the magnitude of policy intervention is higher for the government of the lower cost firm. For example, Neary (1994) and de Meza (1986) show that in the case of Cournot competition, the government of the firm with the lower cost provides higher subsidies. Similarly, Clarke and Collie (2006) show that with Bertrand competition the government of the low cost firm imposes a higher tax.

[15]Here, governments play a role parallel to owners in Section 2 and profit maximization is replaced by welfare maximization.

[16]The bureaucrats' or policymakers' role in the model is similar to managers in Section 2.

managerial delegation, we assume M_i's incentives are based on a linear function:

$$\mu_i = \lambda_i W_i + (1-\lambda_i)R_i = R_i + (1-\lambda_i)\Pi_i \tag{27}$$

Consequently, M_i sets t_i to maximize μ_i, rather than welfare. The timeline is as follows:

Stage 1: Governments select λ_i (non-cooperatively) to maximize W_i
Stage 2: Bureaucrats select t_i (non-cooperatively) to maximize μ_i
Stage 3: Firms select p_i (non-cooperatively) to maximize Π_i

To ensure symmetric information at Stage 2, we assume that each bureaucrat knows the incentive contract in place for the other bureaucrat (that is, λ_j is known to M_i).

As before, we solve the game through backward induction. For given t_i and t_j set by the policymakers at Stage 2, the Stage 3 outcomes as a result of the Bertrand game between firms is, $\forall i, j\{1,2\}, i \neq j$:

$$p_i(t_i,t_j) = \frac{1}{(4-\beta^2)}[\alpha(1-\beta)(2+\beta)+c(2+\beta)+2t_i+\beta t_j] \tag{28}$$

$$x_i(t_i,t_j) = \frac{1}{(1-\beta^2)(4-\beta^2)} [(\alpha-c)(1-\beta)(2+\beta)-(2-\beta^2)t_i+\beta t_j] \tag{29}$$

$$\Pi_i = (1-\beta^2)x_i^2 \tag{30}$$

To save on notation in what follows, we let $x_i(t_i,t_j) = K - \phi t_i + \xi t_j$, where $K = \frac{(\alpha-c)(1-\beta)(2+\beta)}{(1-\beta^2)(4-\beta^2)}$, $\phi = \frac{(2-\beta^2)}{(1-\beta^2)(4-\beta^2)}$, and $\xi = \frac{\beta}{(1-\beta^2)(4-\beta^2)}$.

At stage 2, for any given λ_1 and λ_2 selected at Stage 1, the non-cooperative tax setting game between M_1 and M_2 yields the reaction functions, $\forall i, j\{1,2\}$, $i \neq j$:

$$2\phi\left[\frac{1-\lambda_i(1-\beta^2)\phi}{1-2\lambda_i(1-\beta^2)\phi}\right]t_i = K + \xi t_j \tag{31}$$

Solving the conditions in (31), we get the equilibrium taxes as:

$$t_i(\lambda_i, \lambda_j) = \frac{K(f_j + \xi)}{f_i f_j - \xi^2}, \text{ where } f_i = 2\phi \left[\frac{1 - \lambda_i(1-\beta^2)\phi}{1 - 2\lambda_i(1-\beta^2)\phi}\right]$$

$$\text{and } f_j = 2\phi \left[\frac{1 - \lambda_j(1-\beta^2)\phi}{1 - 2\lambda_j(1-\beta^2)\phi}\right] \tag{32}$$

Plugging the value of taxes in (29), (30) and (25), we get the Stage 2 equilibrium output, firm profits and tax revenues:

$$x_i(\lambda_i, \lambda_j) = \frac{K(f_j + \xi)(f_i - \phi)}{f_i f_j - \xi^2} \tag{33a}$$

$$\Pi_i(\lambda_i, \lambda_j) = (1 - \beta^2)\left[\frac{K(f_j + \xi)(f_i - \phi)}{f_i f_j - \xi^2}\right]^2 \tag{33b}$$

$$\mathrm{R}_i(\lambda_i, \lambda_j) = \left[\frac{K(f_j + \xi)}{f_i f_j - \xi^2}\right]^2 (f_i - \phi) \tag{33c}$$

From Equations (26), (33b) and (33c), we get welfare:

$$\mathrm{W}_i(\lambda_i, \lambda_j) = \left[\frac{K(f_j + \xi)}{f_i f_j - \xi^2}\right]^2 (f_i - \phi)[1 + (1-\beta^2)(f_i - \phi)] \tag{33d}$$

At Stage 1, each government G_i selects λ_i to maximize $\mathrm{W}_i(\lambda_i, \lambda_j)$ in Equation (33d). While the structure and logic of the solution is straightforward, the solution itself is algebraically messy and allows for the possibility of multiple equilibria, depending on parameter values.[17] To obtain less messy results we assume, like much of the literature does, that $\lambda_i \in \{0, 1\}$; that is, the governments choose between providing incentives to policymakers to maximize tax revenues ($\lambda_i = 0$) or to maximize welfare ($\lambda_i = 1$). This simplifies the algebra considerably, and allows for a simple exposition of the counterpart to the paradox outlined in Proposition 2(c) earlier.

---

[17]Recall that f_i and f_j are functions of λ_i and λ_j, respectively, as described in Equation (32).

3.2. *The Stage 1 Delegation Game with $\lambda_i \in \{0, 1\}$*

When λ_i is restricted to a binary choice of 0 and 1, there are four possible outcomes at Stage 1:

Case I: Both governments provide incentives to bureaucrats for welfare maximization; that is, $\lambda_1 = \lambda_2 = 1$. It is evident that this is equivalent to a situation without delegation, since both governments are welfare maximizers anyway.
Case II: Both governments provide incentives to bureaucrats for tax revenue maximization; that is, $\lambda_1 = \lambda_2 = 0$. In this case, both governments use delegation to credibly behave like revenue maximizing Leviathans, even though they are welfare maximizers.
Case III: G_1 provides incentives for welfare maximization ($\lambda_1 = 1$) while G_2 provides incentives for tax revenue maximization ($\lambda_2 = 0$).
Case IV: G_1 provides incentives for tax revenue maximization ($\lambda_1 = 0$) while G_2 provides incentives for welfare maximization ($\lambda_2 = 1$)

Figure 3 summarizes the welfare payoffs for the Stage 1 game (superscripts correspond to the cases above).

		G_2	
		$\lambda_2 = 1$	$\lambda_2 = 0$
G_1	$\lambda_1 = 1$	W_1^I, W_2^I	W_1^{III}, W_2^{III}
	$\lambda_1 = 0$	W_1^{IV}, W_2^{IV}	W_1^{II}, W_2^{II}

Figure 3.

Consider Case I first. From Equation (32), we see that $f_1 = f_2 = \frac{4\phi}{\beta^2}$, which implies that:

$$t_1^I = t_2^I = \frac{(1-\beta)(\alpha-c)\beta^2}{4-2\beta-\beta^2} = t^I \text{ (from Equation (32))} \tag{34a}$$

$$W_1^I = W_2^I = \frac{2(1-\beta)(\alpha-c)^2(2-\beta^2)}{(1+\beta)(4-2\beta-\beta^2)^2} = W^I$$
$$\text{(from Equation (33d))} \tag{34b}$$

Similarly, for Case II, $f_1 = f_2 = 2\phi$, which implies that:

$$t_1^{II} = t_2^{II} = \frac{(1-\beta)(\alpha-c)(2+\beta)}{4-\beta-2\beta^2} = t^{II} \tag{35a}$$

$$W_1^{II} = W_2^{II} = \frac{2(1-\beta)(\alpha-c)^2(2-\beta^2)(3-\beta^2)}{(1+\beta)(2-\beta)^2(4-\beta-2\beta^2)^2} = W^{II} \tag{35b}$$

Comparing (34a) with (35a), and (34b) with (35b), we obtain the following.

Proposition 3 (Panagariya and Schiff, 1994; Clarke and Collie, 2008). *In the third country export model with price completion and strategic delegation:*

(a) *Tax rates satisfy $t^{II} > t^I$. So, tax rates are higher when both governments provide incentives for tax revenue maximization compared to welfare maximization.*
(b) *Welfare is higher with revenue-maximizing taxes than with welfare-maximizing taxes when the degree of product substitutability is high enough; specifically, $W^{II} > W^I$ when $\beta > 0.466$.*

Proposition 3(a) corresponds to the standard observation in the literature that revenue maximizing taxes are higher than welfare maximizing taxes. Proposition 3(b) summarizes the counterintuitive possibility that when governments credibly commit to behaving like Leviathans through the process of delegating tax-setting responsibility, welfare is higher than when they maximize welfare directly (assuming that the degree of product substitutability is high enough). This counterintuitive possibility is highlighted in both Panagariya and Schiff (1994) and Clarke and Collie (2008), and is the natural counterpart to Proposition 2(c) in the managerial delegation game.

To find the Stage 1 Nash equilibrium, we can calculate the welfare in Cases III and IV using Equations (32) and (33c) as well. While we omit the details of these calculations here, based on the payoff matrix in Figure (3) it is straightforward to show, as Clarke and Collie (2008) do, that:

Proposition 4 (Clarke and Collie, 2008). *The equilibrium for the Stage 1 delegation game between governments depends on the degree of product substitutability. Specifically:*

(a) *If* $0 < \beta < 0.466$, *then* $\lambda_i = 1$ *is a dominant strategy for* $G_i, \forall i \in \{1,2\}$. *Consequently,* $\lambda_1 = \lambda_2 = 1$ *is the unique Nash equilibrium. Moreover, in this range of product substitutability,* $W^I > W^{II}$ *holds.*
(b) *If* $0.466 < \beta < 0.862$, *then* $\lambda_i = 1$ *is a dominant strategy for* $G_i, \forall i \in \{1,2\}$, *so that* $\lambda_1 = \lambda_2 = 1$ *is the unique Nash equilibrium. However, in this range* $W^I < W^{II}$, *which yields a Prisoners' Dilemma.*
(c) *If* $0.862 < \beta < 0.983$, *then there exists no dominant strategy for either government. In this case,* $\lambda_1 = \lambda_2 = 1$ *and* $\lambda_1 = \lambda_2 = 0$ *it are both Nash equilibria of the Stage 1 game. Moreover, in this range* $W^I < W^{II}$, *which implies the existence of a potential coordination problem.*
(d) *If* $0.983 < \beta < 1$, *then* $\lambda_i = 0$ *is a dominant strategy for* $G_i, \forall i \in \{1,2\}$, *so that* $\lambda_1 = \lambda_2 = 0$ *is the unique Nash equilibrium. Moreover, in this range,* $W^I < W^{II}$ *holds.*

Proposition 4 outlines a rich set of possibilities in the Stage 1 delegation game. While Proposition 3(b) suggested that when both governments commit to behave like Leviathans welfare is higher than when they maximize profits in the parametric range $\beta > 0.466$, Proposition 4 highlights that this commitment is an equilibrium for a much narrower range of $\beta > 0.862$. In the range $0.466 < \beta < 0.862$, therefore, there exists a Prisoners' Dilemma.

Both (c) and (d) suggest that it is quite possible that countries end up with tax rates consistent with Leviathan-type tax revenue maximization levels even though their governments are welfare maximizers and that, paradoxically (though not surprisingly given Proposition 2), welfare is higher than if governments were to set taxes consistent with welfare maximization.

While interesting, especially as a trade theory counterpart of the managerial delegation game, the differentiated Bertand model examined here has its disadvantages. Specifically, the large set of potential equilibria described by Proposition 4 makes it difficult to extend the model to examine different issues in strategic trade policy. For example, if one wishes to compare tax competition with tax coordination in the presence of strategic delegation, Proposition 4 implies that tax competition itself may lead to one of four situations depending on product substitutability, including the possibility of contending with multiple equilibria in Proposition 4(c). In situations where such extensions need to be examined, it may be worthwhile to consider a different model that yields a single outcome for tax competition. In Section 4, we present a Hotelling version of this delegation game that is based on Mohan and Hazari (2012), which achieves a unique equilibrium for any degree of product substitutability.

4. An Alternative Hotelling Approach

In this section, we examine the impact of delegation while setting strategic trade policy in a Hotelling (1929) framework that is based on Mohan and Hazari (2012). Much of the model remains the same as Section 3. Specifically, we consider the same two firm, two government and two bureaucrat framework, along with the three stage timeline described there. In order to contrast the outcome here with Proposition 4, we focus on the special case where $\lambda_i \in \{0, 1\}$. As before, Figure 3 describes the Stage 1 delegation game between governments.

To introduce a spatial element into the model we assume that consumers are distributed uniformly along a $[0, 1]$ interval. For simplicity we fix the location of the two firms at the endpoints; specifically, we assume that F_1 is located at point , while F_2 is located at point 1. A consumer's location within the interval then indexes the consumer's taste for the differentiated output supplied by the two firms. Each consumer purchases exactly one unit of the output from either of the two firms and receives a utility:

$$u = v - \theta d - p \tag{36}$$

Here, p represents the price of the product, d represents the distance between the consumer and the firm it purchases the product from, and $\theta > 0$ represents the "transportation cost", which in this scenario is the marginal loss in utility from a unit increase in the distance away from ideal specifications of the product based on the consumer's tastes. We assume that $v \gg 0$, to ensure that utilities are positive at equilibrium and that consumers purchase the output.

Based on Equation (36), we can identify the demand for the output of the two firms:

$$x_i = \frac{1}{2\theta}[\theta + p_j - p_i], \forall i, j \in \{1, 2\}, \; i \neq j \tag{37}$$

The demand structure in Equation (37) replaces the one described in Equation (3) for the differentiated oligopoly model presented in Section 3. This is, in fact, the only difference between the two models. In the Hotelling model, $\frac{1}{\theta}$ parameterizes the degree of product substitutability and performs essentially the same role as β in Equation (3), with a higher $\frac{1}{\theta}$ representing a greater degree of product substitutability. However, the Hotelling model has an additional parameter to describe preferences, which is a consumer's location within the $[0, 1]$ interval. This additional degree of modeling freedom allows for a simpler demand structure and, as we shall show below, a unique equilibrium outcome in contrast to Proposition 4.

To develop a close parallel to the model in Section 3, we continue to assume that the marginal cost of production is constant and equal to c for both firms.[18] As before, Equations (24)–(27) describe the profits, tax revenue, welfare and bureaucratic incentives.

Given the tax rate selected by bureaucrats, at Stage 3, firms choose prices to maximize profits $\Pi_i = (p_i - c - t_i)x_i$. This yields the stage 3 equilibrium prices, output and profits:

$$p_i(t_i, t_j) = \theta + c + \frac{2t_i + t_j}{3} \tag{38a}$$

$$x_i(t_i, t_j) = \frac{1}{2} + \frac{t_j - t_i}{6\theta} \tag{38b}$$

$$\Pi_i = 2\theta x_i^2 \tag{38c}$$

For given λ_1 and λ_2 set by the two governments, at Stage 2, bureaucrats choose t_i to maximize μ_i given by Equation (27). The Stage 2 equilibrium taxes are then:

$$t_i(\lambda_i, \lambda_j) = \frac{(3 - 2\lambda_i)(9 - 4\lambda_j)\theta}{9 - 2\lambda_i - 2\lambda_j} \tag{39}$$

Plugging this back in Equation (38b), we get the output as a function of λ_1 and λ_2:

$$x_i(\lambda_i, \lambda_j) = \frac{1}{2} + \frac{\lambda_i - \lambda_j}{9 - 2\lambda_i - 2\lambda_j} \tag{40}$$

At Stage 1, governments select $\lambda_i \in \{0, 1\}$; the payoff structure is described by Figure 3. From (39) and (40), we see that $t_i = 2\theta(3 - 2\lambda_i)x_i$. From this (and Equation 38c) it follows that:

$$W_i = R_i + \Pi_i = t_i x_i + 2\theta x_i^2 = 4\theta(2 - \lambda_i)x_i^2 \tag{41}$$

The welfare levels in the four cases in Figure 3 then follow directly from Equations (40) and (41):

Case I: $W_1^I = W_2^I = \theta$
Case II: $W_1^{II} = W_2^{II} = 2\theta$

[18]Mohan and Hazari (2012) allow for firms to have different costs, and show that a reversal of the traditional result that the magnitude of policy intervention is higher for government of the low cost firm (see also footnote 14) is possible if governments follow different objectives.

Case III: $W_1^{III} = \frac{81}{49}\theta$ and $W_2^{III} = \frac{50}{49}\theta$
Case IV: $W_1^{IV} = \frac{50}{49}\theta$ and $W_2^{IV} = \frac{81}{49}\theta$

Proposition 5 (Mohan and Hazari, 2012). *Consider a strategic trade model with delegation in a Hotelling framework. For both governments, providing incentives for tax revenue maximization by setting $\lambda_i = 0$ is a dominant strategy; consequently $\lambda_1 = \lambda_2 = 0$ is the unique Nash equilibrium of the Stage 1 delegation game for any degree of product substitutability measured by $\frac{1}{\theta}$. Moreover, the equilibrium welfare of both countries by providing incentives for tax revenue maximization exceeds the welfare from setting taxes consistent with welfare maximization; that is, $W_i^{II} > W_i^{I}$, $\forall i \in \{1, 2\}$.*

In contrast to Proposition 4, the Hotelling model yields a unique equilibrium and eliminates the possibility of a Prisoners' Dilemma. The Hotelling delegation model has the attractive feature of being able to justify Leviathan-type tax setting even when governments are welfare maximizers, irrespective of the nature of product substitutability. Moreover, as now expected based on Proposition 2, by providing incentives to bureaucrats for tax revenue maximization, governments are able to achieve welfare higher than that achievable if they were to maximize welfare directly.

5. Related Issues and Extensions

5.1. *Network Effects*

An interesting extension to the basic differentiated Bertrand strategic delegation model involves incorporating network effects. Our presentation here is based on Hoernig (2012), which extends the managerial delegation game in Section 2, and Ghosh and Pal (2017), which extends the strategic trade model in Section 3.

To derive a demand system that allows for network effects, consider a modification of the representative consumer in

Equation (1):

$$U = m + \alpha(x_1 + x_2) - \frac{1}{2}(x_1^2 + 2\beta x_1 x_2 + x_2^2) + n\left[(y_1 + \beta y_2)x_1 + (y_2 + \beta y_1)x_2 - \frac{1}{2}(y_1^2 + 2\beta y_1 y_2 + y_2^2)\right] \tag{42}$$

Here, y_i denotes consumers' expectation about the equilibrium sales of F_i and $n \in [0, 1)$ denotes the strength of network effects. We assume, as before, that $\beta \in (0, 1)$ and that $0 < c < \alpha$. The fact that n captures the strength of network effects can be seen from the fact that $\frac{\partial}{\partial y_i}(\frac{\partial U}{\partial x_i}) = n$; that is, n captures the increase in the marginal utility consumers receive from purchasing F_i's output due to an increase in their sales expectation. Moreover, βn represents the degree to which the goods produced by the two firms are compatible, since $\frac{\partial}{\partial y_j}(\frac{\partial U}{\partial x_i}) = \beta n$. We also note that the utility is highest when expectations are fulfilled and $y_i = x_i, \forall i \in \{1, 2\}$.

From (42), we can derive the demand function, $\forall i, j \in \{1, 2\}$, $i \neq j$:

$$x_i = \frac{1}{(1 - \beta^2)}[\alpha(1 - \beta) - p_i + \beta p_j + n y_i (1 - \beta^2)] \tag{43}$$

Essentially, the presence of network externalities is captured through an extra term added to the demand function in Equation (3).

To begin with, consider the managerial delegation model from Section 2. The Stage 2 optimization of the managers now yields the reaction functions:

$$p_i = \frac{1}{2}[\alpha(1 - \beta) + \beta p_j + c\lambda_i + n y_i (1 - \beta^2)] \tag{44}$$

Now, if we assume the existence of rational expectations (Katz and Shapiro, 1985), then $y_i = x_i$, and we obtain the Stage 2 rational expectations equilibrium:

$$p_i(\lambda_i, \lambda_j) = \frac{1}{(2 - n)^2 - \beta^2} [\alpha(1 - \beta)(2 - n + \beta) + c(1 - n)((2 - n)\lambda_i + \beta\lambda_j)] \tag{45a}$$

$$x_i(\lambda_i, \lambda_j) = \frac{1}{(1-\beta^2)[(2-n)^2-\beta^2]}[\alpha(1-\beta)(2-n+\beta) - (2-n-\beta^2)c\lambda_i + \beta(1-n)c\lambda_j] \tag{45b}$$

$$\pi_i(\lambda_i, \lambda_j) = \frac{1}{(1-\beta^2)}[p_i(\lambda_i, \lambda_j) - c][p_i(\lambda_i, \lambda_j) - c\lambda_i] \tag{45c}$$

The Stage 1 profit maximization programs of the owners the yields the reaction functions:

$$\lambda_i = \frac{(\beta^2-2n+n^2)}{2(2-n)(2-n-\beta^2)}\left[\beta\lambda_j + \frac{\alpha(1-\beta)(2-n+\beta)}{c(1-n)}\right] + \frac{[(2-n)^2-\beta^2]}{2(1-n)(2-n)} \tag{46}$$

In Section 2, we showed that without network effects λ_i and λ_j were strategic complements (substitutes) with Bertrand (Cournot) competition (see Equations (11) and (21)). In Bertrand competition with network effects, however, λ_i and λ_j are strategic complements when network effects are relatively weak ($n < 1 - \sqrt{1-\beta^2}$) and strategic substitutes when network effects are relatively strong ($n > 1 - \sqrt{1-\beta^2}$).

Solving (46) to get the equilibrium weights (that are symmetric):

$$\tilde{\lambda}^B = 1 + \frac{(\alpha-c)(1-\beta)(\beta^2-2n+n^2)}{[4-2\beta-\beta^2-n(2-\beta)](1-n)c} \tag{47}$$

Proposition 6 (Hoernig, 2012). *In the Bertrand model of strategic managerial delegation with network effects*:

(a) $\tilde{\lambda}^B > 1$ *when network effects are weak enough, that is,* $n < 1 - \sqrt{1-\beta^2}$

(b) $\tilde{\lambda}^B < 1$ *when network effects are strong enough, that is,* $n > 1 - \sqrt{1-\beta^2}$

In contrast to Proposition 2(a), we see that $\tilde{\lambda}^B < 1$ is possible when network effects are strong enough, since in this case λ_i and λ_j are strategic substitutes.

Now consider the impact of introduction network effects to the strategic trade model in Section 3, assuming as in Section 3.2, that $\lambda_i \in \{0, 1\}$. While we do not solve the model explicitly here (the interested reader is referred to Ghosh and Pal (2017), whose demand structure is identical to the one developed here), we outline the main result of this extension:

Proposition 7 (Ghosh and Pal, 2017). *Consider the strategic trade model with delegation, Bertrand competition and network effects and the game described in Figure 3.*

(a) *For welfare in a country to be higher when both countries set $\lambda_i = 0$ (Case II) than when both governments set $\lambda_i = 1$ (Case I), we require not only that $\beta > 0.466$, but also that the strength of network externalities is low enough.*
(b) *For $\lambda_1 = \lambda_2 = 0$ to emerge as an equilibrium in Figure 3, we require not only that products are very close substitutes, but also that the strength of network externalities are very weak.*

Proposition 7 highlights that just as network externalities weaken Proposition 2(a), they weaken Proposition 5 as well. In other words, welfare maximizing governments may be less inclined to delegate incentives for tax revenue maximization in the presence of network externalities than in its absence.

5.2. *Managerial Delegation in Strategic Trade Policy*

Our analysis in this survey has focused on a particular aspect of delegation in strategic trade theory: That governments delegate policy responsibility to policymakers such as bureaucrats. This is, however, not the only possible way to incorporate delegation in strategic trade theory. An alternative approach is provided by Das (1997), where owners delegate price or quantity setting responsibility to managers (in a manner similar to Section 2) after governments announce subsidy or tax policy.[19] This model, therefore, directly adds firm level delegation to the third market export model of Brander and

[19] See also Miller and Pazgal (2005).

Spencer (1985) and Eaton and Grossman (1986) and assumes that taxes are set in accordance with welfare maximization.

The logic behind this model can be summarized using the notation developed earlier (where $t_i < 0$ for a subsidy):

> Stage 1: Governments select t_i (non-cooperatively) to maximize W_i
> Stage 2: Owners select λ_i (non-cooperatively) to maximize π_i
> Stage 3: Managers select p_i or x_i (non-cooperatively) to maximize μ_i

It is evident that this model attaches one *ex ante* stage to the managerial delegation model in Section 2 to account for strategic trade policy. The impact of this is that even with identical marginal cost of production c, firms may face potentially different total costs (inclusive of taxes) of $c + t_i$.[20] Since this model reverts to welfare maximizing taxes, we do not elaborate on the modeling details further, except to state the main result in Das (1997): The equilibrium subsidy (with quantity competition) and tax (with price competition) is less when the possibility of managerial delegation is introduced compared to when firms act as traditional profit-maximizers.

6. Conclusions

Strategic trade theory postulates that welfare-maximizing governments can manipulate the outcome of strategic competition between firms through interventionist tax and subsidy policies. In this paper, we survey the literature which argues that welfare-maximizing governments can benefit under certain circumstances from credibly committing to set export taxes that maximize revenues rather than welfare. Given the intellectual antecedents of this argument in the industrial organization framework related to strategic managerial delegation, we have devoted considerable attention to laying out

[20]Though at equilibrium the symmetry of the problem will lead to the outcome that $t_i = t_j$.

the intuition and structure of firm level delegation. An array of possibilities exist in terms of modeling: price versus quantity competition; differentiated oligopoly versus a spatial Hotelling models, and so on. As is typical in the strategic policy framework, results vary depending on the specific model being considered, and our survey has attempted to summarize the underlying principles behind the rich set of outcomes that exist.

References

Bhagwati, J.N. (1971). The Generalized Theory of Distortions and Welfare, in *Trade, Balance of Payments, and Growth: Papers in International Economics on Honor of Charles P. Kindleberger*, J.N. Bhagwati, R.W. Jones, R.A. Mundell and J. Vanek (eds.). Amsterdam: North Holland Publishing Company.

Bhagwati, J.N. and Srinivasan, T.N. (1969). Optimal intervention to achieve non-economic objectives, *The Review of Economic Studies*, 35, 27–38.

Brander, J.A. (1995). Strategic Trade Policy, in *Handbook of International Economics*, Vol. 3, G. Grossman and K. Rogoff (eds.). Amsterdam: Elsevier Science B.V.

Brander, J.A. and Spencer, B.J. (1985). Export subsidies and international market share rivalry, *Journal of International Economics*, 18, 83–100.

Brennan, G. and Buchanan, J. (1980). *The Power to Tax: Analytical Foundations of a Fiscal Constitution.* Cambridge: Cambridge University Press.

Clarke, R. and Collie, D.R. (2006). Export taxes under Bertrand Duopoly, *Economics Bulletin*, 6(6), 1–8.

Clarke, R. and Collie, D.R. (2008) Maximum-Revenue versus optimum-welfare export taxes: a delegation game, *Review of International Economics*, 16, 919–929.

Collie, D.R. (1997). Delegation and strategic trade policy, *International Economic Journal*, 11, 35–46.

Das, S.P. (1997). Strategic Managerial Delegation and Trade Policy, *Journal of International Economics*, 43, 173–188.

de Meza, D. (1986). Export subsidies and high productivity: Cause or effect? *The Canadian Journal of Economics*, 19, 347–350.

Eaton, J. and Grossman, G.M. (1986). Optimal trade and industrial policy under oligopoly, *The Quarterly Journal of Economics*, 101, 383–406.

Fershtman, C. and Judd, K. (1987). Equilibrium incentives in oligopoly, *American Economic Review*, 77, 927–940.

Ghosh, A. and Pal, R. (2017). Welfare ranking of alternative export taxes revisited, *Economics Bulletin*, 37, 1033–1044.

Hoernig, S. (2012). Strategic delegation under price competition and network effects, *Economics Letters*, 117, 487–489.

Hotelling, H. (1929). Stability in competition, *Economic Journal*, 39: 41–57.

Huber, J.D. and Shipan, C.R. (2011). Politics, Delegation and Bureaucracy, in *The Oxford Handbook of Political Science*, R.E. Goodin (ed.). Oxford University Press.

Johnson, H.G. (1950–51). Optimum welfare and maximum revenue tariffs, *Review of Economic Studies*, 19, 28–35.

Katz, M. and Shapiro, C. (1985). Network externalities, competition and compatibility, *American Economic Review*, 75, 424–440.

Miller, N.H. and Pazgal, A. (2005). Strategic trade and delegated competition, *Journal of International Economics*, 66, 215–231.

Mohan, V. and Hazari, B. (2012). Tax policy when countries compete for third market exports, *Pacific Economic Review*, 17, 707–728.

Neary, J.P. (1994). Cost asymmetries in international subsidy games: Should governments help winners or losers? *Journal of International Economics*, 37: 197–218.

Panagariya, A. and Schiff, M. (1994). Can revenue maximizing export taxes yield higher welfare than welfare maximizing export taxes? *Economics Letters*, 45, 79–84.

Schelling, T.C. (1960). *The Strategy of Conflict.* Cambridge, MA: Harvard University Press.

Singh, N. and Vives, X. (1984). Price and quantity competition in a differentiated Duopoly, *Rand Journal of Economics*, 15, 546–554.

Sklivas, S. (1987). The strategic choice of managerial incentives, *RAND Journal of Economics*, 18, 452–458.

Tower, E. (1977). Ranking the optimum tariff and the maximum revenue tariff, *Journal of International Economics*, 7, 73–79.

Trandel, G.A. and Skeath, S. (1996). Welfare effects when strategic trade policy is set to favor producers, *Southern Economic Journal,* 63, 163–171.

Vickers, J. (1984). Delegation and the theory of the firm, *Economic Journal* (Supplement), 95, 138–147.

CPSIA information can be obtained
at www.ICGtesting.com
Printed in the USA
BVHW041204290419
546820BV00004B/8/P